The world's largest collection of visual travel guides

TURKISH COAST

Edited by Metin Demirsar
Editorial Director: Brian Bell

APA PUBLICATIONS

Part of the Langenscheidt Publishing Group

INSIGHT GUIDES

TURKISH Coast

CONTACTING THE EDITORS: Although every effort
is made to provide accurate information in this
publication, we live in a fast-changing world and would
appreciate it if readers would call our attention to any
errors or outdated information that may occur by
writing to us at Apa Publications,
P.O. Box 7910, London SE1 1WE, England.
Fax: (44) 20-403-0290.
e-mail: insight@apaguide.demon.co.uk.

First Edition 1990
Updated 1998, 2000

Distributed in the United States by
Langenscheidt Publishers Inc.
46–35 54th Road, Maspeth, NY 11378
Fax: (718) 784 -0640

Distributed in the UK & Ireland by
GeoCenter International Ltd
The Viables Centre, Harrow Way
Basingstoke, Hampshire RG22 4BJ
Fax: (44) 1256-817988

Worldwide distribution enquiries:
APA Publications GmbH & Co. Verlag KG
(Singapore branch)
38 Joo Koon Road, Singapore 628990
Tel: 65-8651600. Fax: 65-8616438

Printed in Singapore by
Insight Print Services (Pte) Ltd
38 Joo Koon Road, Singapore 628990
Fax: 65-8616438

www.insightguides.com

This guidebook combines the interests
and enthusiasms of two of the
world's best-known information pro-
viders: Insight Guides, whose range of titles
has set the standard for visual travel guides
since 1970, and Discovery Channel, the
world's premier source of nonfiction television programming.

The editors of Insight Guides provide both
practical advice and general understanding
about a destination's history, politics,
culture, institutions and people. Discovery
Channel and its excellent Web site,
www.discovery.com, help millions of viewers
explore their world from the comfort of their
own home and also encourage them to
explore it firsthand.

We would like to introduce you to the
principal contributors of this book.
Project editor **Metin Demirsar** is a
Turkish journalist whose many articles have
appeared in numerous foreign newspapers
and magazines, including *The Wall Street Jour-
nal*. Demirsar also contributed to, and later
revised and updated, both *Insight Guide:
Turkey* and *Insight City Guide: Istanbul*. He
also wrote *Personal Guide to the Turquoise
Coast*. His wife, **Tülay Demirsar** completed
the index and helped compile the Travel Tips.

Alev Alatlı wrote many chapters in the history section and co-authored the feature
about Turkish people. A husband-wife team,
William A. Edmonds and **Anna G. Edmonds**,
wrote several sections, including the feature
on Turkish carpets.

Sevâ Ülman Erten, an Ankara-based
journalist, contributed the features about
holiday villages and Yasar Kemal, Turkey's
best-known novelist.

Jay Courtney Fikes, an American
anthropologist, authored the chapter on Ionia
with related features about Izmir and
Ephesus. Filkes is author of *Step Inside the
Sacred Circle*, a collection of American Indian
allegorical animal stories. He is married to
a Turk and has taught at Marmara University
in Istanbul. He works in Washington D.C. as
an advocate for American Indians.

Demirsar

W. Edmonds

A. Edmonds

Le Cornu

Rossant

Güler

Güner

Laura Le Cornu, and **Juliette Rossant** contributed several features. Le Cornu and Rossant are reporters for Compass News Features. Both are Americans. They also sub-edited *Pnal Guide to The Turquoise Coast*. Le Cornu has a BA in political science from Goucer College in Baltimore, Maryland. Rossant has a BA in classical archaeology from Dartmouth College and an MA in creative writing from the Johns Hopkins University.

British citizens **Robert Love** and **Brenda Wild**, a husband-wife team, joined project editor Demirsar to write the feature on the 1915 military Gallipoli campaign. Love and Wild have both taught physics at Istanbul's Vehbi Koç High School.

Ara Güler, one of the world's most highly estimed photojournalists, provided many of the pictures in this book. Güler is correspondent of *Time-Life Books*, *Magnum Photos* and *Stern Magazine*. Güler's discovery and stunning photography of Aphrodisias in the 1950s has made the ancient Roman city an important destination and paved the way for excavations at the site. Güler's photography also appeared in *Insight Guide: Pakistan* and *Personal Guide to The Turquoise Coast*.

Semsi Güner, the chief photographer of this book, is no new comer to Apa. His superb photography has also appeared in all three previous Apa titles dealing with Turkey – *Insight Guide: Turkey*, *Insight City Guide: Istanbul*; and *Personal Guide to The Turquoise Coast*. A former opera baritone and graphic arts designer, Güner has now been taking photographs of Turkey and the world for the media for well over 30 years.

The article on the Blue Voyage was written by **Galip Isen**, who spends his summers taking well-to-do tourists on cruises along the Greek islands and Turkish Aegean and Mediterranean coasts aboard his yacht.

Selma Manizade, a graphic arts designer, compiled the travel tips at the back of the book. Manizade, a Turk who has lived most of her life in the United States, works for the Türkiye Emlak Bankası bank.

Aliza Marcus and **Yuri Feher** collaborated to write the section about Adana and the East. Marcus, an American freelance journalist who works for *Turquoise* magazine in New York, also penned the article on the late industrialist Hacı Ömer Sabancı. Marcus, who contributed to *The Book of World City Rankings*, is a graduate of Columbia University's School of Journalism. Hungarian-born Feher has a PhD in Anthropology from New York University.

Enis Özbank, who contributed many pictures to this book, is a *Sipa Press* photojournalist whose work has featured in *Time Magazine, Newsweek, Paris Match* and *Epocha*. **Patricia Roberts**, a freelance journalist and writer who lives in Paris, wrote the section on Rough and Smooth Cilicia and the features on Turkey's olive oil industry and water sports.

Nergis Yazgan and **Gernant Magnin** teamed up to write about wildlife and environmental issues of the Turkish Coast. Yazgan is Turkey's leading wildlife conservationist. Magnin is a project officer with the International Council for Bird Preservation (ICBP), a Cambridge UK-based ornithological society. His publications for ICBP include: *Bird Killing in Malta; An Account of Illegal Bird Catching in Cyprus during 1987*; and *Falconry and Hunting in Turkey*.

The project editor also wants to thank Kusadası-based **Demir Ünsal**, director of Vmay Tours Travel Agency, for giving him a personal tour of the ancient sites on the Menderes (Maeander) River Valley. He is also grateful to **Artun Altıparmak**, publisher of Istanbul's *ABC Kitabevi A.S.*, without whose constant encouragement and extremely generous support throughout, this book could not have possibly been conceived, started and finished.

Material for this edition was organised in Apa's London office by update editor **Rachel Parsons** and proofread by **Sylvia Suddes**. The book was updated by **Suzanne Swann**, a freelance journalist living in Turkey who regularly contributes to Insight Guides and other publications on Turkey.

CONTENTS

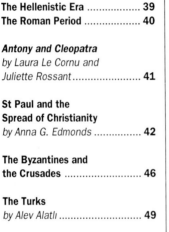

History

A Traveller's Delight
by Metin Demirsar.................... 23

Decisive Dates
by Laura Le Cornu and
Juliette Rossant....................... 26

Early History
by Anna G. Edmonds 28

Alexander the Great 38
The Hellenistic Era 39
The Roman Period 40

Antony and Cleopatra
by Laura Le Cornu and
Juliette Rossant....................... 41

**St Paul and the
Spread of Christianity**
by Anna G. Edmonds 42

**The Byzantines and
the Crusades** 46

The Turks
by Alev Alatlı 49

Islam
by Laura Le Cornu and
Juliette Rossant....................... 57

People
by Metin Demirsar and
Alev Alatlı 65

Discoveries

Cuisine
by Laura Le Cornu and
Juliette Rossant....................... 75

Turkish Carpets
by William A. Edmonds 85

Antiquities Smuggling
by Metin Demirsar.................... 92

Holiday Villages
by Sevâ Ülman Erten 94

Water Sports
by Patricia Roberts 96

**Coastal Wildlife and
Environmental Issues** 100

Places

The Northern Aegean 123

Thrace 124

The Gallipoli Campaign
by Metin Demirsar, Robert M. Love
and Brenda Wild 129

The Troad
by William A. Edmonds and
Anna G. Edmonds 135

Troy and the Trojan War
by Anna G. Edmonds 140

The Southern Aegean 151

Aeolia
by William A. Edmonds and
Anna G. Edmonds 153

The Olive Oil Industry
by Patricia Roberts **156**

Pergamum
by William A. Edmonds and
Anna G. Edmonds **158**

Izmir **167**
Izmir's Minorities **176**
The Ionian Coast **178**

Camel Wrestling
by Metin Demirsar **184**

Ephesus
by Jay Courtney Fikes **187**

The Maeander River Valley **201**
Caria **211**
Bodrum **215**

Sponge Diving
by Metin Demirsar **222**

Blue Voyage **224**
by Galip Isen

Marmaris **231**
by Metin Demirsar

The Mediterranean Coast **241**
The Western Mediterranean ... **244**
Lycia **247**
Saint Nicholas **264**

Antalya and its Environs **267**
by Metin Demirsar

The Eastern Mediterranean **284**
Rough Cilicia **287**
Smooth Cilicia **293**

Adana and the East
by Aliza Marcus and
Yuri Feher **300**

Crusader Castles
by Anna G. Edmonds **304**

Yasar Kemal: Turkey's Top Novelist
by Sevâ Ülman Erten and
Metin Demirsar **308**

**Hacı Ömer Sabancı: The Peasant
Lad who built an Industrial Empire**
by Aliza Marcus **312**

Maps

Turkey 116
Thrace & Marmara 124
The Aegean Coast 150
Pergamum site plan 158
Izmir 168
Ephesus site plan 189
Blue Voyage 224
Western Mediterranean 244
Antalya 271
Eastern Mediterranean 284

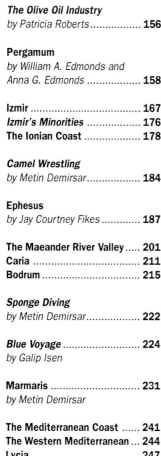

Getting Acquainted

The Place 322
Climate 322
Economy & Government 322
Culture & Customs 322

Planning the Trip

What to Bring 322
Photography 323
Entry Regulations 323
Health 324
Money 325
Public Holidays 325
Getting There 326

Practical Tips

Business Hours 328
Religion 328
Media 328
Postal Services 329
Telecommunications 329
Useful Websites 329
Tourist Information 330
Embassies 331
Emergencies 331
Security & Crime 333
Etiquette 333
Emergency Numbers 333
Women Travellers 334
Travelling with Children 334
Disabled Travellers 335
Religious Services 335

Getting Around

On Arrival 336
Water Transport 336
Inter-City Bus Companies 337
Private Transport 339
Tours 339
Blue Cruises 340

Where to Stay

Types of Lodging 341
The Northern Aegean 342
The Southern Aegean 343
The Mediterranean 349

Where to Eat

Restaurants 354

Culture

Music & Dance 366
Cinema 366
Festivals & Art 367
Nightlife 368

Sports & Leisure

Yachting 369
Golf 372
Horse Riding 372
Lycian Way Walk 372
Turkish Baths 373
Trekking & Mountaineering 373
Watersports 373
Leisure Attractions 374

Shopping

Textiles & Jewellery 375
Leather & Carpets 376
Ceramics & Glass 377
Property 377

Language

Pronunciation 377
Useful Words & Phrases 377

Further Reading

General 382
Other Insight Guides 384

Index 386

TRAVELLERS' DELIGHT

Stretching from the border with Greece to its frontier with Syria, the Turkish Coast has thousands of miles of unspoilt sandy beaches and coves fringed by pine forests, hundreds of pristine fishing villages and market towns, and a wealth of ancient ruins.

The ruins of fabled cities like Troy, Pergamum, Ephesus, Halicarnassus, Xanthus, Side and Karatepe are just a few of the sites of antiquity that dot the coast, waiting to be explored by travellers.

Since the days of Antony and Cleopatra, the southwest corner of Turkey, known today as the Turquoise Coast, has been a playground for yachtsmen. Taking the Blue Voyage into one of these tranquil bays is a sublime form of relaxation.

The Turkish Coast begins in Thracian (European) Turkey at the town of Enez, near the Greek border, and the wide Bay of Saros, which has some of the finest beaches in Turkey. It continues south to the desolate Gallipoli Peninsula, scene of a fierce World War I military campaign, and the Dardanelles, the strategic strait where the legendary Leander drowned while swimming to his lover, the Virgin Priestess Hero. Gökçeada – Turkey's largest island, and Bozcaada, are known for their fine wines and both guard the Aegean mouth of the Dardanelles.

The major part of the Turkish Coast lies in Asia across the Dardanelles. The Asian part begins at the town of Çanakkale and covers a bulging peninsula that in ancient times was known as the Troad. The ruins of Troy, Assos and Alexandria Troas dominate this peninsula. Further south is the Gulf of Edremit, one of Turkey's most picturesque bays. The Gulf is famed for its long stretches of beaches and for its resort towns of Edremit, Burhaniye and Ayvalık, facing the Greek island of Lesbos. Pergamum, one of the country's magnificent sites of antiquity, is just south of the area near the modern town of Bergama. The region from the Gulf of Edremit to Izmir, Turkey's third largest city and second biggest port, was known in the past as the Aeolian Coast.

The area surrounding Izmir was once known as Ionia: the ruins of more than 50 Ionian cities are within a two-hour drive of Izmir. Ephesus, a Hellenistic city just south of Izmir, is one of the world's most frequented ancient sites.

Surrounded by mountains, the area is rich in wildlife and unusual bird species – a delight to nature lovers. More species of fauna and flora can be seen on the Turkish Coast than in most regions of Continental Europe. It is one of the few areas in the Mediterranean where loggerhead turtles come to lay their eggs and endangered monk seals frolic on offshore islands.

Preceding pages: columns of Perge; boat on the lake at Antalya; bejewelled Turkish women; strolling along the beach; the ruins of Aphrodisias; frieze from the Myra theater; windsurfing at Gümbet. Left, the catch of the day.

DECISIVE DATES

Old Stone Age 600,000–7000 BC: Cave-dwellings at Karain.

Neolithic Period 7000–5500 BC: First settlement at Hacılar, earliest agriculture; Çatal Höyük, first cultural centre.

Calcholithic Period 5500–3000 BC: Development of Hacılar and Çatal Höyük; new settlements at Canhasan, Beycesultan and Aphrodisias.

3000–1900 BC: Troy I through Troy IV.

2000–1200 BC: Hittites establish their capital at Hattusa and extend rule over central and western Anatolia; first written history.

1900–1260 BC: Troy V through Troy VII.

circa 1260 BC: Fall of Troy.

circa 1100–1000 BC: Aeolian and Ionian Greek migrants establish settlements along the Aegean Coast.

circa 900 BC: Rise of the Carians, Lycians and Phrygians.

circa 800 BC: Foundation of the Panionic League; rise of Ionian/Aeolian Greek culture in Western Anatolia.

circa 700 BC: Birth of Homer in Smyrna (Izmir); rise of the Lydians.

667 BC: The city of Byzantium (now Istanbul) is founded.

561–546 BC: Reign of King Croesus of Lydia.

546 BC: King Cyrus of Persia defeats Croesus, beginning Persian domination of western Anatolia.

499 BC: Ionian cities revolt against Persian rule. The rebellion is crushed.

490 BC: First Persian invasion of Greece led by Darius defeated at the Plains of Marathon.

circa 484 BC: Herodotus is born in Halicarnassus.

480 BC: Second Persian invasion of Greece by Xerxes ends in defeat at Salamis (480) and Plataea (479).

405 BC: Sparta destroys Athenian Navy in Battle of Aegospotami on the Dardanelles.

386 BC: Persia subjugates Ionia again.

334 BC: Alexander the Great invades western Anatolia.

323–188 BC: Wars between Alexander's successors.

261–241 BC: Eumenes I reigns in Pergamum.

230 BC: Alliance between Rome and Pergamum; Attalus I defeats the Gauls invading Anatolia.

88 BC: Mithridates, king of the Pontus, revolts against Romans.

41–40 BC: Antony summons Cleopatra to Tarsus and begins love affair.

31 BC: Antony is defeated at the battle of Actium. Antony and Cleopatra commit suicide in Egypt (30 BC).

330: Constantine establishes Constantinople as new capital of Roman Empire.

527–565: Reign of Justinian; period of greatest Byzantine power and influence.

677–718: Arab armies sweep across southern and western Anatolia, but fail to conquer Constantinople.

1071: Seljuk Turks defeat Byzantines at the Battle of Manzikert and overrun most of Anatolia.

1071–1238: Seljuks rule Anatolia from Konya; the Sultanate of Rum.

1096: First Crusade of Latin armies invade western and southern Anatolia on their way to Jerusalem.

1204: Latin armies of the Fourth Crusade sack Constantinople.

1240: Ottoman Turks descend on western Anatolia as vassals of the Seljuk Dynasty.

1261: Michael VIII Pelaeologos recaptures Constantinople and restores the Byzantine Empire.

1354: Ottoman armies, led by Ghazi Süleyman Pasha, cross the Dardanelles into Europe.

1402: Mongolian ruler Tamerlane defeats Ottomans under Beyazıt I, setting back Ottoman expansion by a generation.

1453: The Ottomans under Mehmet II capture Constantinople, renaming it Istanbul; the Ottoman capital is established there.

The Ottoman Period 1453–1922

1459–1517: The Ottomans conquer Serbia, Greece, Syria and Egypt. Selim I becomes Caliph (AD 1517).

1520–1566: Reign of Süleyman the Magnificent. Height of Ottoman power; Ottomans conquer Rhodes, Baghdad, Hungary and Libya; the Mediterranean is turned into a Turkish lake.

1571: Turks conquer Cyprus. First Ottoman defeat in the naval Battle of Lepanto by Christian forces.

1669: Crete falls to the Ottomans.

1699: Austria and her allies sign the Treaty of Carlowitz, the first Ottoman admission of defeat; Ottomans lose many central European territories.

1876–1909: Reign of Abdülhamit II.

1878: Turco-Russian wars ends in Ottoman defeat; Serbia, Montenegro, Bosnia, Bulgaria and Rumania become independent; British govern Cyprus.

1911–1913: Balkan Wars; Turks lose Macedonia and a section of Thrace.

1914: Turkey joins World War I as ally of Germany. Russia, France and Britain declare war on Turkey.

1915: The Turkish forces, led by Mustafa Kemal, repel allied landings at Gallipoli.

1918: Turks are driven out of Palestine and Syria by British forces. Turks surrender to the Allied Powers.

1919: Italian forces occupy Antalya and southwest Turkey. French troops seize Adana and southeast Turkey. The Greek army occupies Izmir and invades western Anatolia.

1919–1922: Turkish War of Independence. Greeks are defeated by the Turks and leave Anatolia.

The Republican Period: from 1923

1923: Turkish Republic is declared; the Sultanate and the Caliphate are abolished; Mustafa Kemal Atatürk becomes first President. The Treaty of Lausanne establishes the sovereignty of modern Turkey, determines borders. Exchange of minorities between Greece and Turkey.

1925–1938: Westernizing social reforms introduced by Atatürk include abolition of the *fez*, adoption of the western calendar, introduction of the Latin alphabet and women's rights.

1934: Turkish women granted equal rights with men to vote in all elections – also obligatery.

1946: Turkey becomes charter member of the United Nations; opposition parties founded. First general elections called.

1952: Turkey becomes full member of NATO.

1960: Cyprus becomes independent state; Military coup in Turkey.

1971: Military topples government of Prime Minister Süleyman Demirel.

1974: Turkey annexes and creates Turkish Republic of Northern Cyprus (TCKK) in respouse to increasing Greek nationalistic stirrings.

1989: Turgut Özal is elected President.

1993: Özal dies and Süleyman Demirel becomes President. Turkey's first female Prime Minister, Tansu Ciller of the True Path Party (DYP) takes office.

1996: The Islamic Welfare Party (Refah) and DYP form coalition government, with Necmettin Erbakan as Prime Minister and Tansu Ciller as Deputy Prime Minister.

1998: The Giller-Erbakan, "Refahyol" government is nudged from power by Turkey's secular military.

1999: Veteran politician Bülent Ecevit of the Democratic Left Party becomes Prime Minister. His coalition partner, Devlet Bahgeli, shot to prominence on ultranationalist sentiments. A serious earthquake devastates Turkey's industrial heartland, kills over 20,000 people and highlights flaws in social infrastructure.

2000: Turkey accepts the European Union's invitation to be the 13th candidate for EU membership.

The story of human life in Anatolia is one of successive civilisations superimposed on each other, each altering, fine-tuning or imposing a distinctive cultural trademark on subsequent generations. It is a story of varied and increasingly complex levels of existence, with each group building upon the houses and on the ideas of the previous inhabitants. People added 17 metres (19 yards) to the hill of Troy in the 3,000 years they occupied it. Users of stone tools were followed by users of both stone and metal;

This innovation, which is known as the Neolithic Revolution, meant the difference between savage subsistence and the beginnings of human control of the environment.

More specifically, an important dividing line in the description of human development can be drawn at the time of the Neolithic Revolution, well before the advent of writing. Up until the appearance of the written word, our information is based largely on inference. Before it, we can surmise the

metal workers learned to mint standardised coins, the use of which improved the efficiency of their businesses. Often the groups interacted with civilizations some distance away. The Miletian astronomer Thales was able to predict the eclipse of the sun in 585 BC because he knew about an 18-year periodicity that Babylonian astronomers had observed about eclipses.

Neolithic Revolution: The records of civilisation in the Near East begin with a revolution, a turning point when people changed from being at the mercy of their environment to their becoming herdsmen of wild animals and cultivators of wild grains.

general outlines; after, there is a crescendo of known developments, persons and events. The division is not clear-cut. It may even have been stimulated by the warming of the earth's atmosphere after the last Ice Age.

The major areas of this revolution in the Middle East were the drainage basins of the Tigris and the Euphrates rivers, the Fertile Crescent. Much of this lies further east than the province of this book, but the northwest point of that Crescent extends into the rich farmland of the Cilician Plain (today's Çukurova). Between Antakya and Silifke,

Above, wheat particles found at Karain Caves.

on the slopes of the Taurus Mountains, across the flat land to the west, and extending north along the Mediterranean Coast, archaeologists have found evidence of this change. Here fishermen, farmers and herders have left the clues with which scientists are piecing together the story of human beginnings and achievements. From these clues archaeologists approximate that human life in the Middle East goes back about a million years. Only in the relatively recent past – perhaps 10,000 BC – did people begin using tools. By about 8000 BC, people were shaping tools for specific purposes and controlling food production.

By 5500 BC people had metal tools; the first metal they used in quantity was copper – the Chalcolithic Period. At the same time, the first groups of people to live in primitive settlements perhaps were those who could harvest and store enough food to carry them through winter.

The next advance came with the discovery of how to make bronze. The Bronze Age, commenced around 3200 BC. Copper, lead, nickel and arsenic are all abundant in Anatolia, but archaeologists are not sure where the tin, which was needed to combine with copper to make bronze, came from. It may have been mined in the Taurus Mountains or it may have been imported from Mesopotamia.

Social changes: A metalworking industry meant a permanent settlement, some division of labour and some kind of social organisation along with trading arrangements. With this advance, village life became more complex; buildings were constructed for purposes other than just habitation.

The Bronze Age lasted about 2,000 years. During that time writing was developed and brought into Anatolia by foreign Assyrians around 1900 BC. The use of iron, with its superior strength, was introduced into the area around 1400 BC and established the Iron Age.

The theory associated with iron is that its abundance meant eventually that cheap weapons were available to the masses who then used them against their neighbours. The invading "Sea Peoples" at the turn of the first millennium destroyed civilisations, causing a major regression to a more primitive type of living in western Anatolia – a period described as the "Dark Ages."

Indo-European invaders: The Middle and late Bronze periods (2000 to 1000 BC) are known largely from the finds in Troy. The beginning of the period was marked by waves of Indo-European invaders, some settling peacefully and taking on many of the customs of the indigenous groups, others wreaking considerable destruction on the cities in their paths.

The Battle of Kadesh, which was concluded with a treaty of political alignment between the Hittites and Egypt, was fought on the Orontes River south of Antakya in about 1285 BC. This established the Hittites as an internationally dominant kingdom and set a northern limit to Egyptian influence in the Middle East. The Trojan War between the Greeks and the Trojans ended in about 1250 BC, probably opening up Anatolia to invasion by another wave of barbaric tribes.

Beginning about 700 BC, more accurate dates can be assigned to recorded events. Cimmerians from the Caucasus sacked Gordium around 690 BC; Tarsus was ravaged by the Assyrian Sennacherib at the same time. Lydians plundered Smyrna (Izmir) a hundred years later, and King Croesus was defeated at Sardis by the Persian King Cyrus in 546 BC, beginning the period of Persian influence. Persian control of the western coast and influence of Persian art lasted until Alexander the Great's conquests between 334 and 323 BC.

The written record of past events in Anatolia started in about 1900 BC when the Assyrian merchants living on the outskirts of the Hittite capital of Kanesh (near Kayseri) sent letters to their business associates in Mesopotamia. These letters were inscribed in cuneiform (wedge-shaped characters) on clay and then baked in an oven. In them are references to people such as the Ahhiyawans who were living at the time on the coast.

The earliest group of people living in Anatolia for which we have a name is the Hattians. When they came and where they came from remain a mystery. They were a non-Semitic, non-Indo-European group who were influential enough to give the name of their land to the next invaders who probably called themselves Nesians.

The Nesians, one of the many ethnic groups who invaded the area apparently from the east, established one of their capitals at Hattusa (Boğazköy) and another at

Kanesh (Kültepe). Their ruler styled himself "King of the Hatti", and they and their Indo-European language are known, with some oversimplification, as Hittite.

Lycians of Xanthus: The invasion of these Nesians, or Hittites, coincided with the arrival on the coast of the Ahhiyawans who seem to have come from the west and with whom the Hittites had commercial relations. They may have been the people whom Homer called the Achaeans; if so, more connections – business, military and cultural – between the Hittites, the Trojans and the Greeks may be uncovered. The Ahhiyawans appear to have been an early Greek colony living around Miliwandas. (Can this be Miletus?) Another Hittite influence on the coast shows in the record that during the reign of King Suppiluliumas the Hittites fought the Lukka nation, presumably the Lycians living around Xanthus.

The Hittites were apparently present on the coast as far north as Izmir, although their settlements up to now are known to be single sites. A stone statue of a Hittite still guards the pass at Karabel east of Izmir; there is a relief of a "Mother of the Gods" on Manisa Dağ. This scattering of remains has 'made archaeologists wonder what the Hittites were doing so far from Hattusa or Kanesh.

Another, possibly different, pre-Indo-European group was known as the Pelasgians. They were present in northwestern Anatolia before the Trojan War. Their name suggests that they came from the sea; however, that may merely describe them rather than being what they were actually called. According to Homer, who is the earliest source for such information, the Pelasgians were allies of the Trojans. Herodotus locates their capital on the Sea of Marmara.

At least two other peoples living on the Mediterranean coast of Anatolia at the beginning of this period used Indo-European languages: the Assuwans who spoke Luwian and the Hurrians.

Anatolian coastal districts: The names of the districts in Anatolia at one time indicated political identities and dominance. Today they describe the areas in general geographic and cultural terms. Starting in the north, the coastal regions are usually referred to as Thrace, the Troad, Aeolis, Lydia, Caria, Lycia, Pamphylia and Cilicia.

Thrace originally included all of today's European Turkey and stretched into Bulgaria and Greece. Greek mythology says Orpheus, who charmed open the gates of Hell by playing the lyre, was born on the shores of the Hermus (Meriç) River, the boundary between Turkey and Greece. Thracian invaders – or Phrygians – are probably the ones responsible for the destruction of Hattusa about 1180 BC.

About 1160 BC the Phrygians, known also as the Mushki, appeared and grew in power on the eastern borders of Ionia and Aeolis. They may have brought about the downfall of the Hittites. Their contribution to life on the coast included their improvement of the trade routes known as the Royal Roads, one of which went east from Izmir through Dorylaeum (Eskişehir), Ankara and Boğazkale; another slightly south led from Sardis through central Anatolia and the Cilician Gates; both eventually ended at Susa, now a ruined city in western Iran.

The golden touch: The Phrygian King Midas was so rich that everything he touched turned to gold, including his beloved daughter. To rid himself of this fatal curse, he bathed in the Pactolus River, which flows past Sardis and from which King Croesus got his gold. (British archaeologists have speculated that the ass's ears which Apollo gave Midas when the king preferred Pan's pipes to Apollo's may be an allusion to a combination of two well-documented medical conditions: abnormally long ears, and an excessive growth of hair on the edges of the ears.)

Phrygians are credited with inventing the frieze. They were known for their music; the Phrygian mode was supposed to be stimulating; its cadence may have been preserved through early hymns. (The Lydian mode was considered to be decorous; the Ionian mode, which the Western major scale is based on, was called "wanton." The Aeolian harp is one on which the wind performs.)

Phrygian power was interrupted when the Cimmerians from the north invaded Anatolia briefly about 700 BC. The Cimmerians may have gone off with Midas' treasure since no gold was found in his presumed tomb. The Phrygian Empire was absorbed into the Lydian Empire, and then it passed into Persian control. Under the Attalids it was part of the Pergamene Empire.

The Troad: At one time the northwest corner of Anatolia now called the province of Çanakkale was called Lesser Phrygia. By classical Greek times it was the Troad. The first person to establish a city in the Troad, according to legend, was Teucer, a king who came to the mainland from Lesbos. His son-in-law was Dardanus, the hero of the Dardanelles. (Teucer's great grandson was Tros, to whom we owe the name Troy.) The Dardanians were allies of the Hittite King Mutwatallis in the Battle of Kadesh. They fought a few years later on the side of the Trojans.

The habitation of Troy from 3000 BC to AD 300 has given archaeologists a sequence

against which to measure other sites. Levels I to V in Troy belong to the early Bronze Period. The buildings were made of mud brick on top of stone foundations in the shape of a megaron, a long rectangular building with an entry porch.

From the time of Level II on (*circa* 2400 BC), Trojan potters used a wheel. They probably learned this skill from the people who lived in northern Syria or in Cilicia who had been using it earlier. Pottery similar to what was found first in Troy II has later been discovered in many places near the coast

Above, scene of the ruins of Troy.

north of Izmir. Two kinds of jars are common at this level, one of them in a semi-human form, the other with two shapely handles. Similar kinds of jars are also found in Tarsus and Yümüktepe (Mersin).

The people living in Troy II were skilled in working with metals to make weapons, saws, jewellery and vases. The influence of their artistry spread over western Anatolia, Crete, Thrace and into the Balkans.

By Troy V, potters were using a red or a reddish-brown slip. Sometimes they put a reddish cross on the inside, a mark which has been found on pots in Tarsus (and the Hittite city of Kanesh) and which suggests a link between those places. In addition, bronze was manufactured from this time on.

The fortified city of Troy VI, lasting from about 1900 to 1300 BC, is similar to Hittite forts: the engineering techniques of offsets (ledges) and columns to add strength to the walls were used in Hittite Alisar and Bogazkale. These Trojans seem to have been newcomers to the area, probably one of the Indo-European invaders. Their pottery was a grey "Minyan" ware, perhaps originally an Anatolian rather than a Greek design as was once thought.

Homer's epics: Troy VIIa, built on top of the earthquake ruins of Troy VI, was destroyed during a huge fire in about 1250 BC Most archaeologists identify this event with the war between the Trojans and the Achaean invaders from Greece who are remembered in Homer's epics.

Following that war, several groups of people apparently scattered, founding cities along the Mediterranean Coast. Of these, some Pamphylian cities claimed a Trojan background: Perge, Aspendos and Sillyum (but not Side which is of a later date).

The pottery in Troy VIIb is knobbly and similar in style to that which was being made in central Europe around the same time, rather than anything made in Anatolia; this would seem to indicate that people from Europe were travelling south into Anatolia. Troy VIIb also was destroyed by fire – probably in the course of another war brought on by invaders – around the year 1180 BC.

Troy VIII (700–334 BC) was called Ilion; and today very little exists of it. Troy IX was not an important town to anyone, except perhaps to the pilgrims who came to its

Temple of Athena to pay homage to Homer and his epic.

Aeolis was settled by the first group of people who were uprooted from their land in Greece by invading Dorians toward the end of the second millennium BC. Pushed from Thessaly and Boetia, the Aeolian refugees settled first in the area around Old Smyrna (Izmir). They probably moved in on an already resident group who may have been Hittites, themselves earlier immigrants. Undoubtedly the Aeolians intermarried with these residents. The Aeolian territory extended from the Gulf of Edremit towards the Bay of Izmir.

Its cities included Pitane and Cyme on the coast, but by far its most important city was Pergamum (Bergama), which for 150 years under the Attalid kings rivalled Egypt in political power and cultural brilliance and architecture.

Whoever the natives were, the Aeolians were shortly supplanted by the Ionians who migrated after the collapse of the Achaean kingdom of Mycenae sometime before 900 BC. Their geographic influence extended from just north of Izmir south to Miletus. During the eighth and seventh centuries BC they led in the development of civic organisation with the Panionic League of 12 cities. They sent out a number of colonies to the shores of the Dardanelles, the Marmara and the Black Sea.

Their cultural influence was even more impressive. The Temple of Diana in Ephesus, an architectural masterpiece, and the Mausoleum in Halicarnassus (today's Bodrum) were two of the Seven Wonders of the Ancient World.

The historians: On the coast, the earliest historians were Ionians. They lived at the time of the Persian dominance, but their works contributed not to Persia, but to the importance of the Greek language and to the growth of Greek/Hellenistic analytical thought. Their name in Turkish identifies Greece as "*Yunanistan*," the land of the Ionians. Three of the historians were from Miletus: Cadmus (*circa* 540 BC), sometimes confused with a Phoenician god and credited with inventing letters; Dionysius, and Hecataeus (*circa* 500 BC). The latter began his history remarking, "I write as I deem true, for the traditions of the Greeks seem to me manifold and laughable." Xanthus of Sardis

and Herodotus of Heraclea (Latmus) were precursors of the "Father of History," Herodotus of Halicarnassus (485–425 BC).

Lydia (some historians speculate that this could be the Lud of the Old Testament) was a little inland; its centre was Sardis. Caria was around the Bay of Cos. Lycia is the land south of a line drawn from Antalya across the mountains to Köyceğiz.

The Lycians, who around 1400 BC were raiding Cyprus from Crete, settled temporarily in Miletus. Then they moved south to the area around Xanthus. During the Battle of Kadesh, Lycians fought on the side of their fellow Anatolians. Later, according to Homer, soldiers from faraway Lycia and

"the whirling waters of Xanthus" fought with their leader Sarpedon on the side of the Trojans in Troy.

Native stock Anatolians: The Carians and the Lydians asserted that they were native stock Anatolians. This was probably a legitimate claim, but their importance did not develop until they were stimulated by outside Persian and Greek influences.

The Carian and Ionian centres included Miletus, Knidos and Halicarnassus. Up until 500 BC they dominated Greek rational thought. Besides the historians, a remarkable number of philosophers were born in Miletus. Thales, the forecaster of the eclipse, also confounded his critics, who claimed that philosophers could not be successful in business. He predicted a bumper crop of olives, cornered the market, and made a killing. Anaximenes and Anaximander searched for the basic principle of the universe; the first said it was air, the other claimed it was limitlessness.

As for Halicarnassus (Bodrum), one of its famous sons was Herodotus. Another man whose name still resounds was the good King Mausolus, whose sister-cum-wife built a splendid mausoleum for him when he died about 352 BC. Two queens named Artemisia ruled in Halicarnassus. Both were remarkably adept as captains of their ships in sea

point is well known for its treacherous seas; the new residents constructed a causeway joining the point to the hilly island to the west. In this way they created a double harbour, one south and one north, saving some ships from having to round the point in a storm. About the same time of their move, the Knidians acquired the statue of Aphrodite by Praxiteles which attracted many visitors to their city.

The Lydian capital was Sardis. Lydians appear to be associated around 800 BC with the Etruscans who showed up then in Italy, having come from the east perhaps because of a famine. Three Lydian kings, Gyges, Alyattes and Croesus, are particularly well

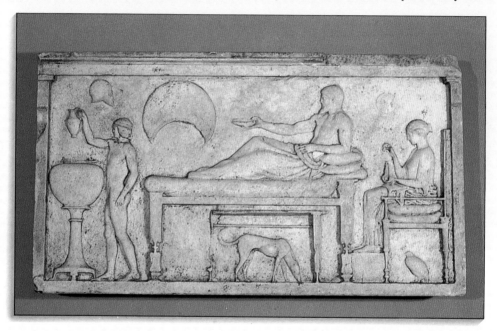

battles, the first (widow of Mausolus) against the Persians in 480 BC, the second against the Rhodians in 351 BC.

Statue of Aphrodite: Knidos was founded by the Dorians, the group who had pushed the Ionians and Aeolians out of Greece and then were pushed out themselves. As a coastal city, Knidos was troubled by pirates, and when it drove the pirates off it sent offerings of thanks to Delphi. In about 360 BC, the city moved from its first location (near present-day Datça) to the tip of the peninsula. This

Left, bust of Hermes, the messenger of God. Above, blissful family life in antiquity.

known: Gyges began his career as a prime minister in about 700 BC, but having assassinated his king in order to save the queen's honour, he took the throne and set about expanding his holdings.

Under King Alyattes, the Cimmerians were defeated. They had invaded Anatolia from the northeast and killed Gyges. (Following their defeat they retreated to the Crimea.) By occupying the Phrygian lands left unattended in the Cimmerians' wake, Lydia came into contact with Persia and aroused the greed of its kings.

Minting coins: The Lydians under King Croesus reformed the monetary system. Previously, coins were an alloy, "electrum," made of varying amounts of silver and gold. The Lydians standardized the values by minting their own coins of pure metal, guaranteeing their quality and thus stimulating business. King Croesus was defeated by the Persian King Cyrus in 546 BC.

Within a few years, most of Anatolia was under Persian control, directed from Susa through their regional governors or satraps. That control continued for about two centuries. In general, it was a benign rule, the Persians mostly recruiting soldiers and levying taxes. One of their satraps, Pharnabazus, built a palace for himself in 546 BC on the shores of Lake Manyas east of Troy. His

Darius to engage them in a naval battle at Lade off their coast in which they were trounced. Darius went on to fight the Athenians only to be defeated himself at the Plains of Marathon in 490 BC.

In 1982, a particularly exciting discovery of a shipwreck was made off the Turkish mainland at Ulu Burun south of Kaş. The contents of the shipwreck, which was dated about 1400 BC, greatly expanded our knowledge of the cargo traded at this period and also of the people who had ties all around the Mediterranean.

The wreck held an amazing variety of objects: tin, glass and ostrich eggshells, for instance. Its cargo in large part was raw

palace garden was distinguished for its "paradise of birds" – a distinction that has lasted into the present time.

South, in Lycia, the many tombs from this period have made the region fascinating. They include pillar tombs (such as the Harpy Tomb in Xanthus with its original frieze now exhibited in the British Museum), house tombs and temple tombs (such as at Myra) and sarcophagi (as in Sidyma, Fethiye and Antiphellus/Kaş).

Ionian uprising: A rebellion by Ionians of Miletus led to their sacking the Persian stronghold of Sardis in 495 BC. This in turn immediately provoked the Persian King

materials. Copper ingots – six tons of them – shaped like animal hides may have been molded in Ugarit in Syria just south of the Antakya border. Ivory may have come from Syria or India. Amber – a puzzle about what its commercial use was – seems to have come from the Balkans.

Nubian ebony: Some pottery came from Cyprus. There were vases from Mycenae and Crete, jewellery from Canaan, seals from Egypt, and ebony from Nubia. Some of the items from the wreck were identified from pictures on Egyptian tombs; one Mycenaean kylix-cup helped date the wreck because of its popularity during the 15th century BC. A gold chalice indicated that part of the cargo may have been intended as a royal present, while a gold scarab was inscribed with the name Nefertiti. The large amount of copper suggested that an army was to be equipped with bronze helmets and swords, but which war they were to be used in and against whom is not known.

The finds are lodged now in the Museum of Underwater Archaeology in Bodrum while study of the wreck continues.

Cave man: Some of the early peoples in Anatolia lived in caves for at least part of the year. These caves, particularly in Beldibi, Karain and Belbaşı in the Antalya region, have preserved much evidence of the trans-

axes have been found from this early period. The stone tools were carefully balanced and shaped to fit neatly in a human hand. Archaeologists have experimented with the harvesting of wild wheat with these types of tools and have discovered that a month's work for a family could bring enough to sustain them for a year, with some to spare for barter.

Among the evidence of the changes that were taking place are the bones of domesticated animals, the sharp stones fashioned to fit sickle blades, the storage pits for harvested grain, and later the first man-built dwellings.

Elephants and hippopotamuses: The caves near Antalya have revealed, along with less

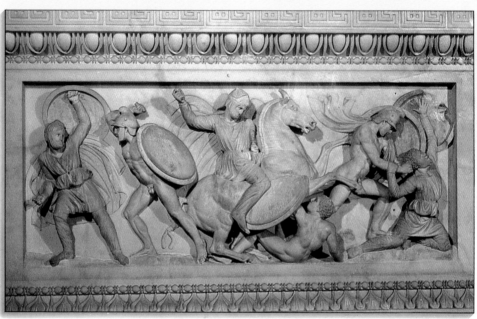

formation in peoples' lives 8,000 years ago.

Stone arrowheads discovered there are shaped to fit into a longer handle; they suggest that the people had begun to use both spears and bows. Tiny, sharp stones probably set along the edges of curved blades made sickles. These indicate the harvesting, but not yet the sowing of, grain. Some of the blades still retain a patina which shows long-time use. In both the Beldibi and Samandağ (west of Antakya) caves, scrapers and hand

Opposite page: left, frieze of a naked man; right, woman with a lyre. Above, a scene of fighting from the Alexander's Sarcophagus.

exotic remains, evidence of species of elephants and hippopotamuses. The Samandağ Cave also contained bones of rhinoceroses, red deer, porcupines, oxen and boars. It is possible that the first hunting by cave dwellers was done as they sailed and fished along the coast.

Pictures painted on the cave walls and scratched on pebbles left in the caves are usually of hunting scenes. These may well have had a religious significance – a prayer for success in the search for food, or an offering of thanks to the spirits of the dead animals. Some have a timeless aesthetic value: a rock carving of a leaping stag at the entrance of the Beldibi Cave shows the grace of a master artist. The painting of hunting scenes seems not to have continued long after the domestication of plants and animals, which lends strength to the hypothesis that the act was related to the need to insure a supply of food by making an appeal to the gods.

Some time later cult statues, particularly of the Mother Goddess, appear in rooms that probably were used for religious or funerary purposes. They seem to have a link with similar symbolism in both Neolithic Çatal Höyük south of Konya and in Crete.

Pottery is predated by stone, wood and woven baskets and bowls. It appears that

Cilicia is today's Çukurova, the fertile plain south of the Taurus Mountains. In Hittite times it was known as Kizzuwatna. Olba (Uzuncaburç) was important in the Hellenistic Period. Among the ruined buildings is a third-century BC Temple of Zeus with columns topped by Corinthian capitals still in place.

Tarsus and Mersin: Excavations at Tarsus and Mersin have unearthed stunning handmade pottery, which is like the early pottery found in the Karain Cave. Some of the earliest of these had patterns made by incising the wet clay.

The lowest level excavated at Mersin (Yümüktepe) revealed items from the Neo-

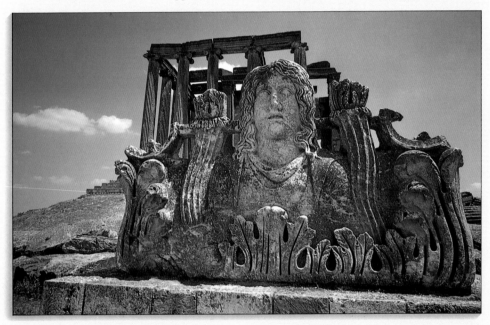

around 6500 BC the people living on the coast learned how to make pottery from those living on the Anatolian plain. There is a strong similarity between the pots found in Çatal Höyük and the first pots from the Antalya region.

Pamphylia was the coastal country that included the cities of Perge, Aspendos, Side and Alanya. Aspendos appears to have had connections with the Lesser Hittite King Asitawandas of Karatepe; its fifth century BC name was Estweddiya.

The city of Side was founded in the seventh century BC by colonists who arrived from Cyme, an Aeolian city just to the north of Izmir.

lithic Period. People had been living there earlier, but those levels have not been explored because they are under water. The walls of the Neolithic city were made of round pebbles perhaps from the stream bed or the sea. No mortar was used in their construction; this technique increased the life of the wall since mud mortar would have washed out in rainstorms, allowing the individual pebbles to be carried away.

Yümüktepe overlooked a trade route along the coast that went into central Anatolia through the Cilician Gates. The village's economy was stimulated by the trade in various items (in particular obsidian, a black volcanic glass), and it must have loaded its own merchandise onto the caravans to be sold in the interior. Perhaps sea shells found in the palace temple in Hattusa came from here.

The importance of obsidian: Obsidian was probably more valuable than sea shells because of its hardness and its quality of flaking with a sharp edge. Obsidian is valuable to archaeologists now for another reason: it is to be found naturally only in specific places around the volcanoes of Hasan Dağ, Erciyes Dağ and Karaca Dağ, which are in the interior of the country. When it appears in the early levels of Mersin and Tarsus, or in the Antalya caves, it indi-

The southern slopes of the Taurus mountains supported a number of smaller kingdoms whose inhabitants used Hittite hieroglyphics for their inscriptions but who themselves did not speak Hittite. Kizzuwatna remained Hittite after the collapse of the central Empire under Phrygian attack.

Lesser Hittite sites: One of these lesser Hittite settlements was at Karatepe on the Ceyhan River north of Adana. Fragments of a Hittite-Luwian and Phoenician bilingual inscription found at the small citadel there have helped to clarify some of the complex relationships among the Assyrians, the Urartians and the Late Hittite kingdoms.

cates both with whom the people were trading and that they had developed some level of commercial skills. Tarsus between 2700 and 2400 BC was a fortified town; its ruler was a minor king. Double-handled pottery produced there is like that found in Troy II and IV. Archaeologists think that this shape probably originated in Cilicia or further east around Islahiye and was carried north from there. A vase from Cilicia was found in the Fourth Dynasty tomb in Egypt, indicating a connection between those two areas too.

<u>Left</u>, the Temple of Zeus at Aizanoi. <u>Above</u>, the amphitheatre at Pamukkale.

Other evidences of the Hittites exist around Karatepe. South, near the village of Babaoğlan, is a castle (probably Roman in origin), and beside it is a rock carving of a man wearing the hat of a Hittite king. This suggests ties between Syria and the region of Hierapolis Castabala (now the village of Bodrum) a few miles beyond a bend of the Ceyhan River. The spectacular Castabala is distinguished now by a medieval fortress. Castabala was its Roman name; its king, Tarcondimotos, fought for Mark Antony and was killed at the Battle of Actium. Castabala was a Roman city built on some earlier Greek and Hittite settlements.

When Alexander the Great began his campaign to conquer the Persian Empire and free the Ionian Greek cities of Asia Minor in 334 BC, he fashioned himself in the likeness of Achilles and Heracles, from whom he claimed lineage. In less than one year Alexander, leader of the League of Corinth and the Macedonian army, swept through Asia Minor, liberated the Greek cities, re-established democracies, and introduced an advanced coinage standard that revolutionised trade and commerce. On his way to conquer the Persian Empire, Alexander paid tribute to his hero, Achilles, at Troy.

After visiting Troy, Alexander confronted his first Persian army at the Granicus River (modern Kocabaş River near the Sea of Marmara). This decisive battle demonstrated his enormous personal valour and the brilliance of his military tactics. The Persians set a trap for Alexander by forcing him to ford the river at a point where the banks were extremely steep so that his troops had difficulty in holding close formations. But Alexander courageously led his cavalry and broke the Persian line. Despite being wounded by a blow to the head, he succeeded in routing the Persians, massacring most of the Greek soldiers who fought with them. Alexander recovered quickly and sent the 2,000 surviving Greek mercenaries to Macedonia to work as slaves.

Persian panoplies: Alexander sent 300 Persian panoplies (sets of armour) taken at Granicus to Athens as an offering to Athena. The armour bore the inscription: "Alexander, son of Philip and the Greeks (except the Spartans) to the barbarians who inhabit Asia." Not only did this dedication omit Sparta but it also omitted the Macedonians who made up the largest part of Alexander's troops. Alexander chose not to call himself King but simply son of Philip, paying respect to the Greek's love of democracy.

From this victory he continued along the coast of Asia Minor, freeing Greek cities from Persian rule. He fought a long and difficult battle against the Persians at Halicarnassus (Bodrum). At Aspendos, the citizens requested not to be garrisoned. For this privilege, Alexander demanded a large sum of tribute as well as horses for his cavalry, for which Aspendos was famous. The citizens refused. Alexander responded by demanding an even higher tribute, and taking all the horses he needed.

However, many cities such as Ephesus, Side and Phaselis willingly opened their doors and treasuries to him. In the Greek cities Alexander won popularity by establishing Greek-style democracies in place of the oligarchies which had ruled under the Persians. He left in place the Persian ruling

system of *satraps* (provincial governers) but financial matters remained in the hands of Macedonians or Greeks.

Alexander's main achievement was to introduce Hellenistic culture to the east and change the ethnographic map forever. He left garrisons in many Greek towns along the coast, encouraging intermarriage and an exchange of culture with local communities. Along with his army and navy, Alexander also brought with him artists, poets, philosophers and historians to record and commemorate his adventures.

Above, bust and statue of Alexander the Great.

THE HELLENISTIC ERA

Even though Alexander failed to establish an empire in Asia that would foster a brotherhood of peoples, he laid the framework for a new era throughout Asia. The centuries following his death are known as the Hellenistic Age. This era, from 323 BC to 30 BC, was characterised by the demise of the Greek city-states and the establishment of large kingdoms, modelled on the Macedonian monarchy. This period saw the spectacular growth of trade and commerce and the development of a common culture made possible by use of the Greek language and the adoption of Greek institutions.

After Alexander's death, his newly established empire declined and the successors, the Diadichi, battled amongst themselves for 20 years.

Finally, three main kingdoms emerged: the Macedonians in Greece; the Seleucids in Syria; and the Ptolemies in Egypt. Control of western Asia Minor, however, fell outside of the three major empires, first ruled by one of Alexander's generals, Antigonus the One-Eyed, and later by another general, Lysimachus.

Monarchies: The new political order of this age was the large monarchical kingdom. These great monarchies, governed by autocratic rulers and vast bureaucracies, conflicted with the Greek love of autonomy.

However, since the Greeks were a major source for the development and defence of the state, the kings allowed the Greek city-states to assume a degree of independence within the monarchical territories. Some Greek city-states combined to form leagues or federations such as the Ionian League.

The large political units encouraged international trade, fostered urban economies and led to the adoption of common law. The most important cross-continental caravan route during the Hellenistic period began in India and stretched across the Persian Gulf to the Tigris, continued to Seleucia, the commercial capital of Asia, and finished at Ephesus. New evidence about trading activity is emerging suggesting that trade patterns were more developed than previously thought.

Modern research suggests that agriculture-based economies yielded a relatively small income as a proportion of total tax revenues. The exceptions were luxury textiles, such as wool and gold-weave cloth, and slaves. Items like olives, wool, grain, wine and timber were export staples but the import and export of slaves was a more lucrative source of revenue. Central regions of Anatolia were rich sources for slaves and slave markets and Side was one of the most important transshipment points.

Sculpture flourished in the Hellenistic Age in Pergamum and along the Aegean Coast. The Gauls who invaded Anatolia in the second century provided material for two innovative schools of art at Pergamum in the first and second centuries BC. Sculptors depicted the Gauls as noble fighters.

Stoics and cynics: Strong interest in philosophy also grew during this period as the old gods of Olympus failed to satisfy intellectual curiosity. Although the Greeks and Hellenised natives continued to follow the old religions there was a concurrent growth of king worship, mystery cults and magic. The Stoics, the Cynics, the Skeptics and the Epicurians evolved reflecting a new growth of individualism and humanism.

The most important instruments facilitating the growth of philosophy in the Hellenistic Era were the new libraries established in Pergamum, Antioch and Alexandria.

Grandiose architecture: There was a trend towards the ornate and the grandiose in architecture during the Hellenistic period in Asia Minor. Due to a declining interest in religion and the city-state there was a significant decrease in the number of temples built. The new emphasis on ornate decoration was reflected in the popularity of the Corinthian order. Hellenised Greeks favoured temples with an increasing number of columns and more elaborate sculptural detail.

In summary, while the Hellenistic Age represented a period of extensive material gain it was also a time of great poverty among the lower classes. The forces of the day nurtured a new spirit of individualism and man believed himself more and more a citizen of the world. Conversely, large kingdoms exerted more control over the lives of individuals.

Although the Roman armies first set foot in Asia Minor in 190 BC for the purpose of defending Greece which was under attack from Antiochus III, this advance set the stage for Rome's eventual domination of the entire Mediterranean basin. For many years, Rome cultivated strong alliances with kingdoms in Asia Minor in order to protect its boundaries. In particular, Rome relied on Pergamum to control smaller kingdoms in Asia Minor and to act as a buffer state between Rome and the Seleucid Empire. Demonstrating its strong allegiance to Rome, Eumenes II of Pergamum supported Rome's campaign in Greece and Asia Minor. In the face of a strong enemy army at the final Battle of Magnesia, Eumenes' troops proved essential for the Roman victory. This decisive battle put an end to Seleucid rule in Asia Minor and Rome acquired the vast territory ruled by Antiochus III.

The Romans were reluctant to take on the governing of yet another large province so soon after acquiring Greece. Therefore they handed the province over to Eumenes who agreed to administer the kingdom and strictly adhere to Rome's foreign policy. This relationship ensured that western Asia Minor was governed in the interests of Rome but the responsibility of rule lay with the Pergamene kings.

The last Pergamene king, Attalus III, was radically different from his predecessors. He was unpopular as a ruler and pursued his personal interests in botany and pharmaceutical sciences rather than his responsibilities as king. He had no heirs. Therefore, to prevent the rise of petty tyrants who would likely take over in the absence of a strong rule, he bequeathed the royal possessions of Pergamum and the supremacy of western Asia Minor to Rome in 133 BC.

Roman province: Rome responded to the bequest by immediately appointing a five-member commission to take control of the new province of Asia. When the commission reached Asia in 132 BC, the country was in a state of civil war. The new government faced resistance from Aristonicus, an illegitimate son of Eumenes, who had the backing of the poor and the landless peasantry. In expectation of greater freedom under the Romans, the free cities refused to support Aristonicus. The cities had fought alone until 131 BC when an army was raised in Rome under the consul Crassus. The support of the city of Ephesus helped turn the war in favour of the Romans. In 129 BC Aristonicus was defeated by the Roman general Aquilius, who put down the final stages of the revolt and set about organizing the new Roman province of Asia.

Rome's political and economic measures for the new province of Asia resulted in hardship for most citizens. Annually appointed governors from Rome were largely uninformed and ignorant of local issues and citizens' needs. Moreover, the people did not feel the same reverence and respect towards the new Roman governors who, unlike their predecessors, were not patrons of the arts.

Exploiting the masses: While some of the governors including Aquilius made contributions to civil life in the province, a large number used their positions to extort taxes from the local people. For example, following the civil war when local governments were in a state of depression, high taxes were levied by the government in order to meet wartime expenses.

Through direct contacts with the Greeks in Asia Minor, Romans were greatly influenced by Greek religion and culture. Children of upper class Roman families learned to speak and read Greek. The Romans, fascinated by Greek literature and philosophy, translated Homer, and copied their forms in writing Rome's epic histories.

The founding of Constantinople as the new capital in AD 330 by Constantine I resulted in a shift of the imperial centre to the east. The division of the Empire into East and West gradually assimilated Roman Asia Minor into the Greco-Anatolian world. By the time the western Roman Empire collapsed in the fifth century, the assimilation was complete, and the Latin Roman Empire had been replaced by the Greek-dominated Byzantine Empire, which lasted until the Ottoman conquest in the 15th century.

Right, Cleopatra captivated men.

ANTONY AND CLEOPATRA

When Antony summoned Cleopatra to Tarsus in 41 BC to confront her with charges of scheming to support his enemies, the stage was set for one of the greatest love affairs in history, Antony's own tragic downfall, and the transformation of the Roman Republic to the Roman Empire. Antony was seeking to enhance his prestige in Rome, secure the eastern boundaries, as well as avenge Rome's only defeat at the hands of the Parthians. He was in desperate need of troops and money to campaign and conquer the Parthians. Cleopatra's objectives were nothing less than the restoration of the Egyptian Empire as it had existed under Ptolemy II Philadelphus. She was willing to trade the wealth of Egypt to Antony for the support of the Roman legions. In his brilliant tragedy, *Antony and Cleopatra*, Shakespeare describes Cleopatra's dramatic arrival at Tarsus to meet Antony:

For her own passion,
It beggar'd all descrip-
*   tion: she did lie*
In her pavilion cloth-of-
*   gold of tissue*
O'er picturing that
*   Venus where we see*
The fancy outwork
nature: on each side her
Stood pretty dimpled
*   boys, like smiling*
*   Cupids*

Antony captivated: If Antony had not been captivated by Cleopatra the first time he met her in Rome when she was Julius Caesar's mistress, he was taken captive now. Antony delayed his plans to conquer the Parthians. The two returned to Egypt where they spent the winter as lovers.

In 40 BC Antony returned to Rome to re-establish his position in the empire and resolve his differences with Octavian, ruler of the western half of the Roman Provinces. Also during this period he married Octavian's sister Octavia. Beginning with his absence in Egypt, Antony's power slowly declined while Octavian fortified his position within the empire, secured the western boundaries and won popular support. In order to re-establish his power in the east, Antony again waged war against the Parthians.

Four years after their last meeting, Antony summoned Cleopatra, this time to Antioch, in order to marshal support for his campaign. In return for Cleopatra's financial backing, Antony gave the Egyptian Queen part of Phoenicia and northern Judea and promised to wed her and legitimise her children. Although defeated, Anthony returned to Cleopatra who provided him with money and supplies. Octavia, sent by Octavian, also came to Antony's rescue, but he sent her back precipitating a break between the two leaders.

Xenophobic fervour: Tensions between Antony and Octavian accelerated in 34 BC when Antony, celebrating victory in Armenia, staged a ceremony in which Cleopatra was pronounced Queen of Kings with Roman territories given to her children. Octavian destabilised Antony's position among the Roman legions by rousing xenophobic fervour against Cleopatra. In 32 BC, Octavian declared war against Cleopatra.

Antony assembled a navy at Ephesus to prepare for battle with Octavian. He was once again assisted by Cleopatra, although she was of little help. She had little to gain from his victory against Octavian, for if Antony won the battle he would return to Rome in triumph, out of her influence and back into the arms of Octavia. What followed was the decisive battle at Actium in 31 BC, where Antony realised his absolute defeat. Conquered and with no hope for a reconciliation with Rome, the lovers returned together to Alexandria where first Antony, then Cleopatra, committed suicide.

All along the Turkish Coast are places where the two lovers supposedly romanced. Antony purchased the city of Coracesium (today's Alanya) for Cleopatra to express his love for her. At Cedrae, an ancient island city in the Gulf of Gökova, Antony was purported to have transported the fine silt sand of its beach (known as Cleopatra's Beach) from the Nile to satisfy his lover. Travellers can also visit Cleopatra's Hamam in the Gulf of the Fethiye where the Egyptian sovereign allegedly built baths, which are now partly submerged as a result of earthquakes. ∎

By foot over hot, dusty roads, by bouncing horsecart and by sailboat, St. Paul the Apostle journeyed the length of the eastern coast of Anatolia from Antioch-on-the-Orontes (Antakya) to Alexandria Troas (Odun Iskelesi south of Troy) during the middle years of the first century.

"I have been constantly on the road," Paul subsequently wrote. "I have met dangers from rivers, dangers from robbers, dangers from my fellow-countrymen, dangers from foreigners, dangers in towns, dangers in the country, dangers at sea, dangers from false friends. I have toiled and drudged, I have often gone without sleep; hungry and thirsty, I have often gone fasting; and I have suffered from cold and exposure."

Beginning with Antioch about AD 40, Paul's influence and that of the early disciples spread Christianity throughout the eastern Mediterranean. Three centuries later Christianity had become the major religion of Asia Minor.

The tentmaker: Paul was born in Tarsus in AD 10, which is today a busy city on the eastern Mediterranean coast. As a boy he learned the trade of tentmaking, subsequently becoming a rabbi and Pharisee. While studying in Jerusalem he was an accomplice in the stoning of Stephen, the first Christian martyr. But later, after seeing a vision of Jesus, he devoted himself to preaching the word of Christ.

Paul's career as a disciple started when a follower of Jesus, Barnabas, called him to work in Antioch (Antakya) in AD 43.

The people that Paul met in Antioch greatly influenced his thinking. Of those attending the synagogue, there were Gentiles who had been attracted to the moral virtues they found in Judaism. Paul held firmly to the prime article of Jewish law: "The lord is our God, one Lord."

While other Jews believed they could be faithful to the law only by keeping to their own community, for Paul, God's very oneness meant that Jesus, who announced God's kingdom, was calling to all the people. Thus Paul's mission came to be focused on the Gentiles.

Paul was not always successful. He re-sented it when his companions, John, Mark and Barnabas, found him overzealous. Even in some of the churches he founded there were many who did not like him. He often ran foul of the law and was imprisoned more than once for his beliefs.

It is often thought that Paul's bitter experiences only reinforced his inner certitude that he could understand and communicate across the ages his insight into Christ's teachings as the fulfilment of the law.

Considering that St. John wrote to the Christians in Laodicea (near Pamukkale), Thyatira (Akhisar), Sardis (east of Izmir), and Philadelphia (Alaşehir), which could have been on Paul's route between Galatia, Phrygia and Ephesus, it is quite possible that Paul had visited them in addition to Ephesus where we know he spent a lot of time. It is also possible that he went to the others of John's "Seven Churches of Revelation" (Smyrna and Pergamum, or Izmir and Bergama as they are called now).

Antioch-on-the-Orontes was an important commercial and educational centre, endowed with handsome public buildings. Known as a sports and recreation centre, celebrations honouring Apollo were held at the Temple to Daphne in a sacred wood southwest of the city.

Its bustling population of nearly a half million people sheltered an influential Jewish element. Some of these people had fled Jerusalem during the persecutions of people who were friends of Stephen. In Antioch, the movement grew, and soon its members began using a name – Christians, the followers of Christ – to identify themselves.

Expulsion: From this church in Antioch, Paul and his companions set out to broadcast their message abroad. Sailing to Cyprus and then to Perge, Paul preached his first sermon to the congregation at the synagogue in Pisidian Antioch (Yalvaç between Konya and Afyon). The crowd he attracted was largely Gentile, and the Jewish members so resented their intrusion that they had Paul and Barnabas expelled from the district.

A prolific writer, Paul also spread the word by writing letters to the Romans and other religious leaders. Many of these are the earliest examples of extant Christian texts.

The disciples then moved to Iconium (Konya). Again they preached to a large group of people, and they narrowly escaped a plot to stone them. However, one young woman of Iconium, called Thecla, was so captivated by Paul's preaching that she braved scorn and danger to follow him.

A 2nd-century book, *The Acts of Paul and Thecla*, was written about her exploits and it names her as Christianity's first female martyr. The book also gives a description of Paul: he was short and bald, had hollow eyes and a hooked nose, but was so full of grace that he seemed sometimes like a man and sometimes like an angel. Thecla later lived

as a nun and established a hospital at Ayatekla, south of Silifke.

In his first journey, Paul concentrated on Anatolian cities. Later, he spent longer periods of time in the major ports, hoping to convert people to Christianity.

Paul was twice in Alexandria Troas, a thriving Aegean port just south of today's Odun Iskelesi. Even though he did not stay there very long, Christian theologians associate this with the dawn of European Christendom, even though believers were already

Above, mosaic of Jesus at Hagia Sophia Museum, Istanbul.

ensconced in Rome. Perhaps it was no mere coincidence that it was at this time that Luke, a devout disciple of Christian gospel, appeared on the scene. It is unfortunate that the records of the other apostles, who worked in Egypt or in the East, have not been preserved as well as Luke's account has been.

One of these accounts describes a time when Paul was back in Alexandria Troas on his third journey. He and his friends were up late into the night discussing Christ's teachings. Suddenly a child who had been perched in a window fell out and landed three floors down on the ground. Paul dashed out to find the boy and was able to reassure his family that no harm was done and he was only badly shaken up. The discussions resumed where they had broken off.

Ephesus attracted pilgrims from all over the Mediterranean because of its Temple to Diana. Its theatre, Temple to Serapis, Celsius library, odeon, and gymnasiums are just some of the grand public buildings that give us today a sense of the wealth of community life when Paul was there.

Performing miracles: For two years Paul stayed in Ephesus teaching the word of Christ, converting people to Christianity, and performing his miracles of healing. By then many people had joined the Christian community.

However, the silversmiths' trade in cult objects was hurt by Paul's condemnation of idols. The merchants created a serious disturbance during which a crowd collected in the theatre yelling, "Great is Diana of the Ephesians!" The demonstration threatened to turn nasty until the town clerk warned the crowd that, while Paul was within the law, they were not.

At the end of Paul's third journey he stopped in Miletus to visit the leading members of the church in that region. His farewell speech to his friends was full of meaning and he reminded them of their long friendship and of how he had taught them everything he knew.

Paul was a controversial figure in the early church, partly because of the mixture in his teachings of Hebraic and Greek thought. In AD 58 he was arrested and sent to Rome, imprisoned and eventually martyred. The controversy over his teachings and his contributions to Christian philosophy continue to this day.

THE BYZANTINES AND THE CRUSADES

In AD 1070, the advancing Seljuk Turks took Jerusalem from the Arab Fatamids, and in the following year they all but annihilated the Byzantine army at Malazgirt (Manzikert) and captured Emperor Romanus IV Diogenes. Within 20 years, the Seljuk armies had overrun most of Anatolia and towered across the Bosphorus, casting a dark shadow over Constantinople itself (1092). The Byzantine Empire, which for seven centuries had held back Asian hordes, could no longer fulfil its historical mission as the European bulwark against eastern invasions. Constantinople itself was threatened.

Fearing the worst, Emperor Alexius I (1081–1118) joined Simeon, Patriarch of Jerusalem, in urging papal aid to drive back the Turks. The appeal was seconded by several prospering Italian cities: Pisa, Genoa, Venice and Amalfi. These Italian cities wanted to end Arab Moslem domination in the eastern Mediterranean and open the markets of the Near East to European trade.

Pope Urban II, dreaming of a united Christendom, took to the road in 1095, sounding out leaders and ensuring support for a crusade against the Moslem Turks. One cold November morning at Clermont in Auvergne, he made one of the most influential speeches in medieval times:

"O race of Franks! Race beloved and chosen by God!… From the confines of Jerusalem and from Constantinople a grievous report has gone forth that an accursed race, wholly alienated from God, has invaded the lands of these Christians, and has depopulated them… Jerusalem, that royal city, situated at the centre of the earth, implores you to come to her aid."

The First Crusade: Now, after centuries of argument, the two great faiths, Christianity and Islam, resorted to war. In the meantime, the Seljuk Turks, "the accursed race", did not speak of Crusades, but of Frankish (French) wars, or of the "Frankish invasions." In July 1096, Kılıç Arslan, whose father, Süleyman, was the first Turk to secure lands from the Byzantines, learned that a huge number of Franks were en route to Constantinople. Not yet 17, Seljuk Emperor Kılıç Arslan already controlled most of Anatolia.

These Occidentals were nothing like the kind of enemy armies to which the Turks were accustomed. There were several hundred knights and a large number of foot soldiers, but there were also children and old people in rags, with strips of cloth in the shapes of crosses sewn onto the backs of their garments. This army looked "more like a wretched tribe evicted from their lands by some invader," thought the Turks.

Walter the Penniless: By the time the Crusaders, who set out from France in 1095

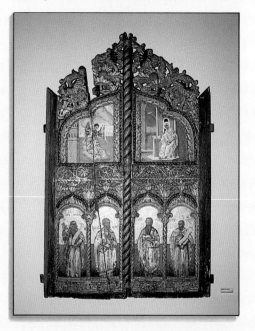

under Peter the Hermit and Walter the Penniless, arrived in Constantinople in 1096, they had been decimated by famine, plague, leprosy, fever and battles on the way. Byzantine Emperor Alexius welcomed them but could not provide enough food, so they broke into the suburbs and plundered churches, houses and palaces. In his haste to free Constantinople from these locusts, Alexius gave them ships to cross the Bosphorus and advance on Iznik where Kılıç

Preceding pages, a caravan passes the remains of the Church of St. John in Pergamum. **Above**, Byzantine icon from the Antalya Museum.

Arslan's bowmen awaited. The Seljuk forces marched out of the city and almost wiped out the First Crusaders. Walter the Penniless was among the slain, while Peter the Hermit fled to Constantinople.

In 1097 new Crusader armies crossed the straits and besieged Iznik. Kılıç Arslan retreated only to face them in Şarhöyük (Doryleaum) near Eskişehir. "The Franks cut the Turkish army to pieces. They killed, pillaged and took many prisoners who were sold to slavery," wrote Ibn al-Qalansi, an Arab chronicler from Damascus. When this event, so shameful for Islam, became known, dread and anxiety swelled to enormous proportions.

In October 1097, the Franks were in Antioch, then Syria's largest city. Two years later, they occupied Jerusalem. "Wonderful things were to be seen," reported the eyewitness Raymond Agiles. "Numbers of Saracens were beheaded. Others were shot with arrows, or forced to jump from the towers; others were tortured for several days and then burned alive. In the streets were seen piles of corpses of men and horses." More than 70,000 Moslems and hundreds of Jews were killed by the Crusaders.

Latin Jerusalem: Thus founded, the Latin Kingdom of Jerusalem lasted 44 years (1099–1143). In 1144, Zengi, a young slave-born *atabey*, or Seljuk military leader, recaptured Urfa for Islam. His successor, Nurettin, of equal courage and greater ability, took over. The Moslem resurgence compelled St. Bernard to appeal to the Pope for a new crusade. In 1147, the German Emperor Conrad III set out with his army followed by French King Louis VII. They took the route of the First Crusade. At Şarhöyük, where the First Crusade had defeated Kılıç Arslan, Conrad's army met the Turkish forces commanded by Seljuk Sultan Mesud I, and was so soundly defeated that hardly one Christian in ten survived.

The French army was decimated by starvation and Moslem raids. The collapse of the Second Crusade stunned Europe.

In the 40 years of peace that followed the Second Crusade, Nurettin spread his kingdom from Aleppo to Damascus. When he died, Selahattin Eyyubi (Saladin the Great) brought Egypt and Moslem Syria under one rule (1175). A four-year truce with the Latin Kingdom came to an end in 1188 when Reginald waylaid a Moslem caravan, taking rich booty and a number of prisoners, including Selahattin's sister. Saladin responded by attacking Reginald's army at Hittin. He then turned to Jerusalem, which fell after a siege.

The Third Crusade: Encouraged by the Italian fleet's domination of the Mediterranean, and Christian control of Tyre, Antioch and Tripolis, Emperor Frederick Barbarrosa set out for Jerusalem in the Third Crusade. The Turks quickly harassed his army and cut off his supplies; hundreds of Christian soldiers starved to death and the Emperor drowned (1190) while bathing in the Göksu River near Adana. Richard I (The Lionheart), the newly crowned King of England, took over. Accompanied by Philip Augustus, the King of France, Richard reached and freed Acre (1191). At this time, Philip, ill with fever, returned to France. After a few indecisive battles Richard was able to advance within 12 miles of Jerusalem, but he too fell ill and sued for peace.

The Fourth Crusade (1202–1204) was led by the Venetian Republic, which agreed to the campaign on condition that it took half of the spoils of the conquest. However, the Venetian Doge had no intention of attacking the Holy Lands. Instead he aimed at conquering Christian Constantinople. The prospect of capturing the richest city in Europe was irresistible, and threats of excommunication fell on deaf ears. The Venetian fleet sailed for Constantinople, capturing the Hungarian port of Zara on the way. In the past, the Greek Orthodox Church of the Byzantine monarchy had offered little help, but had profited immensely from the Latin Crusades: it had regained most of Asia from the Turks and had been happily watching the mutual weakening of Moslems and Latins in their struggle for Palestine. But the time had come for them to pay.

The Venetian armada was before Constantinople on June 24, 1204. The Crusaders landed and set the city on fire. The blaze raged for eight days, spread through three square miles and turned a considerable section of the city to ashes. Soldiers looted homes, churches and shops. St. Sophia's great altar was torn to pieces for its silver and gold. Thousands of art masterpieces were plundered or damaged. The capture of Constantinople by the Latins laid the foundation for Turkish occupation.

THE TURKS

Who, indeed, were these Turks that appeared in the Western world, upset its traditions, changed its course and infuriated Pope Urban II into malediction: "that accursed race!"? Ancient historians called them the "scourge of God," and were terrified. Yet, even the most prejudiced admitted that they were not savages. They had a sense of honour and justice, and often proved themselves "more magnanimous than the Romans". They ate and drank moderately, lived and dressed simply, their only ornamentation being their delicate embroidery.

Steppes people: The Turks originated from the steppes of Central Asia. Geologists tell us that today's arid regions of Central Asia were once much coveted land, nourished with great lakes and rivers. The recession of the last ice age dried up this area and as rainfall was insufficient to support the people, cities were abandoned as they migrated in search of water.

Historical records show the proto-Turkish tribes settled somewhere between the Ural and Altay mountains *circa* 1400–1200 BC, about the time when Jewish tribes appeared in Canaan. They spoke one of the 14 "Turkic" languages, which are neither Semitic nor Indo-Aryan, but agglutinate in structure. Semi-nomadic, the Turks cultivated land, raised animals and worshipped a *Sky Tengrı* (*"tengri"* from "tien," the heavens; *"tanrı"* in contemporary Turkish) and other lesser gods of the sun, the moon, the earth, the ancestors and the fire. Their beliefs differed sharply from Greco-Roman paganism. Turkish cosmology did not offer a scene where gods fought with man to keep him in his place, but provided a serene and fraternal relationship. In his capacity as the elder brother, *Sky Tengrı* taught them every worldly thing they needed for survival, including how to light fire.

As the desert expanded, the steppes shrank, and nomadic tribes were forced to take refuge in oases and adapt to a settled life. Thus the region served as a *"vegina gentium,"* a peoples' womb, which raised kings and sultans to the civilised empires.

Left, a Turkish Zeybek warrior.

However, there was another law at work: that the old empires eventually absorbed the invading Turks who settled to become a minority aristocracy. The two oldest civilisations of the world, the Chinese and the Persians, assimilated them so that within 50 years the invaders had become passionate defenders of their adopted civilisations and religions.

Seljuks: The Empire of the Great Seljuk Turks was based in Persia and thrived from 1037 to 1109 AD. Seljuk armies advanced west and eventually occupied and controlled much of Anatolia. But a new threat appeared in the form of the Mongols. These were a loose assortment of unruly tribes united and disciplined by Genghis Khan (1167–1227) into a superb and terrifying fighting force who would conquer the Seljuks and strike deep into Europe. They could be said to be the first proponents of war as a science.

The Seljuk Empire succumbed but a few remnants survived in Anatolia, most notably in Konya. This was the Sultanate of rum, and the most stunning examples of Seljuk architecture and tile work can be seen here.

A refugee from Iran was Jalal ad-din Rumi, the founder of the Sufi Dervish sect of Nevlana, whose origins are still embodied in Konya. Another who fled the Mongols in Central Asia was Ertuğrul, who had many followers in Bursa. When Ertuğrul died (1288), he was succeeded by his son Osman (Othman), the eponymous founder of the Ottoman Empire. Seeing the Seljuks were too weak to stop him, Osman declared himself an independent *bey* (ruler) of a mini-state in northwestern Anatolia.

Between him and the Sea of Marmara lay a number of Byzantine cities. The most important among them, Bursa, surrendered to his son, Orhan, who made it his new capital (1326). Orhan took the title "Sultan of the Ottomans". The Byzantine Emperors made peace with him, gave him their daughters in marriage and allowed, begrudgingly, his son Süleyman to establish Ottoman strongholds on European soil. When Orhan Bey died in 1359, the Ottomans were well on their way to forming a dynasty.

Murat I (Ameurth) conquered most of the

The Turks 49

Balkans; Dimetoka fell to him in 1361, Filibe in 1363 and Sophia in 1389. He eased their submission by giving them a more efficient government than they had known under Christian rule, and made Edirne (Adrianopolis) his new capital. Beyazıt I, the "Thunderbolt", inherited his father's crown on the battlefield of Kosova, near Mitrovica, Yugoslavia in 1389. He besieged Constantinople four times. In his grandfather's tradition he married a Christian woman, Lady Despoina, sister of Lazerevitch, the ruler of Serbia.

Tamerlane: A new threat appeared from the East in the form of Tamerlane of Genghis Khan's stock. Tamerlane's army had recently taken Baghdad (1393), forcing its Arab sultan, Ahmed, to seek asylum with Beyazıt I. When Beyazıt refused to extradite Ahmed, Tamerlane entered Asia Minor. In 1402, the two kinsmen joined in battle near Ankara. A year later Beyazıt died a prisoner. Constantinople rejoiced, Christendom was saved from the Moslems for another 50 years to come. As Tamerlane's army marched back to Central Asia, Beyazıt's son, Mehmet I, reorganised the Ottoman state, which was in disarray. Mehmet I left his son Murat II to subdue Hunyadi Janos in the Balkans. When Murat II died after 30 years of rule, Christian historians ranked him among the greatest monarchs of his time.

Sultan Mehmet II, "The Conquerer," spoke five languages, excelled in mathematics and engineering, cultivated the arts, supported colleges and pious foundations. He is said to have equalled his father in culture and conquests, political acumen, and even the length of reign. It was to his cannons that Constantinople fell (1453), changing the course of European and Ottoman history.

In conquering Constantinople, the Ottomans took over a feature peculiar to the Byzantine Empire: they allowed the existence in the capital of colonies established by the European city-states of Genoa, Amalfi, Pisa, Venice, Ancona and Narbonn. Granted trading privileges and tax exemptions, these foreign enclaves were allowed to manage their religious and administrative affairs and to conduct their own legal and judicial business. The conquerer would not, however, permit these foreign elements to retain their military strength. He dismantled their fortifications, but did not concern himself with the manner in which these Franks lived and traded. The capitulations of 1521 confirmed those privileges that the Venetians had enjoyed under the Byzantines. This was followed by those concessions granted to France (1536) and England (1580). In addition to commercial and navigational rights, these treaties allowed the European powers to appoint consuls in the Ottoman dominions and gave them jurisdiction in civil matters over their own nationals. Subsequent French capitulations gave the French kings the right to protect every Roman Catholic of non-Turkish nationality in all parts of the Ottoman Empire.

"Millet" system: Thus arose a characteristic administrative feature of the Ottoman Empire: the millet system. Millet is the Arabic word for "nation," and in this case it meant the sultans granted varying degrees of autonomy to their non-Moslem subjects. The millet of Rum (Romans), for instance, consisted of those who obeyed the Greek Orthodox Patriarch, and the Armenian millet consisted of those subject to the Gregorian Armenian Patriarch. The development of the system meant that the Turks themselves became members of a millet – millet of Islam, for sure, but a minority amongst Arabs, Kurds and the rest. The name "Turk" came to denote a vulgar brethren back in Turkestan. In 1828, a Scottish traveller, Charles MacFarlane, would say that the Turks "indeed consider our word Turk insulting. I remember seeing a poor Greek well kicked for exclaiming 'Turkikos!' where he thought no Turk would hear him!"

The steppes had supplied the sultans, but the Ottoman melting pot had engulfed the horsemen so fast that of 292 grand viziers of the Ottoman Empire, only 78 could claim Turkish parentage.

Sultan Mehmet the Conquerer died (1481) at the age of 51, just when his army seemed to be on the verge of conquering Italy. A contest among his sons gave the throne to Beyazıt II, a reluctant warrior who nevertheless managed to build an armada of 270 vessels and destroy the Venetian fleet off the coast of Greece. In 1512, he left his throne to his son Selim I.

The Grim: Sultan Selim I, known in the west as Selim The Grim, despised his father's pacifism. He started out by campaigning against Shah Ismail of Iran who had raided the Turkish frontier. Capturing Tabriz, he made northern Mesopotamia an Ottoman province. He then turned his army against Syria, Arabia and Egypt (1517) and carried the caliphate to Istanbul. Thereafter, the Ottoman sultans, as caliphs, also became spiritual leaders of the Moslem world.

Süleyman the Magnificent succeeded his father as sultan at the age of 26. Francis I had been proposing since 1516 to the European powers that they should utterly destroy the Ottoman state and divide its possessions among themselves as infidel spoils. Süleyman himself supposed that the best defence was offence. In 1521, he captured the Hun-

possessions in the Aegean and the Dalmatian Coast (1540). Four years later, at the age of 72, the master of Egypt, North Africa, Asia Minor, Palestine, Syria, the Balkans and Hungary was dead. The Ottomans were the strongest power in Europe and Africa.

Until Süleyman's death, the only limit to Ottoman advance seemed to be determined by their ambitions. Then there set in, at the end of the 16th century, a period of standstill, when the Christian powers began to challenge Turkish supremacy. Following a temporary revival, under the vigorous Köprülü family of grand viziers, of military ardour and success which terminated in the second siege of Vienna (1683), stagnation

garian strongholds of Szabacs and Belgrade. In 1523 Rhodes fell. Hungary joined the Empire in 1526, amid cheers from Protestants, for Luther had urged the Protestant princes to stay home, "for the Turks were obviously a divine visitation and to resist them would be to resist God." Three years later, Süleyman returned and unsuccessfully besieged Vienna (1539). On the way back to Istanbul, his army ravaged southern Austria. He returned west again (1539), where Venice bore the brunt of his assault, losing its

and decline set in. The Peace of Carlowitz (1699) marked the beginning of the end of the Ottomans. The next blow came with the Treaty of Küçük Kaynarca (1774) signed with Russia, now consolidated under the House of Romanov. Soon the Russians opened up the Black Sea, which for two centuries had been a Turkish lake, to commerce and navigation. Within a decade, Crimea and Caucasia were both under Russian rule.

The decline continued into the 19th century, despite reforms of the armed forces, and establishment of a Council of State, a Penal Code and a State bank, institutions

Above, Ottoman Janissary band plays martial music.

which were to prove abortive in practice.

Iron Fist rule: The 1877–1878 Russian War was a disaster not to be forgotten. The Ottoman empire lost most of its European possessions. Greece had already gained its independence in 1830. With Sultan Abdülhamit, the Ottomans wooed the Moslem nations under their rule and found a new ally in the West: Germany, which helped build the Baghdad Railway, a project that facilitated traffic to the holy cities of Arabia and reinforced the Turkish ruler's position as Caliph. For 30 years he ruled with an iron fist, keeping the country out of major foreign wars, but Abdülhamit could not cure the ills of the empire, and in 1909, he was

began the three-year national struggle for independence.

Under Kemal, Turkish nationalism was ignited, the Greek army was defeated and the French were pushed back. Italy withdrew its troops. The allied powers signed an armistice in 1922. The Treaty of Lausanne (1923) recognised Turkey's present boundaries, and allowed for the exchange of minorities between Greece and Turkey.

The Republic: Turkey was proclaimed a republic on 29 October 1923, with Ankara as the capital, and Mustafa Kemal was elected its first president.

Sweeping reforms were carried out by Kemal to Westernise the nation. The Sultan-

Smyrne

Le port et le Mont Pagus

toppled from power. The Committee of Union and Progress, which replaced him with a puppet sultan, convened Parliament. But soon the empire was plunged into one war after another, culminating with its defeat in World War I, in which it had allied itself with Germany.

Istanbul was occupied by the British, while the Italians seized Antalya and the French occupied the Cilician coast. In May 1919 the Greek army invaded Izmir. Three days later Mustafa Kemal (later named Atatürk), the victorious commander of the Turkish forces at Gallipoli, arrived at the northeast Black Sea port of Samsun and

ate was abolished and the Caliphate suppressed. Atatürk replaced the Sharia, the Islamic Holy law, with civil, trade and criminal codes adopted from the West. Turks adopted last names.

In 1925, the *fez*, the symbol of Islamic Orthodoxy, was banned, replaced by the *şapka*, the Western-style hat with a brim. Atatürk said of the *fez*: "It is a badge of ignorance, indifference, backwardness and hostility to civilisation." He urged Turks to dress like Westerners because "it would help them think like Westerners".

In 1928, the Latin alphabet replaced the Ottoman script, severing Turks' ties with their past. The government in 1934 prohibited the use of the honorary Ottoman titles *ağa, efendi, bey,* and *pasha,* and even banned the playing of Oriental music on Turkish state radio – a ban that was later to be repealed. It also prohibited the wearing of traditional Islamic clothing.

In modern-day Turkey, the subject of headscarves worn by even moderate Islamic women remains a contentious one and has become a powerful symbol of religious defiance.

Womens' rights: Isolated from men and treated as second-class citizens during the Ottoman period, women in the republic were now encouraged to mix with men at parties,

invited to dinner with a Turkish acquaintance, a gentleman of the old school who touched neither alcohol nor coffee and kept his palate additionally uncontaminated by abstaining even from tobacco. For drinks at the meal my friend's host provided only water; but the water was of four different kinds, each served in a different carafe: one from the sweet waters of Europe, one from the sweet waters of Asia, the others respectively from Beykoz and Yeşilköy. He asserted that each of these waters had a special flavour and quality and recommended one for the fish, another for the *pilav*, the third for the sweet and the fourth for the fruit."

Vue des Quais et la Poste Hellénique
Ἄποψις Προκυμαίας, Ἑλληνικὸν Ταχυδρομεῖον

attend public functions, take jobs in the civil service and go to the theatre. Even beauty contests, unthinkable in the past, were encouraged. In 1932, a Turkish woman was crowned "Miss World". Turkish women were granted suffrage in 1934 and 18 women were elected deputies in 1936.

An English observer summed up the changes taking place in Turkey as follows: "One evening between the World Wars, a friend of mine, then representing a leading London newspaper in Constantinople, was

This episode took place during the brief Caliphate of Abdülmecit, when Turkey retained the forms, at all events, of an Islamic state. The host was perhaps exceptional in his connoisseurship of the finer points of water-drinking, but he was still a normal Turk in his abstention from liquor.

A bare quarter of a century later the Turkish government extolled the virtues of alcohol by claiming that in its Anatolian provinces originated some of the earliest and finest wines made by man. The government then inaugurated the export of Turkish wine of good quality, thereby ensuring its place as a permanent national industry.

Left, Izmir in the 19th century. **Above**, "Infidel Izmir" during the Greek occupation.

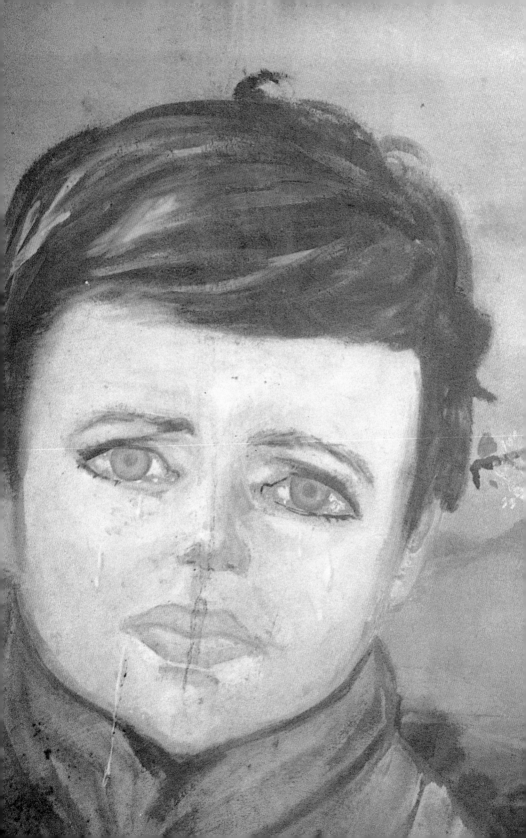

ISLAM

Throughout the tourist towns along Turkey's Aegean and Mediterranean coasts in the quiet early hours of the morning, after the discos and bars have sent their last customers home, another part of Turkish life begins. From the smallest village in the east to the capital of Ankara to the tourist centre of Marmaris, *muezzins* ascend to the tops of minarets to call faithful Moslems to morning prayer *(ezan)*.

The *muezzins* wail from the minarets: "Allah [God] is the great. Allah is great. I do testify that there is no god save Allah." It is a potent message.

According to their birth certificates, the Turkish population is 99 percent Moslem, mostly Sunni. Since the 1920s, due to Kemal Atatürk's religious reforms, Turkey has been a secular state. Therefore religious freedom is guaranteed to all non-Moslems.

During the Ottoman Empire a large number of minorities were free to practise various religions. Today, for example, a small community of Sephardic Jews remains in Istanbul and groups of Greek Orthodox, Armenian Orthodox and Catholics are scattered across the country.

Although Islam is the dominant religion in Turkey, it is practised in a wide variety of ways and rituals. It isn't surprising to see an elderly woman in the traditional Moslem dress, the *çarşaf*, covered from head to toe in black, with her teenage daughter decked out in jeans and a Michael Jackson t-shirt, walking side by side.

While the Koran, the Moslem holy book, forbids alcohol consumption, Turks of all ages drink beer and wine in restaurants and bars. In the southern resort towns, Turks wear the same relaxed and scanty clothing as other Europeans on holiday.

Secular Turkey: Atatürk, the architect of modern Turkey, believed firmly in a secular state. He abolished religious law and instituted in its place secular law. Also Islam was removed as the state religion and the day of rest was changed from Friday to Sunday like the Christian West. He also created a secular

school system. The Roman alphabet replaced the Ottoman script, which was based on Persian and Arabic, further separating Islam from education.

However, since the 1980s there has been an increasing interest in Islam. The 1982 constitution reinstated religious education in primary and secondary schools as a reaction to the growing militancy on university campuses in the late 1970s.

By the mid-1990s, the government and its military backers were becoming alarmed at the growing trend in schools where religion came first and literacy and numeracy skills were relegated to second place. So in 1997 they enacted an 8-year education bill, which raised the school leaving age to 15 years, thereby enraging the clerics, who now found their *imam-hatip* (preacher-parson) schools empty and the religious curriculum replaced by a secular, academic one.

There are two major religious holidays on the Islamic lunar calendar. Since the lunar calendar is approximately eleven days shorter than the Gregorian, Moslem holidays begin earlier each year. *Kurban Bayramı* (Sacrifice Festival), the most important religious holiday of the year, is equivalent to Christmas for Christians.

The festival observes God's intervention when Abraham wanted to sacrifice his son Isaac to God. According to Moslem belief, Allah ordered Abraham to slaughter a sheep instead of his son. *Kurban Bayramı* is a four-day religious affair. Several days prior to *Kurban Bayramı* shepherds drive flocks of sheep into the cities to be sold for slaughter. On the first day of the *bayramı* men go to the mosque early in the morning for prayer. After prayer, the head of the family slits the sheep's throat, skins and butchers it.

A simple meal of lightly spiced sauteed meat from the animal, called *kavurma*, is prepared in most homes. Tradition dictates that one-third of the meat is given to the poor, one-third or less is eaten by the family and one-third is given to relatives and friends. Today, however, many prefer to give money to a good cause instead.

Rigorous fasting: *Ramazan* (Ramadan) is the month of rigorous fasting where nothing

Left, Moslems gather for Friday prayers at Istanbul's Blue Mosque.

is drunk or eaten between sunrise and sunset. The fast is broken with flat round *pide* bread bought hot from bakeries at sundown. This is followed by complex meals of favourite foods, eaten in large quantities.

Just before dawn, drummers wake the faithful so that they can eat before sunrise. Many restaurants and shops will be closed for large parts of the day during *Ramazan* but it is still possible to find food. It's best to be discreet, even though you may see many non-Moslems and moderate Moslems eating in public.

The month of *Ramazan* ends in a three-day national holiday, known as the Sweet Holiday, or *Şeker Bayramı*. Sweets such as

first, and most important, is to bear witness that there is no God except Allah, and Mohammed is his prophet. The others are: to perform the five required daily prayers; those who are rich enough must pay legal alms once a year called *zekat*; fast during the holy month of *Ramazan*; and perform the holy pilgrimage to Mecca at least once in a lifetime if one is in good health and has the financial means.

Whirling dervishes: Whirling men in long white robes, their arms extended, dizzying only to the observer; these are the Mevlevi dervishes, members of an Islamic mystic order who perform the *Sema*, a religious dance accompanied by holy music.

baklava and *lokum* (Turkish Delight) are given as gifts.

Traditionally, prayers start at 4am and are repeated five times a day, becoming a dominant feature of Islamic life. Yet many Turks only go to pray on *bayrams* (religious holidays) or some even less frequently than that. Moslems do not have to go to the mosque to pray. Often shopkeepers and other workers spread out their small prayers mats in the direction of Mecca and pray.

Five pillars: The requirements of Islam, which literally means submission, are few and simple. For a believer to be a perfect Moslem he submits to five principles: the

It is a dance of ecstasy during which they reach a union with God. During the dance, the dervishes turn left around their own axis while circling the ceremonial area symbolising the movements of the planets around the sun. The palm of the right hand faces the sky and the left is turned toward the ground, signifying man receiving from God and contributing to the people.

The eerie ceremony is best seen during the week of the Festival of Mevlana in Konya, south central Turkey, in mid-December. In Istanbul, several groups of

Above, modern women also pray.

Mevlevi men and women perform their dance and mystic music to audiences at the Galata Mevlevihane (also known as Divan Edebiyah Museum) on the last Sunday of each month.

Mevlana Celaleddin Rumi, the great mystic poet, philosopher and founder of the whirling dervishes, was born in Ballkh in Central Asia in AD 1207. He preached to his disciples a union with God through music and dance. After his death in 1273, his followers, the Mevlevis, became closely connected with the ruling Ottomans.

Circumcision: Decked out in a fancy white suit, fur trimmed hat, cape and sparkling attachments, a young boy is led smiling by his mother to become a circumcised Moslem. Boys are typically circumcised between the ages of four and six, but it's more common in large towns to perform the operation at birth and celebrate the occasion later.

After the actual operation, which is performed in a hotel, circumcision house, or even hospital, a lavish party with close friends and family is held. The boy receives many gifts and money which is usually placed in an envelope and tucked under the pillow of his circumcision bed.

Sometimes mass circumcision parties are held, especially for orphans or boys of poor families, with one *fenni sünnetçi* (professional circumciser) carrying out as many as 1,000 operations in one session. The best known *sünnetçi* in Turkey, Kemal Özkan of Istanbul, claims he can perform a "bloodless operation."

Weddings: As varied as religious practices are in Turkey so are marriage traditions. Attending a traditional village wedding is an exhilarating social event which typically lasts three or four days.

The couple is first married by an *imam* (Moslem priest) who comes to the bride's house and performs a short ceremony that includes prayer and an explanation of the marriage vows. All women in the wedding will have the palms of their hands and finger tips reddened with henna *(kına)* to bring good luck.

Separate parties: The women in the wedding have a party separate from the men where they dance and eat to celebrate the marriage of their friend. The men also gather on the same or following day. They also dance, sing, as well as imbibe vast quantities of *rakı*. The Turkish women wash the bride at the village *hamam* or her home and then she is carefully dressed in wedding clothes that include veils and numerous layers of colourful cloth. The groom's friends go to the bride's house to ask for her hand in marriage and are usually refused until they give a gift to the family.

The groom climbs to the roof and breaks an earthenware jug which scares away evil spirits. Finally the bride is shown to her new bedroom where she waits for her husband. When she enters she again asks for a gift, usually a gold bracelet or chain, and then before they sleep they pray together.

In large towns, many of these traditions have been abandoned and replaced by a party for friends and family given in a restaurant or tea garden. All couples must also have a short civil wedding according to modern Turkish law.

Birth and death: A new baby is named only after the whole extended family has been consulted. Usually a baby is named after a relative. The grandparents promise to give the child a gift that will grow, such as a poplar tree *(kavak)*. Babies are always dressed with a piece of blue stone or glass that purportedly wards off the evil eye. This is not part of Islam but of folk belief. Many adult Moslems also wear the blue eye for the same reason. In some village areas, babies are "salted" to ward off evil odours.

When a Moslem dies he or she is carefully washed by someone of the same sex and placed on the bedroom floor. The body is then wrapped in a 16-foot-long white burial cloth. First it is taken to the mosque and put on a special stone catafalque in the courtyard designed for coffins. After the regular prayers, the *imam* leads special services for the dead before the coffin is taken to the cemetery, often shouldered the distance by male relatives of the deceased.

It is common to see religious men with hands behind their backs counting a *tespih* (worry beads) in long and endless motions. Worry beads, similar to Catholic rosaries, come in all sizes and colours. They are sold near mosques or in shops that sell Korans and calligraphy.

Visiting Ottoman Turkey in 1893, Lady G. Max Muller, wife of a British MP, wrote: "We had expected to see all nations here, and we had indeed! It was as if the Tower of Babel has just fallen, and its inhabitants were pouring down the streets of Shinar. The sharp-featured Semites, the almond-eyed Mongols, the Arayans."

A careful eye will note that the modern Turkish are still a culturally mixed group. Not surprising, perhaps, when one considers that the country is not only a bridge between Europe and Asia, but also the former nucleus of an empire which extended from Vienna to Tabriz, and from Crimea to the southern tip of the Arabian Peninsula.

Melting pot: When the World War I defeat resulted in the loss of imperial territory for the Ottoman Empire, forcing the Sultan's subjects to take refuge within the present boundaries of the Turkish state, the ancient melting pot acquired still more ingredients. The refugees from the Balkans, as well as Russia, the Arab states and the Aegean Islands brought with them their ways of life and further enriched the culture.

One important feature that contributes to that variety is that Turkey is a peninsula which occupies a 300,984-square-mile (781,000-square-km) area, approximately three times the size of Great Britain. The major part of the country consists of high plateaux. The topography and the climatic conditions differ widely from one region to another. Temperatures of below zero can occur, while days of over 113° F (45° C) are not uncommon.

Large segments of the population from rural areas may decide to leave their villages after learning of the pleasures of urban life from television or movies, or from direct observation via cheap public transportation. But above all, increasing unemployment and ongoing social and political unrest are the most significant causes of mass migration from eastern provinces into the cities.

After World War II, as urbanisation accel-

erated, housing shortages became severe, and *gecekondus* (squatter houses, shanty towns or overnight houses) sprang up almost overnight around the suburbs of major Turkish cities like Istanbul, Izmir and Adana.

Turkish shanty: Like all social problems, the Turkish *gecekondu* has some aspects that are universal and some that are distinctively Turkish. Perhaps the most distinct thing about the *gecekondu* is that it appears to occupy an intermediate position between the situation in the United Kingdom and the

situation in India. In all three countries migrants from rural areas require housing. In the UK, the government is supposed to build houses for them, administered by the municipal authorities. In India, they camp in the streets. In Turkey, they build their own houses – ramshackle hovels on the peripheries of cities – without asking the state to pay for any of the construction or building materials or for their labour. Whole *gecekondu* cities are known to have been built within two or three years at these sites. But these *gecekondu* towns are built on somebody else's land, most often on state-owned property. "Were it not for the land

Preceding pages: women folk dancers; piggy back ride. **Left**, a village beauty. **Right**, a city beauty.

problem, one can argue that this is the cheapest and most efficient form of low income housing known anywhere in the world," noted Professor C.W.M. Hart of the University of California. These slum houses, however, upset town planning schemes. The frustrated authorities become more and more certain that nothing can be done in these cities unless the newcomers return to their home towns. Unless a reverse migration can be started, municipal officials in many cities argue, the beautiful maps of new housing and town planning projects will perish even before they are completed.

Unbelievable as it may seem to the upper and middle classes of the major developed cities who pass the *gecekondu* areas with a shudder, an overwhelming majority of the people who live in these areas firmly believe they are better off than they were in the villages they came from. They are certain that they have improved themselves as a family. The parents are satisfied with that advance themselves, but they hope and pray and plan for their children to climb up the next rung of the social ladder, from peasant *gecekondu*-dweller to university graduate in two generations.

It does not appear that putting schools in every village in Turkey and factories in half of them would stem the tide. "Why wait a hundred years for that to happen?" say the *gecekondu* people. "It's much easier and quicker to move to the city and build a *gecekondu*. There you will find not only factories for work but decent schools for your younger children."

Nowhere in coastal Turkey is the *gecekondu* problem as acute as in Adana, the country's fourth largest city and the industrial, agricultural and commercial hub of the south. The city's population has been growing at an alarming annual rate of 6.5 percent because of migrations from the rural areas of eastern Turkey. In expectation of a huge increase in its population, Adana's municipal authorities are building a new city to the northwest, rehabilitating the slums and moving some of the urban poor to the new neighbourhoods.

The exodus: In Adana, where 85 percent of the houses are substandard structures without proper drinking water, sewers or electricity and where the highest number of malaria cases is reported in Turkey each year, the majority of the *gecekondu* people are of Kurdish and Arab descent who migrated to the region at one time as seasonal cotton or fruit pickers and decided to stay. They came in waves mainly from the southeast provinces of Diyarbakır, Urfa, Siirt, Mardin, Adiyaman and Van where unemployment figures reach 30 percent of the working population, employment prospects are bleak, and the land is too arid for farming.

The exodus from the rural areas to Adana and other big cities of southern and western Turkey still continues from these and other areas of Anatolia. The migration from that part of Turkey, officials predict, will end only when a series of hydroelectric dam projects on the Euphrates and Tigris rivers, known as GAP, are completed and begin irrigating the arid steppes between the two rivers of southeast Turkey. The first big step in the project, the Atatürk Dam, is already operational.

Travellers to the Çukurova region can see many of these seasonal migrants with their tents pitched along the main highways, always displaced, working for a pittance and exploited by the big landowners, known as the *ağa*. These seasonal agriculture workers – Turkey's Okies and Arkies – follow the farming season, planting cotton and other crops in the spring, picking fruits and vegetables in the summer and harvesting cotton in October and November. They usually return to their families in the villages during the winter after the crops have been harvested only to come back in spring.

An interesting fact is that on the west coast, though nowhere else in Turkey, perhaps over half of the *gecekondu* people do not come from Anatolia at all. There are two other sources for the *gecekondu* population, which when combined at least equal or outnumber the Anatolians.

One of these groups is the *göçmen*, the immigrant group whose members were born, or whose families originated, outside Turkey. The other group are the people who were displaced as a result of extensive road building, slum clearance and urban renewal projects, such as in Izmir.

Balkan Wars' Refugees: The older *göçmen* groups are grandchildren of Turkish refugees who fled their homes in the Balkans as a result of various wars from 1878 onward, and the contracting boundaries of the Ottoman Empire. One can find residues of every conflict that Turkey ever fought since the Crimean War, living in pockets of *göçmen* settlements scattered throughout the country, not only in the *gecekondu* of cities but in the countryside as well. Most of the inhabitants of smaller towns and farmers of Thrace, European Turkey, are of *göçmen* origin. During the Russian-Turkish War of 1878, nearly 1.5 million Turks living in Bulgaria fled to the present boundaries of Turkey and were settled.

A total of nearly 500,000 Turks from Greece were exchanged for Turkey's 1.5 million Greeks in 1923, as part of an

Anatolia, which they were required to cultivate for at least ten years. Some of the farm lands given to these immigrants were either sold or abandoned as soon as the ten-year limitation was up and these Balkan Turks too flocked to the cities.

Migration continues: The migration from Greece, Yugoslavia and Bulgaria to Turkey, which is still going on, is perhaps the most interesting. Typically, these people are Turks by ethnic origin, Moslem by religion, who find residence in the three countries intolerable whatever their economic conditions in their home country. Rather well-off families from the Greek province of western Thrace, where 150,000 Turks still live, have

agreement struck between Ankara and Athens ending three years of bitter hostilities. These Turks were settled all over the country, but mainly concentrated in the western part of Turkey, including the Aegean and Mediterranean where they were given the properties (homes and land) left by the migrating Greeks.

The most recent group are Turks from the Balkan countries of Greece, Romania, Bulgaria, Yugoslavia, Albania and the Aegean Islands who arrived after World War II. Most of them were given farming land in

Above, men celebrate at a circumcision.

been known to sell their farms and move to Turkey because of the Greek government's discriminatory policies against ethnic Turks. Often they move to the city and buy a *gecekondu* for which they pay hundreds of million Turkish lira without a land title deed. The money thus paid represents the life savings of such a family which would be wiped out if their farms were to be demolished by Greek authorities.

The most recent migration was the arrival of nearly 330,000 Turkish refugees from Bulgaria in 1989, in what has been described as the biggest population movement in Europe since World War II. About one million

Turks continue to live in Bulgaria. The Bulgarian government expelled these Turks, who had been protesting their forced assimilation into the Slavic society. Most of these Turkish refugees have been distributed throughout the country, but nearly one-third have moved to Bursa, a province in western Turkey.

Some of these Turks have returned to Bulgaria since the fall of Bulgarian Communist Party chief Todor Jivkov, hoping that the political reforms sweeping that country and Eastern Europe will also benefit them.

In addition to the immigrants from the Balkans there are also recent arrivals from Central Asia, many of whom escaped communist China by way of Pakistan. These East Turkestan Turks, resembling the Turks who conquered Anatolia in the 11th century, with typical oriental features, have moved primarily into the cities of western Turkey, including Istanbul.

The Yörüks: Visitors to the Turkish Coast will sometimes encounter nomadic tribesmen leading their camel caravans along the highways. These are the Yörüks. During the hot summers, to escape the oppresive heat the Yörüks camp out in the high mountain plateaux that surround the coast. Conversely in winter, they come down into the valleys and the coast to leave the cold behind. The Yörüks were nomadic Turcoman warrior tribes who ventured into Anatolia after the Seljuk victory over the Byzantine army in 1071 at Malazgirt and settled in the more remote areas of western and southern Turkey. Their name was derived from the Turkish word "*yürümek,*" to walk, which appropriately describes their way of life as wanderers.

They can be seen principally in the coastal foothills of Muğla and Antalya provinces and also further east in the Mersin and Adana provinces. In spring time, they hold a *panayir,* spring festival that is a continuation of the Greek *panegyria,* or religious holidays. During the *panayir,* the Yörüks pitch tents, sell handicrafts, handmade carpets and food, and play the *davul* and *zurna* (the drum and the oboe) and dance.

The Yörüks are famous for their colourful costumes, tents, delicate embroideries and fancy flat weave wool carpets, the most famous of which are the *kilims.* They also produce fine pillow covers, saddlebags and

sacks. The best collection of Yörük artefacts can be seen in the ethnographic section of the Antalya Museum.

Coastal minorities: Travellers to the Turkish Coast will also from time to time come across members of the non-Moslem minorities: the Jews, the Armenians, the Greeks, and other Catholics.

A few hundred Greek farmer families, all elderly people now, still inhabit the Turkish Aegean islands of Gökçeada (formerly known as Imroz) and Bozcaada (Tenedos) – their existence, their own schools and religious practices are guaranteed by the 1923 Treaty of Lausanne. Some of these families operate pensions and restaurants in these islands and produce wines.

The region's Jewish population is concentrated in Izmir, Turkey's third largest city, where there are about 2,000 Sephardic Jews, but small clusters of Jewish families also exist in Adana and Antakya, near the Syrian border. Jews have lived in Anatolia since Alexander the Great's time, but not until 1492, when Spain expelled Jews during the Inquisition, did large numbers settle in the Ottoman Empire. Welcomed by the sultan partly because of their wealth and business acumen, the refugees became influential merchants and diplomats. For centuries, the Jews went to their own schools, the *Yesivot,* and spoke *Ladino,* or Judeo-Spanish, a mixture of medieval Spanish and Hebrew that in time absorbed words of Turkish, Greek and French origin. Today, older Jews are still fluent in *Ladino* and speak Turkish with a heavy accent. But few young Jews speak *Ladino,* even at home. And many Jewish families send their children to Turkish schools to learn flawless Turkish. Only one course in elementary Hebrew is taught at the *Yesivot,* but no instruction is given in *Ladino,* or Jewish history and literature. Many Turkish Jews are prominent industrialists, businessmen and there are a few politicians. There are also many educators, artists, musicians and distinguished journalists among Turkish Jews.

Esoteric sect: One esoteric sect is the Dönme (which means Apostates in Turkish), a Jewish group that converted to Islam in the 17th century. The Dönmes, who number several hundred in Izmir, are followers of the "False Messiah" Sabatai Zevi (1626–1676), a mystic Jewish leader who preached the Kabala and claimed he would lead the dispersed Jews back to redeem Israel. Zevi's mystical views about Israeli statehood came 200 years before the birth of Theodor Herzl and Zionism. Over one million Jews from every social class and in every country in Europe, Asia and Africa hailed him as their deliverer, though he was disavowed by conservative Jews as a paranoid personality who suffered from hallucinations. Zevi was born in Izmir in a house that still exists in the Kemeraltı shopping district and is considered holy by Dönme adherents. The Sultan, perceiving Zevi's movement as a danger to his empire, imprisoned him and ordered him to abandon his faith or face death with his

because the Latin Church was confined to Christians from the West and was never strong among natives. With the exception of the Armenian Catholics, they were not incorporated into the "millet" system during the Ottoman period, and had to rely on the protection of France, Italy and England. Many Catholics, such as the Italians, Maltese and French, in fact, maintain their European citizenship, though some have adopted dual citizenship. A great many of the British and French Catholics living in Izmir belong to the class known as the Levantines. Nearly all have been born in Turkey and in many cases their families have lived in the country for several generations. Their retention of

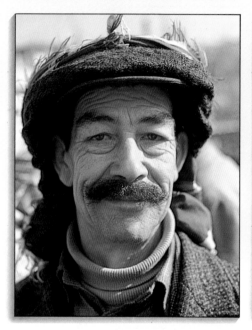

followers. Zevi, to the dismay of his supporters, converted to Islam. His hard core backers followed suit and became Moslems. Dönmes are outwardly Moslem, but in secret observe certain Jewish rites and customs, but in no way do they associate with the Jews, whom they describe as *kafirs* (infidels). The rejection is mutual.

An estimated 2,500 Roman Catholics who live on the Turkish Coast are concentrated in Izmir and Adana. With one or two exceptions, the Turkish state has never considered Catholics as Turkish citizens, mainly

European citizenship is often the only connection with the nation from which they originated.

A final Christian group that lives on the Turkish Coast are the Armenians who number about 5,000. The Armenians, who are Gregorian Orthodox Christians, live mainly in Adana, Iskenderun and Antakya and in other scattered communities in the Hatay province.

Ethnic jokes: The joke that goes around these days in Turkey about the Turks is that they are made up of two essential elements: the leek-eaters and the courgette-eaters. The leek-eaters are those who come from the

Left, a camel trainer and **right**, a peasant girl.

wrong, that is the western, side of the Meriç (Maritsa) River, which separates Turkey from Greece. The courgette-eaters are the Anatolians who are further divided into two: the lovers of *lahmacun*, a pizza-like pastry, and those who claim they would eat anything caught from the sea, even if it were their own fathers! Put in these terms, the coastal line starting from Istanbul all the way down to Antalya, to the point where the hot *kebabs* of southeast Turkey begin to take over, is occupied by the leek eaters. The connotation is that these people are all vegetarians who consume "any thorn or weed" that comes their way. The thorn is of course the artichoke, and the weed is the endive, cooked in

gecekondu in the cities and the hotels and holiday villages of the Turkish Coast. Other Turks say the Laz have the ability to smell where money can be made. Making up affectionate jokes about the mercurial Laz, designed to disprove their claims to be geniuses, is a national pastime. One popular Laz joke is: What did one Laz say to the other Laz who was hammering at the wrong end of a nail? He said, "That nail belongs to the opposite wall, you fool." However, the Laz don't take that lying down. It is said that upon watching a Zeybek, a national folk hero from Muğla, dance the slow rhythm of the *aksak*, a popular dance, a Laz was heard to comment "Given so much time to decide

olive oil, which eastern Turks would not touch. (Try the delicious *istifne salad* in the Isle of Cunda off Ayvalık, on the Aegean, and see for yourself.) Cold food is unthinkable in the east where the diet is based essentially on cereals and *kebabs*.

Consumers of *hamsi* (anchovy) in the eastern Black Sea Coast look down upon both. As far as they are concerned they owe their superior intelligence and agility to that protein-rich seafood. Immediately recognised by their fair skin, red hair, blue eyes, and large noses, the Laz dominate the construction business of Turkey, building the makeshift apartments replacing the

where to place his foot next, even my old father could do this dance, for heaven's sake!"

Turkish women: Nowadays, the ordinary Turk does not keep a harem of women. Nor was the Islamic licence to take more than one wife a rule. That a woman's place was, and to a large extent still is, at home, should not be understood as the patriarchal system of, for example, Rome, where the man, as indisputable head of the family, had the right to be the judge, jury and executioner of members of his family. Latife Tekin, a prominent Turkish woman novelist, explains the Turkish case this way:

"In our society, a woman's place is at home. This means she reigns at home. Man belongs to the streets; he rules in the world outside. Men are alienated, lonely and tense at home. Women feel the same outside. That's why they never leave the house unless fully armoured, that is, dressed to their teeth.

"That the men are seen as extra elements in the house, and that they are shooed to coffee houses are the overt manifestations of this fact. The men's and women's realms compete fiercely, wildly. I remember my mother kissing the door when my father left. My mother, our mothers, may be rightly called radical feminists as they never for-

feited their territory in favour of men's. Anatolian women refuse to buy their final garment, the funeral shroud, with their husbands' money. They bring it with them as part of their dowry, bought for them by their mothers or grandmothers."

Like the ancient Anatolian mother goddess Cybele, the Turkish woman mothers her son and husband. If that means having to provide for them as well, she works outside the home, tilling the fields and har-

vesting crops. The reward is a closely knit family, with children who leave home only upon marriage, and grandparents who do not know what an old peoples' home is.

The young enjoy the loving umbrella provided by their family and just as well, for even today it is often the case that those above the age of 21 are still being taken care of by their families. While this practice is the main deterrent against the current ills of drugs and alcoholism that strike the young in the Western countries, it also demands the upholding of the old values and rules of behaviour. More often than not, you will find that men who have raised children of their own will not, as a sign of respect, smoke (certainly not drink) in the presence of their fathers.

Yet, industrialisation and urbanisation do not allow for niceties and break down the traditional family system. Once out of their realm, women should not expect to be pampered. At the end of a hard day's work, riding at the back of an overcrowded city bus, the young are too tired to give their seats to the elderly who should not be out on the streets at that time of the evening in any case. Urbanisation, which in the final analysis alienates people, masks communal sanctions and codes of behaviour. The result is pollution in both senses of the word.

Left to right: a Turkish girl carries her sister; old woman embroiders new designs; a farmer with gold teeth smiles; a Yörük with his camel.

CUISINE

Adana kebab, Mevlana candy, Izmir köfte and Bodrum's *mantı* are some of the unique regional specialities from Turkey's Aegean and Mediterranean coasts. Today's Turkish cuisine reflects the extent of the Ottoman Empire, which spanned North Africa, parts of the Middle East, the Balkans, and Europe to the gates of Vienna. The legacies of the Ottoman and Seljuk courts include a rich selection of appetisers, soups, meat dishes, vegetable dishes, elaborate desserts and, of course, Turkish coffee.

During the Ottoman Empire, Istanbul, Izmir and Bursa were centres of sophisticated court cuisine due to the influence of European foods and the cosmopolitan lifestyle of the people. However, even though soldiers and administrators from the major cities, particularly the janissaries, travelled and worked throughout the country, they did not promote an exchange of culinary knowledge with people in the countryside. Until the establishment of the Turkish Republic in 1923, cuisine in the rural areas reflected the nomadic lifestyle and meat-eating traditions of the Turkish people who originated from the Asiatic steppes.

After the collapse of the Ottoman Empire in the early 1900s Turkish cuisine underwent a metamorphosis. With the establishment of the new republic, flocks of Anatolian villagers migrated to the major cities and regions along the coast, and took with them their regional produce, cooking and eating habits. In addition, a flood of Turks living overseas returned to Turkey and came home from Crete and Greece bringing new cooking techniques for seafood to the Aegean Coast. Middle Eastern spices and condiments were introduced to the eastern Mediterranean Coast by Turks from Syria.

Fresh ingredients: Turkey is one of the few countries in the world that produces enough food for its own needs. From the major cities in western Turkey to the smallest village near the Russian border, travellers can find open-air markets selling an abundance of fresh produce, homemade yogurt, honeys and jams. The market atmosphere is frantic, jubilant and festive – shoppers give the impression of visiting the market for the first time, greeting each other warmly, enthusiastically selecting their products, and bargaining furiously over every melon and fresh fruit. The crowd is easily moved by the aggressive salesman, whose marketing techniques include tempting the exhausted customers with wedges of juicy watermelon, chunks of soft creamy cheese, and handfuls of shiny, salty black olives.

Dining out in Turkey is a great pleasure. The palate is privilege to a winning combination – the great tradition of the Turkish kitchen and flavour of fresh ingredients. In the early morning hours along almost any coast you can find fishermen gathered on the wharves munching on hot *simit* (a roll of bread shaped like a lifesaver and covered with sesame seeds) and drinking their first tea, guarding the catch of the previous night and exchanging adventure stories like their ancestors have done over the centuries as they wait for seafood restaurants to buy fresh fish directly from them.

Mornings in Turkey begin best on a sunlit balcony with a sumptuous Mediterranean breakfast. A typical breakfast both at hotels and in restaurants is a fairly substantial meal consisting of *beyaz peynir* (feta), honey or jam, black olives, boiled eggs and piles of fresh Turkish bread that resemble Italian loaves. In Antalya, the traveller may be lucky enough to be served a local speciality known as *patlıcan reçeli* (aubergine jam), miniature aubergines preserved in sweet syrup, which is spread on bread or mixed in yogurt.

Eggs menemen: You can easily have a light breakfast of coffee and cheese toast at any cafe. For a more substantial breakfast, visit a *Süt İş* (milk shop). These small restaurants, catering to the morning crowd, specialise in various kinds of milk and egg dishes. One popular breakfast dish is *menemen*, a delicious concoction of eggs, peppers, tomatoes and cheese, served in a pan and accompanied by small buttery buns called *poğaça* and various kinds of cheese *börek* (layered pastry leaves cooked in the oven). *Süt İş* shops also create a variety of smooth milk-based

Preceding pages: grand buffet lunch at a Turkish resort. **Left,** fish and *shish kebab*.

puddings and sweet desserts, such as *sütlaç* (rice pudding), *tavuk göğsü* (breast of chicken pudding) and *aşure* (Noah's pudding), which allegedly contains 99 ingredients.

Turkish black tea, brewed until intensely strong and bitter and then diluted with water, is drunk with plenty of sugar throughout the day from small tulip-shaped glasses. Many visitors find that Turkish tea helps counteract some of the oily Turkish dishes. Tourists will be offered tea wherever they have to wait, from carpet shops to the bus station. It's considered an affront to the host if a guest refuses refreshments. For something lighter, try apple tea, the best of which is made from dried apples and petals already sweetened, or *ıhlamur*, a linden tea recommended as a remedy for upset stomachs.

Turkish coffee, with its peculiar muddy grinds at the bottom of the cup and strong taste, is famous around the world for its use in forecasting the future. However, it is not as readily available as tea. When ordering coffee, the visitor should specify *sade* (unsweetened coffee), *orta* (medium sugar) or *şekerli* (extra sweet). The *çayevi* (tea shops), the social nerve centre of every village and town, are generally frequented by men who leisurely linger over glasses of tea and play backgammon with lightning speed.

Lunch: Lunch is eaten between noon and 2pm in various kinds of streetside restaurants and *büfes* (sandwich stands). The most popular midday meal in Turkey is the *döner kebab*, layered lamb, ground beef and spices roasted on a vertical spit, and served thinly sliced over rice or in a roll with tomatoes, hot peppers and french fries. Generally, lunchtime restaurants in Turkey specialise in one kind of dish or cooking technique. For example, *kebab* houses *(kebapçı)* serve all sorts of grilled or baked meat dishes. The *pideci*, another speciality restaurant, serve freshly baked thick flat bread piled high with delicious toppings such as cheese and eggs, *sucuk* (a spicy salami) or a mixture of the day's offerings.

Another favourite noontime snack is *lahmacun* (Turkish pizza), a thin crisp dough topped with ground lamb, onions, spices and served with ice cold frothy *ayran*, a fortifying drink of beaten yogurt, spring water and a dash of salt. *Lahmacuns* are sold on street corners but the best ones are usually found in *pide* shops – served crisp and hot out of the wood-burning oven. Hot *lahmacuns* from Adana and along the southeast coast are especially good.

For those with a hearty appetite and more time to spend for lunch, a stop-off at a *hazır yemek lokantası* (prepared food restaurant) will guarantee a substantial meal. These restaurants, offering a wide variety of hot traditional Turkish meat and vegetable dishes, don't need to advertise for they are easily found. From the street, the day's selections, unpretentiously displayed, can be viewed. A beaming waiter and other staff members will try to tempt passersby to come inside. First, the tourist should carefully examine the dishes, an array of meats, vegetables, *pilâvs*, bubbling, roasting, and steaming in large steel containers over the stove and steam tables. Menus and price lists are usually unavailable, so your selection must be made by pointing to the dish that you wish to eat.

The kebabs: With great pride and flourish, the chef will serve generous portions, saying repeatedly *afiyet olsun (bon appétit)* and then stand firmly behind the customer waiting for the verdict on his food. The meat dishes include several kinds called *kebabs*, such as *tas kebabı* (mutton with tomatoes and onions), *bahçıvan kebabı* (a gardener's stew), or *köfte* (meatballs) such as *terbiyeli köfte* (meatballs in an egg and lemon sauce). Add to this *pilâv* (rice), or spinach purée with a poached egg, or a dish of homemade yogurt, and the meal will sustain the visitor through hours of sightseeing.

Dinner is eaten anytime between 7pm and 10pm, although many meals last until midnight. Restaurants are classified into two main categories, those serving meat dishes, and those serving seafood. Some, however, will have a combination of both. If you are feeling energetic, visit a *gazino* (a traditional nightclub) where you will be treated to a full night of food and drinks followed by entertaining belly dancers, singing and traditional Turkish music.

When eating at a restaurant, don't bother asking for the menu because usually there is none available and besides, the Turkish method of ordering is much more appetising. It's best to follow the waiter to the kitchen where he will give a special viewing of the evening's choices. All the hungry tourist needs to do is indicate his or her choice by pointing at the dish.

A traditional dinner begins with *meze* dishes (appetisers), a variety of cold and hot food, ranging from salads to savoury pastry to melons. Many Turks make a meal out of these appetisers. The traveller may choose to as well because he may feel stuffed after consuming these rich tidbits. *Meze* dishes are typically consumed along with a glass of *rakı* – the national alcoholic beverage flavoured with anise – which is served with water and ice. Turkey also produces four locally brewed beers: *Efes*, *Marmara*, *Tuborg* and *Venüs*.

(*çoban*), white bean salad (*piyaz*), and *karışık turşu* (mixed pickles). If the restaurant is outside near a harbour, the tourist shouldn't be surprised to find vendors selling peeled fresh almonds and walnuts mounted on a bed of ice, peanuts caked in salt, and of course, lottery sellers plying their wares among the tables or on stands.

One of the best *meze* dishes to look for anywhere along the coast is *çiğ köfte* (raw meatballs) – Turkey's answer to steak tartare. Raw lamb, bulgur wheat and parsley pounded together create a tender, very spicy small meatball that is tempting even to those who don't usually eat raw meat. *Zeytin yağlı*, vegetables cooked in olive oil and served

Appetisers: At a meat restaurant the *meze* usually include only vegetable and meat dishes. Cold *meze* dishes are brought to the table by a waiter as soon as the guest has been seated. The waiter arrives with a tray or trolley piled high with small dishes which he proceeds to put on the table. You should stop him there and choose what you want and send back the rest. Behind him another waiter is carrying a large green salad – you should send this back if you don't think you can eat it. Other salads will be available that are more interesting, like shepherd's salad

Above, the chef slices *a döner kebab*.

cold, make up a large category of *meze* dishes, such as stuffed green peppers, tomatoes, grapevine leaves and mussels. The vegetables or shells come bursting with a mixture of rice, pine nuts, currants and spices. Small lamb's brain served cold with lemon on lettuce are greatly sought after by Turks. There is also a variety of spreads for bread including *ezme* (a fiery hot tomato and onion *salça*, or paste), *haydari* (a thick garlicky yogurt dip), and *cacık*, a thinner version with slices of cucumber, olive oil and parsley, often served like a soup. Turks make amazing pickles out of every kind of vegetable and even some fruits. *Erik*, small green plums, are transformed into sour-sweet pickles that go well with olive oil-laden food. Turks also drink pickle juice. Southerners from Adana are especially fond of a dark red turnip juice, *şalgam suyu*.

Out of the more than 40 ways to cook the humble aubergine most of the best recipes are *meze* dishes. The simple *patlıcan salatası*, coarsely chopped peppers, tomatoes, onions, and of course aubergine, is definitely worth sampling. Diners at traditional Turkish food restaurants should sample the more complicated *imam bayıldı* (literally "the priest fainted"), a whole aubergine stuffed with onions, tomatoes and a sweetish olive oil dressing, often eaten as

tries stuffed with cheese, deep fried and served piping hot. A version called *Avcı* (hunter's) *börek* are Chinese-style spring rolls that are filled with a combination of crisp vegetables or minced meat.

There are also triangle-shaped pastry stuffed with spinach, and *pastırma* (cured beef); the most exceptional are stuffed with fish and mushrooms. One unusual hot *meze* is the *kadın budu köfte* (lady's thigh), an appropriately named meatball shaped like large Italian sausage made from lamb and rice and deep fried eggs. *Rakı* drinkers often eat a great deal of *arnavut ciğeri*, Albanian-style lamb's liver served cubed and sautéed in olive oil and onions.

a main dish. Simple aubergine purée is rendered sublime with bits of smoky aubergine skin mixed in it. Aubergine slices also come fried and topped with yogurt or green peppers.

Böreks: Like many foreign diners in Turkey, you may confuse the arrival of another massive tray of dishes, this time piping hot, with the main course. But these are just some more appetisers. Among the most traditional are the *böreks*. Similarly named cheese and spinach pastries are served at breakfast or lunch in *börekçi* cafes and from street carts. At dinner you should try *sigara böreği*, tightly rolled cigarette-shaped layered pas-

After the *meze* dishes, or as an alternative, the diner may order from a variety of traditional Turkish soups, usually thickened with flour or bulgur wheat and garnished with a fresh squeeze of lemon juice. Throughout the year Turks eat several varieties of lentil soups made with bulgur wheat, rice and vegetables. *Adana çorbası* is a vegetable soup with meatballs and chickpeas. In the summer it's best to try tomato soup, created from the ripe juicy tomatoes of the southern coast, or *balık çorbası*, fish soup. In winter, Turks across the country savour *tarhana çorbası,* made from yogurt curds and flour that is mixed with broth, which is very popular in Denizli. Special restaurants serve an unusual soup called *işkembe çorbası*, made from lamb's tripe and served with plenty of garlic and vinegar. This dish is also highly recommended by the locals as a remedy for a *rakı* hangover.

Meat dishes: If the traveller can resist consuming too many appetisers, the waiter will take orders for meat. In addition to a large number of *köfte* appetisers, a variety of grilled meatballs of various size and spiciness is available, including *kaşarlı* (with cheese) and *sebzeli* (with vegetables). Customers should save some of their cold appetiser dips to use as a good sauce for the main course. Also they can order a mix grill

delicious regional *kebabs* often found at each *ocakbaşı* and meat restaurants. In Adana, the fiery hot mixture of ground meat grilled on a skewer called *Adana kebab* is especially good. If a less spicy version is desired, choose *Urfa kebab*. *Iskender kebab*, named after its creator, the Iskenderoğlu family in Bursa, is another Turkish speciality of layered *pide* bread, slices of *döner*, spicy tomato sauce, yogurt and burnt butter.

Many *kebab* dishes are cooked in the oven (*fırın*) such as lamb *tandır*, leg of lamb cooked slowly until it falls apart and *kağıt kebab*, lamb meat cooked inside a paper package fragrant with thyme, onions and garlic. *Güveç* is the name for various stews

including *pirzola* (lamb chops), *böbrek* (kidneys) and *ciğer* (liver).

An *ocakbaşı* is a restaurant specialising in grilled meat. Similar to a Japanese sushi bar, guests are invited to sit and watch the food being barbecued over coal. The most popular grilled *kebab* is *cöp şiş*, tiny pieces of skewered meat grilled and served with flat thin bread, onions and tomatoes. *Şiş kebab* (*shish kebab*), famous around the world, is made from chunks of lamb or beef – but tourists should look for the unusual and

that are roasted in a slow oven and served in individual earthenware pots, such as layered lamb *güveç* made with onions and aubergine, chicken *güveç* served with baby okra, tomatoes and peppers, and shrimp *güveç* baked in a light tomato sauce and covered in melted cheese. Circassian chicken is a creamy dish made with shredded chicken in a walnut sauce that is reminiscent of the creamy white skin of the sultan's highly prized Circassian harem women.

Seafood: Fish restaurants along the coasts are replete with their own unusual *meze* specialities that have developed from the stock of seafood recipes brought back by

Left, fish, cheese and *rakı*. Above, stuffed grape leaves and radishes.

Turks returning from Greece and innovative chefs enlarging their repertoire of dishes. Visitors to the region will find many of the cold *meze* dishes common in meat restaurants as well as an array of seafood salads, such as octopus salad marinated in lemon juice – particularly good in Bodrum. In Marmaris, pickled sea bream and shrimp salads are highly recommended.

Two popular hot seafood *meze* specialities are golden fried *kalamar* (squid) rings and *midye tava* (mussels) served with a special sauce. In tourist areas various kinds of seafood *börek*, a mixture of the local catch wrapped in leaves of tender pastry, have been added to the menu. Sardines wrapped in

whole. One of the best fish from Izmir is the *trança* (halibut), which is cooked in the oven *(buğulama)* with tomatoes, peppers, onions and *kaşar* cheese and served in the pan. This dish is usually shared by several diners. Another unusual dish, found further down the coast near Mersin, is *balık doldurması*, a stuffed pike with rice, pistachios, and spices bursting from the fish. Along the Mediterranean jumbo shrimp, meaty and tender, are grilled with garlic and butter – these are highly prized by the locals for their unusual size and taste. The Turks also enjoy eating spiny lobsters, which they grill and serve with butter and lemon.

Vegetables find their way into Turkish

vine leaves and grilled is an unusual dish eaten primarily in August when sardines are plentiful.

As a rule, Turkish chefs grill and bake only large firm-fleshed fish. The best season for eating fish is from early autumn to late spring but fish is fairly expensive in Turkey, so the price quoted by the waiter will probably be a per kilo price and not a portion price.

Flatfish: Along the Aegean Coast tasty *ton balığı* (small tuna) are best simply grilled and served with lemon. Swordfish caught in deep water are often grilled on skewers with tomatoes, green peppers and onions, while smaller *dil* (sole or flatfish) are grilled

cooking in *mezeler*, pickles, salads and stews of meat and vegetables. They are also eaten separately in side dishes, such as puréed spinach, broad beans marinated in olive oil and white beans in light tomato sauce. Turks only eat vegetables that are in season and grown locally. Wandering through any village market you will witness Turkish women selecting with care fruits and vegetables that have just been picked. After a tour of the market you will know what to order for a vegetable dish at a restaurant in the evening. If sweet peas are in season as in early summer or baby okra or the sweet pimento peppers of the south in the autumn, order these and you will be highly satisfied. Unusual twists added to the stock of Mediterranean recipes include the Turkish version of Greek *mousaka* made with layers of cauliflower instead of aubergine, stuffed marrow that are spiced with dill and mushroom caps stuffed with *pastırma* and cheese. Marrow is also used to stuff *börek* in Afyon and Denizli, and aubergine *börek* is common in Mersin.

Pilâv is the quintessential Turkish food. *Pilâv*, originating in China, made its way along the ancient silk road west through Turkestan to Anatolia. There are over one hundred recipes for hot rice, bulgur wheat and *kuskus* (semolina in small pellets).

season – figs, watermelons, peaches and apricots – sliced and arranged artfully on a plate, or one of the more elaborate and tempting Turkish desserts. Many restaurants do not make their own dessert and instead diners finish their meal over Turkish coffee while a waiter races to the local *pastane* (pastry shop) to buy something fresh. Most meat restaurants have a selection of milk-based puddings and sweet desserts. Ice cream is popular along the south coast – favourite flavours include regional ripe fruits and nuts. The Bamyacı Ice Cream Parlour in Alanya is perhaps the most well-known ice cream maker in Turkey. The parlour serves two dozen flavours,

Dishes are cooked with butter or olive oil and the simplest is plain rice served with chickpeas called *düğün pilâvı* (wedding rice), popular all over Turkey. If you like liver try *iç pilâv*, rice cooked with currants, nuts, pieces of liver and flavoured with cinnamon. *Mantı*, often called Turkish ravioli, are tiny lamb-filled dumplings cooked in broth and served with a garlicky yogurt sauce and butter steeped in red peppers.

Dessert anyone? After a rich Turkish meal the only room left may be for the fruits in

Left, *Adana kebab.* **Above,** *baklava,* a Turkish pastry.

including *Kahramanmaraş* ice cream. This is made by pounding milk for hours with a long metal peg. In Antalya look for cinnamon cones filled with ice cream and dipped in chocolate. Antalya also hosts some of the best pastry shops specialising in *baklava* with pistachio and *kaymak* (clotted cream) baked inside layers of flaky pastry.

Bodrum specialises in golden morsels called *lokma*, which are fried doughnuts drizzled with syrup sold from stands that line the white streets. With Turkish coffee, the weary traveller can try one of the sweet, heavily flavoured Turkish liquors or the local brandy and cognac for a pick-me up.

TURKISH CARPETS

The words, "Wanna buy a Turkish carpet? Come into my shop, it won't cost you anything. Just have a look," may be the first words a tourist hears in the bazaars or on the streets of Turkey. Whether the salesman knows much English or not, these sentences are spoken eloquently and persuade the sometimes unwary customer into a purchase even when there was no intention of buying. There are basically two types of carpet dealers. The younger "commission" boys stake out a patch of pavement for themselves and will pester practically anybody passing. The older carpet-shop owners are more trustworthy and much less pushy.

Handwoven carpets and flatweaves are perhaps the most available and widespread sale items in Turkey. Admired worldwide, Turkish handwoven coverings – for walls, floors, even tables, are the best known of Turkish export items.

Turkish rugs are most easily found in tourist areas – sold in large commercial shops, small boutiques and even on the street. Carpet salesmen can be the most aggressive and, at the same time, the most hospitable of all salesmen in Turkey.

Tea (either regular or apple) or coffee almost always forms part of the ceremony involved in the purchase of a carpet. The salesmen pull down from the numerous orderly piles literally hundreds of carpets which they throw at the feet of potential customers, one by one, with studied aplomb. And as the traveller soon learns, every salesman is an "expert".

Historical background: Oriental carpets have for centuries been considered works of art. There is much speculation and debate over the origin of knotted carpet weaving and the earliest dates of flatweaves. Suffice to say that in Central Asia the Turkic nomads were most influential in the origin and spread of this art and they maintain that position of prominence even today. Along with the prestige and the exciting designs of the Oriental carpet is the newly discovered and

recognised fame of the less classical flatweaves or *kilims,* as they are generally called.

Unlike its competitors for the tourist market – ceramics, copperware and recently, leather goods – a woven item lives and grows with association. Purchasing a woven item is akin to buying a friend for life.

Each woven piece can be seen as the unique expression of the weaver which in turn becomes the unique expression of the buyer and user. Quality carpets and rugs, like

good bottles of wine, age gracefully if they are taken care of; the colour and gloss become heightened in the carpet, the motifs and colour harmony of the flatweaves mellow and acquire a subtle warmth. Beautiful muted colours often result from the ageing process, a quality that many carpet sellers feel enhance the value.

Learning where to find carpets and *kilims,* and how to judge their authenticity and quality does not require lengthy research or a special knowledge of history, although the more one learns about Turkish carpets the more one will undoubtedly want to know. Here are a few basics about Turkish carpets. These

Preceding pages: at the carpet farm in Milâs. **Left**, weaving a *kilim*. **Right**, nimble fingers work on a rug.

handmade articles, which can be classified as textiles from the weaving and knotting process, are basically of two kinds: the knotted carpet and the woven flatweave. They are highly decorative, both are used as covers, and are produced on a loom with a warp (the continuous threads through the fabric) and a weft (the filler).

Knot power: The knotted carpet is made with the double Turkish or *Gördes* knot, a strong, durable knot that is tied around the warps with its ends clipped to make the resulting pile. Checking whether a carpet has been tied with this knot is very difficult once the carpet has been woven so one can only take it on faith. The *Sina* knot, common in

classified as true *kilims*, *cicims*, *sumaks* or *zilis* depending on the type of weave. A true *kilim* is made with a *kilim* "slit-tapestry" weave. The end result is a slit produced between the different coloured areas of the rug. In the *kilim* technique, motifs and patterns are produced as the weaver winds coloured weft yarn around pairs of warps. *Cicims*, *zilis* and some types of *sumak* are woven using three elements, the warp and weft and coloured extra-weft wrapping or "float" yarns. In the weaving of a *cicim* usually two women work together, one at the back of the rug and one at the front. They pass the weft yarn through the warp threads working simultaneously on both sides in a

Persian carpets, is an alternative and does produce a finer carpet since the knot is tied around a single warp rather than the double warp as in the Turkish knot.

The number of knots per square centimetre is a guide to the fineness of the carpet; the more knots, the finer the weave and the carpet. A silk carpet may have 100 knots per square centimetre and can go up to 900 knots in a square centimetre. Wool carpets will have fewer with only 36 knots per square centimetre.

Flatweaves or flatwoven rugs are generally called *kilims* because of the common weaving technique, but these can be further

"semi-wrapping" technique. The *zili* displays a "weft-float" brocading technique.

Expressing culture: Flatweaves and knotted carpets are expressions of the indigenous culture of Turkey. They are woven throughout Anatolia and the coastal regions by women and girls. They represent a strong cultural tradition of a people and their way of life and still form part of the economy of many Anatolians. The environments out of which flatweaves and knotted-pile carpets come are different. To understand this is to appreciate the richness of each of the

<u>**Above**</u>, **carpet weaving amongst ruins.**

traditions, which developed independently side by side. Those who weave one do not weave the other.

Flatweaves are traditionally woven in the home for domestic use and result from the cultural need for coverings and containers for the nomadic tribal groups. They are lighter and more flexible compared to knotted carpets and besides being useful as wall hangings and floor coverings they appear as numerous other articles: *heybes* (saddle bags), *yastıks* (pillowcases), clothing or grain sacks, seat covers, horse trappings, cradle covers, etc. Unlike the knotted carpet, which has always been a sales item to the West or an investment to the Turk, flatweaves have only recently begun to be produced as a sales item.

Flatweaves in general carry a great deal of symbolism and can reflect a historical context that experts now claim goes back as far as the Neolithic Period in Anatolia. The implications are social, ethnic and cultural. Some of the finest examples of these are still being woven by the Yörüks and the Avşar Turkmen of the Oğuz clan, which came to Anatolia with the Seljuks in the 14th century. These groups, originally nomadic, migrated down the ages throughout Anatolia and in some places still maintain their identity and old customs. To them must be attributed the credit for having preserved some of the finest examples of flatweave art.

Symbols of life: Thus we can see that flatweaves were functional to the way of life of the Turkic nomads who migrated from Central Asia to Anatolia. They were produced to meet the needs of their living conditions – portable, functional for a nomadic lifestyle, and practical. The women worked with products easily available – wool and animal hair, which they collected themselves. In the matter of the decoration and composition, traditionally the end product had to represent the very existence from which they had emerged. The motifs are a reflection of both their creator's life, and their understanding of it. This meant, for example, that a young girl may record in her weaving her concerns about finding a husband, marrying, having a family and living a long life with an assured peaceful death. The motifs traditional on the flatweaves record a story and symbolise a heritage not in writing but in weaving.

Güran Erbek, a Turkish art historian, has put it this way: "According to the Anatolian beliefs, the prayer cloth woven by a young maiden to be used by her future husband has a special meaning. The motifs produced by winding the threads around the warp present an expression of her expectations for the future: happiness, reproduction and a long life. Motifs comprise a language for the women and young maidens. Their happiness, sorrow and desires are expressed through those motifs. It is through those motifs that they display the thoughts which they cannot transform into words, which are considered inappropriate when uttered. A tomb stone on a *kilim*, generally perceived as death, is a way of saying 'I'd die if I ever have to part from my beloved.'"

Times have changed but *kilim* motifs and patterns are still personal – individually and tribally, and have changed little through the ages. Originally they were an expression of the spiritual and religious elements in the lives of the tribal groups. The very names that continue to be used to identify them are an indication of this heritage. The meaning may not have the original significance now but as they have been passed from grandmother to grandchild they become an expression of what the weaver is. This is not as true of carpet weavers who have traditionally woven for middlemen and are given cartoons (patterns on squared paper) to weave from.

Traditional motifs: Some of the common traditional nomadic motifs still being used on flatweaves today bear out this fact: *elibelinde* (hands on hips) – symbol of motherhood and fertility probably derived from the Anatolian mother goddess figure; *koçboynuzu* (ram's horn) – a sign reflecting fertility, heroism, power and masculinity; *aşk ve birleşim* (love and union) – an emblem related to the Oriental ying-yang symbol for the harmony between male and female; *el/parmak/tarak* (hand/finger/comb) – symbols to ward off the evil eye or to ensure protection in birth and marriage; *nazarlık* (evil eye) – a representation against the effect of an evil glance; *çengel* (hook) – another symbol against the evil eye; *yılan* (snake), *ejder* (dragon), *akrep* (scorpion) – all symbols indicate a desire for protection from nature; they are also signs of happiness and fertility; *kurt ağzı, kurt izi* (wolf's mouth, wolf spoor) – protection against the wolves, the predator of sheep; *hayat ağacı* (tree of life) – these stylised trees and plants stand for the desire for immortality and life after death; *çiçek* (flower) – stylised motifs of roses, carnations, tulips and hyacinths reminiscent of the Garden of Eden; and *kuş* (bird) motifs evoke many things – women, love, joy, happiness, power and strength. These and many others are related to the everyday life of rural villagers or nomads and speak of their condition – little wonder that they have continued to be important.

It is interesting to note that the word used by village women for motif is *"gelenek,"* which actually translates as "tradition", a word that evokes considerable meaning and emotion.

In knotted carpet weaving many of the same themes are used but they do not carry the same symbolic intensity of meaning. Those designs most suited to the knotting technique are used. Also, carpet designs have been more formal, emphasising floral and complicated geometric patterns and all of these have been influenced by changing market tastes. Thus they have transformed through the ages.

The dyes: Traditionally, weavers of both the knotted carpet and flatweaves spun their own yarn from the wool of their own sheep, and also dyed it with natural dyes extracted from leaves, bark, roots and fruit. Often the processes were family secrets. This practice has over time given way to the use of chemical dyes. Distinguishing whether the dye used is natural or artificial in a given piece can be determined over a period of time and exposure to sunlight. Natural dyes are more highly treasured by carpet buyers as they are more authentic and don't fade easily. Carpets dyed with artificial colours fade fast. It is a good idea to ask a salesman if the dyes in the piece are natural or artificial, but only a real expert can dare challenge the answer and prove it.

Some experts suggest that when buying a carpet the customer should lick the corner of a handkerchief and rub it over a spot on the backside of the carpet. If it comes off coloured, the dye, whatever its source, is probably not fast. This certainly is an indication that the piece will mellow with age!

The content of the warp and weft is important in the value of a handmade article. Wool – machine or hand spun – cotton, natural silk and artificial (floss) silk, camel or goat hair, can all be used. The inclusion of animal hair is infrequent but is characteristic of the flatweaves of certain tribal groups, whose use of a mixture of elements is more common and is used to give strength and texture rather than artistic effect. Yörük weavers use a great deal of goat hair. Some authorities claim that pure, long-haired lamb's wool makes the best woven pieces. Yörük weavers prefer this. The wool from the sheep, which graze on the high plateau is softer, stronger and more lustrous because of the climate and food.

Types and sizes: The types and sizes of knotted carpets are not strictly uniform although there are general categories. The following dimensions can help serve as a general guide: *yastık* (cushion cover) – 40 x 25 cm (small) or 100 x 60 cm (large); *çeyrek* (medium size) – 135 x 60 cm; *seccade* (prayer rug) – 180 x 120 cm to 200 x 130 cm. A group of larger carpets include *karyola* (bed size) – 220 x 150 cm or *kelle* – 300 x 200 cm; *taban*, which is larger than six square metres; and *yolluk* (runners) come in various widths and lengths.

Flatweaves vary greatly in size and shape depending on the type. Often the shapes are defined because of the maximum width of the horizontal loom, which is portable and particularly suited to the nomadic weaver.

Most carpets and flatweaves have been traditionally related to a geographic area. Sometimes they also carry the name of the group that produces them. However, this is now changing and carpet styles and motifs can now be produced regardless of geographic location. This is particularly true of the flatweaves.

Individual expression: In fact the original geographical designation was probably only partly correct since specific motifs, patterns and colour combinations were likely to be the expression of an individual tribal group and moved with this group as it migrated. There are of course exceptions to this. Furthermore, as commercialism begins to get the upper hand the fusion of different styles will become more common.

The beauty of Turkish weaving design in both carpets and flatweaves is a function of colour, motifs and overall composition. Its common characteristic is the repetition of geometric units. A central theme may dominate, surrounded by complementary motifs. A favourite composition in carpets is one (or more) central diamond or medallion fringed by other motifs. On carpets the central unit is usually contained within a border or borders. In flatweaves motifs generally are arranged on either a diagonal or vertical/horizontal axis and the composition is confined within parallel stripes extending along the length of the piece.

Some nomadic groups known as Yörüks, such as the Karakeçili, Saçkarali, Sarıkeçili and Honamlı, still weave their own styles. The Karakeçili in the Balıkesir-Kütahya region also weave their typical group designs

western flatweaves. The snow-tooth-edged diamond designs common in Eskişehir, Afyon, Kütahya, Nevşehir and surrounding areas continue south to Denizli, Isparta down to Antalya. Some *parmaklı* (finger) *kilims* common in Eskişehir, Afyon and Kütahya continue as far as Isparta and Burdur, but don't go further south. The *elibelinde* motif, widespread in central Anatolia, appears uniquely in a typical theme of the Antalya region. The *gülbudak* rose motif on the other hand appears in the same form throughout the country.

Hereke silk: In Hereke, just east of Istanbul on the Sea of Marmara, the finest woven carpets in Anatolia are produced. That is,

as do the Yüncü Yörüks. The latter group mainly winters in the south on the foothills of the Taurus Mountains but spends the summers in the pasturelands between Eğridir and Lake Burdur. These groups originally moved or were moved from their lands in central and eastern Anatolia during various upheavals in the Ottoman period. Thus the designs have migrated with them.

The effect of these migrations, the heritage of earlier periods – perhaps Neolithic, Phrygian – and those earlier motifs brought in from the western islands can be seen on

Above, giving the sales pitch at a carpet shop.

they are made with quality control and have the most knots per square centimetre. Hereke carpets are of two types, wool and pure silk. The wool carpets generally have 36 knots per square centimetre while the silk carpets range from 100 to 196. Their designs are mainly copies of classical floral Turkish or Persian carpets or new creations by contemporary designers. At one end of each carpet the name Hereke is woven in. In earlier times this was in Arabic script.

Carpets from the Çanakkale region near the Dardanelles are generally woven in the villages of Ezine or Ayvacık. Many still have traditional designs dating to the 16th and

17th centuries famous *"Holbein"* carpets, so called because the rugs were depicted in several of Hans Holbein's paintings. A typical composition consists of one to three rectangular medallions surrounded by geometric motifs usually on a red field or, rarely, on a yellow field.

Bergama carpets have geometric compositions similar to the Çanakkale ones, but the colours are darker shades of red and blue. Kozak carpets are also related but are smaller in size. They may have *mihrap* (prayer) niches, single or mirrored in the middle field. In structure the knots are thick and visible and give the carpets a soft texture.

Brighter colours: Yuntdağ carpets, though

ries. Even today they are known for their finely woven and elaborately designed prayer rugs *(seccade)*. Floral forms dominate not only the prayer niches but also in the borders. Present production, though of good quality, does not match the earlier masterpieces. The weave is always fine, 16 to 36 knots in a square centimetre. Sometimes these carpets have a cotton warp.

Yatak carpets: Çal (Denizli) is famous for its traditional large-sized Yatak carpets. Using strong yellow, black, blue and some red on a cotton warp, they exhibit a long, shiny pile. The field of the carpet is plain with scattered rosettes and squarish forms. The traditional carpets are rare and hard to find.

similar in composition, have brighter colours such as strong green and even sometimes purple. The most familiar design is two by three or four squares of different colours formed by intersecting bands.

Yağcıbedir carpets are woven in the Balıkesir region mainly in the settlements of Yörük tribal groups, the Yağcıbedir. They are easily recognisable because the main colours are dark red, dark blue and ivory. The single or mirrored prayer niches are filled with stylised leaves, flowers and stars. These all have both a wool warp and weft.

The towns of Kula and Gördes were particularly famous in the 18th and 19th centu-

Karakeçeli carpets do not belong to any specific region but are woven in western Anatolia in the Manisa, Kütahya, Balıkesir and Eskişehir regions by tribal segments of the Karakeçeli. The characteristic features of their carpets are a lustrous long and soft pile in red, blue and white and a composition of multi-hooked diamond shapes. Closely related to these are the Yüncü carpets formerly woven by nomad Yörük or Yüncü tribal segments in the Balıkesir region. Generally they are of finer weaves and have double multi-hooked diamond motifs.

Left, an ancient rug. **Right**, a modern silk carpet.

Usually Milâs carpets have either a single prayer niche or two or three narrow mirror image niches with stylised floral forms. The older carpets were bright red, blue, green and yellow but today the common colours are soft brown, beige, yellow and pastel shades. The warp can either be wool or cotton.

Döşemealtı carpets: The most important carpets of the Antalya region come from the villages of Kovacık and Şağıoba in the Döşemealtı region, the latter being the common name for the whole group. The yarn for both the weft and warp is of plateau wool and the predominant colours are red and blue, the dyes being produced from local plants.

The Dobağ Project of the University of the Marmara, which is trying to introduce natural vegetable dyes in the area around Balıkesir has been successful in encouraging the women to continue their home production with better dye stuffs.

With the aid of computers, historic woven pieces have been collected in photographs, coded, classified and catalogued and in some cases reconstructed from museum fragments or even paintings and are being handwoven by expert weavers using natural dyed yarns of Shetland and merino sheep's wool and silk.

Güran Erbek, the author of the beautiful sales catalogue of flatweaves for this project, says that the research on specimens and motifs – in particular their meaning – took the research team all over the region, to 9,000 villages where they interviewed 110,000 weavers. The collecting and bringing to light of the thoughts of these village women in itself is indicative of the high regard now being shown for this unique Anatolian art form.

The Net group: The setting up of commercial centres for the production and sale of carpets and rugs is a way to meet the economic challenge. One such is the Tavas Centre built by the Net Group of Companies, one of the world's largest producers and exporters of carpets, just 24 km (14 miles) from Denizli. The centre, besides its vast sales area, includes dyeing, designing and weaving workshops where local village girls presently weave on 80 looms.

The Net Group, which operates the Bazaar 54 chain of gift shops and carpet sellers, also has a commercial carpet production centre in Sultanköy, near Kuşadası. The Net Group also produces quality pure silk carpets at a workshop in suburban Istanbul. These kinds of centres are not unusual in urban settings, and are now becoming part of the scene in touristic centres.

The most unique carpet display centre in the world is undoubtedly the Ildız Carpet Farm, near Bodrum, 10 km (6 miles) from Milâs. Set up by the Ildız Company, a large producer and carpet exporter, it is probably the world's only carpet farm. Ildız opened the farm in 1984 to revive carpet making in Milâs, a traditional weaving centre. It is located in a dry, almost rain-free region.

At the farm, experts wash and dry under the sun tens of thousands of handmade wool carpets manufactured or bought by the Ildız Company, an Istanbul-based concern which owns the Tribal Art Carpet Shops chain. Ildız, which operates 3,000 looms throughout Turkey, specialises in the manufacture of pastel-coloured Milâs wool carpets, using natural root dyes. The 7-hectare (17-acre) farm has the capacity to dry as many as 20,000 carpets at one time. The best time to visit the farm is in the early summer when thousands of carpets are spread out on the ground, like a huge colourful mosaic.

The carpets are brought there from the different villages of Milâs, Bodrum and other Turkish cities. The reverse sides of the carpets are burned until they become charcoal black. The carpets are then washed with a special shampoo and vinegar, dried in a gigantic centrifuge, and spread out under the sun for as long as three months.

The colours of natural dyed carpets don't fade, but some of the artificial coloured ones do so quite quickly. The carpets are classified into five categories according to the degree of colour fading and then priced. Carpets whose colours have faded sell at lower prices.

A recent survey of changing village social patterns has revealed that instead of a decrease in the number of village women weaving, there has been an increase. With greater mechanisation of the agricultural processes and an increase in demand as well as better labour reimbursement standards, the women are turning to weaving in order to supplement their village income.

This helps them gain a sense of individual worth and security of income in a highly inflationary economy.

ANTIQUITIES SMUGGLING

Since the days of Heinrich Schliemann and his discovery of Troy, Turkey's antiquities have been plundered by treasure hunters, adventurers, crooks and smugglers, all out to make a fast buck. Visitors to such places ranging from the Metropolitan Museum in New York City and the Dumberton Oaks Museum in Washington D.C. to the British Museum in London, the Pergamum Museum in Berlin and the Louvre Museum in Paris will find thousands of ancient artefacts that were illegally exported from Turkey.

As well as the genuine article, fake statues, coins and busts abound, and even experts have difficulty in distinguishing forged objects. These fakes can be found anywhere in Turkey from the Covered Bazaar in Istanbul to various sites along the coast and the Anatolian hinterland. The Turkish mafia has in the past been implicated in the smuggling of antiquities out of Turkey, using peasant farmers and treasure hunters and bribing officials to allow them to dig illegally.

Turkey has been the home of 38 civilisations, ranging from the Hittites to the Turks and the Trojans to the Greeks. With an estimated 20,000 monuments and sites of archaeological importance in Turkey registered with the Ministry of Culture, the country has the world's richest deposits of subterranean and submarine antiquities. Many ancient sites are located in uninhabited, isolated areas. They have not yet been excavated or protected, leaving them open to treasure hunters and smugglers. Turkish officials say that the smuggling of Anatolian antiquities will continue as long as there is a demand for old art objects.

Illicit exports: In some cases in the 19th century, the removal of Turkey's archaeological wealth was tacitly approved by weak Ottoman sultans, kowtowing to western European governments. European diplomats, abetted by their governments, removed statuary, entire buildings and city walls from ancient sites along the Turkish Coast.

Charles Fellows, who served as the British Consul in Asia Minor in the 1840s, with the support of the British Navy, carried off many exquisite pieces of sculpture and entire friezes to the British Museum in London, from ancient ruins on the Turkish Coast. Two of the most magnificent items he stripped and removed that are now exhibited at the British Museum are the Nereid Monument, a magnificent Lycian tomb, and the original reliefs of the Harpies Tomb, both from Xanthus in southwest Turkey.

The Mausoleum: Another collection from Turkey that found its way to the British Museum through government-sanctioned trafficking of antiquities is the remains of the

Mausoleum of Halicarnassus, one of the Seven Wonders of the Ancient World, including 17 slabs of the Amazonamachy (a battle between the Greeks and the Amazons) and the statues of King Mausolus and his wife Artemesia the Younger.

Modern-day Turks deplore the Ottoman government's giveaways and, quite understandably, are making demands that all relics stolen from Turkey should be returned. However, no matter how legitimate their claims may be, foreign

Above, removing amphoras from the sea bottom is considered an act of smuggling.

museums and galleries remain reluctant to give up their treasures, afraid to set a precedent that could seriously deplete their collections. The ongoing saga of the bid to have the Elgin Marbles returned to Greece is another example of this.

Retaliatory steps: The Turkish government has begun to take retaliatory steps to get many of the antiquities back, including taking foreign museums to court and threatening to suspend current excavations by American and European archaeologists. It has tightened regulations governing private treasure hunting and severely increased the penalties for individuals convicted of smuggling antiquities. A person convicted of this crime could face a prison sentence of five to ten years.

It has also restricted scuba diving in the Aegean and the Mediterranean to reduce the smuggling of treasures from shipwrecks. The Institute of Nautical Archaeology, an affiliate of Texas A.M. University, has mapped out more than 125 ancient shipwrecks along the Turkish Coast. Diving is strictly forbidden on sites where ancient shipwrecks exist.

Using diplomatic pressure, the government succeeded, for instance, in getting East Germany to agree to return 7,400 Hittite cuneiform tablets that had been taken out of the country by German archaeologists at the start of the 20th century from the Hittite city of Boğazköy, near the central Anatolian provincial capital of Yozgat, ostensibly for cleaning and coding. In 1940, Germany returned 3,000 of the tablets, but after World War II, the remaining tablets stayed in what then became East Germany.

The Kharun treasures: Another blow against antiques smuggling was accomplished when Turkey, after suing the Metropolitan Museum of Art for seven years for the return of a 2,600 year old collection of gold and silver, known as the "Kharun (or Croesus) Treasures", finally retrieved them in 1993.

Allegedly the richest man of the ancient world, the 6th-century BC Lydian King Croesus' treasure was dug up by villagers near Uşak town in western Turkey; some 260 gold and silver pieces were smuggled to the West in 1966. The Metropolitan Museum of Art paid $1.7 million for what are now valued at $20 million, but denied their possession for nearly two decades. Before the New York Federal Court had reached a verdict, the Met decided to return the collection to Turkey in the summer of 1993. The Kharun Treasure is now on display at the Uşak Museum.

Ankara is also trying to persuade art collectors in the United States to return 1,900 silver coins, known as the "Elmalı Treasures", that were illegally removed from a village near Antalya.

Turkish authorities, however, now stand more chance of recovering "the Treasures of Priam" removed by the infamous German archaeologist Heinrich Schliemann. Convinced that he would find the ancient city of Troy, he excavated around the mound of Hisarlık, unearthed the ruins of a fortified city and smuggled the invaluable antique jewellery to Berlin in the late 19th century. (In fact, he had discovered a much older city, the remains of a prehistoric Bronze Age civilisation.)

In 1945, the Soviet Army carried the collection, deposited at the Berlin Museum, as war booty to Moscow. It was kept in the depths of the Pushkin Museum's store room until the end of the 1980s. A display of the items in 1996 brought protests from Germany. Currently, Turkey, Germany and Russia are negotiating repatriation details but negotiations are expected to continue for some time. It is encouraging that countries who for years denied all knowledge of plundering or hording treasures now take a more conciliatory view. Complicated, expensive legal wranglings are becoming fewer, as détente and globalisation have made parties discuss issues more logically and amicably. A number of individuals have voluntarily returned antiquities to their rightful place.

The Dorak affair: The most spectacular artefacts smuggling of recent years took place in the late 1950s and was known as the Dorak Affair – so named since the unusual gold jewellery was from the village of Dorak near Bursa. The incident tarnished the reputation of James Melaart, a controversial British archaeologist, who claimed that a Greek woman showed him the treasures in Izmir. The treasures were never found, the woman disappeared, and the authorities, suspecting Melaart of smuggling, permanently suspended his excavations at Neolithic sites in Turkey.

"A sense of freedom in the heart of nature" has come to be the motto of a number of holiday villages that have sprouted along the Aegean and Mediterranean shores of Turkey. Not long ago, for most Turks holidaying meant visiting friends and relatives in some other city. With the start of the tourism boom, the concept of taking a holiday began to change. In the summers, Turks started going to seaside resorts in the wake of the construction of hundreds of hotels and pensions on the Turkish Coast.

The four S's: The development of holiday villages started in the 1970s and 80s and continued into the 1990s. In Turkey, as in other Mediterranean countries, the idea of holiday villages was born out of people's longings not only to enjoy the sea but increasingly to get away from the noise, pollution and the humdrum of big cities.

Holiday villages are characterised by their remoteness and holiday makers enjoy the opportunity to get away from stress and return to nature. A large proportion of European visitors tend to go to Turkish holiday resorts in search of the basic four S's: sun, sea, sand and sex.

In the early 1970s, Club Méditerranée of France, Italy's Valtur Tourism Organisation and the Turkish state tourism concern, Turban, were the first to open sprawling, holiday village resorts in what were then little-known, rarely visited romantic settings in Turkey, such as Foça, (north of Izmir) and Kemer (south of Antalya), Kuşadası (south of Izmir) and Marmaris. Today these sites are bustling resorts offering five-star accommodation.

The pioneers: Since the mid 1980s, sparked by Turkey's tourism boom, dozens of holiday villages have sprung up. Most of the villages have been built around Antalya at Kemer to the west and Belek to the east, and the lower Aegean coastal strip, which is famous for its stunning surroundings and favourable climate with an average of 300 days of sunshine a year.

A Tourism Ministry licence is needed to set up a holiday village. Official regulations state that holiday villages must be established "in a suitable touristic area or close to archaeological sites, while providing various sporting and recreational activities next to comfortable accommodations and satisfying food."

Most of the holiday villages offer good sporting facilities, such as tennis, cycling, riding, golf and a whole range of water sports.

Children's heaven: A blessing in most of the Turkish-run holiday villages is that, unlike their foreign counterparts where sometimes children below the age of seven are not accepted, they are heaven for small children. The Tourism Ministry requires the holiday villages to have special play areas and safe, shallow swimming pools for kids.

There are villages to suit a range of tastes and budgets. To protect the guests and maintain a clubbish atmosphere, holiday villages don't allow outsiders to enter the premises and security is strict. Food at the villages is usually a mixture of fresh salad, vegetables and tasty local dishes, served buffet-style.

Left, the Golden Dolphin (Altın Yunus) Hotel in Çeşme. **Right**, relaxing on the beach.

Surf's up in Turkey and there are a dozen ways to make a splash along its coastline as this aquatic playground aspires to be *"California gibi"* (like California, like wow) offering a full range of exciting watersports. Choose your weapon: catamarans, lasers and windsurfers skim in between waterski boats and sea cycles, which dodge bobbing snorkellers who float in fear of careering banana boats, which are themselves forever on a collision course with noisy jet skis, the bane of the beach.

Where the companies do differ, unfortunately, is in their attention to safety. In their haste to attract package tours, many resorts use inadequate equipment and untrained staff. Club Alda maintains safety is its number one rule and is a member of Club Intersport, a Swiss sports organisation that presides over Club Alda's activities and staff. Club Alda prohibits parasailing on its rocky beach, and adventurers can set sail next door at Club Salima or the Ramada Renaissance Resort.

If the water gets too crowded, you can always rise above it all, strapped onto a parachute and yanked to the sky by speedboat, for a gull's-eye view of the flora and fauna below.

Until recently, watersports were mainly the domain of the holiday villages that line Turkey's coast and that offer a wide range of sports activities and instruction patterned after the Club Med concept. Available sports activities include waterskiing, windsurfing, sailing, snorkelling and canoeing. However, now these facilities are offered by many independent and fully qualified outfits dotted along the Turkish Coast.

Sea life abounds: Scuba diving is gaining popularity in Turkey, especially off the coast of Marmaris at the confluence of the Mediterranean and Aegean sea. Foreigners must always be accompanied by a Turkish dive guide and diving must be within posted legal boundaries.

Much of the country's coast is off-limits to underwater activity in order to preserve its rich history, as priceless antiquities and shipwrecks dot the shoreline. To dive within the law, ask the local tourism office for the government's diving *"harita."* Don't push your luck: if you are seen even wearing diving equipment in restricted areas, chances are you'll spend the night in jail.

Dive centres are located along the coastline in major tourism centres but not all are recommended by professional divers, so it might be wise to do some research in your own country before you leave on holiday. Centres that received the thumbs-up include Ayaz Watersports and Bitez Surf School in Bodrum, the European Diving Centre in Marmaris, and the Eurasia Diving Centre in Çamyuva, Kemer.

The PADI-certified staff run all levels of instruction and can arrange your dive excursion or put you in touch with a recommended centre along the Aegean or Mediterranean. Before making a dive with your guide, ask to

three rivers have excellent potential for white-water fun. Köprülü Çay and Göksu River on the Mediterranean coast are ideal for beginners and intermediates; and the Çoruh River in the Black Sea region offers challenging rapids for the more daring. Club Robinson in Side offers one-day "float trips" down scenic Köprü Çayı (Bridge River) near Selge. Guests float down the river in small rubber boats, passing under the shadows of vertical canyons and cliffs and stopping periodically for picnics and water games.

Barbarossa's fate: The Göksu River flows from the Taurus Mountains to Silifke through one of the most beautiful valleys in Turkey. The river is ideal for rafting excur-

see credentials: either a PADI or CMAS card and an updated Turkish diving licence *(Rehber Balık Adam Lisansı)*. Also, as there are now many dive centres popping up all over the place, shop around and go with the people you feel most confident with. Turkey has three decompression chambers, should the unfortunate need arise: in Bodrum, Çeşme and at the naval complex in Çubuklu, Istanbul.

River rafting has become increasingly popular as an organised sport in Turkey, and

sions but tour agencies have been slow to capitalise on its currents, leaving the fun to local children and kayaks. Two sports clubs, Alraft, which operates from Alanya, and Medraft in Antalya, organise trips and rent out rafting gear, but if you have your own equipment, contact Silifke's Tourism Office for assistance in planning a river trip. Find out if a permit is required and take a local guide along who knows the river well. Don't forget Barbarossa's fate – wear a life jacket. (The German Emperor drowned while bathing in the Göksu.)

For further details on water sports, *see Travel Tips*.

Left, scuba divers enjoy Turkey's marine life.
Above, champion windsurfer takes time out.

Whether it's to enjoy the flowers, the birds, the insects, the landscape, or just the silence of a stretch of untouched beach, visitors travelling along the Turkish Coast will get their share of the best of Turkey. Although many areas, especially on the Aegean Coast, have been converted into modern tourist resorts, a score of deserted and mostly clean bays, beaches and real Mediterranean maquis (shrub lands) can be discovered by leaving the well-trodden pathways. It would take many guidebooks to describe all the beautiful natural sites and abundant wildlife found on the Turkish Coast. But what follows are the region's highlights, where nature, rare birds and other wildlife can easily be observed.

Bird-watchers' paradise: Starting off in northwestern Thracian Turkey is Lake Gala, near Enez, on the Meriç (Maritsa) delta, separating Turkey and Greece. The area is rich in rare birds, including the shag *Phalacrocorax aristelis*, the bittern *Bautaurus stellaris*, the glossy ibis *Plegadis falcinellus*, and the greyling goose *Anser anser*. Bird-watchers from all over the world come to this area to observe these endangered species.

Foreigners must get permission from the *kaymakamlık*, the county commissioner's office in Enez, to go on a bird-watching expedition in the border area. The Turkish-Greek border is one of the most heavily guarded regions in the country. Trekkers should also be wary of taking photos in sensitive areas and remember the fate of two eccentric British bird-watchers who were detained in Enez for two months in 1983 on charges of espionage, after they were caught taking pictures of rare birds in a military zone. (The two men were later freed.)

Bird migration route: The Dardanelles is one of the world's main routes for bird migrations. Together with the Bosphorus, it is the only place in Turkey where Europe and Asia are separated by a narrow stretch of open water. This is important for the large migratory birds which, in order to save energy, use uprising warm air, or thermals, to soar to high altitudes and then to glide downwards, thus travelling many miles without beating their wings once. These thermals only occur above narrow straits and this explains why large, soaring migratory birds like storks and birds of prey converge at those bottlenecks. During August, September and October, large numbers of birds may be seen flying over the Dardanelles on their way from northern Europe to warmer climates for the winter. A good pair of binoculars is an essential piece of equipment.

When you cross the Dardanelles by ferryboat, you might notice small groups of flying birds that follow the bends of the strait, flying so close to the water's surface that their wings seem to touch the waves. These are shearwaters, until recently called manx shearwater but now generally referred to as yelkouan shearwater *Puffinus yelkouan*. Although for probably thousands of years these amazing birds have been flying every day from the Black Sea to the Aegean and vice versa, their exact breeding places are still unknown. Ornithologists assume that the yelkouan shearwaters breed on the cliffs of the Black Sea and that their main feeding grounds are in the Aegean, necessitating hundreds of miles of travel each day.

Environment endangered: Travelling further south brings the nature observer to large stretches of maquis, the more original type of Mediterranean vegetation, which covers an area that begins at the Bay of Edremit and continues south as far as Izmir Bay.

Maquis is in fact a low shrub community, consisting of small trees and bushes 2 to 4 metres (6 to 13 ft) high, ideal for nesting of some bird species, such as the little bustard *Tetrax tetrax*. Some typical plant species found in this region are Cistus species, tree heather, rosemary, thyme and juniper. Maquis is used extensively by the local inhabitants as a source of fuel wood, animal fodder and dye for clothing.

Unfortunately, in many places this vegetation has been replaced by more stony areas with low rounded bushes, caused by the irresponsible cutting of original shrubs and subsequent overgrazing by sheep and goats that stunts the recovery of most plants and trees. If this cycle of degeneration intensifies further, environmentalists argue that most of the shrub will disappear, turning the region into steppe. If water were to flush down the top soil quickly, it would create a land that is of no use for humans or wildlife; but fortunately, this stage is encountered only sporadically on the Turkish Coast. Meanwhile, the Association for the Preservation of Nature (Doğal Hayatı Koruma Derneği) and TEMA (the Foundation for the Fight against Erosion) vigilantly work and campaign for the conservation of the natural life of Turkey.

Swampy marshland: One of the least known but richest bird sanctuaries in Turkey is the Çamaltı Tuzlası, a large area of marshland along the northwestern part of Izmir Bay. Heavy industrial pollution in the Bay is

the black-winged stilt *Himantopus himantopus*, unmistakable with long pale red legs and thin, straight bill, and the avocet *Recurvirostra avosetta*, recognisable by its long legs and upturned bill. Izmir municipal authorities have given priority to the clean-up of the Bay of Izmir and have instituted a project that includes a sewage system and dredging the bottom of the bay.

One of the most endangered wetlands on the Turkish Coast is the Küçük Menderes (the Little Maeander) River delta between Izmir and Ephesus, around the district known as Pamucak. The region is a breeding ground for the squocco heron *Ardeola ralloides*, a brownish bird that spends its

threatening the 182 bird species known to live, breed or winter in Çamaltı Tuzlası. This marshland is a wintering ground for the graceful flamingo *Phoenicopterus ruber* – as many as 3,000 flamingos have been counted in the area at one time by Turkish ornithologists, and the dunlin, *Calidris alpina*, large flocks of which come down to the area while migrating from the vast tundra lands in Northern Europe.

Other birds that nest in Çamaltı Tuzlası are

Preceding pages: white pelicans in the Göksu delta. Above, the kingfisher, commonly encountered on the coast.

days perched on tree tops. A dozen hotels have already gone up and others are under construction – activity that is likely to scare away many of the rare bird species that breed in the area.

Anatolian leopard: South of Izmir, after Kuşadası, is the Dilek National Park on the Dilek Peninsula. The area consists of high peaks, deep canyons, and has a rocky coastline. This area was one of the last known habitats of the Anatolian Leopard *Panthera pardus tulliana* that survived in the region up to the 1970s but has become virtually extinct due to human pressure. The booted eagle *Hieraaetus pennatus* is a breeding bird found in the national park's pine forests, and there are several breeding pairs of the peregrine hawk *Falco peregrinus*. Outside the breeding season eleonora's falcons *Falco eleonorae* can be seen nesting on the rocky islands off Dilek Peninsula. Part of the National Park is managed for tourism.

A little further to the south is the Büyük Menderes (Maeander) River delta, a large part of which has been cultivated with cotton as the principal crop. The Menderes River has attractive vegetation, including the characteristic tamarix, trees or shrubs with slender branches and feathery flower clusters, common near salt water and often grown as a windbreak. The Menderes River

Circaetius gallicus, the white stork *Ciconia ciconia* and the little egret are some of the birds that breed and winter along Bafa Gölü, famous for the ruins of Heraclea and the Sanctuary of Endymion. Villagers who inhabit the eastern shores of Bafa Gölü hunt birds on the lake and in the mountains, and pose a threat to local bird populations.

The Bodrum region is a renowned resort that, regrettably, now suffers from uncontrolled building development. The coastline is covered with houses and hotels, some of which drain off their sewage untreated into the Aegean.

Marine turtles: The complex wetland system comprising Köyceğiz Lake, the reed

delta is the breeding place of, amongst others, the dalmatian pelican *Pelicanus crispus*, an endangered species with a world population of less than 2,000. In winter, the delta holds large numbers of wintering waterfowl, including many species of duck, geese and great white egrets *Egretta alba*. The delta is famous for hunting, an activity which has caused immence disturbance to its wildlife.

South of the Büyük Menderes River, but north of Bodrum, is Bafa Gölü, a lake region at the foot of ancient Mount Latmus, known today as the Beş Parmak Dağı (The Five Finger Mountain). The short-toed eagle

beds and marshes between Dalyan and the beach at Iztuzu, form a unique combination of different habitats encountered nowhere else in the Mediterranean. Apart from its ecological importance, the area is also one of the most attractive places on the Turkish coast. The Iztuzu Beach is a major breeding ground for the loggerhead sea turtle *Caretta caretta*, and in 1986 and 1987 the national and international conservation movement succeeded in stopping the construction of a 3,000-bed hotel on the beach.

Noise and lights from the hotel, environmentalists argued, would endanger the newly hatched turtles, which would become disoriented and head inland instead of seeking the safety of the sea.

In 1988, the area was declared a Specially Protected Zone by the Turkish government. During 1989, the state Environmental Affairs Office, in cooperation with a German conservation organisation (AGA) and the Turkish Society for the Protection of Nature (DHKD), took additional measures to protect the magnificent loggerhead sea turtles. A demarcation line on the beach protects the nests with the eggs, buried about 50 cm (20 inches) under the surface, and no-one is allowed at night on the beach during the July-September breeding season. The adult female loggerhead may weigh 136 to 181 kg

A walk along the 4.5-km (3-mile) long Iztuzu Beach is rewarding, starting off on the eastern tip and ending in the west where you can get a lift from a fishing boat to Dalyan village. Here, at the information centre, during the high season, volunteers from DHKD show videos and give out information leaflets on the life of sea turtles.

More turtles: The Dalaman Beach area further southeast holds even more turtles than the Dalyan area. It is completely unprotected, according to a report prepared by the World Wide Fund for Nature. The only tourist development on this long beach is in the Sarıgerme region. But Dalaman River, which empties into the beach area, is being

(300 to 400 lb) The female nests three or four times in a single season.

Any kind of housing or hotel development that would drive away the female turtles and upset the hatchlings is prohibited. In 1989, the breeding success of the turtles was remarkably high, and the Dalyan story can be considered a big victory for conservation that serves now as a model for other areas and countries with important nesting beaches for marine turtles.

Left, pegs show bathers where marine turtles' eggs are incubating and mark the no-entry zone. **Above**, a marine turtle wades ashore.

severely polluted by wastes from the state Seka paper plant. The pollution, the report says, threatens the health of both turtles and humans, requiring an immediate solution.

Just south of Antalya is the Olympus National Park, a large scenic area covered with pine and cedar forests, which is good for trekking and mountain climbing. Until recently, the National Park extended all the way down to the sea to protect one of the last breeding sites of the monk seal *Monachus monachus*, a 3-metre (10-ft) long marine mammal that has become extinct in most Mediterranean countries. The monk seal needs coastal caves with an underwater entrance, and is sensitive to human disturbances such as fishing and dynamiting.

The Turkish population of monk seals is estimated at a mere 30–60 animals, yet Turkey ranks as the second most important country in the Mediterranean for the *Monachus monachus*. Unfortunately, the coastal strip within the National Park has been given away to touristic development, and it is unlikely that the monk seal will be able to withstand the increased human presence. This will be another habitat lost for the monk seal, and one step further towards its extinction in Turkey.

The Bey Mountains southwest of Antalya also contain an abundance of the European ibex *Capra ibex ibex*, an agile wild mountain goat with long, upturned horns. The European ibex population, like many species, is being depleted because of hunting.

Göksu delta: Near Silifke is the Göksu River delta, one of the most prominent wetlands on the Turkish south coast and undoubtedly one of the most important wildlife areas in the entire Middle East. The delta is situated on a peninsula and the beaches are of great importance for two Mediterranean species of sea turtles, the loggerhead sea turtle and the green turtle *Chelonia mydas*. It is also here that the purple gallinule *Porhyrio porhyrio* (a wading bird) has its sole breeding ground. Other rare birds that breed in the delta include the marbled teal *Marionetta augustirostris*, the graceful warbler *Prinia gracilis* and the white-breasted kingfisher *Halcyon smyrnensis*.

For wintering waterfowl the area is of great importance. Two main lakes, Akgöl and Paradeniz Gölü, and adjacent steppe and sand dunes are the main features in the western part of the delta, while large portions of the northern and eastern parts of the delta are under cultivation. Recently the Göksu delta has been threatened by uncontrolled housing projects, mainly holiday villages, and the construction of shrimp and fish farms. Conservation organisations try to stop most of these undesirable developments that will certainly disrupt wildlife. In the long run ecotourism is likely to benefit the local people more than the standard hotel development.

People who want to visit the Göksu delta must follow the main road from Antalya to Adana that passes Taşucu and Silifke. Just after Taşucu, beyond the paper mill, turn right and follow the road along the sea. After about 2 km (1.5 miles), you will see a holiday village on the left, located between Akgöl and the sea. All you need to do is hop over the sand dunes to search for Akgöl and its bird life amongst the reed beds. From the east, Paradeniz Gölü can be reached from the village called Kurtuluş.

The Çukurova delta: The Çukurova delta, south of Adana, was formed centuries ago by sediments carried by the Seyhan, Ceyhan and Berden rivers. Originally the delta was a wild area, large parts of which flooded every spring, and each time a thin layer of fertile sediment was deposited.

In the 1950s many of its marshes and lakes were drained to eliminate malaria and obtain farmland. Today the delta is Turkey's breadbasket, with cotton the chief crop. Extensive irrigation networks and other agricultural measures, such as intensive use of pesticides, have converted the Çukurova delta largely into an artificial area.

Fortunately, however, the Çukurova delta still provides large stretches of unspoiled salt and fresh-water marshes, dunes, beaches and lagoons. The main lagoons, with beautiful scenery, are Tuzla Gölü, Akyatan Gölü (easily accessible from Karataş) and the Yumurtalık Oil Terminal Complex (only reachable from the village of that name, in the east). The total beach length is 110 km (69 miles), and many beaches serve as breeding sites for both the loggerhead sea turtle and the green turtle.

From an ornithological point of view, the Çukurova delta is of immense importance. It is home to large populations of marbled teal, black francolin *Francolinus francolinus*, and one of the largest populations in the Mediterranean of the Kentish plover *Charadrius alexandrinus* with about 3,000 breeding pairs. During April and May the region is extremely good for the observation of the migration of white pelicans *Pelicanus onocrotalus*. In spring, no less than 7,000 pelicans can be seen on their way to breeding grounds in Europe. In winter, a staggering 100,000 waterfowl can be present on the main lakes. Amongst the mammals that make the delta their habitat is the Egyptian mongoose *Herpestes ichneumon*.

The natural parts of the Çukurova delta are threatened by the seemingly inexorable advance of intensive agriculture. Environmentalists believe that the enormous accumulation of chemical fertilisers, herbicides and pesticides used in an uncontrolled way in the farmlands will be seriously detrimental to the environment in the long term. An even greater potential threat may come from the oil refineries and trans-shipment ports in the Gulf of Iskenderun, east of the delta, and leaks from oil tankers plying the Mediterranean. The sea current is westerly, parallel to the coast, and one major accidental oil spill could devastate all natural life in the Yumurtalık lagoons, the largest and most untouched part of the region. The establishment of an action

are that in many cases the big money in newly developed regions is earned not by local people, but by investors from far away cities, and surveys indicate that tourists come to Turkey to enjoy its historical and natural richness.

So for healthy development in the long term, there is the need to be extremely careful with what's left on the Turkish coastline. The example of Spain's Costa Brava, where the tourist boom went wild and local people are left with expensive hotels on a coast that has been destroyed forever, should certainly not be allowed to be repeated. Environmentalists feel strongly that lessons should be learned and careful tourism planning is

plan in case of environmental emergencies is urgently needed.

Quite clearly, there are considerable environmental problems on the Turkish Coast. The natural beauty and wildlife are directly or indirectly threatened by uncontrolled building development, pollution (untreated sewage and industrial wastes), overhunting (mainly in the coastal wetlands) and the increased number and mobility of tourists. Rapid touristic development of the coast is often glossed over by pointing to the needs of local people, but counter arguments to this

needed to protect the environment, develop the tourism industry and maintain the strength of the economy.

One way to control development is through proper legislation. The Turkish government have several coastal management schemes covering this area but they appear to be powerless against rich developers. At Akkuyu, near Silifke, a nuclear power project is planned using "second-hand" imported reactors. Despite protests, thousands of letters and Greenpeace intervention, the project looks as if it will go through in the near future. Sadly, the environment is no match for organised money.

Above, griffon vulture flies overhead.

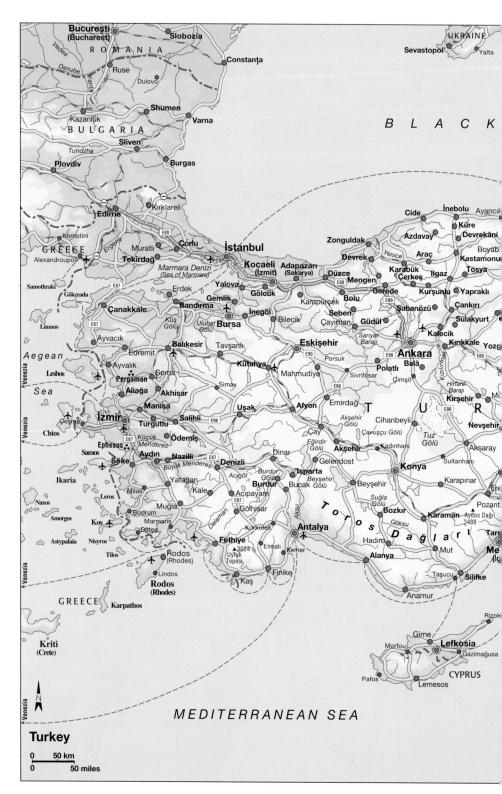

Turkey

0   50 km

0   50 miles

116

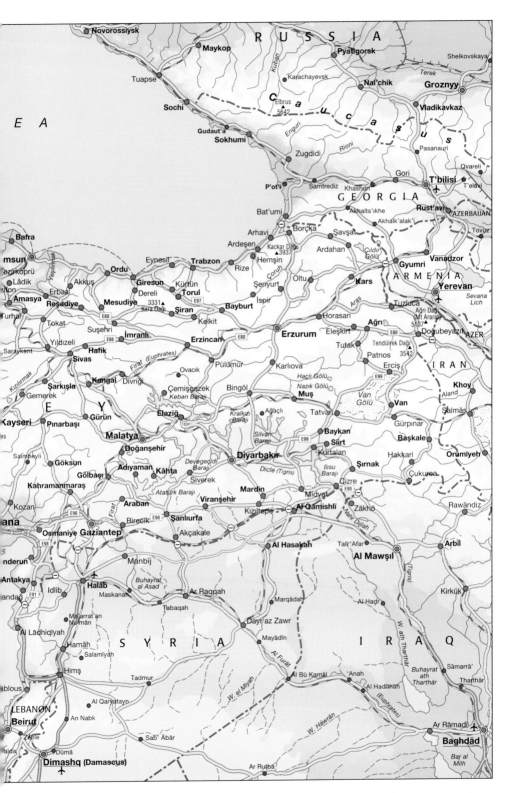

PLACES

The Turkish Coast possesses a wealth of natural beauty, history, sporting and cultural resources and health facilities. You can enjoy the thermal baths of Kestanbol, try hang-gliding around the Assos cliffs, drink the wine of Bozcaada, study the displays in the Çanakkale and Bergama museums, watch the yacht races at Ayvalık, taste spicy *kebabs* in Adana, explore the pits of Heaven and Hell or visit ancient sites like Pergamum, Ephesus and Karatepe. The region includes modern cities like Izmir, Antalya and Adana, and bustling resorts like Kuşadası, Bodrum and Marmaris.

Many resorts along Aegean and Mediterranean Turkey offer all forms of watersports. Scuba diving is particularly popular around Çeşme and Bodrum, while Turkey's main windsurfing centre is at Gümbet. Visitors to Ölüdeniz (the Dead Sea), a lagoon-like inlet on the Mediterranean near Fethiye, can paraglide from the 1,951-metre (6,400-ft) summit of rocky Babadağ, to the beach below.

Since the days of Antony and Cleopatra, the southwest corner of Turkey, known today as the Turquoise Coast, has been a playground for yachtsmen cruising to the deserted coves of the Gulf of Gökova, Hisarönü and Sömbeki bays and the Gulf of Fethiye.

The Turkish Coast begins at the sleepy market town of Enez on the Turkish-Greek border and ends in Antakya, ancient Antioch, near the Syrian frontier. European Turkey includes the wide Saros Bay with its fine beaches and the Gallipoli Peninsula, scene of a World War I military campaign, and the Dardanelles, which separates the European and Asian shores of Turkey's Aegean.

The towns on the Çanakkale Peninsula, such as modern Çanakkale, are located on ancient Troad. The sites of Troy, Alexandria Troas and Assos of antiquity are found in this region. Further south is the Aeolian Coast with the resort towns of Edremit, Ayvalık and Foça.

Izmir, which stands about halfway down Turkey's Aegean Coast, is the nation's third largest city, second biggest port and gateway to Ionian cities such as Claros, Ephesus, Priene, Miletus, and the remains of the monumental Temple of Apollo at Didyma. The resorts of Çeşme and Kuşadası are just two hours from Izmir.

From Kuşadası, travel inland along the Menderes (Maeander) River Valley to the flourishing market towns of Aydın and Denizli. Beyond the Menderes River to the south lies the province of Muğla and the towns of Bodrum, Datça, Marmaris and Fethiye.

An imaginary line east of Marmaris brings you to Turkey's Mediterranean Coast with Antalya as its tourist hub. The ancient cities of Perge, Side and Aspendos, with its stupendous Roman theatre, beckon the traveller. After Alanya, the coast was known as Rough Cilicia because of its jagged, inhospitable shoreline. Rough Cilicia finally gives way to the fertile plain known as the Çukurova with its bustling cities of Mersin, Adana, Iskenderun and Antakya, ending the Turkish Coast.

Preceding pages: beach at the Dead Sea; windmills in Bodrum; the Aegean sunset; Bodrum's streets; an afternoon nap. **Right,** *rakı*-drinking fife players perform at a camel fight.

THE NORTHERN AEGEAN

The Turkish Northern Aegean stands on two continents, Europe and Asia, and is divided by the Dardanelles, the ancient Hellespont. Due to a lack of information about this region, it was one of the least known and less developed tourist areas in Turkey. But since the early 1990s, the famous ruins of Troy near Çanakkale and the ancient sights of Assos have been attracting visitors from all over the world. The Northern Aegean is an enchanting region.

The European part lies on the south-western edge of the landmass known as Trakya or Thrace. It includes the areas around the Bay of Saros, the Gallipoli Peninsula, the Dardanelles and Gökçeada, Turkey's largest island. This area stretches from the farming community of Enez on the Turkish-Greek border to the charming village of Seddülbahir at the tip of the Gallipoli Peninsula—the scene of intense fighting during the 1915 Gallipoli campaign. Gökçeada is one of Turkey's few Aegean islands. The 3,000 Aegean Sea islands, many of which hug the Turkish mainland, are mainly Greek territories.

Inland, Thrace is an agricultural breadbasket with gentle rolling hills and fields of sunflowers, potatoes, mulberry bushes, fruit, vegetables and tobacco. Wine is produced from grapes grown in the region. Most of the inhabitants are farmers and fishermen. There are also descendants of Turkish refugees who fled from the Balkans during various wars fought between the Ottoman Empire and Czarist Russia; a great many are children and grandchildren of Turks who came from Greece during the population exchanges between Greece and Turkey starting in 1923.

Sardalya (sardines), *ton balığı* (Turkish tuna) and *kefal* (gray mullet) are caught in abundance along the Dardanelles and the Bay of Saros, canned at the town of Gelibolu, and then ex-

ported. The Dardanelles is a strategic body of water that connects the Aegean with the Sea of Marmara, the Bosphorus and the Black Sea. Shaped like an S, the 68-km (42-mile) long waterway is known for its swift, erratic currents that make navigation hazardous. Sometimes dense, impenetrable fog descends on the Straits without warning, endangering shipping and the coastal villages. The Dardanelles, which is just over 1 km (less than 1 mile) wide at the narrows, is the only warm water outlet for the Russian Federation and other republics on the Black Sea.

The Asian part of the Turkish Northern Aegean is immediately south and southeast of the Dardanelles, an area that lies within the boundaries of the province of Çanakkale. This bulging landmass, known to the ancients as the Troad, is the northwest corner of Anatolia. Çanakkale, the provincial capital, is the biggest city in the region.

The Troad contains many famous sites from Homer's *Iliad*, including the ruins of Troy, the burial mound of Achilles, which was honoured by Alexander the Great before his invasion of Asia Minor, and Bozcaada (Tenedos), where the Greeks withdrew to induce the Trojans to receive the wooden gift horse. The highest mountain in the area at an elevation of 1,774 metres (5,810 ft) is the legendary Kaz Dağı (Mount Ida), where Paris gave the golden apple to Aphrodite, thus precipitating the ten-year Trojan War.

Many other fascinating sites dot this area, including the ruins of Sestus and Abydos on the Dardanelles. The legendary Leander swam the Hellespont nightly to visit his lover, the priestess Hero, in Sestus, guided by a torch she put on the shore. He drowned one night in a storm when the winds extinguished the torch. Hero, in her sorrow, plunged into the water and committed suicide. Aristotle, the father of logic, taught for three years at Assos, near the quaint village of Behramkale, facing the beautiful bay known as Edremit Körfezi and the Greek island of Lesbos. In the west is Alexandria Troas, once a large, bustling city, but now in ruins.

THRACE

Turkey's Aegean Coast begins at **Enez**, a farming community on the Meriç (Maritza) River along the Turkish-Greek border. In classical times, Enez, or Ainos as it was then called, was a flourishing port city. Now, owing to the silting of the Meriç, Enez is 3 km (2 miles) from the Aegean. In 481 BC, on his way to Thermopylae and Salamis, the Persian King Xerxes visited Enez. Alexander the Great and his army also marched through the city in 334 BC.

Enez, an important commercial centre during Roman times, was linked to the *Via Egnatia*, the overland route that connected Rome to Byzantium. With the fall of the Roman Empire, the city was plundered by various barbarian tribes. In 1384, it came under the rule of Genoese merchants. The Ottoman Turks conquered the city in 1456.

Medieval fortress: The ancient city lies beneath the modern settlement, a town of 3,000 people with a small square and courthouse. There are virtually no remains of the ancient period save for an imposing medieval fortress.

The walls and a column of a cathedral remain standing to the left of the town's gate. The presence of a minaret base and a stone *minber* (an Islamic prayer pulpit) indicates that the structure was previously used as a mosque.

Near the ramparts, travellers can see a deep depression that was once a chapel. Afif Erzen, an Istanbul University archaeologist who excavated the site, discovered two graves beneath the chapel. About 180 metres (590 ft) outside the main gate are the remains of an underground church, and nearby is the **Türbe of Has Yunus**, the tomb of the Turkish naval admiral who conquered Enez.

The **Meriç River** delta with its neighbouring **Lake Gala** is a breeding ground for many unusual and endangered bird species. Its marshlands are favoured grounds for Turkish duck hunters. However, the area is in a mili-

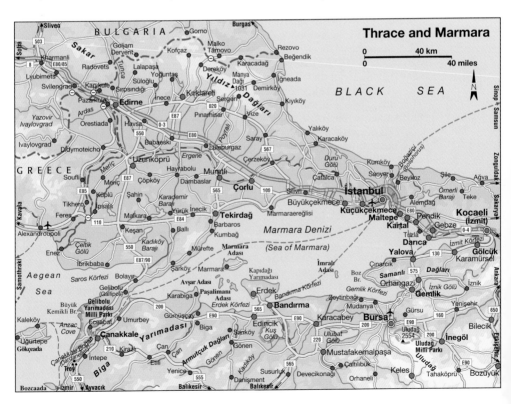

tary zone and photography by members of the public is strictly forbidden.

Enez has few reasonable hotels, and therefore travellers who want to spend the night in the region are advised to stay in **Keşan**, a pleasant town 62 km (39 miles) east.

Enez is best reached by driving from Istanbul, a distance of 260 km (163 miles), which takes about four and a half hours. There are also regular bus services from Istanbul. Motorists follow the Sea of Marmara on E5/100 highway past the town of Silivri, turning left on the E25/110. The road continues inland after Tekirdağ alongside rolling farmlands. They then turn left on route 550 to Keşan and take the secondary road to Enez. Travellers arriving in Turkey from Greece and Bulgaria at Ipsala or Edirne can take route 550 to Keşan to travel to Enez.

NATO war games: A dirt road which follows the **Bay of Saros** back to Keşan has some of the finest beaches in Turkey. The whole region is the setting for annual North Atlantic Treaty Organiza-

In the fertile fields of Thrace.

tion (NATO) war games, beginning the last week of September and lasting about a month. The manoeuvres include amphibious landings along the Bay of Saros, parachute drops near Keşan and mock inland tank battles.

From Keşan, route 550 continues to the narrow, rocky **Gelibolu** (Gallipoli) **Peninsula**. The first town that one comes to is **Bolayır**, which dominates the narrowest point of the isthmus from the top of a hill just off route 550. The Aegean, the Sea of Marmara and the Dardanelles can be seen from Bolayır. A public park with cypress trees off the main square contains the **Tomb of Gazi Süleyman Pasha**, the warrior son of Ottoman Sultan Orhan who led the Ottoman forces across the Dardanelles in 1354, giving the Turks a permanent foothold in Europe. Süleyman Pasha, who died in 1389, is buried with his horse. Nearby is the **Tomb of Namık Kemal** (1840–1888), a nationalist poet, playwright and journalist who spent much of his time in prison and forced exile because of his patriotic views.

The hill is honeycombed with concrete pillboxes that were used as gun emplacements during World War I. A farm road continues along the top of the hill to **Çimpe Kalesi**, a Byzantine fortification which eventually became Süleyman Pasha's stronghold. Further southwest is the promontory known as **Namaztepe** (Prayer Hill), just above the cove where the Ottoman troops first crossed the Dardanelles from Anatolia under Süleyman Pasha's leadership. When the Ottoman soldiers reached Europe, they held a mass prayer at this point, which is now commemorated with a simple monument.

Piri Reis: The road continues for about 16 km (10 miles) to **Gelibolu**, a picturesque town famous for its sardine canneries and numerous Ottoman monuments. A regular ferryboat service takes passengers and cars across to Lapseki on the Asian side of the Dardanelles. The waterfront has a protected wharf, lined with small fishing boats, and the remains of an 8th-century Byzantine castle. In the main square on the waterfront is the **Bust of Piri Reis** (1465–1554), the great Ottoman admiral and mariner from Gelibolu whose map of the coast of the Americas produced in 1513 confounds even today's cartographers because it was drawn only a few years after Columbus discovered the American continent. Piri Reis drew the map, which is now in the Topkapı Museum in Istanbul, in colour on a gazelle hide.

Other sites to visit in Gelibolu are the 15th-century open-air mosque known as the **Namazgah**, located on the lighthouse point. Nearby is the **Tomb of Karaca Bey**, the standard bearer of the Turks as they liberated the town in the 14th century. Near the tomb is the **Cenotaph of Hallacı Mansu**, a famous Moslem dervish whose real grave is in Baghdad. Another landmark is the **French Cemetery**, burial place of French soldiers killed during the Crimean War (1853–1856).

If you plan to cross to the town of Lapseki on the Asian side by ferry from Gelibolu, a delicious fish lunch at one of

The town square at Eceabat.

126

the wharf-front restaurants is a pleasant pastime while waiting for the next ferry.

The road continues along the Dardanelles past **Cumalı Çayı**, a stream formerly known as **Aegospotami**, where the Spartan navy under Lysander defeated the Athenian Fleet in 405 BC, ending the Peloponnesian War in one of the greatest naval battles in history.

Battle sites: Before the road reaches Eceabat, a road forking to the right goes to **Gallipoli Campaign Battle Sites** around the broken Sarı Bayır mountain range and Suvla Bay, and includes numerous Australian, New Zealand, British and Turkish war graves, such as those at **Anzac Cove** and **Lone Pine**, **Conk Bayır** (Chunuk Bair) and **Kabatepe** (Gabatepe). On a slope by the point known today as Akbaş Limanı is the ancient settlement of **Sestus**.

The town of **Eceabat** has several pleasant outdoor fish restaurants and a stunning view of the Dardanelles. A regular ferryboat takes passengers and vehicles across to Çanakkale. The village of **Kilitbahir**, with its heart-shaped fortress, is directly across from Çanakkale, and small ferries take cars and commuters across the Straits.

The road continues along the Dardanelles and then inland to **Alçıtepe** (Krithia), a village that has a privately owned war museum with a collection of mementos of the Gallipoli Campaign. The magnificent **Meh-metçik Anıtı**, the Turkish War Memorial commemorating the 100,000 Turkish soldiers killed during the Dardanelles campaign stands on a hill at Morto Bay. Underneath the memorial is a small war museum, and nearby is the lonely **French War Cemetery**.

The **Tumulus of Protesilaus**, who was the first Greek soldier to have fallen in the Trojan War, is thought to have been located nearby, but is believed to have been destroyed during the 1915 fighting. Several British war cemeteries are located in the Cape Helles region, and the Commonwealth **Cape Helles War Memorial** overlooks the village of Seddülbahir and its castle at the tip of the Gallipoli Peninsula.

Scene from Kilitbahir village.

THE GALLIPOLI CAMPAIGN

The calm blue sea was "absolutely red with blood" for a distance of 50 yards from the shore. It was "a horrible sight to see." Red ripples washed upon the beach and everywhere the calm surface of the water was whipped up into a ghastly discoloured foam by thousands of falling bullets. The sun was shining.

–from Alan Moorehead's *Gallipoli*

Such was the description of the massacre that took place at the Cape Helles Allied landing site known as V Beach, on April 25, 1915. It was given by British Commodore C. R. Samson as he flew in a reconnaissance plane over the battle site where the Turks held up units of the British 29th Division.

Nearly 50,000 Allied troops went ashore that day at seven different beaches along the Gallipoli Peninsula in Europe, and Kumkale, on the Asian shore of the Dardanelles, beginning an eight-month military campaign aimed at defeating the Ottoman Turks in the Great War.

At V Beach, three heavily armed and well-trenched Turkish companies, led by a courageous sergeant called Yahya Çavuş, held back overwhelming numbers of British forces for more than 24 hours, slaughtering the first waves of soldiers as they hit the beach. Entire battalions, including the Royal Dublin Fusiliers and the Royal Irish Rifles, were almost annihilated, losing over 60 percent of their men in the first day of fighting. Yahya Çavuş and all of his men were also killed.

Turkey enters war: Shortly after the outbreak of World War I, Ottoman Turkey sided with Germany and Austria. The Allied powers, Britain, France and Russia, felt that Turkey, weakened by successive Balkan wars, could be forced to accept peace by a decisive show of strength launched against it. The Allies believed that a peace with Turkey would free the stranglehold

against Russia and influence the neutral Balkan states to join Serbia in attacking Austria. The action chosen was to dispatch an Allied fleet to the Dardanelles. The objective was to destroy the Turkish defensive lines and force a passage into the Sea of Marmara and threaten Constantinople.

On February 19, 1915, the fleet took up position and began its bombardment of the outer defences. The attack caused panic in and around Constantinople, the Turkish capital.

Bombardment resumes: On February 25, the fleet resumed its bombardment of the forts with greater precision and effect. By March 4, the outer and intermediate forts had been demolished and the way was open for a major assault on the inner forts.

At the beginning of March the fleet began its attack on the inner defences. At first the shelling caused confusion amongst the defenders but, in fact, little damage was done to the permanent defences. However, by March 12 the situation looked very grim indeed for the

Left, Mustafa Kemal observes enemy positions during the Gallipoli Campaign. **Right**, the Turkish War Memorial at Morto Bay.

Turks, and the German High Command considered defeat imminent. A quote from Admiral von Tripitz summed up the German feelings: "It is a dangerous situation. The capsizing of one little state may affect fatally the whole course of the war."

On the morning of March 18 the British fleet, reinforced by a French squadron, reopened its attack on the inner forts with the intention of forcing a passage through the Narrows. To the Turkish defenders, the sight must have been awesome as it was the largest armada ever assembled. At first, the Turkish defenders retaliated valiantly but were gradually silenced and by mid-afternoon the situation had become critical.

Disaster strikes: With victory in sight, the battleships moved in for the kill, and it was then that disaster struck. First the *Bouvet*, a French battleship, exploded and disappeared with most of her crew. Within minutes, three major British warships had either joined her at the bottom of the sea or had been disabled.

At this point, the fleet withdrew in the belief that it was being attacked by either mobile shore batteries or land-launched torpedoes. Later, it became known that a small Turkish minelayer, the *Nusret*, had penetrated the British screen and had laid mines which had gone undetected. These were responsible for the damage done to the fleet.

Fortunately for the Turks, the Allies were more concerned with their naval losses than with resuming the attack, and did not appreciate how close they were to victory. The assault was abandoned and a new campaign was planned involving a joint operation between the navy and the army. The latter was to land on the peninsula, to overcome the Turkish defenders and then occupy and control the Dardanelles.

Anzac landing: The first landings by Allied troops took place at 5am on April 25, 1915, as the Anzacs (Australian and New Zealand Army Corps) set foot in what proved to be the wrong place. Even so, the troops advanced steadily against light opposition up the ridges of

Scene from Turkish trenches.

the Sarı Bayır Mountain Range. Turkish coastal troops were fleeing in terror. Fortunately for the Turks, at this point, a young Turkish Colonel, Mustafa Kemal, later known as Atatürk, appeared on the scene. Kemal, commanding the Turkish Army 19th Division, arrived ahead of his troops, stopped the fleeing soldiers and asked why they were running away. They replied that the "*Ingiliz*" (British) were coming and they had no ammunition. Kemal's answer was, "You can't run away from the enemy." He quickly ordered them to fix their bayonets and lie down. Seeing this action the Australians also began entrenching. "This was the moment of time that we gained," Kemal was to write in his memoirs.

The Turkish officer was the first commander to recognise the importance of the heights of the Sarı Bayır Mountains as holding the key to the entire Gallipoli Peninsula. He quickly ordered his troops to occupy the heights and then mounted a counterattack with his two best regiments.

The fighting raged on for many days as both sides attacked and counterattacked on the slopes. Although it cost many lives, no progress was made by either side. The Turks held the higher ground and the Anzacs were confined to a small perimeter around the beach, precariously clinging to the sides of the mountain.

Johnnie Turks: Gradually, both sides developed a great respect for each other which bordered on affection, as typified by the Anzacs' description of the enemy as "Johnnie Turks" and their refusal to use gas masks, saying that, "The Turks won't use gas. They are clean fighters." And neither side did.

The landings by the British and the French at Cape Helles had mixed results. On some beaches, such as V Beach, the Turkish opposition was murderous, but on others it was nonexistent. Overall, the landings were successful but the leadership was poor and the advance was uncoordinated. In general no advantage was taken of opportunities offered. Over a period of months, and after many frontal assaults against

enemy trenches defended by machine guns, the Allied line was pushed forward at great cost. However, the Turkish position grew stronger while the Allied attacks gradually weakened until both sides were exhausted and stalemate resulted.

Basically the campaign, like many others in World War I, was marred by unimaginative leadership, culminating in a series of costly mistakes and lost opportunities.

Suvla landings: In August the Allies endeavoured to break the impasse by landing troops at Suvla Bay, just north of the Anzac positions. The landings were a complete surprise and were virtually unopposed. Again, bad leadership ruled the day and the advantage was not seized and, after heavy losses, the position was deadlocked.

By late 1915 the Allied General Command had concluded that further military operations on Gallipoli had very little chance of success and that the army should be withdrawn. The evacuation was probably the most imagina-

Turkish troops prepare to depart for Gallipoli from Istanbul.

tive and successful operation of the whole campaign. Between December 1915 and January 1916, the whole army was evacuated from the peninsula with few casualties, although tons of equipment was abandoned.

So ended a passage in military history that still captures the imagination. It was the baptism of fire for the new nations of Australia and New Zealand, and it demonstrated the courage of the Turkish soldiers. It also created a Turkish hero, Mustafa Kemal, who had a higher destiny to fulfil. For the Allies, Gallipoli was a calamity and saw the fall from favour of many high-ranking officers and politicians. Some reputations were made, but many were lost. The Dardanelles venture was to serve as the model for the evacuation of Dunkirk and the invasion of Normandy during World War II.

The peninsula and its close environs mark the graves of approximately 110,000 men. Of these 34,000 were British or Commonwealth troops, 9,000 French and 66,000 Turkish. (According

to another source, the number of dead is much higher.)

Gallipoli today: In 1918, after the armistice, British troops occupied the peninsula and controlled the Dardanelles until forced by the Turks to leave in 1922. The battlefields of 1915 were, where possible, made safe and the Allied dead laid to rest in carefully prepared cemeteries where they fell. Memorials to the Allied dead were raised at Cape Helles, Lone Pine, Conk Bayır and Morto Bay. There are Turkish monuments all over the peninsula but the largest now dominates the headland at Morto Bay.

The main World War I battlefields are all situated towards the south of the peninsula, Anzac and Suvla Bay on the Aegean shore and Cape Helles on the southern tip. There are several companies in Çanakkale, Eceabat and Gelibolu offering tours of the area but, for the independent traveller, the best way to see the sites is to obtain a map and, using the yellow Commonwealth Graves Commission signs as a guide, locate the cemeteries which mark the main areas of fighting.

Suvla Bay is situated in a natural horseshoe of hills extending south of Anzac Cove. The dominating feature of these hills is Conk Bayır, which overlooks both Anzac and Suvla. On a clear day the **New Zealand Memorial**, which sits on top of this hill, can be seen from long distances.

Lonely beach: Suvla is best approached from the coast road heading north past Anzac Cove and Arı Burnu (the Cape of Bees). Lala Baba, the southernmost extremity of the battlefield is signposted to the left. Further on is another left turn that skirts the salt lake and leads to **Green Hill**, **Azmak**, **Hill 10**, and **Anafarta**, the major foci of the battle in this area. The lonely beach at Suvla is very welcoming with fine, yellow sand and a clear, blue sea. It is an excellent setting for pitching a tent and spear fishing.

The best approach to Anzac is to take the road that leaves the main coastal highway just north of Eceabat. It goes west and is signposted Anzac Koyu, Gökçeada or Kemalyeri. In the distance

Anzac Beach Cemetery.

is the tree-covered ridge marking the site of the Anzac battlefield. On the right hand side of the ridge is the Kabatepe War Museum, which has a good collection of war artefacts and old battle photographs.

Travelling from the museum towards the sea one soon sees the Commonwealth War Graves Commission signposts indicating the various cemeteries. One can follow the high ground which was, in general, held by the Turkish defenders, or go down towards the sea. The former route gradually climbs to Lone Pine and the **Australian Memorial**. Still climbing, the road passes through what was no man's land and the remains of trenches and tunnels can be seen on either side, the Turkish to the right, Anzac to the left.

A short distance further on is the **Nek** with its Turkish Memorial. In the distance and higher up is Conk Bayır and the New Zealand Memorial. Beside the memorial is stacked a pyramid of cannon balls and Turkish trenches, which mark the spot where Mustafa Kemal supposedly gave his legendary order: "I don't order you to attack, I order you to die. In the time it takes us to die other troops and commanders can come and take our places."

Below the brow of the hill is a large Turkish memorial, shaped like an open hand. Conk Bayır affords a complete view of both Suvla Bay and the Dardanelles. It was here that Kemal led the Turkish defence. The tours tend to return back to Anzac Cove. A new Turkish Memorial stands with the following words spoken by Atatürk in 1934 inscribed on its façade:

"Those heroes that shed their blood and lost their lives.
You are now lying in the soil of a friendly country.
Therefore rest in peace.
There is no difference between the Johnnies and the Mehmets to us where they lie side by side here in this country of ours.
You, the mothers,
who sent their sons from far away countries wipe away your tears;

Your sons are now lying in our bosom and are in peace.
After having lost their lives on this land they have become our sons as well."

Cape Helles is best reached from Kilitbahir and Alçıtepe, where there is a private war museum. South of Alçıtepe the British and Turkish War memorials dominate the horizon. The Commonwealth War Graves Commission signposts are up everywhere. The road to the memorial passes the French Memorial.

Westward from Alçıtepe is a track leading to the **Nuri Yamut Turkish Memorial** at Zihindere, or Gurkha Bluff. The centre of intense fighting in 1915, this area claimed 10,000 Turkish soldiers. There is still evidence of the tragedy and it is not unusual to find bones and other relics in the fields.

The Cape Helles Memorial overlooks the village of Seddülbahir and its fortress and V Beach. Nearby is an unpretentious cemetery for the valiant Yahya Çavuş and his men.

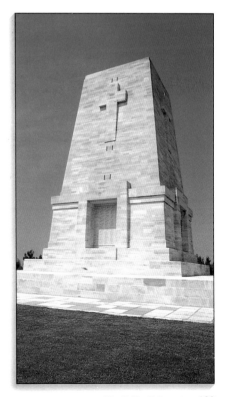

The Lone Pine Memorial commemorates the Australian dead.

THE TROAD

The Troad is the ancient designation for what today is called the Biga or the **Çanakkale Peninsula**. It did not have a firm boundary, but extended inland along the Dardanelles covering about the same area as the present-day province of Çanakkale.

Çanakkale, located on the Asiatic side of the Dardanelles, is the centre of the province of the same name. By car it's now about five hours from Istanbul on the motorway, and there is a marina where passing yachts can moor. The town makes a pleasant base for visiting Troy, the Troad and Gallipoli. The harbour area has recently been refurbished and there is a fine seaside promenade

Çanakkale sets the pattern for the area with its ties to ancient, Ottoman and modern history. First Xerxes and Alexander the Great built bridges of boats as they moved their armies across the Straits (the Hellespont). Probably those bridges reached between the narrowest point of Abydos (Nağra Burnu north of Çanakkale) and Sestus (Akbaş north of Eceabat). The Straits has challenged such swimmers as Leander and Lord Byron to conquer their waters.

The Çimenlik Fortress Museum (formerly the Sultaniye Fortress) that one sees just west of the ferry landing at Çanakkale was built in 1452 by Ottoman Sultan Mehmet the Conqueror. Süleyman the Magnificent repaired it. Later the Queen Mother Hatice Türkhan (who later completed Yeni Cami in Istanbul) restored it and the heart-shaped **Kilitbahir Fortress** directly across in Europe. With these two castles the Turks controlled the passage through the Straits when the Allied Fleet tried unsuccessfully to force its way through in the Çanakkale Naval Battle on March 18, 1915, a prelude to the Gallipoli landings. Reminders of that day are visible in the damaged walls and the cannons placed around the park. A replica of the minelayer, **the Nusret**, is firmly docked on the terrace wall.

On a hill, on the European side of the Dardanelles, facing Çanakkale, is a figure of a giant Turkish soldier with the inscriptions taken from a poem by Necmettin Onan entitled "*Dur Yolcu*" or "*Stop O Passenger*", commemorating the Gallipoli Campaign. Roughly translated it reads:

"The earth you thus tread unawares is where an age sank. Bow and listen.

This quiet mound is where the heart of a nation throbs."

Fresh seafood: Near the ferry landing are restaurants where you can savour fresh seafood specialities in a leisurely meal. A daily ferryboat service takes travellers to **Gökçeada**, the island of **Imroz**, from Çanakkale, as well as from Kabatepe, on the Gallipoli Peninsula. Gökçeada has a military base for commando training but the general atmosphere is relaxed and welcoming for Turkish and foreign visitors. The smaller, sleepy Bozcaada (Tenedos) offers a prettier and more friendly environment and excellent fish and *meze*

Left, relaxing after a hard day's work. **Right**, a Hellenistic vase.

restaurants. Both Gökçeada and Bozcaada still have a tiny Greek population, the original inhabitants of these islands, which are known for their beautiful beaches, fortresses and slow, bucolic existence. Boats to Bozcaada leave from Geyikli, near Ezine town further south from Çanakkale. Regular ferryboats also operate between Çanakkale and the village of Kilitbahir; and Eceabat, across the Dardanelles from the boat landing.

In the main square, the clock in the tower sounds the hours. A tree-shaded promenade extends northeast along the sea front. Stately houses on the hill to the north date from the 19th century when Çanakkale was a busy international commercial centre. The exports of those years (valonia oak [tannin], cereals, lumber, wine and pottery) are still important to the city's economy. The name by which it is now known comes from the quantities of ceramics and terracotta (Çanak in Turkish) that continue to be made in the region.

Travellers to Çanakkale should visit its old **Aynalı Çarşı**, or Bazaar with Mirrors, near the town's centre, for souvenir hunting.

About 1.5 km (1 mile) south of the main part of the city near the E24/500 road to Izmir is the **Archaeological Museum** (open 8.30am–noon and 1.30–5pm daily). Displays include artefacts, sculpture and ceramics from Troy, including a crystal amulet and lion-head (Troy II), a pot cover in the form of a female head (Troy III), goblets (Troy VI) and beautiful terracottas (Troy VIII). There are also collections of costumes, Roman, Byzantine and Ottoman coins and a display of Atatürk's military clothing. In the garden are sarcophagi, stelae and funerary urns.

The Dardanus Tumulus: Leaving Çanakkale and travelling south, the first site that you come to is that of the **Dardanus Tumulus**, indicated by a yellow sign showing a turn off from the main highway (it can also be approached from the road to Güzelyalı.) After following a dirt road for about a mile one finds the walled entrance to the family tomb in the midst of a pleasant pine grove.

Dardanus, the mythical hero after whom the Straits was named, came from Samothrace where he had been caught in a flood. By good fortune he was able to float across to the mainland on a skin bag. His luck continued and he married the daughter of Teucer, the first person to found a city in the region. Dardanus' grandson was Tros; when Tros became king the people and the land took his name. Or so they say.

The beach of Dardanus continues on to **Güzelyalı**; the whole area makes a pleasant summer holiday destination. The hotels, camping spots, pensions and restaurants are varied, good and plentiful, and the swimming and surfing are excellent.

From Çanakkale or Güzelyalı one can make day excursions to various sites; here you can relax on the beach, paint the changing colours of the sea and the mountains, or enjoy the hospitality and stories of the families who have chosen to live here year-round.

Trojan war heroes: A tour west of Troy around the plain begins with the side road that forks off to the right to **Kumkale** just south of Intepe. Keeping close to the shoreline it is possible to see – at least in the distance – several tumuli considered to be monuments of the heroes of the Trojan War. Some of them are in a military zone and therefore not open to tourists; some of them have revealed graves or identities of actual or legendary heroes, and each has enough Hellenistic shards scattered about to keep the legends alive.

The **Tomb of Ajax** is near the village of Yeni Kumkale on the east side of the Küçük Menderes River. Emperor Hadrian believed, when he found the bones of a very large man near here, that he was seeing the mortal remains of Ajax. He picked them up reverently and had a new tumulus cast up over them.

Shortly beyond Yeni Kumkale, and over the dikes that line the river, is the **Castle of Kumkale**, presently a military post. A fierce battle during the Dardanelles campaign in 1915 concentrated on the Kumkale Fortress located on the point where the Dardanelles begins. A monument commemorates soldiers who died fighting here.

Mound of Achilles: The road turns south at Kumkale and at once the two tumuli attributed to Achilles and to his friend Patroclus are visible on the coast (but again the area is in a military zone). South of them is **Cape Sigeon**, and then the **Tumulus of Antilochus**, who carried the news of Patroclus' death to Achilles. On the sea west of Yenişehir is **Beşiğe Tepe**, perhaps the Tumulus of Penelaus, one of the Greek warriors. Items from here in the Çanakkale Museum date from the same time as Troy I – about 2500 BC. They include a necklace of gold and semiprecious stones, some loom weights and a curious four-handled pot.

Not far from **Üveycik** is a prominent dark hump of a much later date than the five Trojan War heroes; it is known locally as **Sivri Tepe** and may possibly be the tumulus of the Emperor Caracalla's friend, Festus.

The port of Odun Iskelesi was the

former jumping-off spot for Bozcaada, the island of Tenedos. Ferries carrying passengers, trucks and passenger cars now leave from Geyikli, just over 2 km (1 mile) north of Odun Iskelesi and take a bit less than an hour for the twice-daily (three in the summer) crossing.

Bozcaada is the island behind which Agamemnon hid his ships while the Trojans tore their city gate down so they could tug the horse inside.

Venetian crusaders: The main harbour of the island in bygone years was guarded by a handsome fortress built perhaps first by Venetian Crusaders. Genoese and Byzantine architects had a hand in it before Mehmet the Conqueror and Süleyman the Magnificent added to it. Besides the towers and curtain walls, it encloses the remains of a mosque, an infirmary, barracks and an arsenal.

The island is 42 square km (26 square miles) with long stretches of golden sandy beaches. Bozcaada wines are famous throughout Turkey, and much of the sunny island is planted with vines. Bozcaada is said to be the most windy part of Turkey. Strong winds start blowing across the island towards the end of August.

For a completely relaxing holiday, the island offers plenty of comfortable hotels and pensions with many restaurants serving fresh fish, excellent *meze* dishes on a par with the best restaurants in Istanbul, and good local wine. Cyclists should enjoy the roads here.

Alexandria Troas: Somewhat less than 5 km (3 miles) south of Odun Iskelesi on the mainland are the scanty ruins of **Alexandria Troas**. The city's founding is a recent relative to most of the other coastal towns. Started at Alexander the Great's orders around 330 BC, it had its heyday under the Roman Empire. Its ancient baths can still be seen today.

St Paul's Journeys: To those who want to trace the missionary journeys of St Paul, Alexandria Troas is of interest because he visited it twice. His first stay was short: here he had a vision of a Macedonian calling to him to come and preach to people across the Aegean. The second time St Paul was in Alexandria

Troas was towards the end of his third journey when he stayed there for a week with some of his friends. From Alexandria Troas St Paul continued his journey by land to Assos.

The thermal springs of **Kestanbol** next to Alexandria Troas have been a centre of healing for centuries. The 150-bed establishment attracts those from the Çanakkale region seeking relief from problems like rheumatism, gout, skin and bone diseases, and heart disorders.

Neandria's ruins lie between Alexandria Troas and Ezine on Mt. Çığrı. The city walls, built probably in the 5th-century BC, can still be identified. Capitals of its 7th-century BC temple are in the Istanbul Museum. Neandria lost its residents to Alexandria Troas when the latter was founded.

Between Kestanbol and **Gülpınar** the road passes several seaside camping spots and another hot spring with colourfully stained rocks at Tuzla. The lack of development there contrasts to that at Kestanbol.

Many yellow signs point to **Apollo Smintheon** (Chryse) where there is a 2nd-century BC temple in the town of Gülpınar. Smintheus is one of Apollo's several names. It means "the killer of mice," and refers to the legend that Teucer (Dardanus' father-in-law) built his first city here where mice gnawed his men's bowstrings.

At the far southwest point of the Çanakkale peninsula stands the dark fortress of **Babakale** (Lefton). An inscription at the entrance to the castle reports that early in the 18th century this was a place where hated and evil pirates dwelt. It adds thankfully that Mustafa Pasha got rid of them, and then went on to build a mosque, a Turkish bath and a fountain in Babakale. Fishing and mining are the main activities of the village now.

One can approach **Assos** (Behramkale) by sea (there is a yacht marina in the harbour at the foot of the hill) or by road from Gülpınar, Ayvacık or Küçükkuyu. The most dramatic way leads from Ayvacık through the pretty

Playing backgammon at Behramkale.

pine forest near Paşaköy from where there is a view of the acropolis in the distance. Near Behramkale is a 14th-century Turkish bridge arching over the stream to the side of the road.

Aristotle and Assos: Assos was established about 1000 BC by Aeolians from nearby Mitylene. It was ruled successively by Lydians, Persians, Pergamenes, Romans, Byzantines and Crusaders until Sultan Orhan took it over for the Ottomans in 1330. During the 4th century BC its ruler was the eunuch Hermias, who was trying to be the philosopher king of his teacher, Plato. Aristotle taught here for three years and finally married Hermias' adopted daughter.

The craggy peak of Assos was surrounded by a wall; the care with which it was built is evident in the sections that stand today. The theatre, council chamber, gymnasium and agora are marked with signs. Archaeologists are reconstructing the Temple of Athena, built about 530 BC. This temple is of interest to art historians because of its combination of Doric capitals and an Ionic frieze. Much of the organisation of Assos resembles that of Pergamum: the main temple was on the acropolis, the gymnasium and the agora with its arcades and the theatre built into the side of the hill were below the temple area.

The wide view from the acropolis is more dramatic than that of Pergamum because you can look out across the deep blue sea to the Greek island of **Lesbos** or **Mitylene** (Midilli in Turkish) about 10 km (6 miles) away.

A fledgling Bodrum: The atmosphere in the restaurants and hotels at the harbour of Assos is that of a fledgling Bodrum. Some of the same elements are present: a historic site, a harbour, an artist's colony, good swimming and lots of sun. An international theatre festival is organised in Assos in late September. An increasing number of aspiring young theatre groups come from different parts of the world to perform in the streets, temple and bridge of the village and the villagers enthusiastically take part in the plays.

The bridge to Assos.

TROY AND THE TROJAN WAR

A beauty contest, a bloody war with lots of heroes on both sides, the best publicity ever written, and then a treasure hunt to find the hidden gold – what a perfect combination Troy makes for a place to fire the imagination.

To see Troy is to share for a moment in the excitement of soldiers clashing swords and shields, of the dust beneath their horses' hooves whitening their faces, of the smell of their sweat at the end of a day of hard fighting.

Schliemann's world: **Troy**, an ancient city in northwestern Turkey, was excavated by a German businessman, Henrich Schliemann, who revolutionised scholars' ideas about classical history. The city is a series of levels, some on top of each other – most levels difficult to distinguish – that go back 5,000 years to the Early Bronze Period. It is where the story of the Trojan War took place. Most significantly, it is remembered as the setting for much of the greatest poetry ever composed, Homer's *Iliad* and *Odyssey*.

Ancient ruins, excavators, Greek myths, epic poetry – there is much to Troy. Each of the parts is fascinating, but none by itself makes full sense.

To see Troy (or Truva in Turkish), it is easiest to start from Çanakkale, a port on the Dardanelles 30 km (20 miles) northeast of the site. You need to take the E24/500 highway toward Izmir. After passing Intepe, you should take the country road that forks to the right with the yellow sign pointing towards Truva.

In ancient times, the low hill of Troy overlooked a plain close to the fork of two rivers, the Scamander (Küçük Menderes) and the Simosis (Dümbrek). Since then the bed of the Scamander has moved slightly west and the hill has risen due to the accumulation of debris over the centuries.

Wooden horse: The approach to the site is protected by a fence, along with gift shops, soft drinks bars and the museum ticket window. Your imagination is immediately teased by the wooden horse at the entrance. You can climb into the horse, pretend that it is about to be tugged inside the walls of Troy and shout as you come to capture the sleeping Trojans. But would anyone now fall for that trick?

Many of the items found in the excavations are presently displayed in the Archaeological Museum in Çanakkale. These include a terracotta sieve from Troy II, graceful stemmed goblets from Troy VI, and a black-glaze vase decorated with an owl from Troy VIII. The latter often reminds visitors of Schliemann's complaints in his book *Ilios* about "innumerable owls, which built their nests in the holes of my trenches; their shrieks had a weird and horrible sound, and were especially intolerable at night."

The general tour around Troy leads first to the massive tower in the strong wall of Troy VI, up through the east gate, and past the carefully constructed houses from Troy VI to those more carelessly made in Troy VII.

The treacherous Trojan Horse, now a symbol of peace.

Wine-dark sea: From the top of the hill you can look out to the Plain of Troy and beyond to Homer's "wine-dark sea", the Aegean. The next thing that comes in sight is Schliemann's great north-south trench. Northwest of a paved ramp and against the wall of Troy II is the place where Schliemann found gold. The part of the treasure that he sent to Berlin disappeared during World War II (after the Berlin Wall was demolished, it was discovered to have been carried off to Moscow's Pushkin Museum) but a few pieces that the Turkish government placed in the Istanbul Archaeological Museum remain. Some speculate that the west gate, beyond where the treasure was found, is the gate that was enlarged so that the wooden horse could be hauled into the city.

The Roman theatre was built on top of the Troy VI walls. The main city gate next to it, the Dardania Gate, was guarded by a tower. This tower, or the one by the east gate, could be where Andromache fainted seeing Achilles drag her husband by his heels in the dust.

Schliemann's biography: Henrich Schliemann had long been fascinated by where Troy had been and what was still there. From early childhood, he was inspired by Homer's epics and determined to prove that Troy was a real city. Poverty, disease, shipwreck, fire and the loss of his sweetheart didn't deter him from his goal. Starting his career as a grocer's helper, Schliemann taught himself several languages including English, French, Russian, Arabic, Latin and Greek.

He memorised the whole of the *Iliad* and the *Odyssey*, and a number of books in other languages, too. He worked hard as an importer of indigo. Then he went to California and struck gold. He happened to be there when the state joined the Union, so he became a citizen of the United States. At last he was an independently wealthy man. In 1871 he began the excavations for which he is most famous.

To see Troy is to exult with Schliemann at his moment of truth when he found the city, and prised out of the dirt what he believed was Priam's glistening goblets and earrings. To see Troy is also to see old stones and dry weeds, to be disappointed that Schliemann left so much rubble and so little order. People are often tempted to ask what all the fuss has been about. To begin to make sense of the site it helps to have a map of the many layers and a good guide.

Nine levels: Schliemann thought that there were seven levels of city in the tumulus which he dug. He recognised two more levels later, and archaeologists have sorted out many more distinct periods; nine levels are still used for reference. However, so much has been built on top of and using bits of previous cities that it is not surprising that Schliemann was confused.

The people who occupied the bottom layer (Troy I) lived in the city around 2500 BC. They left implements of copper, lead, stone, terracotta and bone, enabling archaeologists to determine that they made their pots by hand. Not much else is known about them except that they lost their homes in a huge fire which swept the city.

The residents of the second level (Troy II) who built their city a few years after the fire enjoyed several improvements. They seem to have been the same people or relatives of those who lived in Troy I, although there were important differences. Could the disaster have inspired an emergency relief project that brought in new ideas? Among these were the potter's wheel and the kiln. The artisans of Troy II were skilled in the working of gold, silver, copper and tin – none of which existed in the neighbourhood. Thus they must have been engaged in commerce with other countries.

Treasures of Troy: Troy II is also the level which Schliemann believed was Priam's Troy. His excitement upon seeing the first glimmerings of gold reverberates through his description. Schliemann instructed his workmen to take a break to prevent them from seeing his treasure. He cut into the dirt and rocks with his knife at the risk of the wall collapsing above him. With the help of his wife he packed the treasure they had found into her shawl. Together they smuggled it into their house and later out of the country.

At first Schliemann claimed that someone had collected the hoard in a box and had tried to escape with it. Trapped, perhaps by fire or an enemy, the thief abandoned it at the city wall just as the fire brought the adjacent royal house down on top of it, he said. Later, having found four more caches of treasure nearby, Schliemann decided that the gold had fallen from the upper storey of the palace and been hidden there for centuries.

Schliemann's discovery drew worldwide attention and inspired many archaeologists. People began to accept the idea that, however fictional the ancient gods and goddesses may have been, Homer had told the story of a real event and people.

Schliemann's work opened up the productive field of archaeology. Thenceforth, the search was on to uncover more and more of the treasures hinted at in classical literature.

The obsession: A quotation printed on the title page of Schliemann's book, *Ilios*, hints at how often he recited to himself Homer's *Iliad*, mulling over it for any clues that would lead him to the right place. In Andrew Lang's translation the lines read, "yet will we twain, even I and Sthenelos, fight till we attain the goal of Ilios; for in God's name are we come."

With later, more skilful excavation, archaeologists were able to conclude that Troy II predated Homer's city. It is still not known for certain what destroyed the city Homer wrote about, but one possible explanation is that warriors (perhaps from Central Europe) invaded and conquered it.

Later archaeologists have likewise felt that with Schliemann's huge trench Troy suffered another catastrophe. He was the first to dig there; scientists have profited by what he uncovered. But he destroyed too much in his singleminded purpose of finding only the city. Or was he merely looking for gold?

After Troy II, waves of migrations continued for 400 years while the less prosperous cities of Troy III, IV and V came and went.

Genetic change: Archaeologists have not determined what happened between Troy V and Troy VI that caused the later city to flourish. Some have speculated that some genetic change occurred because of intermarriage between two peoples – the native inhabitants and the invaders?

Troy VI (about 1300 BC) was the height of Troy's splendour. Perhaps a balance had been reached among the different residents in their skills of government and commerce. It was in the city-states which developed during this era that each man learned to exercise his responsibility for the political, ethical and aesthetic life of the community. This was an development in the history of human relations that apparently came out of nowhere.

Stately city: Troy VI was a stately city for its time. It was bigger than the cities it covered up. Its houses were well built and arranged in an orderly fashion. Its walls were sturdy and placed with a keen eye for defence. Its citizens did a lot of trading with Crete and Cyprus and must have been good sailors.

Professor Ekrem Akurgal thinks that Troy VI was the home of Priam of the *Iliad*. He and American archaeologist Carl Blegen think the city came to an abrupt end in 1275 BC due to an earthquake rather than a war.

About a generation later the city of Troy VII (which was less well built) was sacked and gutted, probably by Achaean invaders. Smoke from the fire can be traced on the stones of Troy VII. The late George Bean, who taught classical history and archaeology at Istanbul University for 25 years, and Professor Blegen put Priam's city at this level. Was this time lapse between the earthquake and the fire the reason why Homer thought it was a long war? Akurgal suggests that it was Troy's power and her threat to mainland Greece that brought the war upon her. He also suggests that without the earthquake which weakened her defences the city could not have been taken.

In the two events – the earthquake and

the fire – lie several more puzzles about the story of the Trojan War.

Was the *Iliad* about Troy VII? The epic makes no reference to the final capture of the city. Did Homer not know who won the war? Had the earthquake been forgotten?

The Odyssey: Then there was the *Odyssey*, which does not include the wooden horse and the capture, and Troy VII. Does this mean that Homer did not compose both epics? Or did Homer compose several works – now lost – which covered the whole story?

Was the fall of Troy the critical event which opened the remainder of the Mediterranean to attack by the Sea Peoples and which brought on the Dark Ages, beginning about 1200 BC when civilisations of Anatolia, including the Hittites, were lost? What happened to the well-organised people who had built Troy VI? Was their leader a despot who ruled them with such harsh discipline that the survivors of the earthquake ended up hating him? Did they assign the guilt for their misfortune (translated into the gods' displeasure) to him and thus do everything in their power to revert to former, less sophisticated behaviour?

Myth and reality: Why the wooden horse? Was there a connection between the belief that Poseidon created the first horse and the opinion that the Trojans were famous for taming horses? A connection between the belief that Poseidon caused earthquakes and the story of the downfall of Troy? Would the passage of time have so mixed myth and reality that history reported that the impregnable city (Troy VI) could only be destroyed (Troy VII) by a divinely-related horse (read Poseidon's earthquake)? Or was this simply Homer's poetic licence?

The cities of the next level, Troy VIII, lasted about 500 years, and the most important building during that time was the Temple of Athena.

Troy IX, the city enlarged by the Romans who thought that they were going back to their roots, was inhabited until about AD 400. Its importance

Troy's tiny amphitheatre.

declined when Constantine located his capital city on the Bosphorus rather than on the Dardanelles.

The story: For a romantic, to see Troy is to imagine the most beautiful woman of all time, her bright robes blowing about her, with Paris, hot from battle, leading her to his perfumed bed.

The legendary background of the Trojan War was the curse on the Atreus family (whose sons were Agamemnon and Menelaus) for cannibalism. The more immediate mythical instigator was the goddess Eris (Discord) who did not get invited to a wedding that she wanted to attend on Mount Olympus. Piqued, she tossed a golden apple among the guests inscribed with the words "for the fairest". By rank and prestige, Zeus should have decided who got the apple, but he did not relish handling all the jealous women who would lose. Rather, he turned the honour over to Paris, the handsome son of King Priam of Troy.

Paris had been spending his days on Mount Ida, south of Troy. The three goddesses who most wanted the apple went to find him there. Here, Zeus's wife tried to bribe him to give it to her by offering wealth and power. Athena, one of Zeus's daughters, promised glory and fame in war.

Judgment of Paris: But in the beauty contest Paris decided that the goddess of love, Aphrodite, who was also Zeus's daughter, was "the fairest". The favour she bestowed for receiving the prize was that, instead of being stuck with sweet, innocent Oenone to whom he was pledged, Paris won Helen, the sultry, sophisticated and experienced wife of Menelaus, King of Sparta. Considering the criterion he had to use, and that he was a mere mortal (the most intelligent of animals – and the most silly, according to his fellow Anatolian, Diogenes), Paris made the best of a difficult situation. The story does not say whether or not he knew what his choice would mean.

However, Menelaus must have had some premonition of the trouble he was getting into by marrying a much- **An embankment in Troy.**

sought-after beauty. Helen had her pick of all the eligible men in Greece, and had settled on Menelaus, a much older man. At their nuptials Helen's father had all her suitors swear to stand by her husband if anything happened to her.

Paris sailed to Sparta and was welcomed by Menelaus. In Euripides' *Trojan Women*, Helen called him a "Seed of Fire" and exclaimed, "O, a Goddess great walked with him then." As soon as Menelaus had turned his back, Paris ran off with Helen, "bearing unto Troy destruction for a dower," according to the play *Agamemnon* by Aeschylus.

When Menelaus discovered that he had lost his wife, he called on his friends to fulfil their promise. Not all of them were eager to help him at the outset. Odysseus, king of Ithaca, did not want to leave his wife Penelope and their son so he pretended he was insane. Achilles' mother knew that her son would be killed if he went to Troy so she put him in a dress and made him play with a bunch of girls.

The war begins: It took a couple of years for the Greeks to get themselves organised and outfit all their ships – a thousand by poetic count. As soon as the Greeks reached Troy the war began. Almost at once Hector (the son of Priam and the brother of Paris) killed the Greek Protesilaus. According to an oracle, that death determined the outcome of the war, for the side to lose the first man was destined to be the ultimate winner of the conflict.

The war dragged on for many years turning at times in favour of the Trojans, at times in favour of the Greeks. Homer's *Iliad* takes up the story towards the end of the tenth year. The beginning introduces the brilliant, swift-footed Achilles who is angry at Agamemnon, an anger that was to lead to the deaths of many heroes. Their quarrel was over a slave girl. On the Trojans' side Hector has often been seen as the most sympathetic of Homer's characters. He embodied courage, integrity, tenderness and sorrow as he fought a war that had been thrust on him.

Family bliss: Hector's – and Homer's – kindness is illustrated in a scene between him, his wife Andromache, and their son. As Hector was leaving for the day's battle, Andromache accosted him, to remind him that he faced dangers and he had responsibilities to their family, as demanding as those of the defence of Troy. Hector replied that honour in war (he would have chosen Athena in the beauty contest!) was more lasting than personal comfort. Then – in a very human touch – he reached down for his son. But the boy cried at seeing his father's battle gear. So Hector took off his gleaming helmet with its horsehair crest and, laughing, kissed his son and tossed him in the air.

The end of the war came when the Trojans were so successful that they started to burn the Greek ships. Achilles, who was still sulking about the slave girl and threatening to pull out, finally let his best friend Patroclus wear his set of armour in battle. The sight of Achilles' shield was enough to frighten the Trojans away, but Patroclus was killed by Hector.

Achilles' wrath: Stung, Achilles forgot his anger at Agamemnon. He resumed his soldier's role to avenge his friend's death by killing Hector. Gloating furiously, he tied Hector's feet to his chariot and dragged him around and around Patroclus' tomb.

The *Iliad* ends with the funeral rites for Hector after Priam managed to get through the Greek lines and ransom his son's body. Helen joined Andromache in the dirge, lamenting her involvement in the war and mourning for Hector's gentleness of heart, calling him "of all my brethren of Troy far dearest to my heart!"

Homer picked up parts of the story in the *Odyssey*, reporting that shortly thereafter Achilles himself was shot in the heel – the only vulnerable spot on his body – and killed by Paris.

Paris too was mortally wounded by Philoctetes. He died when Oenone, the nymph whom he had abandoned for Helen, refused to heal his wound.

Horse gift: The death of such a hero appeared to the Trojans reason enough for the Greeks to give up. They had folded up their tents and taken their ships off. As a parting gesture, the Greeks left a toy on the beach for the Trojans to play with: a wooden horse.

Laocoon tried to warn his friends about Greek gifts, but no-one believed him and he and his son were mysteriously swallowed up by a sea monster. The Trojans pulled the horse inside the city for safekeeping and spent the night celebrating their easy victory. In the dark the Greek soldiers slipped out of the horse, the Greek fleet returned and Troy fell in flames. The Greek leaders took many of the Trojan women prisoner. Odysseus, for instance, took Queen Hecuba. Cassandra went to Agamemnon. Polyxena, the daughter of Priam, was taken by the ghost of Achilles and was slain on his tomb. Andromache was claimed by Neoptolemus.

The Greeks scattered to their homes. Menelaus took Helen back with him. Helen, the declared reason for the war, remained uncriticised and as desirable as ever. One explanation of this seeming impossibility was that Helen had really spent the war untouched in Egypt, but it took a lot of convincing even for Menelaus to buy that one. In Euripides' play *Helen*, she greets him effusively on his arrival in Egypt:

Hail to thy wife's restored at last!
upon which Menelaus responds,
Wife indeed! lay not a finger on my robe.

Euripides' more generous portrayal of Helen is in the *Trojan Women* in which she points out to Menelaus that had Paris chosen Athena in the beauty contest, Greece would have fallen to the Trojans:

...thus my love
Hath holpen Hellas. No fierce eastern crown
Is o'er your lands, no spear has cast them down.

Odysseus sailed around for ten years barely escaping many dangerous obstructions as he tried to reach Ithaca. Homer related the events at the end of his journey when he overcame the suitors who had been pestering his clever, patient Penelope to marry again so that one of them could become king.

Homer's life: From ancient times everyone who has spoken Greek or who has been acquainted with the culture of the northeastern Mediterranean has known of Homer. It is generally accepted that he was a poet who lived in 850 BC (about four hundred years after Troy VII) and breathed art into the epics of the *Iliad* and the *Odyssey*. He was a resident of Asiatic Turkey, born in Izmir. His native tongue was Greek. Tradition says that he was blind.

Homer worked with material that was so well known that he had only to refer to Helen or to Hector for his hearers to fill in the rest of the story. Thus there had to be a large body of lore already existing on which he drew. Homer did not use the complete story of the Trojan War; instead he selected what would suit his subject, using the common myth as his framework.

Homer probably intended both the *Iliad* and the *Odyssey* to be recited or sung, not read. Perhaps the occasions for their performances were festivals at court; perhaps they were recited on the presumed anniversaries of Hector's death, or of Odysseus' homecoming; perhaps there were contests for the best recitations. The earliest known written texts existed about 550 BC, which means that for maybe three hundred years they were passed by memory from one person to the next. One wonders how much the original was changed during that time.

Early tourists: Among the early tourist visitors to Troy was Xerxes who made a big sacrifice at the Temple of Athena, but who was then defeated at Salamis. Alexander the Great followed him. He believed that one of his ancestors was Achilles. Alexander, just before beginning his Asiatic campaign, offered a sacrifice at the Tomb of Protesilaus, near Cape Helles, to ensure that he had better luck than the first Greek Prince who fell in the Trojan War. He also picked up a piece of armour in Troy, which he thought had been at the Temple of Athena since the Trojan War.

At the time of Julius Caesar – about 800 years after Homer – Virgil took up the story of the Trojan War. In his *Aeneid*, he followed the hero until Aeneas, a Trojan prince, founded Rome. One of Virgil's last desires was to see the place he had written about.

The Crusaders left Troy alone, but Dante, who was their contemporary, chose Virgil to guide him through the Inferno and into Purgatory. With the Renaissance, no European gentleman was considered educated who did not know the classics. Even more than Dante, Goethe in the 18th century drew on Homer and Virgil. His works, *Iphigenie auf Tauris* and *Achilleis*, and his heroine Helen in *Faust*, were created out of their influences.

The inspiration: The story of Troy presents a number of puzzles. For one, after fighting so hard for so long, why did the Greeks go meekly home? Even the archaeologists see no evidence that they made any use of their conquest. That raises the question of what the war was all about. Was it over the control of

the Dardanelles? Theirs was not the last army to fight over the Straits. Was it because the Trojans were so rich from the commerce that passed through their land that others wanted to rob them? Or was it just over the beautiful Helen – as the story seems to say.

There may be some things about Troy that were easier for ancient Greeks to accept than there are for us. They were closer to the time of the Trojan war. They did not have to be persuaded that Achilles and Hector really lived. They knew exactly where Troy was and where their heroes were buried. They did not have to study hard in school to learn a language that no-one spoke anymore. They could go to a temple-museum and marvel at the trophies from the war: shields, swords, perhaps even Achilles' heel.

The image: That image – perhaps to see Troy at its deepest level is to remember Homer's *Iliad* and *Odyssey*, the epic poetry the ancient world considered so great that it was sacred. On these two works the Greeks based their judgment of human behaviour. On these two great books Western Literature is still judged. No European literature is known to be dated earlier than Homer; few Western writers have come close enough to the richness of his language, the breadth and glory of his humanity, the tenderness and detail of his observations of the world.

Turning point: However overgrown with myth, Troy is a real place. It can be visited today; the stones that were scarred and blackened with smoke from the fire can be seen and touched. No matter how they are interpreted, one or several battles took place here which marked a turning point in Western history and thought.

Of all writers who have been touched by what happened here, Homer most perfectly preserved these conflicts between freedom and responsibility; the weakness and nobility of humanity; evil pride and heroic striving. His portrayals of people, of their emotions and their appetites, grandeur and frailties, above all of his own humanity, have enriched the lives of people throughout the ages.

A path cuts through Troy's walls.

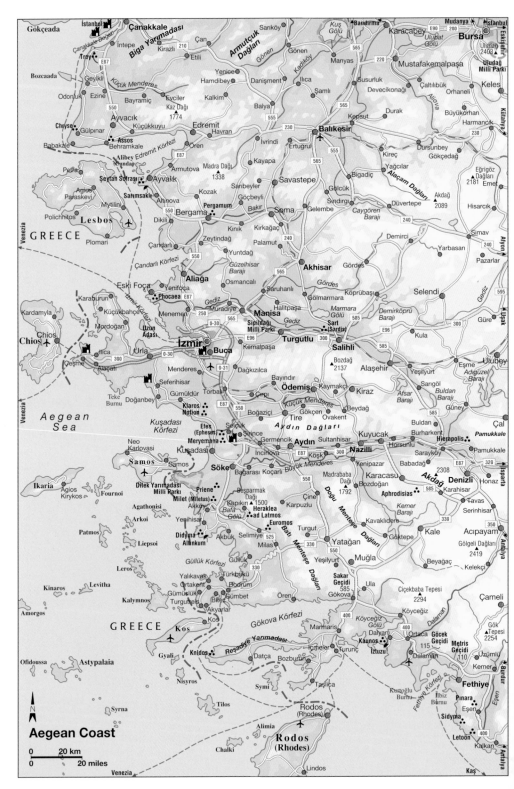

Aegean Coast

0   20 km
0   20 miles

150

THE SOUTHERN AEGEAN

The southern Aegean coast of Turkey begins at the southern slopes of Kaz Daği (Mount Ida) of the Trojan legend and ends at the beautiful Bay of Marmaris. The region has miles of unspoiled beaches, ruins of hundreds of classical sites unmatched anywhere in the world, pristine fishing villages and empty coves ringed by pine forests. It also includes exciting resort boom towns such as Çeşme, Kuşadası, Bodrum and Marmaris. Turkey's third largest city, Izmir, is situated about halfway down the coast.

The northern part of the region was known as Aeolia and had its capital at Pergamum, which was the regional capital of the Roman Empire. **Famous citizen**: Special information is also provided about the towns of Ayvalık, Foça and Çandarlı (Pitane), whose most famous citizen was Arcesilaus, disciple of Plato and founder of the New Academy.

Ayvalık's name possibly means a stand of quinces *(ayva)*; but more likely the source is the name of a local mussel, *ayvada*. The Greek word for the same mussel, *kydonia*, was once the name of the city. This is in keeping with the seafoods that have made Ayvalık a great attraction.

Today Aeolia has become a playground for foreign travellers seeking sun, sand and relaxation. Hundreds of hotels, holiday villages and resorts have opened along the coast, stretching from Edremit (the ancient port of Adramyttium Thebe) to Izmir.

While there are citrus fruit orchards, cotton fields and large stock piles of timber around Edremit and Burhaniye, the major crop of the region is olives. Magnificent groves, some with gnarled trees several hundred years old, stretch for miles along the highway and disappear over the distant hills.

Izmir, Turkey's second largest port, is the gateway to the ancient province of Ionia, which has 55 historical sites, including the ruins of Ephesus, which was a magnificent city during the Hellenistic Period.

In 1952, Dame Freya Stark, a distinguished British travel writer, visited all 55 sites, and came across only one other foreign tourist. Today as many as two million foreign tourists visit Ephesus every year.

Villagers along the southern Aegean Coast raise fighting camels. Camel wrestling is a favourite spectator sport of the region. The Super Bowl of camel wrestling takes place in January when Turkey's top fighting camels slug it out.

The region southeast of Ephesus is the winding Menderes (Maeander) River valley with many significant archaeological sites, including Priene, Miletus and Didyma. One of the world's geographic wonders is located at Pamukkale, which is famous for its white calcified water cascades and hot pools. Aphrodisias, which lies in the heart of the cotton-growing fertile Menderes River Valley, is becoming another Ephesus as archaeologists, funded by the National Geographic Society, make new discoveries at the site that was known as the "Florence of the Roman world".

Native people: The southernmost region of the Turkish Aegean lies within the boundaries of the province of Muğla. In antiquity the region was known as Caria and was inhabited by the Carians, an independent and indigenous people known for their skills as mariners. The Carians fought the invading Persians and Greeks and were conquered by both.

The most important remains of the Carian civilisations are the Mausoleum of Halicarnassus in Bodrum (one of the Seven Wonders of the Ancient World), the Gümüşkesen Mausoleum in Milas and the holy shrine of Labraynda in the hills of Mount Latmus, today's Beş Parmak Daği. Bodrum, considered by many to be the St Tropez of Turkey, is an exciting town with hundreds of nightclubs and discotheques that will appeal to younger visitors.

The southern Aegean offers boating cruises in the Gulf of Gökova. The area is also known for sponge fishing.

AEOLIA

Somewhere between Assos and Edremit the region of the Troad ends and that of Aeolia begins. **Mount Ida** (Kaz Dağı), the home of the nymph Oenone and her childhood sweetheart Paris, has associations with Troy; Mount Ida slopes gently into the Aeolian ports of Küçükkuyu and Akçay.

The Thunder God: Near Küçükkuyu a yellow sign points to a **Temple of Zeus** about 5 km (3 miles) off the highway and just before the village of Adatepe. A bumpy dirt road leads up the mountain to an outlook on the crest of the hill. There, half hidden in pine trees and fluttering talismanic rags, is the tomb of a locally revered holy man. Behind it is an old altar. Zeus the Thunder God would have had a grand view of the entire Bay of Edremit and the Greek island of Lesbos from this perch.

The Edremit coastline, including **Altınoluk**, **Akçay** and **Ören**, has become a summer recreation area with holiday centres scattered among tourist attractions. **Edremit**, a city of more than 30,000 people, is near the ancient port of the Adramttium Thebe. Edremit is twinned with Germany's Piding.

Ayvalık is a large resort town with a picture-book perfect fisherman's harbour overlooking a glistening bay across which some two dozen deep-green islands are scattered like thrown dice. Inexplicably neglected in most guides, Ayvalık is indeed a special find: it possesses not only some of Turkey's most extensive beaches, but also some of the best seafood dining in the country. The pride and joy of Ayvalık is its luscious olives grown on huge plantations in the surrounding area, but the traveller will long remember sitting on the quay while a misty lavender sunset slowly transforms the distant isle of Lesbos into a thing of mystery.

Local lore also has it that the reason for the construction of the maze of narrow back alleys that threads the entire town was to assist smugglers trying to escape from the authorities. Alas, today many of the older houses are falling steadily and surely into dilapidation owing to quarrels over inheritance and the inability of the owners to raise enough cash for repairs. Many are crying out to be turned in to *pansiyons*, which would help the local tourist trade and save the buildings. The Greek Orthodox church in the town centre has some interesting paintings that date back to the first half of the 19th century.

On its beautiful coastline is an archipelago of 23 small islands around **Ayvalık Bay**. One of them, **Alibey Adası** (Cunda), is a picturesque island known in Greek as *Moshonis* (the fragrant one). Regular bus and ferryboat services run between Ayvalık and Alibey Adası.

Another long beach is **Sarmısaklı** souh of Ayvalık, where you can find every kind of popular recreation associated with sand, sun and water, including windsurfing and waterskiing.

Satan's table: Beyond the two-star Murat Reis Hotel a road leads up to **Şeytan Sofrası** (Satan's Table), an area

Left, a blue wagon stands in the street. **Right**, selling the day's catch.

with a delightful panoramic view of Ayvalık, its islands and the bay. The outlook was supposedly named Şeytan Sofrası because of its spellbinding sunrises and sunsets and the belief that devils gathered to dine together every evening at this spot. A giant footprint near the hilltop restaurant is said to belong to Satan.

South of Ayvalık is **Çandarlı**, formerly known as Pitane, a city on a thumb of land located about 10 km (6 miles) west of the main road. Pitane was the northernmost city in the Aeolian League. Little of its history is known beyond the broad outlines of the area. Pottery remains discovered in the excavations at Patane are in museums in Istanbul, Izmir and Bergama.

In Ottoman times the city was the home of the Grand Vizier, Çandarlı Halil Pasha, who opposed Mehmet II's goal to conquer Constantinople. When the city fell, Mehmet executed the Grand Vizier for treason.

On the southwest side of the narrow peninsula a well-preserved Crusader castle built by the Genoese in the 13th or 14th century occupies what may have been part of the ancient Greek wall.

Pergamum's port: Continuing south on the highway you first go past **Elaea**, the port of Pergamum, indicated only by a small yellow sign pointing down a dirt road to Iskele. The city wall parallels the highway. The next Aeolian city is **Gryneum**, identified on some maps as Çıfıt Kalesi. This low promontory has no marking. It can be found between Yenişakran and Çaltıdere. The presumed ruins of a Temple of Apollo are not much to see, but they are far enough off the road from Gryneum to be a pleasant picnic spot.

Myrina is on the north bank of the Güzelhisar river mouth; its double hill is visible from the highway. Hellenistic terracotta statues discovered there are in the Istanbul Archaeological Museum and in the Louvre in Paris.

Amazon legend: Cyme (sometimes spelled Kyme), an important city in Hellenistic and Roman times, derived its name from a legend about an Amazon. Its rulers contributed to the fleets of Darius and Xerxes when the Persians ruled the land. It also paid more taxes than Ephesus or Miletus – a sure sign of prosperity – when it belonged to the Delian League. Excavations by Italian archaeologists have uncovered some old buildings. Parts of the harbour breakwater and the imprint of a theatre are visible.

A scenic, winding road goes past **Yeni Foça** and **Eski Foça**, 38 km (24 miles) off the main road from Aliağa (or more directly from the turn north of Menemen off the main highway). **Phocaea** (Eski Foça) is near the north end of the broad Izmir Bay.

The ancient residents were well-known as navigators. Their ships were powerful, swift vessels, powered by 50 oarsmen capable of carrying 500 passengers. Merchants of Phocaea had business with Egypt, with Amiscus (Samsun) on the Black Sea, and with the colonies of Phocaea, which by the sixth century BC were established in the Mediterranean. Associations with the French continue: the figurehead on the

Sunset at Seytan Şofrası.

prow of Phocaean ships was a rooster, supposedly related to the French *coq gallois*. Club Méditerranée has a resort village just north of the city.

Seals and Phocaea: Different explanations have been offered for the name of Phocaea, which means seal in Greek. One theory is that seals were common in the areas around Phocaea. Others suggest that the outline of one or several of the small offshore islands resembled the marine mammal.

The Genoese who ruled Phocaea in the 13th century built a fortress. In the 14th century the Genoese began alum mining operations at a site about 20 km (13 miles) away and therefore moved to Yeni Foça (New Foça). The Ottoman Turks conquered Phocaea in 1455 and built the **Fatih Mosque**.

Eski Foça, a peaceful little town not much exploited by mass tourism, hosts a music, folklore and a watersports festival in June and has a touch of Old World charm.

Some 7 km (4 miles) east of Eski Foça on the Izmir road next to a stream is a massive, stepped pyramid-like fifth- or fourth-century BC rock tomb called **Taş Kule**.

On a hill behind the town of **Burumcuk** are the ruins of a 5th-century BC city, identified by some as **Larisa**. (It may actually be Cyllene, and the true Larisa may be at Yeniköy on the hill north of Burumcuk.) The site includes city walls, a palace, wells and tombs.

Menemen, population 24,000, is a county capital and market town situated on the Gediz (Hermus) River. There is an old Ulu Cami (great Mosque) and a monument to Kubilay, a soldier who died in a religious uprising in 1930. Menemen is in the middle of a tobacco and cotton growing region, and its many shops sell harnesses, handles for spades, wooden churns and hemp rope. The pots and baskets found in abundance on the highway are well-known Menemen products. Menemen also gives its name to a very tasty local dish made from a mixture of tomatoes, green peppers and scrambled eggs.

The olive-producing town of Ayvalık.

THE OLIVE
OIL INDUSTRY

An olive grove is one of those magical places where it seems you are never alone, as if your footsteps catch woodland spirits at play, sending them hiding among the twisted trunks of every nearby tree.

The olive tree stands firmly rooted in history, with references dating to the sixth millennium BC, and throughout time, ancient cultures tapped the power of this special evergreen and its perfect fruit to produce light, medicine, food, cosmetics and sacred oils.

A staple of the Turkish diet for many centuries, the olive is revered even today for its important role in the country's economy, as Turkey is the world's fourth largest producer of *zeytin yağı* – olive oil.

Nearly 86 million olive trees thrive in Turkey; 75 percent of these blanket the rolling hills along the Aegean Coast, while the remainder grow in pockets on the Mediterranean Coast, Sea of Marmara and southeastern Anatolia.

Big business: Turkey is home to five major olive oil producers, and nearly 4,000 independent producers who operate from neighbourhood factories using old-world methods and machinery.

In towns like Ayvalık, Muğla, Izmir, Edremit and Çanakkale, olive cultivation is a big business requiring serious commitment as farmers wait two to five years for a new tree to bear fruit and almost 20 years before it reaches maturity. Orchards are a long-term investment and regarded as a measure of wealth, with groves handed down through generations.

Turkey's olive producers and farmers are eager to set tourists straight on the subject of authentic Turkish cooking, good naturedly accusing "big city cuisine" of false advertising by using cheaper vegetable oils instead of the real thing – virgin olive oil.

Annually, Turkey produces more than 120,000 tons of olives, many of them for export. The Turkish government is keen to promote the country's agriculture to increase yields, encourage cooperation with its neighbour Greece and, most importantly, bring standards into line with those of the European Union.

Harvest time: In early spring, Turkey's orchards ignite with green flowers which in May bear tiny fruit that is nurtured by sun and *imbat*, the steady warm west wind. In autumn, when the fruit changes colour from green to reddish-orange to black, the harvest begins. The harvest season is heralded by the arrival of workers and their families who travel from inland villages and set up temporary camps on olive farms.

The workers "milk" the fruit off the trees, nimbly handpicking and dropping it into olive baskets. Handpicking is slow, labour-intensive and very costly, but few alternatives exist due to the delicate nature of the olive; even the slightest bruising can result in spoiled fruit and bitter oil.

Upon delivery to the factories, olives are hand-graded to remove debris and damaged fruit. Next a washing and crushing cycle separates the stems and the stones, leaving a thick olive pulp, which is made into a paste and squeezed through a press. The resulting oil and water mixture is then decanted to capture the pure virgin oil. It takes five kilos of olives to produce one kilo of oil.

Oil tasters: Before being placed in underground storage, the oil must pass the final trial: the taste test. No scientific techniques are needed, just a good nose and sharp taste buds determine the oil's fate. Professional tasters are employed by producers just for this purpose. To one oil connoisseur, whose culinary expertise has been called upon for 40 years, olive oil is simple: it's either very good or it's very bad, and it's a smile or a grimace that indicates the thumbs up or down.

Olive oil is sold in two ways in the Turkish consumer market-place. Virgin olive oil, the finest oil from the first pressing, is labelled *Sızma Zeytin Yağı*. This chemical-free oil has an acidity of less than 1 percent. A less expensive oil, labelled Pure Olive Oil, or Riviera Type, is widely distributed in the Turkish market and despite its name, is actually a mixture made up of chemically-refined crude olive oil (from later pressings) and a smaller amount of virgin olive oil.

All is not golden in Turkey's olive oil industry these days, as coastal areas are faced with a pollution problem caused by the indiscriminate dumping of *karasu* (black water), the high nitrogen by-product of olive oil production. Illegal disposal of sewage has residents panicing. Ayvalık is one resort town that is seeking to remedy the situation to protect its tourism business. Present plans call for the relocation of Ayvalık's many small olive oil factories from the city to another site where new plants and a modern treatment facility will be built.

Science is now proving what the ancients knew long ago: olive oil promotes healthy bodies and minds. Olives are an indispensable part of Turkish breakfast and olive oil remains one of the most popular cooking agents in Turkish homes.

Consumption decline: Olive oil has been facing tough competition from lesser oils. Industry officials attribute a ten-year decline in domestic consumption to competition from newer vegetable oils, such as corn and sunflower, which entered the Turkish market with ambitious promotions. Turkey's producers are hard pressed to reverse the trend and have been working closely with the International Olive Council in an effort to launch an advertsing campaign, pitting the high qualities of olive oil against vegetable oils. Olive oil has a clear case as it's the only oil that can be consumed in its natural state, and is medically-proven to help fight cholesterol, as well as aid digestion, bone formation and brain function.

The ancients didn't need science to explain what magic they had contained in their silvery green groves. Sophocles knew what he was talking about when he referred poetically to the olive tree as "the tree that stands unequalled, that can not be surpassed, that bursts forth again and again."

Olives for sale.

PERGAMUM

As the capital of a fast-growing empire, as a centre of art and religion, as a Mecca of healing, Pergamum in the Hellenistic Period was most impressive. That which remains of it now – ruined buildings, history, legends – attracts visitors by the hundreds of thousands. As a walled city on a peak it had a commanding location when it was ruled by Philetaerus and his successors in the third and second centuries BC; as the citadel today, people look up to it from afar wondering at its power; they gaze down from its heights with awe. It was and is a magnificent site.

History: Pergamene kings claimed descent from a certain Telephus who, according to myth, ruled the area at the time of the Trojan War (1250 BC). Archaeological information, including the discovery of shards, shows that the earliest settlement occurred some time later, around 800 BC. The whole area

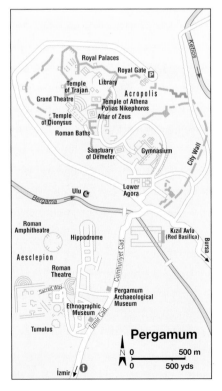

Pergamum

came under Persian control after Cyrus defeated Croesus in 546 BC.

Pergamum's real importance began after Alexander the Great's death in 323 BC when Lysimachus, one of his generals, left a large amount of money there under the stewardship of his officer, Philetaerus. Lysimachus was soon killed in battle, and Philetaerus claimed the treasure as his to use for the good of the city. He also constructed many magnificent temples and new buildings in the city.

Philetaerus' successor, his adopted son Eumenes I (263–241 BC), was able to maintain his position only by buying off the Gauls. They had come from Europe to Anatolia in 279 as mercenary soldiers for the King of Bithynia and had acquired a reputation for being unbeatable, unruly, fierce and warlike. The sculptors of Pergamum were to use the Gauls as models for their many works of art.

Attalus defeats Gauls: Eumenes' adopted son, Attalus I (241–197 BC) decided to take care of his troublesome neighbours, the Gauls. Before the battle, he used a bit of psychology on his own men. In the usual religious service the surprised priests discovered the words, "Victory for the King," written on the sacrificial animal's liver. Only after Attalus' emboldened soldiers had defeated the Gauls did he confess that he had written the words backwards on his hand and stamped them on the liver as he was helping the priest.

It might not be sheer coincidence that the idea and the know-how of writing on skin – parchment – is attributed to a Pergamene ruler at about his time. When Alexandria put an embargo on papyrus to stunt the growth of the rival Pergamum library, scribes found they could use both sides of the parchment sheets and that pages were easier to handle than long rolls.

During Attalus' reign the influence of Rome began to be felt in the area when he gave Rome a sacred black stone from Pessinus that was worshipped as the Mother of the Gods.

Ties with Rome: Attalus' successor was Eumenes II (197–159 BC). He brought Pergamum to its height of power and cultural attainments. To his credit are the Temple of Zeus, the library and gymnasium and the lower agora. Eumenes continued to cultivate good political relations with Rome and reap the benefits. When the Romans defeated Antiochus the Great, the king of Syria, in the Battle of Magnesia in 190 BC, they turned over most of the Syrian lands to Eumenes. Thus in less than 100 years the Pergamene Empire had expanded from a tiny city-state to take in the Aegean Coast of Anatolia as far south as the Maeander River and as far east as present-day Konya.

Eumenes was succeeded by his brother, Attalus II (159–138 BC). Attalus further cemented Pergamum's ties with Rome, consulting with its rulers on major political and economic decisions, regional problems and conflicts.

Attalus spent most of his years warring with his neighbours, including the Kingdom of Bithynia, to the northeast of Pergamum. When Attalus II died at the age of 81, his nephew Attalus III succeeded to the throne of the Pergamene Empire.

Attalus III reigned only for five years (138–133 BC). He was more interested in botany than in politics, writing a book on agriculture which became a reference for the Romans. His specialities were medicinal herbs and poisons, which he tried out on condemned prisoners. He ensured his place in the history books by giving his whole kingdom to Rome, shocking the Pergamenes and effectively ending the Attalid dynasty.

Rebellion: The bastard son of Eumenes II, Aristonicus, led an uprising against Rome, organising disenchanted elements, mercenaries and slaves. At first Aristonicus was successful, defeating a Roman army led by a consul. But within three years the Romans had put down the rebellion.

Pergamum's last attempt at independence took place in 88 BC when it served briefly as the headquarters of Mithridates, King of the Pontus and an avowed enemy of Roman expansion in Asia, who invaded the Aegean Coast of

Modern Bergama as seen from the ruins.

Asia Minor to liberate the Greek-speaking cities. Hundreds of Latins were murdered in the streets. But Roman legions, led by Pompey the Great eventually expelled Mithridates and repossessed Pergamum.

Province of Asia: The Republic of Rome organised the larger part of the Pergamene kingdom into the Province of Asia. However, Rome was not experienced in administering overseas territories, and made a bad job of it at first. Troubled by the insensibility to art in the capital, many of its sculptors moved to Aphrodisias, which became the art centre of the ancient world.

When Rome became an empire, the provinces in Anatolia in general were better administered. The emperors took a more personal interest, and many visited Anatolia, starting with Augustus. Trajan's father had been governor of the province of Asia (which included Pergamum). Caracalla received medical treatment at the Asclepieum after a bad accident at Gallipoli (AD 214). In gratitude he had the Temple of Dionysus covered with marble, and had himself proclaimed the "New Dionysus". In time, the inhabitants of Pergamum moved down from the hilltop fortress to the plain below. The fortress walls were left in a derelict condition and pillaged for stones.

Church of Revelation: Members of the Christian church in Pergamum were criticised by St. John at the end of the first century for various heresies and were told that they lived where Satan's throne was found. Pergamum's reputation, however, grew over the years because one of the Seven Churches of Revelation existed here. Under the Byzantine Empire, Pergamum was a bishopric. Its importance diminished after the centre of power moved to Constantinople in AD 330.

Pergamum was ravaged during the 7th-century Arab invasions. The Crusader Henry of Hainut who was Latin Emperor of Constantinople (1205–1216) took Pergamum in 1212 from the Byzantine Emperor, Theodore Lascaris, who was trying to rule from Nicaea (Iznik).

Early in the 14th century it became a part of the Seljuk Empire and then the Ottoman Empire, at which time Pergamum took its current Turkish name, Bergama. The new city was rebuilt below the acropolis hill after Tamerlane's army destroyed Bergama in 1402 during its brief, bloody rampage through Anatolia. Ottoman control resumed until the town was occupied in 1919 by the invading Greek army for three years.

Since 1923, Bergama has been under the control of the Turkish Republic. Bergama, with a population of some 50,000 today, is the capital of the county of the same name in Izmir Province. Nowadays, the denizens of Pergamum are waging a different kind of battle; one against an international gold mining company. The whole town unanimously campaigns against this new "invader" because it would use cyanide to exploit the gold-rich soil of Bergama, thus destroying agricultural life (once the operation is underway, nobody would buy the peasants' produce for fear of possible poison leakage) and

A Roman statue at Pergamum Museum.

threatening human and animal life.

Archaeology: The historic buildings from the Hellenistic and Roman periods of Pergamum, which are of interest to tourists, are located in three separate areas: the acropolis, the present town and the Asclepieum or medical centre. It is common to start a visit with the acropolis because its height affords a panoramic view of the old city and the relationships of the various parts, and also because the oldest buildings are there.

The highest point of the acropolis in the Hellenistic Period was controlled by the army. Here were placed the barracks and the arsenal, giving the guards maximum viewing power of all sides. The Palaces of the Kings sheltered just below. Those buildings today have not even their bare walls standing.

The **Temple of Trajan** is in striking contrast to the palaces because of restoration work directed by German archaeologists. The white marble columns and flooring of the surrounding enclosure help create a sense of majesty of the people who lived in this part of the ancient city.

The temple is the only building in this area that does not date back to Hellenistic times. It was begun during Trajan's reign (AD 98–117) and completed by Hadrian (117–138). Contemporary practice deified the Emperor; statues of Trajan and Hadrian found there are now displayed in the Pergamum Museum in East Berlin.

Slightly below the Temple of Trajan is the **Temple of Athena**. Its courtyard acted as a kind of museum where works of art and curiosities were displayed, many of which were offerings to the goddess. The Doric temple has six columns on the ends and ten on the flanks. The Temple of Athena, as of those in other western Anatolian cities – Izmir, Miletus and Erythrae – was the most important shrine in the city. In Pergamum, it was related to the Parthenon, according to archaeologist Ekrem Akurgal. Among the bronze statues probably located there were two commemorating the Pergamene battle with the Gauls. Marble copies now in Rome show the "Dying Gaul" and the soldier stabbing himself after having killed his wife to escape capture. Both statues are of the noble foe, the enemy whose courage and devotion raised the struggle above savagery.

Rich library: The entrance to the Library of Pergamum was through the upper entrance of the Temple of Athena, an appropriate association with the goddess of wisdom. Pergamum was one of the centres of ancient learning, and its library once rivalled the great Library of Alexandria, according to ancient chronicles. The library is supposed to have contained 200,000 volumes, but there is a question of where they were all stored since the ruined building seems to have been big enough for only one-tenth of that amount. The library is famous for its rich collection as well as its destruction. Its demise, caused partly by a fire and partly by reactionary Moslem clerics, deprived later generations of much Hellenistic culture. The library continued in its importance as a depository of learning until a love-struck Mark Antony gave most of the volumes away to Cleopatra to take to Alexandria.

In the 7th century, the Moslem Caliph Omar, reasoning that the books were either inconsistent with the Koran and therefore impious or, if consistent then unnecessary, ordered them all destroyed in Alexandria, according to the late historian George Bean.

The Palaces of the Kings stood east of the Temple of Athena and served as the residences of the various Pergamene kings including Eumenes. It was surrounded by the barracks for the kings' guard of honour and soldiers working in his office.

Just 10 metres (30 ft) below the palaces were arsenals, 1.5-metres (5-ft) long buildings constructed parallel to each other, which played a pivotal role in the defence of the ancient city. The barracks and the Command Tower, built during the reign of Attalus I, stood just above the arsenals. Little or nothing remains of these sites.

The Temple of Zeus, the biggest temple in Pergamum, was protected from a fate similar to that which struck the library. Germans in the 19th century took it out of the country stone by stone and reconstructed it in the Pergamum Museum, now in Berlin, saving some of it from being destroyed for construction materials. Turks, however, argue that the temple and other Pergamene relics were smuggled out of the country and should be returned. Nevertheless, German archaeologists are planning to rebuild the Temple of Zeus in Pergamum using casts taken from the original temple in the East Berlin Museum.

The two friezes, that of the mythical adventures of Telephus and that representing the Battle of the Gods and the Giants, were sculpted at the summit of artistic excellence in the Hellenistic Period. The Telephus Frieze interests art students because it is an early attempt to give a realistic perspective and physical setting to the figures. The technical skill exercised in carving the marble with such finesse, the knowledge of anatomy, and the sense of drama vividly conveyed in the scenes place these marbles among the world's most fascinating masterpieces.

The Temple of Zeus is the largest of the buildings on the acropolis. Since it was dedicated to both Zeus and Athena (and perhaps to the rest of the Greek pantheon), it would more correctly be known as the Great Temple. Popular ascription of this as "Satan's Throne" (admittedly a dramatic site at which to point) probably lessens St. John's more general condemnation of the Roman government.

Located next to the Temple of Zeus is the upper agora, which was surrounded originally by two- and three-storey colonnaded porticoes.

The **Pergamum Theatre**, impressive now in its size and acoustics, stretches up the side of the hill for 80 rows of seats and could hold 10,000 spectators. When there was a performance a wooden stage and backdrop were erected above the orchestra; these were dismantled at the end of the performance or at the end of the season. Above the centre of the lower landing stood the king's box, made entirely of marble. The Temple of Dionysus associated with the Pergamum Theatre (immediately north of the stage) was dedicated to Dionysus, the god of wine and entertainment who was believed to have inspired the first drama. Sacrifices for the actors and their performances were held there before the plays began. The building was impressive and pedestrians walking by could gaze with amazement and admiration.

A long promenade runs south of the stage where people walked, conversed, made business arrangements, and enjoyed the view.

City of temples: Below the acropolis on the south side of the hill are less official buildings, among them the **Temple of Hera**, the **Temple of Demeter**, the **Temple of Asclepius**, the lower agora, and the gymnasium on three levels. Perhaps most of the worshippers at the Temple of Demeter were women who held special celebrations at night with torchlight parades.

In the gymnasium the upper building was for young men, the middle building was for adolescent boys, and the lowest was for young boys. As with other gymnasiums, this was a place for both athletics and academic studies. The complex included an auditorium, which seated around 1,000 people and a number of baths. It was in use into the fourth century. There was a ceremonial hall in the eastern part of the gymnasium for receptions, prize givings and other official functions. Next to it was a kind of prayer room where the emperors were worshipped. Water to the gymnasium was pumped from the northern mountains. The middle terrace includes the foundations of a temple dedicated to the patron gods of the gymnasium, Heracles and Hermes.

Remember to pause to look at the construction of the vaulted stairway as you walk down from the gymnasium to the Hellenistic House of Attalus and the lower agora.

Water supply: Consul Attalus was a man of means. The water from the cistern in his house supplied the fountain in the agora below him. Among the official records found in this agora is one that announces the rules concerning the use and maintenance of the water supply – a matter of supreme importance in the defence of a city on a hill, particularly one which can be blistering hot in summer. (The new **Kestrel Dam** northwest of the acropolis is evidence of that continuing importance. Pipes from a water supply in the mountains follow much the same path as the Hellenistic aqueduct.) A hint of the personality of this Attalus can be found in the inscription on the wall of his living room inviting his friends to come and enjoy life with him.

The ancient buildings of the lower city date from the Roman Period. The biggest is the **Kızıl Avlu**, or Red Court, built over the channel of the Bergama Çayı (Selinus River) during the reign of Hadrian. The red colour one sees now is of the bricks that originally were faced with patterned marble rather than all pure white stone.

Even without the brick colour and the heavy walls, the building has a com-pletely different feel to it from the temples on the hill. The many places for ritual ablutions and the paired male-female caryatids, which held up the roofs of the porticoes, indicate that the religious practices observed here may have been to honour the Egyptian gods who were popular in Roman and early Byzantine times, such as Osiris, the god of the underworld and the dead, and the husband of the fertility goddess Isis. Osiris was related to the Greek gods of the underworld, Pluto and Hades. The Kızıl Avlu was constructed in the 2nd century.

During the Byzantine Period the basilica was used as a church dedicated to St. John. One of the towers is now a mosque.

Battles among crocodiles: The Roman amphitheatre, which straddles a tributary of the Bergama Çayı, is one of the very few such structures existing in Anatolia. When realistic sea battles among crocodiles were to be staged, the river was dammed.

Also in the valley of the Bergama

Trees burst through the Great Altar at Pergamum.

Çayı was a stadium and a theatre, both having been constructed during the Roman period. Neither the amphitheatre, the theatre nor the stadium have been excavated by archaeologists. These places are best approached on foot. From one of the gates of the theatre a road began that led southwest about 1 km to the **Asclepieum** or medical centre. (The present road starts in the centre of Bergama.)

As you approach the grounds of the Asclepieum, you will notice the old road and columns (the columns were added during Hadrian's reign), the central courtyard with the small theatre to the far right behind more columns, and on the left the stone and brick ruins of some other buildings. Almost immediately in front of one of the buildings is a rather short broken marble column decorated with snakes twining around a laurel branch – the caduceus, the symbol of the medical profession during ancient times. This symbol is still in use for medical professional associations today.

Psychotherapy: Treatment at the Pergamene Asclepieum consisted of a combination of herbal medicines, physical therapy, psychotherapy, diet, baths, massage, music, sports and intellectual stimulation. A lively account of some of the practices is found in the writings of the hypochondriac, Aelius Aristides, who was a patient in Pergamum for 13 years at the time of the institution's most famous physician, Galen.

Patients at the Asclepieum slept for brief periods on the ground in the sanctuary: this was termed "incubation"; the dreams that they had were interpreted by the doctor-priests who then prescribed a treatment. Among the cures were mud baths followed by running naked around the temples. The theatre and a library housed in the northeast corner of the courtyard helped the patients to while away their recuperation time.

During one bitterly cold night, the staff had Aristides smear himself with mud and run three laps around the temples. He finished by washing off the mud in the sacred fountain.

The institution was so popular that even many Roman senators and merchants came to the Asclepieum for treatment and to see Galen for a check-up or just for plain relaxation. Women who could not bear children would visit the place, hoping medical treatment would result in miracles. One woman, according to a dubious ancient account, was pregnant for five years but could not deliver her child. But after she slept one night at the Asclepieum, and had a vision of the God of Medicine, she at once gave birth to a strapping five-year-old son.

Anatomical procedure: Galen, whose great 16-volume medical treatise, *On Anatomical Procedure*, parts of which have survived to these times, was a specialist in anatomy, human dissection and internal medicine. The bulk of the first nine volumes of his work has survived in Greek and Arabic and constitutes our main knowledge of ancient medical practices. Although he was a highly scientific man, Galen wor-

Haircut for a young lad.

shipped heathen gods like Asclepius, believed in dreams and portents and even subscribed to absurd folk medicines that bordered on quackery.

The circular building to the immediate left of the entrance to the courtyard was the **Temple of Asclepius**, the Roman god of medicine and healing and son of Apollo, the god of music, youth and poetry exemplifying manly youth. It was built as a small replica of the Pantheon, which had been built about 20 years earlier.

South of it and slightly outside the line of the south portico was the round two-storey treatment building with a number of separate rooms. It was linked to the sacred pool near the theatre by an underground passage. Probably people stretched out on its roof (now collapsed) to sunbathe.

The Bergama Museum was built in 1936 to house the finds in the area uncovered since then. It contains a small reproduction of the Temple of Zeus as one would see it in Berlin. A number of pieces of the Hellenistic,

Roman and Byzantine periods collected here merit close attention. The items include statues, friezes, ceramics and coins. The museum also includes an ethnographic section of regional costumes, handiwork and armaments.

The modern city of Bergama is remarkably unaffected by its illustrious past and the large numbers of foreigners who spend their time and money only on its history. While the residents are conscious of this concern, many are engaged in the ordinary businesses which support a city and in the agricultural industry of the area.

The annual International Bergama Festival in early June highlights local crafts, dance, music and food. Good restaurants, hotels, and camping facilities (one in connection with a hot spring) are available. Shops display onyx items; some offer the famous hand-woven *Yağcıbedir* Bergama carpets, produced in the nearby mountain villages. The dominant colours of these carpets are dark blue and red.

Snapshots anyone?

IZMIR

With three million inhabitants, Izmir is Turkey's third largest city and second largest port (after Istanbul). It is a cosmopolitan city created by Turkey's most European-thinking citizens and an influx of rural Turks seeking a better life. In addition to its European ambience, fostered by fine shops, modern hotels, high-rise apartment buildings, and facilities integral to shipping, Izmir offers pleasant surprises to its more independent visitors.

Although Izmir's commercial stature resembles a European town, it remains Turkish in spirit and hospitality. Walking through its less affluent streets you may chance upon a colourful folk dance performed by transplanted villagers or a man prompting his rabbit to select the piece of paper with your fortune written on it.

Izmir's position as Turkey's leading exporter has deep historical roots. Ancient Izmir's commercial development was facilitated by its location on a deepwater harbour at the end of the Golden Road, a trade route which passed through Lydia, Phrygia, the Hittite capital of Hattusa, and then Mesopotamia. Izmir became a centre for shipping in Ottoman times, after the port of Ephesus was abandoned. During the past 500 years, minority groups such as the Greeks, Sephardic Jews and Levantines have been indispensable in expanding Izmir's trade in figs, cotton, olive oil, steel and textiles.

Infidel Izmir: Moslem Turks liked to describe the city as *"Infidel Izmir"* because the city's inhabitants before the 1923 population exchanges were overwhelmingly Christian Greeks. Few Greeks remain here today. With a population educated above the country average in modern, secular Turkey, Izmir could be Turkey's most cosmopolitan and Western-oriented city.

Izmir is home to NATO's Allied Land Forces Southeastern Europe and Sixth Allied Tactical Air Force headquarters, which guard Europe's southern flank.

A walk along **Atatürk Caddesi** north of Cumhuriyet Meydanı is especially interesting at dusk. Along this bayside promenade, known also as Kordonboyu, lined with palm trees, are numerous souvenir shops, hotels, restaurants and government buildings.

Jewish quarter: Continuing along the promenade brings you to the prestigious **Alsancak** district of Izmir. Many of Izmir's most elegant shops and boutiques are concentrated in the area northeast of the Atatürk Museum. Gold, leather, and almost anything else can be purchased in the old **Jewish Quarter** at the western end of the **Kemeraltı Bazaar** near the Hisar Mosque. The Jewish *quartier* was embodied in the Asansör (elevator) district, which has been restored in authentic period style. The Asansör itself is a 50-metre (164-ft) stairway linking an upper and lower shopping precinct.

Izmir also has many civic landmarks worth visiting. Chief among the public monuments is the **Konak Square** with its lavishly decorated Moorish **Clock**

Left, mosaic at Ildırı. **Right**, strolling at Kuşadasi Camp.

İzmir

0 — 1000 m
0 — 1000 yds

N

İzmir Körfezi

ALSANCAK

1456
147
1464

(Atatürk Caddesi)
Şehitler

S. Yasar Resim Müzesi

St Jean Cathedral

Kıbrıs

Kordon
Cumhuriyet

Mahmut Esat Bc Caddesi

Zübeyde Hanım

Atatürk Müzesi

1440

Ali Paşa
Talat
Çetinkaya
Alsancak

Bulvarı

Birinci

B.
Eşref

Alsancak

1391

NATO

Pilevni

Şair
Dr. Mustafa

KÜLTÜR
1382

1383

Caddesi

Vasıf Çınar Bulvarı

Bulvarı

Caddesi
Cumhuriyet

Akademi

Montro Meydanı

KÜLTÜR PA

(Atatürk

Cumhuriyet Meydanı

Atatürk Heykeli

Şehit Nevresbey Bulvarı

Lozan Meydanı

Yolcu Limanı

Gazi Osmanpaşa Bulvarı

Necatibey Bulvarı

Hürriyet

1374

Şair Eşref Bulvarı

1370

Dr. Refik Saydam Bul.

1374

Bulvarı

İSMET KAPTAN

Fethibey
Ziya Bulvarı
Bulvarı

Cumhuriyet Bulvarı

Gazi
Bulvarı

Gazi
Bulvarı

9 Eylül Meydanı

Mürsel

BAS

Şehit
Halit
Kordon

Necatibey
Caddesi

Bulvarı

Basmane İstasyonu

Birinci

Mimar Kemalettin
Caddesi

AKDENİZ

1369

AKINCI

ETİL

Fevzi Paşa Bulvarı

Fevzi Paşa Bulvarı

Sadırvanaltı

Çorakkapı

Mirkelam Kervansarayi

Hisar

Sadırvan

HURSDİYE
Anafartalar

Caddesi

ALTINORDU

967

Konak Meydanı

Belediye Saray

Hasan Tahsin

Bulvarı

Konak
Meydanı

Çarşi
KONAK (Covered Bazaar)
Kemeraltı

929

Kestanepazari

939 NAMAZGAH

Agora

967

KUBİLAY

Saat Kulesi

Konak

Basdurak

GÜZELYURT

816

Konak İskelesi

Millikütüphane Cad.

Devlet Opera ve Balesi

Anafartalar

Kestelli Caddesi

KESTELLİ

919

SAKARYA

817

Patlıcanlı

971

Atatürk Kültür Merkezi

Cumhuriyet Cad.

FEVZİPAŞA

442

803

ALİREİS

981

Mustafa Kemal Yolu

Mithatpaşa

Caddesi

Arkeoloji Müzesi

427

Müftü

Eşref Paşa

Caddesi

ÜLKÜ

746

Hacı Ali Efendi Caddesi

5260

Etnografya Müzesi

NAMIK KEMAL

TUZKU

Kale

Rakim Elkutlu Caddesi

730

Kadı

Tower and its **Monument of Hasan Tahsin**, a Turkish journalist who was the first casualty in the fight against the Greeks who invaded Izmir in 1919. The monument, showing the patriotic Tahsin firing a gun at the Greeks, is also referred to as the **Ilk Kurşun Anıtı** (Monument to the First Martyr). Just north of this statue are the buildings of the **Belediye** (Municipal government), where Turkish art is displayed. Across the street is the **Vilayet Binası** (Provincial Governor's office). From the nearby docks, ferryboats take 15 minutes to cross the bay to Karşıyaka, a busy shopping district.

City mosques: Perhaps the two most interesting of Izmir's many old mosques are the **Kemeraltı Mosque** and the **Hisar Mosque**. Built in 1672, the Kemeraltı Mosque, also known as the **Hacı Mehmet Ağa Camii**, is a modest but attractive building located on Anafartalar Caddesi in the heart of the Kemeraltı Bazaar. The narrow street leaving this mosque is crowded with shoppers looking for all manner of merchandise. Built in 1598, Hisar Mosque is the oldest and largest Moslem shrine in Izmir.

Located just outside the courtyard in front of the mosque are two nurseries and a small tea garden under an old sycamore tree. Locals believe that young women were sold as slaves in the **Kızlarağası Hanı**, a caravansary and market building behind (southwest of) the tea garden. The most delicious ice cream in Izmir is served at **Mennau**, two blocks towards Fevzi Paşa Boulevard from the Hisar Mosque (899 Sokak 30/A, Hisaronü).

Of the seven original Christian churches (communities) of Asia Minor mentioned in Revelations, only Izmir's still flourishes. The church dedicated to Saint Polycarp, martyr and fourth bishop of Izmir, is located at the corner of Necatibey and Kâzım Bey boulevards. The nine-day ritual honouring St Polycarp begins each February 14. The original church at this site dates back to 1625. Today's exquisitely decorated **Church of Saint Polycarp** dates to 1929. Visitors will find the contrast between its humble exterior and opulent interior is unforgettable.

Just 150 metres (492 ft) southwest is the **Santa Maria Church**, built in 1667. Franciscans administer this modest church located at **Halit Ziya Bulvarı**, Number 67, a block south of the **Tourism Information Bureau**.

The Archaeology Museum: Located on a hill southeast of the Government Theatre and Conservatory (opera) and next to the Devlet Hastanesi, or state hospital, the three-storey **Archaeology Museum** contains numerous statues, artefacts, ceramics and frescoes from Greek and Roman sites throughout the region (including Claros, Belevi, Erythrae, ancient Izmir, Sardis and Ephesus). It is advisable to visit the museum before touring such archaeological sites for better appreciation. The exhibit describing Bayraklı, or ancient Izmir, explains the cuneiform tablets excavated at the Hittite site of Kültepe. These indicate that the original name of Izmir was *Tismurna*. Sometime after 1800 BC, the prefix was dropped so that the place-name Smurna remained. Izmir is the Turkish pronunciation of *Smurna* or Smyrna.

Next door is the **Ethnographic Museum**. A two-storey structure which opened in 1985, the museum contains a wealth of old Ottoman and Turkish artefacts, including coins dating to 1389, weapons, carpets, household furnishings, embroidery, jewellery, and exhibits describing production of wood printing, pottery and evil eyes *(boncuk)* made of glass. The exhibits on camel wrestling and military commanders typical of western Anatolia (e.g. *Efe* and *Zeybek*) are fascinating.

The Velvet Castle: Those accustomed to exercise may begin climbing the slopes of **Mount Pagus** from the area near the Basmane Train Station. As one approaches the summit, the winding streets seem to get narrower and the houses smaller. Friendly children and quaint houses make the climb to the **Velvet Castle**, Kadifekale, quite pleasant. Concealed inside the western walls of Kadifekale are large stretches of pine trees, a children's playground, a soccer field and botanical gardens. Doves singing early in the morning make this centre of ancient Izmir especially idyllic. A Byzantine cistern is nestled amid pine trees. From the western ramparts of the ancient fortress there is a splendid view of downtown Izmir and the harbour. At night the tea garden has live music. Just east of the tea garden women weave brilliantly coloured yarn on black-strap looms.

A Hellenistic settlement around Mount Pagus (at the summit of which is Kadifekale) began after 334 BC, as a result of Alexander the Great's command. Kadifekale was connected to the agora by a Roman road. From its northeastern gate the road south led to Ephesus. The western ramparts, with Byzantine watchtowers on a Hellenistic foundation, have been fortified by successive conquerors (Greeks, Romans, Byzantines, and Ottomans). These walls are wonderful places for strolling, watching sunsets over the wide bay, and contemplating ancient Izmir.

Construction of the Hellenistic city on top of Mount Pagus was allegedly commanded by the Goddess of Vengeance (Nemesis) in a dream of Alexander the Great. In 334 BC Alexander, however, didn't apply the goddess' mandate to resettle the Smyrnaeans in the new city. The project began under Antigonus in 300 BC, but it was Lysimachus, conqueror of Ephesus, who completed Smyrna's resettlement by 288 BC. After relocation around Mount Pagus was accomplished, Izmir became the 13th member in a confederation of Ionian cities (the Panionic League). Izmir's population then exceeded 100,000 and the historian Strabo praised it as the "most beautiful city in Ionia."

Agora: The remains of the agora are located on a tract of land in downtown Izmir, 1.6 km southwest of Kadifekale and half a mile north of Konak Square. The original state agora also dates to shortly after Alexander the Great's dream. The agora included a temple, a marketplace and an indoor meeting place where business and politics were discussed. From an altar to Zeus in the centre of the agora fragments of statues

Right, traffic in downtown Izmir.

of Demeter, Poseidon and Artemis (hardly recognisable) have been reassembled. The statues of these three nature deities are now displayed in the Izmir Archaeology Museum.

An unusually severe earthquake in AD 178 forced the Romans to rebuild the Hellenistic agora. In the middle of the agora was a marble square. Along the northern gallery 17 columns of what was once a 165-metre (540-ft) long, three-storey marble edifice remain. Daily business was conducted inside this basilica-style structure. In the centre gallery was the entrance. On the ground floor were arched galleries and 26 shops. The agora itself was on the first floor. The section with columns standing on steps was the second floor. The third floor was all but destroyed, except for fragments of beams connecting two columns. At the northwest corner, a marble staircase takes you underground to an impressive vaulted basement where piped water runs continuously.

Nearby are the remains of the aqueduct built 2,000 years ago. Commercial activity today is especially brisk only 300 metres (984 ft) south of here in the picturesque Kemeraltı Bazaar, which begins in the courtyard of the Kemeraltı Mosque.

Success in exporting and rapid industrialisation have obliterated or transformed the rest of Izmir's legendary sites. The **Baths of Agamemnon**, where the king and his soldiers may have recovered after the Trojan War 2,500 years ago, are still used in treating various ailments. The baths are now administered by the **Balçova Hot Springs**, 13 km (8 miles) west of Izmir, near Inciraltı. Those expecting to visit Homer's birthplace near the banks of the sacred Meles River will find that **Diana's Baths** are now enclosed by Izmir's waterworks, east of the Sümerbank factory off the Altın Yol (Golden Road). Homer is said to have written the *Iliad* and *Odyssey* in a cave near Diana's Baths (Halkapınar Suyu) where a statue of Artemis was discovered.

Izmir's history: Archaeological evidence from Tepekule suggests that Izmir was inhabited by 3000 BC. Now concealed in the industrial zone at the northeast edge of Izmir Bay, the oldest level at Tepekule (Hill Tower) at Bayraklı is contemporary with Troy I. This site was inhabited for 2,000 years by Hittites or Lelegians before Aeolians from the Aegean islands began colonisation about 1000 BC. In 800 BC Ionian Greeks displaced Aeolian Greeks. By 600 BC Tantalos, the tyrant who ruled ancient Izmir, was buried in a round tomb almost 30 metres (100 ft) in diameter and a magnificent Temple of Athena had been built. Following two invasions launched by Lydians before 500 BC, Ionian Izmir lay dormant for 200 years, until Alexander the Great and his successors relocated it.

After 129 BC Izmir was ruled by Rome and it continued to flourish. Christianity was introduced to Izmir by St John, or by St Paul after AD 53. The fourth Christian bishop of Izmir, Saint Polycarp, was a direct disciple of St John. Polycarp, who wrote "the love of money is the root of all evil," was burned at the stake in the Izmir Stadium in AD 153 by order of a Roman administrator. Nevertheless, Izmir's Christian community has persisted until today.

Seljuk Turks controlled Byzantine Izmir from 1078 to 1097, the year Crusaders captured it. In 1261 the Genoese were granted control over Izmir. But, for the next 200 years Izmir was hotly contested by various factions of Christians and Moslems.

Izmir remained under Ottoman rule from the time of Sultan Mehmet I until it was occupied by Greeks in 1919 as part of World War I spoils. The Turkish Republican Army, led by Atatürk, forced Greek evacuation and liberated Izmir on September 9, 1922. The evacuation culminated in a fire that destroyed the city. Izmir has succeeded in blending business and lifestyles and created a modern metropolis. It also plans to stage the Mediterranean Olympics in 2005. Perhaps it is this entrepreneurial spirit that attracts investment and has made Izmir a powerhouse for two technoparks and one environmental technology project.

IZMIR'S MINORITIES

Izmir's affluent ethnic minorities have played an important role in the development of industry, banking and commerce in the city. What follows is a rundown on who these minorities are and their history.

Sephardic Jews: The Jewish community in Izmir may be 2,000 years old. In response to King Ferdinand's order expelling all Jews from Spain in 1492, Sultan Beyazıt II confided to his courtiers that the Spanish King had foolishly "impoverished his own land and enriched ours." Sultan Beyazıt's invitation to settle in the Ottoman Empire was accepted by thousands of Jews exiled from Spain and Portugal. By 1575 most commerce in the Ottoman Empire was controlled by Jews, and Spanish was the trade language of the Mediterranean.

Today the majority of Izmir's 2,500 Jews are still involved in commerce although it is estimated that less than half of them speak fluently the Spanish of Cervantes' era.

There have been two eras of exodus for Izmir's Jewry. During World War I, some 10,000 left Izmir for Latin American countries. Still, in 1927, 17,000 Jews remained in Izmir. After World War II most of them went to Israel.

Beth Israel: There are seven principal synagogues in Izmir. The oldest and best preserved is the **Beth Israel** on Mithat Paşa Caddesi, number 265. Two of Izmir's older synagogues are on **Havra Sokak** (called the street of the synagogues).

A synagogue built in 1821 is located near the gold merchant's quarter of the Kemeraltı. Its amazingly unobtrusive exterior conceals a splendid interior. The monumental synagogue in the suburb of Karataş was built by the famous Rothschild family.

Most scholars of this period agree that Ottoman Jews were better treated than their European counterparts. The Jewish community of Turkey commemorated the 500th anniversary of their residence in 1992 with elaborate festivities held in Izmir and Istanbul.

The Dönme: Sabatai Zevi, born in Izmir in 1626, triggered a scandal of international proportions. Izmir's Orthodox Jews were outraged when Sabatai proclaimed himself the Messiah in 1665. He attracted such an immense international following that the Sultan ordered him to convert to Islam or die. He duly renounced Judaism.

Believers still exist. Sabatai's followers, called the Dönme (turncoats), live secretively in Izmir and Istanbul. Izmir's Jews condemn Sabatai as a "False Messiah" or charlatan who misled the gullible. "His name is cursed among us," one Jewish businessman said. Nevertheless John Freely, an American educator and travel writer who lives and works in Turkey, reported observing a few elderly Dönme worshipping in a house in Izmir which they regarded as Sabatai's birthplace in his *The Western Shores of Turkey*. The house was for years the home of Osman Kibar, the late conservative Mayor of Izmir who was himself a Dönme.

Preceding pages, Izmir's Museum of Ethnography and Archaeology. Left, the Latin Church of St Polycarp.

176

The Levantines: In 1581 an agreement between Sultan Murat III and Queen Elizabeth I granted a seven-year franchise to a group of English merchants known as the Levent Company. These original Levantines were responsible for introducing Europeans to coffee. They also exported figs, currants, dates, lemons, oranges, sultanas, raisins, carpets, textiles, jewellery and copperware. They and their descendants have contributed enormously to Izmir's commercial development.

Today there are 1,500 British residents in Izmir, most of whom are still exporting items such as dried fruits, tobacco, cotton, grapes and motor engines. They meet frequently and many of them worship together at the Church of St John the Evangelist at the northern entrance to **Talat Paşa Bulvarı** in Alsancak. Two other Anglican churches, one at **Buca** and the other at **Bornova**, are still in use.

Italians of Izmir: The term Levantine has been rather loosely applied to all families of European origin, including French and Italian. Italians have long been active as traders throughout the region surrounding Izmir. In 1261 the Byzantine Emperor granted Italians from Genoa full control of Izmir. Although they lost political control of Izmir after 1320, their descendants still survive in the region. Although they are a closed community not conventionally making marital bonds with Muslim Turks, the younger generation of Levantines are more open-minded. One Caroline Giraud, of a wealthy Izmir family, married Mustafa Koç of the biggest industrial conglomerate in Turkey. Money has no religion.

Today only 1,300 Catholics live in Izmir, primarily of Italian descent. Izmir's chief Catholic churches include **Santa Maria**, the **Rosary Church** near Alsancak Iskelesi, **Santa Elena** in Karşıyaka, **Saint Anthony** in Bayraklı, and **Our Lady of Lourdes** in Göztepe. Mass is increasingly said in Turkish. About 100 children attend the private Italian Primary School and receive instruction in Italian.

Jews pray in a synagogue.

THE IONIAN COAST

Heading west from Izmir on the highway to Çeşme one reaches Urla about 35 km (22 miles) after passing Inciraltı and Güzelbahçe. **Urla Iskelesi** is a small picturesque town 1 km right off the main highway. Along its tranquil beach are a few hotels and the ruins of the Ionian port of **Clazomenae**. Greek colonists from Peloponnesus settled on the mainland, just over 2 km (1 mile) southwest of where an indigenous population had lived. After the Ionian revolt in around 500 BC, these Greeks moved out to the island in the bay for fear of the Persians. By order of Alexander a causeway connected the mainland to the island. Today a paved road links the mainland to the **Urla Hospital**. Because of their proximity to the hospital, the ruins of Clazomenae aren't open to the public.

Çeşme, once a quaint fishing village and now a bustling summer town, and neighbouring **Ilıca**, famed for its thermal baths, are booming. Their beautiful white sand beaches entice more visitors every year, who enjoy its daytime sun and night-time fun. In early July, the Çeşme Sea Festival features art, music and sports activities. Çeşme is uncrowded and enchanting between the end of September and early June and there are many small hotels and restaurants to choose from.

Çeşme is windy and picturesque, cooler and less crowded than Izmir. It offers plenty of shopping and sightseeing, with a bit of history to provide a break from sailing, beaches, water sports and discos. Those yearning for excitement can find it easily in nearby Ilica.

Stone castle: A tour of the **Genoese Fortress** overlooking the bay affords spectacular views of Çeşme, its harbour, and the Greek island of Chios. This impressive stone castle was built to protect traders originally from Genoa. Inside the 14th-century castle, a small museum displays Hellenistic and Roman artefacts.

Çeşme as seen from the castle.

Çeşme is easily reached by private transport and there are regular ferry services to the Greek island of Chios and the Italian port of Brindisi.

Near the fortress are the ruins of an 18th-century inn or caravansary. In front of the fortress is a statue of **Cezayirli Gazi Hasan Pasha** and a lion. For Turks the lion symbolises bravery, and this monument commemorates Hasan Pasha's victory over the Russian navy, which attacked the Ottoman fleet in the Bay of Çeşme in 1770. Across the street at the harbour, ferryboats carry passengers about 14 km (9 miles) to **Chios**.

Numerous restaurants are located along the promenade at the edge of the harbour and others are situated along **Inkilap Caddesi**, the main street. At night, after this street is closed to traffic, restaurants like the **Imren** are especially enjoyable.

Turkish ambience: Those seeking more Turkish ambience will find it 3 km (1.6 miles) north at the town of **Dalyan**. This lovely little village sits on a little bay where yachts come in to anchor. The seafood restaurants in this area are particularly good.

The ruins of **Erythrae** can be found near Ildır, a sleepy seaside village northeast of Çeşme. Erythrae is one of 12 Ionian cities mentioned by the historian Herodotus. Principal attractions include the ruins of **Athena's Temple** and a 10,000-seat theatre. Between the temple and Ildır are ruins of a Roman villa, a mausoleum, and a wall belonging to the agora. On top of the hill are remains of a 150-year-old Greek church and Athena's Temple.

Fishing villages: On the way from Çeşme, Kuşadası and Selçuk, there are numerous worthwhile but less publicised sites that can easily be reached by private transport or taxi. Leaving Çeşme and Ildır, travelling east towards Izmir, you reach a junction just before Güzelbahçe. A right turn here (onto route 505) will take you south to **Seferihisar**.

At Seferihisar another right takes one to **Sığacık**, a pleasant little fishing village with an imposing Genoese fortress. Continuing southwest for about 2 km (just over a mile) the road passes the white sandy beach of **Akkum**, before it forks left toward Teos, about 1 km further on.

Teos, a prosperous Ionian port, was situated near one large and one small harbour. By 600 BC its wealth and location at the centre of the Ionian region prompted Thales to propose that it be Ionia's capital city, although his suggestion was never carried out. The inability of Ionian cities, Teos included, to unite politically left them vulnerable to Persian conquest. After the Persians were expelled from Ionia, Izmir lay dormant for 200 years, between 500 and 300 BC, while Teos regained its prominence as a thriving port.

Teos declined after the Romans gained control of Asia Minor, beginning with their naval victory over the Seleucid king, Antiochus III. This decisive battle was fought in 190 BC in the southern harbour of Teos. The best-preserved part of the town is the

Temple of Dionysus, located in an olive grove just off the paved road.

Other visible ruins include traces of the Hellenistic-era city wall, a Roman Period odeon and parts of a theatre.

The prototype for Dionysus, the wine god, may have been Bacchus, of Lydian origin. The Lydians, representing satyrs in processions of Bacchus, dressed in goat skins and sang "goat songs" that may have inspired Greek tragedy. Since Dionysus was their patron, the Artists of Dionysus resided at Teos between 300 and 150 BC. These professional actors and musicians performed at theatres and musical festivals throughout the Greek world.

Myonneus, Mouse Island, is 15 km (9 miles) south of Sığacık. This landmark, known in Turkish as **Çifit Kalesi** (the Jew's Castle) is just north of Cape Doğanbey.

Traces of ancient walls remain on top of this steep and rocky fortress, which once protected pirates from the Romans who attacked Teos. There is a causeway, visible only underwater, connecting the mainland to the citadel.

Lebedos was one of the poorest of the Ionian cities, overshadowed by Ephesus and Teos, with their superior harbours. The ruins are located just south of **Ürkmez**, on a knoll overlooking a sandy cove with a restaurant and camping facilities. There are hotels nearby at Ürkmez and Gümüldür.

From Gümüldür there are 17 km (11 miles) of scenic coastline before reaching the cliffs with the partially excavated ruins of Notium. Its ruins include a **Temple of Athena**, an agora, a theatre and an extensive city wall.

Claros: Homer's hymn to Apollo indicates that the **Temple of Apollo** at Claros, 2 km (1.2 miles) inland from Notium, was a famous sanctuary by the 7th century BC. At the southern entrance to the sanctuary six marble columns have been unearthed in a small canyon. The road entering this sanctuary was 10 metres (30 ft) wide and may have been connected to a harbour at one time.

A short distance north of the entrance is a large altar dedicated to Apollo, and

An Efe, a veteran of the Turkish War of Independence.

a smaller altar to Artemis, his twin sister. Fragments of statues of Apollo, Artemis, and of their mother, Leto, have been recovered.

West of the altars numerous columns, including their Doric-style decorated capitals, are plainly visible.

Colophon: Twelve km (8 miles) north of Claros is the affluent Ionian city of **Colophon**, built on the mountain behind the quaint Turkish village of Değirmendere.

Colophon's strong navy, maritime trade and abundant farmland made it a prosperous member of the Ionian League. Yet even its ferocious warriors and famous cavalry could not protect it from Lydian and Persian conquerors. It was ruled continuously by Persians until Alexander the Great. Although Colophon was rebuilt in 281 BC, it was, even with its coastal ally Notium, unable to compete with the emporium of Ephesus. It disappeared from history leaving only a few ruins.

The territory controlled by the Colophonians extended east to the fertile plain of **Cumaovası**. From Colophon north to Menderes (formerly Cumaovası) it is 16 km (10 miles). **Menderes** is a small town located on a plain where olives, figs, and grapes are grown. From Menderes it is only a few miles to the highway leading north to Izmir or south towards Torbalı and Selçuk.

About 40 km (25 miles) south of Izmir, in the middle of a rich agricultural region, is the town of **Torbalı**, where two small castles are open to the public. Another 15 km (9 miles) south, on top of a hill to the right of the highway, looms **Keçi Kalesi** (the Goat's Castle), a Byzantine fortress built around AD 1200.

Selçuk is a small but thriving tourist centre located near the church of St. John, the Isa Bey Mosque, the Artemision and the ruins of Ephesus. Its main attractions are the museum and the remains of an aqueduct near the train station.

Before visiting the ruins, a trip to the museum (open daily 8.30am–6.30pm) is recommended. In addition to the two

The ruins of Claros.

famous statues of Artemis, there are numerous examples of funeral relics, including Mycenaean bowls dating from 1400 BC, a fresco and marble head of Socrates, a marble head of Eros and a bronze statuette of Eros riding a dolphin. Tours of Ephesus and Meryem Ana, the House of the Virgin Mary, can be arranged from Selçuk or Izmir.

A short drive east of Selçuk is the quaint village of **Şirince**, still unspoiled by tourists. This small village, founded by Christians who left Ephesus around AD 600, is surrounded by pine-covered hills and orchards of olive and peach trees. Homemade wine can be purchased directly from enterprising villagers. There are a few restaurants, plenty of old Greek houses, and two abandoned Greek churches to see.

Only 18 km (11 miles) from Selçuk is the chic coastal playground **Kuşadası**. From here organised tours of Ephesus can also be arranged. Tourist development at Kuşadası has focused on several long sandy beaches and a deluge of lively bars.

Belly dancing: Kuşadası's most unusual lodging is at the **Kervansaray**, situated in the heart of town in what was formerly the Öküz Mehmet Paşa Caravansary. This historic landmark has been lovingly restored and converted into a fine hotel. On the ground floor there are several shops, and a beautiful fountain in the middle of a courtyard. The buffet dinners served here nightly are animated by belly dancing and other forms of entertainment.

From mid-April to October the water is warm enough to make swimming a delightful experience. The most pristine beaches are to be found away from the downtown area, extending from Kadınlar Plajı (Womens' Beach) south to Güzelçamlı, and from the Tusan Hotel north to Pamucak.

Visitors can hire yachts or sailboats at **Kuşadası Marina**. Daily boat tours around the coast are also available. Ferryboats leave daily for the Greek island of **Samos**, only 2 km (1 mile) away. Windsurfing facilities and lessons are also available.

Trees in full bloom with Selçuk Castle in background.

Except for Ephesus, archaeological sites are scarce. The village of **Pygela**, formerly situated a few miles north of downtown Kuşadası, was founded, according to Strabo, by Lelegians and colonised by Agamemnon. The annual meeting place of the 13 Ionian cities comprising the Panionic League was 25 km (16 miles) south of Kuşadası, near the village of Güzelçamlı and the entrance to the **Dilek Peninsula National Park**. After the Byzantines granted trading rights to Italians from Venice and Genoa these merchants shipped silk, saffron and other goods to Europe from Kuşadası. Under Ottoman control the town continued to flourish.

The National Park itself comprises lush forests including laurels, red and black pines, and several types of lime, chestnuts and oaks found only in northern Anatolia. The area is also home to a proliferation of seals, turtles and numerous species of reptiles and birds.

In addition to the Genoese castle on the island, there are two interesting Ottoman era structures built by the architect after whom they are named. The **Öküz Mehmet Paşa Mosque** is near the Town Hall, east of the Öküz Mehmet Paşa Caravansary, which was built in 1613. This impressive stone inn provided safety and hospitality to travellers on the trade route culminating here. The open courtyard housed the animals serving the travellers who were lodged in second-storey rooms.

Connected to the mainland by a causeway 400 metres (1,320 ft) in length is **Kuşadası**, Bird Island, from which this town took its name. This small island offers visitors a restored fortress, several fine restaurants, a disco, a tea garden serving snacks and beverages, and magnificent views of the ocean and bay.

The Genoese Fortress at Kuşadası may have been built by AD 1500. Later it became the home of Hayrettin Barbaros, an Algerian pirate appointed grand Admiral by the illustrious Ottoman Sultan, Süleyman the Magnificent. In 1546 Hayrettin died rich and famous at the age of 70.

Left, Isa Bey Mosque at Selçuk. Right, Kusadası.

CAMEL WRESTLING

Every year in mid-January, the market town of Selçuk is host to the Super Bowl of camel wrestling *(deve güreşi)*, the most popular sport in southern Turkey after football. For the two days of the Selçuk Camel Wrestling Festival, an atmosphere of gaiety and carnival prevails in the town as the top male fighting camels of Turkey vie for honours, prize money and trophies.

Desert ship: Before the advent of automobiles, long-distance lorries, trains and jetliners, camels were the principal means of transport in the Ottoman Empire and the Middle East. Camel caravans carried people and goods from one city to another across miles of deserts and wastelands. Because of its ability to withstand extreme heat and cold, survive long periods of thirst and hunger and stride in a swaying motion, the camel was affectionately described as the "ship of the desert."

Only Yörük Turks, a nomadic people inhabiting the mountain plateaus of coastal Turkey, still prefer camels to cars as a mode of transport. Travellers to the coast can still come across Yörük camel caravans.

Village herdsmen don't race camels, a popular pastime in some Middle Eastern countries, they now train the beasts as fighters.

Camel wrestling is supposed to have started when herdsmen noticed male camels fighting over their females during mating season and turned the battle into a sport.

Weekend tournaments: Camel wrestling meets are held every weekend in many small towns in the provinces of Izmir, Aydin, Denizli and Muğla from January through March. During a weekend tournament, many people from nearby villages descend on the towns to bet on their favourite camels and to sell their produce and display carpets and other handicrafts.

Male camels wrestle as many as 30 times in one winter season, a time when the females are in heat. During the rest of the year they just munch on fodder. The upkeep of a beast costs an enormous amount of money, but ownership of a camel often brings prestige to peasant herdsmen – the same kind of prestige owning a flashy new sports car would bring to a young city Turk.

Not all camels can be trained as wrestlers. "Great wrestlers are born not made," says Hulusi Kanat, a camel trainer for 30 years and a professional announcer at camel fights. The best camels are those from Iranian mother camels, he says. Camels generally begin wrestling at the age of six, but it is not before the age of 15 that they become big and strong enough to be champions. Some old veterans continue wrestling until they are 25.

The bulldozer: Turkey's 250 best fighting camels are known as *tülüs*. These camels can earn up to $1,200 and much more on side bets for their owners during each bout, when one camel is pitted against another. Each *tülü* is an awesome sight, weighing over a ton and standing 2 metres (6 ft) at the shoulders and 2.3 metres (7 ft) at the top of its hump. Each beast is recognised as a superstar in his own right and has a ferocious name, such as the Bulldozer, the Killer, the Warrior, Deli Tülü (the Mad Camel), and the Conqueror.

It is at Selçuk, two hours out of Izmir, where the top camels slug it out. Often, more than 120 camels participate in this extravaganza. Before the tournament begins, the Selçuk-Bodrum Highway, a major thoroughfare, is closed to traffic for about one hour as the owners parade their camels, decked out in colourful blankets, pompons, gold bangles and jewellery, through the main street. The camels also wear large cow bells that jangle as they stride through town.

The camels, frothing at the mouth at the height of the mating season, are muzzled to prevent them from biting jealous rivals or human admirers.

After the opening ceremony in Selçuk, which includes speeches by the provincial governor, the mayor and vote-seeking politicians, the camels are marched to the nearby ancient city of Ephesus.

Gladiators of antiquity?: The fights take place on the grounds of a ruined stadium, used during Roman times to feed Christians to the lions and for fights among gladiators. More than one observer has likened the fighting camels to the "gladiators of antiquity".

Spectators jam the stadium and sit on the stone seats to watch the matches amidst the playing of drums, fife and folklore performances. Vendors sell popcorn, potato chips, nuts and *simit*, a Turkish sesame seed roll shaped like a doughnut.

Two snorting, bellowing male *tülüs* are brought in. They stand at opposite ends of the stadium. The match begins only after a female camel struts between the two rivals to arouse their excitement and aggression. If motivated, the two camels charge at one another like angry bulls, butting heads, bumping sides and kicking with their feet. Often the camels go into a dangerous neck lock or leg lock. The stronger animal tries to crush his opponent with his weight. Each bout lasts about ten minutes after which two nine-men teams, each wearing red- or blue-coloured leather coverings, pull the animals apart with rope in a tug-of-war fashion.

No animals are seriously hurt, and visitors will soon notice that the theory is more brutal than the practice. Many camels refuse to live up to their fierce reputations and, instead, stare at their opponent, spit or just lie down and enjoy the spectacle – and why not, that's what everyone came for? Camels are not naturally aggressive and the efforts of their owners and trainers in getting them to fight are often more entertaining than the fights themselves.

Victory: To win, one wrestler has to knock the other down on his side, chase him out of the stadium or cause him to submit. Otherwise the match is declared a draw. In addition to prize money and earnings from bets, the animal owners get a camel trophy, a plaque and special handmade carpets. It is easy to see why many people prefer nowadays to bet on the horses.

Camels fight it out at Germencik.

EPHESUS

In the sixth century BC, when **Ephesus** was an affluent Aegean port, Heraclitus, the son of an Ephesian priest, dedicated his philosophical treatise called *Nature* to the Temple of Artemis (Nature /Mother Goddess). The eternal flux or constant change he recognised as fundamental in nature was best symbolised by water and rivers. The gradual transformation wrought by the **Kaystros River** (Küçük Menderes in Turkish), which flows into the Aegean, epitomises Heraclitus' theory and explains the demise of Ephesus.

The prosperity Ephesus enjoyed as a trade port connecting Europe, Asia and Africa was dependent on a functioning harbour, and Ephesus declined when its harbour was ruined by centuries of silt accumulating at the mouth of the Kaystros River. Today the city lies 5 km (3 miles) from the sea. The region lay dormant from 1450 to 1950.

Left, the many-breasted Artemis. Below, Priapus, the fearless satrap, and his overgrown phallus.

In its heyday, Ephesus was the most important commercial centre in western Anatolia and had a population of more than 250,000 people. Inscriptions found by archaeologists described Ephesus as the "first and greatest metropolis of Asia."

British and Austrian archaeologists excavated the site in the 19th century. The Austrians smuggled out most of the relics found there, but returned the artefacts when the Ottoman government threatened to ban all future Austrian excavations in the Near East.

In recent decades its ruins have attracted tourists from all over the world. Ephesus is, in a sense, an international city again. Nearly two million foreign tourists visit the ancient city every year. The informed visitor to Ephesus may, with a bit of imagination, relive a moment of world history, but it's wise to go early in the morning before the heat and the hordes of tourists arrive.

This Aegean port turned Asian metropolis has been home to various cultures and religions. Little is known about the earliest inhabitants of Ephesus. The Carians, whose most important city was Halicarnassus (Bodrum), evidently considered themselves natives of the region. Sometime later the Smyrnaians may have colonised Ephesus and Izmir.

Mycenaean pottery: The earliest archaeological evidence of human occupation of Ephesus is painted pottery of Mycenaean origin dating to 1400 BC, which are on display at the Selçuk Ephesus Museum. These elegantly crafted Mycenaean bowls were widely traded, and appear at sites from Troy to Bodrum. It is unclear whether Mycenaeans settled in Ephesus or simply traded with a local population.

The Ionian region of Asia Minor in which Ephesus is located was definitely colonised by 1000 BC. A political struggle for control of Athens prompted the Athenian colonists, led by Androklos, the son of Kodros, king of Athens, to establish Ephesus at the northern end of Mt Pilon. Legend has it that Androklos built a temple dedicated to Athena at the place where a wild boar was killed, in compliance with cryptic instructions received from the Oracle of Apollo, which he consulted. The remains of this temple may be on the small hill just west of the Roman stadium. An effigy of the boar stood on the street in front of the temple for centuries in thanksgiving for the fulfilment of the oracular prophesy.

The Carians fought a losing battle against these Greek invaders but managed to kill Androklos. A shrine to him was built near the **Magnesian** (Manisa) **Gate**. His descendants ruled Ephesus for the next four centuries.

Rapacious king: The prosperity of Ionian Ephesus caught the eye of the rapacious King Croesus of Sardis. In 560 BC this Lydian king captured Ephesus and relocated its inhabitants in the area around the Temple of Artemis. Statues of golden calves and beautiful column capitals, one of which bears his name, were Croesus' chief contribution to the Artemision (Temple of Artemis). He also had a fortification wall built around the city.

After the Persian King Cyrus defeated Croesus in 546 BC, Ephesus was ruled by Persians as a satrapy (province under a governor). Although the citizens of Ephesus continued to trade and practise their religion freely they were obliged to pay extortionate tributes to their Persian masters. From 546 BC until 334 BC, the Ionian region was in turmoil as Greeks and Persians fought each other. When Alexander the Great defeated the Persians on the southern shores of the Sea of Marmara at the Battle of the Granicus in 334 BC, Ephesus was liberated and it became a quasi-democratic city. It was briefly dominated by the Ptolemites of Egypt before being annexed by the Attalid kings of Pergamum.

Roman Ephesus: Roman control of Ephesus began after 133 BC. Although Ephesians joined in a successful revolt against Rome in 88 BC, Roman rule was swiftly reestablished. In 27 BC the Roman Emperor Augustus proclaimed Ephesus capital of the Asian province. It was during this period that Ephesus

The amphitheatre at Ephesus.

became one of the largest cities in the Roman Empire; one of only three cities to have street lighting.

Roman Ephesus was a free city governed by two assemblies: one for ordinary citizens *(Demos)*, the other for the *Boule,* a 300-member elite. Rich Ephesians could attain prestige by sponsoring public works and ceremonies. The most prestigious ceremonial duties, those of the *prytanis*, could be assumed by both sexes. The *prytanis* paid all expenses incurred in carrying out daily animal sacrifices, supervising all cults and insuring that the eternal fire honouring Hestia, goddess of the hearth, always burned in the Prytaneion.

When Emperor Hadrian visited Ephesus in AD 123, it was still a booming emporium and residence of the Roman governor of Asia. Most of the buildings visible today date from the Roman era when Ephesus had nearly 250,000 inhabitants. The buildings, fountains and monuments commemorate Roman administrators and Ephesians wealthy enough to sponsor public works. Following a devastating attack by a large Gothic fleet in AD 262, the grandeur that characterised ancient Ephesus began to wane.

Christians persecuted: During this era of decadence, Christians were persecuted for refusing to sacrifice animals and worship pagan deities. The struggle between the pagan Roman religion and the monotheistic Christianity resulted in Christians being killed by lions in the same stadium where gladiators and wild animals entertained Roman audiences. It is believed that after Christianity was endorsed as the official religion of Rome, all the seats in Ephesus Stadium were destroyed. Today the stadium is the scene for the popular camel wrestling festival and the annual Izmir International Music Festival.

The legend explaining the **Grotto of the Seven Sleepers** illustrates the growth of Christianity. Around AD 250, seven Christian boys took refuge in a cave, located about 500 metres (1,650 ft) east of the **Vedius Gymnasium**. When they awoke, after 200 years of

Modern folk dancing in the ancient theatre.

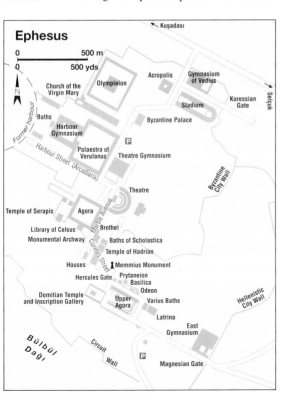

Ephesus

0 — 500 m
0 — 500 yds

N

- Church of the Virgin Mary
- Olympieion
- Acropolis
- Gymnasium of Vedius
- Koressian Gate
- Selçuk
- Stadium
- Former harbour
- Baths
- Harbour Gymnasium
- Byzantine Palace
- Harbour Street (Arcadiana)
- Palaestra of Verulanus
- Theatre Gymnasium
- Byzantine City Wall
- Theatre
- Temple of Serapis
- Agora
- Marble Avenue
- Library of Celsus
- Brothel
- Monumental Archway
- Baths of Scholastica
- Curetes Street
- Temple of Hadrian
- Houses
- Memmius Monument
- Hercules Gate
- Prytaneion
- Basilica
- Odeon
- Domitian Temple and Inscription Gallery
- Upper Agora
- Varius Baths
- Hellenistic City Wall
- Latrina
- East Gymnasium
- Bülbül Dağı
- Circuit Wall
- Magnesian Gate

slumber, Rip van Winkle-style, Christianity had become the official religion and Emperor Theodosius II proclaimed that they had been resurrected. Several hundred graves dating to the fifth century, including those of the seven sleepers, and a church, were excavated in this cave.

Many biblical scholars believe that St Paul's version of Christianity differed significantly from that of St John and his followers. Paul of Tarsus was a Roman citizen and a Benjamite Jew who did not know Jesus in Jerusalem. The fact that Paul persecuted Christians until his blinding vision on the road to Damascus (Acts 9:1–9) distinguishes him from St John.

Flight from Jerusalem: There is evidence to suggest St John and Mary left Jerusalem to escape the persecution that threatened them. If historians are correct in identifying John as Lazarus of Bethany, then the chief priests' decision to kill both Jesus and Lazarus (John 12: 9–11) would make the flight from Jerusalem a necessity. With its commitment to religious freedom and its already thriving Jewish community, Ephesus must have seemed a safe haven. At any rate, both Mary and John are believed to have lived and died here.

Paul's famous confrontation with Ephesians loyal to Artemis is one of a series of conflicts that ended in his decapitatation on the outskirts of Rome in AD 64. It was then than St. John became leader of the **Church of Ephesus**. It is believed that John is buried under the church that now bears his name. By the fourth century, when a modest basilica was built over his grave, the glory of Roman Ephesus was gone. The harbour had silted up. Much of the marble used to build the towers and fortification walls surrounding the **Church of St John** (completed around AD 550), in the town of Selçuk, was brought from the stadium where Christians were once tortured for the entertainment of 70,000 spectators.

It is widely believed that the worship of Artemis was a continuation of the veneration of the Mother Goddess and **Library of Celsus.**

fertility cult suggested by the statues of Cybele scattered throughout Turkey. Statues excavated at the farming community of Çatal Höyük in southcentral Anatolia are 9,000 years old. Yet if Artemis was indeed the mother of all animals, her prototype is likely to have its origins in hunting and nurturing nature. Perhaps the prototype is represented by the Venus figurines and human females depicted in magnificent cave art appearing at numerous sites in Europe and Asia more than 13,000 years ago. The oldest evidence of Cybele-Artemis worship at Ephesus is a plain wooden statue.

Artemis cult: The three well-preserved statues of Artemis on display at the Selçuk Ephesus Museum graphically illustrate the meaning this great mother once had. From the hips down to the toes on both statues, flowers and bees are visible. The belt of the **Great Artemis** (the one wearing the tall crown displayed at the western end of the hall) shows bees and flowers. Next to the **Beautiful Artemis** (displayed at the eastern end of the hall) is a headless statue of Artemis with bees and flowers on her chest. These icons of Artemis imply that the survival of plants and animals requires mutual dependence or symbiosis. Artemis was evidently the chief guardian and personification of harmony in nature. In worshipping Artemis, Ephesians proclaimed that living in harmony with nature was their central concern.

It is frequently asserted that the social structure of bees provided the model for the religious hierarchy entrusted with the worship of Artemis. The Queen Bee, which reproduces the species, is served by all others. At Ephesus there were hundreds of priests, priestesses and guards devoted to Artemis. The chief priest or Megaysos was in charge of receiving donations to and loaning money from the temple treasury. He and the other priests had their reproductive organs removed to become permanent celibates before assuming office. The priestess who assisted the Megaysos in his duties were virgins consecrated to

Temple of Hadrian.

Artemis (reminiscent of the six Vestal Virgins serving the Roman goddess of fire, Vesta).

Testes of bulls: Chastity, fertility and reproduction are key attributes of Artemis. Depicted on the breasts of both statues of Artemis are the testes of bulls that were sacrificed to her. Long misidentified as eggs, these testes symbolise fertility as well.

The necklace that adorns the Beautiful Artemis is comprised of the 12 signs of the zodiac, indicating that she incarnated life and influenced the cosmos. Her association with life was also manifested in the right of asylum granted to criminals who came and sought refuge within the boundaries of the temple. Although such unconditional love of criminals upset many Ephesians, their request in AD 22 for an end of asylum was not granted by Emperor Tiberius. Evidently the great mother was expected to demonstrate love for all her children.

The first Temple of Artemis was evidently destroyed by the Cimmerians who attacked Ephesus in the seventh century BC. The oldest artefacts associated with this temple date to the eighth century BC and are on exhibition in the British Museum.

The Great Temple: Built between 550 and 460 BC, the first major temple honouring this queen of heaven and earth was magnificent. It was the largest marble structure ever built. A total of 127 Ionic columns, each 19 metres (62 ft) high, supported a roof enclosing a courtyard 155 metres (508 ft) long by 55 metres (180 ft) wide.

On all four sides of the temple are two rows of columns. This **Temple of Artemis**, first located in 1869 by British engineer John Wood, was even more impressive than the rival Temple of Hera in Samos and four times larger than the Parthenon in Athens. It was considered to be one of the Seven Wonders of the Ancient World.

Besides the Temple of Artemis, the Seven Wonders included the Pyramids of Egypt; the Colossus of Rhodes; the Statue of Zeus at Olympia; the Hanging

Details from a sarcophagus.

Gardens of Babylon, the Lighthouse at Alexandria and the Mausoleum at Halicarnassus.

The temple was rebuilt after it was burned down, allegedly on the very night Alexander was born in 356 BC, by an Ephesian desperate for publicity. The second major Artemision, built between 350 and 250 BC, was essentially identical to the first except that it was elevated on a base 3 metres (10 ft) high with 13 steps.

The temple had to be reconstructed again after it was destroyed by Goths who attacked Ephesus in AD 125 and again in AD 262. With the growth of Christianity the cult of Artemis declined to be replaced perhaps by the adoration of the Virgin Mary. Marble from the Artemision was used in the construction of **Haghia Sophia** (the grand **Aya Sofya** basilica in Istanbul) and the Church of St John on the hill in Selçuk. Today a single column rising out of a muddy pool is the only reminder of what was once one of the Seven Wonders of the Ancient World.

The **Fortification wall** and the original Magnesian Gate were built in the third century BC by Lysimachus. To appreciate the excellent Hellenistic workmanship on the wall, it's best to climb to the top of the mountain where the city wall is better preserved. After entering via the Magnesian Gate a north turn will bring the tourist to the remains of the **Eastern Gymnasium**, built in the second century. Just east of the Odeon stands the mostly unexcavated **Varius Baths**. Just south of the Odeon are the remains of the **State Agora** and the **Basilica**.

A rectangular temple built around 25 BC was located at the centre of the State Agora. The pediment of this **Temple of Emperor Augustus** is now on display in the courtyard at the Ephesus Museum in Selçuk. The pediment illustrates a legend described by Homer. Three allies of Odysseus are preparing to blind the Cyclops Polyphemus after Odysseus got him drunk with wine. The long 160-metre (525-ft) but narrow Basilica contained the statues of Augustus and his

Relief of a flying goddess.

wife now seen at the Ephesus Museum. Located to the west of the Basilica is the **Prytaneion** where the eternal flame of Ephesus burned and where the two famous statues of Artemis were found.

Modern performances: The small theatre or **Odeon** seated 1,400 and was built by a couple of rich Ephesians in AD 150. Although it was used for concerts, it was the political meeting place for the *Boule*. The people's assembly or *Demos* was convened in the well-preserved 24,000-seat theatre, where today modern folklore shows and plays are frequently performed.

Continuing west towards Curetes Street, north of Domitian Square, is the **Memmius Monument** built in the first century BC. The temple dedicated to Domitian (AD 81–96) is largely unrestored. To the east of the steps at the entrance to the **Temple of Domitian** stands a two-tiered column with reliefs. Just behind it is the cool **Inscription Gallery** where numerous documents pertaining to the history of Ephesus have been found.

About 100 metres (330 ft) west past the **Hercules Gate**, which marks the beginning of Curetes Street, between the Trajan Fountain and the Temple of Hadrian, are the remains of the **Scholasticia Baths**. These heated baths were built in the first century and were repaired frequently thereafter until about AD 400. The last citizen to restore the baths, Christian Scholasticia, is commemorated by a statue. As in all Roman baths, hot, tepid and cold water was available in different rooms. Hot air circulated through baked clay pipes under the floors of the room. The taps provided hot and tepid water.

Next to the baths is a peristyle house that was the brothel, indicating that prostitution was popular and institutionalised in Ephesus. The upper storey of the house has been destroyed and only traces of frescoes remain. A mosaic in the dining room depicts the four seasons while a simple mosaic in the adjacent pool shows three maidens, a servant, a cat and a mouse eating crumbs. A tiny bronze **Figure of**

Mosaic in Ephesus.

Priape, a god with an overgrown phallus, was found in the brothel and now can be seen as an exhibit in the Ephesus Museum.

Public toilets: To the west of the baths is the latrina or public toilets. Across the street from the entrance to the latrina is the western entrance to the baths. Hidden to the right of this entrance is a 50-cm (20-inch) tall relief of Artemis, depicted there with an animal head facing right and holding a staff in her right hand.

The **Temple of Hadrian**, completed in honour of Emperor Hadrian by AD 138, is a visual feast. Behind the bases of four columns that once held statues of four Roman emperors rise four Corinthian columns. A richly decorated arch featuring the face of Tyche, the goddess of chance equivalent to the Roman Fortuna, crowns the two central columns. Above the door behind the central chamber stands a semicircular frontal depicting a bare-breasted maiden surrounded by beautiful flowers and leaves.

On the south side of Curetes Street several elegant houses built on the slopes of **Bülbül Dağı** (Nightingale Mountain) have been excavated. These three-storey structures had courtyards, running water, heating, mosaic floors and walls adorned with frescoes. Originally constructed during the reign of Augustus, these houses were frequently altered until the end of the seventh century. Two of these houses on the slopes are restored and may be entered by climbing the steps just across the street from Hadrian's Temple.

Celsus library: At the end of Curetes Street is the impressive two-storey **Celsus Library**. Because it had to be built between the two older edifices, this structure was cleverly designed to look wider than it really is. When Tiberius Julius Celsus, a famous Roman administrator, died in AD 114 his son had this library built as a monument and mausoleum. Celsus was buried inside an elaborate marble sarcophagus found under a library wall. The interior of the library was spacious

Inscriptions at Ephesus.

and housed 12,000 scrolls kept in niches designed to minimise damage from humidity. Eight Corinthian columns placed on a podium support elaborately adorned frontals.

At the north side of the Celsus Library is the **Mazeus Mithridates Gate**, which leads into the Agora. Its three passages are reminiscent of a Roman victory arch. There is an elegantly decorated frieze above the arch. Upon emancipation, two slaves, Mazeus and Mithridates, built this ornate gate to honour their former master, Emperor Augustus and his family.

Beside the inscriptions in bronze to their master and his family is written the stern warning: "Whoever urinates here will be tried in court." This admonishment reminded Ephesians that the agora or forum was to be entered reverently and not to be sullied.

The **Agora** or shopping centre at Ephesus was a semi-sacred square where various stores were located. Merchandise displayed included locally produced perfume, Arabic herbs, Ana-

tolian wine, jewellery, foods, ceramics, and artefacts of bronze and copper. Women reputed to be the most beautiful in the East were sold here as slaves.

Today only numerous columns standing at the perimeter of this large square meeting- and market-place remind one of the exchange of goods and ideas from three continents that once transpired here. Excavations currently underway will undoubtedly explain more about the original agora built in the third century BC.

The Temple of Serapis is located at the end of a marble road, which begins at the southwestern corner of the agora. This temple, under construction in the second century, was dedicated to Serapis, the Egyptian god of the underworld and judge of the dead. Eight massive marble columns, each weighing 57 tons, lie in front of the temple ruins. After 547 BC, when Ephesus was conquered by Persians, maritime trade between Alexandria and Ephesus must have been brisk. Numerous Egyptian statues and a peace treaty written on

marble also confirm the connection between Egypt and Ephesus. In 299 BC the alliance between Egypt and Ephesus was cemented by the royal marriage between Lysimachus and Arsinos, an Egyptian princess.

From the Celsus Library the sacred or Marble Road goes towards the theatre. Built into the western slope of Mount Pion during the reign of Lysimachus, this impressive, well-preserved theatre seats 24,000 people. Hellenistic plays were quasi-religious, dedicated to Dionysus, the god of wine and entertainment. Prayers and animal sacrifices preceded performances given by masked male actors.

During the Roman era, when St Paul's provocative sermon to Ephesians was delivered here, the theatre was enlarged. St Paul's challenge to Artemis worshippers, and Ephesian silversmiths whose livelihood depended on manufacturing and selling statues of Artemis and her temple, resulted in a riot in this very theatre (Acts 19:24–41). The superb acoustics here, together with concerts by internationally renowned performers, thrill modern audiences each summer at the Izmir Festival. The top tier of the theatre provides a panoramic view of the **Arcadian Way** leading west towards the ancient harbour.

The wide **Harbour Street** testifies to the grandeur that was Ephesus in the first century BC. After docking at the harbour, dignitaries marched 500 metres (1,650 ft) along this marble-paved road lined with statues, porticoes and public buildings. A recently excavated inscription confirms that 50 lamps hung from columned porticoes on both sides of this street at a time when lighted cities included only Ephesus, Antioch and Rome. Between the theatre and the ancient harbour, statues of the four evangelists were, in the fifth century, placed on columns whose shafts are still visible. At the north side of this street are the ruins of the Theatre Gymnasium, the Verlanus Sports Arena and Paleistra, the Harbour Baths and the Church of the Virgin Mary.

Visitors explore streets of Ephesus.

Nestorian heresy: Located to the north of the Harbour Baths, near the **Church of the Virgin Mary**, the first church ever dedicated to the Virgin Mary, is a long extensive ruin where the Third Ecumenical Council proclaimed in AD 431 that Mary was the mother of Jesus, the son of God. This council recorded that Mary lived and died near Ephesus, and branded Nestor, Patriarch of Constantinople, a heretic for his denial of the virgin birth.

The church was converted from a school of higher education to a basilica in the fourth century. Because this basilica underwent two additional alterations, this narrow, elongated edifice now seems confusing. Near the northern apse is the large baptismal pool where the faithful were immersed and baptised inside what was once a circular baptistry covered by a domed roof.

After being expelled from Jerusalem, St John and the Virgin Mary came to Ephesus. It is believed John's grave lies underneath the church erected by Emperor Justinian, who reigned from AD 527 to 565. Even before the construction of the **Church of St John**, which stands near the Citadel of Selçuk, there was a Baptistry in use there. The circular pool where baptisms were performed had a marble floor and was originally covered by a dome with a glass mosaic.

Towards the eastern end of the church, at the end of the central nave just west of the apse, is the **Tomb of St John**. The burial platform, two steps below the floor, used to be covered by a small dome. The marble mosaics adorning the platform have been restored. For several centuries this church was a shrine visited by pilgrims and by the sick and ailing who hoped the dust from the burial chamber would perform miracles and heal them.

The fortification wall that surrounds the church was built in the seventh and eighth centuries to protect Ephesus against Arab attacks. At the main entrance to the church, the **Pursuit Gate** and its adjoining courtyard were built according to an ancient Hellenistic

Praying at the House of the Virgin Mary.

strategy for defence. If the enemy penetrated beyond the gate they were trapped inside the courtyard, which had no exit. In that position they could be killed by men positioned above the courtyard walls.

Turkish conquest: When the Turks arrived in 1304 all that remained of Ephesus was a small Byzantine village, which was easily conquered. The **Isa Bey Mosque** is remarkable and occupies a huge area at the western base of the hill where the Church of St John stands. It was built in 1375 for the Seljuk sultan Isa Bey by the architect Ali Damessene.

The mosque was subsequently toppled by an earthquake. Sometime soon after the Ottomans took over in 1426 Ephesus was utterly deserted. This double-domed mosque has been restored and has three chambers.

Above the main entrance the last of three original minarets still stands. Surrounding the large inner courtyard are unusually high walls that were partially constructed with marble transported from Ephesus.

Magnificent views highlight the 7.5-km (5-mile) ascent from the Magnesian Gate to the souvenir shops and restaurant located on the path leading towards the haven to which St John brought the Virgin Mary after the day of the Crucifixion.

The visionary dream of a German nun, Catherine Emmerich, eventually inspired the search for the **House of the Virgin Mary** (Meryem Ana in Turkish), where Mary lived from AD 37 to 48. In 1891, a search party led by the Father Superior of the Lazarists discovered the House of the Blessed Virgin in a pine forest just before an *ayazma*, a sacred spring. Since its restoration in 1951, this house, which is used as a chapel, has been visited by two popes and millions of pilgrims, both Christian and Moslem.

The building is officially recognised by the Vatican and the Eastern Orthodox churches as the last residence of the Virgin Mary and is considered a holy shrine. The Virgin Mary is also considered a Moslem saint. Pope John

Paul, the Polish pontiff, held Mass in the chapel when he visited Turkey in 1979 for theological unification talks between the Vatican and Orthodox Church Patriarchate in Istanbul.

Each year several hundred thousand pilgrims enter the chapel where Mary's icon stands. After drinking the healing spring water, devout pilgrims attach their prayers to a nearby wall. Chronicles have recorded many miracles, such as the curing of invalids, who entered the chapel on crutches and left discarding them.

In accordance with local tradition, as adopted by Pope Benedict XIV, each August 15 the Mass commemorating the Assumption of Mary is celebrated in the surprisingly modest stone chapel. The 30-minute visit that most Selçuk taxi drivers allow is certainly not sufficient to appreciate fully the serenity this shrine offers. Take a guided tour, which includes Ephesus and the Virgin Mary's house, and you'll have more time and receive better explanations of both places.

The Basilica of St John.

THE MAEANDER RIVER VALLEY

The **Büyük Menderes Valley**, the site of many cities of antiquity including Miletus, Aphrodisias and Hierapolis, is one of the most fertile agricultural regions in Turkey and one of the country's prime sources of food. In summer, this broad, long valley, nurtured by the winding 584-km (365-mile) **Büyük Menderes** (the Maeander River of ancient times), is relatively dry. In winter, torrents of streams irrigate the valley, allowing farmers to grow cotton, olives, citrus fruits and vegetables, graze cattle and sheep and raise poultry. In recent years, Söke, Aydın, Nazilli and Denizli, the main cities in the valley, have become cotton boom towns with high standards of living. The many twists and turns in the Büyük Menderes River have given rise to the verb "to meander" in the English language. According to ancient belief, the river's winding channel inscribed the entire Greek alphabet.

The quickest way to reach the Büyük Menderes Valley from Kuşadası is to take one of two minor asphalt roads through the verdant, undulating hills to **Çamlık**, a village and railroad switch-yard station, on the E24/550 Izmir–Denizli highway. By turning right on the Izmir–Denizli highway motorists can drive to the valley below. A toll motorway links Aydin and Izmir.

Carpets and cuisine: Near Çamlık is the commercial carpet-weaving centre of **Sultanköy**, operated by the Net group, one of Turkey's biggest producers and exporters of handmade Turkish carpets. At **Ortaklar**, the first town in the Büyük Menderes River Valley, turn left, and take the E24/320 highway at the junction towards Aydın and Denizli. The junction is noted for its many one-man *kebab* stands, where you can enjoy a delicious *çöp şiş* lunch or dinner. *Çöp şiş* are tiny morsels of lamb meat roasted on coal barbecues along with tomatoes, peppers and onions.

Aydın, a sprawling provincial capital of over 100,000 people, is 22 km (14 miles) from Ortaklar. Founded originally by an odd group of barbarian tribes from Thrace and the Peloponnesus, Aydın was known in ancient times as Tralles. It came under Carian and Persian domination in the sixth century BC. Tralles passed into the hands of Alexander the Great in 334 BC, and was later acquired by the Kingdom of Pergamum. In 129 BC it became a part of the Roman Empire. The Seljuk Turks ruled the city from AD 1186 to 1300. The Aydınoğulları princes controlled the city for the next 126 years before it was conquered by the Ottoman Turks in 1426. The city was held by the Greek army from 1919 to 1922, until its liberation by Turkish nationalist forces.

Ottoman monuments: Traces of ancient Tralles, which can be seen about 2 km (1 mile) north of the present town, include scant remains of a gymnasium, agora and theatre. The city itself has many Ottoman monuments, the oldest of which is the **Alihan Kümbeti**, a 14th-century tomb with the cemeteries

Left, bathing in the holy pool at Pamukkale. **Right**, peasant woman in the Aegean.

of four Aydınoğlu notables, including Prince Ali Han. This structure is located in the **Üveys Paşa Mahallesi**.

Several 16th-, 17th- and 18th-century mosques are scattered about the town, including the **Ağaçarası Mosque**, the **Süleyman Bey Mosque**, the **Üveys Paşa Mosque**, the **Eski-Yeni Mosque** and the **Ramazan Paşa Mosque**. The 18th-century **Nuh Paşa Medresesi**, a U-shaped Islamic school of theology, can be seen in the city's **Köprülü Mahallesi**. Aydın's main street, **Adnan Menderes Bulvarı**, is named after the Turkish prime minister who was toppled in the 1960 military coup and executed in 1961.

Two towns on the E24/320 highway are **Nazilli** and **Kuyucak**. A country road forks to the right after Kuyucak toward **Karacasu** and Aphrodisias, passing though gentle rolling hills where shepherds graze their sheep.

The ruins of the fabulous Roman city of **Aphrodisias** are located near the village of Geyre, off the right hand side of the road. **Geyre** was once located amidst the ruins, and the villagers used many of the city's stones and statues to construct their houses. The village was relocated in the 1960s as a result of expanded excavations carried out by New York University archaeologists, led by the late Professor Kenan Erim and financed by the National Geographic Society.

School of sculpture: Tourism authorities say that Aphrodisias is likely to surpass Ephesus in size and splendour eventually as a result of Professor Erim's discoveries and excavations. The settlement dates to well before 3000 BC. A Carian city, Aphrodisias made its mark in history during the Roman Period, when it was sponsored by the emperors as a centre of art, sculpture and religion.

The city's School of Sculpture, where many of the Roman Empire's greatest sculptors conducted classes, turned out many fine masterpieces from marble quarried in the foothills of the **Babadağ**, a 2,102-metre (7,000-ft) mountain northeast of Aphrodisias.

<u>Left</u>, a statue of a god in Aphrodisias. <u>Right</u>, a frieze from Roman times.

The **Aphrodisias Museum** houses many of the statues found during excavations by Professor Erim and his team. The most astonishing statue in the museum is of Aphrodite, the patron goddess of the city. Aphrodite's statue bears a striking resemblance to the giant statues of Artemis found in Ephesus, showing a close connection between the two deities.

Aphrodisias was the main centre of the cult of the Carian Aphrodite, from which the town got its name. Pilgrims from all over the Greco-Roman world visited the **Temple of Aphrodite**, parts of which still stand. The temple was transformed into a church after the Roman Empire adopted Christianity as the state religion.

The stadium: The magnificent **Stadium**, built during the early period of the Roman Empire, is perhaps the best preserved in the ancient world. The long, narrow stadium is rounded at both ends and has a seating capacity for nearly 25,000 people. On its northern side is a royal box reserved for visiting dignitaries from Rome. The stadium was the site of many athletic events including foot races. A semi-circular ring on the eastern part was where gladiators fought.

Other buildings of note in Aphrodisias are a small odeon, where theatrical performances and public debates were held, a well-preserved theatre, an agora and a street with columns on each side, and the Baths of Hadrian. Two mounds at the acropolis hill were merely levels of earlier inhabitation. Pottery shards found here showed that Aphrodisias was one of the earliest settlements in the Maeander River Valley, and in western Anatolia.

During the early Christian era, the name of the city was changed to Stavrapolis, or City of the Cross, to wipe out its affiliation with the pagan goddess Aphrodite. A series of earthquakes and invading armies destroyed and sacked the prosperous city. All that remained of Aphrodisias after the seventh-century Arab conquests of Anatolia was a village that took the

Donkeyback-riding through Aphrodisias.

name Caria from the ancient Roman province where it was located. During the Turkish period, the name Caria was corrupted and changed to Geyre.

With a population of 170,000, **Denizli** is an important carpet-weaving, mining and agricultural centre. Specially bred Denizli roosters are world famous. Denizli was founded in the third century BC by Seleucid kings of Syria but it only developed during the Roman period. In 1094, the Seljuk Turks conquered the city, later incorporating it into the Germiyanoğlu Principality. The Ottoman Turks took over in 1428. Denizli (meaning "sea" in Turkish) gets its name from an abundance of streams that wind through the countryside.

The ruins of **Laodiceia**, ancient Denizli, are located 6 km (4 miles) from Denizli. Laodiceia was founded by Antiochus I, king of Syria, and named after his wife, Laodice. The ruins include a stadium, gymnasium, aqueducts and a theatre. The city was the centre for one of the Seven Churches mentioned in the Book of Revelation.

The Cotton Castle: **Pamukkale**, which means Cotton Castle in Turkish, is one of the most spectacular natural wonders in Turkey. Located 22 km (14 miles) north of Denizli, Pamukkale is a cliff of white limestone cascades, tiers of stalactites and natural swimming pools formed over thousands of years by the deposits of mineral and calcium-rich hot streams that run down the hill. The cliffs resemble a fluffy cotton castle from a distance, especially if you are approaching the site from Denizli.

Pamukkale, situated next to the ruins of the ancient Roman city of **Hierapolis**, has always been known for its thermal springs. In order to preserve this wonder for the future, the profusion of tasteless hotels and pensions have been removed and bathing is now forbidden in the pools.

The natural spring waters are believed to be therapeutic for persons suffering from coronary, respiratory and kidney ailments, psoriasis and rheumatism.

Late afternoon in Pamukkale.

204

The Devil's Hole: The source of the springs is believed to be in a cave-like opening known as the **Plutoneum** or the **Cin Deliği** – the Devil's Hole – behind the hotel in the middle of the terrace of Hierapolis. In ancient times, this cave was believed to be the entrance to Hades, the underworld. Entrance to this cave is forbidden today because of its noxious gases and fumes. The cave was linked by a passage to the nearby **Temple of Apollo**. In the past, sooth-sayers and priests were able to operate in the passage by holding onto their breath.

The entire Büyük Menderes River Valley lies on the Anatolian fault, an earthquake-fault zone. This has proved to be both a curse and a blessing: several of the towns in the region, including Denizli and Aydın, have been levelled in the past by land tremors, but many towns in the region have thermal and steam baths thanks to the volcanic activity of the earth's crust below.

Hierapolis was established by the Pergamene kings in the third century BC, but Attalus II, the King of Pergamum, bequeathed the city to Rome in 133 BC. The city prospered during Roman times and three emperors visited Hierapolis during this period. But Hierapolis never fully recovered from three devastating earthquakes that rocked the site in the first century, and from the many wars fought nearby.

St Philip's Martyrium: Other interesting sites in Hierapolis include two theatres, Roman baths and the Martyrium of St Philip, one of Christ's 12 disciples who lived and was martyred there. The necropolis of Hierapolis is one of the most extensive anywhere in Turkey, with hundreds of tombs in the hillside on both sides of the road west of the town. On most days shepherds graze their sheep among the tumbled masonry of the tombs.

About 5 km (3 miles) west of Hierapolis is the Karahayit Thermal, a reddish mineral-water geyser that gushes out of the side of the hill forming red and sulphurous deposits.

The return trip from Denizli to Ortaklar along route E24/320 is a four-hour drive. Halfway to Ortaklar are the unusual geothermal springs at **Çubukdağı** (also known as **Buharkent**, the Steam City). Hot steam gushes out of crevasses on both sides of the highway at Buharkent for several hundred yards, reducing visibility, but neither spas nor stations producing geothermal energy have been built at Buharkent.

To see the other sites of antiquity in the Maeander River Valley, motorists must turn left at Ortaklar on route 525 toward Söke, Milas and Bodrum.

Magnesia on the Maeander: The ruins of Magnesia-ad-Maeandrum (Magnesia on the Maeander) lie 3 km (2 miles) from Ortaklar to the right of the highway. Aeolian soldiers from the original Magnesia in Greece who fought in Agamemnon's army during the Trojan War are believed to have founded the city around 1260 BC. The descendants of the early founders claimed that Magnesia on the Maeander was the first city in Asia Minor to be colonised by the Greeks.

The city was always prosperous because of its closeness to the Maeander River and to the major trade routes. Because of its wealth, the city incurred the jealousy and wrath of its stronger neighbours. It was sacked twice in the 7th century BC, first by the Lydian King Gyges and then by the Cimmerians.

Magnesia became part of the Persian Empire during the 6th century BC, and Xerxes spent some time there preparing for his invasion of Greece. The city capitulated to Alexander the Great without a fight in 334 BC.

Finally it came under the domination of the Pergamene kings and Rome. The city was eventually abandoned during the Byzantine period.

Themistocles: The most important historical figure associated with Magnesia was Themistocles, the Athenian statesman responsible for the big Greek naval victory over the Persians, led by Xerxes, at the Battle of Salamis in 480 BC. Themistocles spent the last years of his life in Magnesia, having fallen from favour in Athens as a result of a political scandal and branded a traitor. Rather than serve Persian interests against his native Greece, the 65-year-old Themistocles committed suicide in Magnesia by drinking the poisonous blood of a bull. All that remains of the city are walls of some buildings, including traces of the Temple of Artemis and a theatre and odeon.

Söke, a lively market town with a population of over 50,000, is off the road. Prosperity has come to the town as a result of an increase in cotton production. The only historical monument of any significance in Söke is the **Ilyas Ağa Camii**, an old Turkish mosque that was restored in 1821. South of Söke, a country road turns right after the town of **Yenidoğan** in the direction of Priene, one of the most outstanding sites of the classical period.

Priene, one of the best-preserved Hellenistic cities in the world, is perched on the side of a mountain off the road. The first thing that strikes visitors is the neat grid pattern layout of the city. Everything has been done on a small scale, compared to its neighbours Ephesus in the north and Miletus in the south, which emphasised size in their architecture. Lord Kinross, a distinguished British diplomat, biographer and travel writer, who visited the site in the early 1950s, had this to say about the city: "Hellenistic in style, unpretentious in scale, Priene has a simplicity which few cities of Greece can equal."

While Miletus, its chief rival, grew fat on commerce and increased its influence with military might, Priene remained modest and unpretentious, devoting most of its time to the worshipping of the gods, sponsoring of sports events and cultural activities. Its population never exceeded 5,000 people at any one time.

Athenian colonists founded the small city-state during the Greek invasions in the 12th century BC. Although a member of the 12-city Ionian League, Priene always felt a particular closeness to Athens, the mother city.

Seven sages: Priene's golden age was in the 6th century BC when the city produced one of the Seven Sages of

Grazing among ruins.

Antiquity, Bias, from whom we get the English verb "to be biased". Bias was instrumental in codifying the laws of the city. Priene suffered severely during the Persian invasion of western Asia Minor. In 545 BC the army of Cyrus sacked the city, burning it down to the ground and enslaving most of its people. Priene joined the Ionian revolt against Persian rule in 499 BC by contributing 12 galleys. Alas the Persians soundly defeated the Ionian fleet off Lade, a small island near Miletus and Priene, in 495 BC, and sacked the city one more time.

During his military campaigns in western Asia Minor, Alexander the Great stayed in Priene for some time and financed construction of the grand Temple of Athena.

After Priene came under Roman domination, the city lost its importance and was finally abandoned in the Byzantine period.

Sacrificial victims: Among the buildings in Priene visitors should see are the small **Greek theatre** with five stone thrones in the orchestra for priests, and a special water clock to time speeches at public assembly meetings; the massive **Temple of Athena** with many of its tumbled elephantine columns sprawled about; the **Council House** resembling a tiny theatre; the **Temple of Demeter**, which had a sacrificial pit, where the blood of the sacrificial victims, often humans, were poured down as offerings to the gods of the underworld; and the **Stadium**, where foot races, boxing, the pentathlon and the pancratium, a competition resembling a combination of today's American-style WWF wrestling and Thai kick-boxing, were regularly held.

The city was once located at the tip of a headland overlooking the Latmian Gulf and was a grand maritime power with a harbour that could hold 200 warships at one time. Today it is 8 km (5 miles) from the sea due to the silting of the Maeander River. Unfortunately, **Miletus** is a big disappointment to travellers visiting the site, for the city isn't as impressive as either Aphrodisias or Priene.

The ruins of Priene.

A Mycenaean settlement existed there between 1400 and 1200 BC. Later it was occupied by a mixture of Cretans and native Carians and was colonised by the Ionians. The historian Herodotus wrote that the Ionians, having brought no women with them, slaughtered all the male inhabitants and married their wives. The women of Miletus vowed never to sit at the tables of their husbands. It was ruled in succession by the Persians, Alexander the Great, the Romans, the Byzantines and the Turks.

By the eighth century BC, Miletus had set up as many as 90 colonies in the Mediterranean, the Dardanelles, the Sea of Marmara and the Black Sea, and traded goods with Egypt, Lebanon, Africa and Greece.

Solar eclipse: Miletus was also a centre for learning and intellectual enlightenment. It was the home of many learned men, philosophers and scientists, including Thales, Anaximenes and Anaximander. Thales, considered by many to be one of the Seven Sages of Antiquity, predicted the solar eclipse

of 585 BC. He also calculated the height of the Egyptian Pyramids by measuring their shadows at the time of day when a man's shadow is equal to his height.

Miletus' steady decline began with the Ionian revolt of 500 BC against Persian rule, which ended in defeat. The silting up of the Maeander was the city's death knell, and it was eventually abandoned. The most significant sites in Miletus are the grand theatre and the Faustina Baths, the Byzantine Citadel, the Heroon (a monumental tomb), the Agora, the Byzantine Church, the Temple of Athena, and the Turkish Caravansary.

Labour strike: The world's first recorded labour strike allegedly took place in Miletus during the construction of the theatre in about AD 100. The construction workers, dissatisfied with the terms and conditions of their contracts, stopped working. The strike was settled when the sides sought the arbitration of the Oracle of Didyma.

Most of the buildings to the east are badly ruined. The city's main sanctuary was the Shrine of Apollo Delphinius, whose earliest levels date back to the 6th century BC. The pinkish Hellenistic building was reconstructed in Roman times. Nearly 200 inscriptions found here have proved crucial in recording the early history of the city.

The **Bouleuterion** (Council Chamber), built between 175 and 164 BC, during the reign of Seleucid king Antiochus IV Epiphanes, is one of the oldest buildings surviving in Miletus. Inside are the remains of an altar dedicated to the Roman imperial cult. Opposite, there was a three-storey **Nymphaeum**, built in the 2nd century AD and elaborately decorated with reliefs of nymphs. It was fed by a now-ruined aqueduct, which distributed water to the entire city.

The **Faustina Baths** are indeed splendid, consisting of a dressing room, cold room *(Frigidarium)*, warm room *(Tepidarium)*, hot room *(Calidarium)*, steam room *(Sudatarium)*, boiler room and exercise areas *(Palaestra)*. A reclining statue of the River God Maean-

dros and a statue of a lion can be seen in the *Frigidarium*.

The most remarkable and popular building in Miletus is the 14th-century **Ilyas Bey Mosque Complex**, built by Ilyas Bey, a prince of the Turkish Menteşeoğulları Dynasty that ruled the area before the Ottoman Turks. It includes a single-domed mosque, an attractive courtyard with cemeteries, an *imaret* (a place where poor people were fed), a convent for dervish mystics, and a public bath.

Didyma: The **Temple of Apollo** at **Didim** (Didyma), 18 km (11 miles) south of Miletus, is one of the most outstanding buildings of the ancient Greek world, both for its size and architectural style.

The oracle dates back to the 7th century BC, long before Ionian settlers arrived in the region. Control of the cult was in the hands of the Branchidae family, who claimed to originate from Delphi, site of the great oracle. The temple was destroyed by the Persians in the 6th century BC and by Alexander the Great in the 4th century BC. The vast structure seen there today dates from about 300 BC, built by Seleucus, king of Syria.

Its decline coincided with the rise of Christianity. Christians finally took control of the pagan building and constructed a large church in its most sacred part. In ancient times, emperors consulted the oracle for advice. Croesus, the king of Lydia, who once consulted the oracle, was told that a great empire would be destroyed if he were to launch an attack against Persia. In fact, it was Croesus' empire that was destroyed.

Little remains of the ancient Greek town of **Notion**, on the coast some 25 km (15 miles) northeast of Kuhadası, but the site is picturesque and makes a good day trip (bring a picnic). At **Klaros**, less than a mile away, there is a little more to see. In ancient times Klaros was known for its temple and oracle of Apollo, and the site of the sacred spring that inspired the oracle can still be identified.

The sprawling Temple of Didyma.

CARIA

The region known as **Caria** in the Greco-Roman world corresponds roughly to the boundaries of the present-day province of **Muğla**, in southwest Turkey. The Carians, the earliest known inhabitants of this region, were a native stock Anatolian people famed for their skills as mariners. Ancient chronicles say Carian sailors served in the navies of the Egyptian pharaohs and of the Persian ruler Xerxes. Homer mentions the Carians in his *Iliad* as being "barbarous of speech". (Coincidentally, linguists have noted that the Turkish dialect spoken in this part of the country is the harshest in western Turkey.)

The region is one of the most popular travel destinations for foreigners and Turks alike. It is rich in archaeological sites and is ideal for yachting, sailing, scuba diving and other watersports. The local inhabitants earn their livelihood from tourism, carpet-weaving and farming. Cotton, olives and citrus fruits are grown in abundance.

To reach the Carian hills from Didyma, motorists should drive along the attractive Akbük Bay to highway 525 and turn right. Lake Bafa, on the edge of the Beşparmak Dağı (Mount Latmus of antiquity), is the beginning of Caria. **Beşparmak** means five fingers in Turkish and indeed the top of the rocky 1,367-metre (4,557-ft) mountain resembles the stubs of five fingers. **Lake Bafa** was once a part of the Aegean Sea. But the silting of the Maeander River left it landlocked and a good 20 km (12.5 miles) from the sea.

The romantic ruins of **Heracleia under Latmus**, one of the least-visited ancient sites of Aegean Turkey, cling to the slopes of Beşparmak Dağı on the eastern side of Lake Bafa, close to the village of Kapıkırı. The ruins can be reached by the road that turns left after Lake Bafa. A yellow sign points in the direction of the ancient city.

Endymion and Selene: Heracleia is associated with the legend of Endymion and Selene and has a **Sanctuary of Endymion**, a horseshoe-shaped temple honouring the shepherd demigod. When the Moon Goddess Selene fell in love with the handsome Endymion, a jealous Zeus put him to sleep. Selene then went to sleep with Endymion and bore 50 children, according to the legend. The sanctuary is located near the lake at the lower part of the village, facing a large trailer camp.

Heracleia also has a partly submerged necropolis of tombs by the lake, an ancient market, a Byzantine church, the Temple of Athena and several miles of well-preserved defensive walls with towers that curve part of the way up Beşparmak Dağı. Monasteries are located on the mountain. Boats can also be hired in the village to visit the Byzantine churches and monasteries on the islands in the middle of Lake Bafa.

The next fascinating site on highway 525 are the ruins of **Euromos**, a Carian settlement just off the road, and its spectacular **Temple of Zeus** with its 16 columns still proudly standing.

Labraynda: Before you enter Milâs, a dirt village road forks left into the rolling hills to the Carian sanctuary of **Labraynda**, a splendid site at the end of a bumpy 10-km (6-mile) drive. The village, built on terraces, dates from the 4th century BC and is 700 metres (2,300 ft) above sea level.

The most important site at Labraynda is the **Temple of Zeus Labrayndus**, the god of the double axe, the patron deity of Caria. Located on an upper terrace, the temple is in ruins with columns and pillars strewn about the site. Behind the temple is the **First Andron**, a well-preserved building with a 2-metre (7-ft) thick wall. The **Androns** – there are several at the site – were men's clubs, where the priests of the shrine gathered for social purposes. Next to it is a **residence** of the clergy.

Fortune-telling fish: The site also has a large tomb, with three sarcophagi inside, on the slope overlooking the temple. Mausolus and other Carian kings maintained at Labraynda a **Summer Palace**, which has not yet been excavated, but is believed to lie near the temple. The holy community also had a **Sacred Pool of Oracle Fish**, which were adorned with earrings and necklaces. According to early chronicles, the goldfish in the pool were capable of making yes and no prophecies by accepting or rejecting food offered after a question. The pool was located in what is now the **Ablution Hall**, along a wall at the lower terrace. Traces of the **Sacred Way**, an 13-km (8-mile) road linking Labraynda to ancient Milâs are still visible. A local villager operates a roadside teahouse at Labraynda and serves drinks, sandwiches and *menemen*, delicious country-style scrambled eggs with peppers and tomatoes.

Milâs, one of Turkey's leading producers of handmade wool carpets, is built on the side of a hill. The market town, known to the ancients as Mylasa, was once the capital of the Carian state, but was ruled successively by the Persians, Alexander the Great, the Romans, the Byzantines and now, finally, the Turks.

The Temple of Zeus Labrayndus.

The most impressive monument in Milâs, visible from every point in town, is the Roman mausoleum known as **Gümüşkesen**, or the "silver purse". Located in a public park overlooking Milâs, the monument is a smaller replica of the Mausoleum of Halicarnassus, with a pyramid roof supported by columns. It was built in the first century AD, and gets its Turkish name from alleged treasures hidden inside its crypt, which was broken into long ago but is now locked. A strange hole exists on the floor of the funerary monument surmounting the sepulchral chamber below. This hole, according to Richard Chandler, an 18th-century traveller, was used by family members of the deceased to pour libations of milk, honey and wine into the chamber to satisfy the spirit of their loved one.

The ruins of a Roman temple can be seen near the **Belediye Binası**, the town hall, but all that remains standing is a fluted column standing on an elevated marble floor.

The double axe: One other fascinating site in Milâs is the **Baltalı Kapı**, or the "Gate of the Axe", located on the main street, just off the state hospital (**Devlet Hastanesi**). Baltalı Kapı derives its name from the frieze of a double axe on its façade, symbolising the divine Kingdom of Caria. The arched gate was in ancient times the beginning of the "Sacred Way" connecting Milâs with the holy shrine of Labraynda.

After leaving Milâs the road reaches a junction. Highway 525 continues east towards the coal mining town of Yatağan and the provincial capital of Muğla. The other road heads towards the resort of Bodrum. A dirt road near the junction leads to **Beçin Kale**, an old Turkish fortification that has a stunning view of Milâs and the valley. Beçin Kale is a 14th-century stronghold of the Menteşeoğlu Beylik, a Turkish dynasty that ruled this area before the Ottoman conquest in 1390. Beçin Kale itself is situated on a flat, rocky hilltop. The fortress, which is in a state of ruin, can easily be toured in 20 minutes. Just inside the gates of the citadel, on the right, is a flight of solid marble steps,

believed to be part of an unknown ancient temple.

Nearby is the interesting **Medrese of Gazi Ahmet Pasha**, an Islamic religious school named after a Menteşeoğlu statesman. The statesman, Ahmet Pasha, and his wife are buried next to each other in an open part of the *medrese*, and today they are considered to be saints by the local inhabitants. Behind the *medrese* are the ruins of a mosque. This is an excellent picnic spot. A one-man beverage stand near the *medrese* provides refreshments.

Probably the world's only carpet farm, the **Ildız Carpet Farm**, is located on the Bodrum-Milâs Highway, 10 km (6 miles) out of Milâs. At the farm, experts wash and sun-dry tens of thousands of handmade wool carpets to test their quality. The carpets are manufactured or purchased by the Ildız Company, one of Turkey's leading carpet exporters and producers. Ildız specialises in the production of pastel-coloured Milâs carpets. Visitors to the carpet farm can ask the attendants to unroll some of the Milâs carpets to view.

Near the carpet farm a road forks right to **Güllük**, a fishermen's town with a pretty port and numerous pensions and small hotels. An airport near Güllük, which provides international connections, opened in 1997, making the area more accessible to tourism.

Boats can be chartered from Güllük for a one-hour trip to the ruins of **Iasus**, a Greco-Roman city. Iasus can also be reached by a rough dirt road that turns west on the Izmir-Milas highway near the ruins of Euromos.

Peloponnesians from Argos, having fought a long and bitter war with the local Carians, colonised Iasus and the surrounding area. But, because of its successful fishing industry and trade, the prosperous city was highly sought after. The town was often sacked by rival powers, being ruled successively by the Persians, the Athenians, the Spartans, Alexander the Great, the Seleucids, the Rhodians, the Romans, the Byzantines, the Knights of St John and now the Turks.

BODRUM

The most international of Turkey's summer towns, **Bodrum** is renowned for its foreign restaurants, party town atmosphere and bohemian lifestyle. This combination appeals especially to young foreigners and Western-oriented Turks, who flock there in summer. Bodrum has a permanent population of only 21,000 people, yet it has some of the best Indian, Italian, and Chinese restaurants on the Aegean coast. The town also has a well developed shopping scene, which attracts both sailors and landlubbers.

Located on the southeastern shore of the Bodrum Peninsula, the town is built on twin bays separated by the massive Castle of St. Peter. Tiny white houses, characteristic of Bodrum, rise from the town and carpet the surrounding hills and mountains. The dark silhouette of Karaada, a virtually uninhabited Turkish island, can be seen at the mouth of the bay with the shadows of the Greek island of Cos visible on the distant horizon.

Sailing centre: Bodrum's harbour is protected by a long jetty, and scores of yachts and sailboats are moored along the quayside. Dozens of restaurants serving enticing seafood, and small outdoor coffee houses line the harbour. With its 125-berth marina, the town is the most important starting point for the Blue Voyage, a yachting cruise into the neighbouring Gökova Bay *(see page 224)*.

Downtown Bodrum, starting from the foot of the castle and winding along the narrow **Dr. Alim Bey Caddesi** and **Cumhuriyet Caddesi**, bustles with activity in summer. These two connected streets are lined with lively bars, restaurants, tavernas, small stores and giftshops selling carpets, leatherware, local jewellery, handmade sandals (for which the town is especially famous), and more. Young artists display their paintings on street corners, old men peddle colourful sponges, and vendors in traditional costumes sell

Kahramanmaraş dondurması, an ice cream speciality from eastern Turkey.

The town has been a centre for boat building since the days of Mark Antony and Cleopatra. Sturdy, luxury yachts, known as gulets, are built all along the Bodrum Peninsula, but the biggest shipyards are located at **Içmeler**, a 10-minute drive from Bodrum.

Knights and conquests: Bodrum has a rich 3,000-year history, replete with military campaigns, naval victories, knights and conquests. In ancient times the city was known as **Halicarnassus**. In 546 BC, like most Anatolian cities, it came under Persian domination. Sixty years later, at the time of the Persian-Greek wars, the city was ruled by a Carian dynasty whose most famous member was Queen Artemesia. When Xerxes, the Persian King of Kings, was preparing his invasion of Greece, Artemesia joined his forces contributing several fighting ships. During a naval engagement in 480 BC in which the Persian fleet was routed, Artemesia displayed unusual bravery, causing Xerxes to exclaim: "My men have shown themselves women and my women men."

The golden age: Halicarnassus saw its golden age under King Mausolus, a Persian-appointed satrap belonging to the Carian dynasty. Mausolus moved his capital (from Mylasa) to Halicarnassus, transforming it into a splendid city. He died in 353 BC and was succeeded by Artemesia the younger, his wife and sister. Artemesia, who ruled for only three years, built a majestic tomb in her husband's memory, from which we get the word "mausoleum."

Alexander the Great arrived in Halicarnassus in 334 BC and conquered the city. After his death the city continued as a Greco-Roman city until AD 654 when it was completely destroyed by the Arab invasions of Anatolia, and wiped from the pages of history until the 15th century.

The Knights of St John revived the city in 1402, when they were given possession of Halicarnassus by Tamerlane, the Oriental ruler whose armies swept through Anatolia. The Knights built the Castle of St Peter, after their patron saint, and named their city Petronium, from which the modern Turkish name Bodrum is derived. The Knights finally abandoned the city in 1522 when the Ottoman Sultan Süleyman the Magnificent conquered Rhodes, their stronghold.

Many Turkish writers and intellectuals have made Bodrum their home, the most famous in recent years being Cevat Şakir Kabaağaçlı (1890–1973), a British-educated Turkish writer nicknamed the "Fisherman of Halicarnassus". Exiled to Bodrum in 1925 because of his unorthodox political views, Kabaağaçlı popularised the town through his essays, short stories and novels, attracting like-minded romantics, writers and artists.

Forsaken and isolated: Bodrum in 1925 was a small, isolated fishermen's village with a population of less than 2,000, which had no road connections with the provincial capital Muğla. Thus it took Kabaağaçlı, accompanied by *gendarmes*, nearly four months to arrive in Bodrum from Ankara, the capital of the new Turkish Republic, trekking part of the way over mountain passes and trails that had not been used since the days of Alexander the Great.

Much has changed in Bodrum since the days of Kabaağaçlı. It was discovered by Istanbul's intellectual crowd in the early 1970s, who made it fashionable. Soon the country's *nouveaux riches* arrived, turning it into their summer hangout. Its fame spread and then came the international jet set. Celebrities like Barbra Streisand, Dustin Hoffman, Clint Eastwood and Jacqui Onassis spent vacations in Bodrum. Ahmet Ertegün, a Turco-American who owns Atlantic Records, one of the world's leading music recording companies, bought a house there, and his guests included rock star Mick Jagger, former World Bank President Robert McNamara and ballet star Rudolph Nureyev. Today the city is compared to Saint Tropez.

The Knights of St John: The most fascinating site to visit in Bodrum is the

Castle, a well-preserved architectural complex. It was built between 1402 and 1503 by the Knights of St John, an international Catholic military monastic order, also known as the Knights Hospitalliers of St John of Jerusalem, the Knights of Rhodes and later as the Knights of Malta. The castle was used by the Knights to carry out raids on the Aegean Coast and served as a refuge for Christians fleeing Turkish captivity. To build the castle, the Knights used green stones, statuary, masonry and marble slabs from the nearby Mausoleum of Halicarnassus, which they found in ruins, destroyed apparently by an earthquake sometime after the 12th century. The castle today houses the **Museum of Underwater Archaeology**.

More than 125 shipwrecks: The museum, located in several buildings in the courtyard, is one of the most impressive of its kind in the world. Opened in 1960, it contains the remains of the world's oldest known shipwrecks, discovered by scientists of the **Institute of Nautical Archaeology** (INA) along the Tur-

quoise Coast. Founded in 1973 by George Bass, a renowned American underwater archaeologist, INA is a research organisation affiliated with Texas A&M University. Using Bodrum Castle as its headquarters, the INA has discovered and mapped more than 125 ancient shipwrecks off the Turkish Coast.

To the right of the courtyard entrance is the **Bronze Age Hall**. It contains rich Mycenaean findings from a land excavation at **Musgebi** on the Bodrum Peninsula, dating from 2500 BC. It also has bronze bars and amphoras recovered by George Bass and his team from a 12th-century BC shipwreck. Bass and his team of divers spent over ten years, up until 1995, excavating the oldest known shipwreck dating from the 14th century BC. The ship was discovered by accident by a sponge diver off the coast of Kaş, at Uluburan.

Across from the outdoor teahouse is **"Shipwreck Hall"**, a large and excellently arranged room that exhibits the hull and cargo of an 11th-century

shipwreck, which was found at **Serçe Limanı**, a shallow cove near Marmaris.

A series of steps behind the Bronze Age Hall lead to the building displaying artefacts from the so-called "**Glass Wreck**". This exhibition contains hundreds of colourful, almost phosphorescent glass jars, bottles and vases, retrieved in 1977 from the Serçe Limanı shipwreck.

The **Italian Tower**, which was the residence of the Italian Knights, houses the **Coin and Jewellery Hall**, a wide collection spanning several centuries. To the left of the Italian Tower is the **French Tower**, where there are two Byzantine shipwrecks, dating from the 4th and 7th centuries.

A relatively recent attraction is the **Hall of the Carian Princess**. Her tomb, discovered by accident in Bodrum in 1989, was found to contain the remains of a woman who lived in about 360 BC, complete with her jewellery and gold appliquéd clothing. A team of British specialists reconstructed the skull and facial features, re-creating the princess from her remains. It is not known who she was, but the richness of her tomb suggested royalty; hence the title of the Carian Princess. Some suggest, with much romance, that she was the wife of Mausolus, the area's most famous ruler. The dates are roughly contemporary, but there is little other justification for the theory. From outside this exhibition room it is possible to climb up to where there are panoramic views of the town and harbour.

In the furthest corner of the castle is the **English Tower**. On its walls are the coats of arms of Edward the Fourth, one of the members of the House of Plantagenet, the dynasty that ruled England from 1154 to 1485, and of the captains of the Knights, Sir Thomas Shefield and John Kendall.

The **German Tower**, where the German Knights lived, is now open to the public. To its left is the structure known as the **Snake Tower**. It gets its name from a snake frieze on its walls, taken from the mausoleum, which

Sailing off Bodrum Castle.

symbolised the serpent shape that Zeus, the supreme deity of the ancient Greeks, took before adopting human form.

The Mausoleum of Halicarnassus can be reached by walking along Neyzen Tevfik Caddesi from the castle along the harbour. Turn right at Hamam Sokak after passing the mosque and left at Turgutreis Caddesi to the Mausoleum of Halicarnassus on the left hand side of the street hidden by a wall. What remains today of the mausoleum – a foundation, a tumble of masonry and columns – belies its original greatness as one of the Seven Wonders of the Ancient World. The structure, built in the 4th century BC, consisted of a high base, 36 columns, a pyramid of 24 steps, crowned by a quadriga (a four-horsed chariot) according to ancient accounts. A small model of the mausoleum can be seen inside the enclosed area. The reliefs and colossal statues of Mausolus and Artemesia uncovered by British archaeologists in the 19th century are now displayed in the British Museum.

A short walk uphill along one of the narrow streets from the mausoleum brings you to the well-preserved Roman **Amphitheatre**, located on the other side of the Bodrum-Izmir Road, with a splendid view of the town and castle.

Gümbet, a village with a long sandy beach, about 5 km (3 miles) from Bodrum, is a well-known windsurfing centre. In addition to windsurfing, water skiing, banana boat riding, canoeing, parasailing and sea biking are also possible.

The modest **Cemetery of Cevat Şakir Kabaağaçlı**, the author who made Bodrum famous through his writings, overlooks Bodrum from a hill between the town and Gümbet.

Chicken princess: Arguably the best restaurant in Bodrum is **Balık Restaurant**. Located on a side street off Dr. Alim Bey Caddesi, Balık Restaurant specialises in authentic Turkish food, including *tandır kebab* – lamb on a skewer cooked on a coal fire and *tavuk prenses* (chicken princess) – a tasty chicken dumpling served with black peppers. It also serves delicious seafood

<u>Left</u>, selling potatoes on market day, and <u>right</u>, inside a private garden.

such as octopus salad and *kalamar*, a fried squid dish.

A pub crawl, involving visits to several of the town's nightclubs, bars and discotheques on the same night, is the best way to enjoy Bodrum's nightlife, starting with the upmarket and immensely popular **Halikarnas Disco and Nightclub**, and working down towards Bodrum Castle. Halikarnas Nightclub, with a grand view of the floodlit Bodrum Castle, caters for glamorous young foreigners and fabulously rich Turks, who dance to loud music from midnight to 5am. The outdoor seaside disco resembles a Greek acropolis with an odeon and an amphitheatre surrounded by columns. A jet of water bursts out of a fountain by the beach near the dance floor while psychedelic lighting is flashed from behind the stage.

The main Cumhuriyet Caddesi, which runs parallel to the shoreline in the south-eastern part of town, offers the greatest number of trendy bars in Bodrum. For something more typically Turkish though, one should visit the so-called **Street of Taverns**, a narrow lane off Dr Alim Bey Caddesi near the castle square. This convivial alley contains a dozen outdoor restaurants/bars that all offer lots of down-to-earth fun, music, fresh fish and tasty *mezes*.

Daily boat trips are available from Bodrum to Cos and Datça. Boats also operate a water taxi service daily to Karaada and nearby beaches and coves for a small fee. Leaving the harbour at 11am, these motor-driven boats, usually Bodrum-built *caiques,* are capable of taking on 30 people at a time.

Karaada, the dark island that guards the town's bay from a distance, is famous for its mud baths. "These baths," the Fisherman of Halicarnassus once wrote, "are almost capable of resurrecting the dead." After allowing passengers a short mud bath and dip in the clear waters, the boat leaves for Ortakent. To the left is the Greek island Cos; Bodrum is to the right.

The boat enters **Ada Boğazı**, a shallow body of water separating a minus-

Left, sandals on display, and **right**, glass bead jewellery for sale.

cule island, Iç Ada, and Bodrum Peninsula. The boat only stops there on the return trip to allow for swimming and snorkelling. Ada Boğazı is often referred to as the "**Aquarium**" because its sandy bottom is rich in marine life. It then passes Çelebi Island and comes to **Ortakent Beach**. Dozens of restaurants and pensions are clustered on this half-moon beach.

On the return voyage to Bodrum, the captain follows the coastline, first passing two promontories on which stands the Aktur Holiday Villas, a luxurious complex. The next wide bay is **Bitez**, one of Bodrum's most popular seaside resorts, with windsurfing, swimming, sunbathing and banana boat riding.

The Hermaphrodite: The last cove before Bodrum is **Bardakçı** (glass maker in Turkish), which has a fine beach. Bardakçı is associated with the legend of the Hermaphrodite, the son of the Olympic deities Hermes and Aphrodite, who fell in love with the nymph Salmacis. It was in Bardakçı that Hermaphrodite and Salmacis were united in a single body, having both male and female sexual characteristics. The cove lives up to its reputation for sexual diversity even today. It was the favourite beach of Zeki Müren, a popular Turkish singer who made his home in Bodrum. Until his death from a heart attack in 1996, in the summer you could see the Liberace-like Müren at his favourite coffeehouse at Bardakçı, surrounded by a flock of admirers.

A number of uncrowded and less noisy towns and villages are located in the vicinity of Bodrum. **Gümüslük**, at the western tip of the Bodrum Peninsula, is a gem of a village with fine fish restaurants and pensions gracing its shore. The ruins of the ancient city of **Myndus** are close by.

The town of **Turgutreis** has a number of fine hotels and pensions. Its name is derived from a 16th-century Turkish naval admiral killed during the siege of Malta, and **Yalıkavak**, a pleasant village, is renowned for its sponge fishers. **Torba**, a quiet little settlement north of Bodrum, has two holiday villages.

Strolling in
Bodrum in
the
afternoon.

SPONGE DIVING

When May comes to coastal villages on the Bodrum Peninsula, most of the men set sail in small wooden-framed boats in search of sponges that will eventually find their way into bathrooms of homes in western Europe, Japan, Canada and the United States. For five months every year, the fishermen comb the entire Turkish Aegean and Mediterranean coast for sponges.

Until quite recently Turkey was a major producer of commercial bath sponges, with annual sponge exports totalling an average of 15 tons. Other producers include Cuba, Mexico, countries in the Antilles, the United States and Greece.

Until the present tourism boom and a fungus epidemic in 1986 that killed many sponges off the Turkish Coast, sponge fishing was the main livelihood of most fishermen and their families around Bodrum. Many former sponge fishermen now prefer chartering their boats to tourists to sending young divers deep down into the sea in search of sponges. Nevertheless, many young Bodrum lads still follow their fathers' footsteps and begin sponge diving at the tender age of 14.

Way of life: Sponge fishing has been a way of life for people of the peninsula for nearly 3,000 years. The ancient Greeks used sponges for bathing, scrubbing tables and floors and for padding armour. The Romans fashioned them into paint brushes, tied them to wooden poles and used them as mops and even substituted them for drinking vessels.

Dubbed the "gold of the sea depths" because of their high value, sponges are porous, multi-cellular marine animals that grow geometrically. They are generally found attached to rocks at depths of between 10 metres (33 ft) and 70 metres (234 ft). Others occur at great depths. More than 5,000 varieties of sponges, mostly marine, are known in the world. A few varieties live in freshwater environments.

Known in Turkey as *sünger*, sponges vary in shapes and sizes and may reach a diameter of 1 metre (3 ft).

"The best sponges for commercial use are those with large holes that return to their original shape when pressed," says Selim Dinçer, a Bodrum marine biologist who has studied sponges.

Lifeline: A sponge fishing team usually consists of five divers, a captain and a cook aboard a 10-metre (33-ft) *tirandil*, a wooden-framed boat that is built in the Bodrum area. Each diver takes a turn under water. The average dive is two to three hours. Equipment consists of a wet suit, mask and regulator. Air is pumped by a regulator to the diver along a lifeline, described as a *nargile*, a hubble bubble or a *hookah*. This allows the fishermen to dive to depths of 150 metres (500 ft). But the further down the sponge divers go, the greater the dangers of getting the dreaded divers' disease, the "bends" – an ailment that can permanently impair, cripple and even kill healthy people. A diver suffering from the "bends" must be treated in a decompression chamber within 24 hours.

Often sponge divers find ancient shipwrecks and amphoras. In 1988, sponge divers discovered in the Gulf of Gökova the remains of two British World War II fighter planes with the skeletons of the crew inside. The two planes had been shot down in 1942 by the Germans.

"A living sponge looks more like a slimy piece of raw liver than like the familiar sponge of the bathroom," Ralph Buchsbaum, a prominent American biologist, wrote in his two volume book, *Animals without Backbones*.

When they are taken out of the sea, sponges are covered by a membrane and a gastric bag full of visceral fluids. They are left in the boat for some time to die, put in plastic bags and lowered into the sea again. After a while, the sponges are brought back up and trampled on to remove the membranes and other fluids. The remaining skeletons are washed, rinsed, dried and chemically treated to give the sponges a pleasant white or yellow colouring.

Right, drying sponges in the sun.

BLUE VOYAGE

The area between Bodrum and Fethiye, which accounts for a good proportion of the yachting activity of the Blue Voyage, can be divided into three main sailing grounds, the Gulf of Gökova, the Gulf of Hisarönü and Sömbeki, and the Gulf of Fethiye. From Bodrum to Marmaris encompasses the ancient Carian Coast. From Marmaris to Fethiye is the Lycian Coast, which extends as far as Antalya.

Planning a cruise: Unless you are prepared to spare at least three weeks on board, don't try to squeeze a Blue Voyage into the three gulfs in one cruise, for you will miss a great deal while making quick leaps from one stop to the next.

A wiser plan would be to divide the area into three separate travel zones and allocate a week to 10 days for each and not less than five days. A fortnight is needed to make the best of two zones. If pressed for time, and if finances allow, it is better to spend it properly in one gulf and return for the others.

The essential spirit of the Blue Voyage *(mavi yolculuk)* is a leisurely communion with nature in the very seas where Western civilisation bloomed. The Blue Voyage is not a glimpse-and-go package trip of lookalike bays. To the sophisticated traveller it is a bridge that leads to the souls and minds of the Pelasgians – the tribes of the sea – as Homer described them, who, though long gone, still haunt these shores.

Unlike yachting holidays in other parts of the world, a Blue Voyage in the Aegean can be a pilgrimage through 3,500 years of Western history, a homage to the past, and lead to a greater understanding and appreciation of ancient civilisations.

Fisherman of Halicarnassus: The **Gulf of Gökova** (also known as the Ceramic Gulf, Kerme Körfezi and Giova), is where it all began. Between the two World Wars, Cevat Şakir Kabaağaçlı, linguist, historian and a student of the

Map of the
Blue Voyage
Regions.

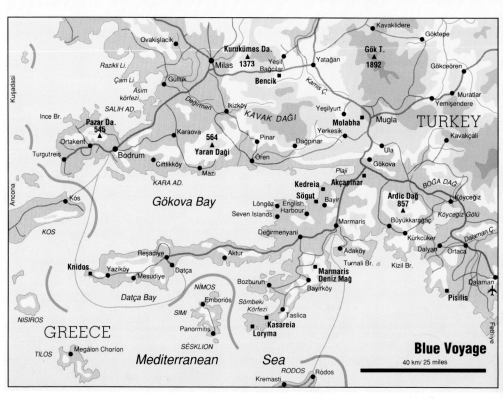

classics, was sent on political exile to Bodrum. It turned out to be a fortuitous move. He fell in love with the tiny fishermen's village, adopted the title "Fisherman of Halicarnassus" as well as the local fishermen's way of life. He wrote continuously of his experiences, especially of sailing in the Gulf of Gökova.

After about 30 years, Turkish intellectuals finally understood what this man was telling them and the Blue Voyage became very fashionable among the well educated elite. Over the years, the voyage has evolved from a trip in a small sponge diver *caique* to a journey in a luxurious Bodrum-built gulet, a 14 to 20 metre long (48 to 67 ft) wooden-framed yacht.

The Gulf of Gökova extends about 56 km (35 miles) from east to west. The main places of interest to visit, however, cover a 32-km (20-mile) strip of territory on the northeastern corner of the Datça Peninsula.

The northern shores of the Gulf of Gökova offer quite a few pleasant, picturesque anchorages dominated by the 900-metre (3,000-ft) Kıran Dağı, a mountain that drops down to sea level in a sheer precipice.

A voyage to the Gulf of Gökova logically starts from Bodrum. Not only can provisions be obtained there and the necessary boats chartered, but there are excellent maintenance facilities and communications networks. The prevailing winds also make it easier to sail southward to Marmaris or eastward into the Gulf of Gökova from Bodrum. (It is also possible to start a voyage in Marmaris, where there are many yachts and skippers available for charter at the marina – *see page 232*.)

Once the loading of provisions, fuelling, watering, selection of cabins and bureaucratic procedures for leaving the port are finished, the yacht is ready to set sail.

Mud baths: The Blue Voyage begins at Karaada, the island famous for its mud baths, 5 km (3 miles) from Bodrum. The mud baths, located in a grotto, are strangely rejuvenating, even though the bottom of the rinsing pool is rather slimy. Bathers emerge from the grotto covered in mud. As well as making your skin lovely and soft, this is an ideal photo opportunity, guaranteed to raise a smile back home.

Just across the northern tip of Karaada is the small **Pabuç Burnu** (Cape Shoe), a good safe haven for late starters from Bodrum to spend the night. Another anchorage is **Kargacık Bükü**, where an extensive and crowded holiday complex has unfortunately marred its beauty.

Another inlet to the south, **Alman Bükü** (German Cove), is somewhat quieter, though gusts of *meltem,* a brisk summer wind, may be disturbing at times. In all of these places, it is best to anchor out and tie a mooring line ashore from the stern of the boat, leaving lots of cable.

Orak Adası (Sickle Island), 16 km (10 miles) east of Bodrum, is famous for its clear waters and abundant marine life. A derelict house stands in the middle of the bay. The island is also notorious for its gigantic rats.

Cruising off the Turkish Coast.

Some 5 km (3 miles) east of Orak Adası is Alakıfla Bay, also called **Kise Bükü**, a corruption of the word "church" *(kilise)*, probably because of the ruins of a monastery in the northwest corner. Monasteries in this part of Turkey were quite frequently constructed on the sites of ruined temples or necropolises of previous civilisations.

The pleasant hamlet of **Çökertme** decorates a picturesque bay near the beginning of the mountain range that culminates in Kıran Dağı. Çökertme, or Fesleğen (Basil) is a stopover either before or after the crossing of the gulf. In the hamlet are several restaurants, whose motorboats accost visiting yachts soon after anchoring and ask whether the yachtsmen wish to make reservations for dinner. The food served at these restaurants is good and reasonably priced. Belly dancing, accompanied by lively music, is the night's usual entertainment. Handwoven carpets can also be obtained in the village.

Threatened environment: Between Çökertme and Akbük there is little else to stop for. The ugly coal-fired **Gökova Thermal Energy Plant** with a gigantic smokestack, built in the mid-1980s despite a vociferous campaign by the international environmental movement, stands at what was once the village of Türkevleri, spoiling an otherwise scenic coastline.

Environmentalists argue that this plant belches low-grade coal fumes into the air and pollutes the entire region. Although the Turkish government on the one hand declared the gulfs of Gökova and Fethiye environmental preservation zones, on the other, it is clearly prepared to destroy what it tries to protect for the purposes of obtaining energy.

Ancient Ceramus, now named **Ören** (which means "ruins") is not a particularly good anchorage, but it has the advantage of being a cheaper centre than Karacasöğüt. Various Carian, Roman and Byzantine ruins can be seen at Ceramus.

Boats tie up for the evening.

One of the most striking, if not the most beautiful, bays in the gulf is **Akbük**. Once past Ören, yachts sail in the shadow of the majestic Kıran Dağı that tints the sea with a barely discernible deep purple in daytime and gives off lapis lazuli shades as the sun sets every evening. Young pine forests thrive on the vertical slopes of the foot hills and Kıran Dağı looms above.

After a 11-km (7-mile) cruise along this breathtaking coast, yachts arrive in Akbük, a fiord-like inlet. Smaller boats may find cosy temporary anchorages in a number of coves in Akbük. These coves, unsuitable for bigger yachts, are the least spoiled in the entire Aegean. Pine forests surround Akbük, and Kıran Dağı stands majestically behind. A beach lies at the end of the bay with a restaurant that is much better than you might expect to find in such a wilderness.

A word of warning: however safe it may look, Akbük is plagued by troublesome gusts and squalls, which deflect from the mountain and can disturb a yacht at anchor. As in all Aegean anchorages, it is advisable to get tern lines ashore after laying a long cable.

Cleopatra's love nest: Did Cleopatra really frolic with Antony on the islands of **Cedreae** (Cedar), south of Akbük? It is not difficult to fathom how such a secluded and beautiful place could be chosen as the venue of an imperial love tryst. The main island has one of the finest and, sometimes, the most crowded beaches in the whole of Turkey, known as **Cleopatra's Beach.** According to one ancient legend, Mark Antony had the beach's fine silt sand transported from the Nile River to satisfy his lover's whims.

It is best to visit Cleopatra's Beach early in the morning or in the late afternoon as it is a regular haunt for tourist hordes arriving daily from Marmaris in their air-conditioned buses.

This group of three islands was perhaps also a holiday resort of antiquity. Little archaeological study has been conducted in the city of Cedreae, on the main island, which has remains of a castle, and an amphitheatre. **Yılan**

Adası (Snake Island) in the north has a necropolis of tombs.

Architectural award: Very few skippers venture east of Cedreae and Akbük to **Gökova Iskelesi**, at the extreme end of the gulf, because of the presence of shoals and insufficient protection from gusts off Kıran Dağı.

Nearby in Akyaka is the residence of Nail Çakirhan, a Turkish architect, which won him the 1983 Aga Khan Award for Architecture.

The most logical place to anchor safely after Cedreae is **Söğüt** (often known as Karacasöğüt or Karaca Limanı), 40 km (25 miles) from Marmaris by road. One of the most magnificent bays in the Mediterranean, Söğüt has already attracted land developers and many private houses have been built near the pier. Several lively and noisy restaurants located along the small harbour keep most yachtsmen up all night with music *alaturka* (Turkish-style) and belly dancing. Another calm wooded anchorage to be found nearby is **Çanak (Bowl) Bay**.

English harbour: According to local lore, British naval vessels hid in **Ingiliz Limanı** (English Harbour), one of the bays interweaving the perfectly sheltered fiord-like **Değirmen Bükü**, during raids against the German-occupied Greek islands in World War II. One fact giving credence to the story is that entrance to the English Harbour is difficult to find. Another was the recent discovery in the bay by Turkish divers of the remains of two World War II British military aircraft with skeletons inside. Villagers say the two planes were shot down in 1942 from the Greek islands by German anti-aircraft guns.

Six good anchorages exist in Değirmen Bükü. One of them is occupied by a restaurant which sells water and other provisions.

Some 5 km (3 miles) west of Değirmen Bükü is the well-sheltered bay known as **Ballısu** (Honey Water, a name derived from the nearby watering hole), which provides a perfect anchorage for visiting yachts.

Secret bays: The entrance to **Löngöz Fiord** is 1 km west of Ballısu. Known also as Kargılı and Gözleme, Löngöz is a narrow tree-lined inlet surrounded by steep rocks ending in a marsh. Throughout the Blue Voyage, you will often hear groans and grunts at night. These are wild bears that once lived by the shore and allegedly used to throw stones at yachtsmen in protest at the noise they were making. They seldom missed. The bears have now taken to the deep forests.

Tuzla, a sheltered bay west of Löngöz, is a good anchorage, protected by a cookie-shaped island from the strong summer winds.

A lovely stop on the Blue Voyage is at **Yedi Adalar** (Seven Islands), a secluded bay south of Tuzla, and an ideal spot for swimming, snorkelling, windsurfing and spear fishing. Visitors here can catch crabs and watch starfish pulsate.

Approximately 5 km (3 miles) south of Yedi Adalar is **Bördübet**, which is said to have been derived from "birdy bed", a name coined by English soldiers in hiding because of its abundance of bird life. It is also one of the safest and most pleasant anchorages in the gulf. To the north of the bay is the area known as **Amazon**, which is now occupied by a camping site. Amazon allegedly gets its romantic name from the race of female warriors who once inhabited these shores.

The **Bay of Büyük Çatı** (Big Roof), not to be confused with Küçük Çatı (Small Roof), a cove to the east, is popular among yachtsmen because it is safe from all winds. This was once a fisherman's watering hole. The remains of a basilica and other ruins that might once have been a monastery are to be found in the hills.

Körmen on the northern shore of the Datça Peninsula is a drab windswept harbour. But it is the main point of contact between Bodrum and Datça. Ferries carrying cars and passengers stop here at least twice a day during the high season.

In late September and early October, when shoals of albacorea, a distant relative of tuna, flock into the gulf, fishermen and yachtsmen in the Bodrum area cast their nets for an easy catch. Körmen then serves as a logical anchorage for the fishermen and yachts.

Another stopping off point towards the end of the Datça Peninsula is **Mersincik**, a quiet, pretty cove.

Knidos, an ancient city situated at the tip of the Datça Peninsula, is usually the last stop before returning to Bodrum from a one-week to 10-day Blue Voyage in Gökova Bay. Knidos, strategically located along the major commercial sea route, was one of the most prosperous cities in the Dorian Hexapolis. It benefited from its safe harbour, which sheltered ocean-going merchant ships. Knidos is famous among other things for the **Statue of Aphrodite**, the first ever of a naked woman. Until the sculptor Praxiteles (390–330 BC) made Aphrodite's statue, the subject matter of all nudes were male gods. Even in ancient times this was a sensation, and tourists flocked to Knidos to see the statue.

The fate of the Knidian Aphrodite is an enigma. Archaeologists can find no trace of her. One view is that the statue must have been destroyed in an earthquake, otherwise it would not have escaped the plundering greed of 19th-century British archaeologists who, supported by the British Navy, removed tons of statuary from Knidos.

The city was the home of Eudoxos, a 4th-century BC astronomer and mathematician who founded an observatory here that operated on the principles of modern geometry. Other wonders include two amphitheatres, the **Temple of Aphrodite** and many other buildings still in the process of being excavated.

The ruins have a grand view of both the Gulf of Gökova in the north and the Gulf of Hisarönü in the south and the boundless open sea in the west. A series of Greek islands, including Cos, Yiali, Nisiros, Khalki and Rhodes can be seen from the headland.

Several modest restaurants serve fresh fish and lobster and often towards the evening's close they become impromptu dance venues.

MARMARIS

Marmaris has come a long way since it was levelled by a devastating earthquake in 1957. The town, once a tiny fishermen's outpost isolated from the rest of Turkey, was completely reconstructed. Today Marmaris is one of Turkey's most popular resorts with hundreds of pensions and hotels and noisy nightclubs.

Often described as the "Pearl of the Mediterranean," because of its magnificent natural surroundings, Marmaris has become an important yachting centre. Located in a long, wide bay, fringed by pine forests and fragrant oleander shrubs that cascade down to the shore from the surrounding mountains, the city lies at the confluence of the Aegean and the Mediterranean. The town is built around a 16th-century Ottoman citadel.

Marmaris is easily accessible to the visitor: it can be reached in two hours by road from Dalaman International Airport, which is about 120 km (75 miles) from the town. A Turkish Airlines shuttle bus operates every day back and forth from the airport to the town. Daily passenger buses carry tourists between Marmaris and most major Turkish cities, including Istanbul, Ankara, Izmir and Antalya. Regular boat services also operate between Marmaris and the Greek island of Rhodes, four hours to the west.

Marmaris has a population of about 15,000, which swells to several hundred thousand (including its environs) during the long summer season when its hotels are completely booked-up and its streets are crowded with both Turks and foreigners.

Like Bodrum, Marmaris is very noisy in the evenings with the steady beat of amplified music coming from dozens of discotheques, bars and pubs. Visitors to Marmaris are advised to stay away from the noisy hub of the town if they want a good night's rest. They can always go into Marmaris by hiring a taxi or a motor launch or by taking the regular munici-

pal trailer train, which is drawn by a big tractor and stops at every main hotel along the bay region. There are hundreds of reasonably priced hotels and pensions around the town and in Içmeler Village.

Turkish character: Despite the many concrete tower blocks built during the 1980s and 90s, Marmaris has retained a distinct Turkish character, unlike Bodrum, and is favoured particularly by German and British tourists and wealthy Turks, who come here to enjoy the warm weather all year round. The 8-km (5-mile) long, 3-km (2-mile) wide **Marmaris Bay** is protected by two islands at its mouth, making it ideal for windsurfing, waterskiing and jet skiing.

Palm trees, banks, restaurants and souvenir shops line Marmaris' **Kordon Caddesi** and **Barbaros Caddesi** at the northwestern end of the bay. The main shopping centre of Marmaris is on several side streets that run off **Cumhuriyet Meydanı** (Republic Square) and the **Atatürk Statue** in front of the citadel. These shops sell a range of

Left, Marmaris Bay, and right, Atatürk's Statue in Marmaris.

goods, from carpets and leatherware to provisions for yachts. Most shops in Marmaris stay open until 9pm.

A good buy in Marmaris, and a delicious souvenir to take home, is honey, sold by bee keepers in the nearby villages, and sold in big jars by street vendors in the town. *Çam balı* produced by bees from the nectar of pine trees, is the tastiest and sweeter than *çiçek balı*, or flower honey.

A number of fine seafood restaurants surround the harbour, where fish and *meze* dishes are served. There are also many restaurants and bars lining Barbaros Caddesi. Those in search of nightlife also congregate around Haci Mustafa Sokaği, with its sophisticated clubs and live music. Venues move swiftly in and out of favour with the locals.

Concrete jungle: Several luxury hotels and holiday villages are located in the more secluded spots of Marmaris Bay. But Marmaris has suffered from the construction of hundreds of tasteless apartment buildings and ugly concrete hotel apartment buildings that hug the shoreline, particularly around the town of Içmeler, on the other side of the bay, 8 km (5 miles) to the west, and Turunç, a village just outside the bay. In its favour, Içmeler does has a cleaner beach to swim in than central Marmaris, and is easily reached by *dolmuş*.

The **Old Quarter**, with its white houses on twisting lanes, is built on different levels on a rocky peninsula around the citadel, and is well worth a stroll. The citadel was originally constructed by Ionians who settled there in 3000 BC. It was repaired by Alexander the Great in the 4th century BC and expanded by the Ottoman Sultan Süleyman the Magnificent in AD 1522 during a military campaign to conquer Rhodes.

The marina, the largest in Turkey, is located on the other side of the peninsula, has 800 berths, and is operated by the Net group, one of Turkey's fastest-growing private tourism outfits.

Flourishing centre: The ancient city of

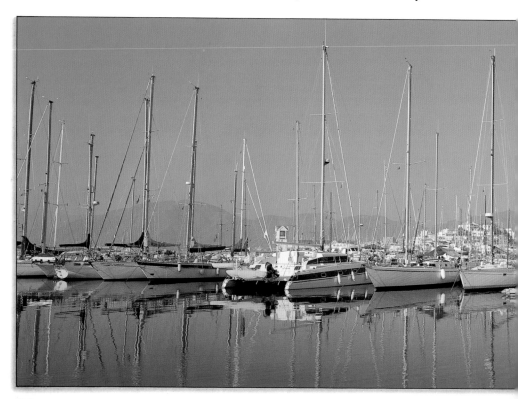

Physcus, a deme (unit of local government) of the Rhodian Peraea, was located at Marmaris and was a flourishing trading centre in its heyday. But nothing remains to be seen of this old settlement save for some walls located at **Aşar Tepe**, on a hill overlooking the town. The ascent to the top of the hill is quite strenuous and recommended only for photographers who want to get some spectacular shots of Marmaris.

Daily excursions: Day excursions by boat can be arranged from the town to the many deserted coves around Marmaris Bay. Yachts can also be chartered easily in Marmaris (there are dozens of travel agencies and charter companies competing for business here) for longer Blue Voyages to explore the neighbouring gulfs of Bozburun, Sömbeki and Hisarönü.

The best way to get acquainted with Marmaris Bay and the outlying areas is to take a boating trip to Çiftlik (the Farm). Motorboat launches, capable of carrying up to 30 people, leave Marmaris quay, along Kordon Caddesi, at 9am. The round trip is very reasonably priced.

It takes two hours to get to Çiftlik, a tiny community outside the bay, which has the best and cleanest beach around Marmaris. The easiest way to reach Çiftlik and the other villages on the rugged Loryma Peninsula is by boat, as road connections are still woefully inadequate, although construction to improve this situation is underway.

The launches cruise along the northeastern part of the bay, hugging the shoreline, leaving behind Marmaris and its marina.

Paradise beach: To the left is **Günnücek Park** with its fragrant conifers. After rounding **Bedir Island**, the boat comes to a stop at a little hidden cove aptly named **Cennet** or Paradise, which is surrounded by a lush forest of pine trees. Resembling a veritable Garden of Eden, Cennet is part of **Nimara Peninsula**, a bulging landmass that shelters the wide bay. The boat stays just long enough for passengers to have

Yachts in the marina.

a quick dive into the water and swim to the sandy beach.

Once all the passengers have returned to the boat, the skipper will continue the voyage, rounding Nimara Peninsula and heading out to the open sea. Often the captain will take passengers behind the peninsula to the **Phosphorescent Grotto**, sometimes referred to as the Pirate's Cave. The boat can only partially enter the tiny cavern where the shiny depths can be seen.

Leaving the grotto, the boat cuts across the sea to **Turunç Bükü**, a once lovely bay that has been ruined by the construction of many ugly hotels, noisy discos and bars, and sails to the next bay, **Kumlu Bükü**, which has fewer hotels and pensions.

Sometimes the boat will stop at both bays to disembark or take on passengers. Next the boat glides by a long, rocky coastline that is completely uninhabited, finally stopping off at **Gerbekse**, a delightful cove with interesting ruins of several Byzantine churches, allowing the passengers to take a quick dip in its clear waters.

Spear fishing: The boat turns back and goes to **Çiftlik**, a bay which is protected by a craggy island on which an Istanbul businessman has built a castle-like summer mansion. The waters of Çiftlik's mile-long beach are crystal clear and clean, a place where snorkelling, swimming and spear fishing along the rocky shoreline are possible. Except for a big hotel, several summer cottages and a few farmhouse eatings places, the bay is deserted. The restaurants serve *shish kebab*, fish, salad and melons. The most pleasant of these is the one operated by the cheerful Mehmet Yılmaz and his large family, who are known for their hospitality and generosity. Yılmaz also operates on the beach an unusual outdoor drinking bar made from the remains of a *caique*. The passengers are allowed two more hours of swimming before the boat begins its return journey.

Environs: One of the most interesting side trips to take from Marmaris is to travel along Datça Peninsula to the ruins of **Knidos**, an ancient Carian city, situated 95 km (59 miles) west of Marmaris *(see page 228)*.

Although difficult, the drive to Knidos is rewarding, just for its splendid scenery. The site itself is almost permanently windy, as it was in antiquity when it was infamous among sailors. It occupies a fascinatingly beautiful location at the tip of the peninsula. Experts are still debating whether this was the sight of the earliest settlement, or whether the town was moved here from present-day Datça. Whatever the case, it is a vast site, only a fraction of which has yet been excavated. Even that is well worth a look.

Among the most interesting features are a stepped street with some dwelling houses and a theatre – situated to the right of the main road as you approach the village. Other ruined buildings overlooking the twin harbours include the foundation of a small round building known as the Temple of Aphrodite, believed to have housed a statue of the goddess, which was created by the Greek sculptor Praxiteles (390–330

An old lady whiles away time by knitting.

BC), and was famous throughout the ancient world. That discovery was made by the American Professor Iris Love whose other, more controversial, claim is that a battered head she found in a basement in the British Museum is that of the Aphrodite statue.

Of the two harbours that served the ancient city, the larger, southern one now benefits tourists with some four or five restaurants. The daily ferry from Bodrum to Datça stops here.

After Içmeler, the asphalt road winds into the mountains for about 20 km (13 miles) only to drop gently to the plains and the **Gulf of Hisarönü** below. The Datça Peninsula, a spiny, 72-km (45-mile) finger-like projection, separates the Hisarönü Bay in the south from the Gökova Bay in the north. The eastern part of the peninsula is covered by pine forest, valonia oak and olive trees.

The easternmost part of the bay is silted and shallow and is known as **Keyif**, meaning "enjoyment and bliss". Soon the narrowest point of the Datça Peninsula is reached. It is named **Balıkaşıran**, and here the isthmus is less than a mile wide. When the Persian army invaded Asia Minor in 546 BC and subdued the Greek cities on the coast, the Knidians began building a deep defensive canal there to separate the Datça (Dorian) Peninsula from the mainland.

To get an outsider's view about the project they consulted an oracle, who replied: "Dig not nor fence your isthmus: Zeus himself had made your land an island, had he so wished." With the oracle's verdict, the Knidians abandoned construction, and the Persian army swept through the peninsula and conquered Knidos.

In the 19th century, English naval Commander Graves, who was surveying the area for charting, reported signs of the canal, but archaeologists George Bean and J.M. Cook, who visited the site in the 1950s could find no traces of the waterway.

Solar energy: The hidden fiord facing the Gulf of Hisarönü is known as **Bencik**, a favoured anchorage among yachtsmen on the Blue Voyage. **Dişlice Island**, which means "Toothy" in Turkish, stands at the entrance of the inlet, resembling bared teeth from a distance. On the eastern end is a meteorological station and an unusual solar energy research institute, which unfortunately blemish the solitude of the otherwise perfect fiord.

For the next 32 km (20 miles) the road is a series of hairpin turns into the mountains from which both bays can be viewed simultaneously from dizzying heights.

Halfway up the peninsula, one reaches **Datça**, which has become a popular stopover for yachtsmen. The town has several colourful seafood restaurants, pubs and discotheques. Across the bay the Greek island of Symi, or Sömbeki in Turkish, is visible only 11 km (7 miles) away. Daily ferryboats carry passengers and cars between Bodrum and Körmen, Datça's harbour village on the Gulf of Gökova. It is possible to take daily excursions from Datça to Knidos by boat on a shared-taxi basis. The boats stop off at a

Night-time in Datça.

number of tranquil bays for swimming, including **Domuz Bükü** (the Bay of Pigs).

Almonds and olives: A few miles out of Datça, the road climbs the rugged vertebrae of a new mountain chain, past small villages, almond orchards and olive groves. It takes about one hour to reach the windswept town of Knidos from Datça.

The sleepy village of **Palamut**, 13 km (8 miles) away, is the next settlement. Palamut, which gets its name from the abundance of fish caught in the bay. The village is the site of the ancient Knidian city of Triopium. It was in that ancient city that Dorian states held competitive sporting events in honour of Apollo, the Greek God of manly youth and beauty, which were the precursors to the Olympic Games. An acropolis and some ruins are to be found above the village, but it isn't really worth walking up the hill to see them. Palamut is famous for its fish restaurants, which serve fresh lobster. Its small harbour provides good shelter for yachts seeking protection from the wind. A long stretch of beach provides excellent swimming.

Another possible excursion from Marmaris is up the Loryma Peninsula to Bozburun, a picturesque village. The road is rough most of the way and motorists are advised to rent Jeeps. The road to Bozburun, southwest of Marmaris, forks left at the end of the Gulf of Hisarönü. The first village one comes to is **Hisarönü**. The village is crowded during the summer months with British and German tourists and has a good selection of pensions and hotels.

The ruins of **Bybassus**, an important Rhodian deme, is located on the other side of the main road. The ruins include an acropolis on a steep rocky hill surrounded by a Hellenistic fortification.

The **Sanctuary of Hemitea**, built in honour of the goddess of healing, is located on a ridge of the mountain known as Eren Dağı (274 metres/900 ft) above the plain of Hisarönü. At this sanctuary pregnant women were treated by a method resembling hypnosis, de-

Temple of Aphrodite in Knidos.

scribed as "incubation," believed to relieve abdominal pains. All that remains of the sanctuary is the temple's platform and crumbling theatre.

About 50 km (30 miles) north of Marmaris, the pretty town of **Mugla** is unique for having clung to its architectural heritage. Only in Safranbolu, in the Black Sea region , have as many old Turkish houses, caravansarays, fountains and mosques been preserved and remain in use by the townsfolk. The tourist office in the centre of town dispenses a handy town plan that helps you to find your way up the hill, where the best examples of domestic Ottoman architecture are to be found.

The **Bay of Orhaniye**, a deep wide inlet of the Gulf of Hisarönü protected by Eren Dağı and clad in olive trees and pine forests, is a popular stopover for yachtsmen. There is a small boat landing and a motel. **Keçibükü** (Goat's Bay), which is at the end of the Bay of Orhaniye, has a boat landing as well. A Byzantine fortress crowns the top of the small island in the bay (**Kizkumu** or

The day's catch.

Maiden's Sand) and a long sand bar runs along the end of it. A pleasant club house and several restaurants are located at Keçibükü.

After Keçibükü, the road gets rough. Another dirt road forks left uphill about 1 km to a shaded grove known as **Şelale** (Waterfalls), where special village *böreks* and grapes are served by a stream. Several waterfalls plunge down the terraces, forming the stream and a deep pool where bathing is possible.

Oregano and laurels: The village of **Bayır**, located in the mountains on the main road to Bozburun, has a pleasant square shaded by a 600-year-old oak tree under which several teahouses provide refreshments for visiting tourists. The villagers are renowned for making *kekik yağı*, the oil of oregano, which grows wild in the mountains of the peninsula. *Kekik yağı*, locals say, has medicinal properties that can help cure anything from stomach ulcers, asthma and eczema, to intestinal worms. The villagers also collect aromatic *defne yaprağı*, laurel leaves, used as a flavouring in the preparation of *shish kebab*.

The most charming village in the area is **Selimiye**, which has a Byzantine fortress at its entrance. The bay forms a natural harbour.

Bozburun is a little town of 2,500 inhabitants. The famous boat-building centre has in recent years become an important stopover for yachts on the Blue Voyage. The town itself does little to distract the eye from the inspiring setting; the area is popular with holidaying Turks.

Cross-Currents: At Datça, the Aegean Sea meets the Mediterranean. Due to differing salt levels and strong underwater currents encountered here, locals claim the air is oxygen-rich and the area healthier than others.

MEDITERRANEAN COAST

The Turkish Mediterranean Coast begins east of Marmaris and ends at the Syrian border south of Antakya. The Turks call the Mediterranean "Akdeniz," the White Sea. The western part of Turkey's Mediterranean Coast includes the eastern part of the province of Muğla and the coastal areas of the provinces of Antalya, Mersin, Adana and Hatay, and is well known. However, the section east of Alanya, despite its rich history, is not so familiar to visitors.

The western Mediterranean Coast is a mountainous region with a narrow coastal strip accommodating many resorts, sunken cities and the ruins of fascinating ancient towns. This area was known in antiquity as Lycia, and the earliest people who inhabited it, the Lycians, were an independent-minded people noted for their bravery and their reverence for their dead. Their impressive tombs, built right into the faces of the mountains, are architectural masterpieces that can't easily be copied even with the advantages of modern technology.

Towns like Fethiye, Kaş and Kemer have already become booming tourism centres, attracting many visitors from all over the world. Travellers to this region come for the excellent yachting, windsurfing and boating, and to explore the hundreds of ancient sites that hug the coast. Saint Nicholas, better known as Santa Claus, lived in Myra in the fourth century.

Five-star hotels: Further east, the Pamphylian Coast, with Antalya as the tourist hub of southwest Turkey, is a breadbasket region, a vast plain surrounded by the towering Taurus and Bey mountains. The region produces cotton, citrus fruits, vegetables and flowers. It is also an important export centre.

It was from Antalya (known as Attalia in antiquity) that St Paul, with Barnabas, set sail on his last journey to Antioch (Antakya) to preach the gospel.

Many cities, including Perge and Aspendos, flourished in Pamphylia. The beaches of the Pamphylian Coast, with their soft, golden sands, are one of the main reasons tourist come here. Many luxury hotels have been constructed along this stretch to accommodate discerning tourists, but there are also many lower-budget establishments to cater for those on a more moderate budget.

East of Alanya is the region that was known as Rough Cilicia, where the Taurus Mountains contrast sharply with the low-lying areas near the coast. In the rugged mountains, goats grow luxurious coats and their hair is woven into a rough fabric used in tent making. The main highway follows the coast and offers drivers stunning vistas of the clear blue Mediterranean sea.

Anamur, the banana-growing capital of Turkey, is one of the quieter resorts in the area, with its long sandy beaches and a magnificent Armenian castle. The mountains eventually give way to the vast Çukurova, a cotton-producing region, once known as Smooth Cilicia.

The first town of note is Silifke – a Turkish version of Cilicia. The town itself is pleasantly quiet and is a useful base from which to see the highlights of the area, including the ruins at Uzuncaburç. Silifke is a popular touristic region with beaches and castles, including the fabled Kızkalesi, which stands on an island near the town. Silifke is located on the Göksu River delta, which is a rich breeding and wintering ground for hundreds of species of birds, including pelicans.

Adana, another important metropolis on the coast, is Turkey's fourth largest city and a major industrial and agricultural centre.

Other cities in the region include the ports of Mersin and Iskenderun, Tarsus and Antakya, all rich in history. Along with other parts of the Turkish coast, this area has a chequered past, living under a succession of empires, from the Hittites, Greeks and Seleucids to the Romans and Byzantines, before it was reclaimed by the Turks themselves.

Preceding pages, Alanya Castle. Left, carrying home the goat.

THE WESTERN MEDITERRANEAN

The western Mediterranean Coast extends from a line east of Marmaris to the resort town of Alanya and covers the ancient Roman provinces of Lycia and Pamphylia. The region has about 60 percent of Turkey's tourist accommodation, with huge hotels, holiday village complexes and thousands of pensions and campsites lining the coastline. Nearly half of the tourists who visit Turkey explore this 400-km (250-mile) stretch of territory.

Fire-breathing monster: The area not only features high profile cities like Antalya, Side and Alanya, but also sites such as Yanartaş, with flames from the mountains thought to be the remains of the fire-breathing monster Chimera; the sunken cities around Kekova Island; Caunos, where archaeologists have unearthed an important city; and Dalyan, one of the last breeding grounds in the

Mediterranean for loggerhead turtles. The town is also famous for its boat rides among the reeds and the rejuvenating mud baths. The high plateaux of Lycia were where townspeople traditionally pitched their tents in the summer to avoid the stifling heat of the coast.

It was along the Lycian Coast that St Paul led some of his early Christian missions. In Patara, he embarked on his last voyage to Palestine. The rock tombs of Caunos, Fethiye and Myra are imposing sites, built into the face of overhanging cliffs – enduring reminders of a people who revered their dead by keeping them alongside the living.

One of the most important events that takes place in this region is the colourful Saint Nicholas Festival held every December 4–6 in the town of Demre to honour the original gift-bearing saint associated with the snowy winters of northern Europe. Saint Nicholas, a prominent Christian figure, was born in Patara in the 4th century and went on to become the Bishop of Myra. The ruins

Preceding pages, rock tombs in Fethiye.

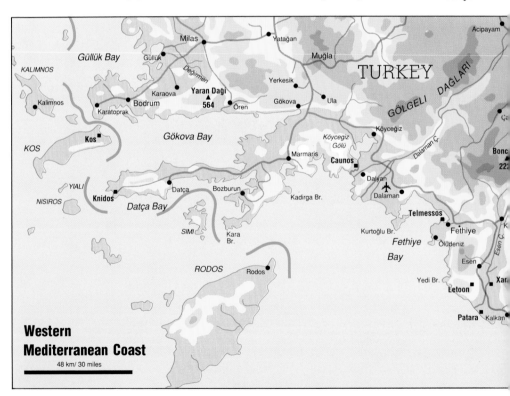

Western Mediterranean Coast

48 km/ 30 miles

of the city of Patara can still be visited *(see page 255)*. His spirit continues to this day with the exchange of gifts during the Christmas season and on New Year's Day.

A "Blue Voyage" exploring the many beautiful islands along this stretch of coast is highly recommended for travellers who want to get away from the stress of modern urban living *(see page 224)*. Daily boat trips from Göcek, an important yachting centre due to its proximity to Dalaman International Airport, take in the sunken city of Kekova, an island just off the coast known in Turkish as Batik Sehir. Travellers in these azure waters can snorkel among the baths that were built for Cleopatra.

Pirate's hideout: The region includes Olympus, a pirates' den that is now in complete ruins in a well-hidden gorge along the rocky Lycian coast. Visitors can also go to Uluburun, a barren cave near the small town of Kaş where underwater archaeologists excavated the world's oldest known shipwreck, discovered by a sponge diver in 1982. The shipwreck has shed light on the complex trade routes that existed some 3,600 years ago in the Mediterranean area.

Some of the most important events of early Western history have taken place along the shores of the Turkish western Mediterranean. Alexander the Great's army thundered across Pamphylian Plain in a campaign to conquer the world and build an empire. Persian and Roman armies clashed with the recalcitrant Lycians. Cleopatra and Mark Antony frolicked in the many coves. Venetian Admiral Andrea Doria raided these shores in the 16th century in a vain effort to prevent the Turks from dominating the entire Mediterranean. From 1919–21, the region was occupied by an Italian army as part of World War I spoils.

Today, this region, with its beautiful beaches and fascinating history, is the pride of modern Turkey and an important area for the development of tourism.

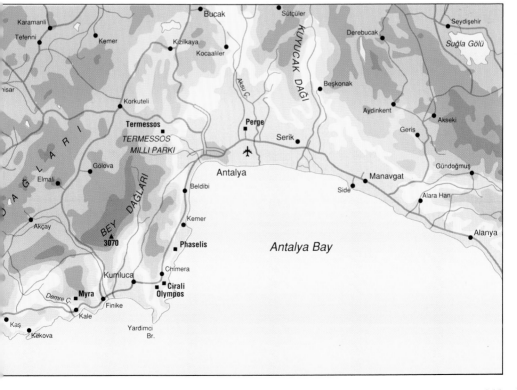

LYCIA

The independent-minded Lycians, believed to be of Cretan origin, settled and defended the wide peninsula between present-day Fethiye and Antalya from around 1,400 BC, and were the first known inhabitants of the region. They had their own language, still to be seen on inscriptions though as yet not fully understood, but are best known today for their spectacular tomb designs. They were a fierce sea-going people feared by the Phoenicians and Saracens for their exceptional bravery. They had their own 12-god Pantheon, and revered their dead in magnificent tombs cut into the mountain face.

From the 6th century BC onwards, at least 20 cities in this urbane, sophisticated region banded together in a loose federation, known as the Lycian League, each city voting according to its wealth and status. In 540 BC however, Cyrus II conquered western Anatolia, and Lycia fell under Persian rule. The Hellenistic era began when Alexander the Great arrived in about 333 BC and the cities of Lycia surrendered one by one, some with positive glee. Shortly afterwards, the league was revived, acquiring economic as well as political prominence. The Lycian language died out gradually, to be replaced by Greek.

In 197 BC Lycia was conquered by Antiochus III of Syria. In turn, he was defeated by Rome in 189 BC and Lycia joined the empire. It was an unhappy relationship and, within 20 years, the Senate had given its troublesome cities autonomy. After the Battle of Philippi in 42 BC, control passed to Mark Antony, who gave the territory its freedom, leaving it the only part of Asia Minor not under Roman domination. A century later, the emperor Vespasian (AD 69–79) brought the joint province of Lycia and Pamphylia back under Roman control.

For the next 2,000 years, Lycia remained a remote, backward area, largely cut off from the mainland by its soaring mountains. Only in the 1980s were its spectacular coastal bays connected to the rest of the country by proper roads. Now the background song of the winter months is the beat of the hammer and the whine of the power drill as every available scrap of land is covered with hotels.

Lycia can be reached from Marmaris by driving along route 400 past Köyceğiz, a town on the Köyceğiz Lake famous for its green houses, and taking the country road that forks to the right. This road leads to the village of Dalyan and to the ruins of Caunos, the first city of Lycia. Dalyan can also be reached by daily boating excursions from Marmaris; the journey takes about four hours.

Dalyan, an unspoiled, cosy little resort on the Dalyan River, faces the spooky rock tombs of Caunos. Its nights are lazy and calm and its riverside fish restaurants are superb. Dalyan means fishing weir and takes its name from the many fisheries along the river, which trap *kefal* (mullet) and *levrek* (seabass).

Left, the "Turtle Beach" at Dalyan. **Right**, enjoying a mud bath.

These unusual breeds can live in both salt waters and fresh waters. They are caught when returning to the sea after spawning at Köyceğiz Lake. Visitors who decide to spend some time in Dalyan should try *kefal*, a long grey fish, best served grilled. They should also sample *yengeç* (crab) as an appetiser. The waiter usually brings a small hammer to crack the shell to extract the delicious meat.

The most pleasant hotels and pensions in Dalyan are those located along the river banks.

A boat can be rented for a few hours to take tourists across the river to the ruins of **Caunos**, located on two separate levels. An ancient Carian and Lycian city, Caunos was once a thriving port. But like many ancient riverside cities along the Turkish Coast, its downfall came with the silting up of its harbour by the Dalyan River. In the fourth century BC, the town was known to be rife with malaria, which also contributed to its demise. Among the ruins are an amphitheatre, ancient walls, an acropo-lis hill, and of course the rock tombs, hewn into the cliffs. Motorboats also travel upstream to some invigorating mud baths.

Marine turtles: Motorboats can be hired from Dalyan to Iztuzu Beach, popularly known as **Turtle Beach**, at the mouth of the river. It takes about an hour to reach the 10-km (6-mile) long beach, which resembles a long sand bar. Travellers can also reach the beach by car. A road from Dalyan to Iztuzu Beach winds along the marshes for 15 km (9 miles). The water is shallow and safe, especially suitable for children, and the beach is ideal for tossing frisbees, playing volleyball and building sandcastles. Iztuzu Beach is one of the last remaining breeding grounds in the Mediterranean for the Loggerhead Marine Turtle *Caretta caretta*.

During the June–September turtle-breeding season, the beach is closed to the public from 6pm to 9am to prevent tourists from trampling on the turtles' nests. Resembling amphibious landing craft and each weighing 140 kilos (300

Rock cemeteries at Caunos.

lb), hundreds of female turtles, travelling there from as far as the West African Coast, invade the shore in June and July, almost always at night, and lay about 100 leathery eggs that resemble golf balls in the sand. The female turtle may lay eggs four times during the breeding season. Before lumbering back to the water, the females cover their eggs with sand to protect them from predators. Nevertheless, predators such as foxes living in the hills come down to the beach at night and often find the nests by scent.

Crawling seaward: It takes about six to eight weeks for the baby turtles to hatch. Once out of their shells, they cling to one another and claw their way up the sand for air and make their fateful journey to the sea. Hundreds of turtles are eaten alive by ghost crabs that lay traps for them in the sand. Hawks and other predatory birds catch those turtles that fail to reach the sea by daylight.

The Turkish environmental movement, assisted by Germany's Green Party, won its first major victory at Turtle Beach in 1987 when it successfully pressurised the Turkish government into halting the construction of a large Turkish-German hotel near the beach, asserting that it would endanger the newly hatched turtles. The beach today is an environmentally protected zone, and guards patrol at night to prevent trespassing.

From Dalyan, another road leads through fertile farm lands of orange and tangerine groves to **Ortaca**, a cotton-producing town, and links up to route 400. The town of **Dalaman**, just off the Muğla-Fethiye highway, has an international airport

Göcek: From Dalaman the east-bound road climbs over pine-covered mountains before descending to the town of **Göcek**, on the northwestern end of the Gulf of Fethiye. Göcek is 30 km (19 miles) from Dalaman International Airport. Despite its small size, it is a town of true international character.

From Göcek it is possible to charter yachts to the 12 Islands of the **Gulf of Fethiye**, one of the most secluded and

Bays of the Turquoise Coast.

beautiful areas on the Turquoise Coast. Daily motorboat excursions to the **12 Islands** leave Göcek quay in the mornings. The day trip can also be made from Fethiye. Fares for the round trip are very reasonable. You can also charter a *caique*, inclusive of its captain if you want to be alone and have complete privacy, although obviously this is much more expensive.

As the boat heads away from Göcek, the first two islands you encounter are **Göcek Adası**, famous for its verdant pine forests, and **Zeytinli Adası**, a privately owned estate with thousands of olive trees.

Soon you reach **Yassıca Adaları**, an archipelago of small islands good for mooring and swimming, and the larger **Hacıhalil Adası**. The boat doesn't usually stop at any of these islands, but continues to the big island on the left, **Tersane Adası**, which has a protected cove suitable for anchorage. The boat will stop there for about half an hour, permitting passengers to swim ashore and explore the verdant island. The ruins of several buildings, which were most likely inhabited by Greek families before the 1923 population exchanges, face the cove. Tersane means "shipyard" in Turkish, and the Greek families who once lived there built wooden-framed boats.

The Pig's Island: From Tersane, the boat crosses the narrow strait to **Domuz Adası** (Pig's Island, which is privately owned).

The boat continues to **Hamam Cove**, which has several partially submerged ruins of buildings that some locals claim were the **Baths of Cleopatra**. The structures sank as a result of earth tremors. The skipper of the boat will stop for 90 minutes in the bay, allowing passengers to have lunch at one of the alfresco restaurants, open only in the summer. The break will also give visitors time to swim and explore the ruins using a mask and snorkel.

From Hamam Cove, the captain will take you to the westernmost point of the Gulf, **Bedri Rahmi Bay**, which gets its name from the cubist painting of a fish

Selling watermelon from a horse-drawn carriage.

on a rock by the shore. It was painted in 1974 by the late Bedri Rahmi Eyuboğlu, a well-known painter and writer who popularised the Blue Voyage with his great paintings and poetry. The region is also known as Taşyaka, or **Tombs Bay**, because of the many Lycian cemeteries and pigeonhole rock tombs along the jagged shoreline. The site was identified by the late George Bean as the ancient Lycian city of Crya. The boat stops to let passengers swim ashore and visit the rock tombs and admire Eyuboğlu's painting.

The next bay on the way back to Göcek is **Boynuzbükü**, a sheltered bay surrounded by pine trees where sail boats can anchor safely. A river, lined with reeds and oleander shrubs, empties into the bay.

Fethiye: A one-hour drive east from Göcek brings the traveller to **Fethiye**. Once a small market village, Fethiye has become a thriving tourism centre. The town is immensely popular among French, German and British tourists and yachtsmen. However, unlike Bodrum and its peers, Fethiye has managed to retain much of its orignal Turkish ambience. It is also a yachting centre for day cruises into the Gulf of Fethiye, and the 12 Islands. Blue voyage cruises also go from here to Kaş, Kekoya and Antalya.

Telmessus: Fethiye dates back to the 6th century BC. It was once a grand Lycian city called **Telmessus**. Traces of the ancient settlement can be seen about the town, including the awesome rock tombs on the face of a cliff east of the city and several scattered heavy sarcophagi, including one next to the Town Hall (**Belediye Binası**). The town, however, is modern, having been reconstructed after the earthquakes of 1950 and 1957 levelled it.

Situated at the eastern end of the big Gulf of Fethiye, the town is surrounded by tall mountains that are snowcapped in winter. A bulging headland and an island, popularly known as **Şövalyeler Adası** (The Knights' Island), protect the town, forming a lake that is an ideal shelter for yachts.

Oludeniz Bay.

Temple tomb: The rock tombs are just behind the city. Cars can be left on the base of the cliffs and the tombs can be reached by walking up a steep path. The most magnificent of these monuments is the **Temple Tomb of Amyntas**. A sarcophagus, weighing several tons, stands smack in the middle of the road, near the rock tombs. Neither the rock tombs nor the sarcophagus were damaged or even budged during the earthquakes that flattened Fethiye in 1950 and 1957. The local denizens have never considered pushing the sarcophagus off the middle of the road, claiming that if they were to move it even slightly "the whole world would shake." An acropolis hill at the back of the town is occupied by a castle, believed to have been constructed by the Crusader Knights of St John.

Environs: Numerous excursions can be made to different resorts, towns and ancient Lycian cities from Fethiye. One of these excursions is to the ghost town of Kaya and the resort of Ölüdeniz. A dirt road, on which the massive sarcophagus stands, curves into the mountains behind the town for about 10 km (6 miles), passing dense pine and cedar forests, and winds down to a fertile plain.

Kaya, formerly known as Kormylassos, stands on the side of a hill overlooking the plain and was once a wealthy Greek town of 5,000 people, the most populous in the region. The Greeks abandoned Kaya as part of the general population exchanges between Greece and Turkey in 1923. (Nearly 1.5 million Greeks living in Turkey switched places with 500,000 Turks living in Greece.) Kaya today is an eerie ghost town that is worth an early morning or late afternoon stroll. Hundreds of houses, with their roofs crumbled from the quakes that rocked the region, remain standing along rock paths. Two churches, one built in 1888 with frescoes depicting biblical scenes, remain intact. Several chapels exist below the church on the hill. An enterprising local tour company now offers nuptial tours for lovers who want to tie the knot in a unique, biblical setting.

The same road continues on to **Ölüdeniz**, the "Dead Sea," another 10 km (6 miles) from Kaya. (Ölüdeniz can also be reached directly from Fethiye. The turn-off to Ölüdeniz is on the Muğla-Antalya Highway.) Ölüdeniz is a misnomer. Although it resembles a perfectly calm lagoon, it has a small mouth opening to the sea through which boats could once enter. Ringed by mountains, pine trees and a long sandy beach, Ölüdeniz was an ideal shelter for boats seeking protection from the stormy sea, but it was closed to yachts back in 1984 to prevent further pollution of its waters.

The **Belcekız Beach**, along the lagoon, is one of the best sand beaches of Turkey. The water becomes deep very quickly, however, and is not suitable for toddlers or children learning to swim. The beach area is crowded and noisy in the summer. Scores of camp sites and motels have opened in the past decade along the beach, and more are being built in the mountains.

Paragliding: In addition to swimming at Belcekız Beach, visitors can parasail at one of the parasailing clubs available along the beach. They can also try paragliding from the top of Baba Dağı, a rocky peak of 1,976 metres (6,520 ft) dominating the coast.

Excursions can also be made from Fethiye to the ruins of five Lycian cities in the Xanthos valley, the main area of settlement in Lycia: Tlos, Pinara, Letoon, Xanthos and Patara.

Pinara, southeast of Fethiye, located near the village of Minare, can be reached by a short dirt road that branches off the Fethiye-Kaş Highway south of Kemer. Once a great city, Pinara is believed to have existed since the Trojan War (1200 BC) and perhaps even earlier. The town is built on two acropolis hills. Only a few traces of the earliest city are visible, including several cisterns and rock-foundations of wood and mud-brick houses, built on a hill honeycombed with pigeonhole tombs. Many sarcophagi are scattered about the main acropolis hill, including one that is the largest in southwest Turkey.

To the south are rock-cut house tombs and the remains of a Christian church, an odeon theatre, and a large house-type tomb dubbed the **Royal Tomb**, believed to be the funerary monument of a prince. The interior of the Royal Tomb is decorated with the reliefs of different Lycian cities. Nearby are the agora and the main theatre.

A 20-minute drive south from Pinara brings the motorist to **Letoon**, the ancient sanctuary of the Goddess Leto, mother of both Artemis and Apollo. The turn-off to Letoon is past the town of Esen and the village of Hazırlar. The shrine is about 5 km (3 miles) off Fethiye-Kaş highway. Leto was the principal Goddess of the Lycians.

The ruins contain the foundations of three temples, the main one dedicated to Leto, and the others to Artemis and Apollo. They also contain a nymphaion, a kind of public bath, that is partially submerged in water. The site contains a well-preserved amphitheatre too. In the middle of the **Temple of Apollo** you can see a mosaic of a lye, the sun, a bow and arrow: the only known mosaic of the Lycian civilisation.

Hera's wrath: According to popular Lycian myths, Leto was the mistress of Zeus. She incurred the wrath of Zeus' jealous wife, Hera, who hounded her and sent her into exile. In her peripatetic wanderings, Leto came upon a water fountain where she wanted to quench her thirst, but three nasty shepherds drove her away. After giving birth to Artemis and Apollo, according to the same myths, she returned to the site and turned the shepherds into frogs as a punishment.

The ancient city of **Xanthos** is just 5 km (3 miles) away, off the Fethiye-Antalya highway, near the village of Kınık. It can be reached from the bypass and is signposted from the right. Xanthos has a thrilling history and atmosphere but is in a great state of disrepair and its hard to visualise its former glory.

On the left-hand side is an outstanding amphitheatre, and next to it two tombs. The so-called **Harpies Tomb**,

The ghost town of Kaya, near Fethiye.

an elevated funerary monument, gets its name from its reliefs showing the mythological harpies, half-birds, half-women monsters, carrying away dead children to the underworld. Next to it is the **Pillar Tomb**, a squat Lycian sarcophagus on top of a long, rectangular pillar. Facing the amphitheatre is the agora on which stands the famous **Xanthian Steele**, a pillar tomb whose frame is covered with 250 lines of Lycian script, the longest ever discovered, and a Greek poem. On the other side of the road are ruins of two Byzantine basilicas and a monastery.

Mass suicides: Xanthos made its mark in history during Persian General Harpagus' invasion of the southwestern coast of Asia Minor around 540 BC. The Persian army swept into Lycia from Caria and was opposed by the Lycians. Defeated by Harpagus in battle, the Lycians retreated into their besieged city. Rather than surrender Xanthos, the Lycians gathered their wives and children into the acropolis, which they set ablaze in a defiant act of mass suicide.

They then marched out to fight the Persians and were killed to the last man.

The Lycians re-enacted the tragedy 500 years later during the Roman civil wars. In 42 BC, when Brutus arrived in Xanthos to raise money for his army for the coming showdown with Antony and Octavian, the Lycians withdrew into the city and slaughtered their families, built a huge funeral pyre in the centre of the city and threw themselves into the flames to die. The city was repopulated by descendants of the Lycians during the Byzantine period. But its end most likely came during the Arab invasions of Anatolia in the 7th century.

The great plunder: Xanthos was discovered by Sir Charles Fellows in 1838. Four years later, sailors from the British Navy, under Lieutenant Thomas Spratt's command, removed hundreds of statues and friezes from the site and were even helped by Turks to do so. Fellows was knighted for his deeds. All the statuary removed from Xanthos is now exhibited at the British Museum in London in the Xanthian Hall, including

View of the Lycian shrine.

254

the sculptures of the magnificent **Neried Monument**, a beautiful tomb.

About 10 km (6 miles) south of Xanthos are the ruins of **Patara**. A sign points towards the ancient site of the Antalya-Kaş road. Patara is the supposed birthplace of Saint Nicholas, the gift-bearing Santa Claus. Patara was once a great commercial port, but today is partly covered by sand dunes and hidden by an almost impenetrable forest of thick bushes and trees, about 728 metres (2,390 ft) from the sea. An archaeology team from Akdeinz University in Antalya, sponsored by the Culture Ministry, has been excavating at Patara for many years searching for lifestyle clues of ancient Lycians. A unique milestone consisting of 49 blocks was unearthed bearing Greek inscriptions. Also 100 metres (328 ft) of a Roman high street have been exposed.

Local developers, with less than scrupulous backers, have waged a so-far unsuccessful drive to oust the archaeologists from the area.

Motorists pass an arch as they enter Patara and vehicles can be parked in front of the restaurant behind the beach. The nearby amphitheatre is half filled with sand. On the knoll between the beach and the theatre stands an unusual structure believed to be a water cistern. Next to it are ruins of what may be a lighthouse for guiding boats into the harbour, which is now silted up. Next to the harbour is the **Granary of Hadrian**, which is well preserved. An agora and a tomb are nearby.

Patara's beach: Patara's stretch of sandy beach 18 km (11 miles) is a postcard dream – it is one of the most extensive stretches of sand anywhere in Turkey, but it is difficult to swim, as the water is so shallow. If you get to swimming depth, there can be undertows, and the beach itself is often windy. It is also lonely and not a place to wander off on your own to dream, however tempting.

The road to Kaş winds along the coast, passing **Kalkan**. This tiny town has become one of the most exclusive

Parasailing over the beach.

and sought-after resorts on the Mediterranean coast, with narrow streets of overhanging Ottoman houses clinging precipitously to narrow alleys that swoop down into a harbour carefully restored to attract the yachting crowd. In spite of its size and the absence of a proper swimming beach, Kalkan has some delightful *pansiyons*, upmarket boutiques for wealthy shopaholics and a proud collection of some of the best restaurants outside Istanbul. The mosque near the harbour appears to have been converted from a Greek church by little more than the addition of a minaret.

The waters around Kalkan are a favourite for spear fishermen, with many natural freshwater springs providing the opportunity for a freshwater shower when divers surface at the shore; offshore this strange phenomenon makes the surface much colder than deeper waters. For those in search of sand, regular *dolmüs* run the 19 km (12 miles) west to Patara.

The dramatic cliff-hugging route eastwards winds around several small sandy coves, linked to the road above by steps. The best is tiny Kaputah Beach, 6 km (3.5 miles) east, which also acts as the official beach for Kah. From here, you can swim round to beautiful blue-green phosphorescent sea caves.

The resort of **Kaş** (pronounced somewhat like "cash") is about 60 km (38 miles) east of Patara on the Fethiye-Antalya highway. Like most towns on the Lycian coast, Kaş is wedged between mountains and the sea. In recent years, it has become a popular stopover for yachts on the Blue Voyage. Kaş faces the tiny island of Kastellorizon (Meis in Turkish), the furthest Greek island from mainland Greece. Meis, a resort island, gets all its supplies from Kaş, and all its hotel owners speak fluent Turkish. Each morning, several motorboats come to Kaş to carry food and other supplies to Meis.

Kaş was the location for the ancient city **Antiphellus**, but few remains of the old settlement have survived to this day. There are several sarcophagi about the

The sand-filled theatre at Patara.

town, including one by the port and an elevated one on the square above Uzunçarşı Caddesi, which features the heads of lions coming out of its sides. A Hellenic amphitheatre is situated a short distance from the town.

Hero carpet shop: Kaş has an extensive bazaar area, where there are numerous gift shops. The best carpet dealers in town are **Kaş and Carry** and **Magic Orient**, both of which supply a large and tasteful collection of old and new carpets and kilims, handmade saddlebags and other beautiful textiles.

Kaş has many fish restaurants by the port, lined with visiting yachts, and surprisingly, for such a small town, there are a few gourmet international restaurants like the **Chez Evy** French restaurant, **J P Spaghetti House** and **Smiley's**, popular for its garlic bread. Guests will find plenty of chicken and meat dishes, as well as freshly caught fish from the bay.

The restaurants of this region are also famed for serving goat's meat, a local delicacy, instead of mutton or beef. But beware: those unaccustomed to goat meat may experience painful indigestion. Visitors should make certain that food prices are clearly listed at the front entrance of each restaurant and compare prices with other restaurants. Several restaurants in Kaş have a reputation for overpricing food. The town also has several discotheques and late-night bars. Check out **Mavi** and **Red Point**.

Oldest known shipwreck: A short boat trip from Kaş brings you to Ulu Burun, where a team of Turkish and American underwater archaeologists have been excavating the oldest known shipwreck since 1984. They are members of the Institute of Nautical Archaeology (INA), affiliated with Texas A&M University. The team is led by Dr George Bass, founder of INA, and Cemal Pulak, a Turkish marine archaeologist of international repute. The 14th-century BC vessel was discovered in 1982 at a depth of 45 metres (150 ft) by a sponge diver, who spotted what appeared to be "metal biscuits with ears," bringing the INA

Sailboats in Kalkan.

divers to the scene. The metal biscuits turned out to be huge copper ingots shaped like ox hides.

The discovery has shed considerable light on rather sophisticated Bronze Age Trade in the Eastern Mediterranean. The 15-metre (50-ft) vessel was carrying a hoard of goods from one port to another when it sank, possibly in a storm. Many of the relics that have been discovered are now in Bodrum's Underwater Archaeology Museum. Besides copper ingots, the scientists recovered Baltic amber beads, the first to be discovered outside Greece, a Mycenaean vase, Canaanite amphora, ebony from Nubia, unworked ivory, stone anchors, tins and glass.

Because the shipwreck is at such great depth, the recovery work has taken many years. Divers who go down are in constant danger of getting nitrogen narcosis or worse, the "bends".

Bass has had a few mishaps. Once he ran out of air at 45 metres (150 ft) deep. "I was sure I was going to drown. But as I clawed my way to the surface, a Turkish friend grabbed me and gave me air," Bass once told the *National Geographic Magazine*.

The island of **Kastellorizo** (Meis in Turkish), just out to sea from Kaş, is the easternmost of the Greek islands. Elderly Greek women who have made the day-trip to Kaş may be seen shopping or sitting on the benches along the harbour, waiting for the ferry home. It is easy to do daytrips by boat, with many of the operators in Kaş harbour offering excursions. But be warned that an overnight stay will cancel your Turkish visa and you may have problems getting back in.

Sunken cities: Kaş is also the centre for boating trips to the nearby sunken cities around Kekova Island and the fishing village of Kale, famous for its necropolis of Lycian tombs.

This is a full-day trip – boats leave for Kale from Kaş each morning at 8am and return around 6pm. With stopovers in numerous bays, it takes five hours to reach Kaleköy, the last destination. (Kekova Sound can also be reached by boat from Demre's port.)

The first site one comes to is **Aperlae**, east of Kaş, on the Sıçak Peninsula. Yachts can anchor in the bay and motorboats can tie up by the boat landing, known as **Sıçak Limanı**. The village of **Sıçak** is located in the hills about an hour's walk away. The boat landing is built along the ruins of Aperlae, an ancient Lycian city. The ruins include an acropolis, city walls, a necropolis of tombs and ruined houses.

The most remarkable sights in Aperlae are the harbour, quay and many streets which are now submerged by water near the boat landing. This was caused either by a rise in the sea level or by a major earthquake. Visitors are advised to snorkel with a mask to see the astounding sunken city.

East of Aperlae is **Kekova Sound** with several deep bays, protected by the elongated Kekova Island and several smaller islands. Francis Beaufort, a British naval commander who surveyed the region in the early 19th century, recommended Kekova Sound as an anchorage for a naval fleet. "Its great extent, its bold shores and the facility for defence may hereafter point it out as an eligible place for a rendezvous of a fleet," he wrote in his book of surveys, *Karamania*.

Submerged houses: Numerous submerged houses and their foundations can be seen all along the northern shore of **Kekova Island**. At the western tip of the island, visitors can see the apse of a lone Byzantine church and remains of some houses. This was the Greek settlement of Tersane (shipyard), whose inhabitants are believed to have been boat builders.

A narrow channel across from Tersane leads to a wide hidden bay. On the shore stands the farming community **Uçağız**, with small, pleasant boat landings. Australian writer Rod Heikell, who visited the hamlet in the late 1980s, reported seeing cattle wandering about the streets. East of Uçağız are the ruins of **Teimiussa**, a Lycian city, with numerous sarcophagi and rock tombs, and remains of a fortification.

The most charming village in Kekova Sound is **Kaleköy**, opposite the island.

A medieval castle overlooks the village.

A 300-seat theatre is inside the castle. This was the site of ancient **Simena**. The villagers make their living from the sea catching fish and lobsters. The community has three jetties, which double as restaurants during the tourism season. A lone Lycian sarcophagus standing in the water lures visitors to pose beside it for photographs. Nearby, in the middle of the bay is a rock with steps cut into it. This may have been part of a house or perhaps some kind of ancient lighthouse.

St Nicholas Church: About 50 km (23 miles) east of Kaş is the farming community of **Demre**, famous for its many green houses. It was at Demre that Saint Nicholas, the original Santa Claus, worked in the fourth century. Demre has little to offer, but where else in Turkey can you find Christian churches almost intact? Most guide books gloss over the church but it is a gem and, even though surrounded by stories and legends, its easy to be a believer once inside.

The ruins of **Myra** are north of the town. Myra's big amphitheatre, the first structure one comes to, is of Roman style. In the west gallery are the inscriptions "Place of vendor Gelasius", and this was probably the stand where theatre-goers could buy popcorn, nuts and other edibles to nibble on while watching a performance. Myra has the most impressive rock tombs on the entire Lycian Coast. The cliff facing Myra is honeycombed with rock graves, giving it a gloomy sepulchral atmosphere. Many of these tombs, to which one can climb following the trail up to the cliffs, have friezes of human figures or graffiti. The most striking cemetery is known as the **Painted Tomb** with friezes of a man and his family, presumed to have been buried there.

Finike, Turkey's leading orange-producing community, is 40 km (25 miles) east of Demre. Finike is an unexciting market town by a river. In recent times, it has become a popular stopover for yachtsmen. Just before entering the town you come to a wide cove, known

A Gypsy with his dancing bear.

as **Andrea Doria Bay**, named after the 16th-century Venetian admiral who is said to have concealed his flagship there while fighting the Ottoman navy.

Most visitors pass through Finike and some write it off as uninteresting. However, Finike has a civic gloss lacking in other places and it is extremely prosperous without the rampant development seen in other places. The Marina, green areas and general well-groomed look are in distinct contrast to rowdier, racier resorts. Income from citrus fruits is considerable, making tourism less pushy.

Apart from Gögek and Kemer, this is the only marina that can cater appropriately to luxury yachts on most of the Mediterranean coast.

Finike marks the southern end of one of the few roads to cross the mountains to the interior of Lycia, offering what is either a spectacularly beautiful excursion, away from the madding crowd, through the rugged Taurus Mountains and across the Anatolian plains, taking in ancient Limyra and Arykanda, or an alternative route through to Antalya.

To take the first route head north from Finike on the N-635. After 7 km (4 miles), when you reach Turunçova, turn right for **Limyra**, which is 3 km (1.5 miles) off the main road, along a narrow road through the villages. This was the 4th-century BC capital of Pericles, founder of the revitalised Lycian League, whose tomb, the **Heroön**, elaborately carved with scenes from the hero's life, tops the highest point of the most extensive necropolis in Lycia (open access). It is a steep 40-minute climb up, but the views of the coast are astounding. Less energetic visitors have plenty to occupy themselves with the mausoleum to Gaius Caesar, grandson of Augustus, who was destined to be emperor but died here of battle wounds before he could wear the purple robe. Near the theatre is the free-standing 4th-century BC Tomb of Catabara, with reliefs of a funeral banquet and the judgement of the dead. Many of the other tombs are painted. The buildings near the river belonged to a Byzantine convent.

Afternoon in Kaş.

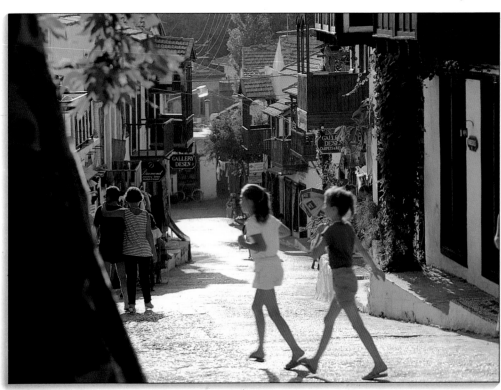

Return to the main road for a further 21 km (13 miles) to the mountain hamlet of Arif and the stunningly beautiful Roman city of Arykanda (open access). This is one of the most remote and least-known of all Turkey's ancient cities, sited at the end of a plunging valley sprinkled with wild flowers and surrounded by snow-capped peaks in spring. The lower area is centred on a bath house built in the 4th century AD from recycled materials. The sheds above cover the mosaic floors of a large Byzantine basilica, while further up the hill are the odeon, theatre, stadium and agora of the 1st–2nd century AD Roman city. From here, the path twists round the mountain to a superb bath house and gymnasium with 10-metre (33-ft) high arched ceilings, picture windows with views that stretch forever, and mosaic floors. Beyond that are a temple and the cemetery.

Return to the main road which continues north, crossing the huge shallow lake of Göltana Gölü, which dries to a shimmering pan in summer, to the market town of Elmalı, on the slopes of 2,269-metre (7,442-ft) Elmalı Dag ("Apple Mountain"). The town has a tiled 15th-century mosque and creaking but elegant timber-framed Ottoman mansions. There were several important Bronze Age settlements nearby, at Karatah-Semayük, Kızılbel and Karaburun, but none are open to the public; most of the finds are in the Antalya Archaeological Museum.

From here, the road continues through Korkuteli to the Karain Cave, Termessos and Antalya.

Offbeat site: For the next 50 km (32 miles), the road twists along the coast past the town of **Kumluca** and then winds up into the mountains blanketed by tall pine and cedar trees. To reach the ancient pirates' hideout of Olympus, motorists must turn right off the old Finike-Antalya highway followed by another right at a sign showing Çavuş and Olympus. After driving for about 2 km take a left turn at the Olympus sign.

Olympus, a city in ruins, is located in a gorge between two steep mountains.

Sailing off on a "Blue Voyage" from Kaleköy.

A stream runs through the town, once a pirates' hideout, and the ruins are on both banks, covered by a jungle of bushes and trees. A Turkish guard sits near the entrance of the ancient site. Olympus, which probably means mountain in a pre-Greek language, is one of 20 sites and mountains in the eastern Mediterranean with that name. The town has never been excavated. Nearly 2,000 years ago, pirates controlled this settlement, raiding and plundering commercial ships plying the coast, but the Roman general Pompey finally succeeded in stamping out piracy in the region after a military campaign.

Parts of a quay on the southern bank of the stream, and remains of a theatre across the knee-deep water can be seen. On the northern bank was the main section of the city, and an acropolis on the hill by the beach is still visible. Several tiny sarcophagi, probably of children, stand with their lids partly open on the side of the hill. The walls of what were probably residential houses also stand on the northern bank along the river. The main necropolis is on the southern side of the river bank and has many ornate tombs.

The sea, with a pounding surf, is just about 200 metres (650 ft) from the entrance of the settlement and the beach is a fabulous place to take a break from sightseeing, swim and have a picnic.

The eternal flames of Yanartaş (the Burning Stone) are near the village of **Çıralı** on the face of a mountain. The climb to Yanartaş takes about 45 minutes. Flames shoot out of a dozen or more holes in these rocks.

The Chimera: The fires have been burning for thousands, perhaps millions, of years. The flames, according to myths, are the remains of the Chimera, the fire-snorting monster that once terrorised the coastal area. The Chimera, which had a lion's head, a goat's body and a serpent's tail, was slain by the mythical Lycian hero Bellerophon who flew over the mountains with his winged horse Pegasus. But Turkish scientists claim, more prosaically, that the

Sitting at the Chimera.

fires are caused by a build up of underground methane gas that can't be extinguished. If the flames are doused with water, they will come back burning bright in seconds. The area is volcanic by nature and may have considerable oil reserves. In the past, the state Turkish Petroleum Corporation has searched the area with some success.

Just below the Yanartaş are some unusual ruins believed to be a sanctuary for the fire god Hephaestus. One of the ruins, strangely, resembles a weird Byzantine chapel.

The Finike-Antalya road from the turn-off to Yanartaş swings through **Olympus National Park** over 70 km (44 miles), passing through verdant pine forests. The range is good for climbing, trekking and hunting.

Phaselis: Shortly after passing the village of Beycik a dirt road forks right leading to **Phaselis**, an ancient Greek city, situated on the tip of a peninsula. There is some confusion about the early history of the town. Some say the city was founded by Rhodian colonists in 690 BC. Others claim it was founded much earlier by the seer Mopsus, who led Greek colonists to the southern coast in the wake of the Trojan War. Whatever its origins, the city today offers the visitor the chance to wander among Roman and Byzantine ruins of two harbours, a main avenue, aqueducts, baths, a theatre, an agora and a temple. Pine tree-lined bays are the favourite haunt of those who seek to swim in the Mediterranean waters or to sunbathe and windsurf.

The **Beldibi Caves**, where people of the Stone Age once lived, are located between Kemer and Antalya. In 1960, Turkish archaeologist Enver Bostancı discovered flint stones, bits of pottery, and a wall painting of a wild goat and other animal figures, indicating that the inhabitants were hunters. The ancient findings are housed in the magnificent Antalya Museum.

The highway continues on its path north and soon the cliffs of Antalya come into view, beginning the wide plain of Pamphylia.

A sarcophagus stands in the water at Kaleköy.

SAINT NICHOLAS

Each 4–6 December, church scholars and amateur historians worldwide invade the farming community of Demre (ancient Myra), famed for its delicious red tomatoes and juicy oranges, to attend the only Santa Claus Symposium in the world.

Saint Nicholas, the original Santa Claus, a legendary man of good deeds, worked and preached in Demre 1,700 years ago, and his reputation as a gift-bearer spread throughout the Christian world, many church scholars say.

Rattling bones: Although much controversy rages in church circles over his very existence, the Christian Church officially recognises Saint Nicholas as an authentic historical figure, the first Bishop of Myra.

While sceptics still assert that Saint Nicholas never lived, others argue he was present at the Council of Nicaea of AD 325 where he slapped the heretic Arius with such force that the victim's bones rattled.

Born in the nearby city of Patara about AD 300, Saint Nicholas came to Myra as a young man. Not long after, he was elected the town's bishop.

Since Myra was a port as well as a farming town, Saint Nicholas first became the patron saint of sailors. The abandoned Saint Nicholas Church, where he purportedly delivered sermons, is located on one of the two main streets of Demre. The church is a Christian as well as a Moslem shrine. Saint Nicholas is known among Turks as Noel Baba, or Father Christmas. A statue of the saint, surrounded by children, stands in the courtyard.

Pirates remove remains: His marble sarcophagus lies inside the church, but his remains were spirited away in the 11th century to Bari, a town on Italy's Adriatic Coast, and deposited in a church named after him. Turkish mythology has it that some of the bones were preserved and are those found in the Antalya Museum.

When his fame reached northern Europe, his name was abbreviated to Claus, and Saint Nicholas became Santa Claus. The traditions of reindeer, elves, toys, sleigh and red, fur-lined attire were derived from the snowy winters of northern Europe. The giving of gifts associated with the Christmas season may have come from many tales of the original Santa. One story had him give a bag of gold each to the three daughters of a poor man as dowries so they could marry. Another tale tells how he restored to life three boys murdered by a local butcher.

The Dutch, who were the first to corrupt the name to Sinterklaas, honoured the saint by filling children's clogs with presents. The custom was soon attached to Christmas and the shoe became a stocking. The modern icon of the old man, dressed in red with a long white beard was actually an invention of the Coca Cola company – the image was used in their advertising campaigns.

Divine nature: Various stories have Nicholas saving shipwrecked sailors, resurrecting the dead, parting the waters of a wide river Moses-style, and recouping lost property. He is said to have saved Myra from famine, securing the arrival of corn-bearing ships to the port in time to prevent mass starvation. While inspecting a church under construction, the building collapsed on him, but the saint emerged unhurt.

During the three-day Saint Nicholas symposium and seminar, scholars and clergymen discuss the character and the life of the saint and trace his development as a Christian figure.

On December 6, the traditional date of Saint Nicholas' death, priests from the Orthodox Church Patriarchate hold two-hour liturgical services at the small Church of Saint Nicholas. The services and symposium coincide with the Saint Nicholas festival held in Demre.

The Festival has a light-hearted appeal but attracts high profile clerics and believers from many faiths. It also fosters much good will and understanding in a country where religious tolerence does not always come easily.

Left, the statue of St Nicholas; and **right**, Myra's theater.

ANTALYA AND ITS ENVIRONS

Each year, ever increasing numbers of tourists pour into ever larger hotels along this relatively flat stretch of coastline, which provides good beaches and building land. The results are mixed. The influx has been good for conservation, with several of Turkey's finest Graeco-Roman cities on proud display; but while larger cities such as Antalya are flourishing, smaller towns are being swamped; there are few hideaways left in ancient Pamphylia.

Antalya is the tourism centre of southwest Turkey. Surrounded on three sides by snowcapped mountains, the Bey Dağları in the west and the Toros Dağları (Taurus Mountains) in the north and east, Antalya is situated on a vast fertile plain. Antalya is also the region's agricultural and commercial hub. Antalya's farmers grow everything from cotton and citrus fruits to watermelons, fresh vegetables, flowers and ostriches, which they supply to diverse markets.

Its long, clean sandy beaches, unpolluted waters, ancient ruins, long summers and mild winters have made Antalya province appeal particularly to travellers from northern Europe. During March to April, it is possible to ski at **Saklıkent** (The Hidden City) and swim in the Mediterranean on the same day. The ski resort, which operates in the winter season, is only 50 km (30 miles) from the city and takes about an hour to reach.

Cave men: In addition to all forms of watersports, Antalya also offers travellers special tours for hunting, mountain climbing, trekking and cave exploration. The Beldibi and Karain caves, once inhabited by people from the Stone Age, are the most interesting.

Bayindir International Airport, where hundreds of charter flights arrive daily in the summer, is only 15 km (10 miles) from the city centre and within two hours' driving distance of most of the resorts and historical sites in the region. A 160-km (100-mile) stretch of territory around Antalya has the greatest concentration of hotels in Turkey – these comprise nearly half of the country's bed capacity. Some 50 five-star hotels and holiday villages and thousands of smaller hotels and pensions have opened in the past ten years to accommodate tourism expansion, and many more big hotels are being built to meet demand.

The city, which has a population of 1 million, is located on cliffs that drop into the Mediterranean. Antalya is a garden city with two parks lined with palm trees. These are **Atatürk Park** and Karaalioğlu Park. Both offer stunning views of the mountains and the Mediterranean.

The city's main streets, Kenan Evren Bulvarı, Cumhuriyet Bulvarı and Atatürk Caddesi, are lined with apartment buildings and clothing shops, selling international designer fashion.

The ancient city: The Old Quarter, known as Kaleiçi, is separated from the new city by a series of Roman walls, and

Left, Antalya's Fluted Minaret. Right, a deserted beach.

faces the marina. Most of the buildings in this part of the town are 18th- and 19th-century traditional wooden Turkish houses. Many have been nicely restored or turned into pretty hotels or pensions but most are still hoping for a new lease of life.

Antalya was founded by Attalus II, king of Pergamum (159–136 BC), during the early days of his rule, and was named Attaleia after him. The town was ruled successively by the Romans and the Byzantines. During the Crusades, the Crusaders used the port to carry out raids against Moslems in the eastern Mediterranean. The city was conquered by the Seljuk Turks in 1207 and ruled by their vassals, the Hamitoğlu tribe. But in 1361, Peter de Lusignan, King of Cyprus, captured the city. It fell to the Ottoman Turks in 1391. In 1918, the Italian army occupied the city after the Ottoman Empire's defeat in World War I but withdrew in 1921 when the Turkish nationalists, under Kemal Atatürk, put up armed resistance to the Allied occupation.

The most charming place to stay in town is the Kaleiçi Old Quarter where travellers have a choice of many delightful, modestly priced hotels and pensions. This district can be reached by car taking the modern road downhill from Cumhuriyet Bulvarı. There is a public park just above the marina where cars must be left. Bed and breakfast at a Kaleiçi pension is very reasonably priced. **Doğan Pansiyon**, a smartly renovated house on the Mermerli Banyo Sokak, is highly recommended. The upmarket **Marina Hotel** and **Tütav**, both on Mermerli Sokak, and **Turban Adalya Hotel** near the marina are the best hotels in the Old Quarter.

More luxurious hotels in town are the **Talya Hotel** (on Fevzi Çakmak Caddesi), which is favoured by businessmen; the **Club Hotel Sera** (near Lara Plajı), which attracts wealthy German tourists; the **Dedeman Hotel Antalya** (on the road to Lara Plajı), which has a stupendous view of the Mediterranean; and the Bey Dağları and Falez, overlooking the Konyaaltı Beach.

Antalya has a number of first-class restaurants. The **Hisar Restaurant, Kral Sofrası** and **Kirk Merdiven Restaurant** in the Old Quarter combine traditional Turkish dishes and seafood with an array of *meze* appetisers.

A compact city: Most of the city's historical sites can be seen in a two- or three-hour walk. A stroll through the town can start at Kaleiçi with a walk down to the marina, a former fisherman's wharf, now a bustling port with many yachts, schooners and motorboats. Street vendors sell juicy *ajur*, locally produced long cucumbers, and *frenk yemişi*, a cactus fruit that tastes like a cross between watermelon and cantaloupe (and is said to have properties that alleviate kidney stones).

A short walk uphill from Iskele Caddesi, a narrow winding street, brings you to the new town. Along this street are many souvenir shops. One shop with a courtyard sells colourful handmade *Döşemealtı* carpets, and young girls show how they produce the carpets on looms. *Döşemealtı* carpets get their name from the village near Antalya where they are produced.

On street corners tradespeople sells local teas, spices and edibles, including aromatic *ada çayı* (island tea), *dağ çayı* (mountain tea) and *papatya çayı* (dandelion tea), and *tirmis*, which looks like corn but tastes like hazelnuts.

Fluted minaret: Soon the twisting street reaches one of the main squares of Antalya, the **Kaleiçi Square**, which is now used as the **Clock Tower**, once a part of the ancient city walls. To the left is the **Yivli Minare** (Fluted Minaret), a brick tower that today is the symbol of Antalya. The 37-metre (122-ft) high tower was constructed in 1230 by Alaeddin Keykubat, a Seljuk Sultan. The original mosque to which it was attached was destroyed and replaced in 1373 by the **Alaeddin Mosque**.

The **Eski Cami** next door was built in 1373 by Mehmet Bey. In the grounds, a huge, ancient olive tree has grown up to enclose the grave of a wise muezzin. If you write your request on a piece of

Antalya's Marina and Old Quarter.

paper, wrap it in an olive leaf and leave it in the hollow trunk, your wish will, of course, be granted.

Just south of the Fluted Minaret towards the marina at a lower level is the **Karatay Medresesi**, an Islamic religious school built in 1250 by a Seljuk notable. Near it, but on higher ground, are two tombs: **Zincirkıran Mehmed Paşa Türbe** built in 1378, and the **Nigar Hatun Türbe**, constructed in 1502. The two Islamic theological seminaries, **Atabey Armağan Medresesi** and the **Ulu Cami Medresesi** nearby are in ruins.

Immediately behind the Clock Tower is the 17th-century **Tekeli Mehmet Paşa Mosque**. The mosque is unique because the Son Cemahat Yeri (the last place of assembly) is inside the mosque, covered by domes, instead of being on the outside. Foreigners can enter mosques, but must take off their shoes at the entrance, like all Turks. Women have to cover their hair and arms with scarves. You cannot enter wearing shorts and shoes as it would be disrespectful toward worshippers and would sully the old prayer carpets inside.

Chic clothing shops: Cumhuriyet Bulvarı, which eventually becomes Orgeneral Kenan Evren Bulvarı, is the long street that runs on an east-west axis through the city. A left turn at the clock tower takes you to the main shopping district of the town with chic clothing stores and fancy seafood restaurants. To the left is the Mediterranean with the Bey Dağları in the horizon. Higher up, you arrive at **Cumhuriyet Meydanı** (The Republic Square) with the equestrian **Statue of Kemal Atatürk**.

The **Antalya Arkeoloji Müzesi** (Archaeological Museum) at Kenan Evren Bulvarı, Konyaaltı, 2 km/1 mile west of the town centre (tel: 0242-241 4528; open Tues–Sun 8.30am–5pm; entrance fee) is one of the finest in Turkey, with magnificent exhibits, beautifully displayed, and a children's room with a model village and tables where children can play safely under supervision.

Most of the finds come from the surrounding area, including many millennia of prehistory from the Karain Caves, Bronze Age jewellery and toys from Elmalı, and exquisite classical statuary from Perge and Aspendos. The Hall of the Emperors and Classical Art displays statues of the Greek gods, emperors Hadrian and Septimus Severus and their Empresses.

Other exhibits include part of a stunning mosaic collection from Xanthos depicting the infant Achilles being dangled by his mother into the River Styx. The bits of dust and bone, said to be the remains of St Nicholas from his tomb in Demre, are third generation: his grave had already been robbed twice during the Crusades, making the claim that the display holds the remains of Santa Claus about as believable as the claim that the Topkapı Museum really does have 64 strands of the Prophet Mohammed's beard. There is also a broad-based ethnographic collection with displays on Turkish lifestyle, dress, musical intruments and carpets. Allow plenty of time: this museum is a real treat, with an excellent gift shop.

Hadrian's Gate.

Pickle juice: Right of the Clock Tower is Atatürk Caddesi, an avenue that cuts Cumhuriyet Bulvarı on a north-south axis. Several *lokantas* (traditional Turkish restaurants) in the alleys near the intersection serve good *kebab* dishes. Shops nearby sell a variety of unusual jams, jellies and pickles. One of the most interesting jams being aubergine marmalade. Ice-cold pickle juice *(turşu suyu)* is an excellent thirst quencher.

A right turn along Atatürk Caddesi brings the traveller to **Hadrian's Gate** (Hadrianus Kapısı), a magnificent three-arch marble gate erected in AD 130 in honour of Roman Emperor Hadrian's visit to the city.

Further down the street is the **Belediye Binası** (The Municipality) and the entrance to Inönü (or Karaalioğlu) Park, which is lined with palm trees. The park, named after Ismet Inönü, the second President of Turkey, has playgrounds for children, pleasant outdoor coffeehouses and benches to sit down and admire the stunning beauty of the sea and the mountains in the distance.

Roman tomb: A stroll to the eastern end of the park brings you to the **Hıdırlık Kulesi**, a rotund tower that is believed to be a tomb of a Roman Senator from Antalya. The tower is a miniature version of Hadrian's Tomb in Rome. Walk up the street that intersects the tower and you approach the **Kesik Minare** (the Truncated Minaret). This odd structure stands next to the **Korkut** or **Cumanın Mosque**, now in complete ruins. Built originally in the fifth century as the **Panaghia Church**, it was converted into a mosque by Korkut, the son of Sultan Beyazıt II, who added the minaret. The mosque and the minaret were destroyed in a huge fire during the 19th century.

The marina, just 10 minutes away from the Kesik Minare, has many pubs and discotheques.

Antalya is also well known to hunters. The surrounding Bey Dağları and Taurus Mountains are host to several species of large game including the European Ibex *(yaban dağ keçisi)*.

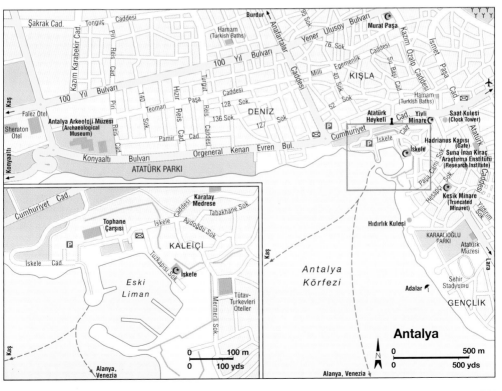

Excursions from Antalya: Numerous ancient sites, caves and resorts are reachable from Antalya. One site to visit near Antalya is the **Düden Şelalesi**, a series of waterfalls set in a woodland park about 10 km (6 miles) outside the city near the village of Varsak. The waterfalls are situated on the **Düden River**, one of several rivers that nurture the fertile Antalya Plain. The best time to visit the site is in the morning or late afternoon when it is not crowded. Several tea houses and outdoor restaurants, shaded by plane trees, are in the park. A Turkish version of *Snow White and the Seven Dwarfs* was once filmed in this setting.

The Düden River empties into the Mediterranean, plunging off Antalya's cliffs east of the city. A half-hour boat trip can be arranged from the marina to this site for a small fee. A smaller inland waterfall east of the city is the **Kurşunlu Şelalesi**, which has a 17th-century water mill that was recently restored. The site is 15 km (9 miles) from Antalya and can be reached by taking a road off highway E24/400 on the way to Alanya.

Nomadic carpets: The village of **Döşemealtı**, famous as a carpet-weaving centre, is north of Antalya on highway E24/650 to Burdur. The colourful pure-wool Döşemealtı carpets are made by nomadic Yörük tribesmen who inhabit the Taurus Mountains. These carpets have geometric patterns and a colour harmony of blues, dark greens and reds.

Nearby is a road that forks left to the **Karain Caves**, where Stone Age man lived from as early as 600,000 BC to the 7th century BC. Turkish archaeologists who excavated at Karain discovered the skull of a Neanderthal man and the fossil remains of an ancient elephant, hippopotamus and bear, and tools dating back to the Paleolithic Period. Many of the findings are in the small **Karain Museum**, but some are also exhibited in the Antalya Museum. The cave is situated on the slope of the mountain above the museum. It covers a vast area and consists of several interconnected sections.

It is a two-hour walk up to **Kocain Magarası**. Take the Burdur road for 27 km (16 miles), then turn off to the village of **Ahırtah**. This is Turkey's largest cave, an awe-inspiring 633 metres (2,000 ft) long and 35 metres (100 ft) high, with giant stalactite pillars. At present, you can only visit on your own, with a good torch and good boots, but there are plans to improve access.

The **Kırkgöz Han**, a Seljuk inn with 40 rooms, is located on the Burdur Road, 24 km (15 miles) north of Antalya. Before reaching Döşemealtı highway 350, turn left towards **Korkuteli** off route E24 to Burdur. This road leads to **Evdir Han**, another Seljuk inn or caravansary. Evdir Han was built in 1219 and consists of a courtyard surrounded on four sides by porticoes. The southern entrance is magnificent with stalactites and geometric designs. Nearby are the ruins of the Byzantine settlement **Eudoxia**, with several water channels and scattered sarcophagi.

Güver Uçurumu, a vast gorge form-

Selling fancy patience beads and spoons.

ing a 160-metre (705-ft) drop down the cliffs, is located about 3 km (2 miles) north of Evdir Han. Formed millions of years ago, the gorge is a stunning site.

The ruins of **Termessus**, one of the few cities in Asia that Alexander the Great could not conquer, are located in the mountains west of Güver Uçurumu. To get there take the road that forks left and has the sign reading Güllük Dağı Termessus Milli Parkı. The narrow, twisting road climbs into the mountains to the site. All cars must be left in a car park and the rest of the way about 2 km (1 mile) must be ascended by foot. The region is a national park. Termessus, built on the slopes of several mountains, resembles an eagle's nest. During the Hellenistic and Roman periods it was a flourishing city with a population of 150,000 people. Now it is in complete ruins, abandoned in the fourth or fifth century.

Termessus was a Pisidian city. The Pisidians, who inhabited the mountainous region north of Antalya, fought many wars against the invading Greeks.

The site includes numerous city walls, King Street, an observation tower, water cisterns, a necropolis, a gymnasium, bathhouses, a colonnaded street, an agora and an astounding **theatre** overlooking the surrounding mountains. The theatre, built during the Hellenistic Period, has a seating capacity of 4,200. The orchestra is covered with rubble, which probably tumbled down because of earthquakes. A smaller odeon or assembly hall on the upper reaches of the city could seat 600 people. The most important site in Termessus is the **Tomb of Alcetas**, a general of Alexander the Great who was defeated by Antigonas in 319 BC and sought refuge in the city. He committed suicide, preferring death to being returned to his enemies. The ruins of three temples are visible, including the **Temple of Zeus Solymeus**, the **Minor Temple to Artemis** and the **Major Temple of Artemis**. The **Soldier's Tomb**, which gets its name from the shields, spears and helmet carved on the frieze, is in the necropolis. The **Found-**

Theatre at Termessus in ruins.

er's House, west of the agora, is a Roman-type house in good condition.

Ancient cities: Scores of ancient ruins are east of Antalya, including Perge, Sillyum, Aspendos, Selge, Side and Seleucia in Pamphylia. Alarahan, on the road to the resort of Alanya, is famous for its castle and golden beaches.

The E24/400 highway can be reached eventually by driving east from Antalya on Cumhuriyet Bulvarı and Sudi Turel Caddesi, named after a former Energy Minister from Antalya.

The first major destination east of Antalya is **Perge**, which is in the hills on a dirt road off the Antalya-Alanya highway, 20 km (12 miles) from Antalya. Signposted in yellow, the ancient Roman site lies just after a turn on the left.

Vaulted stadium: As you enter Perge, the first building you drive past is a second-century Roman amphitheatre with a seating capacity of 17,000. The main ruins are less than 1 km (900 yards) off the amphitheatre. Visitors can park their cars and walk past the stadium, which is one of the best pre-served in the eastern Mediterranean. The 234 by 34 metre (772 by 112 ft) stadium could seat about 12,000 people. The vaulted sections at the sides were probably shops.

The main city, just off the stadium, was once encircled by walls, some of which are still standing. The walls once had 30 towers. The city was laid out in a grid pattern with two main intersecting streets. Entrance to the ruins is by the **Later Gateway**, which leads to the **City Gate Complex**, a horseshoe-shaped courtyard flanked by two towers. This area is the most fascinating part of the city. Niches built inside the complex walls contained statues of gods and local heroes, such as Mopsus and Clacas, the mythic founders of the city. This complex was turned into a kind of memorial by Plancia Magna, a wealthy Pergaean lady. Just behind this complex is the **Monumental Gateway**, a three-arched structure of two storeys, which was also adorned with statues. To the right of the circular courtyard is the agora, the city's main shopping centre.

The Gate Towers of Perge.

The main thoroughfare of Perge is a colonnaded street with a water channel running through the Later Gateway and the City Gate Complex. The water was brought to the city from a source at higher ground. About halfway up this avenue on the left is the **Church of Perge**, which was once a bishopric. At the end of the street, past the intersection, near the acropolis hill, is a **Nymphaion**. Turn left at the intersection to come first to a gymnasium, then a bath. A necropolis of several tombs is situated at the end of this street. Perge once possessed a famed temple dedicated to the Pergaean Artemis but its whereabouts today is still unknown.

Nebulous early history: Perge is believed to have been founded by Greek migrants after the Trojan Wars. When Alexander the Great arrived in Pamphylia in the 4th century BC, the Pergaeans submitted without a struggle. Alexander used Perge as a base for mopping up operations on the coast of southwest Asia Minor. St Paul stopped in the city during his missionary adventures. The city continued as a Greco-Roman city, and was a bishopric during the early Byzantine Period. As a result it contains a fine example of a Roman stadium. However, the city as a whole was probably abandoned after the Arab invasions in the 7th century.

The ruins of **Sillyum** are 10 km (6 miles) east of Perge. A dirt road forking left from the Antalya–Alanya highway leads to Sillyum, built on a high acropolis hill. Although it hasn't been excavated and isn't often visited, Sillyum is more impressive than many of its neighbouring Pamphylian cities, according to the late George Bean. Greek settlers, possibly led by the seer Mopsus and his mixed multitudes, the same tribes that established Perge, founded the city after the fall of Troy around 1200 BC.

Alexander the Great, during his sweeping campaign through southern Asia Minor in the 4th century BC, besieged Sillyum, but abandoned his plan to conquer it, as control of the city would be of no strategic advantage.

The Roman theatre at Aspendos.

Ramps: The first structure travellers encounter as they ascend the acropolis hill at Sillyum is the **Lower City Gate**, a horseshoe-shaped edifice consisting of two towers and a small courtyard. Further on are the ruins of a palace and a stadium. The most impressive ruins in Sillyum are the ramps that lead up to the acropolis. The lower one, constructed in Hellenistic times, is the best preserved.

Near the top of the acropolis hill is the **Upper City Gate**, from which one can see the necropolis below as well as the city tower. Several interesting buildings are located on the acropolis, including a well-preserved Byzantine structure, a public hall and a smaller building that has the most interesting feature in Sillyum: an inscription in the local Pamphylian-Greek dialect, dating from the 3rd century BC. Other buildings to be seen on the acropolis hill are an odeon, two theatres, a few houses, a 10-metre (33-yard) long underground water cistern and several temples.

The Roman Theatre: The next destination in the direction of Alanya worth visiting is **Aspendos**, located near the village of Belkız, about 50 km (30 miles) from Antalya. A dirt road with the sign Aspendos forks to the left. The road continues over the **Köprüçay** (the Eurymedon River) for about 5 km (3 miles). The first ruins you come to are the remains of two public baths. Next is the great **Aspendos Amphitheatre**, one of the best-preserved Roman theatres in the world, which holds over 20,000 spectators. The Aspendos Opera and Ballet Festival, held in June each year in the theatre, is the Antalya region's most prestigious cultural event. Visitors can test the acoustics by walking up to the very top of the gallery of the theatre. Somebody whispering on the stage below can be easily heard.

A grisly but unsubstantiated tale surrounds construction of this grand theatre in the second century. There was once a king of Aspendos who had a lovely daughter, named Belkız. As the young woman had many suitors, the king announced he would wed his daughter to the man who would construct the greatest public structure in the city. The king could not decide between the two rival contractors who sought the marriage of Belkız. One of them built the spectacular theatre. The other constructed the important and equally impressive aqueducts to supply the city with water. In the end, the king cut his daughter in half, giving each man a part of her body.

A half hour is enough to explore the theatre. The other buildings do not warrant more than a quick walk by. Near the theatre, and on the same level, is a 215-metre (710-ft) long stadium. In the vicinity of the stadium are some sarcophagi and tombs, including one hewn out of the rocks.

An acropolis behind the amphitheatre can be entered through three gates, of which the northernmost is best preserved, although it is half-buried. The structures there include an agora, a market hall with several shops intact, a 3rd-century basilica, a nymphaion, a council chamber and aqueducts. The aqueducts that carried water to the city from the mountains north illustrate the Romans' superior knowledge of hydraulics.

Visitors to Aspendos can return to the Alanya highway by crossing over the stone **Köprüçay Bridge**, built in the 13th century by the Seljuk Turks. The bridge is narrow but sturdy, and can accommodate one car at a time.

Selge: Soon another road forks left from the Antalya-Alanya Highway leading to the astoundingly beautiful, cool, green Köprülü Kanyon, a high mountain gorge sliced through by the tumbling milky turquoise Köprü Irmagi (Eurymedon River). The tarred road ends at Behkonak after 43 km (26 miles). Fishing for brown trout here is technically illegal, but the authorities seem to turn a blind eye.

The gaggle of waterside restaurants are eager to feed you on pellet-fed rainbow trout, while teenage guides urge you to follow them on walking trails to the dramatic Roman bridge, which gave the canyon its name (a little way downstream on the far side of the river). Behkonak is also the base for several whitewater rafting companies offering half and full day trips (most will collect people from hotels throughout the Antalya area).

If your vehicle has good suspension, continue carefully up the dirt road for a further 14 km (8 miles), across a high plateau, its soft volcanic rock carved and twisted into columns ("fairy chimneys") by the wind, to the village of Altınkaya (Zerk) and the ruins of **Selge**. This road continues for the next 55 km (34 miles), passing Beşkonak, crossing a narrow Roman bridge, after which a side road to Karabuk must be taken.

Selge itself is on the Zerk-Altınkay road. Built on three hills, it was a Pisidian city. Pisidia was the name of the mountainous lake district north of Pamphylia. Selge has numerous ruins, including a theatre, a stadium, a customs house, tombs and sarcophagi and temples to Zeus and Artemis. A 3-km (2-mile) wall encircled the city, parts of which still stand today. In ancient times Selge was famous for its wines and olives.

Aqueduct at Side.

To reach the resort village of **Side**, a captivating settlement, motorists must return to the Antalya-Alanya highway. Side is located next to the ruins of one of the most impressive ancient settlements in Turkey. The ruins are situated on a peninsula 80 km (50 miles) east of Antalya. A road forks right to Side near a service station before reaching the town of Manavgat.

Romantic setting: The presence of an inhabited village next to the ancient ruins makes the site even more romantic. To get the full visual impact of the town and the deserted ruins, and escape the crowds, visitors should try to arrive either early or late in the day. Alternatively it may be well worth visiting during the November–March off season.

Side, which means "pomegranate", is a pre-Greek word that symbolised fertility. The city is believed to have been founded by migrants in the 13th or 14th centuries BC. In the 6th century, the city was dominated by the Lydians and then the Persians. It was conquered by

Alexander the Great in 334 BC, and later controlled by the Ptolemites and the Seleucids. Between 188 and 78 BC, the Kingdom of Pergamum gained hegemony over the city, transforming it into an important commercial port, the remains of which can still be seen today. It became a Greco-Roman city, and an important Christian centre, but it was abandoned in the 12th century. The present inhabitants of Side are the descendants of Turkish refugees who fled Crete during the uprising of 1898 and settled in this village.

Pulitzer prize winner: Side was made world famous by the late Alfred Friendly, former managing editor of the *Washington Post* and Pulitzer Prize-winning American journalist who lived there many years. A foundation set up by Friendly's wife has helped finance the restoration of many sites in Side, including the temples by the harbour.

The first ruins to be seen are the aqueducts, the remains of city walls and a Nymphaion. The **Side Amphitheatre** looms up on the left, next to the agora. Across is the **Bathhouse Museum**. Visitors enter the city by driving past the Vespasian Monument and the Later City Gate, an arched structure. Cars aren't allowed in the town.

The best way to see the town is to walk down the main street to the harbour, once the commercial hub of Pamphylia, now a simple fisherman's cove. To the left are the **Temple of Apollo** and the **Temple of Athena**, both dating from the second century, and a 9th-century Byzantine basilica. The eastern shore of the town brings one to the **Temple of Men**, a moon Goddess. A crescent-shaped sandy beach extends east of the site for many miles. Soon one comes back to the amphitheatre. The **State Agora** and **M-Building**, which resembles a palace, are just behind the well-preserved theatre.

Stupendous view: Much of the wall around the city is either submerged in the sand or partly sunken in the sea. For a spectacular view of Side, visitors should climb to the top row of the amphitheatre. The Museum is housed in an ancient bath that has been restored. It contains many fine Roman statues and sarcophagi, several of which are in the courtyard. The bathhouse, built during the Roman Period, is well preserved. It contains an *Apodyterium* or changing room, a *Caldarium* or hot room, a sweating room and a cooling room. The bathhouse was a place where men socialised and discussed local and political affairs.

The next town on the Antalya-Alanya highway is Manavgat, situated on the Manavgat River. Other than the pleasant riverside teahouses, there isn't much to see in the town itself, except for the bustle of the wholesale market from where trucks deliver the produce of the region, including giant melons, to other parts of Turkey. But a road forks to the left before the entrance to the town towards Manavgat Şelalesi (Falls), the ancient town of Seleucia in Pamphylia and Oymapınar Barajı (Dam). This road goes 17 km (11 miles) to the **Oymapınar Dam**, one of the biggest hydro-electric dams in Turkey. A visit to the dam and its lake is worthwhile if per-

It's all in the family.

278

mission to enter is granted by the guards. Some 5 km (3 miles) from the Antalya-Alanya road is the turnoff for **Manavgat Şelalesi**. A short walk leads to the falls. One of the best places in this area to have lunch is by the picture-postcard falls, along which there are several restaurants serving *alabalık* (trout) or *piliç şiş* (chicken on a skewer) or *piliç çevirme* (barbecue chicken) and tasty appetisers. The **Manavgat River** is one of Turkey's main sources for trout fishing. It is also one of the few places in Turkey where river rafting has been tried by sports enthusiasts. Motorboat rides up the Manavgat River from Side and Manavgat are possible to a point further downstream. Besides sports, this tropical, verdant river is an attraction in its own right.

Seleucia in Pamphylia is one of several cities in Anatolia named after the Seleucia kings of Syria. The most famous of these is Seleucia in Pieria, the ancient port of Antioch. Seleucia in Pamphylia is located about 5 km (3

miles) north of Manavgat Falls and is reachable from the village Şıhlar. A turnoff points in the direction of Selevkiye (the Turkish for Seleucia). The ruins to see in Seleucia include an aqueduct, an ancient bridge, city walls, a bathhouse, an agora and an odeon.

Alanya is about 50 km (30 miles) from Manavgat along the E24/400 highway. The road follows the sea closely, passing many fine deserted beaches along the way to Alanya, including the **Incekum Beach**. About 30 km (19 miles) east of Manavgat a village road forks to the left and continues to the **Alarahan**, an inn constructed in 1232 by the Seljuk Turks, consisting of a courtyard surrounded by vaulted rooms and corridors. The inn also has a fountain and a *mescit* or small mosque. Nearby is the fortress of **Alarakale**, built to protect the inn from marauders. Nearly halfway to Alanya is a 13th-century Turkish caravansary, **Serapsu Han** on the left.

Giant gastropod: **Alanya** (formerly Coracesium) is built around a rocky

The Manavgat Waterfalls.

peninsula that resembles a gigantic gastropod from a distance. Jutting out to the sea like an immense mollusc, the red peninsula is crowned by a long crenellated fortress that was built by the Seljuk Turks in the 13th century to dominate the Mediterranean Coast. In ancient times, the peninsula served as the headquarters of Pamphylian pirates who raided passing commercial ships for booty and slaves.

Alanya has some of the finest beaches in Turkey, and it is pleasant to spend some time swimming and sunbathing on the long beach that lies before Alanya. The first site in Alanya to be seen is the **Damlataş Cave**, on the edge of the peninsula before entering the city. The damp air in this claustrophobic cave with thousands of colourful stalactites is believed to be beneficial for those suffering from asthma and other respiratory diseases. But elderly people and those with heart ailments should avoid entering it.

Alanya is a pleasant touristic town, located at the foot of the peninsula, with many seaside restaurants and hotels. The town's symbols are the 13th-century **Red Tower** (Kızıl Kule), a crenellated defensive building, and its ancient **shipyards**.

Alanya Castle, perched on top of the peninsula at a dizzying height of 243 metres (800 ft), dominates the coast, and overlooks the town and the majestic cliffs that plunge into the sea. The ancient walls around the old city wind 7 km (4 miles) uphill like the Great Wall of China, to **Içkale**, the citadel, capped by three towers. Inside is a courtyard with the Byzantine **Church of Saint George** (Aya Yorgi) and a pleasant outdoor coffeehouse.

A small outdoor shop in the courtyard sells baby dolls made from squashes, a particular art in this part of Turkey. At the northeast corner of the courtyard is the spot called the **Adam Atacağı**, (the place from where men are thrown). It was there that condemned men were hurled down the cliffs to their deaths. A condemned man would be pardoned, according to one legend, only if he

A minaret spikes the sky in old Alanya.

could toss a pebble from that height into the sea, an impossible task. Next to it is a deep open pit covered by railings that some people suggest was a dungeon where the prisoners were kept.

From the citadel, the **Cılvarda Burnu**, a rocky promontory on which there are the ruins of three buildings, including the town's mint (**Darphane**), a tower and a monastery complex, is visible. The only way to reach these buildings is to take a boat ride along the peninsula from Alanya to the promontory and walk up.

The Old Quarter: The inhabited **Old Quarter** of the city is in the middle section of the castle. A left road as you are about to leave the castle leads to the Old Quarter, passing the fortress known as the **Ehmedek**. In the Old Quarter, you can visit the **Akçebe Sultan Mescidi** (small mosque) and **Türbe** (Tomb). These structures, built in 1230 by the Seljuk Sultan Alaeddin Keykubat I, consist of three sections, two of which contain tombs. Other buildings of note in this quarter are the

Frolicking on the Turkish Riviera.

Mecdüddin Cistern, which is still in use; a caravansary (a type of inn) that is comprised of a rectangular courtyard surrounded by rooms, a depot and the **Bedesten** (an ancient version of a shopping centre). Nearby is the **Alaeddin Mosque**, a 13th-century structure that was reconstructed by Ottoman Sultan Süleyman the Magnificent in the 16th century. Alanya is also famous for its ice cream and **Bamyacı Ice Cream Parlour** in both Güler Pınarı Mahalesi and Keykubat Caddesi makes the best in town.

The Kızıl Kule, a five-storey, 33-metre (10-ft) high octagonal tower that now houses the **Ethnographical Museum** is within walking distance from downtown Alanya along the harbor. The museum displays various exhibits, including Yörük tents, rugs and armour. Walk further down to the **Shipyards** (Tersane) nearby. Used by Seljuks to build their fleet, the dockyard is still used today to construct small boats. During the Ottoman Period, Alanya was one of the Turks' main naval bases.

ΕΙΛΗΤΙΟΩΕΕΙΝΕΤΙCΕΥ
ΕΚΦΗΝΑΣΤΗΓΗΝΤ
ΠΟΙΜΕΝΙΟΝΓΙΝΩΟ
ΚΕΝΗΣΩΝΕΙΕΡΗΝΑ

THE EASTERN MEDITERRANEAN

Turkey's eastern Mediterranean coast begins east of Alanya and ends along the Syrian frontier south of Antakya, stretching for 672 km (420 miles). The region was known to the Romans as the Cilician Coast. The area can be roughly divided into three distinct geographical zones: the rugged, mountainous terrain that stretches from Alanya to Silifke, which was known as Rough Cilicia; the vast fertile plains to the east, which was known as Smooth Cilicia, today's Çukurova; and the areas east of Adana, which extend into the Hatay, a province bordering Syria, with Antakya its capital.

Banana capital: In Rough Cilicia, the Taurus Mountains plunge into the Mediterranean over precipitous cliffs. Here and there are tiny valleys where bananas and olives are grown. The Alanya-Silifke highway winds along the ridges of the mountains. The banana capital of Turkey is Anamur, a town with a population of 35,000 halfway along Rough Cilicia. Anamur's banana growers are fond of saying their bananas taste better than the popular imported Cikita brand of South America. Anamur has miles of uncrowded golden beaches, dominated by a magnificent Armenian Castle. The ancient ruins of Anemurium are west of the town.

Rough Cilicia ends east of Taşucu and Silifke. The name Silifke is a Turkish version of Cilicia. Numerous sites of historic interest are near this coastal town, including the ghastly pits known as Heaven and Hell and the Kızkalesi (the Maiden's Castle), which stands on an island.

Neolithic settlement: Mersin, today Turkey's third biggest port after Istanbul and Izmir, started out as a neolithic settlement, rivalling in antiquity the oldest archaeological finds in Egypt and Mesopotamia.

The town of Tarsus, further east, was the birthplace of St Paul the tentmaker,

<u>Preceding pages, the mosaic of the Three Maidens in Silifke.</u>

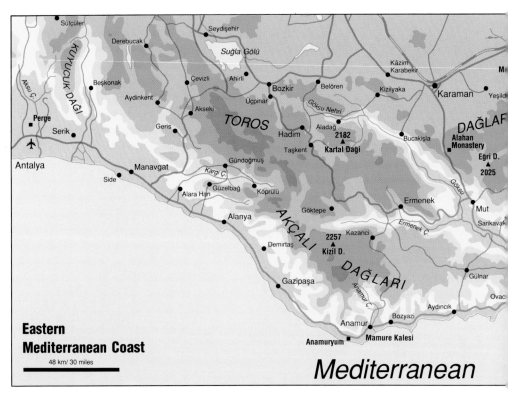

Eastern Mediterranean Coast

48 km/ 30 miles

Mediterranean

whose missionary journeys helped spread Christianity westward into Anatolia from Judea. Today it has become a booming market town. It was also in Tarsus that Antony summoned Cleopatra for their first meeting that began their big romance and ended in their tragic deaths.

North of Tarsus, high up in the Taurus Mountains, engineers nearly 3,000 years ago built an East–West short cut through Asia Minor known as the Cilician Gates. The armies of Cyrus the Younger, Alexander the Great and the Crusaders marched through this mountain pass. A modern highway today crosses the Taurus Mountains at Ulukışla east of the Cilician Gates, connecting the Anatolian steppes with the Cilician Coast.

Industrial hub: Adana, Turkey's fourth largest city and cotton boom town, stands in the centre of the vast Çukurova. It is a large industrial city, which produces cotton fabrics, tractors and harvesters and processed food, such as margarine. Numerous towns and cities can be reached from Adana, including Yumurtalık, which is the terminal of the 980-km (612-mile) Iraq–Turkey crude oil pipeline. The town has a big port that is usually lined with ocean-going oil tankers.

The port of Iskenderun, where a huge Soviet-built iron and steel complex operates, is east of Adana, surrounded by the Amanos Mountains.

From Iskenderun, the road climbs the mountains to Belen Pass, the ancient Syrian Gates, to Antakya (the former Antioch). This was the site of St Paul's first ministry, the third largest city of the Roman Empire, outranked only by Rome and Alexandria. It was also in Antioch that the term Christians was first applied to the followers of Jesus. Today Iskenderun and Antakya (both of which belong to the province of Hatay) are the principal Arab-speaking cities of Turkey.

Antakya has an important museum which contains some fine mosaics from the Hellenistic, Roman and early Christian periods.

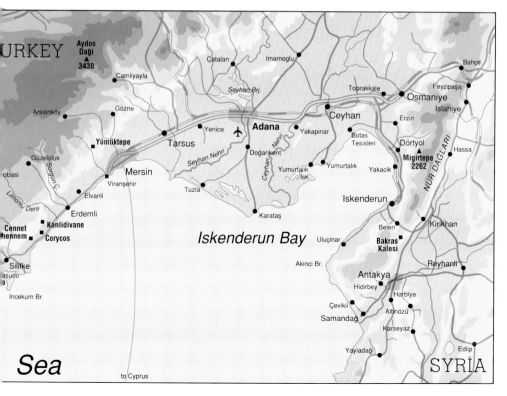

ROUGH CILICIA

Heading east beyond Alanya the highway takes to the sky on the arms of the Taurus Mountains as the first reaches of the **Cilician Coast** begin. For the next 672 km (420 miles), Cilicia's history unfolds like a colourful tapestry, its length textured with tales of conquests, corsairs and Cleopatra.

This stretch of the Mediterranean offers some of the country's most spectacular scenery and uncommon diversions. Where else can one end a day of castle-hopping with a sunset swim to a Crusader fortress, or drink from the Fountain of Knowledge after a sneak preview of Heaven and Hell?

Land of contrasts: Cilicia is a land of contrasting natural beauty that both beckons and repels. In ancient times the western region was known as "Cilicia Tracheia" (Rough Cilicia) as here, the Taurus Mountains crowd the coast, sending craggy slopes plunging into the Mediterranean. Cilicia Tracheia appeared so intimidating to the ancients that even Alexander the Great crossed it off his list after one look at its impenetrable terrain.

The eastern region, known as Cilicia Campestris (Smooth Cilicia), begins at the Lamus River, past Silifke, where the Taurus pull back from the coast, leaving a vast fertile delta that has long sustained civilisation.

Cilicia was forever caught in the tug-of-war between rival kingdoms and aspiring powers and a succession of peoples ruled the land including the Phoenicians followed by the Greeks who fought in the Trojan War.

Pirates terrorise coast: The Roman Empire claimed Cilicia as one of its provinces and the Romans embarked upon a successful mission to wipe out Cilicia's most famous denizens: pirates. These buccaneers fed the Roman slave trade during the first century BC, terrorising the coastal cities and plundering Syrian ships as they passed on their way to Aegean trading ports. They ruled the waves unhindered until 67 BC when General Pompey put an end to the motley lot and piracy disappeared until Arab ships pestered the Byzantines in the seventh century.

In the 12th century, the kingdom of Lesser Armenia flourished along the coast, allying itself during the next 300 years with the invading Crusaders, who left their Frankish touch in the string of medieval coastal castles. When Armenian rule faltered, the Lusignans arrived from Cyprus, only to be overwhelmed by the fierce Seljuk and Karamanid Turcomen tribes.

Prosperity and progress eluded Cilicia and the region succumbed to Ottoman rule in the 15th century, eventually receding into anonymity. It was only in the mid-20th century that Cilicia re-emerged, fuelled by a drive to play a role in the country's economy.

Sustaining industry: The lowland of Cilicia Campestris is now called the Çukurova Plain and is the centre of Turkey's cotton crop, which sustains a thriving textile industry. Two commercial ports were built, in Mersin and Taşucu, opening trade lines with the outside world and hoping to establish the region as an industrial base.

A government agriculture project transformed the rugged slopes of Cilicia Tracheia into patchwork valleys, crisscrossed with banana plantations and olive, lemon and fig orchards. And best of all, centuries of obscurity have left most areas of Cilicia untouched. Cilicia Tracheia appears much the same as it did in Alexander's day: beautiful, unspoiled and treacherous.

Treacherous is just one way to describe the 217-km (136-mile) drive from Alanya to Silifke as the coast road twists its way above pine forest gorges and turquoise coves of Rough Cilicia.

Hairpin turns: Drivers should limit their travel to the daytime when the region's beauty can be appreciated and the hairpin bends seen!

Public bus companies serve the coast frequently and have terminals (*Oto Gar*) in Antalya, Side, Alanya, Anamur, Silifke, Mersin and Adana. Reservations need to be made a day in advance as the buses are always packed with

Left, women work while men relax.

locals, tourists and *asker* (soldiers) on their way to assignments.

Travellers should try and reserve a seat with a sea view, but they should prepare for the sun: only some of the buses have smoked-glass windows.

Seleucid fortress: The first remains of ancient civilisation in Cilicia lie in **Aydap**, known in the past as Iotepe. This was one of three fortress-cities established in the second century BC by Seleucid King Antiochus IV to protect Seleucid interests from invading pirates and mountain tribes. **Gazipaşa**, the next town, is the site of the king's second city (Selinus) now marked by meagre ruins by the beach. Selinus made the social column in AD 117 when Roman Emperor Trajan died while passing through after the Parthian War. His death was considered by many to be symbolic and is believed to mark the very beginning of the decline of the Roman Empire.

The third and best-preserved city is **Antiochia-ad-Cragum**, and it's exactly as its name suggests – on a crag.

Ruins run helter-skelter onto a rocky promontory that once bore the brunt of continuous pirate attacks.

Leaving behind the ghost of Antiochus to fend for himself, the highway glides into a magnificent valley overgrown with terraced banana plantations, which embroider the mountainside and run to the shores of a beautiful bay. This is **Kaledıran**, known in the past as Calendiris, above which the skeleton of a Byzantine fortress keeps watch from a rocky ledge. The settlement is a good place to stop for a swim and sample the sweet *muz* (bananas).

Tasty carobs: Cilicia's forest is one of the most beautiful and well-tended in Turkey. Sleepy men sell *muz* under straw huts while young girls work the dangerous roads, balancing trays of nuts and fruit on top of their heads hoping to tempt tourists. The weird-looking brown pod stacked on a string is the carob *(keçiboynuzu)*.

With Kaledıran in the distance, the road descends to a wide fertile delta, the Anamur Plain.

Straight ahead is **Anamur**, a town with about 35,000 residents, many of whom are unhappy that they have been ignored by travel books and tourists. Despite little historical significance, Anamur is a convenient base from which to visit surrounding sites. The town has an interesting Seljuk period mosque dating from the early 14th century and pleasant beach-front camping.

Phoenician colony: About 7 km (4 miles) from the ancient city of Anemurium (Greek for windy place), sits **Anamur Burnu** (Cape Anamur). Originally a Phoenician colony, it later became a Hellenistic city and was incorporated into Roman Cilicia in AD 72. After continual harassment by pirates and mountain tribes, Anemurium was abandoned in the 7th century, when the Arabs showed up.

A defensive wall climbs to a citadel and two aqueducts run parallel to the main road through town. It's worth hiring a guide to help you uncover the many mosaics and frescoes that are hidden throughout the site of domed tombs and churches.

Cape Anamur is Turkey's closest point to Cyprus, only 64 km (40 miles) away. On a clear day one can easily distinguish the Beşparmak Dağları (the Pentadaktylos or Five Finger Mountains) that run along the northern coast of the Mediterranean island. Gigantic radars on Cape Anamur sweep the eastern Mediterranean for enemy aircraft and naval vessels.

Crusader fortress: The massive outline of **Mamure Castle** commands the coastline 3 km (2 miles) east of Anemurium. One of the largest and best-preserved Crusader fortresses in Asia Minor, it was first mentioned in the third century as a Roman stronghold before becoming a pirates' den. During the 12th century the castle was incorporated into Armenia's defence system, and later passed to the Lusignans of Cyprus, the Seljuks and the Karamanid Turcomens. The Ottomans moved in, added the mosque and other restorations and remained there until the sun

The Castle of Anamur dominates the coast.

set on their empire in 1923. The circular stairway leads up the huge defence tower to a great view of the castle's 36 towers and massive ramparts. Matches are needed to light its paths.

The **Köşebükü Mağarası**, one of Cilicia's famous wishing and asthma-curing caves, is 17 km (11 miles) from Anamur in a lovely pine forest in the Taurus foothills. Locals believe the cave's air cures asthma, while others make pilgrimages to the cavern depths to throw money into a pit and ask for Allah's blessing.

Taxis are found at the bus station but meters seem out of fashion and price haggling is a necessary evil.

Softa Kalesi (Scholar's Castle) looms high on a ridge just 12 km (8 miles) east of Anamur. A hardy hike is required to reach the massive defensive walls of this 12th-century fortress. Before Softa Kalesi, the road winds through a beautiful forest and passes the government-run **Pullu Camping Grounds**, situated in a pine grove on its own private beach.

Aydıncık sits on a bay tucked between the arms of the Taurus Mountains 57 km (35 miles) from Anamur. Also known as Gilindere, it is the impressive site of ancient Kelenderis, one of the oldest colonies in Rough Cilicia, founded in the 5th century BC by Greeks from Samos.

Further on, the village of **Boğsak** rings a turquoise bay punctuated by the ghostly **Provencal Island**, a perfect Hallowe'en haunt as the island is blanketed with tombs, sarcophagi and medieval ruins. The Gothic arches of a Crusader chapel, built by the Knights of St John, add to the general gloom.

On the western reaches of the bay sits **Liman Kalesi** (Harbour Castle), another medieval fortress built by the Armenians in the 14th century.

Taşucu, once a small village, is now a commercial port and one of two coastal departure points for the Turkish Republic of Northern Cyprus (the second is Mersin). Hotels and restaurants line the bay and on the edge of town a sprawling paper factory makes use of the Cilician timber. Travellers who want to take the ferry to Northern Cyprus should stay here. Those travelling to Greece or to the Greek-controlled Southern Cyprus should not have their passports stamped for Northern Cyprus (officials will stamp a separate sheet of paper instead). A 14th-century Turkish fortress guards the pretty beachhead.

Before Silifke, a sign points to **Aya Thekla** (Meryemelik in Turkish), a Christian pilgrimage site devoted to St Thekla, St Paul's first convert and Christianity's first female martyr. Thekla became one of Byzantium's most popular saints and her life story was the basis for the *Acts of Paul and Thekla*.

According to the Acts, Thekla met Paul in Iconium (Konya) and was so moved by his preaching on the virtues of chastity that she cried out, "I shall cut my hair and follow thee whithersoever thou goest." With that pious promise, she ended her engagement and incurred the wrath of a jilted fiance who plotted revenge.

Divine intervention: Upon his orders, Thekla was stripped naked, set upon a pyre in a crowded amphitheatre, and wild lions were sent in for the kill. Divine intervention prevailed, and as the Acts report, "there was about her a cloud, so that neither the beasts did touch her nor was she seen naked."

Thekla was released, became St Paul's chief follower and founded a convent in a cave in Seleucia. One story has Thekla living to a ripe age; another claims she was murdered by thieves. Two basilicas were built in her honour. The first by Constantine after his conversion to Christianity and the second, located over the cave, was built in the 5th century by Emperor Zeno.

The underground chapel has frescoes and mosaics and has been turned into a small museum exhibiting locally found sculpture.

Just 1.6 km (1 mile) inland is **Silifke**, the ancient Seleucia-ad Calcynum, founded in the 3rd century BC by Seleucus I Nikator. Silifke is the largest town in Rough Cilicia and is divided by the **Göksu River**.

Silifke's **Archaeological Museum** is very close to the bus station and opens daily. Numismatists will revel in the large collection of Hellenistic coins. Nearby is the ruin of a Roman temple dedicated to Zeus.

Silifke is renowned for its folk dancers and each May hosts the international Music and Folklore festival.

The town's most visible site is a massive medieval fortress which looms atop a flat hill. This citadel was built by Byzantines in the seventh century as a bulwark against Arabs, and passed to the Crusaders, Armenians and Seljuks before finally becoming Ottoman property in 1471.

Byzantine cistern: Below the hill lies **Tekir Ambarı**, a Byzantine cistern built from an ancient cave. Restaurants offering Silifke's famous creamy yogurt and a "*manzara*" (a view) have invaded the grounds. One detour from Silifke must not be missed: the road winds through the **Göksu Valley** along one of the most scenic drives in Turkey and leads to the Alahan Monastery.

Alahan Monastery is perched on a narrow mountain terrace nearly 2,100 metres (7,000 ft) above sea level and overlooks a fabulous view of winding the Göksu Valley.

About 45 km (28 miles) out of Silifke the pine forests give way to olive groves as life takes on a harsher edge and the first reaches of the Anatolian plateau begin. This is the domain of the nomad, whose straw huts line the roadside, their sides bulging with colourful *kilim* cushions *(yastıks)*.

Mut, the proverbial town-in-the-middle-of-nowhere, appears on the horizon. The site of ancient Claudipolis, it was founded in 50 BC by Marcus Aurelius Polemo, who undertook the unenviable and daunting task of uniting the wild mountain tribes under one kingdom.

After Mut, the Taurus range reappears and 15 minutes later a sign marks a 2 km (1.3 mile) road to the 5th-century Alahan Monastery. A one-hour trek through the pine forest to the mountain ledge in the early morning is an exhilarating experience. Before the final bend, north towards Aloda, one can see early Christian cave churches carved into the cliff sides.

The Evangelist Church is the first part entered from the western terrace. The church's surviving portal has detailed friezes symbolising the triumph of Christianity over paganism. A close examination shows saints Gabriel and Michael trouncing the likes of Cybele, the Anatolian mother goddess, as well as a bull and a priest of Isis.

The portal leads to a circular baptistry, which is next to the Eastern Church, a simple yet beautiful doomed basilica crafted by expert masons in the early 6th century. Three interior arches, held by Corinthian columns, grace the central aisle.

Tempting trails offer short-cuts down the mountain, but a carpet of pine needles makes the going rather slippery, so unless you're very sure-footed it's probably wise to stick to the beaten path. Buses passing from Konya to Silifke will stop to pick up travellers who wait by the road at Alahan.

Alahan Monastery, north of Silifke.

SMOOTH CILICIA

The second detour from Silifke is to **Uzuncaburç**, just 30 km (19 miles) to the north. This is the site of the former Olba/Diocaesarea, founded in the 3rd century BC by Seleucis I Nikator. It is a peaceful and impressive site, displaying a medley of Hellenistic, Roman and Byzantine ruins.

It's business as usual in Uzuncaburç as villagers tend to vineyards, goats and apple orchards. Enterprising women have set up black wool nomad tents under which they sell their much-prized handiwork – ancient crafts at thoroughly modern prices.

Corinthian Order: After paying the attendant, you enter the city through the Roman parade gate. Head down the colonnaded street to the **Temple of Zeus Olbios**, which was erected at the end of the 3rd century BC, making it the oldest known structure of the Corinthian Order in the world. Thirty of its columns still stand; four are topped with Corinthian capitals. In the grassy square to the side of the temple, sculpted friezes display the exaggerated visages of lions, bulls and monsters.

To the west stands the **Temple of Tyche**, goddess of fortune. Five Corinthian columns, each reportedly cut from a single slab of Egyptian granite, tower above a massive foundation. To the north rises an original city gate with three well-preserved arches; one proclaims the town's name, Diocaesarea. Out by the entrance, the road leads north past a small cafe where the village men play perpetual games of *okey*, a simplified version of *mahjong*, between glasses of *çay* (tea).

The Long Tower: To the right stands a five-storey, 22-metre (73-ft) Hellenistic tower, which once served as a priest's tomb and later formed part of a defence and communication network with other towers throughout the region. Uzuncaburç means "long tower" in the Turkish language.

The road to Uzuncaburç winds through pine forests, passing through Demircili, the first-century Roman city of Imbrogin. Several unusual temple-like tombs can be seen, the most interesting is the double-decker **Çifte Anıt Mezarları** (Twin Monument Tombs), which are visible from the road.

Taxi anyone? *Dolmuş* depart for Uzuncaburç at 11am daily across from Silifke's Tourism Office. If you miss the *dolmuş*, share a cab. A private taxi will cost you as much as five times the shared amount.

Back on the coast road, stop at **Yapraklı Eşik** (The Cove with Leaves), a perfectly sculptured cove with enticing turquoise water. Its currents are of two different temperatures: the top layer is a chilly 8°C, but the bottom layer is a soothing 23°C.

Susanoğlu, the next village, has a wide bay and long beach. Local holidaymakers have turned this once-pretty setting into an eyesore. Military-style barbed wire fencing encloses the beach and the clutter of pensions, motels and cafés along with the people crowding it.

In kinder days, Susanoğlu was known as Corasium, a major Byzantine port specialising in the trading of salt. Traces of salt pans and catch basins are carved into the rocks on the east side of the bay.

Phallus of Priapus: A detour 12 km (8 miles) north through Susanoğlu leads to the ancient city of **Paslı**, the best-preserved Roman site in the region and home of the famous **Mezgit Kalesi**, the **Temple Tomb of the Fearless Satrap** (Persian governor). From the monument's right side appears a remarkable relief – the outstanding **Phallus of Priapus**, the god of fertility and vitality, whose glorious presence bears testimony to the courage and fearlessness of the deceased. As the tale goes, Priape was the illegitimate son of Zeus and Aphrodite, and Hera, in a jealous fit, deformed the child, giving him a phallus equal to his height.

Priape, also known as God Bes, ranked high with the ancient Anatolians who erected temples and sacrificed donkeys in the deity's honour. Sacred wishing rocks, scattered throughout the countryside, were visited by young women who begged the God of Fertility for a good husband.

Rumour has it that village girls still make the pilgrimages to the monument in Paslı, and whisper, "Wake up oh my good fate, before my roses fade." Tiny bronze Priape statues and colourful postcards were once extremely popular with tourists who tittered at the prospect of amusing their friends.

Narlıkuyu (Pomegranate Spring), is a sliver of a bay lined with lively seafood restaurants and a small hotel, but it's the **Kızlar Hamamı** (the Bath of the Maidens) that lures visitors. This 4th-century Roman bath has a lovely floor mosaic depicting the **Three Graces**, Aglaia, Euphrosina and Thalis, the daughters Zeus had with Eurynome, daughter of the Ocean. The bath itself is housed in a small nondescript shed in the village and is open daily. A small entrance fee is charged, and it's well worth the money.

On the shore a spring sprouts fresh

A farmer drives his tractor through a colonnaded field.

water into the sea – this is the **Fountain of Nus** (the Fountain of Knowledge). Its powers must be taste-tested!

Across Narlıkuyu await the other-worldly sites of Cennet Deresi and Cehennem (Heaven's Stream and Hell), which form the **Corycian Cave Complex**. These massive sink-holes were created centuries ago when the ground collapsed from chemical erosion by an underground stream.

Cennet (Heaven) is an enormous pit, measuring 250 metres (820 ft) long and 70 metres (230 ft) at its deepest point. The stairway to heaven is lined not with "pearly gates" but with sagging trees, littered with paper talismans and peti-tions placed by superstitious visitors asking for cures and good luck. Obvi-ously, anything will suffice, as snack bags and candy wrappers join hundreds of ribbons and shredded tissue paper strewn on the branches of the trees. It isn't a heavenly sight.

Descending the 452 rock steps into heaven's bowels may convince the visi-tor that he has accidentally landed in hell. The descent is foreboding as the air becomes stifling and the sun is blotted out by trees. A roaring sound, which grows louder with each step, does noth-ing to soothe the nerves.

At the grotto's end, the **Church of St Mary** guards the entrance to the gloomy cavern, which according to mythology, was the Home of Typhon – the monster with 100 dragon heads and snakes for feet. The roaring sound comes from a river deep inside the cav-ern, which ancients believed was the River Styx, the river encircling Hades over which boatmen known as Charon ferried dead bodies.

Symbolic assurance: When the Byz-antines arrived in the 5th century they were uneasy with the site's evil conno-tations and ascribed it heavenly powers, building a basilica to honour the Virgin Mary at the cave's entrance as symbolic assurance that Typhon was put to rest forever. The Church of St Mary has well-preserved frescoes showing Christ with two saints.

Venture into the cave with the help of

The church in Heaven.

a guide and a lantern, but save your breath because the climb back to the real world is definitely challenging.

Cehennem (Hell) lives up to its reputation. The path to this chasm is lined with littered trees sporting paper petitions, this time asking to keep the hounds of hell at bay. The chasm resembles the open jaws of a monster; it is the perfect façade for the entrance to the underworld, as the ancients believed.

If the stairs of Heaven together with the sight of Hell leave you gasping for breath, you should head to the **Wishing and Asthma Caves** (Dilek Astım Mağarası), which are also part of the Corycian Cave complex. The descent into the cave purports to provide relief for asthma sufferers. But the descent is only for the sure-footed and the cave itself is a bit claustrophobic. Sufferers known to be cured have yet to manifest themselves.

The tiny resort village of **Kızkalesi** (Maiden's Castle) lies a few minutes east. Known as Corycus in ancient times, the Turks call it Kızkalesi after the Byzantine fortress of the same name, and it floats in a storybook setting 200 metres (660 ft) offshore. Its land-locked partner, the massive 12th-century Corycus, rambles on the coast just east of the sea castle. At one time the fortresses were connected to each other by a sea wall that formed a secure port for Corycus.

Pirates' haunt: Corycus is believed to have been settled before the 4th century BC and during the second and third centuries BC it was a strategic harbour and a famous pirates' haunt. The region prospered under Roman and Byzantine rule but declined slowly over the following centuries and was eventually abandoned; only during the past 50 years have people returned.

However, Kızkalesi of today, with its wild frontier town atmosphere, is far from its former days of splendour. The beach is crowded with hotels, motels and pensions – many only half-finished, and in the peak summer months the streets are filled with holidaymakers –

Left, the Guardian to Hell. Right, a frieze at Kanlıdivane.

mainly locals from Adana, with a sprinkling of curious foreigners. Club Barbarossa offers a decent escape from the maddening crowd and has a pleasant beach, nice pool and good view of the Maiden's Castle.

Taxis are rare but a *dolmuş* leaves every 15 minutes from the main Mersin-Silifke road in either direction. There are good places to swim all along the coast and they are best tested in late spring or early autumn when the crowds are thinner. To explore the sea castle, you should either swim to it (a brave feat), rent a canoe from the public beach, or hire a guide and row a boat across.

Maiden's legend: Although built for military reasons, the fortress carries the standard medieval castle legend involving a maiden and the premise that neither love nor care can change the course of human fate.

The tale describes the King of Corycus, who upon learning that his daughter's fate was to die by a snake bite, shipped her off to the island castle, far away from the world's dangers. Naturally, a lowly reptile made its way to the princess (in a basket of figs sent by a well-intentioned suitor) and the princess met her fate.

Some 3 km (2 miles) from Kızkalesi is **Ayas**, ancient Elaeusa-Sebaste, founded partly on an islet, and known to the Romans as Elaeusa (Olives) and Sebaste (Augustus) to the Greeks. Three columns, a theatre and necropolis can be seen.

The entrance to **Kanlıdivane**, the ancient settlement of Kanytelis, lies 7 km (4 miles) east in Kumkuyu. A 3 km (2 mile) road leads to the city, which was founded around a huge sacred chasm. Houses, churches, cemeteries and cisterns remain. A Hellenistic tower, like that in Olba/Diocaesarea, stands at the hellish pit's southwest corner. Carved into the cliff underneath is a rock bas-relief showing a family of six. Of the five churches, the most impressive is the **Church of Papylos** at the northeast end of the hole.

Necropolis: Visitors must see the necropolis which lies in a small valley 300 metres (985 ft) away. Walk down the road that leads to **Çanakçı** and head left down the footpath to the south side of the gorge. There, nine reliefs glow from the red rock; one tomb shows a woman fashionably dressed in a tight gown; another is of a man reclining with a glass of wine.

The road to Mersin is dotted with aqueducts in almost every valley, which long ago tunnelled water from the **Lamas Çayı** (the ancient Lamus River) to the ancient cities, before winding through the Cilician Plain and flowing into the Mediterranean. Although many ancient geographers placed Smooth Cilicia east of the Göksu River (the Calycadnus), Strabo, the most famous of Greek geographers, considered the Lamus River the boundary between Rough Cilicia and Smooth Cilicia, as here the Taurus disappears into the backdrop, leaving a wide fertile delta stretching to the foothills.

A right turn at Mezitli will take you to **Viranşehir**, 1.6 km (1 mile) away. Viranşehir was founded in the 7th

The Banana Man in Anamur.

century BC by settlers from Rhodes who set up an important trading post. Shortly after, Attic colonisers took over, naming it Soli ("sun" in Greek). These people spoke a strange harsh dialect that both puzzled and amused their neighbours, giving birth to the word "solecism", which translates as incorrect speech or grammar.

The Stoic School: Soli was also the birthplace of Chrysippus, a founder of the less-than-fun Stoic School of Philosophy, who in the 3rd century BC wrote 750 books on stoicism, decreeing that "the wise man should be free from passion, unmoved by joy or grief and submissive to natural law." Stoicism, according to Dionysus of Halicarnassus, was a "monument of dullness."

In 91 BC the Armenian Tigranes chased the population out of Soli, and then pirates wreaked havoc until 67 BC when Pompey cleaned the coast of corsairs, burning 1,300 pirate ships and ending the buccaneering business in just three months. He repopulated Soli with his prisoners of war – demanding they behave – and renamed the city Pompeiopolis. The city originally was entered through a 150-metre (500-ft) long Via Sacra (Sacred Way), lined with 200 Corinthian columns that led to the harbour. Today twenty columns remain, standing firmly in a field of raspberry bushes.

Mersin is capital of İçel Province. Its earliest inhabitants were the Hittites. It has undergone positive changes in the past years, transforming itself from the sleepy fishing village of old. A new harbour (the largest in Turkey), an oil refinery and international trade has boosted its stature as a modern industrial city.

There isn't much history to see in Mersin unless you are a fanatic about excavation sites. About 3 km (2 miles) away is the terraced mound of **Yümüktepe** – the original site of the city, which was excavated in the 1930s and 1940s. The oldest stratum dates back to the Stone Age.

Mersin has many quality hotels, like the five-star Merit and the good old Hilton, which dot a lovely palm-lined boulevard. English is spoken at the Tourism Office, located on the east side of the harbour, and its personnel provide information about the Turkish Republic of Northern Cyprus. There is a regular ferryboat service from Mersin to Gazimagosa (Famagusta) in Cyprus. *Dolmuğ* buses run frequently through the city to Mersin Bus Station. From there, buses leave for all points east, west and north.

Soap opera: Some 25 km (16 miles) east of Mersin, **Tarsus** languishes on the banks of Tarsus Çayı, the ancient River Cydnus. The city commands a strategic position on the rich, fertile Cilician Plain and has a long history dating back to the 14th century BC. Ancient Rome was impressed by Tarsus and proclaimed it the capital of its Cilician province in 64 BC. And it was here that the world's first docu-soap opera unfolded, as Mark Antony summoned Cleopatra to Tarsus with intentions of slapping her hand for supporting the rival Cassius. But poor Antony succumbed at the first sight of Cleo-

Farmers pile cotton in sacks.

patra floating up the Cydnus in her gleaming golden barge under purple sails, swathed in flowing silks and reclining under the attentions of fawning slave boys.

Tarsus is best known as the birthplace of Paul the Apostle, who worked as a tentmaker in the city until his preachings took him on the road. Although not much to look at, the well that marks the site has great religious significance and is popular with visitors.

A few reasonable sites remain in Tarsus. There's **Cleopatra's Gate** (Kancik Kapisi), one of the city's original six entrances. Little is known of the Gate's connection to Cleopatra herself although she was believed to have visited the area. Down from the gate is the "**Özgürlük Anıtı**", an inscription of independence carved into a stone, which dates from the reign of Emperor Severus Alexander and proclaims that Roman civil law will apply in Tarsus.

The local museum is worth a quick trip. Located in the **Kutupaşa Medresesi**, it contains numerous friezes, statu-

ary and a Roman sarcophagus. The forbidding-looking mosque to the north was once a Gothic church. Most noticeable in Tarsus are the carts, stands and markets overflowing with fruit and vegetables, adding a welcome splash of colour against the greyness of the town. Against this oriental backdrop sits a 19th-century American high school.

The **Cave of the Seven Sleepers** is 14 km (9 miles) from Tarsus, and legend says early Christians hid here to avoid persecution by the Roman governor Dacianus. After awakening from a 100-year slumber they returned to town and attracted attention with their out-of-date fashions.

About 50 km (31 miles) north of Tarsus, after the town of Ulukişla, are the infamous **Cilician Gates** (Gülek Boğazı), actually a 1,286-metre (4,160-ft) narrow passage blasted through the Taurus range. It was one of the most important, and dreaded, mountain crossings in history and until recently was the only main connection between Tarsus and the Anatolian highlands.

Harvesting the crop in the Çukurova Region.

ADANA AND THE EAST

In the middle of the Cilician Plain, now called Çukurova, lies **Adana**, Turkey's fourth-largest city with 1.2 million inhabitants. This fertile region 40 km (25 miles) east of the Taurus Mountains owes much of its wealth to the Ceyhan and Seyhan rivers, which for centuries have irrigated the vast fields. But the area's prosperity has only recently trickled down to the majority of the population, whose grinding poverty as virtual serfs to rapacious landowners is so aptly described by Adana's favourite scribe and perennial Nobel Prize nominee, Yaşar Kemal.

In fields near the city people continue to toil as they have for hundreds of years, backs bent and heads covered to protect them against the harsh Adana sun. Yet here and there are signs of change: brightly painted houses, cars parked alongside the fields, and an increasing number of schools and markets.

Economic boom: In Adana, the economic boom is unmistakable. The city's location as a major transport hub to Syria and Iraq, coupled with the growth of Turkey's textile industry and the nearby presence of a US Air Force base have all contributed to the growing economy. The construction industry is thriving, particularly five-star hotels and new apartment blocks – and the old village character of Adana has given way to a city feel.

Downtown Adana exudes a pleasant large-town small-city ambience with its spacious, tree-lined boulevards, elegant clothing shops and the latest European and Japanese cars.

Unfortunately, a major earthquake in 1998 put the lid on many ambitious schemes, as well as leaving the injured and the homeless to pick up the pieces.

As with most eastern cities, Adana's population increased as it absorbed growing numbers of rural farmers who flocked to urban areas to escape clashes between Turkish government forces and a terrorist group, the Kurdistan

Left, emptying red peppers. Right, downtown Adana.

Workers Party (PKK). Many of these refugees struggle to make a success of their lives, lacking the skills required for modern city life.

Sectarian violence has abated somewhat after the capture of PKK leader, Abdullah Ocalan in March 1999 and eastern regions are at the top of a government priority list to receive aid and investment. But it will be hard to redress the social burden placed on the cities.

The Cilician Plain is steeped in history from the Hittites onward, but in Adana itself there are few ancient sites. The Roman Bridge **Taşköprü** is a fine example of antiquity built by Hadrian in the second century.

Few people outside Turkey know of the city's most awe-inspiring sight – the Merkez Cami (New Mosque), an enormous, beautiful new mosque whose white marble reflection sparkles in the Heyhan River. Opened in 1999, it is second in size only to the Sulimaniye Mosque in Istanbul, with six minarets, a 51-metre (167-ft) high dome and space for 30,000 people, while the elaborate tiles and gold leaf inside are based on the spectacular interior of the Blue Mosque. Future plans include a huge open plaza and museum of Islam.

The most impressive structure in the city has to be the **Ulu Cami**, located in the historic district between an uninspiring bazaar and the auto repair and spare parts district. The exact date of the mosque's construction is debatable. Some say it was built in 1507 by Halit Bey, emir of the Ramazanoğlu Turks, and ruler of the region until the Ottomans conquered Adana in 1517. However, a plaque above the door puts the date of completion at 541, attributing it to both Halit Bey and his son, Mehmet Pasha.

Iznik tiles: The mosque has an interesting squat minaret and the tiles inside are said to come from the famed Iznik kilns. Adjacent to the mosque is a charming if a bit dilapidated park containing Halit Bey's Iznik-tiled mausoleum, a perfect place to sit and wait for an attendant to unlock the door and allow you into the mosque.

Adana during the Ottoman Period.

Across the street from Ulu Cami is a little teahouse, set in the midst of an old complex for religious studies. Despite its proximity to the mosque, the only thing being studied there now is backgammon and the fine art of conversation beneath shady trees.

Two other sites of interest are close by. The Ethnographic Museum, located on a small alley just off Inönü Caddesi and Ziya Paşa Bulvarı, houses a small collection of *kilims*, jewellery, weapons, musical instruments and clothing. The building may have been built by the Crusaders as one of their numerous churches, but an inscription above the entrance dates it in Greek letters to 1845.

Roman ruins: The **Adana Regional Museum** is an airy modern construction on Fuzuli Caddesi, the main road running along the Seyhan two blocks west of Inönü Caddesi. There is a generous collection of Roman ruins and a little garden filled with more ruins and old tombstones.

Apart from cotton, this region is best known for spicy *Adana kebab*. Although every restaurant menu features this dish, the best ones are clustered on **Atatürk Bulvarı**, across the street from the Tourism Office. Those longing for an American-style snack can find comfort in the neighbourhood around the US Consulate, where restaurants offer hamburgers, french fries and lots of Coca-Cola memorabilia.

One other dish worth trying in Adana is *piliç şiş* (a *shish kebab* made from chicken instead of mutton). Visitors to the city should also try *şalgam suyu*, a salty, crimson drink made from the juices of turnips, beets and carrots, served in most Adana restaurants.

Adana is also famous for *bici*, a dessert of crushed ice, rice pudding, rose water and powdered sugar. Served in pretty glass bowls by men with pushcarts, *bici* is a nice change from the gallons of water you have to drink in the hot, hot weather.

Adana has several first-class hotels, including the **Büyük Sürmeli** and **Zaimoğlu**, both on Özler Caddesi,

Marco Polo's town: Some 50 km (31 miles) south of Adana on the delta formed by the Ceyhan and Seyhan rivers lies **Karataş**, a sleepy port and summer resort town with little attraction save for its bathing beach. Another 40 km (25 miles) east of Karataş is the port of **Ayas**, noted by Marco Polo in the early 13th century as a bustling market spot for spices and fabrics, although little of this atmosphere remains.

Much more splendid are the sites east of Adana off the E-5 highway on the way to Ceyhan. About 30 km (19 miles) past fields of cotton and more auto repair shops lies **Yılan Kalesi**, or Snake Castle. In an area where castles and fortresses are so numerous as to almost become mundane, this eerie structure high atop a hill that looks black from the road should not be missed. Reportedly built by the Armenians in the early 13th century, it was extended by the Crusaders. The origin of its name is unknown, although this area is rife with snake legends and possibly snakes.

Just beyond Yılan Kalesi, a road turns

Holding up the prizefighter.

north, forking left after 35 km (22 miles) to the farming village of **Kozan Â**, shrunk from former glories as capital of Cilician Armenia. An unmarked road in the middle of town leads steeply upwards and turns through a series of outer walls to the gate of the castle, built by Leo II (1187–1219). The main walls, ringed by 44 towers, form a saddle linking the twin summits of the long, narrow hill. The capture of the castle and King Leo VI by Egyptian Mamelukes in 1374, marked the end of the southern Armenian kingdom.

Continuing on E-5, turn inland towards Kadirli at the intersection for Ceyhan on the right to reach **Anavarza**, founded by the Romans in the first century BC. Driving on this narrow road you are thrust back decades, passing miles of cotton fields broken up by the occasional splash of colour as people arduously pick the ripe cotton by hand, or clusters of houses with sun-bleached clothing hanging on the line to dry.

Anavarza is a picturesque village of 1,000 people living amidst Roman ru- ins. Just across from the ancient walls, which are more or less intact, is a small sign saying "Museum". It looks more like a private house, which in fact it is, but the few Roman ruins and tombstones in the front garden are misleading as to the quality of the exhibits inside.

A small bath that has been excavated contains a fine mosaic in honour of ancient gods, and when water is thrown on it – as surely will be done by some of the people sitting around a table outside – it takes on an almost new character. A short hike through the family's backyard leads to another bath: this one is slightly larger with a fish mosaic design on the bottom.

A little way past the museum is the ancient city gate, still standing, beyond which lie seemingly indistinguishable rocks. Some of the young boys who hang around the arched gate will show the visitors where the amphitheatre was and so on, but the area has never been properly excavated. In the distance loom a few castles atop a hill ➡**306**

Placing bets at the cockfights.

CRUSADER CASTLES

Even in their ruined state, the silhouettes of Crusader castles beckon explorers and hint of ancient glory and adventure. They inspire dreams of knights in shining armour, stirring battles and colourful pageantry. The stone buildings that stand along the western coast of Turkey also provide a real history lesson as witness to the skill, energy and artistry of their successive owners, in particular the Crusaders who invaded Anatolia from Europe in the 12th and 13th centuries.

Precision-made: The castles were precision-made instruments of military strategy. Generally they were composed of two concentric curtain walls interrupted with towers, a main gate and one of several postern gates in the outer wall. In the central area were living quarters for the lord, his accompanying knights, squires and the farming community who would retreat behind

the walls during an attack, a chapel, cisterns, storage space and stables for the animals.

During the time of the Crusades, knights, because of their versatility, were often indispensable to any army. The armoured knight on horseback wielding a sword, coupled with courage and resourcefulness, was capable of overwhelming opponents with more formidable weapons. Castles, in a way, were the knights' armour.

Battering rams: The varieties of forces employed against the men and their castles included catapults, archers' fire, battering rams, siege towers and sappers' tunnels. Under the protection of the archers' fire, men wielding a metal-pointed log could pick at the loose mortar in the wall, changing the point for a battering ram when the stones started to come apart.

Protected by towers: Entrances to castles posed special security problems. Often they were at the end of a sloping ramp to make the attackers work uphill. At Silifke (southwest of Mersin) the ramp was protected by a tower that exposed anyone approaching the gate to fire from behind. There might be several turns in the entrance to foil the rush of a battering ram, as at Bağras (south of Iskenderun). The confusion could be impounded by the entrance being dark, thus temporarily blinding those who had broken through.

Wooden siege towers higher than the ramparts of a castle that could be rolled up to its wall gave the attackers the advantage of firing down on the defenders. They, however, were subject to fire and being toppled by well-placed missiles from the castle.

More frightening in the long run to the defenders, because they could not see them, was the steady thud of sappers digging a tunnel below their walls. As the sappers proceeded, they shored up the tunnel with wooden struts which they set fire to when they had reached their goal. The collapse of the burning tunnel brought down the walls above it. This method was employed successively by the Arabs against Edessa (Urfa) in 1144.

Villagers and Anavarza Castle.

Maximising control: The castle was always sited to maximise the owner's control of his territory. It also was placed so that friends could communicate. From Yılan Kalesi, which dominates the Cilician Plain above a curve in the Ceyhan River, one could see at least eight other castles in a 50-km (31-mile) radius, including Sis (Kozan), Anavarza and Toprakkale.

Castles were often on cliffs in mountain passes. **Güllek** stood above the Cilician Gates; the watchman there could spot the dust of an approaching horde two days away to the south, giving the defenders time to lay down their supplies. Its rock base made it invulnerable to attack by sappers.

The surrounding rugged countryside was part of the defence of seaports such as **Corycus** (Kızkalesi), which was linked by a sea wall to the offshore castle for military reasons.

Blind spots: The height of the walls was enhanced by a moat, usually filled with water. The moat gave protection to the archers on the walls who, without it,

were hampered by the blind spots at ground level.

Towers that jutted out from the curtain walls enabled the defenders to outflank the attackers. In Yılan Kalesi, the natural contours of the hill were incorporated into the angles of the walls to give the best advantage from several sides for defence.

The walls and entrance could be further protected by openings in the upper floors, as at Silifke, through which defenders dropped stones and boiling oil on the attackers.

Military architecture: The last of the Crusader castles to be built in Turkey is that of the Knights of St. John at Bodrum. Dating from 1402 and built using stones from the Mausoleum of Halicarnassus, it survives as a magnificent example of 15th-century military architecture. Construction was stopped in the 16th century, for with the advent of gunpowder as a propellant, castles had quickly become obsolete. Today a museum of underwater archaeology enhances its attraction. ∎

Yılankale in Adana.

whose ascent is not easy, which is probably why the climb is used as an exercise course for soldiers at Adana's **Incirlik Base**.

Frustrating trip: In theory the road slicing between the two hills should lead straight to **Karatepe National Park** about 20 km (13 miles) southeast of Anavarza. In practice, driving along this road is more than likely to end in frustration and failure as the dirt roads, zig-zagging through the endless cotton fields, are confusing and unmarked. The various villages amidst the fields contain helpful residents, but few of them possess vehicles, so you are likely to be given conflicting directions. The best plan is to return to Anavarza and from there continue on to Ceyhan.

Safely back on the E-5, the trip is straight to **Osmaniye**, where you turn left at the junction for Iskenderun south and Karatepe north. From here the road is well marked, although a few miles up it turns to dirt and gravel, but the scenery of lush green and rolling mountains makes the pain worthwhile.

Karatepe, situated in a forest overlooking a breathtaking lake formed by a dam on the Ceyhan River, is a major site of Hittite remains dating approximately to the 12th century BC. Knowledge of this culture is still fairly scant as only a few records have been unearthed.

In fact, the existence of this group of people – at the height of their power (they ruled Anatolia from the 19th–13th century BC) they had clout and an imperialistic appetite matching that of the Egyptians – was discovered only a century ago.

The open-air museum houses some two dozen sculptures and reliefs, all restored and exhibited one after the other under shady trees. The pieces seem in very good condition and some are extremely beautiful; there are animals, domestic scenes including a mother suckling an infant, and figures holding menacing-looking spears. For archaeologists, one of the more fascinating aspects of the discoveries here was the unearthing of tablets containing the first known examples of Hittite writ-

Village girls skip rope during a Sunday outing.

ing. Sadly, it is forbidden to take pictures, but postcards can be bought at the entrance of the site.

Another memorable site in the area is **Kadirli**, north of both Anavarza and Karatepe and situated on the banks of the Ceyhan River. Development has been slow in coming to this spot, which is perhaps why a wealth of ancient ruins remains. There are neolithic mounds, almost a dozen castles nearby and some Hittite reliefs. The road is rather tortuous and, given the number of ruins elsewhere and the surfeit of castles, you can give this a miss.

The Earth Castle: Leaving the national park and heading back to the E-5, you pass **Toprakkale**, or Earth Castle, built in the 10th century by Byzantine Emperor Nicephorus II Phocas. This castle was bitterly fought over by the Armenians, the Crusaders and the Arabs as it was a vital outpost guarding the route leading from the Cilician Plain to the Hatay region, the same route travellers must still follow to reach Iskenderun and beyond.

Toprakkale also signals the beginning of the Plain of Issus, where Alexander the Great defeated the Persian armies under Darius III in 333 BC. Darius is said to have fled the field, leaving behind even his harem. The victory thus gave Alexander room to begin his sweep of Syria and finally ancient Palestine. Turning south at the intersection at Osmaniye and Toprakkale, the E-5 road enters the Hatay, Turkey's southernmost province.

The **Hatay** was given to Syria under a French mandate after the collapse of the Ottoman Empire, but was returned to Turkey in 1939. For many years Syria has wistfully claimed the Hatay as part of its territory, saying that Turkey's sovereignty over the province is illegal. Contrary to international realities, Syrian maps still show the Hatay as part of its national boundaries. Turkish authorities find Syrian claims absurd. But because of its proximity to Syria and its historic importance as a major port and trading centre, the Hatay attracted numerous minorities and nationalities, bequeathing to the region a rich heritage of languages, cultures and religions.

Cheap accommodation: In general, this region tends to be very inexpensive for the traveller. The price of food can run as low as half of what one would pay in Istanbul, while the best hotels (so far nothing available higher than four-stars) often cost $60 for a double. Partly because the Hatay draws few tourists, and partly because it is a region noted historically for a mix of peoples, the locals are friendly because they are pleasantly surprised to see a stranger. While there is little in terms of local crafts to buy (unless one counts boxes of laundry detergent and cigarettes smuggled from Syria), in Antakya particularly it is possible to find interesting pieces of carved wood.

The northern part of the Hatay is now dominated by oil refineries and steel plants, which fill the sky with evil-smelling smoke. The first town is **Dörtyol**, the end of the line for the oil pipeline travelling from the Kirkuk oil fields in Iraq.

Dörtyol is followed by the ➠**310**

Mecca or Elvis Presley rugs for all faiths.

YAŞAR KEMAL

Yaşar Kemal, Turkey's most eminent novelist and a perennial candidate for the Nobel Prize, likes to emphasise his rural roots. "I am a peasant," says the burly, 1.8-metre (6-ft) tall author. "I was born in a village."

Best known for his novels of social protest that take place in the rural settings of his native Çukurova (Cilician Plain), Kemal has been compared to William Faulkner and Nikos Kazantzakis for his depth and keen observations, and penetrating factual accounts of changing village life in Turkey and of his rich use of the Turkish language. His use of colloquial language, dialect and curses, taken straight from the villages of the Çukurova Plain, is extraordinary and natural.

The transformation of the Çukurova from an underdeveloped rural farm belt to an industrial region, where feudal ownership of land still prevails, is a theme widely used in Kemal's novels. His chief characters are the common people: cotton farmers, peasant villagers, seasonal migrant workers, and brigands, fighting against an oppressive class of feudal landlords, who own entire villages.

Kemal was also the first writer in Turkey to describe in detail rural blood feuds between rival family clans, instigated by conflicting claims over women and property.

The Financial Times once described Kemal as "a man who tells, like no other, the tale of Turkey under change."

His best-known novel, *Memed, my Hawk*, has been translated into many languages. The four-book epic tells the life story of Memed, a young Çukurova lad who escapes his village, controlled by a tyrannical, exploitative feudal landlord, to become a Robin Hood-like bandit. From his hideout in the Taurus Mountains, Memed leads a pack of *eşkiya* (brigands) who steal from the rich and give to the poor and plots his revenge against the evil landlord who murdered his loved one, a young village girl he tried to elope with. Of Memed, the protaganist, Kemal says: "I can't kill the son of a bitch. He has taken me over. When I started writing *Memed, my Hawk*, I was 24 years old and he was 21. When I completed the fourth book on him, I was 65 and the bastard was still 24."

Yaşar Kemal is a pen name he started using in the 1950s. He was born Kemal Sadık Gökçeli in the village of Gökçeli near Adana in 1922. His father came from a line of feudal landlords and his mother from bandits. He was five years old when he witnessed the murder of his father in a mosque, a shocking event that was to propel him towards a career as a writer.

As a young lad, he worked as an apprentice to the *aşıks*, the travelling bards of Anatolia who roamed the countryside with their *saz*, a banjo-like instrument, singing songs about love and heroism and religion. From these traditional minstrels, Kemal learned the art of story-telling.

Kemal dropped out of high school to take an odd assortment of jobs, including working as a cotton picker, factory worker, and as a petition writer. He worked three years as a night watchman in a public library in Adana, where he read every book on the shelves during the long, lonely nights and memorised some of the great Greek classics, including Homer's *Iliad* and the *Odyssey*. In 1950, he migrated to Istanbul to start a journalism career with the newspaper *Cumhuriyet*, where he quickly became a star feature writer.

His first novel, *Memed, my Hawk*, brought him national recognition and international acclaim. In the early 1980s Peter Ustinov made a motion picture based on the book, filmed in Yugoslavia.

In his book *Iron Earth, Copper Sky*, Kemal describes the sufferings and hardships of the seasonal migrant workers arriving in Çukurova from nearby impoverished mountain villages to harvest cotton.

In *A Murder in the Iron Workers Market*, written in 1974, and *Yusufcuk*

Yusuf, published a year later, Kemal tells of the emergence of a new type of feudal land ownership system, influenced by the arrival of industrial development in the region. The new landowners, cunning as ever but not as effective as in the past, fear that the workers will one day unite to undermine them. These landowners attempt to dominate the workers by inciting conflict between them.

More than 112 editions of his books have been published overseas, and his works have been translated into English, French, German, Russian, Spanish and other languages.

In 1982, the French Critics Association awarded him the *Del Duca Prize*, a $30,000 award whose earlier recipients included Jean Anouilh of France, Argentinean poet Jorge Luis Borges, Italian novelist Ignazio Silone and Senegal's former President, the poet Leopold Sedar Senghor.

Two years later, French President François Mitterrand presented him with the *Légion d'Honneur*, an honour he shared with Italian film director Federico Fellini, the late Dutch documentary film maker Joris Ivens and Elie Wiesel, a Nobel Prize-winning American novelist who achieved fame through his books about the Jewish holocaust during World War II.

Many of his novels have been translated into English by his wife Thilda, a woman Kemal describes as "my most important and trustworthy friend in the whole world."

He despises many of the inevitable changes taking place in Çukurova where mechanised agriculture has replaced the horse and plough.

In an interview given to a journalist at the *International Herald Tribune*, he described how these changes are altering the environment for the worse: "In the 1920s there were 10 large marshes in Çukurova, filled with all kinds of birds – there were even flamingos. There were gazelles. Then in the 1950s the tractor arrived and nature changed immediately – no more marshes, no more gazelles." ∎

Novelist Yaşar Kemal.

ancient port of **Payas**, now alternatively referred to as Yakacık on most maps but Payas on road signs. The harbour has long since been filled up, but is still worth visiting because Payas is the site of an extremely well-kept 16th-century Ottoman mosque complex reportedly built by Yavuz Pasha under advice from the most celebrated of all Ottoman architects, Mimar Sinan.

Truck route: It is easy to drive right past Payas town, as you will probably be boxed in between precariously balanced trucks journeying to the Syrian border. From the road, the town looks uninteresting, filled with car repair shops, grubby teahouses and down-at-heel hotels.

There are no signs off the main road pointing to the complex, so it is best to turn right after the first block of shops, and then simply head towards the sea and the castle, slightly visible in the distance. For all the dirt and traffic of the main road, the back of Payas is remarkably clean and quiet. Sheep and cows graze idly by the walls of the caravansary, while olive tree groves, wandering bushes and flowers give the area a sleepy character.

As you enter the caravansary, immediately on the right are the old baths, now boarded up and guarded by wayward cows. Beyond the squat roof of the *hamam* is a 13th-century Crusader castle, later repaired by the Ottomans and used as a sort of housing complex centuries ago. In surprisingly good condition, the huge iron door will be opened by the elderly watchman, who can usually be found in the bazaar opposite the *hamam*. It is best to ascend to the top of the castle walls, from where you have a spectacular view out to the Mediterranean and across the town. Little remains within the castle grounds save for a few ruins of old houses now partly obscured by overgrown grass.

Islamic schooling: As you leave the castle, you will see, almost straight ahead, a courtyard framed by a mosque and a students' quarters. Whether official or not, the mosque is back in use, and visitors are likely to see a group of

Planting crops in the Çukurova.

young children busy studying the Koran. The students' quarters have been transformed into latter-day apartments, with laundry drying from trees and women squatting by the courtyard's walls, chopping vegetables and playing with babies.

Coming out of the courtyard you turn right to enter the covered bazaar, a narrow hallway with a vaulted ceiling. The bazaar has been refurbished fairly recently, and all the shops are newly numbered and framed by plate-glass windows. If you exit the bazaar from the entrance, you will see on the right buildings that were probably used to house the soup kitchen and more apartments.

In order to reach Iskenderun, drivers must double back and return to the E-5. Driving at night is perhaps one of the best times to make the one-hour trip. By sunset, the road clears a bit of cars, and what during the day is a horribly crowded, polluted site is transformed after dusk: puffs of smoke from steel plants disappear gently into the night against a backdrop of blinking factory lights and bright red, yellow and white flames.

Iskenderun: At first sight **Iskenderun** is not very exciting. The streets are narrow and crowded with cars, pedestrians and fruit sellers pushing wooden carts. The city is bordered on one side by a busy port – whose position is slowly being usurped by Mersin – and on the other side by the Amanos Mountains rolling into Syria.

Iskenderun was known as Alexanderatta after its founder Alexander the Great, and Iskender is the Turkish equivalent for Alexander. The 175,000 people in the city are a mix of the multinationals who populate the Hatay.

Now Turkey's southernmost port, it was originally founded as a port town by Alexander the Great to celebrate his victory over Darius III, but its importance dwindled after the founding of a rival Seleucid port near Antioch a few years later.

Tasty prawns: There isn't much to see or do in Iskenderun, although there is a wide promenade along the ➠**314**

➠**314**

The port of Iskenderun.

HACI ÖMER SABANCI

If Yaşar Kemal is the man who introduced central Anatolian life to the world through his vivid portrayals of a young peasant boy struggling against an exploitative landowner in *Memed, my Hawk*, then Hacı Ömer Sabancı is the man who showed that it is possible to overcome these harsh conditions.

Hacı Ömer started life as a peasant boy toiling in the region of Çukurova, a fertile plain whose vast expanses of cotton turned into great wealth in the late 1800s as American and European demands for cotton could no longer be met by their own farmers. But unlike Memed and other peasants who fill Kemal's novels, Hacı Ömer's fight against poverty ended not in gunshots and mountain pursuits, but in the creation of the renowned Hacı Ömer Sabancı Holding Company.

In the New York-based *Fortune Magazine*'s list of 500 top overseas corporations, Sabancı Holding repeatedly ranks among the top 200, one of two Turkish groups to make the list. With huge assets, thousands of employees, more than 600 bank branches and holdings in education, health and cultural institutions in addition to over 100 factories in textiles, food, plastics, tyres, automobile parts, cement, paper, electronics, pharmaceuticals and agribusiness, Sabancı Holding is a testament to one man's ability to conquer the greatest odds.

In many ways, Hacı Ömer's life mirrored that of the dissolution of the Ottoman Empire and the founding of the Turkish Republic. Born in Akçakaya village in Kayseri province in 1906 or 1903 (there is some dispute over the exact date), he left to seek his fortune in Adana in the early 1920s, just after Turkey's eventual founder, Mustafa Kemal (Atatürk), delivered the region from its three-year occupation by the French following the Ottoman Empire's defeat in World War I.

The whole country was reeling from the shock of defeat and the threats to its ever-diminishing borders. Hundreds of thousands of Turkish men were wounded or died in the war, and the economy lay in tatters. Hacı Ömer's father had been killed in the war too, fighting the enemy in some distant battlefield. But in the Çukurova region there was great hope, for the world still wanted cotton and the fields were still blooming. So like many other young men who trooped off to Adana in search of a livelihood, Hacı Ömer started off in a cotton factory, washing cotton for 85 piasters a day. But this young man, who not only had the desire to make money but also had the will, slowly became well known in Adana for his thriftiness and his commercial drive and good sense. Soon, he was acting as an employment agency, matching workers with job openings. After the founding of the Republic in 1923, Hacı Ömer was recruited to restart factories abandoned in Adana by Armenian and Greeks during the intercommunal strife both before and immediately following the end of the French occupation.

Industrialist Hacı Ömer Sabancı.

When it was legislated in 1934 that all people must take a surname, Hacı Ömer, by then a wealthy factory owner, took the name Sabancı – meaning ploughmaker – so he would never forget his roots.

By the end of World War II, the country embarked on a modernisation programme through the help of the Marshall Plan, and businessmen were at the forefront of the changes. Hacı Ömer, already a millionaire, was never a man to pass up a business opportunity and he quickly realised that if he wanted to expand his holdings even further, he would need a bank. With a bank, he could easily obtain money for his new enterprises and still practise his renowned thriftiness by encouraging others to save their money, which in turn could finance his new operations.

At that time, banking was still a profession mainly left to foreign minorities, and the general public was usually too poor to worry about savings, or kept their money hidden under their beds or stashed somewhere else. But Hacı Ömer, with an appetite for risk and the insight that made him a successful businessman, realised that a stronger economy would support and need banks, and so he became a founding partner of Akbank in 1948. Akbank today ranks among the 200 largest banks in the world in assets and profits.

By the mid-1950s, he had moved into apartment construction and textiles, establishing in Adana the giant Bossa factory, one of the world's largest textile mills. A few years later he acquired majority shareholding in the bank and started up an insurance company.

In his personal life, he was just as demanding, teaching his six sons the value of thrift, insisting they take advantage of the formal education he could not pursue. His wife, Sadıka, whom he married in 1928, stood by him as he dreamt and built his family fortune. In 1949, Hacı Ömer acquired a mansion along the Bosphorus in Istanbul, which continues to serve as the family home.

Hacı Ömer never forgot his Anatolian roots, but he also remembered that modern Turkey grew out of the splendours of the Ottoman Empire, and this fanned his love for fine antiques and furniture. Each piece to him symbolised more than sheer economic or utilitarian value – it represented a story much like his own: creation, use and appreciation for fine craftsmanship. If he had one spendthrift side to him – and tales of him avoiding taxes to save money even when he was a wealthy man are legendary – then it was in the pursuit of collecting pieces of the past. His love of art was best exemplified at the Sabancı Villa on the Bosphorus, where many objects of master painters and sculptors can still be seen today. His only other pastime was chatting with friends about business or smoking a *nargile*, or hookah, in Emirgân, a town on the Bosphorus near his home.

An earthy man who spoke with a strong rural accent, Hacı Ömer always dressed like an Anatolian peasant and never wore a tie in his life, even when meeting the President of the Republic. He hung up on the wall of his house a harness he had used while working as a young *hamal* – a beast of burden – to carry huge bales of cotton on his back, as a reminder to himself and his family of his humble origins as a cotton worker.

Hacı Ömer died in 1966, but the fortune he so carefully amassed and the friendships he maintained with people from peasants in Adana up to high government officials did not disappear. Thousands mourned his passing and Adana today has countless signs of his love for Turkey, from his factories and banks to a cultural centre and educational institutions established by Sabancı Holding.

His eldest son died in 1979, but the other five sons continue to work in the company now headed by Sakıp Sabancı, the second oldest son.

It is virtually impossible to travel anywhere in Turkey today without seeing the SA initials in front of a factory or company name, a symbol now not only of one man's ability to amass great wealth, but of Turkey's growing economic power. ∎

Mediterranean that offers a pleasant walk and numerous beer and teahouses. Across the street from the promenade are large, outdoor restaurants serving traditional Turkish *meze* dishes with fresh fish and giant-sized prawns. One *meze* dish that must be tried in Iskenderun is *humus*, an appetiser made from crushed chick peas, flavoured with lemon and parsley. This and other Arabic dishes found in Iskenderun have been influenced by the city's proximity to Syria.

Iskenderun is also an important naval base. A boot camp for Turkish naval infantry, with a live-sized concrete destroyer in its midst, can be found on the road to Antakya.

After leaving Iskenderun, a right turn off the E-5 will take the motorist along the Gulf of Iskenderun to **Arsuz**, a little resort village thought to be the site of the Seleucid town of Rhosus, built in 300 BC. The hamlet, which has a pleasant beach, contains the remains of several ancient buildings and city walls. Many of the old mansions in Arsuz were built by the French when they ruled the area under a League of Nations mandate from 1919–1939. A Crusader castle stands further south near the promontory known as **Hınzır Burnu** (the Cape of Pigs), which is the western side of the peak known as **Musa Dağı** (The Mountain of Moses). The mountain was the scene of intense fighting in 1915 between insurgent Armenians and the Turkish army. The stand of the Armenian rebels was made famous by Franz Werfel in his acclaimed novel, *Forty Days in Musa Dagh.*

Returning to the E-5, the road turns away from the sea and into the **Amanos Mountains**. A road forks to the right to **Soğukoluk**, a breezy plateau town where many of Iskenderun's wealthy families have summer villas.

The Syrian Gates: Back on the E-5, the road narrowly winds its way around the Amanos Mountains, from which you have a terrific view of the **Orontes Valley** – part of the **Amik Ovası** – whose flowing fields and generous greenery attest to the area's fertility and

A young woman carries her baby on her back.

source of the region's wealth. This section of the road is called the **Belen Pass**, formerly known as the Syrian Gates for its strategic location between the sea and Antioch (modern day Antakya). **Belen** itself is a small village whose fame rests upon the belief that its waters hold curative powers. For those who dare, open water fountains in the city centre offer the traveller a cool, refreshing drink.

As you drive towards Antakya, you will notice that the sides of the road are dotted with ancient Roman walls and mounds, all unexcavated sites of earlier life. After the pass there is a turn-off for **Bağras Castle**, a medieval fortress reportedly built by the Byzantines in the 10th century. This fortress passed through the hands of the numerous empires that stormed the region, finally falling to the Crusaders in 1097. After the Ottomans conquered the region in the 16th century the fortress was abandoned.

The road continues its slow dip into Antakya – set on the banks of the **Asi Nehiri** (the Orontes River) – through the fertile Amik Plain. Virtually every hill along the way contains stone outcroppings from previous civilisations, but most are unmarked and barely visible, so it is best to wait until Antakya for your exploration.

Antakya, better known by its ancient name of Antioch, was founded in 300 BC by Seleucus Nikator, a lesser general in Alexander's army. Following Alexander's death, Seleucus added Syria and Mesopotamia to his empire that started in Babylonia. Antioch became the capital city of the Seleucid Empire and made a name for itself as a busy commercial centre.

Antioch passed to the Romans in 81 BC, and in 64 BC it was made capital of the Roman province of Syria. Antioch's splendour became known throughout the Hellenistic world and the population grew to almost half a million. Numerous Roman rulers, including King Herod of Judea, gave public buildings to the city, and spacious villas and temples cropped up in the area. Many of the beautifully detailed mosaics that were so popular with the Romans – used as bath floors and as decorations in salons and gardens – are now on display in the **Antakya Archaeological Museum**.

Antioch was the scene for St Paul's first ministry. It was here that the term "Christian" was first used to describe the followers of Jesus.

But the city suffered from devastating earthquakes and, as the Roman Empire began to disintegrate, Antioch came under attack. It was sacked numerous times by the Persians and the Arabs, the latter of whom captured the city in AD 638. The Byzantines took it back in 969, only to lose it again – this time to the Crusaders who once again made it their capital. Finally however, in 1268, its glorious history ended in tragedy when the Mamelukes of Egypt sacked the city and drove out the remaining inhabitants.

Virtual decay: For centuries Antioch lay in a state of virtual decay. Old engravings made by 19th-century travellers show Antioch as a scattering of ruined buildings along the Orontes,

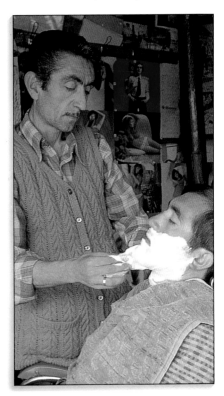

Having a close shave.

with shepherds the only sign of life in the once-bustling city.

Since the founding of the Republic and the development of this region as an important farming and rejuvenated commercial centre, Antioch's population has grown to over 200,000 and the city is full of new apartment blocks and streets crowded with boutiques selling fashionable designer gear.

Excavations conducted in the 1930s discovered numerous ancient sites within and around the city, most famous of which are the many mosaics dating from early Roman times, now on display in the Archaeological Museum. It is worth travelling to Antakya just for a viewing of them. The majority date to the second and third centuries, and the collection is the world's most extensive gathering of Roman mosaics. Many were found virtually complete and the colours are almost as brilliant in hue as they were when new. The museum also includes an interesting collection of Roman coins, along with pottery and jewellery.

In addition, Antakya is filled with various sites of Christian and Roman significance. Within the city itself is a Roman bridge (circa AD 200) crossing the Asi River, a very small but charming bazaar in the centre of town, and numerous beautiful mosques. The circumference of the ancient city walls, about 30 km (19 miles) in length, gives some idea of the city's former fame.

Daily tours: Primarily because of the amazing mosaics found in the museum, and because of the city's location on the road to Syria, Antakya has built itself up as a tourist centre, and almost daily tour buses disgorge their many passengers outside the Büyük Antakya Hotel, located across the street from the museum. The people who work at the Tourist Information Office off **Atatürk Caddesi** at the first roundabout into the city are usually very helpful and will often offer to accompany visitors personally if they have trouble locating a specific site.

The food tends towards *humus*, *shish kebab* and *meze* dishes, served in the

The Hittite Lions in Antakya Museum.

best restaurants found along **Hürriyet Caddesi**, which runs from the left bank of the Asi River south. On the streets, vendors sell fresh fruit drinks and *bici*. The refreshing *bicis* are best eaten with lots of ice. The best accommodation in town is the four-star **Büyük Antakya** Hotel on Atatürk Caddesi.

Like the whole of the Hatay, Antakya's population is mixed, and Arabic vies with Turkish as a first language. The majority of Arabs in Antakya are Alevis, members of Turkey's Shiite community. There is a small Jewish population living here, numbering about 150 people, and an equally tiny Christian population.

Jewish community: The **synagogue** is located on the eastern bank of the Asi River, right behind the **Old Market District** on KurtulusCaddesi. It is only open on Saturday mornings and Jewish holidays. Disguised as a government building with a picture of Atatürk above the doorway, it is not easy to locate. Walk to the Habib Naccar Camii and then ask directions of one of the trades-

men sitting outside their shops drinking tea. The **Habib Naccar Camii**, constructed in the 17th century, is one of the finer mosques in the city and is well worth a visit.

Kurtuluş Caddesi itself is the new version of ancient Antioch's famed main street. The ancient street, constructed around 30 BC with colonnades running on either side of the street that were supposedly over 9 metres (30 ft) wide and 3 km (2 miles) long, has been replaced by modern buildings, *hans* (commercial centres) and pavements.

The first Christian community: Antakya is famous for the grotto **Church of St Peter**, just outside the city on the road to Halep (Aleppo). This is allegedly the oldest working church in existence, and it is here that St Peter together with St Paul and Barnabas reportedly preached from a cave around AD 47 and the world's first Christian community was founded. The grotto church is said to have a secret tunnel through which believers could escape when they were under threat of persecution.

A mosaic of the sea god Poseidon at the Antakya Museum.

During Antioch's heyday, it was renowned for its **Shrine of Daphne**, now located in Harbiye, a cool verdant plateau 13 km (8 miles) south of Antakya on the road to Samandağ.

According to myth, this is the spot where Apollo pursued Daphne and she was changed into a laurel. There is some contention over whether this was really the setting, but its beauty – cascading waterfalls set among small ledges of pine trees above the Asi River – makes it an appropriate spot.

The conqueror of the region, Emperor Seleucus, built a temple and oracle complex to Apollo here, and later Roman rulers added even more temples and palaces. It was allegedly here that Cleopatra and Antony were married and where the Antioch Games, precursor of the Olympics, took place. But Daphne fell along with Antioch, and although it remains a favourite holiday spot for locals and visiting Arabs, one's imagination must be put into full force to see its former beauty.

The grove itself is filled with little open-air *kebab* restaurants whose patrons sit around tables balanced precariously on rocks along the bubbling, torrential streams. Above Daphne is a street of hotels and fish restaurants, except that fish is rarely on the menu and the ones available look like they swam too long near the oil terminal of Dörtyol.

The area was also made famous during the Roman-Byzantine reign by the activities of St Simeon the Elder, who around AD 420, having decided that the way of faith was to avoid the world, climbed up to a mountain top east of Antioch, and perched himself on a pillar. He kept moving to higher and higher pillars before finally settling on a point falling across the Syrian border near Yayladağı.

But his style of faith proved popular, and his most faithful disciple, St Simeon the Younger, ascended **Samandağ** (the Mountain of St Simeon) reportedly at the age of seven, to preach and pray around AD 520, remaining chained to his pillar for 25 years. The two churches dedicated to him on the mountain top remain in a state of disrepair owing to frequent earthquake activity, and reaching them is not easy.

Samandağ (also the name for the city), about 19 km (12 miles) from Antakya, is Turkey's southernmost city where the Asi River feeds into the Mediterranean. This city is the modern town of Antioch's ancient port, **Seleucia ad Peiria**. Seleucia was the original capital of the Seleucid Empire until 281 BC, when Seleucus was assassinated and his son Antiochus took the throne and moved the capital to Antioch. It was originally one of four cities founded by Seleucus.

Ruined harbour walls still dot the beach front, while nearby is the **Tunnel of Vespasian**, a huge series of water sluices carved out of rock near the sea and dated to AD 79. You can hike around in the water tunnels, enjoying the solitude of the spot, which makes for a refreshingly pleasant change from the noisy beach below.

As a resort area, Samandağ is less than attractive, although it is quite popular with Arab visitors. The sea is polluted and the undertow is treacherous.

From the centre of the town itself there is an interesting albeit rough road that leads to **Hıdırbey**, a tiny village that boasts **Hıdır's Tree**, reportedly sprouted from the staff of the Moslem Prophet Hıdır. Legend has it that the Old Testament Prophet Moses met with Hıdır for instruction near this spot. In Turkish, Hıdır – or Hızır – refers to an extraordinary being who wanders the earth performing miracles.

Facing Musa Dağ, Hıdırbey is set in a sort of valley through which runs a pretty creek. The tree is definitely there, although it is not quite as large as some people say. After the long, hot drive, it is best just to buy a refreshing drink from the nearby shop and, like all locals, sit and stare at the tree and the creek. Unless you are very adventurous and have a full tank of petrol, it is better to return on the same road you have come in on, for it is unclear where the road goes after Hıdırbey.

Right, old men with watermelons.

INSIGHT GUIDES

TRAVEL TIPS

Insight Guides Website

www.insightguides.com

Don't travel the planet alone. Keep in step with Insight Guides' walking eye, just a click away

✵ INSIGHT GUIDES

The world's largest collection of visual travel guides

Insight Guides – the Classic Series that puts you in the picture

Alaska	China	Hong Kong	Morocco	Singapore
Alsace	Cologne	Hungary	Moscow	South Africa
Amazon Wildlife	Continental Europe		Munich	South America
American Southwest	Corsica	Iceland		South Tyrol
Amsterdam	Costa Rica	India	Namibia	Southeast Asia
Argentina	Crete	India's Western	Native America	Wildlife
Asia, East	Crossing America	Himalayas	Nepal	Spain
Asia, South	Cuba	India, South	Netherlands	Spain, Northern
Asia, Southeast	Cyprus	Indian Wildlife	New England	Spain, Southern
Athens	Czech & Slovak	Indonesia	New Orleans	Sri Lanka
Atlanta	Republic	Ireland	New York City	Sweden
Australia		Israel	New York State	Switzerland
Austria	Delhi, Jaipur & Agra	Istanbul	New Zealand	Sydney
	Denmark	Italy	Nile	Syria & Lebanon
Bahamas	Dominican Republic	Italy, Northern	Normandy	
Bali	Dresden		Norway	Taiwan
Baltic States	Dublin	Jamaica		Tenerife
Bangkok	Düsseldorf	Japan	Old South	Texas
Barbados		Java	Oman & The UAE	Thailand
Barcelona	East African Wildlife	Jerusalem	Oxford	Tokyo
Bay of Naples	Eastern Europe	Jordan		Trinidad & Tobago
Beijing	Ecuador		Pacific Northwest	Tunisia
Belgium	Edinburgh	Kathmandu	Pakistan	Turkey
Belize	Egypt	Kenya	Paris	Turkish Coast
Berlin	England	Korea	Peru	Tuscany
Bermuda			Philadelphia	
Boston	Finland	Laos & Cambodia	Philippines	Umbria
Brazil	Florence	Lisbon	Poland	USA: Eastern States
Brittany	Florida	Loire Valley	Portugal	USA: Western States
Brussels	France	London	Prague	US National Parks:
Budapest	Frankfurt	Los Angeles	Provence	East
Buenos Aires	French Riviera		Puerto Rico	US National Parks:
Burgundy		Madeira		West
Burma (Myanmar)	Gambia & Senegal	Madrid	Rajasthan	
	Germany	Malaysia	Rhine	Vancouver
Cairo	Glasgow	Mallorca & Ibiza	Rio de Janeiro	Venezuela
Calcutta	Gran Canaria	Malta	Rockies	Venice
California	Great Barrier Reef	Marine Life ot the	Rome	Vienna
California, Northern	Great Britain	South China Sea	Russia	Vietnam
California, Southern	Greece	Mauritius &		
Canada	Greek Islands	Seychelles	St. Petersburg	Wales
Caribbean	Guatemala, Belize &	Melbourne	San Francisco	Washington DC
Catalonia	Yucatán	Mexico City	Sardinia	Waterways of Europe
Channel Islands		Mexico	Scotland	Wild West
Chicago	Hamburg	Miami	Seattle	
Chile	Hawaii	Montreal	Sicily	Yemen

Complementing the above titles are 120 easy-to-carry Insight Compact Guides, 120 Insight Pocket Guides with full-size pull-out maps and more than 60 laminated easy-fold Insight Maps

CONTENTS

Getting Acquainted

The Place 322
Climate 322
Economy & Government........322
Culture & Customs................322

Planning the Trip

What to Bring.........................323
Photography 323
Entry Regulations..................323
Health 324
Money....................................325
Public Holidays 325
Getting There 326

Practical Tips

Business Hours 328
Religion 328
Media 328
Maps 328
Postal Services 329
Telecommunications 329
Useful Websites 329
Tourist Information 330
Embassies 331
Emergencies...........................331
Security & Crime 333
Etiquette 333
Emergency Numbers..............333
Women Travellers...................334
Travelling with Children.........334
Disabled Travellers................335
Religious Services..................335

Getting Around

On Arrival 336
Water Transport.....................336
Inter-City Bus Companies......337
Private Transport...................339
Tours 339
Blue Cruises..........................340

Where to Stay

Types of Lodging...................341
The Northern Aegean 342
The Southern Aegean............343
The Mediterranean 349

Where to Eat

Restaurants 354

Culture

Music & Dance......................366
Cinema 366
Festivals & Art.......................367
Nightlife 368

Sports and Leisure

Yachting.................................369
Golf.......................................372
Horse Riding 372
Lycian Way Walk 372
Turkish Baths 373
Trekking & Mountaineering ...373
Watersports 373
Leisure Attractions 374

Shopping

Textiles & Jewellery 375
Leather & Carpets 376
Ceramics & Glass..................376
Property.................................377

Language

Pronounciation.......................377
Useful Words & Phrases 377

Further Reading

General 382
Other Insight Guides..............384

Getting Acquainted

The Place

With a population of more than 60 million and territory totalling around 300,000 square km (780,000 square miles), Turkey is geographically and demographically one of the largest countries in Europe. The size of France and Britain combined, it is surrounded by the Mediterranean, the Aegean and the Black Sea. Three percent of Turkey lies in Europe, while ninety-seven percent of the country lies in Asia. The former region is known as Trakya, or Thrace, while the latter is called Anatolia, a rugged region covered by mountainous terrain surrounding vast fertile plains and steppes, nurtured by several winding rivers.

Most of the population of Turkey lives in the west along the verdant coastal plains. Six out of ten Turks live in cities while the rest inhabit villages. Antalya has been the fastest growing city in Turkey and the population has ballooned to over one million.

Time Zone

Turkish Standard Time is seven hours ahead of Eastern Standard Time and two hours ahead of Greenwich Mean Time.

Electricity

Electricity in Turkey is 220 volts. Two-round prongs are the standard plugs for normal appliances.

Geography

Turkey is a vast country that is sandwiched – both politically and geographically – between East and West. It is bordered by Greece and Bulgaria in the northwest, Georgia and Armenia to the northeast, Iran to the east and Iraq and Syria to the southeast. At Istanbul, the continents of Europe and Asia are separated by the Bosphorus and Sea of Marmara.

Turkey's volcanic nature makes much of the country prone to earthquakes. In 1999, the Marmara and Black Sea area suffered three major tremors, killing thousands, making many homeless. South coastal areas are less prone to such disasters, although Izmir frequently records minor tremors and Adana and Fethiye have both had quakes in the past.

Climate

The Aegean and South Coastal regions of Turkey have a typical Mediterranean sub tropical climate, with mild, rainy winters and hot summers. However, over the last four or five years, summers have become increasingly humid and oppressively hot. April/May or Sept/October are the best months to visit Turkey.

Temperatures (°C/°F)

	Jan	April	July	Oct
Izmir	9	20°	32°	27°
	48	68°	90°	80°
Antalya	11°	22°	38°	26°
	52°	72°	100°	78°

Economy

For years Turkey's economy has been growing too fast. Inflation and internal debts are chronic problems. However, Turkey is a major exporter, particularly of ready-to-wear clothing and home textiles, to Europe and the United States. In December 1999, Turkey was accepted as the 13th candidate for membership in the European Union, but the economy has a long way to go if it is to reach its full potential. Many concerns are still state-run and, despite recent attempts at privatisation, civil servants and others are continuing to resist change.

The coastal region around Antalya is best known for floral exports (particularly carnations), fruit and vegetables

Turkey produces automobiles, high level defence systems and aircraft, and is a key exporter of appliances and electronic equipment. Izmir has no less than three technoparks in action or on the drawing board.

Government

Turkey is a republic governed by a 555 member national assembly. This is a multi-party political system with democratic ideals, but there are still many problems. Turkey has a President (Ahmet Necdet Sezer, elected in May 2000), but the daily running of the country is the job of the Prime Minister. There are a plethora of political parties but it is rare that any one party has a clear majority come election time. This has meant that coalition politics predominate in Turkey. Bulent Ecevit, a veteran centre-left politician, fronts a 3-party coalition government formed in April 1999.

Politics is taken very seriously in Turkey and many people identify friends (and enemies) by their political affiliations.

Turkey has been a loyal and active NATO member since 1952 and entered the European Customs Union in 1990. In the long term, EU membership is likely to lead to substantial changes in government policies as well as adjustments in national laws and the Turkish Constitution. The government has promised to maintain its secular status, guarantee human rights and freedom of the press.

Culture & Customs

Much emphasis is placed on the family in Turkey. Children are very important and are expected from every couple. Although the economics of supporting a family in Turkey are strained, the average family has two or three children. In rural areas, families are often much larger and it is not unusual for couples to have eight or nine children.

Women are still expected to marry by the time they reach 25, but their roles in society are changing. In larger cities there are plenty of women in the work force, serving in all the professions including teachers, doctors, lawyers, scientists, administrators and business managers. But in many Turkish families the tradition of the male breadwinner and the female housewife lives on.

Because Turks are so family-oriented, the Turkish language has provided for the specific naming of each family (gender is always evident) member. For example, an older brother is an *agabey*. An older sister is an *abla*. An aunt from the mother's side is a *teyze*, while an aunt from the father's side is a *hala*. An uncle from the mother's side is called *dayı* while an uncle from the father's side is known as an *amca*.

Some words clarify age. An older person is usually addressed as *siz* (the formal you), while a younger person is *sen*.

Family structure is still very cohesive and retirement homes are rare in Turkey. Often three generations live together under one roof, partly because it is more economical but also because the displacement of an older member is seriously frowned upon by society.

Planning the Trip

What to Bring

CLOTHING

Dress differs from region to region. In the cities, shorts are not very common, but in coastal towns and resorts, colourful beach shorts and T-shirts are popular. Beachwear and light cotton clothing are recommended.

During the hot, sultry summer months, it is a good idea to wear a hat or cap, and use plenty of sunscreen. Rubber sandals and slippers can also be worn on the beaches of southern Turkey. In January and February, Antalya has been known to go down below freezing at night.

Most Turkish women in the cities adopt western dress. Women wearing *çarsafs*, black veils covering the body from head to toes, are usually peasant villagers or Saudi tourists. As a sign of respect for Islam, women must wear head scarves and cover their arms and legs when visiting mosques. Women should also dress conservatively in rural areas and small towns away from coastal resorts.

PRESCRIPTIONS

Except for addictive drugs and opiates, all medicines are obtainable over the counter from a pharmacist *(eczane)* without a doctor's prescription. They usually cost less than from western chemists and some people stock up on items that require repeat prescriptions at home. Many well-known generic medicines and

antibiotics are produced locally in Turkey. Birth control pills and condoms are usually available at pharmacists but not at obvious 'impulse buying' points: you will have to ask.

Photography

Taking photographs is perfectly acceptable in almost any context. Turks are generally pleased to be included in photographs, and of course if on holiday themselves will be snapping away. It is polite, however, to ask first and to respect their wishes if they say no. Veiled women sometimes prefer not to be photographed. Some people may ask for a copy of any photographs you take of them: if you take their address, do send the pictures.

The country is immensely photogenic, so take more film than you expect to need; it will get used.

Museums sometimes charge for the use of cameras or videos; flash photography may not be allowed as it can damage paints and textiles.

Mosques usually allow discreet flash-free photography – be tactful.

Developing is readily available and of good quality; fast developing shops have sprung up everywhere. The prices for processing are high, though, and comparable with the equivalent express service at home.

Film is expensive, but prices are lower in photographic shops than at tourist sites (which usually have only a limited supply).

Entry Regulations

VISAS & PASSPORTS

The requirement for visas for foreigners who come to Turkey is based mainly on reciprocity. Citizens of countries who impose visas on Turkish nationals are, generally, expected to obtain a visa before entering Turkey, either at a Turkish Embassy or Consulate before departure or at the border. All travellers must have a valid passport. Citizens of the UK, the United States, Canada, Austria,

Italy, Israel, Portugal and Spain require visas.

Visas can be obtained at customs entry points and you must have the required money at hand in foreign currency (they don't give change). Citizens of some countries, namely Germany and Australia, do not need a visa. However, everybody gets a stamp and a tourist visa for three months: this is a multiple entry visa but the fine is high if you leave after the three months expires and it increases on a daily basis. You must have your passport stamped on the way out as well.

It is essential to check the regulations and cost of the visa before departure, as the rules can change quickly and arbitrarily. You can do this on the Turkish government Foreign Office web site (www.mfa.gov.tr) or alternatively by contacting the nearest Turkish Consulate or Embassy (see below for details).

IDENTIFICATION

You must have identity with you at all times in Turkey, and a driver's licence is not acceptable for most foreigners. A passport is the most useful and widely accepted form of identification. Police and Jandarma frequently board buses and ask to see everyone's identity cards, so make sure that you have yours to hand.

CUSTOMS

Visitors to Turkey may bring in the following duty free: 400 cigarettes, 50 cigars, one kilogram (2.2 pounds) of tobacco, one kilogram (2.2 pounds) of coffee, 1.5 kilograms (3.3 pounds) of instant coffee and up to seven bottles of spirits, of which no more than three may be of the same brand.

Valuable items, particularly cars, may be entered in your passport on arrival to ensure that you don't resell them in Turkey. But, as prices of electronic items are more or less

what they are everywhere else, it is rare that you will receive this kind of stamp, except for your car. If you have a car stamped in your passport, remember that you cannot just park it and make day trips to Rhodes or Meis. The car must be left in a Customs Area and this is not recommended.

Sharp instruments such as knives cannot be transported in hand luggage in transit to Turkey. They should be placed in check-in baggage.

Gifts not exceeding $285 in value may be brought into the country duty free. Gifts up to $285 may be sent by mail one month before and after the *Kurban Bayram*, *fieker Bayram* (following Ramadan), Christmas, New Year and Easter.

Taking antiques (100 years or older) out of Turkey is illegal and considered an act of smuggling. Make sure that carpet sellers or jewellers give you your Museum Certificate proving the item is not an antique and can be legally taken out of Turkey at the time you purchase the item. It will be more difficult trying to get this later on or when you reach customs! Remember that animals like Van Cats and Sivas Kangal Dogs are now included in the category of items that cannot be exported from Turkey.

Health

No vaccinations are required when travelling to Turkey, but it is a good idea to have cholera shots if you are planning to travel in the country-side. Be aware also that the change in bacteria content in food may cause diarrhoea.

Fruits and vegetables should be washed well. Tap water can be used for washing but should not be drunk. Always use bottled water for drinking wherever you go in Turkey.

Be cautious with local animals, such as dogs and cats, since many will not have had rabies shots.

Make sure you have medical travel insurance that covers you for Turkey. There are few reciprocal arrangements with other countries'

Turkish Embassies

Turkish Embassy in London
43 Belgrave Square, London
SW1X 8PA.
Tel: (020) 7393 0202.
Fax: (020) 7393 0066.

Turkish Consulate General
Rutland Lodge, Rutland Gardens,
Knightsbridge, London SW7 1SW.
Tel: (020) 7584 1078.
Fax: (020) 7584 6235

The Turkish Embassy in the United States
1714 Massachusetts Avenue
NW, Washington DC 20036.
Tel: (202) 659 8200.
Fax: (202) 659 0744.

health systems and, even if such provisions exist, you must pay for treatment first and claim on your return.

Turkey has some excellent private clinics with top-notch equipment and technicians, and some have air ambulances. State hospitals, although crowded, also have good facilities. Most now take credit cards but, again, you must pay before receiving any treatment. The cost of private medical treatment varies widely but is often considerably cheaper than in Europe or North America.

ANIMALS

If you wish to take animals into Turkey, a rabies vaccination certificate for domestic pets and hunting dogs is required. It must be issued 48 hours before departure for Turkey and translated into Turkish by a Turkish Embassy or Consulate.

POSSESSION OF DRUGS

It is hoped the visitor to Turkey hasn't been introduced to the country through the film *Midnight Express*. Penalties are heavy for possession of drugs and other addictive substances (which includes hashish). Incidents of drug abuse and alcoholism are very low in Turkey.

Money

The Turkish Lira (TL) comes in coins of 5, 10, 25 and 50 thousand, and the notes in 50, 100, 250, 500 thousand, and 1, 5 and 10 million.The 100,000 silver coin is gradually replacing the paper 100,000 TL note. Take great care not to confuse the 100,000 TL note with the 5-million note. They are uncannily similar and it is easy to confuse the two, but their values are vastly different. Don't change money until you need it, as the exchange rate rises almost daily. Turkey has an inflation rate varying between 80 percent–120 percent. Foreign exchange rates are published daily in newspapers (including the English-language *Turkish Daily News)* and posted in banks.

There is no limit on the foreign currency that can be brought into or taken out of Turkey.

Money transfers can be withdrawn as Turkish Lira with no problems. If a transfer is withdrawn as a foreign currency, a commission of up to three percent is usually charged.

Money can be changed almost any time at the airports. Banks have 24-hour operations at Istanbul Atatürk Airport; and there are plenty of automatic teller machines in larger towns and sightseeing areas. ATM's of major Turkish banks, such as Is bankası, Yapı Kredi Bankası and Pamukbank, give cash advances against major international credit cards.

Traveller's cheques can be cashed at banks and post offices and can be used when making purchases. However, many places do not cash Travellers Cheques or will want a hefty commission for doing so, and offer a less favourable rate of exchange. You must have your passport and may be asked for additional forms of identification.

Public Holidays

Jan 1	New Year's Day
April 23	National Sovereignty and Children's Day
Beginning of Feb	Şeker Bayramı (The Sweet Holiday). This Moslem holiday, which follows the Ramadan fasting period comes 10 days earlier each year.
Early April	Kurban Bayramı (The Sacrificial Holiday). This Moslem holiday is observed after the pilgrimage to the Islamic holy lands and comes ten days earlier each year.
May 19	Youth and Sports Day
Aug 30	Victory Day
Oct 29	Republic Day

Religious Festivals

Mid Jan	Camel Wrestling Festival, Selçuk
18th March	1915 Sea Victory Celebration and Memorial Ceremonies, Çanakkale
May	Efes International Festival of Culture and Tourism, Selçuk
May	International Music and Folklore Festival, Silifke
May	International Yachting Festival, Marmaris
Late May	International Beach Volley Tournament, Alanya
June	International Offshore Races, Istanbul-Izmir
June	Foça Music, Folklore and Watersports Festival, Foça
June	Marmaris Festival, Marmaris
June	Bergama Festival
June	International Sea and Music Festival, Çeflme
June	International Song Competition, Pamukkale
June	Finike Festival, Finike
June–July	Istanbul International Music Festival, Istanbul
June–July	Izmir International Music Festival, Izmir and Ephesus
June–July	Traditional Kırkpınar Grease Wrestling Festival, Edirne
July	Tourism and Culture Festival, Iskenderun
July	Tourism Festival, Kufladası
Aug	Troy Festival, Çanakkale
Sept	Izmir International Fair, Izmir
Sept	Kemer Carnival
Sept	International Fair, Mersin
Sept	Altın Portakal (Golden Orange) Film Festival, Antalya
Sept	Yağcı Bedir Carpet Festival, Sındırgı, Balıkesir
Late Sept	Assos International Theatre and Dance Festival, Assos, Behramkale (Ayvacık)
Sept–Oct	International Fine Arts Biennale, Istanbul
Sept–Oct	Akdeniz Song Contest, Antalya
Sept–Oct	Art and Culture Festival, Mersin
Oct	International Regatta and Cup, Bodrum
Oct	International Gullet Biennale, Bozburun, Marmaris
Late Oct	International Triathlon Races (swimming, biking, running), Alanya
Nov	International Yacht Races, Marmaris
Dec	International St Nicholas Symposium, Demre
Dec	Mevlana (Whirling Dervishes) Commemoration Ceremonies, Konya

Getting There

BY AIR

Many major airlines have flights to Bodrum, Izmir and Antalya, with most of them being routed through Istanbul. There is increasing pressure for more direct flights to all of these places. Flight time from London to Istanbul is about 3.5 hours and from New York, 9 hours. For scheduled flights, the two main carriers are Turkish Airlines (THY) and British Airways. Turkish Airlines has one of the most modern fleets in IATA and service, food, safety and comfort are good.

Istanbul Airlines also flies to Antalya and is usually a bit cheaper but their arrangements for transfer passengers challenge even those who know Turkish and the stopover time is long. If this does not bother you, then this is an efficient airline with an excellent safety record.

As more tourists come to Turkey, there are numerous charter and package holiday companies. Most of these are use Antalya airport, as well as Bodrum, Dalaman and Izmir.

AIR TRANSPORT

Turkish Airlines
Reservation Offices
Adana
Stadyum Caddesi 2.
Tel: (0322) 457 0222.
Fax: (0322) 454 3088.
Ankara
Atatürk Bulvarı.
231/A, Kavaklıdere.
Tel: (0312) 419 2800/468 7340.
Antalya
Özel Idare Işhanı.
Cumhuriyet Caddesi.
Tel: (0242)-243 4383.
Fax: (0242)-248 4761.
Airport: (0242)-330 3221/330 3230 (bookings and reservations): (0242)-330 3030 (Information only).
Bodrum
Neyzen Tevfik Caddesi.
No.208, Milas Airport.
Tel: (0252) 313 3172/73.
Fax: (0252) 313 3174.

Dalaman
Dalaman Airport,
Tel: (0252) 692 5899.
Istanbul
Cumhuriyet Caddesi.
199-201, Harbiye.
Tel: (0212) 247 1338.
Hamidiye Caddesi.
Dogubank 27, Sirkeci.
Tel: (0212) 522 8888/663 6385
Izmir
Gaziosmanpaşa Bulvarı.
Underneath Büyük Efes Hotel.
Tel: (0232) 484 1220/445 5363.
Fax: (0232) 483 6281.
Marmaris
Atatürk Caddesi 50/B. Tel: (0252) 412 3751.
Mersin
Istiklal Caddesi.
27 Sokak, Çelebi Iflhanı.
Tel: (0324) 231 5232.

Other Domestic Airlines
Reservation Offices
Istanbul Airlines
Selekler Carşişi, Güllük Caddesi.
Tel: (0242) 243 3892/3.
Fax (0242) 248 4761.
Flights to Bodrum, Antalya, Dalaman.
Top Air
Ataturk Airport, Yeşilkoy.
Tel: (0212) 613 8150/599 0227.
Flights to Bodrum and Antalya.

Travel to and from the airport
If you are coming on a package tour, or on a charter flight your transfer to your hotel will probably be arranged for you. If you are on a scheduled flight from abroad, then taxis are about the only option at most of the coastal airports. Turkish Airlines' ground service, Havaş, has a shuttle bus service at the main airports but this only serves the domestic terminal and usually only meets incoming and outgoing Turkish Airline flights. Taxis know they have a captive clientele and far too many overcharge accordingly. Many incoming tourists who only want to go to the local bus station are told by drivers that the bus no longer runs or does not depart for another six hours. The average cost for a 200-kilometre journey (Antalya airport to Kaş, for example) is

between $60 and $70, expensive if you are travelling on your own, but good value if you are sharing with other people.

BY SHIP

From Izmir (Çeşme) and Antalya, ferries run a regular weekly service to and from Brindisi and other Italian ports in the summer season. Also from Izmir, there is a service to Patras passing via the Corinth Canal. The Antalya to Turkish Northern Cyprus service opened in 1999, run by Fener Tours. Ferries to Northern Cyprus also run frequently from Taşuçu and Mersin to Girne. From Marmaris, many ferry companies go daily to Rhodes. Between Bodrum and the Greek island of Kos, and from Bodrum to Datça, services run twice a day in the summer. In winter months, some services continue but less frequently. Details are best obtained from local tourism information offices. Alternatively, ring the **Turkish Maritime Lines** in Karaköy in Istanbul: tel: (0212) 245 5366 and (0249) 7178. Fax: (0212) 251 9025. Their Antalya telephone number is: (0242)-241 1120. Fax: (0242)-242 3322. In Izmir/Çeşme: tel (0232)-464 8864. Fax: (0232)-464 7834.
Fener Tourism, Travel and Shippıng Agency
Fevzi Çakmak Caddesi, Işıklar, Antalya
Tel: (0242) 242 0860.

BY TRAIN/BUS

With flying so convenient and bus travel so comfortable, the appeal of a train journey hinges more on romanticism and the nostalgia of steam trains. If you come to Turkey by train, you have to get out at Sirkeci Station on the European side anyway, as trains do not cross the Bosphorous. From Izmir's Basmane station, train lines go east to Aydın but are very slow.

Due to the Taurus mountain range, there is no train line on Turkey's south coast. Turkish Railways (TCDD)

Entry by Yacht

Upon docking the yacht at a Turkish port, the captain must meet with the authorities and make necessary declarations. Entry into Turkish waters will be recorded in the captain's passport and . cancelled upon departure. Ports acceptable for entry are: Trabzon and Samsun (on the Black Sea); Tekirdağ and Bandırma (on the Sea of Marmara); Istanbul (on the Bosphorus); Çanakkale (on the Dardanelles); Akçay, Ayvalık, Dikili, Izmir, Çeşme, Kusadası, Güllük, Bodrum, Datça and Marmaris (on the Aegean); and Fethiye, Kafl, Kemer, Antalya, Alanya, Anamur, Taşucu, Mersin and Iskenderun (on the Mediterranean).

Registration must be renewed if yachts depart from Turkey. Yachts have to be moored for winter lay-up, replacement of person registering, or completion of the specified sailing route. Registration of the log is valid for three months.

Yachtsmen must adhere to their registered sailing routes. Health certificates issued for foreign yachts are valid for three months under condition that no foreign port has been entered. In the case of death or contagious disease, port authorities must be notified.

Foreigners entering Turkey may leave their vessel at a licensed marina for up to two years for winter lay-up, repair and maintenance services, and can leave the country by other means. Yachts over 30 NRT must pay a lighthouse fee.

runs an Istanbul to Antalya service one day per week but you have to get out at Burdur and a bus takes you the last 100 kilometres (60 miles) over the mountain passes and down into Antalya. There is an Antalya to Istanbul leg of the journey as well. If you have time and don't mind a certain amount of disorganisation, this is a lovely journey and the dining car is fitted out with linen cloths and silver cutlery. TCDD food is usually very good and amazingly cheap. Details and bookings from TCDD Hydarpafia Station: Tel: (0216) 336 0655/336 0475 and (0216) 348 8020, or Ankara: (0216) 312-311 4200.

BY ROAD

Some people choose to come to and from Turkey by bus. Long distance bus travel these days is no longer a nightmare: buses are comfortable and have every convenience. Varan, Bosfortur and Ulusoy are the companies with regular scheduled routes to and from Athens, some European cities, (mainly Frankfurt and Munich) and Bulgaria. All of these come into Istanbul's seething terminal at Esenler, in the western part of Istanbul, and you can then book for other points on the south coast, Izmir and Bodrum (see details of Bus Travel in Getting Around, page 338). Motorists can also drive to the eastern Turkish Mediterranean from Aleppo, Syria.

PACKAGE TOURS

Unless you are planning to move around a lot, package holidays are usually much more reasonable than booking independently, particularly if you want to stay in a top hotel. The choice of packages is enormous, whether you are looking for a villa holiday, an adventurous mountaineering or white-water rafting vacation or a simple flight/accommodation deal. It's worth shopping around, though, for best deals on flights and hotels.

Specialist Agents/Operators
United Kingdom:
Sunquest
23 Prince's Street, London W1R 7RG.
Tel: (020) 7499 9991.
Britain's largest specialist operator to Turkey, which caters mainly for mass-market, budget-mid-range one or two-centre holidays. There are a huge range of hotels to choose from.
Simply Turkey.
Chiswick Gate, 598-608 Chiswick High Road, London W4 5RT.
Tel: (020) 8541 2204.
Self-catering from rural cottages to villas with pools. Also gülets, scuba, kayaking, paragliding, archaeology and painting.
Metak Holidays.
70 Welbeck Street, London W1M 7HA.
Tel: (020) 7935 6961.
Fax: (020) 7224 3675
Hotel-based packages in a range of coastal resorts. This is one of the few companies which flies direct from Stanstead to Antalya on Northern Cyprus Turkish Airlines.
Tapestry Holidays.
24 Chiswick High Road, London W4 1TE.
Tel: (020) 8742 0055.
Good small hotels and pansiyons, yachting and watersports.

United States:
ATC Anadolu Travel & Tours.
420 Madison Avenue, Suite 504, New York, NY 10017.
Tel: (1-800) ANADOLU/(212) 486 4012.
Escorted tours, city breaks, gület cruises and customised itineraries.
Blue Voyage Turkish Tours & Travel.
323 Geary Street, Suite 401, San Francisco, CA 94102.
Tel: (1-800) 81-TURKEY/(415) 392 0146.
Tailormade tours including fly-drive, gület charters and escorted tours.
Club America.
51 East 4nd Street, Suite 1406, New York, NY 10017.
Tel: (1-800) 221 4969/(212) 972 2865.
Escorted and independent tours including historic sights, yacht charters and special interest.
Wilderness Travel.
1102 Ninth Street, Berkeley, CA 94710.
Tel: (1-800) 368 2794/(510) 558 2488.

E-mail: info@wildernesstravel.com
Internet: www.wildernesstravel.com
Adventure tours, including *gulet* cruising, hiking and touring.

Geographic Expeditions.
2627, Lombard Street
San Francisco, California 94123.
Tel: (415) 922 0448.
Fax: (415) 346 5535
E-mail: info@geoex.com
Internet: www.geoex.com
Upmarket operator offering luxury yacht cruise (Blue Voyage) along the Mediterranean coast.

Canada:
Orchard Park Travel.
2365 Gordon Drive, Suite No. 1
(Guisachan Village)
Kelowna,
British Columbia BCV1Y 3C2.
Tel: (250)-860 3409.
Fax: 250-860 4305 Toll free within North America: 1-800 661 3409.
Small groups organised by company that promotes intercultural relationships almost as much as sightseeing.

Within Turkey
Gino Marine.
Netsel Marina
Marmaris
Tel: (0252) 412 0673/412 0680
Fax: (0252) 412 0674/412 2066
e-mail: ginoy@superonline.com
Internet: www.ginogroup.com
Experienced yacht brokerage firm with offices in Kuşadası, Bodrum, Göçek, Antalya and Marmaris.

Practical Tips

Business Hours

Government offices are open from 8:30am to noon and 1:30pm to 5:30pm. Commercial banks are open from 8:30am to noon and 1:30pm to 5pm. The main post offices in cities and resorts, from where you can make phone calls, are open 24 hours, even during public and religious holidays. In resorts, some banks have exchange offices which are open till late in the evening, and 24-hour ATM's give Turkish Lira or hard currency cash against most major credit cards.

Religion

Turkey is 99 percent Moslem, but small pockets of Christians and Jews live in the big cities and in the rural areas of eastern Turkey. Turks are predominantly Sunni, but one out of every six Turks is *Alevi* (Shiite). Pious Turks pray in mosques which conduct services five times a day. The call to prayer, known as the *ezan*, is sung by *muezzins*, and sometimes even played on tape, from minaret tops. Izmir, Istanbul, Adana, Iskenderun and Antakya have churches serving different Christian denominations and there are also synagogues for the Jewish community.

Media

NEWSPAPERS & MAGAZINES

English, American and European daily papers can be found easily during the summer season at all the major coastal resorts. They are usually on sale the day after

publication. Most of the magazines and tabloids that you find at home are on sale in Turkey. Turks love magazines, and publications like *Cosmopolitan* and *House Beautiful* are available in Turkish editions.

The Turkish Daily News is the only English language paper available. It is a middle of the road daily with a few original stories and news from main wire services. They have opinions on many things and, although the writing style usually leaves a lot to the imagination, many foreigners rely on it for cinema listings and classified advertisements etc. The sports section is particularly lively. A web site (www.turkishdailynews.com) has summaries of the main stories. *Turkish Business World* is the only English-language business magazine on the market. It features a range of economic, trade and corporate stories with very good photographs and graphics. It is published monthly and available from Dunya outlets. Tel: 216-318 3592. E-mail: euras@ superonline.com

Cornucopia is a beautifully illustrated English-language

Maps

Maps are notoriously difficult to come by in Turkey. There are no publicly available large-scale maps as distributing these is seen as a threat to national security. The best at present are the 1:800,000 sheets and road atlas published in Germany by R.V. Verlag, and the 1:500,000 sheets published as a joint production of the Turkish Ministry of Defence in Ankara and the Kartographischer Verlag Reinhard Ryborsch in Frankfurt. These may be available in UK from Stanfords in London (tel: (020) 7836 1321) and other good travel bookshops, or alternatively from specialist bookshops in Turkey.

Tourist maps are available from tourist offices all along the coast.

magazine featuring Turkish arts, history and culture. It is stocked at Turkish bookshops selling foreign-language publications or you can subscribe on the web at www.cornucopia.net.

RADIO

Like television, radio was state run up until the mid 1990s, with only Turkish Radio and Television (TRT) having broadcasting rights. Nowadays, legality is a fuzzier issue but hundreds of regional radio stations thump out music and chit-chat and fill in the late night hours with call-in shows. TRT3 is the government-run classical music station. The station also has English, French and German-language news broadcasts regularly throughout the day. VOA (Voice of America) is one of the strongest signals going. It features American-based news, views and commentaries.

The BBC World Service is available if you have a good short wave radio. Reception varies according to your location. It provides a great deal of information which might be of interest to the tourist. You can get up to date information on frequencies, problems and reception from foreign missions and consulates and from organisations like the American Cultural Association.

TELEVISION

More than 15 television channels now operate in Turkey. Most of them are privately owned by a few media giants. S how TV, Interstar, ATV, Kanal D and TRT channels are among the most popular with Turk-ish viewers. The state-owned TRT 2 Television runs the news in English, French and German every night at 10pm. The home-TV channel, Cine 5, shows live first-division Turkish football matches and the latest Hollywood films, which are some-times broadcast in the original language, with Turkish subtitles.

INTERNET

Turks have a passion for new technology, and are currently conducting a love affair with the Internet. Government offices, media, universities and even modest businesses have websites, and late at night the youth of Turkey log on and chat.

Some of the newest additions to coastal café life are the selection of cyber cafés which have sprung up almost everywhere. They are often owned by smart yuppies and tend to drift in and out of business. You can always ask at the local Tourism Information Office to find out the ones nearest to you.

Sometimes, travel agencies let you log on to check your e-mail for a small charge. Average costs are about $1.00 for half an hour's use.

Postal Services

Turkish postal services are among the most reliable in the world. A post office is called a PTT. In addi-tion to mailing letters and sending telegrams from a PTT, you can make local, long distance and foreign phone calls.

Telecommunications

TELEPHONES

Public Telephones

In Turkey there are both token (jeton) and card based (telefon kartı) public phones. Some are situated in post offices, which also have metered phones (you pay for your call when you have finished); others are located in the streets or grouped in busy areas such as bus and railway stations and airports.

Tokens and phone cards can be bought from PTTS, news-stands and vendors near phone booths.

Card phones are more reliable (the equipment is newer), and the cards are readily available and easier to use for long-distance calls. They come in denominations from 30 to 180 units.

Jeton telephones are gradually being phased out. The telephones

that take the plastic phone cards sometimes accept credit cards – look for the credit card logo.

There are also many enterprising offices and booths which have sprung up all over the country. The proliferation of such facilities is about the closest the authorities have come to privatising phone services. These are called kontur telefon and are located almost everywhere. You can call abroad and also send faxes using this service. *Kontur telefon* do not usually accept payment by credit card – you must have cash. These services are more expensive than calling from standard PTT phones, but are often more convenient.

Mobiles

Like everybody else, Turks are mobile-mad. The main operators are Turkcell and Telsim, regulated by, the state-owned monopoly Turk Telekom. Other networks are gradually being allowed to operate.

Turkcell has over 6 million subscribers and has roaming agreements with about 80 other countries. If you bring your mobile or cell phone with you, check with your operator before you leave that you can log onto the Turkcell network. If you key in the network selection manually on your phone, Turkcell's code is 28601. If you bring a two-band phone from the USA, you will need to change your handset or your SIM card to be compatable within most of Europe, including Turkey. If you own a newer, 3-band phone, then there should be no protocol problems.

The other solution is to go into a local Turkcell office (there are lots of them everywhere) and take out a prepaid card. This is called Hazır Kart and involves minimum formalities and beaurocracy.

TELEGRAMS AND FAX

Telegrams can be sent from any post office. The number of words and the speed required determine the cost. There are three speeds: normal, *acele* (urgent) and *yıldırım* (flash). This can be done at PTTs or over the phone by dialling 141 (but you will probably encounter language difficulties).

Faxes can also be sent from many post offices, hotels and photocopy shops.

International Codes

Australia	61
Canada	1
United Kingdom	44
United States	1

Turkish Telephone Codes

The following are the international telephone code numbers of Turkey's major cities and resorts on the Aegean and Mediterranean. To use the codes within Turkey itself, the numbers must be preceded by 0.

City Name Telephone Codes

Adana	322
Alanya	242
Anamur	324
Ankara	312
Antakya	326
Antalya	242
Aydın	256
Ayvalık	266
Balıkesir	266
Bergama	232
Bodrum	252
Bursa	224
Çanakkale	286
Çesme	232
Çesme-Ilıca	232
Dalaman	252
Dalyan (in Mugla province)	252
Datça	252
Denizli	258
Eceabat	286
Edirne	284
Enez	284
Fethiye	252
Finike	242
Foça	232
Gelibolu	286
Ipsala	284
Iskenderun	326
Istanbul	European side 212
	Asian side 216
Izmir	232
Kalkan	242
Kaş	242
Kemer	242
Konya	332
Köycegiz	252
Kuşadası	232
Manisa	236
Marmaris	252
Mersin	324
Mugla	252
Pamukkale	258
Selçuk	232
Silifke	324

Other Useful Numbers

110	Fire
112	Emergency Ambulance Callout
115	International Telephone Operator (for reverse charge calls)
118	Directory Enquiries
135	Wake up Call
154	Traffic Police (Alo Trafik)
155	Police (for emergencies only)
156	Gendarmerie
184	Health Information

Local Tourist Information Offices

Government-run tourism bureaux are located in prominent positions and, in larger centres, are marked with the international "i" symbol. In other places, they have a sign that says Turizm Danıflma Bürosu or Tourism Information. They are open seven days a week, often until late, in the high season, but work an 8.30am–5pm routine Mondays to Fridays between the end of October until early May.

Don't expect much from them in the way of sophisticated tourist data or service. Rumour has it that tourism will become less centralised, and increasingly hived off to regional offices with specific touristic interests. Still, it may be a while before this happens. Most of the tourism offices do have adequate local knowledge and try to be as helpful as they can.

Adana, Atatürk Caddesi 13, tel: (0322) 359 1994/352 4886.

Alanya, Çarsı Mahallesi, Kale Arkası (behind citadel), tel: (0242) 513 1240; also, next door to Damlatas Magarası, tel: (0242) 513 1240/513 5436.

Ankara, Gazi Mustafa Kemal Bulvarı 121, Tandogan, tel: (0312) 229 2631/231 5572.

Antakya, Vali Ürgen Alanı 47, tel: (0326) 216 0610.

Antalya, Selçuk Mahallesi, Mermerli Sokak, next door to Ahi Yusuf Mosque, tel: (0242) 247 5042/247 0541; also Cumhuriyet Caddesi, Özel ıdare Altı, No. 2, tel: (0242) 241 1747.

Ayvalık, Opposite Yacht Marina, tel: (0266) 312 2122.

Bergama, Zafer Mahallesi, Izmir Caddesi 54, tel: (0232) 633 1862.

Bodrum, Barıs Meydanı, tel: (0252) 316 1091/316 7694.
Çanakkale, Iskele Meydanı (Harbour Square) 67, tel: (0286) 217 1187.
Çeşme, Iskele Meydanı (Harbour Square) 8, tel: (0232) 712 6653/712 6653.
Dalaman, Airport, tel: (0252) 692 5220.
Datça, Hükümet Binası, Iskele Meydanı (Marina), tel: (0252) 712 3546/712 3163.
Edirne, Hürriyet Meydanı 17, tel: (0284) 225 1518.
Fethiye, Iskele Karflısı 1 (opposite the marina), tel: (0252) 614 1527.
Foça, Atatürk Bulvarı, Foça Girifli

Public Holidays

1,tel: (0232) 812 1222.
Izmir, Gazi Osmanpasa Bulvarı, under Büyük Efes Hotel, tel: (0232) 489 9278; Atatürk Caddesi 418, Alsancak, tel: (0232) 422 1022; Airport, tel: (0232) 274 2214.
Kaş, Cumhuriyet Meydanı 5, tel: (0242) 836 1238/836 1695.
Kemer, Belediye ve Turizm Binası, tel: (0242) 814 1112/814 1537.
Köycegiz, Atatürk Kordonu, tel: (0252) 262 4703.
Kuşadası, Liman Caddesi 13, tel: (0256) 614 1103. Fax: (0256) 614 6295.
Marmaris, Iskele Meydanı 2 (Harbour Square), tel: (0252) 412 1035/412 1277.
Mersin, Ismet Inönü Bulvarı 5/1, tel: (0324) 238 3271.
Mugla, Marmaris Bulvarı 24, tel: (252) 214 1261; Cumhuriyet Meydanı, Belediye Atapark Sitesi, tel: (0252) 214 3127.
Pamukkale, Ören Yeri (Archaeological Site), tel: (0258) 272 2077.
Selçuk, Atatürk Mahallesi, Agora Çarsısı 35, tel: (0232) 892 6945/892 6328.
Side, Side Yolu Üzeri, Manavgat, tel: (0242) 753 1265.
Silifke, Gazi Mahallesi, Veli Gürten Bozbey Caddesi 6, tel: (0324) 714 1151.

Overseas Tourist Offices

The following is a list of the overseas bureaux of the Turkish Tourist Information Department.
United Kingdom
170–173 Piccadilly, First Floor, London W1V 9DD.
Tel: (020) 7629 7771.
USA
821 United Nations Plaza, New York N.Y. 10017.
Tel: 1-212-687 2194.

Embassies

Listed below are the foreign embassies and consulates located in Ankara, Istanbul, Adana and Izmir.
Australia,
Nene Hatun Caddesi 83, Gaziosmanpafla, Ankara.
Tel: (0312) 446 1180
Tepecik Yokuflu 58, Etiler, Istanbul.
Tel: (0212) 257 7050.
Canada,
Nene Hatun Caddesi 75, Gaziosmanpasa, Ankara.
Tel: (0312) 436 1275.
United Kingdom,
Sehit Ersan Caddesi 46/4, Çankaya, Ankara.
Tel: (0312) 468 6230.
Mesrutiyet Caddesi 34, Tepebaflı, Beyoglu, Istanbul.
Tel: (0212) 252 6436/293 7540.
Kızılsaray Mah. Dolaplıdere Caddesi, Pırıl Sitesi, 1st floor, Antalya.
Tel: (0242) 247 7000.
Atatürk Caddesi, Adliye Sokak 12/C, Bodru.
Tel: (0252) 316 4992.
USA,
Atatürk Bulvarı 110, Kavaklıdere, Ankara.
Tel: (0312) 468 6110/426 5470.
Mesrutiyet Caddesi 104-108, Tepebası, Beyoglu, Istanbul.
Tel: (0212) 251 3602.

Consuls and Honourary Consuls
Antalya
Austria
Namık Kemal Bulvarı 82.
(Balcılar Ticaret)
Tel: (0241) 1622

Germany
Atatürk Caddesi 9/9.
Tel: (0321) 6914/322 9466
Italy
Işıklar Caddesi
1321 Sokak No. 3.
Tel: (0348) 5090 93
Norway
Liman Mahallesi
Akdeniz Caddesi 528.
Tel: (0241) 1622
Russia
Ofo Caddesi, Blok 1/1.
Tel: (0349) 0423
Spain
Tel: (0241) 7770/7773
Sweden
Konyaaltı Bulvarı 78.
Tel: (0242) 248 9061.
Fax: (0242) 241 5222
Switzerland
Tel: (0247) 2246/243 1500
(Pamfilya Travel)
Turkish Republic of Northern Cyprus
Yacht Harbour.
Tel: (0248) 9847
United Kingdom
Fevzi Çakmak Caddesi
1314 Sokak 6/8, I ıklar.
Tel: (0244) 5313 Fax: (0243) 2095
e-mail: britconant@celik.net.tr

Izmir
United Kingdom Vice Consulate
Mahmut Esat Bozkurt Caddesi
1442 Sokak No. 49
Alsancak
Izmir.
Tel: (0232) 463 5151.
Fax: (0232) 421 2914
United States Consulate
Kazım Dirik Caddesi
Atabay I_ Merkezi 13-8.
Tel: (0232) 441 2203.
Fax: (0232) 441 2373

Bodrum
United Kingdom Consulate
Atatürk Caddesi
Adliye Sokak 12C, Bodrum.
Tel: (0252) 316 4932. Fax: (0252) 313 0052

Emergencies

Violent crime is rare in Turkey. Theft by pickpockets is however on the rise in crowded urban settings. Cars with cassette players and radios are also a popular target. In larger cities, parking in well-lit places is a wise precaution against these sort of crimes.

MEDICAL SERVICES

Pharmacies

These should be your first port of call for treating minor ailments. There is a rota system whereby one pharmacist in every district stays open 24 hours for emergencies. This is referred to in Turkish as a *nöbetçi*, and the address will be noted in pharmacists' windows.

Most standard drugs are

Foreign Exchange Offices are called Döviz Para and are located everywhere. Rates for all the well known currencies are posted prominently. You get a better rate from these places than from banks. No commission is charged for cash, but you will need to negotiate if you want to cash travellers' cheques. Exchange offices are open longer hours than banks and often on weekends too.

Some banks have machines that change foreign notes. This is not recommended, as notes must be in pristine condition before being inserted into the machine. If they are not, the machine tends to retain them without giving you your Turkish Lira notes! The rate is also less than a change boutique. Shops and stores will also often give you cash against your credit card on request.

Izmir:
Bamka Döviz, Cankaya (inside the old flea market).
Tel: (0232) 441 5859.
Izmir Döviz, Çankaya.
Tel: (0232) 441 8886.
Kaynak Döviz, Konak.
Tel: (0232) 489 0474.

available in Turkey without a prescription. Routine medication cane be obtained at any pharmacy *(eczane)* should it be necessary. It is a good idea to show the pharmacist the empty container, to be sure that you are being given the right drug.

Doctors and dentists

Though some doctors and dentists in the cities do speak English or German, and many are highly trained, unless it is an emergency, it is better to wait until you return home for treatment. Most four and five-star hotels have a doctor on call with some English and/or German.

Alanya

Hayat Hastanesi, (Private), Yeni Hastane Caddesi, Yayla Yolu Civarı, tel: (242) 512 1455.

Antalya

Akdeniz University Medical School Hospital, Kepez Mahallesi, tel: (0242) 227 4343.
Antalya Private Hospital, Bayındır Mahallesi, 325 Sokak 8, tel: (0242) 335 0000. (English- and German-speaking doctors).
Antalya Private Clinic, Iflıklar Caddesi 55/2, tel: (0242) 243 3159.
Akdeniz Hospital, (Private), Sorgun Yolu, tel: (0242) 746 0013.
Specialists' Polyclinic, (Private), 100 Yıl bulvarı, Devlet Hastanesi Kavflagı, tel: (0242) 241 3187.

Bodrum

Bodrum State Hospital, Turgutreis, Caddesi, tel: (0252) 313 1420.
Bodrum Clinic, Saglık Ocagı, Turgutreis Caddesi, tel: (0252) 316 1353.
Halikarnas Clinic, Kıbrıs Sehitleri, Caddesi 97, tel: (0252) 316 3635.
SOS International, tel: (0532) 215 3780.

Izmir

American Hospital, 1375 Sokak, Alsancak, tel: (0232) 484 5360.
Karakas Jewish Hospital, (Musevi Hastanesi), Inönü Caddesi 336 Sokak 30, tel: (0232) 484 9832.

Below are the contact details for the major credit card companies:
American Express
Tel: (0212) 224 4363/235 9500
Diners' Club, MasterCard, EuroCard and Visa
Tel: (0242) 2487892.

Finding a Doctor Abroad

Travel medicine is now a major industry worldwide and there is no shortage of people out there to help you should you fall ill or have an accident away from home. Below are a few of the larger organisations. As they are web-based, your country of origin is not so important but where there is a subscription fee, you will need to pay in US dollars or by credit card.

International Association for Medical Assistance to Travellers (IAMAT).
www.sentex.net/iamat/index.html
Based in Canada.
Tel: (519) 836 0102.
All doctors listed speak English or French and their local language. Operates in 125 countries. Membership is free but they appreciate a donation.

HighwaytoHealth
www.highwaytohealth.com
HighwaytoHealth is a fee paying service to help you find and pay for a doctor or medical care while you are abroad. They list more than 18,000 physicians in 80 countries. It works a bit like an auction "best offer" system and you can select the doctor who suits your location, needs and budget. They are based in the USA and also offer a profile of emergency numbers for 350 travel destinations and airports. The firm runs a medical insurance scheme through a big-name insurance underwriter.

The International Society of Travel Medicine
www.istm.org
The International Society of Travel Medicine compiles up to date news

on health precautions, epidemics or health hazards from the World Health Organisation and the Atlanta-based Centers for Disease Control and Prevention.

Security and Crime

Turkey has an enviably low crime record. This reflects Turkish society: restricted access to guns, low incidence of drug use, respect for law and order and most important of all, close-knit communities and enduring family ties. Foreigners and tourists are regarded as guests, and as such are well treated; in normal circumstances you can expect the police to be polite and helpful towards you.

Tourist areas are regularly patrolled by special *Turizm* or "Foreigners' Police", who will do their best to help you. Most speak some French, English, German or Arabic.

Inevitably, there is still some crime, especially in urban areas where there is pronounced poverty and unemployment. Car crimes and break-ins regularly occur, and purse-snatching and pickpocketing are on the increase in crowded places. There have even been instances of tourists being drugged and robbed.

Take the same precautions as you would at home – don't leave valuables visible in a car, use a handbag with a long strap slung diagonally over the shoulder and don't walk down dark streets on your own at night.

Make sure that your holiday and medical insurance covers you for both the European and Asian sides of Turkey.

Drugs

The film *Midnight Express* is always brought up in this context, much to the annoyance of the Turks. But although the script may have been exaggerated, heavy penalties are exacted on anyone found in possession of drugs. A foreigner on a narcotics charge can expect a lengthy custodial sentence.

Military zones

These are normally clearly marked, often by a sign with a picture of an armed soldier. You should keep clear, and also avoid photographing anything with a military content.

Tourist crime

The Turks take a very dim view of drunken tourists scaling the statues of Atatürk, or being anything other than respectful to their national icons, their religion or their women.

Etiquette

There are few don'ts in Turkey; there is little interference in the personal lives of foreigners as they are regarded as a law unto themselves. Your visit is governed by the rules of hospitality intrinsic to Turkish society. While you are in Turkey, you will be regarded as a guest by the Turkish people. This will show itself in the extent to which people will offer endless cups of tea, personal hospitality and invitations to private homes, all of which can be gracefully and tactfully refused if you wish, without giving offence.

Feet are regarded as unclean, so don't put them on a table, or where someone might sit. Remove your shoes inside a Turkish home.

On the beach

Beachwear is worn only on the beach, and topless sunbathing is frowned on, although all too many tourists strip off at the first patch of sand. At some family resorts women enter the water fully clothed.

In Mosques

Non-Muslims should not enter a mosque during prayer time, and not at all on Friday, the holy day. The call to prayer from the minaret comes five times a day between dawn and nightfall.

Both men and women should be modestly dressed. For women this means a longish skirt or trousers, and covered shoulders. For men, shorts are not acceptable. Before entering remove your shoes. You can leave them outside, carry them

Emergency Numbers

Ambulance	112
Police	155
Fire	110
Emergency:	115

with you or you may be given plastic shoe covers instead. Women may be asked to cover their heads, so always carry a scarf or hat.

Off the beaten tourist track there may not be an attendant to supervise you, but do follow these guidelines to avoid giving offence.

Take care not to disturb, touch or walk in front of anyone who may be at prayer. The larger, more famous mosques will be open throughout the day from the first prayer to the last one at night. Smaller ones may only open at prayer times; you may have to find a caretaker (*bekci*) or wait for prayer time, and enter as the worshippers leave.

In Turkish Baths

The traditional Turkish bath (*haman*) has its own etiquette. The sexes are segregated, either in different parts of the bath or by different times or days, though some tourist *hamams* allow mixed bathing.

Contrary to popular belief, the vast majority of *hamams* offer a relaxing experience which is nothing to be afraid of. Both sexes should keep their underpants on and cover themselves with a wrap *(pestemel)*.

The easiest way to enjoy it is to go with someone who has been before; otherwise just watch your neighbours and copy them.

You don't need to have anything with you, but you can of course take along your own wrap, towels, washmitt and toiletries.

See also page 410 for a list of *hamams* worth a visit.

Turkey's toilets

You will probably find Turkish toilet facilities disconcerting. Arm yourself with a supply of paper (which goes in the bin, not the hole, as the drains can't cope with it); if possible use the more commonly available squat toilet.

The standard of public lavatories varies greatly, but special nappy-changing or baby rooms are rare. You will find clean western-style facilities in the more upmarket hotels and restaurants

Women Travellers

Turkish attitudes towards women are liberal in cosmopolitan cities and tourist areas, and are more restrictive in provincial towns.

Country women in rural regions cover their heads with scarves more as a means of protecting their hair from dust and dirt than because of religious conservatism, although religious fundamentalism has prevailed among certain groups in recent years. In big cities you will see women wearing anything from a full black veil to the latest fashion.

Travelling Alone

The major cities in Turkey and tourist areas are liberal and westernised, and are very safe compared with many other countries. Leers and suggestions may be common, but physical attacks are rare. Women visitors should not be afraid to travel alone, or to go out at night, though provocative dress may create problems, and at night you might feel more relaxed with a companion or two.

Turkish culture does segregate the sexes, however: on buses you will not be permitted to sit next to a male stranger. Restaurants often have a designated *aile salonu* (family room), and sometimes establishments prefer a lone woman to sit there.

No woman, whether on her own or with a male partner, is welcome at a traditional coffee or tea room (*kahvehane* or *çayhane*) – they are male preserves.

Harassment

You should expect Turkish men to chat you up, often in an outrageously flamboyant fashion, but you can reduce harassment to a minimum by dressing respectably

and looking as if you know where you are going. Turkish women get some degree of harassment, too, but they cope by sticking together and giving a firm brush-off.

If you are groped by a stranger, speak up loudly; the shame will usually be enough to fend him off and everyone nearby will probably make it a point of honour to rush to your defence.

Travelling with Children

Turkey has very few obvious facilities for children, but the Turks adore babies and children and will be delighted you have brought yours with you. They will undoubtedly make a huge fuss of them.

City streets are far from buggy-friendly, however; high kerbstones and steep and uneven surfaces make them almost impossible to push. Buses are often crowded and their entrances are high and awkward. Bring a rucksack-style baby carrier or papoose; you will quickly realise why most Turkish babies are simply carried in their parents' arms.

Discounts

In Turkey, child discounts are different from elsewhere: normally you pay for children over seven years old on public transport, but you may not pay at all for children up to 12 years of age at museums. It seems often to be at the whim of the attendant. Hotels will offer discounts of up to 50 percent off room rates and set-meal charges.

Accommodation

Hotels will almost always put up extra beds if there is space in your room. Most places have family rooms, sometimes for as many as six, and even *pansiyons* may have small apartments/suites with a mini-kitchen included at no extra cost. You need to ask in advance if you need a cot.

Food

There are plenty of plain dishes in Turkish cooking that western

children will find acceptable, without having to resort to fast food, although pizzas, burgers and chips can be found easily.

Restaurants rarely offer meals specifically for children, but they will do their best to find something for them to eat, even if you can't see anything obvious on the menu. If you would like something plain, ask for *çok sade* (very plain), or *acısız*, (not peppery hot). *Çocuklar için* means "for the children".

Dishes children may like include grilled *köfte* (meatballs), and any grilled meat, lamb or chicken *şiş kebabs*, grilled steak or chicken (*tavuk or piliç ızgara*); all kinds of Turkish bread; *sade pilav* (rice); and *pide* (Turkish pizza) – the one topped with goat may not appeal to everyone. Chips are *patates tava*.

For dessert, Turkish rice pudding is excellent (*sütlaç*), or you can always ask for a plate of sliced fresh fruit (don't forget to peel it, though, to be on the safe side), melon in season or ice cream.

Babies

Breastfeeding mothers need not feel shy, but as Turks are modest in public, you should be discreet. Wear something loose, or use a large scarf or beach wrap to screen yourself and your baby – this is what rural Turkish women do, and it will also protect you from hot sun.

There is almost no ready-made babyfood, but restaurants will be happy to heat milk for you.

What to Bring

You will need good sunblock, hats and long light clothes for children in summer. July and August will be too hot in southern resorts for children unused to such heat, and it can be difficult to get them to sleep.

Disposable nappies and other baby gear such as Johnson's toiletries are readily available, if expensive.

Sightseeing

Very little in Turkey is specifically devised with children in mind, but there are one or two attractions intended for them. Holiday villages,

Disabled Travellers

Turkey has very few facilities of any kind for the disabled. Even manoeuvring a wheelchair in Istanbul, for instance, is a strenuous challenge. There are next to no disabled toilet facilities, and mosques will usually not allow wheelchairs in. However, as with everything in Turkey, people are exceptionally friendly, kind and helpful, and will do their best to assist you in getting in to a museum or building.

The powers that be are aware that they have to do something about this situation, so things may improve. There are now a very few low level telephone booths and buses with wheelchair access. The Turkish Tourist Office in London issues a guide to facilities for the disabled in Turkey, and there is a Turkish Association for the Disabled in Istanbul; tel: (0212) 521 4912.

For information before you travel:

UK: RADAR (Royal Association for Disability and Rehabilitation), 12 City Forum, 250 City Road, London EC1V 8AF.
Tel: (020) 7250 3222.
Fax: (020) 7250 1212.
US: SATH (Society for the Advancement of Travel for the Handicapped), 347 Fifth Avenue, Suite 610, New York NY10016.
Tel: (212) 447 7284.
fax: (212) 725 8253.

Bougainville Travel Agency in Kaş is one of the few that belongs to the International Association for Diving for the Disabled and they are fully licensed for instruction and courses, and employ trained specialists.
Bougainville Travel
Tel: (0242) 836 3737
e-mail: info@bougainville-turkey.com
www.bougainville-turkey.com

with facilities geared towards families may still have only minimal play equipment.

Depending on their age and interests, children should enjoy some of the sightseeing. Palaces can be difficult, as you may have to join a guided tour (even if your children like that sort of thing, the guide's English is often difficult to understand).

Cappadocia

With its incredible lunar landscape, underground cities to explore and hundreds of caves and rock churches, plus the possibliity of pony trekking and seeing pottery made at Avanos, Cappadocia is packed with interest for children, and they normally enjoy days spent here enormously. Adults will find the scenery fascinating too.

The Coast

Sand, swimming pools, the sea and watersports will all appeal to the older ones. Ancient cities are usually good value as there are plenty of things to climb on, space to run around, and, if the parents have done their homework, some great stories about ancient times.

Gay Travellers

Turkish attitudes to gays, or to overtly gay behaviour, are contradictory. On the one hand, they adore their own amazingly exhuberant transvestite or transsexual singers; on the other, they can be publicly intolerant of respectable middle-aged gay couples. However, like many things in Turkey, there are practices amd traits that are accepted and condoned by Turks but are viewed less tolerantly in foreigners,.

Homosexual acts between adults over 18 are legal, and in coastal resorts such as Alanya, you'll find greater tolerance and even some gay bars and discos.

Religious Services

Turkey is officially a secular state, although 98 percent of the population are Muslim. Jewish, Armenian and Greek minorities are concentrated in Istanbul and Izmir. Due to its vast history of mixed races and cultures, the country has hundreds of non-Muslim places of worship which have now become places of historical interest. Istanbul, Ankara and Izmir, still have some functioning churches and synagogues. Attending a service can be a way of meeting people who live and work in the place you are visiting.

IZMIR

Anglican
St John's, Talatpasa Bulvarı, Alsancak; tel: (0232) 463 6608.

Catholic
Notre Dame de St Roserie, 1481 Sokak, Alsancak; tel: (0232) 421 6666.
Santa Maria, Halit Ziya Bulvarı 67; tel: (0232) 484 8632.
St Polycarpe, Gaziosmanpaşa Bulvarı 18 (across from Büyük Efes Hotel); tel: (0232) 484 8436. The oldest church in the city, dedicated to a mid-first century saint crucified in Izmir.

Protestant
St Mary Magdelena, Hürriyet Caddesi 18, Bornova; tel: (0232) 388 0915.

Orthodox
Orthodox Church, 1374 Sokak 24, Alsancak; tel: (0232) 483 3601.

Jewish
Bet Israel, Mithatpasa Caddesi 265, Karatas; tel: (0232) 425 1628.
Hevra, 937 Sokak 4/17, Kemeraltı, Konak.
Shaar Ashamayam, 1390 Sokak 4, Alsancak; tel: (0232) 425 1083.

ANTALYA

The St. Paul Cultural Center
Kılıçarslan Mahallesi
Yeni Kapı Sokak No. 24, Kaleiçi,
Antalya; tel: (0242) 244 6894; fax:
242-244 6895
e-mail: stpaul@akdenizk.net.tr
The permanent home of the
International Church of Antalya.
Citizens of any country or religious
denomination can attend the
Church service on Sundays at
11:00 am. The center houses a
church for Christian Turkish
speakers, as well as a library and
computer center for visitors and
students (agape777@hanmail.net)

Getting Around

On Arrival

Taxis are readily available at all airports 24 hours during the summer
months. Most car rental services
have offices at the major airports
along the coast, and at major
tourist destinations and in Istanbul.
   Regular shuttle buses also operate at Istanbul Atatürk Airport and
the other major airports, carrying
people to the main Turkish Airlines
ticket offices in the cities. A regular
service bus operates from Dalaman
Airport to Marmaris, situated
approximately two hours away.

Water Transport

The Turkish Maritime Lines (Türkiye
Deniz Yolları or TML) operates a
regular passenger line service to the
Turkish Aegean and Mediterranean
from Istanbul, with stops at major
ports and resorts. They provide first-
class accommodation and service
and excellent opportunities for
sightseeing. All boats depart from
Sirkeci or Eminönü, and it is best to
make early reservations.
   One of the best and cheapest
ways to reach Izmir from Istanbul is
a combination boat and train trip.
Every day except Sunday, passenger boats travel from Sirkeci to
Bandırma, a pleasant town on the
Asian shores of the Marmara Sea in
the south. Departure time is 8pm
on Fridays and 9am on other days.
You can then pick up a train from
Bandırma to Basmane Station in
Izmir. The trip takes 10 hours.

Çanakkale Car Ferry Service

Regular passenger and car
ferryboats operate on the
Dardanelles every hour between
Çanakkale on the Asian side and
Kilitbahir on the European side.
Ferryboats on the Gelibolu-Lapseki
line operate every two hours. Daily
ferryboats also go to the Turkish
Aegean island of Gökçeada (Imroz)
from Çanakkale and Kabatepe on
the Gallipoli Peninsula. The Turkish
Aegean island of Bozcaada
(Tenedos) can be reached by daily
ferryboats from Geyikli Iskelesi,
south west of Çanakkale. Bozcaada
is a pretty (and usually sleepy) little
island whose main livelihood is
wine production. Gökçeada is both
residential and a military base.
Both islands welcome foreign
visitors and you do not have to get
permission to visit the island.

Izmir Ferry

The pleasant and comfortable car
and passenger ferryboats leave for
Izmir from Istanbul weekly on
Fridays at 5.30pm. Arrival is early
next morning.
   From Izmir (Çeşme) and Antalya,
there is a regular weekly service to
and from Brindisi and other Italian
ports in the summer season. There
is also a service from Izmir to
Patras, passing via the Corinth
Canal. The Antalya to Turkish
Northern Cyprus service opened in

Private Cruise Boats

The following companies offer
luxury cruises for small groups
and have a luxury feel different
from most coastal marinas.
HALAS M/S.
Iltur A.Ş.
Tel: (0212) 287 1014.
An historic restored Bosphorus
ferry, redecorated and fitted with
15 cabins, and now a luxurious
yacht which has hosted royalty
and many celebrities. Daily and
weekly rentals.
Hat-Sail Tourism & Yachting Inc.
Maçka.
Tel: (0212) 258 9983.
Bosphorus cruises for groups or
executive meetings with
lunch/dinner and cocktails, also
yacht cruises on the Aegean and
Mediterranean Seas.

Major inter-city bus companies

Kamil Koç (Istanbul, western and southern destinations and Ankara):
Istanbul Otogar: (0212) 658 2000
Izmir Otogar: (0232) 472 0058
Izmir, Basmane.
Tel: (0232) 489 5910.
Antalya.
Tel: (0242) 241 9292.
Bodrum.
Tel: (0252) 313 0468.
Alanya.
Tel: (0242) 511 0678.
Pamukkale (Istanbul, western and southern destinations):
Istanbul, Taksim.
Tel: (0212) 249 2791.
Istanbul, Kadıköy.
Tel: (0216) 336 5413.
Istanbul, Esenler.
Tel: (0212) 658 2222.
Antalya.

Tel: (0242) 331 1020.
Izmir, Basmane.
Tel: (0232) 484 0800.
Alanya.
Tel: (0242) 513 2204.

Ulusoy (Istanbul, Ankara, Black Sea region, Izmir and the Aegean, Antalya and the Mediterranean, plus international destinations):
Istanbul, Ulusoy Turizm head office.
Tel: (0212) 658 0270.
Istanbul, Taksim.
Tel: (0212) 249 4373.
Ankara, Söğütözü.
Tel: (0312) 286 5330.
Ankara, Kızılay.
Tel: (0312) 419 4080.
Izmir, Efes.
Tel: (0232) 441 7150.

Izmir, Karşıyaka.
Tel: (0232) 369 3949.
Antalya.
Tel: (0242) 242 1303.
Alanya.
Tel: (0242) 512 2868.

Varan (Istanbul, Ankara, western and southern destinations, international):
Istanbul, Varan Turizm head office.
Tel: (0212) 658 3000.
Istanbul, Taksim.
Tel: (0212) 251 7481; reservations: (0212) 527 5615.
Izmir, Efes.
Tel: (0232) 489 1917.
Antalya.
Tel: (0242) 242 3618.
Bodrum.
Tel: (0252) 316 3103.

1999, run by Fener Tours (see page 326 for details). Ferries to Northern Cyprus also run frequently from Ta fluçu and Mersin to Girne. From Marmaris, many ferry companies go daily to Rhodes. Between Bodrum and the Greek island of Kos, and from Bodrum to Datça, services run twice a day in the summer. In winter months, some services continue but are less frequent. To find out timetables, enquire at local tourism information offices for details or contact Turkish Maritime Lines in Karaköy in Istanbul (see page 326 for contact details).

Passenger Ferries
Apart from the numerous cruises by Turkish Maritime Lines in the Mediterranean, several foreign shipping companies have regular boat services to the ports of Istanbul, Izmir, Kuşadası and Bodrum.

Car Ferries
Turkish Maritime Lines (TML) operates an Izmir–Venice line weekly during the summer. The boat leaves Izmir on Wednesday at 4pm, and arrives in Venice on Saturday. The return trip to Izmir is on Saturday at 9pm, arriving on Tuesday. From June to October, TML also sails to

Venice from Antalya, leaving every other week.
Ferryboats operate between Mersin and Magosa (Famagusta in the Northern Cyprus) three times a week. A private ferry company operates boats regularly between Tasucu and Girne (Kyrenia) in Northern Cyprus.

Ferry Lines between Turkey and Greece:
Ayvalık–Lesbos: April through October daily boat service except Sundays. Price $15 adult single; $25 same day return; $15 motorcycles; $120 caravans. Crossing: two hours.
Bodrum–Cos: Daily service in summer. Price $10 adult single; $15 return same day return; $25 open return; $15 motorcycles; vehicles $40 up to 1,650 pounds (750 kg); $60 up to 2,200 pounds (1,000 kg); $80 up to 2,750 pounds (1,250 kg); and $100 for caravans. Crossing: one and a half hours.
Marmaris–Rhodes: Daily service in the summer. Price $20 adult single; $50 motorcycles; $65 cars; $100 minibus; $150 caravan. Crossing: three and a half hours.
Kusadasi–Samos Island: every day in the summer.

Long Distance/Intracity Bus Travel
Turkey has excellent bus services, both within and between cities. Not surprisingly, this is the preferred method of long-distance travel since it is cheap, reliable and generally comfortable. You can leave from Istanbul Otogar at 9pm and be in Antalya by 7 or 8am the following morning, and the same bus will take you on to Alanya.

There are many horror stories about buses. Stick to the names who run regular scheduled services (some of them have kept the same route for decades). Although other companies may be cheaper, it is better to pay a few more dollars for safety. Kamil KoÁ now attaches your portion of an insurance policy to your ticket. As well as this company, Varan, Ulusoy and Pammukale companies are reputable, and have two or three drivers to share the driving on each journey. Cheaper, less esteemed companies have been known to rustle up a driver at short notice (occasionally from the pub!) when there are sufficient passengers to fill the bus on an unscheduled run, so beware.

Dolmuş

An economical and enterprising method of travelling around a city or to a neighbouring town is by dolmuş (which means "full", sharing the same root as the Turkish word for the country's stuffed vegetables).

This is a kind of shared taxi which, in some cities, takes the form of a large car (such as the 1950s vintage American cars for which Istanbul was once famous), a Skoda station wagon in Adana or a regular taxi or minibus in some other towns.

The dolmuş travels along a fixed route for a fixed fare, paid to the driver. At the start of the route, it may not set off until it is full, which may entail a wait. After that, passengers can get on and off whenever they want.

Long distance bus travel is supremely comfortable and the new, modern buses have everything except automatic pilot. Service staff offer refreshments and cologne, and there are usually videos and stops every four hours or so for meals and toilets. Buses do have toilets but passengers are discouraged from using them, as they are meant for the drivers.

You are not allowed to drink alcohol, take your shoes off or use your mobile phone when travelling with any of the well known companies. All buses are non-smoking but this does not seem to include the driver. Air systems are so sophisticated nowadays that you may not even notice if he smokes or not.

Buses are usually segregated and women and men who don't know each other or are not related sit with their own sex. All companies run a free shuttle service between city centre sales offices and the main otogar, which is usually outside the city centre.

As Turks are becoming more prosperous and like to travel, the main companies do get booked up quickly. Previously one could simply show up for a long distance journey. Now, even out of season, seemingly remote destinations are often full. It is essential to book, and the further ahead the better.

Local and City Bus Travel

Bus is a convenient and extraordinarily cheap way to get around cities and smaller towns. Most drivers do not speak English

and it can be a bit tricky getting to the right place. But it beats a taxi any day if you have a spirit of adventure. In larger cities, it is easier to find someone who speaks at least a little English and will be more able to help.

Many bus companies run hourly local services along the coast. These are usually mini buses. Some can be comfortable but if you plan to go more than 60 miles/100 km, they can be agony. The journey from Fethiye to Antalya (220 miles/350 km) is a nightmare in the summer months. Because of local infighting and politics, buses are small, cramped and not air conditioned. They are also very crowded and, whilst it may be part of your travel philosophy to see as much local culture as you can, after a few hours of intimate contact with peasants, produce and children, you might decide that there are better ways to experience rural Turkey.

From Finike, a modern, comfortable, air conditioned service runs several times per day to and from Antalya. At about 10am, Kamil Koç and Pamukkale bus companies stop for 20 minutes at Fethiye on the daily Istanbul to Kaşrun. They are usually empty after Fethiye. This is a good and quick way to get to Kaş, even if it costs a bit more., Ask at the well known long distance bus companies for their local schedules.

Antalya now has a tramway system which runs from Konyaalti to outside the Dedeman Hotel. It is not very frequent but it is a jolly and

cheap way to see the main part of Antalya. Stops are clearly marked on the main route.

Taxis

Turkish taxis (taksi) are bright yellow with a light on top. They are reasonably priced and plentiful. In the cities and big towns, it is often unnecessary to look for one; they will find you, signalling by slowing to a crawl alongside you or by hooting.

You should check the meter is switched on (one red light on the meter for day rate and two for evening).

Sadly, there are inevitably drivers who do their best to multiply the fare by driving round in circles or simply by claiming that the meter is broken; try and check roughly how much it should be before getting in. There are also a few very dishonest drivers, who generally operate from the airport and in the old area of Istanbul. Their trick is to take advantage of visitors' confusion with Turkish currency and numbers. Most taxi drivers will however try their hardest to help you, though, even if they speak little or no English.

It helps to have your destination written down in case of difficulties in comprehension, and also because your driver may himself be new to the area. State the area location first, and go into detail later. When your driver gets close to your destination, he will ask for directions. You will be expected to pay on top of your fare the fee for crossing places (like Antalya Otogar) where cars pay an entrance and exit toll.

Most taxis operate independently around a local base, which may be no more than a phone nailed to a telegraph pole. There are few radio-controlled networks. Hotels and restaurants will always be able to find you a taxi.

Tours For long distances or sightseeing tours with waiting time built in, prices can be negotiated.

By train

Turkish Railways (TCDD) runs an Istanbul to Antalya service one day per week, but you have to get out at Burdur, where a bus takes you the last 60 miles (100 km) over the mountain passes, down into Antalya. There is an Antalya to Istanbul leg of the journey as well. If you have time and don't mind a certain amount of disorganisation, this is a lovely journey and the dining car is fitted out with linen cloths and silver cutlery. TCDD food is usually very good and cheap *(for contact details, see page 327).*

Private Transport

Driving within Turkey requires the utmost alertness of the driver at all times. Winding coastal roads, while breathtakingly scenic, can be dangerous. Above all, beware of aggressive male drivers.

You may feel you have the right of way if you are on the main road and other traffic is coming in from the left or right. Turkish rules agree with you, but it is common practice to allow other drivers in who are accessing the road from minor junctions. Even on the motorway, many drivers roar into the main lanes without looking. Many accidents involve foreigners who do not realise the dangers of this risky practice.

If you are unlucky enough to have a prang, even a minor one, people usually stop to look and will try to help you move your car off the road if it is obstructing other traffic. Until the police arrive, do not move your car, however inconvenient it is for others. If you have moved the car to a safe place at the side of the road, the police will often refuse to give you an accident report. Without this report, it will be difficult to pursue insurance claims within or outside of Turkey.

Numerous car rental agencies, such as Avis, Hertz, Europcar, Budget and Airtour have offices in major cities and resort towns on the Turkish Coast. Renting a car costs about twice as much in Turkey than in Europe and the US.

CAR RENTAL SERVICES

Avis Offices

Adana, Ziya Pasa Bulvarı, Hürriyet Apt. 11/B, tel: (0322) 453 3045; Airport: tel: (0322) 435 0476.
Alanya, Atatürk Caddesi 13, tel: (0242) 513 3513/513 4990.
Antalya, Fevzi Çakmak Caddesi, Talya Apt. 67/B, tel: (0242) 242 5642/241 6693; Airport, tel: (0242) 330 3073.
Ayvalık, Talatpasa Caddesi 67/B, tel: (0266) 312 2456.
Bodrum, Neyzen Tevfik Caddesi 92/A, tel: (0252) 316 1996/316 2333; Imsık Airport, Bodrum, tel: (0252) 373 5707.
Çesme/Izmir, Cumhuriyet Meydanı, underneath Rıdvan Hotel, 11/1C, Çesme, tel: (0232) 712 6706.
Dalaman, Airport, tel: (0252) 692 5410/692 5588.
Fethiye, Fevzi Çakmak Caddesi 1/B, tel: (0252) 614 6339/612 1385.
Göcek/Mugla, Setur Travel Company Office, Göcek Village, Mugla, tel: (0252) 645 2079/645 1323.
Iskenderun, Pac Meydanı, Pınarbası Caddesi 1/A, tel: (0326) 615 4949.
Istanbul, Hilton Hotel Arcade, Elmadag, tel: (0212) 246 5256/241 7896; Selamiçesme (Asian side), Bagdat Caddesi 162/7, tel: (0216) 355 3665/350 4878; Airport, International Lines, tel: (0212) 663 0646; Chauffeur-drive service, tel: (0212) 241 7896.
Izmir, Sair Esref Bulvarı 18/D, Alsancak, tel: (0232) 441 4417; Airport, tel: (0232) 274 2172.
Kemer/Antalya, Atatürk Bulvarı 8/G, Kemer, tel: (0242) 814 3936/814 1372.
Kuşadası, Atatürk Bulvarı 26/A, tel: (0256) 614 4600.
Marmaris, Atatürk Caddesi 30, tel: (0252) 412 2771/412 6412.
Mersin, Ismet Inönü Bulvarı 100, Uysal Apt., tel: (0324) 232 3228.
Selçuk/Ephesus, Atatürk Caddesi, Belediye Pasajı 7/10, Selçuk, tel: (0232) 892 2226/892 2469.
Side, Fatih Caddesi 25, tel: (0242) 753 1348/753 2813.

Budget Rent-a-Car Offices

Alanya, Saray Mahallesi, Atatürk Caddesi, Oral Apt., tel: (0242) 513 7382.
Antalya, Gençlik Mahallesi, Fevzi Çakmak Caddesi 27, tel: (0242) 243 3006; Airport, tel: (0242) 330 3079.
Bodrum, Neyzen Tevfik Caddesi 86/A, tel: (0252) 316 7382.
Bursa, Çekirge Caddesi, Kültür Park Karsısı, Kerem Apt., tel: (0224) 222 8322.
Fethiye, Karagözler Yokusu, tel: (0252) 614 6166.
Izmir, Sair Esref Bulvarı 22/1, Alsancak, tel: (0232) 441 9224; Airport, tel: (0232) 274 2203.
Kusadası, Saglık Caddesi 58, tel: (0256) 614 4956.
Marmaris, Ulusal Egemenlik Caddesi 12, Girginç Apt., tel: (0252) 412 4144.
Side, Side Girisi (at the entry to Side Town), tel: (0242) 753 1486.

Speed Limits

- **Urban areas** 50 kph (30 mph)
- **Open roads**
90 kmh (55 mph) for saloon cars
80 kmh (50 mph) for vans
70 kmh (40 mph) if towing a trailer or caravan
- **Motorways** 120 kph (70 mph) for cars

Tours

Tours of the Aegean include visits to Ephesus, Sardis, Pergamon, Aphrodisias and Izmir, plus the beautiful resorts of Bodrum, Fethiye and Marmaris.

On the Mediterranean, you can visit the ancient ruins of Perge, Aspendos, Alanya, Antalya, Side, Termessos and the beaches of Kaş, Silifke.

You may be interested in taking a long tour along the Aegean and Mediterranean coasts, or into the plains of Anatolia, or Ankara and Cappadocia and eastern Turkey.

AEGEAN COAST

Bodrum
Duru Turizm
Atatürk Caddesi 20.
Tel: (0252) 316 1413.
Era Turizm
Neyzen Tevfik Caddesi 4.
Tel: (0252) 316 2310. 2054
Uncle Sun
Atatürk Caddesi 6.
Tel: (0252) 316 2659.5501
All three offer a variety of local
tours including historic sightseeing,
cruises and scuba diving.

Izmir
Akintur
Kızılay Caddesi, Alsancak, Izmir.
Tel: (0232) 422 6569.
Tours of Izmir, Ephesus, Pergamon,
Sart (Sardis) and Hierapolis, as well
as trips to Cappadocia, Antalya or
Istanbul with overnight stays.

Kusadası
Yücel Tour
A. Menderes Bulvarı, Kuşadası.
Tel: (0256) 614 6827.
Excursions to Didyma, Milet
(Miletus) and Priene, plus yacht
charters, vehicle hire and safaris.
Sun Wind
Celai Atik Sokak No 10, Kuşadası.
Tel: (0256) 614 9268.
Local excursions and safaris by jeep
or on horseback.
Panda
Sağlık Caddesi, Kuşadası.
Tel: (0256) 614 8631.
As well as the usual local
excursions, the company offer ferry
tickets to Samos and car and
motorbike hire. A hotel reservation
service is also available upon
request.

Marmaris
Turmaris
Atatürk Square, No 48/2,
Marmaris.
Tel: (0252) 413 2610.
Located in the centre of town, this
is a useful place to book a ticket on
an air-conditioned catamaran to
Rhodes.
**Yeflil Marmara Turizm (Yacht
Charter and Daily Tours)**
Marmaris.

Blue Cruises by Gulet

A Blue Cruise *(Mavi Yolculuk)* is a
delightful way to visit the coastal
sights of the southwestern shores
of Turkey – sailing on a traditional
wooden schooner, or *gulet*, at a
leisurely place, stopping to swim
or sightsee at places of interest
on the way. This can be the best
way to visit the classical sites,
many of which were originally only
accessible by sea.
   The boats are fully crewed, and
are usually very comfortable, with
every need catered for. You can
either choose to book as a group,
taking over a whole boat (they vary
in size and number of berths), or
individually, in which case you will
not be able to choose your
travelling companions.

Cruises start from many
different ports, large and small,
on the Aegean and Lycian coasts;
you can more or less choose
where you would like to begin.
   July and August are the most
expensive months and very
popular, but it can be too hot,
especially for ruin-tramping on
shore. Spring is quieter, but the
sea can be extremely cold.
Aficionados often choose to take
their holidays in September or
even October, when the crowds
have gone but the sea is still
warm for swimming.
   Blue Cruises are bookable
locally, or through your travel
agent. (*See also page 371 for
contact details.*)

Tel: (0252) 412 6486 and 412
2290/91
Fax: (0252) 412 5077
Very professional agency with many
international contacts.

Gino Marine
Netsel Marina
Marmaris
Tel: (0252) 412 0673/412 0680
Fax: 252-412 0674 and 412 2066
e-mail: ginoy@superonline.com
Internet: www.ginogroup.com
Tours, rentals, transfers,
consultancy and yacht brokerage
with offices in Kuşadası, Bodrum,
Göçek, Antalya and Marmaris.

MEDITERRANEAN COAST

Adana
Adalı Turizm
Stadyum Caddesi 37/C, Adana.
Tel: (0322) 453 7440.
Full-service travel agency handling
flights, packages, accommodation,
car hire and local excursions.

Alanya
Airtour Turizm
Atatürk Caddesi No. 100
Suite 1
Tel: (0242) 512 7420.
Fax: (0242) 513 3985

One of the reputable agencies along
the coast. They arrange
adventurous jeep safaris as well as
the usual rentals, transfers and
other agency business.

Antalya
Pamfilya
30 Ağustos Caddesi 57/B
Tel: (0242) 243 1500/242 1404
Sightseeing tours, yacht charters,
rafting, and trekking.
Stop Tours
Dr. Burhanettin Onat Caddesi,
Yılmaz Sitesi, A Blok, No. 14.
Tel: (0242) 322 6557.
Some of the activities on offer
include mountain biking, horse
riding, yacht tours and visiting
historic sights.
Skorpion Turizm
Fevzi Çakmak Caddesi 26/A.
Tel: (0242) 243 0890/91
Fax: (0242) 243 0892
Sightseeing tours and a host of
outdoor activities, including
mountaineering, jeep safaris,
trekking and village tours.

Finike
Diving Cruises
Tel: (0242) 825 7120.
E-mail: lucas@escortnet.com
A brand new venture on the Turkish
Coast for 2000 is a diving cruise for

a select group (maximum of eight people) of experienced divers. A unique 20-metre (66ft) boat has been purpose built for luxury cruising and will be based in Finike. There is a decompression chamber on board. Contact managing partner and ex sponge diver, Tosun Sezen, for details and brochures:

Fethiye
Light Tours
Atatürk Caddesi 104.
Tel: (0252) 614 5143.
Sightseeing, cruises and jeep safaris, as well as flights, accommodation and other travel agency services.
Simena Travel
Atatürk Caddesi, PTT Santral Sokak, Urantaş Sitesi, Kat 4.
Tel: (0252) 614 4957.
Island and moonlit cruises, historic sightseeing and jeep safaris.

Kaş
Bougainville Travel
Ibrahim Serin Cad. 10
Tel: 242-836 3737. Fax: 242-836 1605. E-mail:
bougainville@superonline.com or
info@bougainville-Türkiye.com
www.bougainville-Türkiye.com
The best in the area for archaeological and cultural tours conducted by specialists. One of Kaş' premier diving schools and also a trained Diving For the Disabled instructor. Features bicycle tours with a professional cycling guide.

Where to Stay

Turkey offers all conceivable varieties of accommodation, from basic campsites to the most luxurious of hotels.

Not long ago, most visitors to Turkey were independent travellers, and outside the capital and Istanbul, accommodation was simple, even spartan. It is still true that there is most choice in the most developed resorts and cities, but the more unusual destinations can offer unique places to stay. On the coast, there are rapidly increasing numbers of huge resorts (in the main indistinguishable from each other), populated with equally anonymous small concrete blocks for those on a tight budget.

Types of Lodgings

HOTELS

Choosing a Hotel
In busy resorts and cities, noise may be a factor: if you are choosing your hotel on the spot, ask to see the room first – this is quite normal, and will not cause offense. If choosing a hotel during the day, think about the proximity of nighttime activity; somewhere that is peaceful at 10am may be throbbing with disco music through the night.

Hotel Categories
The Ministry of Tourism classifies all hotels from one to five stars, with the majority in Turkey between one and three.

At one-star level you will get an en-suite room that is basic but modern and reasonably comfortable. A three-star hotel will usually have a restaurant and a bar, minibars and TVs in the rooms

and possibly a swimming pool too.

The five-star hotels at the top end of the market include the luxury flagships of the major international hotel chains, such as Inter-Continental, Hilton, Hyatt and Swissotel. As well as some of the big-name hotels in Antalya and Alanya, the Belek, Side and Serik area, west of Antalya, has a cluster of first class holiday resorts. This region was developed as a golf tourism area and great care has been taken to protect the environment here. If you are travelling in a group, or during the low season, there are bargains to be had at most of these places.

Apart-hotels
Apart-hotels offer the independence of having your own flat and the option of either catering for yourself or eating out. These can be private apartments or part of a hotel complex. Apart-hotels are well equipped, with every convenience you would enjoy at home. They are fully furnished and, if you book in advance, check to make sure what is and what is not included as standard items. Many now offer TV, telephones and air conditioning as well as a balcony barbecue/grill.

PENSIONS

A Turkish *pansiyon* is halfway between a simple hotel and a bed and breakfast. They can be lovely places to stay, especially if they are run by a family. At the seaside resorts, you will find that they are often used by Turkish families on their summer holidays, and only offer full-board or half-board terms in high season. The more expensive will have en-suite facilities in every room. In some, hot water is heated by solar panels on the roof – and may run out. The difference between a hotel and a pension is sometimes indistinguishable. This is a sort of grey area with no fixed rules, but let your comfort quotient and budget decide what you want regardless of the name.

YOUTH HOSTELS

Accommodation is so reasonable in Turkey that there are very few youth hostels. It is possible, out of term-time, to stay in empty student dormitories, halls of residence or in the teachers' accommodation (oğretmen evi), but the rooms will be spartan and often no cheaper than a pansiyon or hotel.

SELF-CATERING

There is plenty of choice, but rapid development does mean that you should check that your holiday spot is not in the middle of a building site. Some agents specialise in providing quiet, rural, more genuinely Turkish locations, but these may not have pools.

CAMPING

The best camping areas (kampink) are close to the seaside resorts, and have all the necessary facilities, including showers, shops and restaurants. Camping is considerably cheaper than staying in an hotel but, as it is becoming increasingly popular, it is wise to book in advance in order to make sure you get a choice spot. You should camp only in designated areas and not by the side of the road. You should also avoid public harbours or beaches.

Hotel Listings

"SL" indicates "special licence" hotels, which are housed in restored historic buildings. They normally have a limited number of rooms available to stay in with many of the luxuries offered by the larger hotels.

The Northern Aegean

THRACE & MARMARA

Bursa
Çelik Palas Oteli
Çekirge Caddesi 79.

Tel: (0224) 233 3800.
Fax: (0224) 236 1910.
Bursa's finest hotel is open all year round. It is air-conditioned, has its own mineral water bath, hammam and sauna, an excellent restaurant and beautifully decorated public rooms. Service and atmosphere are excellent. **$$$$**
Safran Hotel
Ortapazar Caddesi, Kale Sokak 4, Tophane.
Tel: (0224) 224 7216.
Fax: (0224) 224 7219.
Lovingly restored wooden house in the old town. Rooms have modern amenities, TV and minibars. Those preferring to stay out of town could try one of the many ski lodges nearby. **$$**

Uludag
Beceren Hotel
Oteller Bölgesi,
Uludağ, Bursa.
Tel:(0224) 285 2111.
Fax: (0224) 285 2119.
E-mail: beceren@turk.net.tr
www.berceren.com
80 rooms and all facilities including baby sitting, market and emergency generator. **$$**
Grand Hotel Yazıcı
Gelişim Bölgesi, Uludağ Bursa.
Tel: (0224) 285 2050.
Fax: (0224) 285 2048. **$$$$**
Ergün Hotel
Oteller Bölgesi,
Uludağ, Bursa.
Tel: (0224) 285 2100.
Fax: (0224) 285 2102.
More like a chalet with 25 rooms and 100 beds. No restaurant. **$$**

ASSOS

Assos
Behramkale Iskele, Ayvacık.(SL).
Tel: (0286) 721 7092.
Fax: (0286) 721 7249.
36 rooms with shower and toilet, direct-dial phone, TV, minibar, air conditioning. Restaurant, bar. **$$$**
Bayram Motel
Kadırga Koyu, Behramkale, Ayvacık.
Tel: (0286) 721 704.
Fax: (0286) 721 7141.
30 rooms with shower and toilet,

direct-dial phone, central heating. Restaurant, bar, campsite, beach, parking. **$$$**
Behram
Behramkale Iskele, Ayvacık, (SL).
Tel: (0286) 721 7016.
Fax: (0286) 721 7044.
17 rooms with shower and toilet, direct-dial phone and central heating. Restaurant, bar. **$$$**
Nazlıhan
Behramkale Iskele, Ayvacık, (SL).
Tel: (0286) 721 7064.
Fax: (0286) 721 7387. 37 rooms with shower and toilet. Restaurant, bar. **$$**

BOZCAADA (TENEDOS) ISLAND

Ege Bozcaada
Kale Arkası, (SL).
Tel: (286) 697 81 89.
Fax: (286) 697 8389.
36 rooms with toilet and shower. Bed and breakfast. Bar and TV room. Garden. **$$**
Thenes
Igdelik Mevkii.
Tel: (0286) 697 8888.
Fax: (0286) 697 8367. 28 rooms with toilet and shower, direct-dial phone, central heating. Restaurant, bar, water sports. **$$**
Ümit
Igdeli Sokak 14.
Tel: (0286) 697 8880.
Fax: (0286) 697 8278.
Six rooms with direct-dial phone, bathroom, central heating. Bed and breakfast. **$$**

ÇANAKKALE

Akol
Kordonboyu Caddesi.
Tel: (0286) 217 9456.
Fax: (0286) 217 2897.
135 rooms with bathroom, balcony, direct-dial phone, air conditioning, minibar, TV, central heating. Restaurant, bar, swimming pool. **$$$$**
Anzac
Saat Kulesi Meydanı 8.
Tel: (0286) 217 7777.
Fax: (0286) 217 2018.
27 rooms with bathroom, phone,

TV, central heating, minibar.
Restaurant, bar, meeting room. **$$**

Büyük Truva
Cevatpasa Mahallesi, Mehmet Akif
Ersoy Caddesi 2.
Tel: (0286) 217 1024.
Fax: (0286) 217 0903.
66 rooms with toilet and shower,
direct-dial phones, TV, minibar,
central heating. Restaurant, bar,
meeting room. **$$$**

Güleç
Cevatpasa Mahallesi, Velibey
Sokak 6.
Tel: (0286) 217 2500.
Fax: (0286) 217 6409.
Pension with 21 rooms with
shower and toilet, direct-dial phone,
TV, central heating. Bed and
breakfast. **$$**

Kestanbol
Hasan Mevsuf Sokak 5.
Tel: (0286) 217 0857.
Fax: (0286) 217 9173.
26 rooms with shower, toilet,
phone, TV, central heating. Bed and
breakfast. **$**

EDIRNE

Balta
Talatpasa Asfaltı 97.
Tel: (0284) 225 5210.
Fax: (0284) 225 3529.
75 rooms with bathroom, direct-dial
phone, TV. Restaurant, bar, meeting
room. **$$**

GELIBOLU

Abide
Morfo Bay, Alçıtepe Köyü, Eceabat,
Gelibolu Peninsula.
Tel: (0286) 844 6158.
Hotel and restaurant, next to
stunning beach.

Boncuk
Sütlüce Kale Köyü, Gelibolu.
Tel: (0286) 576 8292.
Fax: (0286) 576 8158.
48 rooms with toilet and shower,
direct-dial phone, central heating.
Restaurant, bar, swimming pool,
sports. **$$$**

Kum Motel & Camping
Birinci Pasa Mahallesi, Evren Sokak
2/2, 16km from Eceabat, Gelibolu.

Price Guide

Prices are per night for a double
room during the high season.
$$$$ = above $100
$$$ = $50 to $100
$$ = $30 to $50
$ = below $30

Tel: (0286) 814 1455.
Fax: (0286) 814 1917.
56 rooms withshower, phone,
heating. Camping, restaurant,
beach, sports and parking. **$$$**

GÖKÇEADA (IMBROS) ISLAND

Gökçe Hotel
Town centre, Gökçeada Island.
Tel: (0286) 887 3473.
Rooms with toilet and shower,
direct-dial phone, central heating.
Bed and breakfast. **$$**

KEŞAN

Yener
Yukarı Zaferiye Mahallesi,
Demirciler Caddesi 18.
Tel: (0282) 714 3660.
Fax: (282) 714 5755.
68 rooms with bathroom, direct-dial
phone, TV, central heating. Restau-
rant, bar, meeting room. **$$$**

The Southern Aegean

AKÇAY-ALTıNOLUK-EDREMIT

Afrodit Holiday Village
Altınoluk.
Tel: (0266) 378 5380.
Fax: (0266) 378 5222.
25 apartments, 12 suite rooms.
Restaurants, bars, beach, Turkish
bath, fitness centre, swimming
pool, disco, market, sports. **$$$**

Günes
Buruncu Mevki, Altınoluk.
Tel: (0266) 396 1313.
Fax: (0266) 396 1370.
83 rooms with toilet and shower,
direct-dial phone. Restaurant, bar,
beach, pool, disco, sports. **$$$**

Idaköy Çiftligi
Çamlıbel Köyü, Edremit.
Tel: (0266) 387 3402.
Istanbul office tel: (0216) 337
1962; fax: (0216) 347 2224).A
farm house/pension with a small
number of rooms, set on the outskirts of the village of Kaz Dagları
(Mt Ida). **$$**

Linda Hotel
Barbaros Meydanı, Akçay.
Tel: (0266) 384 3500.
Fax: (0266) 384 2524.
Pension with 18 rooms all with
toilet and shower, direct-dial phone,
TV, heating. Restaurant and bar. **$$**

ALIAGA

Afacan Motel
Incirlik Mevkii, Aliaga.
Tel: (0232) 628 7030.
Fax: (0232) 463 0975.
36 rooms with bathroom. Restaurant, bar, swimming pool, garden,
playground, campsite, disco,
sports. **$$**

AYVALıK

Billurcu
Sarımsaklı, Ayvalık.
Tel: (0266) 324 1188/89.
Fax: (0266) 324 1751.
60 rooms and 38 apartments, with
bathroom, direct-dial phone, TV.
Restaurants, bars, swimming pool,
sports, meeting room. **$$**

Florium
Lale Adası, Ayvalık.
Tel: (0266) 312 9627.
Fax: (0266) 312 9631.
135 rooms with air-conditioning,
minibar and balcony. Restaurants,
bars, swimming pool, Turkish
bath, sauna, pâtisserie,
sports. **$$$$**

Club Washington
Tuzla Mevkii, Ayvalık.
Tel: (0266) 343 7395.
Fax: (0266) 343 7399.
230 rooms with bathroom, direct-
dial phone, air conditioning, central
heating. Restaurants, bars,
swimming pool, playground, disco,
game room, shops, sports, meeting
room, parking. **$$$**

Taksiyahis
Maresal Fevzi Çakmak Caddesi 71,
Ayvalık.
Tel: (0266) 312 1494.
Pension with five rooms. Shared
bathrooms and kitchen, washing
machine, Turkish bath. **$$**

Yalı
Behind PTT building 20, Ayvalık.
Tel: (0266) 312 2423.
Pension with five rooms. Shared
bathrooms and kitchen, hot water,
washing machine. **$$**

AYVAÇIK

Behram Hotel
Behramkale Iskele.
Tel: (0286) 721 7016/721 7044.
One of the oldest decent hotels in
the resort, the Behram has 17
comfortable rooms with bathroom
and phone; seaside fish restaurant.
Open all year. **$**

Eden Beach
Kadırga Koyu.
Tel: (0286) 762 9870.
Fax: (0286) 762 9404.
On a pebbled beach, with 68 rooms
equipped with phone, central
heating and music. Restaurant, bar
and watersports. **$$$**

Nazlıhan
Behramkale Iskele.
Tel: (0286) 721 7385/7386.
Fax: (0286) 721 7387.
Restored from an early 20th-century
stone mansion, it houses 37 rooms
with balconies and private
bathrooms overlooking the harbour.
Two bars and a disco. **$$**

BERGAMA

Berksoy
Izmir Asfaltı 19, Bergama. Tel:
(0232) 633 2595.
Fax: (0232) 633 5346.
57 rooms with bathroom, phone,
TV, minibar, central heating. Restaurants, bars, meeting room, swim-
ming pool, playground, sports. **$$$**

Böblingen
Asklepion Caddesi 2, Bergama.
Tel: (0232) 633 2153.
Pension with 11 rooms with shower.
Bed and breakfast. **$**

Efsane
Izmir Asfaltı 86, Bergama.
Tel: (0232) 632 6350.
Fax: (0232) 632 6353.
24 rooms with toilet and shower,
phone, central heating. Restaurant,
bar, swimming pool. **$$**

Tusan Motel
Yolçatı Mevkii, Bergama.
Tel: (0232) 633 1173.
Fax: (0232) 632 6284.
44 rooms with bathroom, central
heating. Restaurant.

BODRUM

Aksu
Cumhuriyet Caddesi 159, Bodrum.
Tel: (0252) 316 8883.
Fax: (0252) 316 9111.
21 rooms with toilet and shower,
phone, fan, central heating. Restaurant, bars, swimming pool, beach,

Ambrosia
Bitez Yalısı.
Tel: (0252) 343 1886.
Fax: (0252) 343 1879.
84 rooms minibar, balcony, central
heating. Restaurant, bars, conference rooms, Turkish bath, gym,
jacuzzi, health room, swimming
pool, beach, shop, sports. **$$$**
garden. In city centre. **$$**

Anka
Eskiçesme Mahallesi, Asarlık
Mevkii, Gümbet.
Tel: (0252) 316 8217.
Fax: (0252) 316 6194.
90 rooms with toilet and shower,
phone, balcony. Restaurant, bars,
swimming pool, beach, garden,
disco, health cabin, sports. **$$**

Antique Theatre Hotel
Kıbrıs şehitleri Caddesi 243.
Tel: (0252) 316 6053/54.
Fax: (0252) 316 0825
A small luxury hotel with all the
personal touches. Located opposite

the antique theatre, it is a
refreshing change in Bodrum's
touristy landscape, and a write-up in
a US paper has made it very
popular. The restaurant enjoys
similar rave reviews. **$$$**

Bodrum Cesars
Okaliptus Sokak 4, Gümbet.
Tel: (0252) 316 9571.
Fax: (0252) 316 9570.
100 rooms with air conditioning,
minibar. Restaurants, bars, swimming pool, Turkish bath, health
club, shop, casino, night club,
sports. **$$$$**

Bodrum Maya
Gerence Sokak 49, Bodrum.
Tel: (0252) 316 4741.
Fax: (0252) 316 4745.
72 rooms with toilet, shower,
phone, air conditioning, central
heating. Restaurant, bars, pool,
gym, sauna. City centre. **$$**

Bona Dea
Bardakçı Koyu, Bodrum.
Tel: (0252) 313 0371.
Fax: (0252) 313 0375.
138 rooms with air conditioning,
minibar, balcony, central heating.
Restaurants, bars, meeting room,
pools, medical room, health centre,
baby sitter, beach. **$$$**

Club Hotel M Holiday Village
Degirmen Mevkii, Haremtan,
Bodrum.
Tel: (0252) 316 6100.
Fax: (0252) 316 2581.
209 rooms with bathroom, TV,
minibar, air conditioning, phone.
Restaurants, bars, conference
room, swimming pools, beach,
Turkish bath, gym, health cabin,
sports. **$$**

Club Med Palmiye Holiday Village
Çiftlik Köyü Yalısı.
Tel: (0252) 368 915.
Fax: (0252) 368 9138.
176 rooms with toilet and shower,
phone, air conditioning.
Restaurants, bars, conference hall,
swimming pool, beach, Turkish
bath, gym, health cabin, shop,
sports. **$$**

Club Yalıkavak Boydas
Tilkicik Köyü, Yalıkavak.
Tel: (0252) 316 3548.
Fax: (0252) 316 1365.
123 rooms with toilet and shower,
phone. Restaurants, bars,

swimming pool, beach, health cabin, shop, sports. **$$$**
Kariye Princess
Canlıdere Sokak 15, Bodrum.
Tel: (0252) 316 8971.
Fax: (0252) 316 8979.
E-mail: princess@superonline.com
52 rooms all fitted with air conditioning, minibar, central heating. Restaurant, bars, meeting room, swimming pool, Turkish bath, gym, garden, casino, night club. **$$$$**
Hotel Palmira Deluxe
Köyaltı Mevkii
Türkbükü.
Tel: 252-377 5601.
Fax: 252-377 5951
e-mail: palmira@turk.net
60 rooms and five suites, in this luxury setting. The low-rise natural stone accommodation is a bonus. Comfortable, well-equipped rooms have balconies overlooking pool. Beach is 500 metres away. **$$$**
Medisun
Yahsi Yalısı, Ortakent.
Tel: (0252) 348 3207.
Fax: (0252) 348 3487.
75 rooms with air conditioning, minibar, safe, central heating. Restaurant, bars, garden, Turkish bath, sauna, gym, swimming pool, garden, hairdresser, shop, disco, sports. **$$$**
Mylasa Hotel
Cumhuriyet Caddesi 2
Azmakbaşı.
Tel: (0252) 316 1846
Fax: (0252) 316 1254
Small, 14 rooms, no-frills hotel but lovingly done up and cared for in Med style. Terrace bar and dining room. **$$**
Mylasa Pension
Cumhuriyet Caddesi 34, Azmakbaşı .
Tel: (0252) 316 1846.
Fax: (0252) 316 1254.
16 rooms with toilet and shower, phone. Breakfast room, bar, TV room. Bed and breakfast. In city centre. **$**
Myndos
Mindos Caddesi 1, Bodrum.
Tel: (0252) 316 3080.
Fax: (0252) 316 5252.
51 rooms with toilet and shower, phone, central heating. Restaurant, bars, swimming pool, TV room. **$$$**

Olfiya
Yalıçiftlik Mevkii.
Tel: (0252) 368 9111.
Fax: (0252) 368 9112.
200 rooms with air conditioning, minibar. Restaurants, bars, conference rooms, pool, beach, sauna, health cabin, hairdresser, shops, disco, children's club, sports. **$$$$**
Yaprak
Kadıkalesi, Turgutreis.
Tel: (0252) 382 2017.
Fax: (0252) 382 4982.
43 rooms with toilet and shower, phone, balcony. Restaurant, bar, swimming pool, beach, sports. **$$**
Yasemin Evleri Apart
Yeni Devlet Hastanesi Yolu.
Tel: (0252) 313 4374.
Fax: (0252) 313 4377.
E-mail: yaseminevleri@superonline.com
Lovely secluded setting 22 miles (35 km) from Bodrum city centre. Own pool and 38 self-contained apartments with microwave ovens, children's playground and air conditioning. The beach is 2½ miles (4 km) away but you might skip it for the peace and quiet of this (so far) unspoiled corner. **$**

BURHANIYE-ÖREN

Artemis Holiday Village
Ören.
Tel: (0266) 412 5420.
Fax: (0266) 422 1317.
112 rooms. Restaurants, bar, disco, beach, swimming pool, shops, sports, playground. **$$**
Konak Lale Hotel & Fer-Tur Villas
Ören.
Tel: (0266) 422 1343.
Fax: (0266) 422 2366.25
Suite rooms and 15 apart-villas. Restaurant, bar, garden, sports, disco. **$$**
Urut 1
Hürriyet Meydanı 14, Burhaniye.
Tel: (0266) 422 1105.
Fax: (0266) 412 5250.
72 rooms with bathroom, phone, central heating. Restaurant, bar, meeting room. **$$$**
Urut 2
Meco Caddesi, Ören.
Tel: (266) 422 1205.

Fax: (266) 412 5250.
34 rooms with toilet and shower. Restaurant, bar, garden. **$$**

ÇESME-ILıCA

Altın Yunus Holiday Village
Boyalık Mevkii, Çesme.
Tel: (0232) 723 1250.
Fax: (0232) 723 2252.
514 rooms. Restaurants, bars, conference rooms, casino, indoor and outdoor pools, beach, multifunctional health club, hydrotherapy, sports, shops. **$$$**
Altın Yunus Tatilköyü
Kalemburnu Boyalık Meydanı, Ilıca.
Tel: (0232) 723 1250.
Fax: (0232) 723 2252.
E-mail: info@altinyunus.com.tr
Attractive, low-rise resort built around a sandy bay, with luxurious fittings and all possible mod cons and entertainments. **$$$**
Çesme Marin
Hürriyet Caddesi, Çesme.
Tel: (0232) 712 7579.
Small, pleasant seafront hotel. **$**
Club Kardia Holiday Village
Çiftlik Mahallesi, Çesme.
Tel: (0232) 722 1111.
Fax: (0232) 722 1227.
257 rooms with toilet and shower, phone, fan, balcony. Restaurants, bars, meeting rooms, Turkish bath, fitness centre, indoor and outdoor swimming pools, beach, children's club, sports. **$$**
Framissima Boyalık Beach
Boyalık Mevkii, Çesme.
Tel: (0232) 712 7081.
Fax: (0232) 712 7331.
210 rooms. Restaurants, bars, meeting rooms, swimming pool, beach, play ground, disco, shops, sports. **$$$$**
Golf Holiday Club
Çiftlik Mahallesi, Çesme.
Tel: (0232) 722 1003.
Fax: (0232) 722 1225.
62 suite rooms with toilet and shower, balcony. Restaurant, bars, swimming pool, beach, garden, disco, sports. **$$$**
Inkim
Izmir Caddesi, PTT Karsısı, Ilıca.
Tel: (0232) 723 3900.
Fax: (0232) 723 3904.

71 rooms with toilet and shower, phone, central heating, balcony. Restaurant, bar, swimming pool, beach, sports. **$$**

Kanun Kervansaray
Çeşme Kalesi Yanı.
Tel: (0232) 712 7177.
Fax: (0232) 712 2906.
Romantically restored 16th-century *caravansaray* based around a fountain courtyard, with 32 rooms and 2 suites, some with a sea view. **$$$**

Kaptan
Yeni Çevre Yolu, Çeşme.
Tel: (232) 712 6186.
Pension with 40 rooms with toilet and shower, phone. Swimming pool. Bed and breakfast. **$**

Omarland Holiday Village
Narlıca, Ildırı, Çesme.
Tel: (0232) 715 2153.
Fax: (0232) 715 1421.
75 apartment villas with bathroom, phone, TV, refrigerator, fireplace, air conditioning, balcony. Restaurant, bars, swimming pool, beach, night club, disco, sports. **$$$**

Dalyan

Evim Pansiyon
216 Sokak 40.
Tel: (0232) 812 1360.
Renovated old house with 7 rooms and a beautiful garden. **$**

Göl Hotel
Waterfront, near marina.
Tel: (0252) 284 2096.
Fax: (0252) 284 2555.
Pretty but basic lakeside hotel with a pool, restaurant and bar. **$**

Hanedan
Sahil Caddesi.
Tel: (0232) 812 1515.
Fax: (0232) 812 1609.
A basic, but comfortable 4-storey building on the harbour. **$**

Karaçam
Sahil Caddesi 70.
Tel: (0323) 812 3216.
Fax: (0232) 812 2042.
A charming old Greek house with 24 rooms. Popular with tour groups, so book well ahead. **$$**

Sultan Palace
Tel: (0252) 281 2103.
Ten minutes upriver from Dalyan, this exceptional traditional Turkish hotel is totally isolated on its

hillside, set in gardens by a large pool. On an island, accessible only by boat from Dalyan waterfront. **$$**

DATÇA

Fuda Yalı
Dr. Turgut Dündar Caddesi, Datça.
Tel: (0252) 712 2237.
Fax: (0252) 712 4066.
20 rooms with toilet and shower, phone. Restaurant, bar, garden, beach, sports. **$**

Mare
Sükrü Efendi Caddesi, Datça.
Tel: (0252) 712 3211.
Fax: (0252) 712 3396.
50 rooms with toilet and shower, phone, balcony. Restaurant, bar, swimming pool, garden, beach, shop, sports. **$$$**

Soytok
Yalı Caddesi 5, Datça.
Tel: (0252) 712 2160.
Fax: (0252) 712 3065.
39 rooms with toilet and shower, central heating. Restaurant, bar and attractive garden. Bed and breakfast. **$$**

DIDIM

Club Patio Ligamar Holiday Village
Çamburun Mevkii, Akbük, Didim.
Tel: (0256) 856 4273.
Fax: (0256) 856 4281.
134 rooms with air conditioning, balcony. Restaurants, bars, health cabin, swimming pool, garden, shops, disco, children's club, sports. **$$$**

Grand Didyma
Üç Mevsim Sitesi, Altınkum, Didim.
Tel: (0256) 813 2038.
Fax: (0256) 813 3468.
63 rooms with toilet and shower, air conditioning. Restaurant, bars, swimming pool, playground. **$$**

Holipark Swan,
Akbük Mevkii, Didim.
Tel: (0256) 846 1830.
Fax: (0256) 846 1797.
197 rooms with air conditioning, balcony. Restaurant, bars, Turkish bath, pool, beach, garden, hairdresser, disco, sports. **$$$$**

DIKILI

Mysia
Geren Mevkii, Dikili.
Tel: (0232) 671 7010.
Fax: (0232) 671 4987.
136 rooms with bathroom, phone, TV, air conditioning, minibar. Restaurants, bars, meeting room, pâtisserie, swimming pool, garden, health cabin, shop, sports. **$$$$**

Sinka
Iskele Caddesi, Park Karsısı 2, Dikili.
Tel: (0232) 671 4433.
Fax: (0232) 671 4717.
24 rooms with bathroom, phone, central heating. Restaurant, bar. **$$**

FOÇA

Club Mavi Holiday Village
Çanak Mevki, Foça.
Tel: (0232) 825 1002.
Fax: (0232) 825 1030.
250 rooms with bath, phone and refrigerator. Restaurant, bars, health cabin, playground, sports . **$$**

Club Mediterranee
Eski Foça.
Tel: (0232) 812 3691.
Fax: (0232) 812 2175.
350 rooms with bathroom, safe. Restaurants, bars, Turkish bath, swimming pool, disco, children's club. **$$**

Evim Pansiyon
216 Sokak 40.
Tel: (0232) 812 1360.
Renovated old house with 7 rooms and a beautiful garden. **$**

Hanedan Holiday Resort
IV Mersinaki Foça Izmir.
Tel: (0232) 812 3650.
Fax: (0232) 812 2451
64 rooms with TV, balconies and private bathroom. Beachfront ▸ location. One VIP suite and 80 well equipped holiday villas. **$$**

Hotel Club Phokaia
Ismetpaşa Mahallesi
II Mersinaki Köyü.
Tel: (0232) 812 4041
In a world of its own in a dream setting. 164 rooms and 4 presidential suites. Bars, restaurants and activities for all age groups and social sets. **$$$**

Karaçam
Sahil Caddesi 70 (SL)
Tel: (0232) 812 1416
Fax: (0232) 812 3216.
A charming old Greek house with
24 rooms. Popular with tour groups,
so book well ahead. **$$**

GÜLLÜK (BODRUM)

Labranda Corinthia
Sıralık Mevkii, Güllük, Milas.
Tel: (0252) 522 2911.
Fax: (0252) 522 2009.
138 rooms with air conditioning,
minibar, balcony, central heating.
Restaurants, bars, swimming pool,
beach, meeting rooms, shops, gym,
health cabin, disco, sports. **$$$**

GÜMÜLDÜR

Denizatı Holiday Village
Büyükalan Mevkii, Gümüldür.
Tel: (0232) 793 1333.
Fax: (0232) 793 1692.
70 rooms with toilet and shower,
balcony. Restaurant, bars, beach,
swimming pool, garden, health
cabin, disco, shop, sports. **$$$**
Euro Sun Club
Atatürk Mahallesi, Gümüssu
Caddesi 17, Gümüldür.
Tel: (0232) 793 1407.
Fax: (0232) 793 1850.
173 rooms with bathroom, phone,
air conditioning, refrigerator, central
heating. Restaurants, bars, health
cabin, beach, swimming pool,
garden, disco, sports. **$$$**

IZMIR

Atlantis Hotel
Gazi Bulvarı No. 128.
Tel: (0232) 483 5548.
Fax: (0232) 0699.
Close to the railway station at
Basmane, this is a comfortable
hotel with a good dining room. **$$**
Balçova Termal
Vali Hüseyin Ögütgen Caddesi 2,
Balçova.
Tel: (0232) 259 0102.
Fax: (0232) 259 0829.
198 rooms with bathroom, phone,

air conditioning. Restaurants, bars,
meeting rooms, garden, physical re-
habilitation centre, indoor and
outdoor swimming pools, health
cabin, sauna, jacuzzi, sports. **$$**
Ege Çınar
9 Eylül Meydanı 2, Basmane.
Tel: (0232) 441 3113.
Fax: (0232) 489 5068.
35 rooms with bathroom, phone,
TV, air conditioning, minibar, central
heating. Bed and breakfast, bar. **$$**
Ege Palas Hotel
Cumhuriyet Bulvarı 210 Alsancak,
Izmir.
Tel: (0232) 463 9090.
Fax: (0232) 463 8100.
www.egepalas.com.tr
In city centre with 112 rooms, many
overlooking Izmir Bay. Good
restaurants, sauna, fitness centre
and indoor parking. **$$$**
Hisar Hotel
Fevzipaşa Bulvarı No. 153, Izmir.
Tel: (0232) 484 5400.
Fax: (0232) 425 8830.
Not much to look at but its 63
comfortable rooms, excellent buffet
breakfast and central location make
up for drab exterior. Rooms facing
the main street can be noisy. **$**
Izmir Palace
Vasıf Çınar Bulvarı 2,
Alsancak.
Tel: (0232) 421 5583.
Fax: (0232) 422 6870.
Sea-front hotel. 152 rooms with
bathroom, phone, minibar, TV, air
conditioning, central heating. Res-
taurant, bar, meeting room, 24-hour
room service. **$$**
Mercure
Cumhuriyet Bulvarı 138.
Tel: (0232) 489 4090.
Fax: (0232) 489 4089.
168 rooms with air conditioning,
minibar, hairdryer. Restaurants,
bars, meeting rooms, night club,
casino, shops, indoor and outdoor
swimming pools, gym, sauna,
solarium, hairdresser. **$$$$**
Thermal Princess
Balçova, Izmir.
Tel: (0232) 238 5151.
Fax: (0232) 239 0939.
300 rooms with thermal bath, air
conditioning, minibar, hairdryer, safe.
Restaurants, bars, pâtisserie,
meeting rooms, Turkish bath, sauna,

Price Guide

Prices are per night for a double
room during the high season.
$$$$ = above $100
$$$ = $50 to $100
$$ = $30 to $50
$ = below $30

gym, hairdresser, shops, indoor and
outdoor swimming pools, casino,
night club, disco, sports. **$$$$**

KÜÇÜKKUYU

Çetmi Han (SL)
Yesilyurt Köyü, Küçükkuyu,
Kazdagları (Mt Ida), Çanakkale.
Tel: (0286) 752 6169.
Fax: (0286) 752 6170.
10 rooms with toilet and shower,
central heating. Restaurant, bar
with fireplace, garden.

KUŞADASI

Club Solara
Güzelçamlı Mevkii, Kuşadası.
Tel: (0256) 646 1988.
Fax: (0256) 646 1483.
90 rooms with toilet and shower,
phone, balcony. Restaurant, bar,
meeting room, pool, garden, night
club, playground, sports. **$$**
Dias Hotel
Candan Turhan Bulvarı 64
Kuşadası.
Tel: (0256) 612 3315.
Fax: (0256) 612 3316.
A budget hotel with 47 rooms in the
city centre. Some rooms are en
suite and 22 are air conditioned. **$$**
Efe Hotel
Güvercin Ada Caddesi 37,
Kuşadası.
Tel: (0256) 614 3660/61.
Fax: (0256) 614 3662
E-mail: hotelefe@wec.net.com.tr
This is a dandy, small hotel open all
year round. All 44 rooms have a
sea view. Live music every night
including winter months. **$**
Fantasia De Luxe
Söke Yolu, Yavansu Mevkii, Kuşadası.
Tel: (0256) 614 8550.
Fax: (0256) 614 2765.

324 rooms, air conditioning, minibar, balcony. restaurants, bars, indoor and outdoor pools, beach, disco, casino, Turkish bath, health club, shops, sports. $$$$
Grand Blue Sky
Kadinlar Denizli.
Tel: (0256) 612 7750.
Fax: (0256) 612 4225.
A sea-facing hotel, offering the full range of watersports, (including diving) and private beach. Open all year. $$
Imbat
Kadınlar Denizi Mevkii.
Tel: (0256) 614 2000.
Fax: (0256) 614 4960.
One of Kuşadası's big resort hotels with all the amenities one would expect from a 5-star hotel: disco, pool, watersports, restaurant and bar. Ladies' Beach end of town and easily reached by *dolmuş* from the town centre. Open all year. $$$$
Kısmet
Akyar Mevkii, Türkmen Mahallesi, Kuşadası.
Tel: (0256) 614 2005.
Fax: (0256) 614 4914.
102 rooms with bathroom, phone, TV, air conditioning, balcony. Restaurants, bars, beach, garden, sports. $$$
Korumar
Gazi Begendi Mevkii, Kuşadası.
Tel: (0256) 614 8243.
Fax: (0256) 614 5596.
E-mail: korumar@koru.com.tr
www.koru.com.tr/koru/korumar
248 rooms with air conditioning, minibar, balcony, central heating. Restaurants, bars, conference rooms,Turkish bath, fitness centre, shops, indoor and outdoor pools, beach, disco, casino, sports. $$$$
Martı
Kadınlar Plajı, Kuşadası.
Tel: (0256) 614 3650.
Fax: (0256) 614 4700.
112 rooms with bathroom, phone, balcony. Restaurants, bars, night club, sports. $$
Öküz Mehmet Pafla
Kervansarayı (SL)
Atatürk Bulvarı No. 2, Kuşadası.
Tel: (0256) 614 4115.
Fax: (0256) 614 2423.
E-mail: caravanserail@kusadasi.net

www.kusadasihotels.com/caravanserail/
The glamourous exterior of this establishment is accompanied by professional and efficient service. 40 rooms with toilet and shower, phone. Restaurant, bar, nightclub, laundry, garden.
Turistik Hotel Kelebek
Sogucak Köyü, Kuşadası.
Tel/fax: (0256) 681 0653.
20 rooms with toilet and shower, phone, TV, refrigerator, balcony, central heating. Restaurant, bar, garden, swimming pool.

Price Guide

Prices are per night for a double room during the high season.
$$$$ = above $100
$$$ = $50 to $100
$$ = $30 to $50
$ = below $30

MARMARIS-HISARÖNÜ-BOZBURUN

Aqua
Içmeler, Marmaris.
Tel: (0252) 455 3633.
Fax: (0252) 455 3650.
A landscaped garden leads down to the beach, while indoors there is a fitness centre and a tennis court. Open all year. $$$
Efendi
Kenan Evren Bulvarı, Içmeler, Marmaris.
Tel: (0252) 455 2053.
Fax: (0252) 455 3313.
30 rooms with toilet and shower, phone, air conditioning, balcony. Restaurant, bar, swimming pool. $$
Golden Key Villas
Off Datça Road, Hisarönü.
Tel: (0252) 466 6211.
Fax: (0252) 466 6042.
Small villas with 30 rooms, with bathroom, air conditioning, phone, TV. Restaurant, bar, swimming pool, beach, garden, sports. $$
Hotel Begonya
Acı Mustafa, Sokak 101, Marmaris.
Tel: (0252) 412 4095.
Fax: (0252) 412 1518.
Attractive, stone-built converted barn with a courtyard garden.

Unfortunately it is close to the local disco. $$
Hotel Laguna
Içmeler, Marmaris
Tel: (0252) 455 3710.
Fax: (0252) 455 3622.
E-mail: reserv@lagunahotel.com
www.lagunahotel.com
Don't be fooled by the shoebox concrete exterior. The Laguna is comfortable and homey inside and they do everything very well. Winner of the Hotelier Association's 'Golden Key' Award in 1997. $$$
Interyouth Hostel
Tepe Mahallesi 42, Sokak 45, Marmaris.
Tel: (0252) 412 3687.
Fax: (0252) 412 7823.
Budget accommodation in the main covered market of Marmaris but with some single and double rooms as well as the basic dorms. There is another hostel with the same name on Kemeraltı Mahallesi (tel: (0252) 412 6432), outside the centre, which should offer a more peaceful night's sleep. Open throughout the year. $$$
Kavala
Turunç Köyü, Marmaris.
Tel: (0252) 476 7211.
Fax: (0252) 476 7213.
38 rooms, 6 flats, with toilet and shower, phone, air conditioning, balcony. Restaurant, bars, swimming pool, beach, garden, TV room. $
Lidya
Siteler Mahallesi 130, Marmaris.
Tel: (0252) 412 2940.
Fax: (0252) 412 1478.
336 rooms with toilet and shower, phone, air conditioning, central heating, balcony. Restaurants, bars, indoor pool, beach, garden, health cabin, casino, disco, sports. $$$
Magic Life Der Club Marmaris Holiday Village
Yalancı Bogazı, Marmaris.
Tel: (0252) 412 0700.
Fax: (0252) 412 0708.
247 rooms with air conditioning, balcony. Restaurants, bars, pool, beach, garden, Turkish bath, fitness centre, shop, sports. $$
Mares (formerly Altın Yunus)
Pamucak, Marmaris.
Tel: (0252) 455 2200.
Fax: (0252) 412 1214.

420 rooms with air conditioning, minibar, balcony. Restaurants, bars, conference rooms, swimming pool, garden, beach, marina, Turkish bath, gym, casino, disco, shops, sports. **$$$$**

Marti Resort
Içmeler, Marmaris.
Tel: (0252) 455 3440.
Fax: (0252) 455 3448.
E-mail: marti@escortnet.com
www.marketweb.net.tr/marti
One of the key-note holiday clubs in Marmaris. Big, bold and beautiful and more like a village. Pets are welcome and they offer every sport imaginable. Several rooms are specifically designed for the physically challenged. **$$$$**

Merit Laguna
Altın Sahil Mevkii, Içmeler, Marmaris.
Tel: (0252) 455 3710.
Fax: (0252) 455 3622.
64 rooms with air conditioning, minibar, balcony. Restaurant, bar, pool, beach, garden, Turkish bath, gym, shop, sports. **$$$**

Moonlight Apart Hotel
Turgut Reis Caddesi 10/1, Içmeler, Marmaris.
Tel: (0252) 455 2529.
14 flats with bathroom, refrigerator, kitchen, balcony. Bar, garden, swimming pool. **$**

Munamar Vista
Kayabal Caddesi, Içmeler, Marmaris.
Tel: (0252) 455 3360.
Fax: (0252) 455 3359.
Spacious rooms and lots of facilities, including a pool, disco and a beach on the doorstep with plenty of watersports. The water *dolmuş* from Marmaris makes a stop here. Open all year and suitable for anyone seeking a location that is relatively peaceful yet close to Marmaris. **$$**

Yunus Hotel
Kemal Elgin Bulvari 288, Sokak No.5, Marmaris.
Tel: 252- 412 1799/3888.
Fax: 252-412 3877.
A small, budget conscious hotel in the city centre with 50 rooms. Air conditioning and a swimming pool for children. **$$$$**

PAMUKKALE (DENIZLI)

The Pamukkale region does not strictly fall within the coastal area but there are many classical ruins and attractions in the area that make a detour worthwhile. A word of warning – most of the hotels close to the "Cotton Castle" of Pamukkale have been closed. In fact, almost all of them were built without official planning permission, and their future is precarious. You cannot stay near the limestone falls, nor can you swim or wade here, despite the enticing photographs!

For accommodation, choose either Denizli or Aydın. Neither offers much except that Denizli is a good place to pick up quality pure crystal glassware from the Denizli Glass Shop in the city centre.

SEFERIHISAR

Çakıraga
Sıgacık Mahallesi, Akkum Caddesi, Seferihisar.
Tel: (0232) 745 7575.
Fax: (0232) 745 7023.
32 rooms with bathroom, phone, TV, refrigerator, central heating, balcony. Restaurant, bars, swimming pool, garden, shop. **$$$**

Club Teos Holiday Village
Seferihisar.
Tel: (0232) 745 7467.
Fax: (0232) 745 7475.
130 rooms with toilet and shower, phone, balcony. Restaurant, bars, swimming pool, garden, children's club, shops, disco, sports. **$$**

Selçuk (Ephesus)Kalehan Hotel (SL)
Antique House, Atatürk Caddesi 49, Selçuk.
Tel: (0232) 892 6154.
Fax: (0232) 892 2169.
E-mail: ergir@superonline.com
www.kalehan.com
The only upmarket place to stay near Ephesus. Restored in auberge style by the owners. Customers from around the world return here. 54 rooms with toilet and shower, phone, central heating. Restaurant, bar, pool, garden. **$$$**

Sirince Evleri (SL)
Sirince Köyü, Selçuk.
Tel: (0232) 421 3467.
Tel/fax: (0232) 898 3099.
5 rooms with bathroom, phone, minibar, fan. Bed and breakfast, garden, laundry. **$**

The Mediterranean Coast

ADANA

Hotel Seyhan
Turhan Cemal Beriker Bulvarı 30.
Tel: (0322) 457 5810.
Fax: (0322) 454 2834.
Shiny-new, ultra-modern mirror-plated towerblock in the town centre, with several restaurants and bars, pool, health club and nightclub. **$$$$**

Inci Hotel
Kurtuluş Caddesi 40, 01060 Kuruköprü.
Tel: (0322) 435 8234.
Fax: (0322) 435 8368.
Large business-style hotel situated in the city-centre, with friendly staff and a lively nightclub in the basement. **$$$$**

ALANYA

Alaaddin Incekum
Incekum, Avsallar, Alanya.
Tel: (0242) 517 1491.
Fax: (0242) 517 1317.
232 rooms with air conditioning, minibar. Facilities include pool, beach, Turkish bath, fitness centre, shops, playground. **$$$$**

Alara
Yesilköy, Alanya.
Tel: (0242) 527 4740.
Fax: (0242) 527 4166.
120 rooms with bathroom, phone, balcony. Restaurant, bar, pool, beach. **$$$**

Alya Hotel
Oba Göl Mevkii.
Tel: (0242) 514 0695.
Fax: (0242) 514 0698.
Away from the bustle of central Alanya, with private beach. **$$**

Ananas Altınyunus
Alanya.
Tel: (0242) 514 0900.
Fax: (0242) 514 0850.

176 rooms with air conditioning, minibar. Facilities include swimming pool, beach, meeting rooms, casino, fitness centre, children's playground. **$$$$**

Aspera
Fugla Koyu, Incekum, Alanya.
Tel: (0242) 517 1797.
Fax: (0242) 517 1723.
180 rooms with air conditioning. Restaurant, bars, pool, beach, Turkish bath, gym, disco. **$$$**

Club Hotel Serda Altınyunus
Telatiye Mevkii, Konaklı, Alanya.
Tel: (0242) 565 2535.
Fax: (0242) 565 2537.
100 rooms with air conditioning. Facilities include pool, beach, disco, health cabin, sports. **$$$**

Club Justiniano
Okurcalar Koyu, Karaburun Mevkii, Alanya.
Tel: (0242) 527 4955.
Fax: (0242) 527 4682.
296 rooms with air conditioning. Facilities include indoor and outdoor pools, beach, Turkish bath, gym, sports. **$$$**

Club Oasis Beach Vista Holiday Village
Konaklı, Alanya.
Tel: (0242) 565 1451.
Fax: (0242) 565 1449.
836 rooms with bathroom, phone, balcony. Swimming pool, beach, disco, sports. **$$$**

Crown
Güller Pınarı Mahallesi, Yenilmez Sokak 6, Alanya.
Tel: (0242) 513 2830.
Fax: (0242) 513 5850.
40 rooms with bathroom, phone, central heating. Restaurant, bar. **$**

Dimçay Mevkii
Tel: (0242) 518 1740.
Fax: (0242) 518 1756.
www.alantur.com.tr
The granddaddy of the holiday club set, but still popular after 35 years. Rooms, suites, bungalows and duplexes available. The huge expanse of private beach and green area on offer are now almost impossible to find elsewhere in Alanya, and the beach has the European Blue Flag environmental certification. **$$$**

Hamdullah Pasa Holiday Village
Bölge Trafik Karsısı, Konaklı, Alanya.
Tel: (0242) 565 1520.
Fax: (0242) 565 1531.
311 rooms with bathroom, phone, air conditioning. Pool, beach. **$$$**

Ladin
Karasaz Mevkii, Keykubat Caddesi, Alanya.
Tel: (0242) 514 1217.

Fax: (0242) 514 1221.
44 rooms with bathroom, balcony. Restaurant, bar, pool. **$$**

Liberty
Konaklı, Alanya.
Tel: (0242) 565 2625.
Fax: (0242) 565 2627.
82 rooms with air conditioning. Facilities include pool, beach, Turkish bath, disco, health cabin, sports, diving school. **$$$**

Mesut
Oba Kasabası, Göl Mevkii, Alanya.
Tel: (0242) 514 0485.
Fax: (0242) 514 0486.
100 rooms with bathroom, balcony; 70 with air conditioning. Restaurant, bars, pool, beach. **$$**

Serapsu
Konaklı Kasabası, Alanya.
Tel: (0242) 565 1476.
Fax: (0242) 565 1072.
218 rooms with air conditioning, minibar. Facilities include pool, beach, disco, fitness centre, diving school, shops, sports. **$$$$**

Sunny Hill
Çarsı Mahallesi, Damlatas Mevkii, Sultan Alaaddin Caddesi 3, Alanya.
Tel: (0242) 511 1211.
Fax: (0242) 512 3893.
73 rooms with air conditioning. Facilities include pool, health cabin, garden. **$$**

Campsites in the Western Mediterranean

Bambus Motel & Camping
Lara Yolu.
Tel: (0242) 241 5263.
Many consider this one of the best camping spots in Turkey. They seem to get things right for vast numbers of nationalities and enthusiastic campers. Children's playground and tea garden. **$**

Beldibi Camping,
30km west of Antalya in a 'detour' village.
Tel: (0824) 81 05.
The campsite is situated close to the beach and equipped with showers, supermarket and restaurant. **$**

Denizer Camping
Sarısu (turning and sign next to the Mobil Station).
Tel/Fax: (0259) 0871.

On the outskirts of Antalya going west towards Kemer. This is a well-run site with high standards right on the sea front. It is near the commercial port for Antalya but this does not detract from its appeal. Pool, bungalows, Turkish nights and space for 50 caravans and tents. **$**

Kındlıçeşme Camping Area
9 miles/15km west of Antalya before Kemer.
Tel: (0242) 814 1075.
Open May to October only.
This is a gorgeous wooded area west of Antalya with its own sandy beach. Clean, well run facilities for caravans, tents and RV's. Barbeques and picnic tables. Popular in the high season, so booking is advisable. **$**

ANTALYA

Altun Pension
Marina, Kaleiçi (Old Quarter).
Tel: (0242) 241 6624.
Bed & breakfast. **$**

Antalya Prince
Lara Yolu, Karpuzkaldıran Mevkii.
Tel: (0242) 349 3868.
Fax: (0242) 349 3873.
114 rooms with bathroom, phone, TV, air conditioning, minibar. Facilities include restaurant, bars, pool, beach, fitness room, Turkish bath, disco, shops, sports. **$$$**

Argos (SL)
Opposite Atatürk Ortaokulu, Kaleiçi (Old Quarter).
Tel: (0242) 247 2012.
Fax: (0242) 241 7557.
15 rooms with bathroom, phone, TV, air conditioning, minibar. Restaurant, bar, pool, garden. **$$**

Bagana Ranch Motel
Yukarı Karaman Köyü (village),
Antalya.
Tel: (0242) 425 2270.
Fax: (0425) 2444.
10 rooms with bathroom, TV, radio,
refrigerator, air conditioning,
balcony. Restaurant, bar, pool,
garden. Riding, trekking, mountain
biking, table tennis. **$$$**

Cender
30 Agustos Caddesi.
Tel: (0242) 243 4304.
Fax: (0242) 243 3987.
154 rooms with air conditioning,
minibar. Facilities include pool, gym,
Turkish bath, disco. **$$**

Club Hotel Sera
Lara.
Tel: (0242) 349 3434.
Fax: (0242) 349 3454.
223 rooms, 10 bungalows with air
conditioning, minibar. Facilities include swimming pool, garden,
Turkish bath, gym, casino, disco,
shops, sports. **$$$$**

Dedeman Antalya
Lara Yolu.
Tel: (0242) 321 3930.
Fax: (0242) 321 3873.
482 rooms with air conditioning,
minibar. Facilities include indoor
and outdoor pools, fitness centre,
Turkish bath, casino, disco, shops,
many sports. **$$$$**

Dogan Pension
Kılıçarslan Mahallesi, Mermerli
Banyo Sokak 5, Kaleiçi (Old
Quarter).
Tel: (242) 241 8842.
Fax: (242) 247 4006.
Bed & breakfast. **$**

Hadriyanus Pension
Kılıçarslan Mahallesi, Zeytin
Çıkmazı, Kaleiçi (Old Quarter).
Tel: (0242) 241 2313.
Bed & breakfast. **$**

Lara
Lara Yolu.
Tel: (0242) 349 2930.
Fax: (0242) 349 2936.
75 rooms with bathroom, phone,
TV, air conditioning. Facilities
include restaurant, bar, indoor and
outdoor pools, beach, health cabin,
sauna, shop, disco, sports. **$$**

Magic Mount (SL)
Tünektepe, Antalya.
Tel: (0242) 345 7998.

Fax: (0242) 345 0945.
Hilltop hotel outside of downtown
Antalya. 35 rooms with bathroom,
phone, air conditioning. Restaurant,
bar, disco, garden, pool. **$$$**

Marina (SL)
Mermerli Sokak 15, Kaleiçi (Old
Quarter).
Tel: (0242) 247 5490.
Fax: (0242) 241 1765.
Email: marina@antalya.teknet.com.tr
42 rooms with bathroom, phone,
TV, air conditioning, minibar,
heating. Restaurant, bar, swimming
pool, garden. **$$**

Ninova Pension
Barbaros Mahallesi, Hamit Efendi
Sokak 9, Kaleiçi (Old Quarter).
Tel: (0242) 248 6114.
Fax: (0242) 352 0479.
Bed & breakfast. **$**

Perge
Perge Sokak 5.
Tel: (0242) 244 0025.
Fax: (0242) 241 7587.
26 rooms with bathroom, phone,
TV, air conditioning, minibar. Res-
taurant, bar, beach, garden. **$$**

Sheraton Voyager
100 Yıl Bulvarı.
Tel: (0243) 2432.
Fax: (0243) 2462.
E-mail: www.superonline.com/
hotelguide
409 luxurious rooms including 22
suites surrounded by lush tropical
greenery. The service and
friendliness of this large hotel set it
apart from some of its grander
cousins. **$$$$**

Villa Perla
Barbaros Mahallesi
Hesapçı Sokak No 26, Kaleiçi.
Tel: (0242) 248 9793.
Fax: (0242) 241 2917.
In the centre of the old city, 10
carefully restored rooms and one
suite. Customers, both local and
foreign, return time and again. **$$**

DALYAN

Göl Hotel
Waterfront, near marina.
Tel: (0252) 284 2096.
Fax: (0252) 284 2555.
Pretty but basic lakeside hotel with
a pool, restaurant and bar. **$**

Sultan Palace
Tel: (0252) 281 2103.
Ten minutes upriver from Dalyan,
this exceptional traditional Turkish
hotel is totally isolated on its
hillside, set in gardens by a large
pool. Situated on an island,
accessible only by boat from Dalyan
waterfront. **$$$$**

FETHIYE-ÖLÜDENIZ

Club Tuana Vista Holiday Village
Yanıklar Köyü, Fethiye.
Tel: (0252) 633 6316.
Fax: (0252) 633 6324.
244 rooms with bathroom, phone,
TV, air conditioning, balcony. Res-
taurants, bars, pool, beach, garden,
Turkish bath, gym, shop, disco,
sports. **$$$**

König Pension
Barbaros Sokak 113, Çalıs Yolu,
Fethiye.
Tel: (0252) 613 1904.
Fax: (0252) 613 1299.
18 rooms with toilet and shower,
balcony. Restaurant, bar, pool. **$$**

Lykia Botanik Holiday Village
Kargı, Yanıklar Köyü, Fethiye.
Tel: (0252) 633 6151.
Fax: (0252) 633 6142.
Inside a large botanical garden,
beach, pool. **$$$**

Meri
Ölüdeniz.
Tel: (0252) 616 6060.
Fax: (0252) 616 6456.
75 rooms with toilet and shower,
phone, TV, balcony, air conditioning,
central heating. Restaurant, bar,
garden, beach, TV room. **$$**

Montana Pine Resort
Ovacık Köyü, Ölüdeniz.
Tel: (0252) 616 6252.
Fax: (0252) 616 6451.
90 rooms with toilet and shower,
phone, air conditioning, balcony.
Restaurant, bars, pool, garden,
shop. **$$$**

Prenses
Iskele Meydanı 7, Fethiye.
Tel: (0252) 614 1305.
Fax: (0252) 614 4479.
Located in city centre. 65 rooms
with toilet and shower, phone, TV,
balcony, air conditioning, central
heating. Restaurant, bar, TV room,
meeting room. **$$**
Ocakköy Holiday Village
Ocakköy, Ovacık, Fethiye.
Tel: (0252) 616 6155.
Fax: (0252) 616 6158.
8 rooms, 30 villas, rooms for
disabled travellers, with toilet and
shower, fan, minibar, balcony.
Restaurant, bar, pool, garden, shop,
sports. **$$$**
Telmessos
Hisarönü, Ölüdeniz.
Tel/fax: (0252) 616 6888.
85 rooms with toilet and shower,
phone, balcony. Restaurant, bars,
pool, garden, sports. **$$**
Villa Doffodil
Karagözler, Fevzi Çakmak Caddesi
115, Fethiye.
Tel: (0252) 614 9595.
Fax: (0252) 612 2223.
Pension with 15 rooms, all with
bathroom, phone. Restaurant, bar,
swimming pool. **$**

FINIKE

Anadolu Hotel
Sahil Yolu, Finike.
Tel: (0242) 855 3804.
Fax: (0242) 855 3805.
25 rooms with toilet and shower,
phone, balcony. Restaurant. **$**
Bahar Hotel
Cumhuriyet Caddesi.
Tel: (0242) 855 2020.
Fax: (0242) 855 2093.
A small, family-run mid range hotel
with 24 rooms right in the city
centre. Quiet location and willing,
friendly service. **$**

GÖKOVA BAY

Dedegil,
Akyaka Beldesi, Gökova, Mugla.
Tel: (0252) 243 5054.
Fax: (0252) 243 5301.
51 rooms with toilet and shower,

phone, balcony. Restaurant, bar,
pool, garden. **$$**
Yücelen
Akyaka Beldesi, Gökova, Mugla.
Tel: (0252) 243 5108.
Fax: (0252) 243 5435.
75 rooms with toilet and shower,
phone, balcony, central heating.
Restaurant, bar, pool, garden, shop,
sports. **$$**

KALKAN

Club Xanthos
Kalamar Koyu, Kalkan.
Tel: (0242) 844 2388.
Fax: (0242) 844 2359.
52 rooms with bathroom, phone,
TV, air conditioning, minibar,
balcony. Restaurant, bars, pool,
garden, disco, Turkish bath, fitness
room, beach. **$$$**

Price Guide

Prices are per night for a double
room during the high season.
$$$$ = above $100
$$$ = $50 to $100
$$ = $30 to $50
$ = below $30

Dionysia
Cumhuriyet Caddesi, Kalkan.
Tel: (0242) 844 3681.
Fax: (0242) 844 3139.
23 rooms with toilet and shower,
phone, fan, balcony. Restaurant,
bar, pool. **$**
Enerhan Hotel
Kalamar Road.
Tel: (0242) 844 3162.
Fax: (0242) 844 3449.
32 rooms overlooking the sea.
Interesting blend of contemporary
and classical architecture
about ½ mile/1 km from the city
centre. Restaurant, plus
conference rooms available on
request. **$$**
Kalkan Han Pension
Köyiçi, Kalkan (village centre).
Tel: (0242) 844 3151.
Fax: (0242) 844 2048.
16 rooms with toilet and shower,
ceiling fan. Restaurant, bar and
terrace. **$**

Kelebek
Mentefleoglu Mahallesi, Kalkan.
Tel: (0242) 844 3770.
Fax: (0242) 844 3771.
20 rooms with toilet and shower,
phone, air conditioning. Restaurant,
bar, garden, pool. **$$**
Pirat
Marina, Kalkan.
Tel: (0242) 844 3178.
Fax: (0242) 844 3183.
126 rooms with bathroom, phone,
air conditioning. Restaurant, bar,
shop, pool, diving centre. **$$$**

KAŞ

Aquapark
Çukurbag Peninsula, Kaş.
Tel: (0242) 836 1901.
Fax: (0242) 836 1992.
124 rooms with bathroom, phone,
air conditioning, balcony.
Restaurants, bars, pool, beach,
garden, disco, shop. **$$$$**
Begonvil Hotel
Küçük Çakıl Mevkii
Tel: (0242) 836 3079
Typical whitewashed and lattice-
balcony Med style, but this is a
clean, pretty and well-run hotel. Just
15 rooms but most overlook the
sea. **$$**
Club Phellos
Dogruyol Sokak 4, Kaş.
Tel: (0242) 836 1953.
Fax: (0242) 836 1890.
81 rooms with bathroom, air
conditioning, balcony. Restaurant,
pool, garden. In city centre. **$$$**
Hamarat Pension
Çukurbag Peninsula, Kaş.
Tel: (0242) 836 1547.
8 rooms. Kitchen. **$**
Kekova Hotel
Atatürk Bulvarı
(entrance opposite the bus station).
Tel: (0242) 836 1950.
Fax: (0242) 836 1952.
24 rooms in a quiet part of town
with upmarket amenities. **$**
Korsan Hotel
Çukubağ Yarımadası.
Tel: (0242) 836 3145.
A small (20-bed) hotel on the
Peninsula. Great sea views and
smart service. Moderately priced
but with many extras. **$$**

Mimosa
Elmalı Caddesi, Kaş.
Tel: (0242) 836 1272.
Fax: (0242) 836 1368.
24 rooms with toilet, shower,
phone, fan. Restaurant, bar,
disco. **$$**

Puya Pension
Meltem Sokak 6, Kaş.
Tel/fax: (0242) 836 2163.
12 rooms with toilet and shower,
phone. Restaurant, bar. **$**

Uzun Pension
Yeniyol Mahallesi, Kaş.
Tel: (0242) 836 1721.
Fax: (0242) 836 1697.
17 rooms. Breakfast room, bar. **$**

Medusa Hotel
Küçük Çakıl Mevkii No. 61.
Tel: (0242) 836 1440.
Fax: (0242) 836 1441.
Forty rooms overlooking the
sea with own beach, pool, bars
and restaurants. Very popular
hotel, advance booking
advisable. **$$$**

Rhea
Küçük Çakıl Mevkii
Tel: (0242) 836 3084.
Fax: (0242) 836 1788.
Upmarket pension with
wonderful sea views and air
conditioning. **$$**

Sardunya Hotel
Hastane Caddesi, Kaş.
Tel: (0242) 836 3080/81.
Fax: (0242) 836 3082.
Clean, neat rooms, many
overlooking the sea. The hotel does
not look much different from most
others in Kaş, but it is cheerful and
efficient, and many tourists return
for repeat holidays. **$$**

Yalı Pension
Hastane Caddesi 11, Kaş.
Tel: (0242) 836 1132.
Küçük Çakıl Mevkii.
Tel: 242-836 3062/64.
Fax: 242-836 3063
E-mail: herahotel@superonline.com
Classical grandeur but with
columns hand-carved circa 1997!
Open all year round. 40 rooms,
suites, fitness centre, pool and
jacuzzi. The only Turkish Bath
(hamam) for miles around and
many locals use it. This is now
Kaş' only luxury hotel of any note
and reliability. **$$$$**

KEMER

In many districts around the
Mediterranean coast west of
Antalya City (including Kemer,
Çamyuva, Göynük, Beldibi and
Tekirova), accommodation
facilities mainly consist of holiday
villages, club/resorts and large
hotels. These have, almost
invariably, extensive gardens,
large swimming pools, many types
of sea and land sports, nightclubs, fitness centres, Turkish
baths, children's clubs, etc. The
rooms usually have air
conditioning and minibars.
   To save space, we are listing only
addresses, phone and fax numbers
and number of rooms. For smaller
hotels and pensions, facilities will
be stated for each place.

Ambassador Plaza Apart Hotel
Kavaklı Caddesi 14, Kemer.
Tel: (0242) 814 5030.
Fax: (0242) 814 5035.
67 flats with bathroom, phone, air
conditioning, kitchen, refrigerator,
balcony. Restaurant, bar,
babysitting, swimming pool, beach,
garden, Turkish bath, fitness
centre, shops. **$$**

Belhan
Çifte Çeşmeler, Beldibi, Kemer.
Tel: (0242) 824 8054.
Fax: (0242) 824 8733.
21 rooms with toilet, shower,
phone, air conditioning. Restaurant,
bar, pool, garden, beach. **$$$**

Club Alda
Beldibi, Kemer.
Tel: (0242) 824 8151.
Fax: (0242) 824 8159.
Large holiday village with 364
rooms. **$$$$**

Club Aldiana Milta
Göynük, Kemer.
Tel: (0242) 815 1650.
Fax: (0242) 815 1680.
Large holiday village with 394
rooms. **$$$$**

Club Hotel Sato-Montana
Beldibi, Kemer.
Tel: (0242) 824 8460.
Fax: (0242) 824 8462.
90 rooms with toilet and shower,
phone, air conditioning, balcony.
Restaurant, bar, pool, garden,
health cabin, disco, sports. **$$$**

Club Phaselis
Kemer.
Tel: (0242) 815 1631.
Fax: (0242) 815 1637.
Holiday village with 296 rooms. **$$$**

Club Turtle's Marco Polo
Çamyuva, Kemer.
Tel: (0242) 824 6336.
Fax: (0242) 824 6346.
Holiday village with 404 rooms. **$$$**

Dragos
Deniz Caddesi 37, Kemer.
Tel: (0242) 814 2489.
Fax: (0242) 814 3241.
58 rooms with toilet, shower,
phone, air conditioning, balcony.
Restaurant, bars, pool. **$$**

Elit Hotel
Çifte Çeşmeler Mevkii, Beldibi,
Kemer.
Tel: (0242) 824 8629.
Fax: (0242) 824 8453.
43 rooms with toilet, shower, phone,
TV, air conditioning, minibar, balcony.
Restaurant, bar, pool, disco, garden,
health cabin, beach, sports. **$$$**

Favori Aqua Resort
Çamyuva, Kemer.
Tel: (0242) 824 6214.
Fax: (0242) 824 6210.
133 rooms. **$$$$**

Gelidonya Club
Atatürk Bulvarı, Kemer.
Tel: (0242) 814 5041.
Fax: (0242) 814 5045.
51 rooms with toilet and shower,
phone, air conditioning, minibar,
balcony. Restaurant, bars, pool,
garden, beach, TV room. **$$$**

Grand Hotel Kemer Vista
Göynük Beldesi, Kemer.
Tel: (0242) 815 1700.
Fax: (0242) 815 1697.
318 rooms. **$$$$**

Kiris World Magic
Kemer.
Tel: (0242) 824 6800.
Fax: (0242) 824 6820.
410 rooms, 60 villas. **$$$$**

**Naturland Eco Park and Resort
Hotels**
Çamyuva, Mevkii, Kemer.
Tel: (0242) 824 6214.
Fax: (0242) 824 6210.
A tourist complex devoted to
environmentally friendly tourism.
Rooms, suites, aqua paradise,
organic farm and ranch with horse
riding. **$$$**

Park Kimeros Holiday Village
Göynük, Kemer.
Tel: (0242) 815 1663.
Fax: (0242) 815 1671.
244 rooms. **$$$**
Pirate's Beach Club
Tekirova, Kemer.
Tel: (0242) 821 4001.
Fax: (0242) 821 4003.
Holiday village consisting of 256
rooms. **$$**
Phaselis Rose
Tekirova, Kemer.
Tel: (0242) 821 4780.
Fax: (0242) 821 4792.
300 rooms. **$$$$**
Seagull
Çifte Çesmeler Mevkii, Beldibi,
Kemer.
Tel: (0242) 824 8465.
Fax: (0242) 824 8466.
50 rooms with toilet and shower,
phone, air conditioning, balcony.
Restaurant, bars, pool, beach,
sports. **$$$**

KÖYCEGIZ

Kaunos
Cengiz Topel Caddesi, Köycegiz.
Tel: (0252) 262 4288.
Fax: (0252) 262 4836.
40 rooms with toilet and shower,
phone, balcony. Restaurant, bar,
pool, lake sailing, disco. **$$**
Özay
Kordon Boyu 11, Köycegiz.
Tel: (0252) 262 4300.
Fax: (0252) 262 2000.
32 rooms with toilet and shower,
phone, balcony, central heating.
Restaurant, bar, pool, garden, lake
sailing, disco. **$$**
Panorama Plaza
Cengiz Topel Caddesi 69, Köycegiz.
Tel: (0252) 262 3773.
Fax: (0252) 262 3633.
28 rooms with toilet and shower,
phone, TV, balcony. Restaurant,
bars, pool, garden, health cabin,
sports. **$**

PATARA

Beyhan Patara Resort Hotel
Gelemiş Köyü. Patara.
Tel: (0242) 843 5096.
132 rooms with bathroom, phone,
air conditioning, TV, minibar.
Restaurants, bar, swimming pool,
garden, Turkish bath, gym, disco,
sports. **$$$**
Golden Pension
Patara, Kalkan.
Tel: (0242) 843 5162. **$**
Hotel Mehmet
Patara, Kalkan.
Tel: (0242) 843 5032.
Fax: (0242) 843 5078.
Pension. **$**
Patara View Point
Gelemiş Köyü, Patara.
Tel: (0242) 843 5184.
Fax: (0242) 843 5022.
Pension. **$**

SIDE-MANAVGAT

There are thousands of big, bold,
beautiful and ugly hotels and
holiday clubs in and around Side.
They all seem to have thought of
absolutely everything that you might
want on holiday, as well as many
things you might not, but you're not
likely to get the blues in this
bustling metropolis.

Apollo Pension
Near the Temple of Apollo, Side.
Tel: (0242) 753 1941.
Bungalows. **$$**
Arkaç Hotel
Manavgat, Side.
(On the sea side of the main road
before turning off to Side)
Tel: (0242) 742 3983.
Fax: (0242) 742 3395.
This is a wonderful hotel
with just 34 rooms built in
caravanserai style. Pool and air
conditioning. A stylish and
modern *hamam* (Turkish Bath).
Beauty treatments also available.
Most business focuses on day
trips for this alone and the rooms
are seldom used for overnight
stays. Front rooms face onto the
main coastal road and it can
be noisy. **$$$**

Büyük Sürmeli
Özler Caddesi 175, Kuruköprü,
Adana.
Tel: (0322) 352 3600.
Fax: (0322) 352 1945.
166 rooms with air conditioning,
minibar. Facilities include swimming
pool, casino, night club, Turkish
bath, gym. **$$$$**
Caesars Resort
Kumköy, Side.
Tel: (0242) 753 2480.
Fax: (0242) 753 1852.
175 rooms with air conditioning,
minibar. Facilities include, pools,
beach, beauty and fitness centres,
Turkish bath, conference centre,
casino, disco, sports. **$$$$**
**Dedeman Club Blue Waters
Holiday Village**
Sorgun, Manavgat.
Tel: (0242) 756 9464.
Fax: (0242) 756 9556.
312 rooms with air conditioning.
Pool, beach, disco, Turkish bath,
health cabin, shop, sports. **$$$$**
Excelsior Corinthia
Titreyengöl Mevkii, Sorgun,
Manavgat.
Tel: (0242) 756 9110.
Fax: (0242) 756 9114.
151 rooms all with air conditioning.
Pools, beach, disco, Turkish bath,
fitness centre, shops, sports. **$$$$**
Hotel Cats Garden
Yalı Mahallesi
1010 Sokak No. 1.
Tel: (0242) 753 2352.
Fax: (0242) 753 3029.
A simple but pretty hotel in a quiet
area, ½ mile/1 km from Side town
centre. 65 rooms and 30 suites.
The 35 apartments are well fitted,
neat and clean. Pool and
restaurant. Beach 500 metres. **$$**
Hotel Tropic and Apartments
Deniz Bükü Mevkii. Side.
Tel: (0242) 753 1304/2296.
Fax: (0242) 753 2297.
Excellent hotel and self-catering
flatlets close to the sea. The same
enterprising owner runs the ostrich
farm just outside Manavgat.
Hotel Turquoise
P.O. Box 70, Side.
Tel: (0242) 756 9330.
Fax: (0242) 756 9345.
418 rooms and 30 apartments.

Private beach and a myriad of water sports. Four rooms for disabled visitors. **$$$**

Kleopatra
Manavgat.
Tel: (0242) 753 1033.
Fax: (0242) 753 3738.
42 rooms with bathroom, phone. Restaurant, bar. **$$**

Morning Star Pension
Barbaros Sokak, Side.
Tel: (0242) 753 1134.
Fax: (0242) 753 1389.
6 rooms. **$**

Novotel Turquoise
Acısu Mevkii, Sorgun, Side.
Tel: (0242) 756 9330.
Fax: (0242) 756 9345.
272 rooms with air conditioning, minibar. Facilities include pools, beach, Turkish bath disco, gym, shops, sports. **$$$$**

Paradise Apart Hotel
Titreyengöl Mevkii, Sorgun, Manavgat.
Tel: (0242) 756 9210.
Fax: (0242) 756 9269.
Holiday village with 285 apartments and 50 studios with kitchen, air conditioning. Pool, beach, nightclub, fitness centre, shops, sauna, sports. **$$$$**

Resit Ener Tesisleri Mocamp
Girne Bulvarı 138, Adana.
Tel: (0322) 321 2758.
Fax: (0222) 321 2775.
16 rooms with toilet & shower, phone, air conditioning, minibar. Restaurant, garden, swimming pool, camping. **$$$**

Seyhan
Turhan Cemal Beriker Bulvarı 30, Adana.
Tel: (0322) 457 5810.
Fax: (0322) 454 2834.
140 rooms with air conditioning, minibar. Facilities include pool, casino, night club, Turkish bath, gym. **$$$$**

Sidelya
Çolaklı Beldesi, Manavgat.
Tel: (0242) 763 6370.
Fax: (0242) 763 6114.
271 rooms with balcony. Pool, beach, shop, sports. **$$$**

Sunrise Golf Hotel
Kızılagaç Mevkii, Manavgat.
Tel: (0242) 748 2610.
Fax: (0242) 748 2635.

501 rooms with air conditioning, minibar. Pools, beach, Turkish bath, gym, disco, sports, golf. **$$$$**

Sunrise Queen Hotel
Side.
Tel: (0242) 753 4783.
Fax: (0242-753 4760
Rather tacky exterior, but the complex has an enormous variety of rooms, including honeymoon suites, jacuzzi suites, 20 non-smoking rooms and 3 rooms for disabled guests. Health centre, tennis courts and beauty parlour. **$$$$**

ANAMUR

Hermes
Iskele Civarı Mevkii, Anamur.
Tel: (0324) 814 3950.
Fax: (0324) 814 39 95.
70 rooms with air conditioning. Restaurant, bars, pool, beach, disco, sauna. **$$$**

Vivanco
Kaledibi Mevkii, Bozyazı, Anamur.
Tel: (0324) 851 4200.
Fax: (0324) 851 2291.
66 rooms with air conditioning, minibar. Facilities include pool, beach, disco, sports. **$$$$**

Yan
Anamur Iskele Mahallesi, Yalı Evleri, Anamur.
Tel: (0324) 814 2123.
Fax: (0324) 816 4888.
24 rooms with bathroom. Facilities include restaurant, bar and swimming pool. **$$**

ANTAKYA

Büyük Antakya
Atatürk Caddesi 8, Antakya.
Tel: (0326) 213 5860.
Fax: (0326) 213 5869.
72 rooms with air conditioning, minibar, phone. Restaurant, bars, disco, shops, games room. **$$$**

Orontes Hotel
Istiklal Caddesi No 58.
Tel: (0326) 214 5931/32.
Fax: (0326) 214 5933.
A comfortable mid-range choice in the city centre with 61 rooms and two well-equipped suites. **$$**

BELEK AND SERIK REGION

The Belek area was a dream of the Turkish Tourism Ministry in the 1980s. They examined the Mediterranean Coast in detail at the beginning of the 1990s and brought Japanese and other investors to the area. But, eventually, they settled on Belek and Serik as the 'Golden Rectangle' where man's skill could complement the environment. Superb championship golf courses with all the related facilities are now on offer, and are world-renowned.

Adora Golf Resort Hotel
Belik, Serik.
Tel. (0242) 725 4051.
Fax: (0242) 725 4071
E-mail: adora@verisoft.com.tr
www.leonardo.com.tr
Everything you would expect of a 425 room luxury complex with a golf course on your doorstep. This was one of the original 'golf' hotels built before there was even a golf course! **$$$$**

Altis Golf Hotel
Belek, Serik
Tel: (0242) 725 4242.
Fax: (0242) 725 4234.
E-mail: info@altis.com.tr
Internet: www.altis.com.tr
A mature, world class resort. **$$$$**

Antbel Belek
Üçkum Tepesi Mevkii, Belek, Serik.
Tel: (0242) 725 4102.
Fax: (0242) 725 4268.
Another Belek institution, this is the tourism arm of an industrial concern. But this luxury complex has kept much of the individuality and personal touch emphasised by the original owner. **$$$$**

Gloria Golf Resort
Acısu Mevkii, PO Box 27, Belek, Serik.

Tel: (0242) 715 1520.
Fax: (0242) 715 1525
www.gloria.com.tr
One of the main golf resorts on the coast. Villas, suites, Junior suites and accommodation for physically challenged guests. Tennis, squash and fitness centre. **$$$$**

Merit Arcadia
Iskele Mevkii
Belek Tourism Centre, Belek
Tel: (0242) 715 1100.
Fax: (0242) 715 1080.
E-mail: merithotels@turk.net
www.merithotels.com
This establishment offers everything you could want or dream of. Situated on the Mediterranean coast with service to match the location. **$$$$**

Sirene City
Belek, Serik.
Tel: (0242) 725 4130.
Fax: (0242) 725 4149/4150.
As the name says, not a resort but a city. Olympic pool and pubs jostle with facilities for children. All amenities and even locals come here to chill out. **$$$**

Tatbeach Golf Hotel
PO Box 01, Belek Tourism Centre, Serik.
Tel: (0242) 725 4076.
Fax: (0242) 725 4099.
E-mail: info@tatbeach.com
www.tatbeach.com
This resort changes hands on a regular basis between large conglomerates, but maintains a good standard and has excellent facilities. It is one of the founding members of the National Golf Club in Belek. **$$$$**

ISKENDERUN

Grand Hotel Ontur
Muammer Aksoy Caddesi 8, Iskenderun.
Tel: (0326) 616 2400.
Fax: (0326) 616 2410.
95 rooms with air conditioning, minibar. Restaurant, bars and a disco. **$$$$**

Arsuz
Arsuz (Uluçınar), Iskenderun.
Tel: (0326) 643 2444.
Fax: (0326) 643 2448.

104 rooms with bathroom, phone, central heating. Restaurant, bars, beach, sports. **$$$**

KIZKALESI

Club Barbarossa
Kızkalesi, Erdemli.
Tel: (0324) 523 2364.
Fax: (0324) 523 2090.
103 rooms with air conditioning, TV. There is a restaurant, bars, swimming pool, beach and a variety of sports on offer. **$$$**

Kilikya
Kızkalesi, Erdemli.
Tel: (0324) 523 2116.
Fax: (0324) 523 2084.
63 rooms with air conditioning, minibar. Restaurant, bars, pool, beach and sports available. **$$$**

Yaka
Kızkalesi, Erdemli.
Tel: (0324) 523 2041.
Fax: (0324) 523 2448.
17 rooms, all with bathroom. Restaurant and a bar. **$$**

MERSIN

Gondol
Gazi Mustafa Kemal Bulvarı 20, Mersin.
Tel: (0324) 234 1200.
Fax: (0324) 234 1207.
78 rooms with air conditioning, minibar. Pool, gym, disco. **$$$$**

Hilton Sa
Adnan Menderes Bulvarı, Mersin.
Tel: (0324) 326 5000.
Fax: (0324) 326 5050.
E-mail: salesflmersin@hilton.com.
www.hilton.com
189 rooms with air conditioning, minibar. Facilities include pool, casino, disco, fitness centre, conference hall. **$$$$**

Sahil Martı
Silifke Caddesi, Mezitli, Mersin.
Tel: (0324) 358 3700.
Fax: (0324) 358 1716.
61 rooms with air conditioning, minibar. Restaurant, bar, pool, beach, disco, gym. **$$$**

Ölüdeniz

Belcekiz Beach Holiday Village
Tel: (0252) 617 0077.
Fax: (0252) 617 0372.
E-mail: belcekiz@superonline.com
www.belcekiz.com
Tel: (0252) 616 6009.
Fax: (0252) 616 6448.
Colourful, low-rise holiday village with a pool and jacuzzi, shopping mall, hamam and two restaurants, on the beach within easy walking distance of the lagoon. Closed in winter. **$$$**

Hillside Holiday Village
Kalemya Köyü on the road to Ölüdeniz, Fethiye.
Tel: (0252) 614 8360.
Fax: (0252) 614 1470.
E-mail: hbc@hillside.com.tr
www.hillside.com.tr/hbc
A holiday haven surrounded by pine trees and mountains. Theme attractions, sporting activities. **$$$**

Hotel Meri
Inside the Ölüdeniz National Park.
Tel: (0252) 617 0001.
Fax: (0252) 617 0010.
Comfortable 75-room hotel over-looking the lagoon, with two pools, a private beach and watersports. Closed in winter. **$$**

Hotel Montana Pine Resort
Ovacık Mah., Ölüdeniz Beldesi.
Tel: (0252) 616 7108.
Fax: (0252) 616 6451.
Charming hotel in the pine forests overlooking the lagoon. Three pools, tennis courts and a gym and games room. Shuttle bus to the beach. Closed in winter. **$$$**

Ocakköy Holiday Village
Ovacık Köyü, on the road to Ölüdeniz.
Tel: (0252) 616 6155/56
Fax: (0252) 61661 58
30 natural, comfortable stone low-rise cottages here. Wheel chair access. Peace and quiet. **$$**

Yumak Apart
On the way to Babadaş
Ovacık Köyü. Ölüdeniz.
Tel: (0252) 616 6995.
Fax: (0252) 616 785.
E-mail: karayumak@superonline.com
Modern apartments for up to four
people with pool and garden. **$$$**

SILIFKE

Altınorfoz Banana
Atakent, Silifke.
Tel: (0324) 722 4211.
Fax: (0324) 722 4215.
112 air conditioned rooms. Pool,
beach, Turkish bath, sports. **$$$**
Pinepark Holiday Club
Yeşilovaçık, İçel.
Tel: (0324) 747 5518/5519.
Fax: (0324) 747 5066.
E-mail: info@mesa.com.tr.
www.mesa.com.tr
58 rooms, 20 villas and 38
apartments. Private beach and
pool. **$$$**
Tolya Hotel
Atakent. Silifke.
Tel: (0324) 722 2144.
Fax: (0324) 722 2145.
Private hotel in the city centre with
30 rooms and private beach. **$$**

Where to Eat

Choosing a restaurant

It is difficult to go hungry in Turkey.
From the sesame sprinkled bread
rings *(simit)* sold in every street to
the most elaborate Ottoman palace
cuisine, there is something here for
all appetites.

There are also plenty of foreign
restaurants. Urban Turks have also
taken to the international fast-food
chains such as Pizza Hut and
McDonald's. Here, these chains
have an upmarket image, since for
Turks they are relatively expensive.
Many affluent Turks have travelled,
with the result that they love more
sophisticated eating out too, so you
can find fashionable restaurants
offering anything from sushi to
spaghetti.

The best hotels often have
excellent restaurants, and lavish
buffets are often available in their
coffee shops. However, don't
assume that fancy décor and well-
dressed waiters necessarily mean a
good meal; often you will find the
simpler restaurants give you better
service and tastier food.

Restaurant Types

The word *restoran* is applied to
almost anywhere where food is
served. Turkish restaurants fall into
clearly defined categories:
● **Balık lokantası:** fish restaurants
serving hot and cold *meze* (a mixed
selection of starters, which can
make up a whole meal), freshly
caught fish and shellfish. You can
look at the fish available to help you
decide what to choose. Fish is more
expensive than other food in Turkey,
and is normally priced by weight.
● **Çayhane/Kahvehane:** local tea or
coffee houses. Some Turkish men

seem to spend their lives in them,
smoking and playing backgammon,
but these are not places where
foreigners would be welcome.
● **Et lokantası:** restaurant
specialising in meat dishes.
● **Kebapçı:** a kebab house, offering
various kinds of kebabs.
● **Köfteci:** a meatball specialist.
● **Lokanta:** the basic
neighbourhood restaurant, feeding
local businessmen at lunchtime, as
well as visitors. These are reliable
places to eat, and it is easy to see
what you are getting as the food
displayed in hot cabinets. Once you
have chosen, a waiter will bring your
food to your table.
● **Mantı/Gözleme Evi:** serve
Turkish ravioli and filled pancakes.
● **Meyhane:** translated somewhat
inadequately as "tavern". Some of
these places are smoky drinking
dives, dedicated to wine (and
sometimes song) over food, but the
best are also famous for their
delicious cooking. *Meze* are often
especially good here.
● **Muhallebici:** Turkish pudding
shop – for milk puddings and
baklava, plus chicken dishes.
● **Ocakbası:** grill restaurants, where
you can sit at a table set around a
charcoal fire and cook your own
choice of meat (though, of course, if
you prefer, the restaurant will do it
for you). Breads, rice and salads
will also be on offer.
● **Pastane:** at a Turkish pastane –
the word *pasta* means pastry or
gateau in Turkish – you can buy
flaky *su böreği* (baked layers of
pastry with cheese and parsley),
gateaux and desserts, and often sit
and eat on the premises. Coffee
and tea are not always available.
● **Pideci/Lahmacun:** these
establishments specialise in the
Turkish equivalent of pizza.

Restaurant Listings

Eating on the run is a national
characteristic. If Turks are hungry,
they do not believe in waiting or
hanging on until the next meal
Convenient places to grab a
sandwich, *tost* or *pide* are on every
corner. Eating on the street is

common and many street sellers make their living catering for compulsive snackers. Street sellers sell a range of foods, including stuffed mussels (*midiye*), simit, pilav and chicken pieces kept warm over a gas-fired oven. Köfte sellers dish out small hamburgers cooked to order as you wait. Baked potatoes are another favourite and come with a choice of enticing sauces and embellishments.

Usually these are fine to eat but, in summer months, try to avoid foods with mayonnaise or egg, which can cause serious stomach upsets. Turks have expressed some concerns of their own that some of their street cuisine culture may not exactly conform to European Union health and safety standards.

Thrace & Marmara

On the whole, restaurants in this area are average provincial establishments with no frills, quite unlike the luxury restaurants found in Istanbul, Ankara and the coastal resorts. Telephone reservation is unusual and rarely necessary.

BURSA

In addition to several restaurants in the Kültürpark, which serve traditional Turkish food, there are several fish restaurants tucked away behind a fishmonger's in Alt Parmak in the city centre. These restaurants serve alcohol and have something of the lively atmosphere of Istanbul's *meyhanler*.

Cumurcul
Çekirge Caddesi.
Tel: (0224) 235 3707.
Attractively converted old house in Çekirge, with the usual range of *meze*, kebabs and grills. Reservations at weekends. **$$**
Inegol Köfteci
Atatürk Caddesi 48.
For a change from kebabs, try the *Inegol köfte* (grilled meatballs served with raw onion rings). Open all year. **$**

Kebabçi Iskender
Unlü Caddesi 7, Heykel.
Tel: (0224) 221 4615.
Popular with the people of Bursa. The owners claim to be descended from the inventor of the famed *Iskender kebab*. Open all year. No credit cards. **$**

ÇANAKKALE

Akol Hotel Restaurant
Kordonboyu Caddesi.
A varied menu of Turkish and international dishes, and fine views of the ships that pass through the straits. Open all year. Major credit cards accepted. **$$**
Aussie & Kiwi
Yalı Caddesi, 32,
Antipodean haven serving homesick backpackers with such staples as Milo and Vegemite. **$**
Bizim Entellektüel ("Our Intellectuals" Restaurant)
On the quayside.
Meze, meat or fish and salad. Popular with Turkish diners. Open all year. **$**

The **Otel Anafartalar** (**$**), which is conveniently close to the ferry and has a wide range of *meze*, kebabs and fish, is also worth investigating. The **Anzac Hotel** is a popular meeting and eating place for backpackers, a few minutes' walk from the ferry, and serves good snacks and light meals. **$**

GELIBOLU (GALLIPOLI)

Gelibolu Restaurant
Near the harbour.
Famed for its fish dishes, particularly Gelibolu's speciality, *sardalya* (sardines). Open all year. **$–$$**
Ipek Urfa Kebab Salonu
Towards the town centre.
Tasty, spicy kebabs at reasonable prices. **$**

Aegean Coast

Look also at the hotel list for many of the best local restaurants Alternatively, head for the harbours.

Most are lined with small fish restaurants with outdoor terraces.

AYVALIK

Öz Canlı Balık
Gazinolar Caddesi.
Excellent *meze* and fish, near the seafront. No credit cards. **$$**

BERGAMA

Sağlam
Cumhuriyet Meydanı 29.
Tel: (0232) 632 8897.
A short distance from the tourist office on the other side of the street, with regional specialities, a courtyard and a second dining area upstairs. Open till 8pm all year. **$$**

BODRUM

Bodrum is Turkey's most sophisticated and well developed resort. Here you will also find some of the finest restaurants along the coast and many big-city eateries. None of them is cheap, but a few are reasonable and all represent good value for money. No other area offers such a variety of cuisines.
Alarga
Türkbükü Village, Bodrum Peninsula.
Tel: (0252) 377 5006.
A gourmet fish restaurant, popular with Turkish holidaymakers for its food as well as its spectacular sea view. Booking is essential. **$$$**
Amphora
Neyzen Tevfik Caddesi 172.
Tel: (0252) 316 2868.
Housed in an atmospheric old olive press building, Amphora serves Turkish dishes including seafood. **$$**
Bar-B-Q House
Bitez Village, Bodrum Peninsula.
Tel: (0252) 343 1724.
A stylish restaurant serving grilled dishes in a charming garden populated with citrus trees. **$$**
Buğay
Türkuyusu Caddesi.
Tel: (0252) 316 2969.
Serves outstanding vegetarian and organic dishes. The restaurant and

Price Guide

The following price categories are an indication only, based on a two-course meal for one (such as *meze*, kebab, salad and bread, with non-alcoholic drinks).

The top hotels tend to be expensive but food quality and service are consistent and reliable. The cost of alcoholic drinks can often be little different to what you would pay elsewhere.

Fish is now an expensive commodity and it is increasingly difficult to find a clean, simple and cheap hideaway with grilled fish and rakı. Expect to pay Western prices or close to. Restaurant prices vary from place to place. Some resorts regulate prices closely; others do not. Credit cards are widely accepted at most places except fast-food outlets or bufé stands.
$$$ = $20–35
$$ = $10–20
$ = $8–10

its owners are heavily into the Eco scene. Only home-made wine available. Open all year. **$$**

Bura
Atatürk Caddesi,
Dere Sokak No 18.
Tel: (0252) 313 2042.
A fashionable watering hole for gourmets. Elegant style complements international cuisine with Turkish touches. The bar gets crowded and is as popular as the restaurant. All credit cards accepted. **$$$**

Epsilon
Türgüt Reis Caddesi,
Keleş Çıkması 5.
Tel: (0252) 313 2964.
Top-notch chef recreates Ottoman and classic Turkish delicacies. Gourmet meals are enhanced by a lovely, secluded garden and a classy art gallery also on the premises. Expensive, but the lunch-time menu is more economical. Open all year round. **$$$**

Han
Kale Caddesi 23.
Tel: (0252) 316 7951.

Housed in an old *caravanserai* with an inner courtyard, Han is one of the oldest restaurants in Bodrum. The restaurant features Turkish music and belly dancing.

Ibo's
Meyhaneler Sokak, off Dr Alimbey Caddesi.
Locally known as the *Street of Taverns*, this alleyway is lined with many small restaurants and bars offering a jovial ambience, Turkish music, *meze* and fish dishes. Ibo's is one of the oldest and most popular venues on this street. **$$**

Kocadon
Neyzen Tevfik Caddesi 160.
Tel: (0252) 316 3705.
Lovely location near the marina with romantic Bodrum-style architecture. One of the best known addresses when it comes to seafood, and the accolades are well deserved. Expensive. **$$$**

Kortan
Cumhuriyet Caddesi 32.
Tel: (0252) 316 2141.
Great fresh seafood and a lovely view of the castle are offered at this terrace restaurant. **$$**

Ladda's
Neyzen Tevfik Caddesi
Tel: (0252) 313 1504.
One of Bodrum's several oriental cuisine restaurants, Ladda's is owned by a Thai woman, and the food is prepared by chefs from Bangkok. **$$$**

Mausolus
Neyzen Tevfik Caddesi.
Tel: (0252) 316 4176.
This downtown restaurant offers fish and *meze* dishes, and a view of the castle. **$$**

Nur
Cumhuriyet Caddesi, Eski Adilye Sokak 5.
Tel: (0252) 313 1065.
Meat and fish dishes served for lunch and dinner in this smart restaurant with a Mediterranean atmosphere. Open all year. **$$**

Pancho's
Cumhuriyet Caddesi, opposite Halikarnas Disco.
Tel: (0252) 316 0893.
Pancho's serves Argentine-style steaks and tasty salads. **$$$**

Picante
Türkkuyusu Mah. Külcu Sokak 8.
Tel: (0252) 316 0270.
It is worth seeking out this place for its intimate setting and appealing Mexican cuisine. The margaritas and Spanish tapas attract aficionados. Credit cards accepted. Closed out of season. **$$$**

Sandal
Atatürk Caddesi 74.
Tel: (0252) 316 9117.
Renowned for its Thai and Chinese food, the Sandal offers set meals and à la carte. Open all year. **$$**

Salmakis.
Cumhuriyet Caddesi, Bodrum Town, and at Bitez Village.
Authentic Chinese cuisine. **$$**

Secret Garden
Kumbahçe Mahallesi,
Sanat Okulu Sokak and 1019 Sokak.
Tel: (0252) 313 4479/5021.
Classic Mediterranean setting and outstanding imaginative cuisine by foreign chef/owner. Excellent wine list (said to be one of the best in Turkey) with sound advice on selections. Reservations essential. Closed Mondays. **$$$**

Sunny's
Cumhuriyet Caddesi.
Tel: (0252) 316 0716.
Sunny's serves British-style dishes, as well as some unusual Turkish *mezes*. **$$**

Bodrum Environs

There is no doubt that Bodrum is a heaving resort. When you tire of the crowds, head for the harbours of Yalıkavak and Gümüşlük, villages outside the centre, further down the Bodrum Peninsula. The style here is casual and sometimes the ambiance can be better than the food, but the village atmosphere is soothing.

Batı
Gümüşlük.
Tel: (0252) 394 3079.
You will not be disappointed by the meat or fish choices available here, served in a rustic setting.

Denizhan
Konacık
On the Türgüt Reis Road
Tel: (0252) 363 7674.

Price Guide

Based on 2-course meal for one:
$$$ = $20–35
$$ = $10–20
$ = $8–10

Specialising in the spicy dishes of Eastern Turkey, there are some unusual and little known regional specialities on the menu. Splendid setting. Fresh produce from own garden. Open all year. All cards. **$$**

Etobur
Ortakent.
On the Türgüt Reis Road close to turnoff to Yalıkavak
Tel: (0252) 358 5633
Very good meat restaurant with mouth-watering desserts. They specialise in grilled meat, and prices are moderate. **$$**

MB
Gereflaltı 101, Yalıkavak Village, Bodrum Peninsula.
Tel: (0252) 385 4959.
This is an upmarket, chic restaurant which serves good food in a comfortable, relaxing atmosphere. Gets extremely busy at times, so reservation is essential. **$$$**

Samdan
Yalıkavak Village, Bodrum Peninsula.
Tel: (0252) 364 4424.
The Bodrum branch of the elegant, gourmet restaurant chain, serving international cuisine. Advance reservations essential. **$$$**

Ship Ahoy
Türkbükü Village, Bodrum Peninsula.
Tel: (0252) 377 5070.
Set on a private jetty, Ship Ahoy is popular with the trendy set. An ideal place for people-watching, for winding down and for the good music at the bar. **$$$**

ÇESME

Körfez
On the waterfront.
Tel: (0232) 712 6718.
This popular restaurant has a good range of *meze* and fish dishes. Western dishes are also available,

but they may prove disappointing. Open all year. **$**

Other dependable restaurants on the same street are **Meydan, Sahil** and **Yalı**.

IZMIR

Bordo
Mustafa Kemal Sahil Bulvarı No. 44 (½ mile/1km after Tansas hypermarket), Narlıdere, Izmir.
Tel: (0232) 239 3870.
Located quite a long way from the central eating district of Izmir in a leafy, upmarket suburb. Splendid Turkish food served on the patio in summer and by the fireplace in winter. Moderate prices. Reservations essential. **$$**

Chinese Restaurant
1379 Sokak.
Tel: (0232) 483 0079.
The largest Chinese restaurant in town, offering a wide range of dishes. Easy to find on the street that runs behind the Hilton Hotel. Credit cards accepted. Open all year. **$$**

Deniz
Atatürk Caddesi 188-B.
Tel: (0232) 422 0601.
Very highly regarded by the citizens of Izmir, who return here regularly for the specialist fish dishes. Reservations often necessary. Cards accepted. Open all year. **$$$**

La Folie
Şehit Nevres Bulvarı No. 5/A, Alsancak, Izmir.
Tel: (0232) 463 5858.
Fax: (0232) 464 3338
In the city centre behind the Büyük Efes Hotel, this restaurant is away from the bustle of the Kordon eateries and serves adventurous food with Italian flavours. The sun dried tomatoes can be a bit overdone, however! **$$$**

Seçkin
M. Kemalettin Caddesi 16/A, Konak.
Tel: (0232) 489 2404.
Upstairs is an Internet café, while at street level there is an efficient restaurant offering a host of Turkish dishes and desserts. Open all year round. **$**

KUSADASı

Club Cappello
Akyar Mevkii.
Tel: (0256) 614 4043.
Within walking distance from the town centre, just before the Korumar Hotel. Intimate atmosphere. Local fish and meat dishes. Open all year. Reservation advisable. **$$**

Golden Pizzeria
Ismet Inönü Bulvarı 19.
Tel: (0256) 614 5417.
In the centre of town, this pleasant and clean restaurant serves a wide range of pizzas; also open for breakfast. Open all year. **$**

Istanbul Meyhanesi
Kaleiçi Kışla Sokak No. 7.
Tel: (0256) 613 1677.
Lively and noisy taverna atmosphere with Turkish music. Recommended primarily because of the excellent traditional Turkish starter menu accompanied by rakı or wine. **$$**

Kazım Usta
Balıkçı Limanı (Fisherman's Harbour).
Tel: (0256) 614 1266.
An enduring seafood legend in and around Kuşadası, which means it trades heavily on tradition. Flashes of brilliance and a stunning selection of *mezes*, even if served by deadpan staff. **$$**

Sultan Han
Bahçe Sokak 8.
Tel: (0256) 614 6380/614 3849.
Touristy, but so what? A variety of local dishes and an appetising selection of *meze* in a restaurant that aims to evoke a traditional Turkish-style atmosphere. Credit cards accepted. Open all year. **$$$**

MARMARIS

Alba
Kaleiçi 30, Sokak 10.
Tel: (0252) 412 4299.
Delicious European cuisine, complemented by a wonderful panoramic hilltop view. **$$$**

Birtat Restaurant
Barbaros Caddesi 19 (on the yacht harbour).
Tel: (0252) 412 1076.

Beautiful setting and standard Turkish fare at affordable prices. **$$**

Begonya
Hacı Mustafa Sokak No. 101 (bar Street).
Tel. (0252) 412 4095.
Better known as a hotel but the restaurant, added in 1998, has quickly achieved recognition for its unusual Turkish dishes and imaginative European fare. Closed in winter. All cards accepted. **$$**

Dede
Barbaros Caddesi.
Tel: (0252) 413 1289.
Fairly typical of the sea-facing restaurants lining the promenade near the tourist office. Large menu featuring familiar Western dishes as well as local fish selections. Open all year. **$$**

Napoli
Barbaros Caddesi, Barlar Sokak 70.
Tel: (0252) 412 6555.
Offers a good selection of pizzas. **$**

Pineapple
Netsel Marina.
Tel: (0252) 412 4999.
A stylish restaurant for good meat and fish dishes. From here, you can relax and watch the trendy yachting crowd at play. **$$**

Sandra's
Barbaros Caddesi 183-B.
Tel: (0252) 412 6932
Comprehensive menu that doesn't always succeed, but there are many interesting home-made specialities. Closed in winter. All credit cards accepted. **$$**

Yakamoz
Kemeraltı Caddesi, opposite Selen Otel.
Tel: (0252) 412 5160.
A well-established fish restaurant serving delicious food. **$$**

PRIENE

Şelâle
Güllübahçe.
Tel: (0256) 547 1009.
A pleasant place for lunch, situated close to Kuşadası; choose from the kebabs, meatballs and range of fish dishes displayed at the counter. Open all year. **$**

SELÇUK

Kalehan
Kalehan Hotel.
Tel: (0232) 892 6154.
Turkish dishes served as set meals or à la carte in this comfortable restaurant. Air-conditioning, reasonable prices and character. Open all year. **$–$$**

Şelçuk Köftecisi
Vergi Dairesi altı 37/J.
Tel: (0232) 892 6696.
This café specialises in meatballs, though the kebabs are good as well. It is often not found by visitors (partly due to its unassuming décor). Open all year. **$$**

Mediterranean Coast

FETHIYE

Anfora
Paspatur Hamam Sokak 5.
Tel: (0252) 612 1282.
Trendy décor, good Turkish and continental food, popular with groups. There are many other good restaurants in this buzzing old town street; take time to stroll and read the menus. **$$**

Fedir
Tutum Sokak 3.
Tel: (0252) 614 1095.
Good Turkish dishes offered at reasonable prices. **$$**

Çiftlik Restaurant
Islamlar Köyü.
Tel: (0242) 838 6155
There is not much else on offer except the trout here, which you can choose yourself. They will cook it any way you want. Rakı and other alcoholic drinks, salad and fruit are served on the oil-cloth table tops.

Meğri Lokantası
Ordukan Aş, Eski Cami Geçidi, Likya Sokak 8-9.
Tel: (0252) 614 4046.
Excellent seafood, *meze* and grills served al fresco. Open all year round. **$$**

Pizza Villa
Çarflı Caddesi 36.
Tel: (0252) 614 6451.
Offers tasty and inexpensive fare, including hot chicken wings. **$**

Cafés and Bars

Many smart cafés turn in to bars at night. In the cosmopolitan cities and resorts these are as subject to fashion as they would be in London or New York. Some will have live music.

Expensive hotels have glamorous, expensive bars: sometimes offering a spectacular view, for which you pay through the inflated price of the drinks. Others offer themed nights to bring in custom. In some of these bars you can find snacks; full meals may also be available.

● **Cafés** There are plenty of elegant European-style cafés springing up, offering Turks an experience that is not quite Turkish. The cafés offer French-style baguette sandwiches, Italian cappuccinos and American cheesecake. You'll find the "ladies who lunch" here as these are places to be seen..

Rafet Restaurant
Kordon Boyu.
Tel: (0252) 614 1106
On the harbour in the city centre, this restaurant has been going for almost 50 years and is well patronised for its wide range of meat, fish and meze dishes. **$$**

Yaka Park
Yaka Köyü (village).
Tel: (0252) 638 2011.
Yaka Park offer delicious fresh fish from their own trout farm. **$$**

Yat
Yat Limanı Karşısı, near Hotel Likya.
Tel: (0252) 614 7014.
A splendid seafront setting opposite the marina, with excellent fish and grills; Live music and belly dancing on occasions in summer. **$$**

KALKAN

For such a small place, Kalkan has a very comprehensive selection of fine restaurants. Try any of the attractive locations along the harbour front. Prices are well regulated here and menus display prices clearly. Everyone is friendly and even if you just want to watch the sunset and sip a beer, you'll be treated the same as if you order a four-course meal.

Alternatif
Yaliboyu Mah.
Tel: (0242) 844 3571.
The English owner here has been attracting clientele for over ten years with her adventurous and stylish cooking. With a bit of notice, special orders can be catered for. Closed in winter. **$$**

Belgin's Kitchen
Yaliboyu Mah.
Tel: (0242) 844 3614.
It looks a bit gimmicky with floor-level dining and Ottoman trappings, but there is no mistaking the home-style Turkish cooking. This is a serious kitchen with smart service to match. Closed in winter. **$$**

KAS

Bahçe
At the top of the main shopping street, opposite the sarcophagus.
Tel: (0242) 836 2370.
Outdoor garden open in summer only. Imaginative and cheerful home cooked meals but don't be fooled by the casual atmosphere. Oya Beceren is a serious professional cook and the service reflects this. Booking is essential. **$$**

Blue House
Ilkokul Sokak No. 9.
Tel: (0242) 836 2171.
Fazilet hanım is the most gracious of hostesses, and you eat right in her house on the terrace overlooking the harbour. How much more honest can you get than that? Open evenings only but, by request, she sometimes cooks lunch for special groups. Closed in winter. **$$**

Café Corner and **Merhaba Café** are two perennial favourites along the street from the PTT. Full breakfasts, brunch or a cappuccino with a gooey home-made cake pull in the customers. **$**

Chez Evy
Terzi Sokak 2.
Tel: (0242) 836 1253.
A unique blend of French country cooking and Turkish staples make this small backstreet restaurant one of the most popular on the Lycian coast; essential to book ahead. Closed in winter. **$$**

Çınar
Ibrahim Serin Sokak.
Tel: (0242) 836 1735.
A long-established Turkish restaurant with outdoor seating and reasonable prices. **$**

Eriş Lokantası
Cumhuriyet Meydanı
Gursoy Sokak.
Tel: (0242) 836 2134.
Fax: (0242) 836 1057.
Congenial French-speaking owner, leafy location and occasionally brilliant dishes make up for school-boy service and notable culinary lapses. Refuse any wines from the decorative overhead racks! **$$**

J.P. Spaghetti House
Öztürk Sokak (next to Orman Çay Bahçesi).
Tel: (0242) 836 1733.
Tasty spaghetti, ravioli, lasagne and tiramisu are offered in this friendly restaurant. **$$**

Mediterranean Café
Prominent corner location in the main square.
Tel: (0242) 836 1262.
Same owners as Bahçe (above) with the accent on fresh and well presented food. Open April to November and sometimes at New Year or other Turkish holidays. **$$**

Mercan
Harbour Front.
Tel: (0242) 836 1209.
The setting and cuisine are unbeatable, and the food, particularly the fish, is very good indeed. **$$**

Oba Ev Yemekleri
Çukurbağli Caddesi.
Tel: (0242) 836 1687.
Charming, laid-back family-run restaurant with a shady garden terrace and ever-changing variety of nourishing stews. Open all year. **$**

Smiley's
Uzun Çarsı Sokak 11.
Tel: (0242) 836 2812.

An attractive restaurant which offers garlic and cheese on *pide* bread in addition to a good selection of seafood dishes. **$$**

Sun Café and Restaurant
Hükümet Caddesi.
Tel: (0242) 836 1053.
Fax: (0242) 836 1924.
E-mail: suncafe@hotmail.com
Despite several moves, the owner has the same chef and turns out top-class Turkish food at very good prices. Ask if you want something special and they will cook it for you. Open all year round. Attractive terrace for summer dining. **$$**

Kemer
Derya Türk Mutfaği
Liman Caddesi.
Tel: (0242) 814 4775.
Basic local café with excellent food, Formica tables and friendly staff; some might like to avoid a few specialities, which include lamb's brains and tripe soup. Open all year. **$$**

Kemer Marina
Yat Limanı (on the edge of the marina).
Tel: (0242) 814 1192.
Upmarket, slick restaurant catering mainly to the international yachting crowd, with good Turkish food and a small bar. Summer only. **$$**

Olympos
Park Restaurant
Ulupınar Village (Köyü) on old road between Kemer and Olympos, Ulupınar, Kemer.
Tel: (0242) 825 7213.
A converted mill provides the ideal setting in which to eat their speciality, fresh trout. The lower level seating is down many flights of stairs next to a stream. Open all year. Fireplace in winter. **$$**

Patara
Golden Restaurant
Gelemiş Köyü.
Tel: (0242) 843 5162.
Best of a number of basic Turkish restaurants in the village, serving fish and grills. Closed in winter. **$**

SAKLıKENT

The sun and heat are fine but you will find that Turks often escape the suffocating summer temperture by heading for higher ground and fresh water. Saklıkent Gorge is about 50 km (30 miles) outside of Fethiye but is worth a visit.

Hidden Paradise (Kayıp Cennet)
Saklıkent.
Tel: (0252) 636 8406/8777.
Trout and other specialities. **$$**
Hüseyin Güseli'in Yeri
On the approach road to Saklikent Gorge.
Tel: (0252) 636 8113.
Turkish pancakes and grills cooked over an open fire are the highlights here. Closed in winter. **$**
Saklıkent Restaurant
(Within the gorge).
Tel: (0252) 636 8555
Turkish *mezes* and fresh trout is the stock in trade here. **$$**
Yaka Park
Yaka Köyü.
Tel: (0252) 638 2011.
Trout so fresh they swim up to the table at this trout farm/restaurant based in a restored windmill in cool, green parkland. Closed in winter. **$$**

ADANA

Anatolian Restaurant and Bar
Atatürk Caddesi 182, Incirlik.
Tel: (0322) 332 8022.
Hollywood-style Turkish restaurant adorned with carpets and cushions. A buffet designed to cater for the appetites of the American airforce personnel next door. **$$**
Büyük Onbasilar Restaurant
Gazipasa Bulvarı.
Airy first-floor restaurant with good food and service, overlooking one of the city's main squares. **$$**
Mesut
Vali Yolu, Ekin Sk, Vizon Apt Alti.
Tel: (0322) 453 3468.
Quiet suburban indoor restaurant, famous for classic Turkish food, a wide range of *meze* and wonderful kebabs. Open all year. **$$**

ALANYA

Arzum Mantı Evi
Atatürk Caddesi.
Tel: (0242) 513 9393.
Simple but delicious home cooking, with *mantı* and vegetarian dishes. **$**
Garden Restaurant
Keykubat Caddesi 5.
Tel: (0242) 513 8561.
Peaceful haven with live guitar or jazz, good food and a garden. Open all year. **$$**
Iskele Bar and Restaurant
Iskele Caddesi.
Tel: (0242) 513 1822.
Noisy, brash but immensely popular harbourfront hangout with a wide range of Turkish and international food, seafood and live music. **$$**

ANTAKYA

Anadolu
Hurriyet Caddesi 50/C.
Tel: (0326) 215 1541.
Drab town favourite where delicious food more than makes up for the poor décor. Broad range of *meze*, grills and kebabs. Open all year. **$$**
Didem Turistik Tesisleri
Reyhanli Yolu Uzeri.
Tel: (0326) 212 1928.
A good range of Turkish dishes. **$**
Sultan Sofresi
Istiklal Caddesi 18.
Tel: (0326) 213 8759.
Local neighbourhood restaurant on the river; good range of *meze*, and excellent soups, casseroles and kebabs. Open all year. **$$**

ANAMUR

Astor Restaurant
Iskele Mah, Inönü Caddesi.
Tel: (0324) 814 2280.
Shady beachfront terrace, serving simple *meze*, grills and fish. Closed in winter. **$**
Çelıkler/Kale
Mamure Kalesi Karşışı, Iskele.
Tel: (0757) 71358.
One of several small terraced restaurants near the castle, which are ideal for lunch before the chef turns tour guide. Shady parking is a

major benefit in summer. Open all year; small *pansiyon* in summer. **$**

ANTALYA

As one would expect, the harbour restaurants specialise in seafood. In addition to such standards as sea bass, red mullet and swordfish, you can sample the Turkish version of bouillabaisse, *tarança sis* (not skewered fish, as the name would suggest, but a stew using grouper, grida or sea bass as its base).

Near the corner of Atatürk and Cumhuriyet Caddesi is an alley of outdoor restaurants serving a variety of Turkish dishes, including *tandır*, or oven-baked lamb served with flat *pide* bread. Sold by weight, a 150g portion of *pide* should satisfy a sightseer's hunger.

The colourful jars lining the windows of the pickle seller *(turşucu)* are proof of the ingenuity of Turkish cuisine. There is a wide range of Turkish pickles, sold by the piece so sampling is simple. Jams and jellies find favour in Antalya, thanks to the enormous variety of local fruits. A speciality is rose jam.

As well as neighbourhood and harbour-front restaurants, all the big hotels have excellent dining rooms with international dishes. Expect to pay high prices but it's worth it for the service and professional touches.

Ahtapot
Kaleiçi, Yacht Marina, 38.
Tel: (0242) 247 1141.
A fish restaurant right on the harbour. **$$**
Alp Paşa Hotel
Barbaros Mahallesi,
Hesapçı Sokak No. 30–32, Kaleiçi.
Tel: (0242) 247 5676/243 0045.
Fax: (0242) 248 5074.

Natural Internet Café
Cumhuriyet Meydanı, Antalya.
E-mail: vural@antintercafe.com.tr
Talya Hotel
Classy place to browse in comfortable surroundings but slightly pricy.
Ayda Pastanesi
Opposite Turkish Airlines Office on Cumhuriyet Caddesi.
Cyber café which combines surfing the net with snacks and sticky buns. Stays open until midnight.

Non residents are welcome at Alp Paşa for lunch or dinner. Imaginative menu with Turkish cuisine and western dishes à la Turk. It is cosy in winter and al fresco in summer. $$$
Club 29
Kaleiçi, Yacht Marina, Antalya.
Tel: (0242) 241 6260.
Housed inside a restored warehouse with a superb view overlooking the harbour, this restaurant serves gourmet international and Turkish dishes. Complete with a terrace swimming pool, 29 turns into a disco after midnight. $$
Deniz
Karaalioglu Parkı, 1311 Sokak 7.
Tel: (0242) 241 5799.
Hidden away on a side street, this restaurant has exceptional sea views and equally good Turkish dishes. It regularly features Turkish dancing and floor shows later in the evening. $$$
Develi Restaurant
Konyaaltı.
Tel: (0242) 22912 00/01.
Part of a chain of kebab restaurants but they offer many other Turkish specialities and will cook almost anything you ask for. Service in the best Turkish tradition is formal and efficient. Attractive beach front location, generous portions and fair prices. $$
El Toro
Atatürk Caddesi 50/A.
Tel: (0242) 247 1024.
Italian pizzas and ice creams, steak dishes, fresh vegetables and salads

in a warm and attractive atmosphere. $$
Gaziantep
Konyaaltı Sahil Seridi 6.
Tel: (0242) 242 4250
Balbey Mahallesi, 410 Sokak 4, (in the Old Bazaar, situated opposite the Clock Tower).
Turkish grilled meat specialities, mezes and seafood dishes, served attentively. $$
Hisar Touriskik Tesisi
Cumhuriyet Meydanı, Tophanealtı.
Tel: (0242) 241 5281.
Still trading on its superb location, and locals complain that it is overpopulated with Russian girls. But it is an Antalya landmark and serves good, sometimes brilliant, food. The high prices have not affected its popularity. $$$
Kırk Merdiven
Musalla Sokak 2, Kaleiçi.
Tel: (0242) 242 9686.
Set in a cosy corner inside the fortress walls in the Old Quarter of Kaleiçi, this is an excellent restaurant. Fish and meat dishes and traditional Turkish mezes in a homely atmosphere, made warmer in winter with a fireplace. Piped classical Turkish music. $$
Kral Sofrası (King's Table)
Yacht Marina, Kaleiçi.
Tel: (0242) 241 2198.
Housed in a charming old building, Kral Sofrası is one of the most popular restaurants in Antalya. It serves delicious regional mezes, fish and meat dishes in a traditional and cosy decor. Not much sea view, but friendly and comfortable ambience more than compensates. $$
La Trattoria
Fevzi Çakmak Caddesi 3/C (opposite the Belediye).
Tel: (0242) 243 3931.
Trendy Turkish-English owned Italian restaurant. Heaps of delicious pasta and stodgy puddings. Friendly and efficent service. $$$
La Notte Fish
Iskele Caddesi 1, on the Marine Parade.
Tel: (0242) 243 2751
Still the best place to enjoy fish in the city. Romantic setting and all the trappings. No bargains to be had but everything is fresh and

beautifully cooked and presented. There is live music occassionally in the evenings. $$$
Maritime Bar and Restaurant
Sheraton Voyager Hotel, 100 Yıl Bulvarı.
Tel: (0242) 243 2432.
Gourmet international dishes and seafood are accompanied by live guitar music in the luxurious, lush green atmosphere of the largest five-star hotel in Antalya's city centre. $$$
Mermerli
Banyo Sokak 25, Kaleiçi.
Tel: (0242) 248 5484.
Established more than 50 years ago, the Mermerli Restaurant overlooks the Antalya Harbour and serves tasty food that has been popular with locals and visitors alike, at reasonable prices. $$
Met Fish Restaurant
Lara Yolu.
Tel: (0242) 321 1828/322 5879. .
One of Lara's best, offering delicious fish, sea views and a friendly family atmosphere. $$
Parlak
Behind Yapı Kredi Bankası, Clock Tower end of Kazım Özalp Caddesi 7.
Tel: (0242) 241 9160.
A typical Turkish lokanta (traditional restaurant) and tavern, Parlak serves tasty mezes and barbecued chicken in a welcoming ambiance. $$
Sıla
Iskele Caddesi 25, Kaleiçi.
Tel: (0242) 244 1910.
Inside a restored old building, with traditional decor and cool interiors. Large menu of Turkish dishes. $$
Sini
Hükümet Caddesi 34.
Tel: (0242) 244 4683.
The restored building still needs a bit more work, but this is a bustling city-centre eatery, and it gets very crowded at lunchtime. Salad bar, Turkish specialities and lots of cosmopolitan chatter. Near the Clock Tower.
Sırrı
Selçuk Mahallesi, Uzunçarsı Sokak 25, Kaleiçi.
Tel: (0242) 241 7239.
This original 19-century wooden building with 14 rooms and a court-

Price Guide

Based on 2-course meal for one:
$$$ = $20–35
$$ = $10–20
$ = $8–10

yard now serves as a restaurant and family home. **$$**

Tropic Terrace
Sheraton Voyager Hotel, 100 Yıl Bulvarı.
Tel: (0242) 243 2432.
The terrace restaurant of the Sheraton serves a wide menu in a luxurious atmosphere. **$$$**

Yalı Balıkevi
2061 Sokak No. 4, Eski Lara Yolu.
Tel: (0242) 323 1823.
Fax: (0242) 323 7700
Outside the mainstream of core eateries, this is a refreshing corner of solitude and an outstandingly good restaurant. Fish is a speciality but this restaurant does everything very well. **$$$**

Yat
Yacht Marina, Kaleiçi.
Tel: (0242) 242 4855.
Turkish and international dishes served in a lively atmosphere. **$$**

Yedi Memet
Konyaaltı Plajı.
Tel: (0242) 241 1641.
A long-established, traditional Turkish meat restaurant, Yedi Memet is very popular with the locals and always crowded, so it is advisable to book. **$$**

Yelken.
Yacht Marina 6.
Tel: (0242) 242 9789.
Another seafront restaurant serving well prepared Turkish dishes. **$$**

Yörükoglu.
Yenikapı (opposite Belediye).
Tel: (0242) 247 5171.
A traditional and popular Turkish restaurant with a nice garden. **$$**

Aspendos

Belkis Restaurant
Belkis Köyü, on road to the ruins.
Tel: (0242) 735 7263.
Simple riverfront restaurant near the ruins, specialising in traditional Turkish stews. Closed in winter. **$$**

Iskenderun

Hasan Baba
Ulucami Caddesi 43/E.
A good, simple kebab house. **$**

Köprülü Kanyon

Ada Insel
Köprülü Kanyon Yolu Üzeri, Beşkonak.
Tel: (0242) 765 3389.
Shady riverside terrace, before you reach the hubbub of Beşkonak. The food is simple (trout, kebabs and salad) but well cooked, with friendly, helpful owners. They also arrange rafting trips. Open all year. **$**

Mersin

Ali Baba Restaurant
Uluçarşi Otopark Girisi Karşısı.
Tel: (0324) 223 3088.
Good standard Turkish menu. Right by the main car park. **$$**

Pizzeria Ocin
Bahri Ok Ishani 39, off Atatürk Caddesi.
Rustles up spaghetti, pizzas etc. for a young crowd. **$$**

Side

Liman
71 Liman Caddesi (towards the temple).
Tel: (0242) 753 1168.
This is one of the best of the many fish restaurants lining the waterfront. Open all year. **$$**

Nergiz
Liman Caddesi, Selimiye Köyü.
Tel: (0242) 753 1467.
This large restaurant, on the main square beside the harbour, is where most tourists gravitate. The décor is attractive, and it has a large terrace and good seafood. Prices are marginally higher than others along the strip, but not exorbitant. Open all year. **$$**

Tarsus

Şellale
Tel: (0324) 624 8010.
The poshest of several restaurants and cafés clustered around the waterfall where Alexander the Great supposedly caught a chill that put his campaign back two months. The nicest place to eat in the hot, dusty city – either here or at the simple café next door, which confusingly shares its name. Open all year. **$$**

Hibeş

Antalya is well known for its citrus fruit and carnations but less for any specialty cuisine. However, *hibeş* is a dish found in Antalya but nowhere else in Turkey. It is a hot and very spicy sesame seed starter that uses tahini, the oil from the sesame seeds. The tahini is blended with garlic, lemon juice and hot red peppers and is spread on bread or crackers. If the seeds are roasted the traditional way over a wood fire and processed laboriously by hand, the dish has a distinctive earthy flavour. Almost every restaurant in Antalya makes it, but few promote it as a local delicacy! Its rather unattractive colour is not a culinary come-on but, if you try it, you will wonder why it is not more universally available.

Culture

Developing the Turkish people's interest in Western arts and culture was an important part of Atatürk's raft of reforms in the early years of the Republic. The most fundamental change was the switch from Arabic to Roman script, together with modernisation of the language; others included the introduction of Western art forms such as classical music, ballet and opera.

Cinema is very popular, and contemporary Turkish film-making is interesting, though of course you won't find English subtitles on Turkish films. Antalya and Izmir also host film festivals.

Traditional Turkish folk music is a living art, and immensely popular – you will hear some form of it everywhere. It has blended inextricably with Western pop and rock. As a result, Turkish pop has a decidedly ethnic flavour.

Music & Dance

CLASSICAL

Western art forms such as ballet, classical music and opera are now well established among the educated, secular classes. The opportunities for seeing performances vary from city to city. Istanbul, Ankara and Izmir have large cultural centres and their own symphony orchestras, ballet and opera companies, which tour elsewhere. The standard is variable, especially for opera and ballet.

It is not easy to find out about programmes much in advance, and tickets are often hard to obtain. Seats can be sometimes sold out or given away to sponsors before the public gets an opportunity to buy them.

If you are travelling inland from the Turkish Coast area, the annual cultural highlight in Turkey is the Istanbul Festival (April–July), which incorporates four linked festivals of music, theatre, cinema and jazz. It is organised by the Istanbul Foundation for Culture and Arts, which also runs the International Istanbul Biennial art exhibition. Banks and institutions sponsor other jazz, blues and classical festivals, which attract top performers. At international festivals you will get the opportunity to hear world-renowned soloists, orchestras and conductors, plus the cream of home-grown talent.

TRADITIONAL TURKISH

Turkey has an exceptionally rich musical tradition. Academics and folklore groups sponsor interest in *halk müziği* (folk music), which is still played at village weddings and festivals. Visitors are most likely to encounter this form of music at a concert or dance display organised for tourists. A "village" music and dance performance will often include a belly dancer.

Although some of the shows put on for tourists can be shoddily done, some of the more expensive hotel restaurantsl put on high quality folk music and dancing to accompany your Turkish dinner.

Types of music

Sanat and *Fasıl* music (both traditional Turkish styles) are best heard live, and are played in numerous bars and *meyhanes*.

Arabesk, melancholic and sentimental oriental pop ballads, will probably be the first thing you hear in Turkey, and will emanate from every taxi and minibus.

Classical Ottoman and religious music is played by distinguished groups such as those of the Istanbul Municipal Conservatory. This type of music can be heard in concert halls and on radio and

television, where it is sometimes perfomed live.

At some Dervish *tekkes* or lodges, visitors are permitted to watch the remarkable meditational whirling dance.

JAZZ, ROCK AND POP

Turkey is beginning to creep on to the international rock-band circuit: the Rolling Stones and Sting have recently played here. Home-grown bands thrive and live jazz plays in bars, nightclubs and concert halls.

Cinema

Screens are dominated by international films, mostly recent releases from the US. These are usually shown in the original language with Turkish subtitles (*alt yazılı*) – though the title of the film will be translated into Turkish. If the film has been dubbed, *Turkçe* (Turkish) or *ilk gösterim* (dubbed) will appear on the programme listing or poster outside the cinema – this will usually be the case with cartoons and films suitable for children. At any one time there will be a choice of a dozen or so foreign films in Izmir and Antalya. Most places of any size have a cinema.

If you want to see the latest Turkish movies with English subtitles, come during one of the major international film festivals. These include the Golden Orange Festival in Antalya (autumn) and the Istanbul Film Festival (spring).

There is a weekly free sheet in Turkish, *Sinema*, which you can pick up at any cinema; it lists the current week's programme.

Antalya
Altın Portakal
Kaleiçi.
Tel: (0242) 248 6302.
Kent
Şarampol Caddesi.
Tel: (0242) 243 2342.
Kültür Sineması
Atatürk Caddesi.
Tel: (0242) 241 6239.

Megapol Sineması
Özlem Sokak.
Tel: (0242) 237 0131.
Prestige
Metin Kasapoğlu Caddesi, Metropol
Çarşısı.
Tel: (0242) 312 0543.

Bodrum
Karya Princess
In the basement of the Karya Hotel.
Tel: (0252) 316 6272.
Sinema Bodrum
Outdoors; shows start 10pm.

Izmir
AFM
EGS Park.
Tel: (0232) 373 7320.
Deniz.
Tel: (0232) 381 6461.
Petkim
Kultur Merkezi.
Tel: (0232) 616 3240.
Şan
Şan Pasajı, Konak
Tel: (0232) 483 7511.

Cultural Festivals

January
Ağrı – Troubadour Celebration.

February
Izmir – Camel Wrestling.

March
Çanakkale – 1915 Sea Victory
Celebration.
Izmir – European Jazz Days.

April
Çanakkale – Anzak Days.

May
Alanya – International Rafting and
Triathlon Organization.
Aydın – Erik Culture and Arts Festival.
Ciğli (Izmir) – Bird Sanctuary
Celebration.
Ephesus (Selçuk) – Festival of Art
and Culture.
Marmaris – International Yacht Week.
Silifke – Music and Folklore Festival.

June
Adıyaman – Tourism and Cultural
Festival.
Antakya – St. Pierre Mass.

Foca (Izmir) – Music, Folklore and
Watersports Festival.
Istanbul – International Classical
Music Festival.
Kemer (Antalya) – International
Golden Pomegranate Festival.
Marmaris – International Music and
Arts Festival.

July
Antakya (Hatay) – Tourism and
Culture Festival.
Çesme – Sea Festival and
International Song Contest.
Foça – Watersports Festival.
Iskenderun – Culture and Tourism
Festival.
Kuşadasi (Izmir) – Music Festival.

August
Alanya – International Beach
Volleyball.
Antalya – 30 August, Zafer Bayrami
(Victory Day).
Bozcaada (Troy) – Arts and Culture
Festival.
Çanakkale – Troy Festival.

September
Izmir – International Fair.

October
Alanya – Arts and Culture Festival;
Triathlon Competition.
Antalya – Golden Orange
International Film Festival.
Bodrum – International Sailboat
Race.
Bozburun (Izmir) – International
Gület Sailing Festival.
Istanbul, Ankara, Adana – Akbank
Jazz Festival.
29th – Cumhuriyet Bayrami
(Republic Day). Everywhere.

November
Marmaris – International Yacht
Races.
10th, anniversary of Ataturk's
death. Everywhere.
24th, Teacher's Day. Everywhere.

December
Demre (Kaş) – St Nicholas' Festival.

Art

The huge Biennial Exhibition
brings together a heady mix of
international contemporary
artists; with the emphasis also
on showcasing Turkish artists.
   Turkish painting and
sculpture have a short history,
but Turkish artists are now
experimenting with conceptual
art and video. In architecture
and design, some contemporary
or recent buildings and interiors
will be of interest to the visitor
to Turkey.
   Many financial institutions
sponsor modern art, including
decorative arts and art
jewellery. As a result, you will
find many small art galleries in
the somewhat strange settings
of corporate office
headquarters in the big cities.
Here, the art exhibited may or
may not be for sale. There are
many other small commercial
galleries, some of which double
up as bars or cafés.
Art Galleries in Antalya include:
Antalya Güzel Sanatlar Galerisi
Cumhuriyet Caddesi.
Art House
Pamir Caddesi 26/A.
Tel: (0242) 242 4141.
Falez Hotel Gallery
Konyaaltı Falez Mevkii.
Tel: (0242) 248 5000.
Turkuaz Sanat Galerisi
Tel: (0242) 242 0176.

Nightlife

Nightlife traditionally revolves around *meyhane* (taverns), bars, restaurants and *gazinos*. In these places, *meze* are served with accompanying Turkish cabaret or dancing. In the major cities and resorts, though, discos and clubs exert a powerful pull on the young and more affluent.

You'll find a range of bars from the simple to the exotic and elegant; some with live music.

The best dance clubs play the most up-to-date music. Along the coast, the larger hotels have their own discos and cabarets, most of which are open to non-residents.

Thrace & Marmara

Apart from a few local discos, there is little or no nightlife – as westerners understand the term – in Thrace or Marmara. Notices of occasional concerts and plays appear on posters and in shop windows. In Bursa the really desperate might like to try:

Bongo Bar
Clup Altınceylan, Kültür Park.
Karagöz Theatre
Çekirge.
Details of performances and tickets from Ienal Çelikkol at the Karagöz Antique Shop, Eski Aynalı Çarşı 1-17.
Tel: (0224) 222 6151.
The Club S
Kültür Park (Ipekiş entrance)
Weekends only.

Aegean Coast

Bodrum
Halikarnas
Cumhuriyet Caddesi.
Tel: (0252) 316 8000.

The most famous disco on the Turkish Aegean coast. Midnight laser and light show.
M&M Dancing
Dr. Alim Bey Caddesi.
Tel: (0252) 316 2725.
The closest rival to the Halikarnas in terms of popularity. The lively music keeps on playing until around 4am.
Ora
Dr Alim Bey Caddesi 19/21.
Tel: (0252) 614 3903.
Attracts a lively crowd of young people intent on enjoying themselves until the early hours of the morning.

Çeşme
Lowry's Irish Pub
Izmir Caddesi, Ilica.
Tel: (0232) 723 0425
Authentic Irish-managed pub with live music and food.

Izmir
Windows on the Bay
Hilton Hotel, Gaziosmanpaşa Bulvarı.
Tel: (0232) 441 6060.
Looking out over the city from the 31st storey and open till the early hours of the morning with live music.

Kuşadası
Emperor
Barlar Sokağı (Beer Street) 21.
Tel: (0256) 612 2575.
Elbow space is at a premium in this very popular disco in the heart of Kuşadası's entertainment area, surrounded by pubs.

Mediterranean Coast

Alanya
Auditorium Open Air Disco
Dimçayi Mevkii.
Noisy, lively open air disco. Summer only.
Janus Restaurant and Café-Bar
Rıhtım Girişi.
Tel: (0242) 513 2694.
Large, vivid pink harbourfront café/restaurant/bar through the day, with late night dancing. Open round the clock.

Antalya
Birdland Jazz Club
Hıdırlık Kulesi Arkası, Hesapçı Sokak 78, Kaleiçi.
Tel: (0242) 242 01507.
This trendy jazz club in a restored *konak* (mansion) oozes cool.
Club 29
Yat Liman, Kaleiçi.
Tel: (0242) 241 6260.
The trendy venue in Antalya, this upmarket restaurant beside the old harbour transforms itself late at night into a huge disco and music venue, with live performances by some of Turkey's top bands. There are dance-floors indoors and out, and a large pool for cooling off in. Restaurant open all year; disco closed in winter.
No Name Bar
Old Marina.
Tel: (0242) 241 0538.
Popular harbour-front bar with live American-style rock and roll and karaoke in nine languages. There is also an Internet café, satellite TV, an English-language library and regular theme nights.
Şaziye Bar
Cumhuriyet Caddesi, 59 Sokak.
Classy, bar designed for those with the wealth and years to support it.

Fethiye
Disco Marina
Yat Limanı Karşısı, opposite the Yacht Harbour.
Tel: (0252) 614 9860.
Popular with the young Turks and tourists; an odd but entertaining mix of modern music, mirror balls and professional dancers (including belly dancing).
Ottoman Café
Karagözler Caddesi 3/B.
Tel: (0252) 612 1148.
Ottoman style. Live Turkish folk music and tour groups. Visit in the afternoon or early evening.
Yes!
Cumhuriyet Caddesi 9.
Tel: (0252) 614 9289.
Trendy and highly successful English-Turkish venture mixing traditions, ages, disco and live shows. Entrance free; happy hour 9pm–midnight; open until 4am.

Kalkan
Aquarium Bar
Town centre.
Tel: (0242) 844 3453.
Three floors of entertainment, a lively bar, excellent music, games room and live shows with transvestite belly dancers.

Kaş
Fullmoon Disco
Fullmoon Hotel, 1 km (½ mile) out of town, on the Kalkan road.
Tel: (0242) 836 3241.
MDC
1 km (½ mile) east of town, on the Demre road.
Tel: (0242) 836 2491.
Both are popular, seafront open-air discos whose brain-numbing beat is carefully sited away from the town.
Red Point Bar
Topçu Caddesi.
Huge, noisy overcrowded bar that has become an essential stopping place for anyone out on the town.

Side
Blues Bar
Cami Sokak.
Tel: (0242) 753 1197.
Friendly bar that prides itself on being safe for single women. Sit on the outdoor terrace and choose from 100 different cocktails.

Sport

In the early days of tourism, sun, sand, sea and social life were the main attractions for visitors. Nowadays, tastes are more sophisticated and travellers want action and adventure when they come to Turkey. The country has responded extremely well to these new demands, and now offers many variations on sport and leisure themes.

Yachting

Arranging a Blue Voyage: Many European and some American travel agencies specializing in trips to Turkey organize yachting holidays to the Turquoise Coast – the area from Bodrum to Antalya.

However, chartering through a local agency in Bodrum, Marmaris, Fethiye and Antalya not only cuts down costs but also offers a wider selection of yachts and fares. These agencies also arrange transfers from airport to hotels in Turkey. Any travel agent in Bodrum or Marmaris can make reservations for a Blue Voyage, a cruise along the Turquoise Coast.

As a rule, one third to half of the boat's charge is paid at the time of reservation. Alternatively you can rent a yacht yourself. This is much cheaper, but you need to know what you are choosing.

BODRUM CUP

If you wish to cruise in a *gulet*, you might consider participating in the Bodrum Cup, a regatta held at the Gulf of Gökova. The Cup is held in last two weeks of October. This is not only a race in which you can crew, but it is also a chance to get

acquainted with Turkish wooden-framed yachts and Turkey's magnificent sailing grounds. The programme includes stops in Gökova, Knidos, Datça, Bencik, Serçe and Ekincik; a sampling of anchorages as good as any express tour allows. For reservations, contact Era Yachting in Bodrum.

Major bareboat agencies are usually connected with foreign agencies and are mostly sold out in the summer. So, do not leave it to chance, and reserve early.

RENTAL PRICES

Bareboat prices change according to the size of the yacht and the season. In March or November, a 47-foot (14-metre) *Sun Kiss 47* is priced at $1,200–1,500 per week. The highest price is in July or August, when a one-week rental of the same nine-berth yacht is $2,400–2,700. A small, 26-foot (eight-metre) four-passenger *Gib Sea 27* in March or November costs $400–450 per week and in July and August the same boat costs $1,000.

Bodrum-built *gulets* (the name derives from the French *goélette*, meaning schooner) are priced on a daily basis. A 39–48 foot (12–15 metre) boat with two or three cabins sells for around $225–275 a day in May and October. In July, prices soar to $300 and in August climb to $400. A more luxurious 19–20 metre (63–66 foot) *gulet* can be rented for $600–800 a day in August or for as little as $300 in October. Maximum-size luxury yachts over 20 metres (66 feet) go for as much as $1,250–1,300 in August and $600–800 in the lower season.

QUAYSIDE BARGAINING

Just call any travel agency in Bodrum or Marmaris to find out about prices. During the low season, quayside bargaining can lower prices by as much as half. Certain agencies market the Blue

You can voyage on a per cabin basis as well. That means if you can't find enough friends to share a boat, you can join a group on the same boat. You will have your own cabin, probably with a bathroom. The passengers eat together and conform to the program of the boat. Depending on the season, costs range from $275–400 per person.

FLOTILLA CRUISE

Though it somewhat dampens the sense of adventure and individuality that is the essence of being at sea, a middle-of-the-road solution for those who want to steer their own ship but lack the skill and/or the courage to go it alone is chartering a bareboat in a "flotilla cruise". Three to 12 yachts will form a group, headed by a guide who leads the way and will attempt to solve any problems you may encounter, ranging from broken transmission gear to bee stings.

Turkish bareboat operators favour French-made yachts. The majority of the fleet consists of Jeanneaus and Benettaux with occasional Moodys and a few German and Scandinavian models. The yachts are kept in good condition, and the better known companies change the bulk of their yachts every five years.

BAREBOAT CRUISE

For all practical purposes, a bareboat is the charterer's own yacht. The boat is easy to sail shorthanded. Inside, it is cosy and comfortable. Hiring a bareboat leaves you free to explore and experiment as you wish.

CHARTERING WITH CREW

Wooden charter yachts with crew vary in size from 10 metres (33 ft) to 25 metres (83 ft). They have anything up to ten double cabins, sometimes with upper bunks. The interiors are generally decorated with wood and make for pleasant

Gulets

Yachts are classified according to their rigs in the tradition of seamanship: schooners, sloops, ketches and others. A *gulet* was actually a schooner with a rounded stern. Turkish yachting agencies applied the term to any boat whose rounded rump resembled a *gulet*. In the last few years, owners began building yachts with transom sterns, *aynakıç* (mirror ass), which gave them more room below decks to squeeze more cabins into.

The term *gulet* then expanded to describe yachts of any shape, except the smaller, double-ended triandils. A *gulet* in the strict sense

bedrooms. Lockers and drawers solve the problem of storage in the cabins. Lighting is usually natural with sunlight flowing in from the portholes. A proper wooden yacht carries no less than 2.5 tons of freshwater, at least five times more than a bareboat. That means the voyagers can often have two showers a day – a blessing in hot weather and salty seas, and virtually impossible to have on a bareboat. Heated pressurized water is often a standard item on *gulets*.

Crews, according to the size of the boat, vary from two to four. They do all the work, including preparing the meals. However, many captains are willing to allow an eager guest to play with the ropes and lines, steer the boat or enter the galley and mess it up in the name of cooking a "special".

Activities available in an anchored *gulet* include skin diving, fishing, windsurfing, rowing or motoring in a dinghy. At additional cost, you may also be able to try your hand at water skiing or waterbiking – though the agency should be forewarned if you want it to provide such options.

Blue Voyagers must enjoy hiking. Taking to the densely vegetated hilltops at every anchorage is a joy. The backdrop of an embroidered coastline, the azure sea and the clear blue sky also mean great

is considered superior to the *aynakıç* because it has to have more overall length per cabin. Secondly – and perhaps this is the most important feature of this type of boat – in the farthest astern of the deck, there is a small aftcastle embellished with soft mattresses and cushions in the shade of the awnings, known as a "pigeon nest." To many connoisseurs, the essence of a Blue Voyage is enjoying the journey lying on the pigeon's nest.

Since almost all meals are taken in the open air, too, a *gulet*'s wide deckspace is a welcome comfort.

photography, so don't forget to take a camera. Afterwards, it is possible to lie in the back of the *gulet*, eating sandwiches and drinking tea from tulip-shaped glasses. The Blue Voyage is the ultimate in relaxation.

YACHT CHARTERING

Antalya
Air Tour
Kızılsaray Mahallesi, 79 Sokak,
Emin Apart. 9/A.
Tel: (0242) 248 3422.
Akay Travel
Cumhuriyet Caddesi 54.
Tel: (0242) 243 1700.
Fantazi Marine Centre
Esentepe, Göynük (between Kemer
and Beldibi on the main road).
Tel: (0242) 815 1833.
Maki Tur
Tuzcular Mahallesi, Uzun Çarsı
Caddesi 16/B, Kaleiçi.
Tel: (0242) 243 1402.
Pamfilya
30 (Otuz) Agustos Caddesi 57/B.
Tel: (0242) 243 1500.
Rosemary's Yacht Charter
Kemer Marina, Kemer.
Tel: (0242) 814 3404.
Setur
Fevzi Çakmak Caddesi 12/5.
Tel: (0242) 241 6938.
Tantur
Atatürk Caddesi 31, Ulusoy Ishanı.
Tel: (0242) 426 2530.

Bodrum
Aegean Yacht Services
Pasatarlası Caddesi 21
Tel: (0252) 316 1517.
Bodrum Pruva Yachting
Neyzen Tevfik Caddesi 48/B.
Tel: (0252) 316 0443.
Era Tour
Neyzen Tevfik Caddesi 160/A.
Tel: (0252) 316 2054.
Fora Yachting
Neyzen Tevfik Caddesi 220.
Tel: (0252) 316 3046.
Giz Yacht Services
Neyzen Tevfik Caddesi 230/A.
Tel: (0252) 316 8799.
Nautilus
Neyzen Tevfik Caddesi 224/A.
Tel: (0252) 316 6835.
Pupa Yachting
Firkateyn Sokak 19.
Tel: (0252) 316 2398.
Uncle Sun
Ondört Evler Sitesi 4, Sanayi Sitesi Yanı.
Tel: (0252) 316 2659/316 5501.

Marmaris
Ekin Tour
Iskele Meydanı (at the Harbour Square).
Tel: (0252) 412 2552.
Gino Tour
Netsel Marina.
Tel: (0252) 412 0676/412 5220.
Mengi Yachting
Hacı Sabri Sokak 7/A.
Tel: (0252) 412 1307.
Setur
Barbaros Caddesi 87.
Tel: (0252) 412 4608.
Venüs Yachting,
Talatpasa Sokak, Demirtas Apt. 24.
Tel: (0252) 412 8535.
Yesil Marmaris Tourism
Barbaros Caddesi 11.
Tel: (0252) 412 2290.
Yüksel Yachting
Netsel Marina
Tel: (0252) 412 1016.

Fethiye
Alesta Yachting and Travel Agency,
across from the Marina, Korbey Apartment 21.
Tel: (0252) 612 2367.
Lama Tours
Hamam Sokak 3/A
Tel: (0252) 614 4964.

Light Tours
Atatürk Caddesi 104.
Tel: (0252) 614 4757.
Simena Travel
Atatürk Caddesi, PTT Santral Sokak, Urantas Sitesi.
Tel: (0252) 614 4957.

YACHT MAINTENANCE

Antalya
Setur Marina
Commercial Dockyard, Free Trade Zone.
Tel: (0242) 229 1494.
Turban Marina, Kaleiçi, Customs Building, Yacht Harbour.
Tel: (0242) 243 4750.

Bodrum
Agantur
Içmeler Mevkii.
Tel: (0252) 316 1708.
Canel Ticaret
Cevat Sakir Caddesi 48/A.
Tel: (0252) 316 1650.
Nautilus
Neyzen Tevfik Caddesi 224/A.
Tel: (0252) 316 6835.
Yat Lift
Içmeler Mevkii.
Tel: (0252) 316 7842.

Marmaris
Netsel Marina
Harbour.
Tel: (0252) 412 2708.

Spectator Sports

Soccer is the national obsession; the fortunes of favourite teams are closely followed, with raucous celebrations after a victory. Galatasaray, Beşiktaş and Fenerbahçe are all Istanbul-based teams with a national following. Small boys wear the strip, and you'll see coloured scarves and flags flying and hear car horns blaring on the night of a match. A Turkish soccer match is a thrilling event, and the atmosphere inside the ground dramatic and emotional. Trouble is always anticipated, so you can expect to see armoured vehicles and water cannons in readiness outside the ground.

Basketball is also a popular spectator sport, and is played by youths all over the country.
Volleyball: The Alanya International Beach Volleyball Tournament is held annually in the second week of June, the tournament reflects the growing appreciation of volleyball as a spectator sport for both men and women. They get wide media coverage and some sponsership.

LOCAL SPORTS

Grease Wrestling
Soccer may get all the kudos and sponsorship money but traditional grease wrestling is Turkey's national sport! It is usually a summer sport and the top teams compete at Edirne in July, but local events can be staged in any month or season. The contestants wear *kıspet*, specially designed leather pants , and the making of these is a time-honoured, albeit dying, art. . . The grease is real olive oil.

The competitors are judged in different weight groups from flyweight up to heavyweight and the whole spectacle is thrilling. Much is made of fife and drum music and traditional costumes. Many local grease wrestling bouts raise money for worthy projects like a new school wing or a new mosque.

For dates and times of fixtures taking place between Fethiye and Antalya, telephone (0242) 345 5567 or ask at the nearest Tourism Information Office.

Camel wrestling
An annual camel-wrestling festival takes place at Selçuk in January, when two adult male camels are pitted against each other. Other bouts take place in the Aydın region in December and January.

Birdwatching

Although not strictly a sport, bird-watching is an increasingly popular outdoor activity, attracting Turks and tourists alike. Several places in Turkey are designated as a "bird

paradise" *(kuş cenneti)*, a
flamboyant name for a sanctuary.
You will find them in or near many of
the areas already attracting tourists,
but they are of variable interest.

Golf

From humble beginnings and not a
few misgivings, golf has become a
serious game and there are
certainly some serious resorts.
These are the main courses and
their facilities. All the courses are
located in the Belek Tourism
Centre, near Serik.
National Golf Club
Tel: (0242) 725 5400.
Fax: (0242) 725 5522.
E-mail: national@golfturkey.com
www.golfturkey.com/national
18-hole championship course and a
9-hole academy course.
Gloria Golf Club
Tel: (0242) 715 1520.
Fax: (0242) 715 1523.
E-mail: maltuntaslar@gloria.com.tr
www.gloria.com.tr

Lycian Way Walk

An ambitious project has now
been completed to waymark the
Lycian Way Walk, 320 km (200
miles) of mountain trail from
Fethiye to Antalya. There is an
accompanying guide book in
Turkish and English detailing key
sites of historic interest,
pathways and comprehensive
trekking and survival tips. At the
time of writing, the Turkish Army
had not yet given permission for
the publication of the detailed
maps which are meant to be
included in the book. Up to date
information and details of guided
tours or trekking expeditions can
be found at Bouganinville Travel
in Kaş, who also stock the Lycian
Way Guide book:
Tel: (0242) 836 3737
E-mail: info@bougainvilleturkey.com
www.bougainville-turkey.com
Also available frrom Mithra Travel
in Antalya:
Tel: (0242)248 7747.
Fax: (0242)247 0553.

18-hole championship course and a
3-hole practice course.
Tatgolf International Golf Club
Tel: (0242) 725 5303.
Fax: (0242) 725 4129
E-mail: reservation@tatgolf.com.tr
www.tatgolf.com.tr
27-hole championship Course.
Nobilis Golf Club
Tel: (0242) 715 1987.
Fax: (0242) 715 1985
E-mail: nobilisgolf@superonline.com
www.golfturkey.com/nobilis
18-hole championship course.

Horse Riding

Riding schools abound along the
Turkish coast and many are first-
class stables with Arabian and
thoroughbred horses. They offer a
range of lessons, trail riding,
jumping, as well as ponies for
children. Many also have
accommodation, bars, pools and
related activities. Below are the
stables that look after horses well
and cater for a variety of riding
skills.
Alanya/Avsallar
Tel: (0242) 517 2023.
Mrs Eni Schranke has Arabian horses
and one donkey. She caters for riding
holidays for children as well as adults
but accommodation is limited.
Manavgat/Sorgun
Tel: (0242) 756 9248/766 9021.
First-class ranch. Eight Arabian and
English horses. Riding instructor,
lessons and forest tours. No
accommodation.
Belek
Club Aldiana.
Tel: (0242) 756 9263.
The Club's own ranch has excellent
horses, instructors and German
discipline.
Beldibi
Pine Resort.
Tel: (0242) 824 9390.
Opened in 1999, they have 10
Arabian and English horses, English-
speaking staff, accommodation, bar
and restaurant. Everything here is
luxury and upmarket.
Kemer
Berke Horse Ranch, Çamyuva.
Tel: (0242) 818 0532.
Fax: (0242) 818 0093.

www.berkranch.com.
Forest tours, jumping,
accommodation, swimming pool
and mountain biking on offer.
Çamyuva
Naturland Country Resort.
Tel: (0242) 824 6214.
Fax: (0242) 824 6210.
E-mail: info@naturland.com.tr
www.naturland.com.tr.
Five-star hotel and all activities with
12 Arabian and English horses.
Upmarket eco activities and good
accommodation.
Fethiye
Tel: (0252) 616 6285.
Klaus and Inge Thienger have 12
Arabian and English horses. They
give riding lessons, forest trail rides
and offer limited accommodation.
English, German and Turkish are all
spoken.

Skiing

Turkey has a number of ski resorts
and the sport is gaining in
popularity. Above Antalya at
Saklıkent, there are several ski
slopes, lodges and restaurants.
These are not luxurious but most
people come here for the day.
Skiing goes on from about
December until March and this area
is great fun, although no challenge
for experienced skiers. Skis and
equipment can also be rented (call
Bakırlı Motel on the slopes (0242)
446 1279/1280 or Ideal Sport in
Antalya (opposite the main PTT) on
(0242) 247 0109.)

Tennis

Most of the resort hotels have
tennis courts and a few top-name
professionals have come to chill out
and practise at Belek and Serik.
Antalya has an upmarket tennis
club; you must be a member or a
member's guest to play here, but in
the summer months it is usually too
hot to play tennis anyway.

Trekking and Mountain Climbing

Trekking and walking tend to be
undertaken by organised groups

Turkish Baths (Hamams)

As a spectator sport, nothing surpasses a *hamam* – be sure to visit one during your stay. Many people are put off the idea because they simply don't know what to expect (or what to do). Don't worry. The locals will happily fill you in.

The rules are simple, based on the old Roman baths or the Scandinavian sauna. The sexes are usually segregated either in different baths or by set hours for each. Nudity is not the norm, so wear a swimming costume or ask for a sarong *(peştamal)*. You will also be given a towel and wooden clogs *(takunya)*.

Change in the reception area *(camekân)*. From here, you move through to a private side-room to wash down before entering the central hot steam room *(hararet)*. In the old baths, this is often a spectacular chamber with domes, arches, marble and tiles, at the centre of which is a large marble slab. You lie face down on this and are given an energetic face, foot and/or full-body massage, or a scrubdown with a camel-hair glove.

Most five-star hotels offer luxurious, modern *hamams*, but some more traditional bath houses are well worth a visit, and may be more atmospheric.

Aegean Coast
Bodrum
Haman, Dere Umucra Sokak. Surprisingly traditional for touristy Bodrum, with some afternoons set aside for women.
Marmaris
Sultan Turkish Bath, Taşlik Centre. Tel: (0252) 413 6850.
A modern and clean bath that provides mixed bathing as well as single-sex sessions.

Mediterranean Coast
Alanya
Mimoza Turkish Bath, Sugözü Caddesi 19.
Tel: (0242) 513 9193.
All-in-one experience for the body, mind and social life; with a café.
Antalya
Antalya Yeni Hamami, Sinan Mah. 1255, Sokak, No. 3/A.
Tel: (0242) 242 5225.
Modern, shiny and professional. You may not experience the atmospheric delights of Ottoman marble, but you will certainly come out clean.

Fethiye
Old Turkish Bath, Hamam Sokak 2, Paspatur Bazaar.
Tel: (0252) 614 9318.
Unusually there are some hours for mixed bathing at Fethiye's 16th-century bath house, in the middle of the bazaar, now geared almost entirely towards tourists.
Side
Arkaç Hotel (On the sea side of the main road before turning off to Side) Manavgat, Side
Tel: (0242) 742 3983.
Fax: (0242) 742 3395
This is a *caravanserai* style hotel but they have a luxurious and modern Turkish Bath on the lower level. Beauty treatments and massage in brightly tiled surroundings. Booking advised.
Kaş
Hera Hotel
Küçük Çakıl Mevkii.
Tel: (0242) 836 3062/64.
Fax: (0242) 836 3063
E-mail: herahotel@superonline.com
This is a lovely *hamam* on the outskirts of Kaş and if nothing else should convince you that luxury and pleasure are better than grottiness and atmosphere when it comes to *hamams*.

who know the paths and peaks. Most travel agents can arrange this, whether it is along the Taurus Mountain ridge or in some of the National Parks. In Antalya, the Taurus Nature Sport Club (TODOSK) concentrates on weekend outings for nature lovers with all skill levels accommodated (tel/fax: (0242) 244 0883). They are associated with the Turkish Mountaineering Federation, based in Ankara (tel/fax: (0312) 310 1578.

Watersports

Turkish resorts can now offer sailing, surfing, windsurfing, scuba diving and snorkelling, paragliding and waterskiing to a much higher and safer standard than was previously the case. Diving in

particular has become extremely popular in Turkey.

Swimming

Swimming in the sea should always be undertaken with caution. There are some areas where seemingly inviting beaches harbour dangerous currents. Plenty of places offer perfect conditions, but check first.

Some areas are also home to sea urchins, so a pair of plastic sandals or espadrilles for wading may be a good investment. Turkish beach hygiene can leave a lot to be desired, too, and busy beaches will be marred by litter.

The big resort hotels all have pools. In winter, indoor hotel pools can be fun, though expensive (with luxurious towels and service).

Diving

The larger resorts have clubs and schools offering properly supervised instruction leading to internationally recognised certificates. In some places underwater attractions include archaeological remains or ancient sunken vessels, though since these are often unexcavated, diving is strictly controlled by the government. Guides must be certified by the Ministry of Tourism. You should bring any international certificates with you. For simple snorkelling, you can normally hire a boat for the day to take you to secluded spots.

Alanya
Active Divers Club
Iskele Caddesi 80.
Tel: (0242) 512 8811.

Diving tours, underwater photography and PADI courses, from the Pasha Bay Hotel.
Active Diving Centre
Tel: (0242) 511 3662.
Dolphin Dive
Tel: (0242) 512 3030.

Antalya
Ilter Diving Centre
Tel: (0242) 311 8677.

Fethiye
European Diving Centre
Atatürk Caddesi.
Tel: (0252) 614 9771.
Run by Englishmen with US and UK trained intructors; PADI courses.

Kemer
Eurasia Diving Centre
Tel: (0242) 814 3250.
British intructors.

Marmaris
European Diving Centre
Içmeler.
Tel: (0252) 455 4733.
A British-owned diving school offering a one-day introductory course, plus complete PADI courses.

Kaş
Kaş has become a very active diving centre with over 15 schools . Baracuda Diving Club, Bougainville and Sun Diving are the pioneers, with safety rating high on the agenda. Booking in advance is not necessary for individual dives but they appreciate advance notice from groups. Daily diving trips only. All give beginner instruction and sometimes have night diving. Bougainville also caters for disabled divers.
Baracuda Diving Club.
Tel: (0242) 836 2987/836 2996
Bougainville Travel
Tel: (0242) 836 3737
E-mail: info@bougainville-turkey.com
Internet: http://www.bougainville-turkey.com
Sun Diving.
Tel: (0242) 836 2637

Bodrum
Ayaz Watersports, Gümbet Beach.
Bitez Surf School, Bitez Village,

about 6 miles (10kms) from Bodrum Town.
Club Ersan, Içmeler.
Zulu Turizm, Güvercinlik Village, about 12 miles (20kms) from Bodrum Town.

Diving Cruises

In 2000, diving cruises for a select group (8 maximum) of experienced divers began. A unique 20-metre (66ft) boat purpose built for luxury cruising is used, and is based in Finike. It has a decompression chamber on board. Contact managing partner and ex-sponge diver, Tosun Sezen, for details and brochures (tel: (0242) 825 7120. E-mail: lucas@escortnet.com).

White Water Rafting

White water rafting has caught the imagination of many visitors and is not only adventurous but can be a welcome relief from roasting on the beach. You also get to see some marvellous natural sites which would otherwise be inaccessible. The best known rafting areas are Köprülü Canyon near Antalya and Dim Çayı, near Alanya. Köprülü Canyon is more sedate and ideal for a daily outing for all the family. Dim Çayı can be pretty challenging and experts will find it more exciting. Safety standards are much improved of late but insist on a helmet if it is not offered.

Paragliding

This sport is ideally suited to the high mountains which offer perfect plateaux for taking off and good updraughts. Fethiye is one of the more attractive areas for this sport but there are reports that it is encroaching somewhat on environmentally protected areas.

Jeep Safaris

These are an excellent way of seeing many local sights if you don't want to set out by car on

your own. In fact,they are often more like a Jeep convoy, but companies like Airtour have some very adventurous outings for those who really like to get off the beaten track. Note that these are light-weight touring jeeps and not 4x4 or off-road vehicles.

Leisure Attractions

Ostrich Farms
There are over 100 ostrich farms in Turkey. They are all privately owned and, when quantities are sufficient, they will provide high protein, low cholesterol meat for mass consumption. Hides and skins are for upmarket leather accessories. Tropic Ostrich Farm was the first in Turkey and is an innovator in regulating trade and environmental protocols. The farm is open as a tourist attraction and the owner, known locally as the Ostrich King, welcomes visitors. The ostriches put on their own show for guests and there is a bar and information centre.

Tropic Ostrich Farm
Çeltikçi Village, Manavgat.
Tel: (0242) 753 2296.
Fax: (0242) 753 1304.
E-mail: tropical@superonline.com

Aqualand
Dumlıpınar Bulvarı, Antalya (next to Yedi Mehmet restaurant).
Tel: (0242) 243 4544.
Fax: (0242) 247 0255.
Theme parks came late to Turkey but they are keen to make up for lost fun time. Aqualand is wild, wet and wonderful and tourists like it as much as the locals. A free shuttle service calls at several key city centre points and most public transport passes by the entrance at the western end of Antalya.

Golden Orange Film Festival
Held every September/October in Antalya, this is a trendy festival, much boosted now that Antalya has something like 30 cinemas. However, troubles plague it even after decades.

Aspendos International Opera and Ballet Festival

If you see nothing else in Antalya, try to get out to Aspendos, about 45 kilometres east of the city, during the month of June. Programs can be obtained from tourist offices and the Town Hall tel: (0242) 243 7640; fax: (0242) 243 8827. It is not the Met or the Royal Opera House but the authentic Roman theatre and good orchestra make for a thrilling evening.

Casinos

Casinos were very popular up until the mid 1990s, when a religious-oriented government put a stop to it. There are plans to restore this activity and make it better regulated.

Shopping

Turkish shopkeepers assume that, as a foreigner, you have come to Turkey to shop and, in particular, to buy from them. Sometimes looking at rival shops to compare goods and prices does not go down well.

Tourism has not been buoyant over the last few years and, unfortunately, many merchants still have old stock around but at new prices. They are, understandably, very keen to get this off their hands. Unless you really think it has no equal, don't be bamboozled into buying. Remember, many shops employ staff on a commission basis only and some know little or nothing about the product they are selling.

In Turkey, haggling and bargaining are widely advertised as the way to conduct business. Certainly bargaining can be fun if you know that you are getting a good deal in the end but an increasing number of tourists find beating down prices boring and time-consuming. Many people would rather find something they like at an honest price, pay for it and leave. Others, on the other hand, have come to believe they can bargain for anything and everything and, in supermarkets and post offices, this is highly offensive. Similarly, it is very bad form to try bargaining for products such as bread, where prices are set by the government. Many visitors still do this believing that they are being overcharged in the first place.

The good news is that there are wonderful things to buy at all the coastal resorts. The following are general guidelines and brand names to look for that are well known locally for quality and value. Specific traders' names are only given if they are known to have a number of satisfied international customers.

Textiles

Turkey turns out good-quality blue jeans at half the price of other places. The ubiquitous T- and sweat shirt is a favourite, but check quality and stitching: these can be super or awful. Printed viscose skirts in blinding prints are popular at beach resorts and can be bought anywhere along the coast. Zeko Triko is the biggest and most flamboyant name in swimsuits anywhere and a good selection of styles can be found at most upmarket resorts. These are not cheap, but are worth the price for the saucy, original designs.

Men's shirts in top quality cotton poplin are a dream. Abbate, Provva, Bisse and Bilsar are the names to look for that are made in Turkey. All are major exporters to European wholesalers.

Turkey is a major world supplier of textiles to export markets. Bed sheets and duvet covers are in wonderful local cotton and can be teamed with matching curtains, pillow slips and other accessories. For towels and terry towelling bathrobes, Özdilek is one of the best-known names. Hundreds of firms make bed linens. Çalışkan of Bursa is a reliable one; so is Çukurova, who have retail outlets in several cities, including Antalya.

Jewellery

Turkey is traditionally known for gold jewellery but many silver items are just as attractive and popular. Note that they may not always be Turkish even though they have an ethnic style. Semi-precious stones are a wonderful buy. Amber, agate, lapus and coral are offered from many jewellers. Many will sell the stones and custom design a setting for you. As anywhere else, prices vary widely and cater to all budgets.

Like buying jewellery anywhere else, exercise caution. Few local jewellers are members of any

Carpets/Kilims

Unquestionably one of the things to buy in Turkey. Even if you do not like shopping, at least try to make time to see something that is part of Turkish cultural heritage. A reputable carpet dealer will give you a summary about how carpets are produced and maybe a smattering of history of where carpets are made and the significance of the many patterns and motifs. When you buy a carpet or kilim, you are taking home a souvenir or heirloom that will give enduring pleasure.

There is a downside and this is that so many places sell carpets it is almost impossible to know which are reputable and offer good value for money. Many tour groups take in one of the big carpet warehouses as part of a daily sightseeing tour, but remember you don't have to buy if you don't want to.

Reputable dealers will give a Museum Certificate showing that the carpet you purchased is not an antique and can legally be taken out of Turkey. Make sure you get this certificate at the time of purchase. If a dealer refuses or says he will send it on later, chances are he is not a legitimate carpet specialist.

The two professional dealers below have been in business for over 20 years, have many local and international customers who return and remain personal friends and are not surly if you decide you don't want to buy after all. This is not to say that there are not many other excellent carpet professionals along the coast: just bear in mind that there are far too many disreputable ones.

Kaş and Carry
Bahçe Sokak, Kaş.
Tel: (0242) 836 1662/836 1663.
Fax: (0242) 836 2389.

Magic Orient
Hükümet Caddesi, Kaş.
Tel: (0242) 836 1610/836 3150.
Fax: (0242) 836 1620.
www.magicorient.com

international organisations and some may not even be jewellers at all. Guarantees may prove worthless once you get home.

Places like Xtra and Topika in Kaş are the exception to most rules. As well as a staggering range of stones and silver jewellery and accessories, Topika sells good quality diamonds. Xtra is a specialist in classical gold pieces and, like any professional jeweller, takes queries or complaints personally.

Leather

Leather garments have always been a good buy in Turkey. The only problem is that too many of the outlets on the Aegean and Mediterranean coastal regions have stocked the same models for years. Compared to some of the stunning designs coming out of Istanbul fashion houses, these cumbersome jackets and stiff vests look dated.

Sometimes there is little choice. In Antalya, Kırcılar is the exception to this and have some good contemporary fashions. Desa is also located in some of the big resort areas and they have superb garments, mostly for women. This is the Turkish firm that produces Marks and Spencers' top selling collection of suede garments. They also sell quality footwear for men and women.

Small leather accessories, briefcases, handbags and shoes are all good value and make wonderful gift items. If you are paying in cash you can always get a discount.

Avoid the tawdry rustic-look bags and carry-alls that are sold as "camel hides" These are the cheapest end of split calf leather and are designed to dupe – they will not last and are next to worthless. Plenty of smarter styles are available and the names who offer the best quality and value are Matraş, Tergan, Gön and Desa. These are the top names in Turkey and many have smart shops in tourist areas and big cities.

Ceramics/Porcelain

The colourful, painted ceramic dishes and bowls on display everywhere are mostly from Kütahya, an area that produces almost nothing else except decorative dinnerware and gift items. Not all the designs are to Western tastes, but look carefully through the vast selection and you will find some stunning contemporary designs with a more understated eastern touch. The large plates and bowls are often more decorative and are sold as wall hangings and collectors' pieces, not table pieces. Nothing for sale is antique, so be suspicious of any shop selling them as such.

Many resort areas also have local producers who turn out highly original designs, often in their own studios. If time permits, some of these will make to order for an economic quantity. Again, originality and one-of-a-kind designs do not come cheaply but you are unlikely to find anything like this at home.

Glass

There is only one name in glass in Turkey. Paşabahçe is a partially state-controlled glass works with good quality mid range glasses, tumblers, bowls and ovenproof cookeryware. They also do a more upmarket range of good quality crystal. They have shops everywhere and the staff are helpful and friendly. The bigger shops sell home décor accessories.

Spices

Spices are another item that seems to have crept into the tourist repertoire, as traders found there were profits to be made. Not all of these are made in Turkey, and a huge variety of spices and herbs are sold either loose and weighed or in attractive gift packs. Flavoured and herbal teas are usually included in the range. Use your nose and common sense to check items.

Turkish Delight

This is the classic and best known Turkish sweet. A favourite with everybody, it tastes delicious and, even better, has few calories! It is called *lokum* in Turkish and can be bought loose by weight or boxed. The top name to look for in the boxed variety is Hacer Baba, which has a creamy texture but is easier on the teeth than some over-sugared varieties of *lokum*.

CDs and Cassettes

These are good value and the choice is vast, but many are pirated copies. If you buy from an upmarket specialist music store, they will be imported originals, but street vendors often sell cheap copies.

Markets

Local markets are a wonderful source of shopping inspiration. Many of these travel around from village to village but each village awaits "market day" in a festive spirit. Fresh produce, unusual highland cheeses, home-produced olive oil, live chickens and freshly gathered free range eggs are just a few of the items on sale. Markets provide a wonderful opportunity for some creative photography. But you can also find gifts here to take back home, and stands sell factory seconds in jeans, T-shirts and other clothing items at bargain prices.

Property

Many visitors who come to Turkey for the first time are enchanted by its energy, easy-going life style and the invigorating Mediterranean joie de vivre and decide to go for the dream house or sea-side villa for holidays or retirement. There will be no shortage of agents offering their services. These may be builders, waiters, travel agents, foreigners married to Turks or anybody else who wants to make a quick buck. Think very carefully before taking a costly step that you might live to regret.

If you are serious about settling in Turkey, deal with one of the large global real estate firms, like Colliers, who know the market, are up to date with current market prices, residence permit requirements and who know which nationalities can and cannot purchase property in cities or rural areas. Many properties carry over title deeds (or 'promised' ones) and personal debts from one owner to the next. This is legal in Turkey but many foreigners find they cannot later sell their house as it did not really belong to them in the first place. It is best to employ an international lawyer or a reputable Istanbul or Ankara one, as local lawyers tend to have local interests at heart.

Language

Atatürk's great language reform took place in 1928, when Arabic script was replaced by the Roman alphabet, and Persian and Arabic vocabulary was ousted by words of Turkic origin, with the intention of simplifying the language to boost literacy levels.

One legacy of the flowery elaborations of late Ottoman speech is in the way Turkish people exchange formal greetings: these pleasantries and politenesses follow a set routine in which both sides of the exchange follow formulaic patterns of questions with set answers.

Turkish is undoubtedly a difficult language for Europeans to learn. Although the grammar is consistent and logical, with few irregularities, and pronunciation follows phonetic spelling, both the vocabulary and structure are very different from any language that English-speakers may have tackled before. The vocabulary in particular is very difficult to remember and use, especially over a short visit. There are a few words, mainly of French or English origin, that you will recognise once you have deciphered the Turkish spelling.

It is probably most useful to try to master basic pronunciation, so you can say addresses and place-names correctly, and read and use some set phrases. Off the tourist track English is hardly spoken, so you will need to know a little more.

Pronunciation

As spelling is phonetic, pronunciation is the easy, once you have mastered the different Turkish vowel and consonant sounds.

Letters are always pronounced in the same way. There are only a few difficult ones . "C" is always pronounced "j" as in "jump", so the Turkish word *camii* (mosque) is pronounced "jah-mi", and *caddesi* (road, street) is pronounced "jah-des-i". The soft "ğ" disappears in speech, and is never voiced, but it lengthens the preceding vowel. Also, look out for the dotless i, which makes an "er" sound; it is quite different from the dotted i. Compare *ızgara* (grill, pronounced uh-zgara) with *incir* (fig, pronounced in-jeer). Double consonants are both pronounced. Each syllable in a word carries equal stress, as do words in a phrase.

The basic rules are:

c "dj" as in jump
ç "ch" as in chill
s s as in sleep
fl "sh" as in sharp
g g as in good
ğ is silent, lengthens the previous vowel, never begins a word
a ah as in father
e e as in let
i with a dot as in sit
ı without a dot is an er or uh sound, like the second e in ever
o is pronounced "o" as in hot
ö with diaeresis is similar to ur as in spurt, or German "oe" as in Goethe
u is pronounced like "oo" as in room
ü is like the ew in pew, or u-sound in French 'tu' (impossible without pursing your lips).

Useful Words & Phrases

DAYS OF THE WEEK

Monday *Pazartesi*
Tuesday *Salı*
Wednesday *Çarşamba*
Thursday *Perşembe*
Friday *Cuma*
Saturday *Cumartesi*
Sunday *Pazar*

MONTHS

January *Ocak*
February *Şubat*
March *Mart*
April *Nisan*

May *Mayıs*
June *Haziran*
July *Temmuz*
August *Ağustos*
September *Eylül*
October *Ekim*
November *Kasım*
December *Aralık*

NUMBERS

1 *bir*
2 *iki*
3 *üç*
4 *dört*
5 *beş*
6 *altı*
7 *yedi*
8 *sekiz*
9 *dokuz*
10 *on*
11 *on bir*
12 *on iki*
20 *yirmi*
21 *yirmi bir*
22 *yirmi iki*
30 *otuz*
40 *kırk*
50 *elli*
60 *altmış*
70 *yetmiş*
80 *seksen*
90 *doksan*
100 *yüz*
200 *iki yüz*
1,000 *bin*
2,000 *iki bin*
1,000,000 *bir milyon*
To make a complex number, add the components one by one eg: 5,650,000 = *beş milyon altı yüz elli bin* (in Turkish these would normally be run together). Managing huge numbers has become routine for Turks in dealing with their currency.

Greetings

Hello *Merhaba*
Good morning (early) *Günaydın*
Good day *İyi günler*
Good night *İyi geceler*
Good evening *İyi akşamlar*
Welcome! *Hoş geldiniz!*
Reply: **Happy to be here!** *Hoş bulduk!*
Please, with pleasure, allow me, please go first (multi-purpose,

polite expression) *Buyrun*
Don't mention it *Rica ederim*
Pleased to meet you *Çok memnun oldum*
How are you? *Nasılsınız?*
Thank you, I am/we are fine *Teşekkürler, iyiyim/iyiyiz*
My name is... *Adım...*
I am English/Scottish/American/Australian
Ben İngilizim/İskoçyalım/Amerikalım/Avustralyalım
We'll see each other again ("see you") *Görüşürüz*
God willing *İnşallah*
Goodbye *Hoşça kalın* or *Allaha ısmarladık*
Reply: **"go happily"** *Güle güle* **(only said by the person staying behind)**

Essentials

Yes *Evet*
No *Hayır/yok*
OK *Tamam*
Please *Lütfen*
Thank you *Teşekkür ederim/sağolun/mersi*
You're welcome *Bir şey değil*
Excuse me/I beg your pardon (in a crowd) *Affedersiniz*
Excuse me *Pardon*
Leave me alone *Beni rahat bırak*
Get lost *Çekil git*
I don't speak Turkish *Türkçe bilmiyorum*
Do you speak English? *İngilizce biliyor musunuz?*

Emergencies

Help! *İmdat!*
Fire *Yangın!*
Please call the police *Polis çağırın*
Please call an ambulance *Ambulans çağırın*
Please call the fire brigade *İtfaiye çağırın*
This is an emergency *Bu acıldır!*
There has been an accident *Kaza vardı*
I'd like an interpreter *Tercüman istiyorum*
I want to speak to someone from the British Consulate *İngiltere konsoloslugundan biri ile görüşmek istiyorum*

I don't understand *Anlamıyorum*
I don't know *Bilmiyorum*
Please write it down *Onu benim için heceleyebilir misiniz?*
Wait a moment! *Bir dakika!*
Slowly *Yavaş*
Enough *Yeter*
Where is ...? *Nerede?*
Where is the toilet? *Tuvalet nerede?*
What time is it? *Saatiniz var mı?*
At what time? *Saat kaçta?*
Today *Bugün*
Tomorrow *Yarın*
Yesterday *Dün*
The day after tomorrow *Obür gün*
Now *Şimdi*
Later *Sonra*
When? *Ne zaman*
Morning/in the morning *Sabah*
Afternoon/in the afternoon *Oğleden sonra*
Evening/in the evening *Akşam*
This evening *Bu akşam*
Here *Burada*
There *Şurada*
Over there *Orada*
Is there a newspaper? *Gazete var mı?*
Is there a taxi? *Taksi var mı?*
Is there a phone? *Telefon var mı?*
Yes, there is *Evet, var*
No, there isn't *Hayır, yok*
There is no ticket *Bilet yok*
There is no time *Zaman yok*

Common Phrases

Afiyet olsun *Enjoy your meal/drink*
Çabuk ol *Hurry up, be quick*
Defol!/git! *Beat it, get lost*
Bir dakika (bir daka) *Wait a minute*
Boş ver *Let it go, forget it*
Gidelim mi? *Shall we go?*
Ne kadar? *How much is it?*
Tuvalet var mı? *Is there a toilet here?*
Şerefe *Cheers*
Teşekkür ederim *Thank you*
Bir şey deşil *Don't mention it, not at all*
Kendine iyi bak *Look after yourself*
Kolay gelsin *Take it easy*
Kusura bakma *Excuse me, sorry*
Saat kaç? *What time is it?*
İnşallah *Hopefully, God willing*
Maalesef *Sorry, there isn't any*
Sakın ol *Keep your cool, calm down*

Sana ne? *What's it to you?*
Tamam mı? *Agreed? Ok?*
Gel buraya *Come here*
Tabi ki *Certainly, of course*
Gözünüz aydın *Congratulations (after a happy event)*
Hayırlı olsun *best of luck*

Sightseeing

Directions
How do I get to Bodrum? *Bodrum'a nasıl giderim?*
How far is it to...? *...'a/'e ne kadar uzakta?*
Near *Yakın*
Far *Uzak*
Left *Sol*
On the left/to the left *Solda/sola*
Right *Sağ*
On the right/to the right *Sağda/sağa*
Straight on *Doğru*
North *Kuzey*
South *Güney*
East *Doğu*
West *Batı*

Sights/places
City *Şehir*
Village *Köy*
Forest *Orman*
Sea *Deniz*
Lake *Göl*
Farm *Çiftlik*
Church *Kilise*
Mosque *Camii*
Post Office *Postane*
What time does it open/close? *Kaçta açılıcak/kapanacak?*

Travelling

Car *Araba*
Petrol station *Benzin istasyonu*
Petrol/gas *Benzin (super/normal)*
Fill it up, please *Doldurun, lütfen*
Flat tyre/puncture *Patlak lastik*
My car has broken down *Arabam arzalandı*
Bus station *Otogar*
Bus stop *Emanet*
Bus *Otobüs*
Train station *Gar/İstasyon*
Train *Tren*
Taxi *Taksi*
Airport *Havalimanı/Havaalanı*
Aeroplane *Uçak*
Port/harbour *Liman*

Road Signs

Dikkat *Beware/Caution*
Tehlike *Danger*
Yavaş *Slow*
Yol ver *Give way*
Dur *Stop*
Araç giremez *No entry*
Tek yön *One way*
Çıkmaz sokak *No through road*
Bozuk yol *Poor road surface*
Tamirat *Roadworks*
Yol kapalı *Road closed*
Yaya geçidi *Pedestrian crossing*
Şehir merkezi/Centrum *City centre*
Otopark/Park edilir *Parking*
Park edilmez *No parking*

Boat *Gemi*
Ferry *Feribot/Vapur*
Quay *İskele*
Ticket *Bilet*
Ticket office *Gişe*
Return ticket *Gidiş-dönüş*
Can I reserve a seat? *Reservasyon yapabilir miyim?*
What time does it leave? *Kaçta kalkıyor?*
Where does it leave from? *Nereden kalkıyor?*
How long does it take? *Ne kadar sürüyor?*
Which bus? *Hangi otobüs?*

Health

In an emergency it can be quicker to get to hospital by taxi.
Clinic *Klinik*
Dentist *Dişçi*
Doctor *Doktor*
Emergency service/room *Acil servis*
First aid *İlk yardım*
Hospital *Hastane*
Pharmacist *Eczacı*
Pharmacy *Eczane*
I am ill *Hastayım*
I have a fever *Atesim var*
I have diarrhoea *İshallım*
I am diabetic *Şeker hastasıyım*
I'm allergic to... *Karşı alerjim var...*
I have asthma *Astim hastasıyım*
I have a heart condition *Kalp hastasıyım*
I am pregnant *Gebeyim*
It hurts here *Burası acıyor*

I have lost a filling *Dolgu düştü*
I need a prescription for... *İçin bir reçete istiyorum...*

Accommodation

Hotel *Otel*
Pension/guesthouse *Pansiyon*
Single/double/triple *Tek/çift/üç kiflilik*
Full board *Tam pansiyon*
Half board *Yarım pansyon*
With a shower *Duşlu*
With a bathroom *Banyolu*
With a balcony *Balkonlu*
With a sea view *Deniz manzaralı*
Lift *Asansör*
Room service *Oda servisi*
Air-conditioning *Havalandırma*
Central heating *Kalorifer*
Key *Anahtar*
Bed *Yatak*
Blanket *Battaniye*
Pillow *Yastık*
Shower *Duş*
Soap *Sabun*
Plug *Tıkaç*
Towel *Havlu*
Basin *Lavabo*
Toilet *Tuvalet*
Toilet paper *Tuvalet kağıdı*
Hot water *Sıcak su*
Cold water *Soğuk su*
Dining-room *Yemek salonu*

I need/...is necessary *lazım/...gerek*
I have a reservation *Reservasyonım var*
Do you have a room? *Odnız var mı?*
I'd like a room for one/three nights *Bir/üç gece için bir oda istiyorum*
I'm sorry, we are full *Maalesef doluyuz*

Shopping

Price *Fiyat*
Cheap *Ucuz*
Expensive *Pahalı*
No bargaining (sign) *Pazarlık edilmez*
Old *Eski*
New *Yeni*
Big *Büyük*
Bigger *Daha büyük*
Small *Küçük*
Smaller *Daha küçük*

Very nice/beautiful *Çok güzel*
This *Bu*
These *Bunlar*
That *Şu*
I would like... *İsterim...*
I don't want *İstemem*
There isn't any *Yok*
How much is it? *Ne kadar?*
Do you take credit cards? *Kredi karti alır mısınız?*
How many? *Kaç tane?*

Eating Out

Basics
Table *Masa*
Cup *Fincan*
Glass *Bardak*
Wine glass *Kadeh*
Bottle *Şişe*
Plate *Tabak*
Fork *Çatal*
Knife *Bıçak*
Spoon *Kaşık*
Napkin *Peçete*
Salt *Tuz*
Black pepper *Kara biber*
Starters *Meze*
Soup *Çorba*
Fish *Balık*
Meat dishes *Etli yemekler*
Grills *İzgara*
Eggs *Yumurta*
Vegetarian dishes *Etsiz yemekler*
Salads *Salatalar*
Fruit *Meyva*
Bread *Ekmek*
Peppery hot *Acı (a-je)*
Non-spicy *Acısız (a-je-suz)*
Water *Su*
Mineral water *Maden suyu*
Fizzy water *Soda*
Beer *Bira*
Red/white wine *Kırmızı/beyaz sarap*
Fresh orange juice *Portakal suyu*
Coffee *Kahve*
Tea *Çay*

A table for two/four, please *İki/dört kişilik bir masa, lütfen*
Can we eat outside? *Dışarıda da yiyebilir miyiz?*
Waiter! *Garson!*
Excuse me (to get service or attention) *Bakar mısınız?*
Menu *Menü*
I didn't order this *Ben bunu ısmarlamadım*

Some more water/bread/wine, please *Biraz daha su/ekmek/ şarap, rica ediyoruz*
I can eat... *Yiyorum...*
I cannot eat... *Yiyemiyorum...*
The bill, please *Hesap, lütfen*
Service included/excluded *Servis dahil/hariç*

Menu Decoder

Kahvaltı/Breakfast
Beyaz peynir White cheese
Kaflar peyniri Yellow cheese
Domates Tomatoes
Zeytin Olives
Salatalık Cucumber
Reçel Jam
Bal Honey
Tereyağ Butter

Extra dishes which you may order for a more substantial breakfast:
Haşlanmış yumurta Boiled egg (hard)
Rafadan yumurta Soft-boiled eggs
Menemen Scrambled egg omelette with tomatoes, peppers, onion and cheese
Sahanda yumurta Fried eggs
Pastırmalı yumurta Eggs fried with pastırma, Turkish cured beef, like pastrami
Sade/peynirli/mantarlı omlet Plain/cheese/mushroom omelette

Çorbalar/Soups
Hafllama Mutton broth
Tavuk çorbası/tavuk suyu Chicken soup
Düğün çorbası Wedding soup (thickened with eggs and lemon)
Ezogelin çorbası Lentil and rice soup
Mercimek çorbası Red lentil soup
Domates çorbası Tomato soup
İşkembe çorbası Tripe soup
Paça çorbası Lamb's feet soup
Şehriye çorbası Fine noodle soup
Yayla çorbası Yoghurt soup
Tarhana çorbası Soup made from a dried yoghurt base

Soguk meze/Cold starters
These are usually offered from a large tray of assorted dishes, or you can choose from a cold cabinet.
Beyaz peynir White cheese
Kavun Honeydew melon
Zeytin Olives

Patlıcan ezmesi Aubergine purée
Piyaz/pilaki White bean salad with olive oil and lemon
Acı Spicy hot red paste or salad of chopped peppers and tomato
Taramasalata Purée of fish roe
Çerkez tavuğu Shredded chicken in walnut sauce
Haydari Dip of chopped dill and garlic in thick yoghurt
Fava Purée of beans
Dolma Vegetables or other things stuffed with rice mixed with dill, pinenuts and currants
Yalancı yaprak dolması Stuffed vine leaves
Midye dolması Stuffed mussels
Biber dolması Stuffed peppers
Lakerda Sliced smoked tuna
Hamsi Fresh anchovies in oil
Zeytinyağlı Vegetables cooked with olive oil, served cold
Zeytinyağlı kereviz Celeriac in olive oil
İmam bayıldı Aubergine stuffed with tomato and onion, cooked with olive oil

Sıcak mezeler/Hot starters
Sigara böreği Crisp fried rolls of pastry with cheese or meat filling (can also be triangular: *muska*)
Arnavut ciğeri Albanian-style fried diced lamb's liver
Kalamar tava Deep-fried squid rings
Midye tava Deep-fried mussels
Tarator Nut and garlic sauce served with above, or with fried vegetables
Patates köfte Potato croquettes

Salata/Salads
Karışık Mixed
Çoban salatası "Shepherd's salad" (chopped mixed tomato, cucumber, pepper, onion and parsley)
Yeşil salata Green salad
Mevsim salatası Seasonal salad
Roka Rocket/arugula
Salatalık Cucumber
Domates Tomatoes
Marul Cos/romaine lettuce
Semizotu Lamb's lettuce/purslane
Söğüş Sliced salad vegetables with no dressing

Et yemekleri/Meat dishes
Kebap Kebab
Döner Sliced, layered lamb grilled on revolving spit

Tavuk döner *As above, made with chicken*
Şiş kebap Cubed meat grilled on skewer eg *kuzu şiş* (lamb), *tavuk şiş* (chicken)
Adana kebap Minced lamb grilled on skewer, spicy
Urfa kebap *As above, not spicy*
Bursa/İskender/yoğurtlu kebap Dish of döner slices laid on pieces of bread with tomato sauce, melted butter and yoghurt with garlic
Pirzola Cutlets
Izgara Grill/grilled – usually over charcoal
Köfte Meatballs
Köfte ızgara Grilled meatballs
Bıldırcın ızgara Grilled quail
Kuzu tandır/fırın Lamb baked on the bone
Hünkâr beğendili köfte Meatballs with aubergine purée
Kadınbudu köfte "Ladies' thighs", meat and rice croquettes in gravy
Karnıyarık Aubergines split in half and filled with minced lamb mixed with pine nuts and currants
Kavurma Meat stir-fried or braised, cooked in its own fat and juices
Çoban kavurma Lamb fried with peppers, tomatoes and onions
Saç kavurma Wok-fried meat, vegetables and spices
Etli dolması Dolma stuffed with meat and rice (eaten hot)
Etli kabak dolması Courgettes stuffed with meat
Etli nohut Chickpea and lamb stew
Etli kuru fasuliye Haricot beans and lamb stew
Kağıt kebabı Lamb and vegetables cooked in paper
Kıymalı with minced meat
Güveç Casserole

Balık yemekleri/Fish dishes
Most fish is eaten plainly grilled or fried, and priced by weight. Always ask the price, "ne kadar?" before ordering.
Balık ızgara Grilled fish
Balık kızartması Fried fish
Balık şiş Cubed fish grilled on skewer
Alabalık Trout
Levrek Seabass
Lüfer Bluefish
Hamsi Anchovies
Sardalye Sardines

Karagöz Black bream
Uskumru Mackerel
Palamut Tuna
Kalkan Turbot
Gümüş Silverfish (like whitebait)
Barbunya Red mullet
Kefal Grey mullet
Kılıç balığı Swordfish
Dil balığı Sole
Karides Shrimp, prawns

Karides güveç Prawn casserole with peppers, tomato and melted cheese
Hamsi pilav Rice baked with anchovies
Levrek pilakisi Sea bass stew with onion, potato, tomato and garlic
Kiremitte balık Fish baked on a tile
Kağıtta barbunya Mullet (or other fish) baked in a paper case

Other things that may be on menus:
Makarna Macaroni, noodles
Patates puresi Mashed/puréed potatoes
Patates kızartması/tava Chips/french fries.
Pilav Cooked rice, can be a rice dish with meat, chicken, pulses or noodles
Tost Toasted cheese sandwich
Turşu Pickles – Turkish pickles are sour and salty, sometimes spicy.

Tatlı/Desserts
Baklava Layers of wafer-thin pastry with nuts and syrup
Ekmek kadayıf Bread pudding soaked in syrup
Güllaç Dessert made with layers of rice wafer, sugar and milk
Tavuk göğsü Milk pudding made with pounded chicken breast
Kazandibi Glazed, with browned, caramelised top
Dondurma Ice cream
Muhallebi Rice flour, milk and rosewater blancmange
Sütlaç Rice pudding
Aflure "Noah's pudding" made with dried fruits, nuts, seeds, pulses
Kabak tatlısı Candied pumpkin
Ayva tatlısı Candied quince
Kaymaklı with clotted cream
Komposto Poached fruit
Krem caramel crème caramel
Pasta Gâteau-style cake, patisserie

Soft or cold drinks

Su Water
Memba suyu Mineral water
Maden suyu gazoz/soda Sparkling water
Ayran Yoghurt whisked with cold water and salt
Meyva suyu Fruit juice
Visne suyu Sourcherry juice
Kayısı suyu Apricot juice
Taze portakal suyu Freshly squeezed orange juice
Şerbet Sweetened, iced fruit juice drink
Limonata Lemon drink
Buz Ice

Hot drinks

Çay Tea
Açık Weak
Demli Brewed
Bir bardak çay Glass of tea
Bir fincan kahve Cup of coffee
Ada çayı "Island tea" made with dried wild sage
Elma çayı Apple tea
Kahve Coffee
Neskafe any instant coffee
Sutlu with milk
Şeker Sugar
Türk kahvesi Turkish coffee
Az flekerli with little sugar
Orta Medium sweet
Şekerli Sweet
Sade without sugar
Süzme kahve Filter coffee
Sahlep Hot, thick sweet winter drink made of *sahlep* root, milk and cinnamon

Alcoholic drinks

Bira Beer
Siyah Dark (beer)
Beyaz Light (beer)
Cintonik Gin and tonic
Votka Vodka
Yerli Local, Turkish
Şarap Wine
Şarap listesi Wine list
Kırmızı şarap Red wine
Beyaz şarap White wine
Roze şarap Rosé
Sek Dry
Antik Aged
Tatlı Sweet
Şişe/yarım şişe Bottle/half bottle
Rakı Turkish national alcoholic drink, strongly aniseed-flavoured
Yeni Rakı Chief brand of rakı

Further Reading

General

There are plenty of books about all aspects of Turkey in English: such a complex country with so many layers of history and culture couldn't fail to generate a wealth of histories, memoirs, poetry, fiction, biographies and travel writing. Not much Turkish writing has been translated into English, however. Some good books in English have been written and issued by Turkish publishers, but are difficult to obtain outside Turkey.

History

Black Sea, The Birthplace of Civilisation and Barbarism, by Neal Ascherson (Vintage, 1996). Compelling, brilliantly written book about the cultures surrounding this great inland sea; from Herodotus to the fall of Communism.
Byzantium, three volumes: *The Early Centuries*, *The Apogee* and *The Decline and Fall*, by John Julius Norwich (Penguin, 1993–1996). Thorough, accessible, readable and entertaining account of the history of the empire up to the Ottoman conquest of 1453.
Constantinople, City of the World's Desire, 1453–1924, by Philip Mansel (Penguin, 1997). Outstandingly researched portrait of the imperial city. Scholarly and gripping, with a mass of information, anecdote and analysis.
Istanbul, The Imperial City, by John Freely (Viking, 1996). Illustrated introductory "biography" of the city and its social life through 27 centuries by a long-time resident and lover of Turkey.
Orientalism, Western Conceptions of the Orient, by Edward W. Said (Penguin, 1995). Highly acclaimed overview of Western attitudes towards the East, analysing literature, arts and culture.

On Secret Service East of Constantinople, by Peter Hopkirk (Oxford Paperbacks, 1995). Brilliant account of Turkish and German conspiracies against Britain and Russia after 1914, by the author of *The Great Game*.
The Fall of Constantinople, 1453, by Steven Runciman (Cambridge University Press, 1965). Great British medieval historian, also author of the classic three-volume history of The Crusades.
The Hittites by O.R. Gurney (Penguin). Classic history of the earliest Anatolian civilisation suitable for non-specialists. Gurney practically invented Hittite studies single-handed.
The Ottomans, Dissolving Images, by Andrew Wheatcroft (Penguin, 1995). Colourful, readable account of the development of Ottoman power and empire, with good detail about social life.
Sultans in Splendour, by Mansel, Philip (Andre Deutsch, 1988). The last years of the Ottoman Empire in photographs, many unpublished and from imperial collections.
Turkey Unveiled, Atatürk and After, by Nicole and Hugh Pope (John Murray, 1997). Excellent, readable account of the intricacies of Turkish political affairs in the recent past, written by journalists who have been living in and covering the country for the past 10 years.

Lives & Letters

An English Consul in Turkey, Paul Rycaut at Smyrna 1667–78, by Sonia Anderson (Clarendon Press, 1989). Rycaut spent 17 years in Turkey, 11 as consul in Smyrna, whose contemporary English community is vividly described in this biographical study.
Portrait of a Turkish Family, by Irfan Orga (Eland Books, 1993). Vividly and movingly describes the author's family life and his growing up first as a child in Ottoman Turkey before World War I, then through the war and the years of Atatürk's reforms.
The Imperial Harem of the Sultans, The Memoirs of Leyla Hanımefendi (Peva Publications, 1995, available

in Istanbul). The only contemporary account of daily life at the Çirağan Palace during the 19th century, originally published in French in 1925, which gives a vivid portrait of this hidden world.

The Turkish Embassy Letters, by Lady Mary Wortley Montagu (Virago, 1995). Newly edited edition of these lively and intelligent letters, written in 1716 when the writer's husband had just been appointed ambassador. One of the most fascinating of early travel writers.

Embassy To Constantinople, by Lady Mary Wortley Montagu (Century, 1988). Lady Mary's observations and comments in letters to English friends during her husband's tenure as Ambassador to the Sultan's Court circa 1720.

Lords of the Horizons: A History of the Ottoman Empire, by Goodwin, Jason (Henry Holt, 1999). With a few notable historical ommissions, a comprehensive modern approach to a country still coming to terms with its empirical past.

Atatürk, by Mango, Andrew (John Murray, 1999). The most recent biography of Atatürk to replace Lord Kinross' of 1964.

Portrait of A Turkish Family, by Orga, Irfan (Eland, 1988). First published by Victor Gollancz Ltd. in 1950, the second edition contains an epilogue by the author's son. Somewhat melodramatic but heart-rending story of how World War I and the demise of the Ottoman era affected a well-to-do Turkish family.

The World Behind the Veil, by Croutier, Alev Lytle (Bloomsbury, 1989). Turkish expatriate returns to her homeland to research her past. The book is a treasure of harem history with stunning and original photographs and portraits.

Art & Architecture

A History of Ottoman Architecture, by Godfrey Goodwin (Thames and Hudson). Comprehensive and definitive, covering every kind of building all over Turkey. Goodwin's other great book is a monograph on Sinan, the greatest of the Ottoman architects (Saqi Books).

Ancient Civilizations and Ruins of Turkey, by Ekrem Akurgal (Haset Kitabevi, 1973, available in Istanbul).

Hattusa, The Capital of the Hittites, by Kurt Bittel (Oxford University Press, 1970).

The Palace of Topkapı, by Fanny Davis (Scribners, 1970).

Turkish Art and Architecture, by Oktay Aslanapa (Faber and Faber, 1971).

Carpets

Halı Magazine (Halı Publications). Six issues a year dedicated to rug commerce and scholarship, with frequent articles on Turkish textiles and carpets. They also publish *Istanbul, The Halı Rug Guide* and *Orient Stars*, by E. Heinrich Kirchheim, lavishly illustrated with 250 colour plates of classical Turkish carpets.

Travel Writing

A Fez of the Heart by Jeremy Seal (Picador, 1996). The author travels around Turkey in search of a real fez, the red felt hat banned in 1925; and offers a perceptive alternative view of modern Turkey.

From the Holy Mountain, A Journey in the Shadow of Byzantium, by William Dalrymple (Flamingo, 1998). Starting from Mount Athos in Greece, the author follows the trail of Eastern Christianity, travelling into Eastern Turkey and beyond. Dalrymple has been hailed as a successor to Patrick Leigh Fermor; he is certainly adventurous and his writing is lively and erudite.

In Xanadu by William Dalrymple. Flamingo Books. London, 1990. Tracing Marco Polo's footsteps through Asia Minor, Easy style and acerbic observations related to the present make good reading.

The Crossing Place, A Journey among the Armenians, by Philip Marsden (Flamingo, 1994). Travels in search of this remarkable people, one of Turkey's most important minorities, the remaining traces of their culture and their diaspora.

Under a Crescent Moon, by De Souza, Daniel (Serpent's Tail, 1989). Rich, sometimes humourous, vignettes of Turkish prison life in the foreigner's block, without bitterness or retribution.

Anthologies

Istanbul, A Traveller's Companion, selected and introduced by Laurence Kelly (Constable). A wonderful collection of extracts from 14 centuries of writing, arranged around landmark buildings. Acts as a background guide, bringing to life sites that visitors can still see.

Istanbul, Tales of the City, selected by John Miller (Chronicle Books, 1995). Pocket-sized eclectic collection of prose and poetry, including pieces by Simone de Beauvoir, Disraeli and Gore Vidal.

Fiction

Greenmantle, by John Buchan. (Penguin). First published in 1916, the immortal Richard Hannay adventures across the Balkans into Anatolia. Based on a true story.

Mehmet My Hawk, by Yasar Kemal (Harvill). The best-known Turkish novelist in translation. This is just one, the most famous, of many novels. Some are set in and around Istanbul, some are set in rural Anatolia.

The Rage of the Vulture, by Barry Unsworth (Granada). Historical novel by the best-selling author, set in the twilight years of the Ottoman Empire and focusing on the sultan Abdülhamid.

The White Castle, The Black Book, The New Life. Novels by Orhan Pamuk, translated by Güneli Gün (Faber). Introspective, perceptive, sometimes over-complex but much lauded contemporary Turkish writer. *The New Life* was the fastest selling book in Turkish history.

Food & Cooking

Classic Turkish Cookery by Ghillie and Jonathan Basan, introduced by Josceline Dimbleby (Tauris Parke

Books, 1997). A beautifully illustrated book which places Turkish cooking in its geographical and cultural context; the recipes are a practical and authentic introduction to the best of Turkish dishes, gleaned from sources all over the country.

Timeless Tastes, Turkish Culinary Culture, project director Semahat Arsel (Vehbi Koç Vakfı and Divan Istanbul, 1996). Published to celebrate the 40th anniversary of the Divan Hotel, long renowned for its kitchen and its patisserie. The book has several authors: experts on culinary art and history, and professional chefs who give their recipes. This history of Turkish cooking at the most elevated level is illustrated with Ottoman miniatures and engravings.

The Art of Turkish Cooking, by Neşet Eren (Hippocrene Books, 1996). Written in 1969, the excellence of this book lies in its simple instructions, and the use of simple ingredients that are readily available (a characteristic of Turkish cooking anyway). The style is a little dated, but the recipes are authentic. A less lavish choice than the above two books.

Guides

Aegean Turkey, Lycian Turkey, Turkey's Southern Shore, Turkey Beyond the Maeanders, by George E. Bean (John Murray). Scholarly specialist guides to the archaeological sites of Turkey, compiled from Professor Bean's research.

Blue Guide Turkey, by Bernard McDonagh (A&C Black, 1999). Latest edition of the classic fount of all wisdom on history and archaeology.

The Companion Guide to Turkey, by John Freely (Harper Collins, 1996). This was first published in 1979 but revised in 1992. Freely's knowledge of and affection for the country is palpable in its pages.

Other Insight Guides

Three distinctive series from Apa Publications are designed to meet your varying travel needs.

The 194-strong **Insight Guides** series, companions to this title, includes titles on *Turkey, Istanbul, Crete* and *The Greek Islands*.

The **Insight Compact Guide** series, which packs easily accessible information into a small format, together with carefully referenced pictures and maps, includes titles on *Turkey, The Turkish Coast and Rhodes* and *Crete*.

The **Insight Pocket Guides** series contain personal recommendations from local hosts and includes an invaluable full-size, fold-out map. Titles in this range include: *Istanbul, The Turkish Coast, Crete, Rhodes* and *Athens*.

Feedback

We do our best to ensure the information in our books is as accurate and up-to-date as possible. The books are updated on a regular basis, using local contacts, who painstakingly add, amend and correct as required. However, some mistakes and omissions are inevitable and we are ultimately reliant on our readers to put us in the picture.

We would welcome your feedback on any details related to your experiences using the book "on the road". Maybe we recommended a hotel that you liked (or another that you didn't), as well as interesting new attractions, or facts and figures you have found out about the country itself. The more details you can give us (particularly with regard to addresses, e-mails and telephone numbers), the better.

We will acknowledge all contributions, and we'll offer an Insight Guide to the best letters received.

Please write to us at:
Insight Guides
APA Publications
PO Box 7910
London SE1 1XF
Or send e-mail to:
insight@apaguide.demon.co.uk

ART & PHOTO CREDITS

Index

a

Ablution Hall, Labraynda, 212
Abraham, 59
Achaeans, 23, 30, 31
Achilles, 38, 141, 145, 147
Actium, Battle of, 26, 37, 41
Ada Bogazı, 220
ada cayı (island tea), 269
Alanya, 280
Adana, 27, 37, 47, 66, 68, 69, 104, 285, 287, 300, 301, 302
Adatepe, 153
Adıyaman, 67
Adnan Menderes Bulvarı, Aydın, 202
Adramittium Thebe, 153
Aegean Coast, 23, 26, 43, 51, 59, 65, 93, 94, 95, 96, 151, 184, 211, 222
Aegospotami, Naval Battle of, 26, 137
Aeolia, 30, 32, 153, 154, 155, 181
Aeolians, 26, 30, 32, 33, 36
Afyon, 42
Africa, 51, 208
Aga (German Conservation Organization), 103
Agamemnon, Baths of, Izmir, 173
Agiles, Raymond, 47
Aglaia, 294
Agora, Izmir, 172
Ahhiyawans, 29, 30
ajur (sweet cucumber), 269
Akbank, 313
Akbas Liman, 127
Akbük, 127
Akbük Bay, 211
Akçakaya Village, Kayseri, 312
Akçay, 153
Akdeniz, Akdeniz Song Contest, 276
Akhan Caravansary, 204
Akhisar, 42
Akkum, 179
aksak (Turkish folk dance), 70
Aksaz Liman (Nato Naval Base) 247
Alanya, 23, 41, 272, 279, 280, 281, 287
Alarahan, 279
Alasehir, 42
Alçitepe, Gallipoli, 127, 133
Aleppo, 47, 315
Alexandria, 158
Alexandria Troas, 23, 39, 43, 123, 138

Alexius, 46
Aliaga, 154
Alihan Kümbeti, 201
Alisar, 31
Allied Powers, (World War I) 27, 129, 131
Alman Büku, Gulf of Gökova, 226
al-Qalasi, Ibn, 47
Alsancak, Izmir, 169
Altar of Zeus, 93
Altay, 49
Altın Kum, 209
Altınoluk, 153
Amalfi, 46, 50
Amazonamachy, 93
Amik Ovası, 310
Anafarta, Gallipoli, 132
Anamur, 23, 287, 288, 289
Anamurium, 289
Anatolia, 23, 26, 27, 28–37, 42, 46, 49, 67, 68, 92, 93, 156, 158, 216
Anavarza, 302, 303, 305, 306
Ancona, 50
Andrea Dorea Bay, Finike, 260
Anaximander, 32, 208
Anaximenes, 32, 208
Andirons, Labraynda, 212
Andromache, 141, 145
Ankara, 30, 50, 52, 59, 216
Antakya, (Antioch) 26, 28, 29, 34, 35, 39, 41, 42, 47, 68, 285, 314–318
Antalya, 23, 27, 35, 36, 37, 52, 69, 93–95, 103, 105, 225, 256, 261–274, 287
Antalya Free Zone, 267
Antalya, Gulf of, 251
Antalya International Airport, 267
Antilles, 222
Antioch Games, 315
Antiochia-ad Cragum, 288
Antiphellus, Kas, 256
Antiquities Smuggling, 92, 93
Anouilh, Jean, 309
Anzac (Australian and New Zealand Army Corps), 130
Anzac Battlefields (Gallipoli), 132
Anzac Cove (Gallipoli) 127, 132
Aperlae, 258
Aphrodisias, 26, 60, 202, 203, 204
Aphrodite, Statue of (Knidos) 33, 229
Apollo, Oracle of, Didyma, 256
Aquilius, 40
Arabic, 59
Arabian Peninsula, 51, 65
Arabs, 23, 26, 67, 216, 287, 291, 307, 314

Arcadian Way, 197
Arı Burnu (Gallipoli), 132
Arıstides, Aelius (the hypochondriac), 164
Aristonicus, 40, 160
Aristotle, 139
Arius (the heretic), 264
Armenians, 41, 50, 59, 68, 69, 302, 305
Arsuz, 313
asker (Turkish soldiers), 288
Asclepium, 161, 164
asıks (Anatolian minstrels), 306
Aspendos, 23, 31, 36, 38, 275, 276
Aspendos Theatre, 275, 276
Assuwans, the, 28
Assyrians, 29, 37
Assos, 23, 138, 139, 153
Asartepe, 233
Atatürk, Mustafa Kemal, 27, 52, 53, 59, 131, 132, 173, 268, 312
Atatürk Caddesi (Antalya) 267; (Izmir) 169
Atatürk Monument (Izmir) 167
Atatürk Park, Antalya, 267
Atatürk Square, Marmaris, 231
Atatürk Statue, Antalya, 270
Athens, 26, 34, 38, 127, 188, 192, 207
Atreus, Family of, 144
Attalid Kings of Pergamum, 30, 32, 188
Australia, 127, 132
Australians, 131
Australian War Memorial, Gallipoli, 133
Austria, 157
Auvergne, 46
Ayaz, 297, 302
Ayathekla, 43, 290
Aydın, 23, 201, 202
Aydıncık, 290
Aynalı Çarsı, 136
Ayvacık, 138
Ayvalık, 23, 100, 153, 156, 157
Ayvalık, Bay of, 153
Azmak, Gallipoli, 132

b

Babaoglan, 37
Babylon, 28, 315
Baghdad, 27, 50
Balçova Hot Springs, Izmir, 173
Balıkasıran, Datça Peninsula, 235
Ballisu, 228
Ballkh, 58
Balkans, 34, 50, 51, 65, 67, 123

Balkan Wars, 27, 129
Baltalı Kapı, Milâs, 213
Barbaros, Hayrettin, 183
Bardakçı, Bodrum, 221
Bari, Italy, 264
Barnabas, 42
Basmane Train Station, Izmir, 169, 194
Bass, George, 217, 218
Baskara (Bactra), 49
Baths of Hadrian, Aphrodisias, 203
Baths of Cleopatra, Gulf of Fethiye, 251
Bayır Village, Marmaris, 237
Bayraklı, Izmir, 173
Bean, George, 142, 161, 235, 274
Beçin Kale, Milâs, 213
Bedesten, Alanya, 281
Bedri Rahmi Bay (Gulf of Fethiye), 251
Behramkale, 123, 138, 139
Belbası Cave, Antalya, 35, 36, 263, 267
Belcekız Beach, 253
Beldibi Cave, Antalya, 35,36, 263, 267
Belen Pass (Syrian Gates), 310
Belkız, Aspendos, 275, 276
Bencik, Datça Peninsula, 235
Benedict XIV, Pope, 199
Bergama, 23, 161
Berlin, 141
Besige Tepe, 137
Beth Israel Synagogue, Izmir, 176
Beycesultan, 26
Beykoz, 53
Bias, 207
Biga Peninsula, Çanakkale, 135
bird varieties of the Turkish Coast
    Avocet, 101
    Bittern, 100
    Black Francolin, 104
    Black-winged Stilt, 101
    Booted Eagle, 101
    Dalmatian Pelican, 102
    Dunlin, 101
    Eleonara's Falcons, 102
    Flamingo, 101
    Glossy Ibis, 100
    Graceful Warbler, 104
    Great White Egrets, 102
    Greyling Goose, 100
    Kentish Plover, 100
    Little Bustard, 100
    Little Egrets, 102
    Marbled Teal, 104
    Peregrine Hawk, 102
    Purple Gallinule, 104
    Squocco Heron, 101
    Stork, 100
    Turtle Doves, 271
    White Pelican, 104
    Yelkoan Shearwater, 100
Bitez, Bodrum, 221
Bithynia, 158, 159
Black Sea, 32, 51, 52, 123
Blegan, Carl, 142
Blue Voyage, 23, 215, 217, 225–229, 233, 251, 256
Bodrum (near Castabala), 37
Bodrum (Halicarnassus, Petronium) 23, 32, 33, 35, 38, 75, 93, 96, 184, 187, 215–225, 236, 257
Bodrum Peninsula, 215, 222
Boetia, 32
Bogazkale, 30, 31
Bogsak, 290
Bolayır, 125
books
    A Murder in the Iron Workers Market (Yasar Kemal), 306
    Acts of Paul and Thekla, 290
    Agamemnon (Euripides), 145
    Aeneid, the (Virgil), 146,147
    Animals Without Backbones (Ralph Busbaum), 222
    Faust (Goethe), 147
    Helen (Euripides), 145
    Iliad, the (Homer), 140, 141, 142, 145, 146, 147
    Iphigenie auf Tauris (Goethe), 147
    Iron Earth, Copper Sky (Yasar Kemal), 306
    Karamania, 259
    Kitabı Bahriye (Piri Reis), 153
    Memed, my Hawk (Yasar Kemal), 308
    Old Testament 32
    Odyssey, the (Homer), 140, 141, 143, 145, 146, 147, 306
    On Anatomical Procedure (Galen), 164
    Trojan Women (Euripides), 145
    Yusufçuk Yusuf (Yasar Kemal) 308, 309
    Western Shores of Turkey (John Freely), 176
Borges, Jorge Luis, 309
Bornova, Izmir, 177
Bosphorus, the, 313
Bozburun, Marmaris, 236, 237
Bozburun, Gulf of, 233
Bosphorus, the 52, 100, 122, 143
Boston, 139
Bouvet (French Battleship) 130
Boynuzbükü (Gulf of Fethiye), 251
Bördübet Liman (Gulf of Gökova) 229
Britain, 47, 129
British Army (at Gallipoli), 129, 130, 131
British Navy, 92, 130
Bronze Age, 26, 29, 31
Bronze Age Hall (Bodrum Museum) 217
Buca, 177
Buharkent (The Steam City), 205
Bulgaria, 27, 30
Burak, Aytaç, 301
Burdur, 272
Burhaniye, 23
Bursa, 49, 93
Burumcuk, 155
Bushbaum, Ralph, 222
Bybassus, Hisarönü, 236
Byron, Lord, 135
Byzantine Empire, 26, 47, 49, 160, 177, 274
Byzantines, 40, 46, 139, 208, 213, 287, 291, 315

C

Cadmus, 32
Calcholithic Age, 26, 29
Caliphate, 23, 52
Çakırhan, Nail, 228, 247
Çamaltı Tuzlası, Izmir, 105
Çambalı (pine honey), 232
camel wrestling, 184, 185
Çamlık, 201
Canaan, 34, 49
Canada, 222
Çanak Bay, Gulf of Gökova, 228
Çanakcı, 297
Çanakkale, 23, 31, 132, 135–138, 156
Çanakkale, Naval Battle of, 135
Çanakkale Peninsula, 127, 135
Çandarlı (Pitane), 153, 154
Çandarlı Halil Pasha, 154
Canhasan, 26
Cape Crio, Knidos, 236
Cape Doganay, 180
Cape Hellas (Gallipoli), 127, 128, 131, 132, 133, 146
Cape Hellas War Memorial, 127, 133
Cape Sigeon, 137
Caria, 23, 30, 32, 198, 207, 212, 213, 235
Carians, 23, 26, 208, 211, 215
Carlowitz, Treaty of, 27, 35
Çarsaf, 59
Çatal Höyük, 26, 38, 191
carpet motifs 87–88, 90
carpet varieties
    Bergama carpets, 90

Dösemealtı carpets, 91, 269, 272
Gördes carpets, 90
Hereke silk carpets 89
heybes, 87
Holbein carpets, 89
Karakeçili carpets, 90
kilims (flatweaves), 68, 85, 87,
    88, 89
knotted carpets, 88
Kozak carpets, 90
Kula carpets, 90
Milâs carpets, 90
Parmaklı *kilims*, 89
sumaks, 86
Yagcıbedir carpets, 90
Yüntdag carpets, 90
zilis, 86
Cassandra, 146
Castabala Hierapolis, 37
Castabus, Festival of, 236
castles
Alanya Castle, 280
Alarakale, 279
Bagras Castle (Iskenderun),
    304, 315
Bodrum Castle (Castle of St
    Peter) 215, 216, 217, 218,
    219, 305
Çesme Kalesi (Genoese
    Fortress) 178
Çifit Kalesi, 180
Çimpe Kalesi, 126
Gülek Kalesi, 305
Kadife Kale, Izmir, 172
Keçi Kalesi, Selçuk, 181
Kilitbahir, Çanakkale, 29
Kızkalesi, Silifke, 305
Kumkale, Dardanelles, 129, 139
Kuşadası Castle, 183
Liman Kalesi, 290
Mamure Kalesi Anamur, 289
Mezgit Kalesi, 294
Sis Kalesi, 305
Softa Kalesi, Anamur, 290
Toprakkale, 305
Yılan Kalesi, 302, 305
Catholics, 50, 59, 59, 68, 69
Caucasia, 51
Caucausus, 29
Caunos, 247
Cehennem (the Abyss of Hell), 296
Celsus Library, Ephesus, 43, 195
Cennet (Paradise Beach), 233
Cennet (Heaven), 295
Cenotaph of Hallacı Mansur,
    Gelibolu, 126
Cervantes, 176
Çesme, 23, 101, 178
Çesme, Bay of, 179

Çesme Sea Festival, 178
Cezayirli Hasan Pasha, 179
Chimera, 23, 262
China, 68
Chinese, 49
Christianity, 26, 42, 43, 46, 173,
    203, 290
Christians, 59, 182, 184, 311
Chrysippus (Stoic), 298
churches
Evangelist Church, Alahan
    Monastery, 291
Haghia Sophia, Istanbul, 43, 193
Our Lady of the Lourdes, Church
    of, Izmir, 177
Panaghia Church, Antalya, 291
Perge, Church of, 273
Rosary Church, Izmir, 177
Santa Elena, Church of, Izmir, 177
Santa Maria, Church of, Izmir,
    170, 177
St Anthony, Church of, Izmir, 177
St George, Church of, Alanya, 280
St John, Church of, Selçuk, 181
St John the Evangelist, Church of
    of, Izmir, 170, 177
St Mary, Church of (Heaven), 295
St Peter, Church of (Antioch), 317
Çiçek Balı, 232
Çiftlik, 233, 234, 235
Cılvarda Burnu, Alanya, 281
Cilicia, 30, 31, 52, 287
Cilician Gates (Gülek Bogazı), 25,
    30, 36
Cimmerians, 29, 33, 192
Çıralı, 262
Clacas, 273
Claros, 181
Claudiopolis, 291
Clazomenae, 178
Cleopatra's Beach, 41, 227
Cleopatra's Baths (Hamam Cove),
    41
Cleopatra's Gate, Tarsus, 299
Clermont, 46
Clock Tower, Antalya, 269
Clock Tower, Izmir, 169
Coin and Jewelry Hall, 218
Çökertme, Gulf of Gökova, 226
Columbus, Christopher, 126
Colophon, 181
Commonwealth, the British, 132
**Commonwealth War Graves
    Commission**, 132
Cook, J.M., 213, 235
Conk Bayır, Gallipoli, 127, 132, 133
Coracesium, 41
Corycian Cave Complex, 295, 296
Corycus, 296

Cos, 32
Costa Brava, Spain, 109
Covered Bazaar, Istanbul, 93
Crassus, 40
Crimea, 51, 65
Crimean War, 27, 67, 126
Crusaders, 47, 49, 139, 147, 287,
    291, 307
Crusades, 27, 46, 47, 49, 268
Cuba, 222
Çubuklu, 101
Çukurova (the Cilician Plain), 23, 28,
    30, 36, 37, 104, 105, 287, 300
Culture Ministry, 92, 93, 138
Cumaovası, 181
Cumhuriyet (Turkish newspaper), 326
Cumhuriyet Meydanı, Antalya, 270
Cumhuriyet Meydanı, Izmir, 167
Cydnus, 299
Cyme, 32, 36, 154
Cynics, 39, 91

d

dag çayı (mountain tea), 269
Dalaman, 249
Dalaman Beach, 107
Dalmatian Coast, 51
Dalaman International Airport,
    231, 249
Dalan, Bedrettin, 251
Dalyan, 102, 103, 179, 247
Damascus, 47,190
Damlatas Cave, 280
Dante, 147
Daphne, shrine of, 315
Dardanelles, the, 23, 26, 27, 31,
    32, 100, 122, 125, 126, 127,
    129, 132, 133, 135, 136,
    143, 147,
Dardanians, 31
Dardanus, 31, 136, 138
Dark Ages, the, 26, 29
Darphane, (the Mint), 281
Datça, 33, 220, 235
Datça Peninsula, 225, 234, 236
davul, 68
Degirmen Bükü, 228
Degirmendere, 181
defne yapragı (laurel leaves), 237
Del Duca Prize, 309
Delphi, 33
Delian league, the, 154
Demre, 258, 259, 264, 265
Demirçili, 293
Demirel, Süleyman, 27
Denizli, 23, 204
Despoina, Lady, 50
Development Bank Of Turkey, 139

Diana's Baths, 173
Didyma, Oracle of, 208, 209
Diyarbakır, 67
Didyma, 29, 211
Dilek Peninsula National Park, 101, 183
Dimetoeki, 50
Dinçer, Selim, 222
Diogenes, 144
Dobag Carpet Project, 91
Domuz Büku, 236
Dorak Affair, 93
Dorians, 32, 33
Dönme, 68, 69, 176, 177
Dörtyol, 305
Dösemealtı, 272
Dr Alim Bey Caddesi, Bodrum, 215
Dunkirk, 132
Düden Selalesi, 272

e

Eceabat, 127, 132, 136
Ecumenical Council, 198,
Edirne, 50, 125
Edremit, Gulf of, 23, 32, 123, 153, 156
Edremit (city), 23, 153
Efe, 172
Egypt, 26, 27, 32, 34, 37, 39, 41, 43, 45, 51, 154, 188, 208, 311
Egyptians, 304
Ekincik, 247
Elaea, 154
Elaeusa, 297
Elmalı Treasures, 93
Emirgan, Istanbul, 313
Endymion Sanctuary, 211
Enez, 23, 100, 122, 125
English Harbour, Gulf of Gökova, 228
English Tower, Bodrum Castle, 218
Ephesus, 23, 28, 39, 40, 42, 43, 101, 154, 167, 180, 181, 187–199, 203, 206
Epicurians, the, 39
Erbek, Güran, 91
Erim, Kenan, 202, 203
Eros Riding the Dolphin, Statue of, Ephesus Museum, 183
Ertegün, Ahmet, 217
Erythrae, 161, 179
Erzen, Afif, 125
Erzurum, 65
Eski Foça (Phocaia), 154
Eskisehir (Dorylaeum), 30, 47
Esteddiya, 36
Etruscans, 33
Eudoxia, 272
Eudoxos, 229

Euphrosina, 299
Euromos, 211
Evdir Han, 272
Evren, Kenan, 27
Ezan, 59
Ezine, 138

f

Fatamids, the, 46
Fellini, Federico, 309
Fellows, Charles, 92
Fertile Cescent, the, 28
Festus, 137
Fethiye, 23, 34, 94, 224, 251
Fethiye, Gulf of, 23, 41, 224, 250, 251
fez, the, 27, 52
Filibe, 50
Finike, 260, 261
Foça, 23, 94
food 75–81, 357, 380
France, 27, 50, 129
Franciscans, 170
French Critics Association, 309
French Tower (Bodrum castle), 218
French Crimean War Cemetery (Gallipoli), 126
French War Memorial (Gallipoli), 127, 153

g

Galatia, 42
Galen, 164
Gallipoli Campaign, 127, 128, 129–133
Gallipoli Peninsula, 23, 27, 52, 125, 129, 131, 132
Gelibolu, 126, 129
Gauls, the, 26, 145, 158
Gazimagosa (Famagusta), 298
Gazi Pasa, 288
gecekondu (squatter housing), 65, 66, 67, 172, 300
Genoa, 46, 50, 177, 178, 183
Genoese, 173
Gentiles, 42
Gerbekse, 234
German Tower, Bodrum Castle, 218
Germany, 27, 52
Germiyanoglu Principality, 204
Geyre, 202
Glass Wreck, the, Bodrum Castle, 218
gods of mythology
    Aphrodite, 144, 203, 294
    Apollo, 30, 39, 181, 315
    Artemis, 181, 191, 203, 256, 276

Athena, 38, 144
Bacchus, 180
Cybele, 71
Dionysus, 180
Endymion, 211
Eris, 144
Hephaestus, 262
Hera, 144, 254, 294
Heracles, 38
Hermaphrodite, 221
Isis, 163
Leto, 181
Oenone, 144, 153
Osiris, 153
Pan, 30
Priapus, 195, 294
Salmacis, 221
Selene, 211
Tyche, 196
Zeus, 144, 153, 211, 218, 254, 276, 294
Golden Road, 167, 173
Gordium, 29
Göcek, 241
göçmen (refugees), 67
Gökova, Gulf of, 23, 41, 222, 225, 229
Gökova Iskelesi, 227
Göymen, Koral, 237
Granicus, Battle of, 188
Greece, 23, 27, 30, 31, 32, 33, 39, 40, 52, 67, 68, 100, 144, 208, 222
Greek Orthodox, 47, 59
Greeks, 29, 30, 50, 55, 67, 68, 123, 140–147, 160, 167, 173, 178, 287, 298
Green Hill, Gallipoli, 132
Gregorians, 50, 163
Gryneum, 154
Gurkha Bluff, Gallipoli, 133
Güllük, 213
Gümbet, Bodrum, 23, 97
Gümüldür, 181
Gümüskesen Mausoleum, Milâs, 212
Gürkan, Hülya (Camp Operator), 254
Güven Uçurumu, Antalya, 273
Günücek Park, 233
Güzelbahçe, 178
Güzelçamlı, 182, 183
Güzelyalı, Çanakkale, 136, 137

h

Hacı Ilyas District, Milâs, 213
Hacılar, 26
Hacı Ömer Sabancı Holding Company, 312

Hadrian's Gate, Antalya, 270
Hadrian's Granary, Patara, 256
Halas (cruise ship), 250
Halit Bey, 301
Hamitoglu Tribe, 268
Hattians, 29
Hatay, 307
Hattusa (Bogazköy), 26, 29, 30, 37, 93, 167
Havra Sokak (Street of Synagogues), 176
Heaven, the Pit of, 287, 296
Hebrew, 68
Hecatataeus, 32
Hector (Trojan Hero), 145, 147
Hell, the Abyss of, 287
Helen (Trojan War), 144, 145
Hellenistic Period, 26, 38, 39
Hemitea, Sanctuary of, 236
Heraclea under Latmos, 102, 211
Hereke, 89
Hero, 23
Herodotus, 26, 30, 32, 33, 179
Heroon, 208
Herzl, Theodor,69
Hıdır, 318
Hıdırbey Village, 318
Hıdır's Tree, 318
Hınzır Burnu (The Cape of Pigs), 308
Hierapolis, 205
Hisarönü, Gulf of, 23, 225, 229, 233
Hisarönü Village, Marmaris, 236
Hittites, the, 26, 29, 30, 32, 36, 37, 47, 92, 93, 167, 173, 301, 304
holiday villages 94
Homanlı Turks, 89
Homer, 26, 30, 31, 32, 40, 173, 194, 211, 225
House of Romanov, 53
Hungary, 27, 53
Hunyadi, Janos, 52
Hurrians, the, 30
Hürriyet (Turkish newspaper), 251

i

Iassus, 213, 307
Ice Age, the, 28
Ildır, 179
Ildız Carpet Farm, Milâs, 91, 213
Ildız Company, 213
Ilıca, Çesme, 178
Imam (Moslem priest), 61
Imbat (west wind) 156, 169
Ibrogin, 293
Incekum Beach, 279
Incirlik Base, Adana, 303
Industrial Free Zone, 154

Institute of Nautical Archaeology, the, 93, 215
Intepe, Çanakkale, 137
Ionia, 23, 30, 178–182
Ionians, 26, 32, 33, 34
Ionian League, 39, 181, 207
Ionian Revolt, 178, 207
Ipsala, 125
Iraq, 51, 300
Iraq-Turkey Crude Oil Pipeline, 23
Iran, 30
Iskenderun, 23, 69, 96, 309
Iskenderun, Gulf of, 105, 309
Islam, 46, 52, 59, 60, 61, 70, 308
islands
    Alibey Ada, (Cunda), 153
    Bedir Adası, 233
    Bozcaada (Tenedos), 23, 123, 135
    Cedrae, Gulf of Gökova, 227
    Chios (Greek island), 177, 179
    Crete, 27, 31, 32, 34, 142, 153, 278
    Cyprus, 27, 32, 42, 142, 287, 289
    Dislice Adası, Gulf of Hisarönü, 235
    Domuz Adası, Gulf of Fethiye, 250
    Gökçeada (Imroz), 68, 122, 127, 132, 135
    Hacı Halil Adası, Gulf of Fethiye, 250
    Karaada, Bodrum, 215, 220, 225
    Keçi Adası, 234
    Kekova Adası, 251, 258, 259
    Khalaki (Greek island), 229
    Lesbos, 139, 153
    Meis (Kastellorizon), 256
    Nisiros (Greek island), 229
    Orak Adası (Gulf of Gökova), 226
    Provencal Island, 290
    Rhodes, 51, 229, 233, 231
    Samos (Greek island), 183
    Samothrace, (Greek island) 136
    Symi (Greek island), 234
    Twelve Islands, Gulf of Fethiye, 248
    Yedi Adalar, Gulf of Gökova, 229
    Yilan Adası, 227
    Tersane Adası (Gulf of Fethiye), 250
    Yassica Adasi (Gulf of Fethiye), 250
    Yiali (Greek island), 229
    Zeytinli Adası (Gulf of Fethiye), 250
Israel, 69
Istanbul (Constantinople, Byzantium), 26, 27, 47, 50, 51, 52, 59, 125, 126, 129, 135, 139, 197, 272,

Istanbul University, 125
Italians, 46, 47, 177, 183
Italian Primary School, 177
Italian Tower (Bodrum Castle), 218
Ivens Juris, 307
Izmir (Smyrna), 23, 26, 27, 30, 31, 32, 36, 42, 52, 66, 68, 93, 94, 101, 156, 161, 167–184, 187
Izmir, Bay of, 32, 101
Iztuzu (Turtle Beach), 248

j

Janissary, 51
Japan, 222
Jerusalem, 27, 46, 47
Jewish Quarter (Izmir), 169
Jews, the Sephardic, 42, 47, 49, 68, 167, 176
Jivkov, Todor, 68
John Paul, the Pope, 197
Judaism, 42
Judea, 41

k

Kabaagaçlı Cevat Sakir (The Fisherman of Halicarnassus), 216, 219, 220, 225
Kabala (Jewish mysticism), 69
Kabatepe, Gallipoli, 127, 133
Kadesh, Battle of, 29, 31, 32
Kadınlar Plajı, Kusadası, 97, 182
Kadirli, 302, 306
Kafirs, 69
Kaledıran, 288
Kaleiçi (Antalya), 268
Kale Köy (Kekova Sound), 258, 259
Kalkan, 256
Kannesh (Kültepe), 29, 30, 31
Kanlıdivane (Kanyetelis), 297
Karabel, 27
Karabük, 276
Karacasu, 202
Karahayıt Thermal Resort, 205
Karain Caves, 23, 26, 35, 36, 267
Karakeçili Turks, 89
Karamanid Turks, 287
Karatas, 104, 176, 302
Karatay Medresesi, 269
Karatepe, 23, 36
Karatepe National Park, 303, 306
Kargacık Bükü, 225
Karsıyaka, 170
Karun Treasures, 93
Kas, 34, 218, 254, 256, 258
Kaya Ghost Town, Fethiye, 252
Kayseri, 29

Keçibükü (Gulf of Hisarönü), 237
kekik yağı (oregano oil), 237
Kekova Sound, 258
Kemel, Yaşar, 308, 309, 312
Kemalyeri (Gallipoli), 132
Kemer, 23, 94, 95, 263
Kemeraltı (Izmir), 68, 169, 170, 172, 176
Kendall, John, 218
Kesik Minare (Truncated minaret), 291
Kestanbol (spa), 138
Kestrel Dam, 163
Kesan, 125
Keyif, 235
Kına (henna), 61
Kınık (Xanthus), 255
Kırkgöz Han, 272
Kızıl Avlu, 163
Kızıl Su, Pamukkale, 205
Kızkalesi, Silifke, 23, 296
Kızlar Hamamı (the Maidens Bath), 294
Kirkük Oil Fields, 305
Kıdzlaragası Han, 170
Kibar, Osman, 177
Kilitbahir, 127, 136
Kisebükü, Gulf of Gökova, 226
Kizzuwatna, 36, 37
Knidos, 32, 33, 229, 235
Knights of St. John, 213, 216, 252, 290
Koç Group, 231
Konak Square, Izmir, 169, 172
Konya, 27, 36, 42, 43, 49, 61, 290, 291
Konyaaltı Plajı, Antalya, 267
Koran (Islamic holy book), 59
Kordon Boyu, Izmir, 169, 252
Korkuteli, 272
Köprüçay Bridge, 276
Köprülu Family, 51
Körmen, 229, 236
Kösebükü Magarası, 290
Köycegiz, 32
Kula, 90
Kumlubükü, 234
Kumluca, 261
Kumlukuyu, 297
Kurban Bayramı (Sacrifice Festival), 59
Kurds, 50, 67
Kutupasa Medresesi, 299
Kursunlu Selalesi, 272
Kurtulus Village, 104
Kuşadası, 23, 94, 97, 179, 182, 183
Kuşadası Marina, 183
Kuyucak, 202

Kücük Kaynarca, Treaty of, 51
Küçükkuyu, 159

l

Labraynda, 212, 213
Ladino (Judeo-Spanish), 68
Lacoon, 146
Lade, 207
Lade, Battle of, 34
lakes
Akgöl, 104
Akyatan Gölü, 104
Lake Apolyont, Bursa, 93
Lake Bafa, 102, 211
Lake Gala, Enez, 100, 125
Lake Köycegiz, 102, 247
Lake Manyas, Bandırma, 34
Paradeniz Gölu, 102
Tuzla Gölü, 104
Lala Baba (Gallipoli), 132
Laodice, 204
Laodiceia, 42, 204
Lapseki, Çanakkale, 126
Lara Plajı, 267, 268
Larisa, 138, 155
Latin Alphabet, 176
Latin America, 176
Latin Kingdom, 41
Lausanne, Treaty of, 27, 52, 68, 153
Laz, 70
Leander, 23, 135
Lebedos, 180
Lelegians, 173
Lepanto, Battle of, 27
Lesbos (Greek island), 23, 31
Lesser Phrygia, 31
Letoon, 254
Levant Company, the, 177
Levantines, the, 69, 167, 177
Library of Alexandria, 161
Library of Pergamum, 161
Libya, 27, 147
lokanta (basic restaurant), 270
Löngöz Fiord, Gulf of Gökova, 228, 229
Lone Pine (Gallipoli), 127, 132
Loryma, 237
Loryma Peninsula, 233, 236
Lud, 32
Luke, 43
Lukka, the, 30
Lusignans, the, 287, 289
Luther, Martin, 51
Luwian, 30
Lycia, 23, 30, 32, 34, 225, 247–263
Lycians, 26, 30, 32

Lydia, 30, 32, 138
Lydians, 26, 29, 30, 33, 34, 139, 180, 181

m

Macedonia, 27, 38, 153
MacFarlane, Charles, 50
McNamara, Robert, 217
Magnesia, Battle of, 159
Magnesia on the Maeander, 205
Mamelukes, 311
Manavgat, 278, 279
Manavgat Falls, 278
Manzikert, Battle of, 27, 46, 68
Marathon, Battle of, 34
Marco Polo, 302
Mardin, 67
Marmara, Sea of, 32, 38, 39, 122, 125, 129, 156, 158, 188, 208
Marmara University, Istanbul, 91
Marmaris, 23, 94, 95, 96, 218, 225, 231–237
Marmaris, Bay of, 231, 233
Marshall Plan, 313
Marsailles, 154
Martyrium of St. Philip, 205
Mausoleum of Halicarnassus, 32, 93, 212, 217, 218, 219
Mazeus Mithridates Gate, 136
Mediterranean Coast, the, 23, 27, 30, 40, 42, 43, 46, 59, 93, 94, 95, 96, 285, 286
Medrese of Gazi Ahmet Pasa, Milâs, 213
Mehmetçik Abidesi (Turkish War Memorial, Gallipoli), 127
Melaart, James, 93
meltem (summer sea breeze), 226
Memmius Monument (Ephesus), 194
Menderes Adnan, 27
Menemen, 155
Menteseoglu Principality, 213
Mermerli Cafe, Antalya, 291
Mersin, 23, 36, 37, 285, 287, 290, 297, 298, 309
Mersincik (Gulf of Gökova), 229
Mevlana Celaleddin Rumi, 60
Mevlana Festival (Festival of the Whirling Dervishes), 60
Mexico, 176, 222
Mesopotamia, 29, 157, 311
Mezitli, 298
Middle East, the, 28, 29
Milâs (Mylasa), 23, 208, 209
Miletus, 30, 32, 34, 39, 43, 154, 206–209
military coups, 27
Miliwandas, 30

Millet System, 50
Mimar Sinan, 305
Miss World, 53
Mitterrand, François, 307
Mitrovica, 50
Monumental Gateway, 273
Monument of Hasan Tahsin, 169
Mopus, 273
Morto Bay, Gallipoli, 127, 132
Moses, 316
Moslems, 50, 59, 73, 173
mosques
    Agaçarası Mosque (Aydın), 202
    Akçebe Sultan Mosque (Alanya),
        281
    Alaeddin Mosque, Antalya, 269
    Alaeddin Mosque, Alanya, 281
    Blue Mosque, Istanbul, 59
    Fatih Mosque, Eski Foça, 155
    Firuz Bey Mosque, Milâs, 213
    Habib Nacaar Camii, 317
    Hacı Mehmet Aga Mosque, Izmir,
        170
    Hisar Mosque, Izmir, 170
    Ilyas Aga Camii, 206
    Ilyas Bey Mosque Complex,
        Miletus, 209
    Ilyas Bey Camii, Selçuk, 181
    Isabey Camii, 199
    Kemeraltı Mosque, Izmir, 170
    Korkut Mosque, Antalya, 291
    Namazgah Mosque, Gelibolu, 126
    Orhan Bey Camii, Milâs, 213
    Öküz Mehmet Pasa Mosque, 183
    Süleyman Bey Mosque, 202
    Tekeli Mehmet Pasa Mosque, 270
    Ulu Cami, Adana, 301
    Üveys Pasa Mosque, 202
    Yeni Cami, 135
mountains
    Amanos Mountains, Hatay, 314
    Babadag, Ölüdeniz, 23, 202, 253
    Besparmak Dagı, Turkish
        Republic of Northern Cyprus,
        289
    Besparmak Dagı (Mt. Latmus),
        106, 211
    Bey Dagları 23,104, 263, 267,
        269, 270, 271
    Bülbül Dagı, 195
    Çıgrı Mountain, 138
    Erciyes Dag, Kayseri, 37
    Hasan Dag, 37
    Karaca Dag 37
    Kaz Dagı (Mt Ida) 123, 144, 153
    Kıran Dagı (Gulf of Gökova), 225,
        226, 227
    Manisa Dag, 30
    Mount Pagus, Izmir, 172

Mount Pilon, 188
Musa Dagı, Hatay, 309, 316
Sarı Bayır Mountain Range,
    Gallipoli, 127, 131
Taurus Mountains (Toros
    Dagları), 23, 29, 89, 267,
    271, 272, 287, 291
Yayladagı, 318
Mücdüddin Cistern, 281
mud baths, Karaada, 225
Mugla, 23, 70
Muller, Lady G. Max, 65
museums
    Alanya Ethnographical Museum,
        281
    Antakya Archaeological Museum,
        310, 311
    Antalya Museum, 46, 68, 263,
        265, 270
    Aphrodisias Museum, 202
    Bergama Museum, 165
    British Museum, London, 34, 92,
        192, 256
    Çanakkale Museum, 137
    Çimenlik Fortress Museum,
        Çanakkale, 135
    Dumberton Oaks Museum,
        Washington, D.C., 92
    Ephesus Museum, 187, 191,
        193
    Istanbul Archaeological Museum,
        136, 138
    Izmir Archaeology Museum, 170,
        172
    Izmir Ethnographical Museum, 170
    Kabatepe War Museum, Gallipoli,
        133
    Karain Museum, Antalya, 272
    Louvre Museum, Paris, 92, 154
    Metropolitan Museum, New York
        City, 92, 93
    Museum of Underwater
        Archaeology, Bodrum, 217
    Pergamum Museum (East Berlin),
        96, 97, 161, 162
    Side Museum, 278
    Silifke Archaeological Museum,
        290
    Topkapı Museum, Istanbul, 126
Mugla, 23, 156, 211
Musgebi, 217
Mustafa Pasha, 138
muz (Turkish mini bananas), 288
Müren, Zeki, 221
Mycenae, 32, 34
Myndos, 221
Myonneus, 180
Myra, 34, 260, 264, 265
Myrina, 154

n

Namaztepe, Gallipoli, 126
nargile (hookah), 313
nargile (sponge fisherman's air
    lifeline), 222
Narin, Halit, 95, 234
Narlıkuyu, 294
National Geographic Magazine,
    258
North Atlantic Treaty Organization
    (NATO), 27
NATO Regional Headquarters,
    Izmir, 27, 169
NATO War Games, 125
Nazili, 202
Neandria, 138
Near East, 28
Nek, the (Gallipoli), 127
Neolithic Period, 26, 28, 93
Nesin, Ahmet, 257
Nessians, the, 29, 30
Nestor, 198
Nestorian Heresy, 198
Net Group, the, 95, 201, 233
New Zealand, 127, 132
New Zealand War Memorial,
    Gallipoli, 132, 133
Nicaea, 160
Nicaea, Council of, 264
Nice, 154
Nile River, 227
Nimara Peninsula, 234
Normandy, the invasion of (World
    War II), 132
Northern Cyprus, 298
Notium, 181
Nubia, 34
Nuh Pasa Medresesi (Aydın), 202
Nuriyev, Rudolph, 217
Nuri Yamut Turkish Memorial,
    Gallipoli, 133
Nusret, the, (Turkish World War I
    minesweeper), 135
Nymphaion, 274

o

Ocakköy, 254
Odeon, Ephesus, 194
Odun Iskelesi, 43, 137, 138
okey (Turkish mahjong), 293
Öküz Mehmet Pasa Caravansary,
    182
Olba, 36, 293, 297
Old Market (Antakya), 314
Old Quarter (Alanya), 281
Old Stone Age, 26

olive oil, 156, 157
olive oil industry, 156, 157
Ölüdeniz (The Dead Sea), 23, 252, 253
Olympus, 23, 39, 261
Olympus National Park, 107, 108
Onan, Necmettin, 135
Onassis, Jacqueline, 216
Önder, Mehmet, 92
Ören, 153, 227
Orgeneral Kenan Evren Bulvarı (Adana), 301; (Antalya), 267
Orhaniye, Bay of, 237
Orion-Tur Travel Agency, 265
Orontes Valley, 310
Ortaca, Mugla, 249
Ortakent Beach, Bodrum, 220, 221
Ortaklar, 201, 205
Orthodox Churches of the United States, 265
Orthodox Church Patriarchate, Istanbul, 50, 199
Osmaniye, Adana, 304, 305
Ottoman Empire, 27, 65, 73, 129, 176, 268,
Ottomans, 40, 50, 51, 57, 122, 139, 183, 291
Oymapınar Dam, Manavgat, 278
Özal, Turgut, 27
Özgürlük Anıtı (Tarsus), 299

p

Pabuç Burnu, 225
Paçaraz Peninsula, 252
Pakistan, 68
Palamut (Gulf of Hisarönü), 236
Palestine, 27, 51
Pamphylia, 23, 30, 31, 36, 267–281
Pamucak (Aydın), 101, 182
Pamukkale, 42, 204, 205
panayır, 68
panegyria, 68
Pan Hellenic League, 26, 32
Paris (Trojan Hero), 139, 144, 145
Parthenon, 161, 192
Parthian War, 288
Parthians, 41
Paslı, 294
Pasaköy, 138
Patara, 254, 256
Patroclus, 145
Payas, 307, 310
Pelesgians, 30, 225
Peloponnesus, the, 127, 178
Peloponnesians, 213
Penelope, 145, 146
Pergamene Empire, 30

Pergamene Kings, 40, 139
Pergamum, 23, 26, 32, 39, 49, 93, 158–165
Pergamum Theater, 162
Perge, 23, 31, 42, 273
Persia, 26, 29, 32, 33, 206
Persian-Greek Wars, 215
Persians, 32, 38, 49, 59, 178, 207, 209, 277, 305
Pessinus, 159
Peter the Hermit, 46, 47
Pharnabozus, 34
Pharoahs of Egypt, 211
Phaselis, 38, 263
Philestaeros, 158
Philadelphia II, 42
Phoenicia, 41
Phoenicians, 32, 287
Phrygia, 37, 42, 167
Physcus, 233
Piding, 153
Pınara, 254
Piri Reis, 126, 153
Pisa, 44, 50
Pitane, 32
Plantagenet, House of, 218
Plataea, Battle of, 218
Plato, 139
Plutoneum (Hierapolis), 205
Province, 40
Prytaneion, 194
Pisidia, 273, 276
Ptolemias of Egypt, 41, 277
Pullu Camping, 290
Pumpelly, 49
Pyramids of Egypt, 49, 208

r

Ramazan (Ramadan), 59
Ramazanoglu, 301
Red Tower, Alanya, 280, 281
Reginald, 47
Rhodian Peraea, 233
Rhodians, 33, 213
rivers
  Berden River, 104
  Akçayı, 272
  Asi River (the Orontes), 29, 310, 311, 315,
  Bergama Çayı, 163
  Büyük Menderes River (the Maeander), 102, 201, 205, 208, 211
  Ceyhan River, 37, 104, 300, 302, 304
  Cumalı Cayı (Aegospotami), 127
  Dalaman River, 103, 244
  Dalyan River, 247

  Düden River, 272
  Euphrates River, 27
  Göksu River, 47, 97, 104, 290, 291, 297
  Hermais River, 139
  Karaçayı, 272
  Kocabas River, 38
  Küçük Menderes River (Kaystros River), 187
  Lamas Çayı (Lamus River), 298
  Manavgat River, 272, 279
  Meriç River (the Maritsa), 30, 70, 100, 125
  Pactolus River, 30
  Seyhan River, 104, 300, 302
  Tarsus Çayı, 298
  Tigris River, 28
  Xanthus River, 255
Romans, 26, 40, 49, 125, 139, 180, 184, 202, 208, 213, 222, 287, 289
Rome, 26, 43, 159, 160, 161, 206, 207
Rothschild Family, the, 176
Rough Cilicia, 23, 248, 287–291
Royal Roads, 30
Rulers
  Alexander the Great, 23, 26, 29, 38, 39, 125, 135, 138, 158, 178, 181, 188, 207, 215, 233, 274, 277, 305, 309
  Antigonus the One-Eyed, 39
  Antony, Mark, 23, 26, 37, 41, 215, 227, 299, 315
  Cassius, 299
  Cleopatra, 23, 26, 41, 215, 227, 287, 299, 315
  Emperor Carcalla, 137, 160
  Emperor Constantine the Great, 26, 143
  Emperor Frederick Barbarossa, 47
  Emperor Hadrian, 137, 161, 270, 301
  Emperor Justinian, 26, 198
  Emperor Marcus Aurelius Polemo, 291
  Emperor Michael VIII Pelaeogos, 27
  Emperor Nicephorus III, Phocas, 305
  Emperor Romanus IV Diogenes, 46
  Emperor Severus Alexander, 299
  Emperor Theodore Lascris, 160
  Emperor Theodosius II, 190
  Emperor Tiberius, 192
  Emperor Trajan, 160, 161, 285
  Emperor Zeno, 290
  Ertugrul (Seljuk warror), 49

Julius Caesar, 41, 146, 147
King Agamemnon, 144, 146
King Alagttes, 33
King Antiochus I, 204
King Antiochus III, 40, 180
King Antiochus the Great, 159
King Asitawandas, 36
King Attalus I, 26, 158
King Attalus II, 40, 159, 205, 268
King Croesus, 26, 29, 30, 33, 34, 158, 188, 209
King Cyrus, 26, 29, 34, 158, 188
King Darius, 26, 34, 154, 305, 309
King Peter de Lusignan of Cyprus, 268
King Edward IV, 218
King Eumenes I, 26, 158
King Eumenes II, 40, 159
King Herod of Judea, 311
King Ferdinand of Spain, 176
King Gyges, 33
King Louis VII, 47
King Mausolus of Caria, 33, 93, 215, 219
King Mausolus of Sparta, 144
King Midas, 30
King Mithridates of the Pontus, 26, 159
King Mutwallis, 31
King Philip, 38
King Philip Augustus, 47
King Priam of Troy, 31, 141, 142, 144, 145
King Richard I (the Lionheart), 47
King Seleucus I Nikator, 290, 293
King Seleucus of Syria, 209, 315
King Tarcondimotos, 37
King Xerxes of Persia, 26, 125, 135, 146, 154, 206
Lysimachus, 39, 159
Nurettin, 47
Odysseus (King of Ithaca), 145, 146
Octavian, 41
Pompey the Great, 160, 287
Philadelphus, 41
Queen Artemesia the Younger, 33, 93, 215, 219
Queen Hecuba, 146
Saladin the Great, 47
Sennacherib, 29
Sultan Abdülhamit II, 27, 52
Sultan Alaeddin Keykubat, 269, 281
Sultan Beyzait I (Thunderbolt), 27, 50
Sultan Beyazıt II, 176

Sultan Kılıç Arslan, 46, 47
Sultan Mehmet II, the Conqueror, 27
Sultan Mesud I, 47
Sultan Murat I (Ameurth), 50
Sultan Murat III, 177
Sultan Orhan, 49, 50, 125, 139
Sultan Osman (Othman), 49
Sultan Selim I, the Grim, 27, 51
Sultan Süleyman the Magnificent, 27, 138, 183, 216, 233
Tamerlane, 27, 50, 160, 217
Tigranes, 288, 299
Zengi, 47
Rumania, 27, 67
Rum (Greeks of Turkey), 50
Russia, 27, 51, 52, 65, 122, 129
Russian Navy, 179
Russian-Turkish War of 1878, 67

S

Sabancı, Hacı Ömer, 312, 313
Sabancı, Sadıka, 313
Sabancı, Sakıp, 313
Sacred Pool of Oracle Fish, Labraynda, 212
Sacred Way, Labraynda, 212, 213
Saçkarali Turks, 89
St Bernard, 47
St Gabriel, 291
St John, 42, 160, 173, 176, 186, 198
St Joseph's School, Izmir, 177
St Michael, 291
St Nicholas, 260, 264, 265
St Paul, 23, 26, 42, 138, 139, 173, 190, 274, 290, 315
St Polycarp, 173
St Simeon the Elder, 316
Saklıkent, 27, 267
Salamis, Battle of, 26, 206
Salmacis, 221
Samandag, 35, 317, 318
Samson, C.R., 129
Samsun, 56, 154
Santa Claus Symposium (Demre), 264, 265
Sapka, 52
Sardis, 27, 30, 34, 42
Sarhöyük, 47
Sarıkeçili Turks, 89
Sarimsaklı, 153
Saros Bay, 23, 122, 125
Sayın, Emel, 236
saz (Turkish banjo), 366
Sceptics, 39
Schliemann, Heinrich, 31, 92, 93, 140, 141, 142

Scholastica Baths, 194
Sea Peoples, 29
Sebaste, 297
Seddülbahir, 122, 127
Seferihisar, 179
Seka Paper Plant, Dalaman, 103, 250
Selale, 237
Selçuk, 179, 184, 193
Seleucia, 192
Seleucia in Pamphylia, 279
Seleucid Empire, 313, 316
Seleucids, 204, 277
Seljuk Empire, 59
Seljuk Turks, 27, 46, 49, 68, 173, 204, 268, 279
Selge, 276
Selinus, 288
sema (Dervish dance), 58
Serapsu Han, 279
Serbia, 27, 50
Serce Liman, 218, 237
Serepedon, 32
Sestus, 127
Seven Churches of Revelation, 160, 204
Seven Sages of Antiquity, 207, 208
Seven Sleepers, Cave of the, 299
Seven Wonders of the Ancient World, 93, 192, 219
Seytan Sofrası, Ayvalık, 153
Shakespeare, William, 41
Sharia (Islamic Holy Law), 52
Shefield, Sir Thomas, 218
Shinnar, 65
shipyards, Alanya, 281
Shipwreck Hall, the, 217, 218
Sigacık, 179
Sıçak Limanı, 258
Sıçak Peninsula, 258
Side, 23, 31, 36, 38, 276, 278, 287
Side Amphitheater, 278
Sidyma, 34
Sıhlan, 279
Siirt, 67
Silifke, 23, 28, 43, 97, 287, 290, 291, 293, 297
Silivri, Istanbul, 125
Sillyum, 31, 274
Simena, 259
Simeon, 46
Sina Knot, 86
Sirince, 182
Sivritepe, 137
Snake Tower, Bodrum Castle, 218
Sogukoluk, 310
Sophia, 50
Southern Cyprus (Greek-controlled), 290

Söke, 206
Sögüt, 228
Sömbeki, Gulf of, 23, 225, 233
Sparta, 144, 158
Spartans, 127, 213
Spain, 176
sponge (sünger), 222
sponge fishing, 222
Stoics, 39
Strabo (Geographer), 172
Strabo, 297
Sultanköy, 201
Susa, 34
Sultanate of Rum, 27
Sunni Moslems, 59
Susa, 30
Susanoglu, 293
Suvla Bay (Gallipoli), 127, 131, 132, 133
Süleyman Pasa Gazi, 27
Syria, 34, 39, 47, 49, 68, 157, 159, 300, 305, 309, 311, 314
Syrian Gates (Gülek Bogazı), 314, 315

t

Tabriz, 65
Tantalos, 173
Taris, 156
Tarsus, 26, 29, 31, 37, 41, 42, 298, 299
Tasyaka (Tombs Bay), 251
Tas Köprü, 301
Tas Kule, 155
Tasucu, 290, 287
Tavas Carpet Center, 91
Taylor, Elizabeth, 43
TEH Project, 91
Teimiussa, 259
Tekin, Latife, 70
Tekirdag, 125
Tekkeköy, Denizli, 204
Telmessus, 251
Telephus, 158
tespih (worry beads), 61
temples
    Aphrodite, Temples of;
        (Aphrodisias), 203
        (Knidos), 229
    Apollo, Temples of;
        (Letoon), 254
        (Claros), 181
        (Hierapolis), 205
        (Didyma), 209
        (Side), 278
    Asclepius, Temple of, Pergamum, 162, 165
    Artemis, Temples of;

(Ephesus), 181
(Termessus), 273
Athena, Temples of;
    (Assos), 139
    (Erythrae), 179
    (Izmir), 173
    (Heraclea Under Latmus), 211
    (Notium), 181
    (Pergamum), 161
    (Priene), 207
    (Side), 278
    (Troy), 32, 146
Demeter, Temples of;
    (Pergamum), 162
    (Priene), 207
Diana, Temple of, Ephesus, 32
Dionysus, Temple of, Pergamum, 160, 162
Domitan, Temple of, Ephesus, 194
Hadrian, Temple of, Ephesus, 195
Hera, Temple of, Pergamum, 162
Men, Temple of, Side, 278
Serapis, Temple of, Ephesus, 196
Trajan, Temple of, Pergamum, 161
Zeus, Temples of;
    (Adatepe), 153
    (Euromos), 212
    (Pergamum), 159, 162
    (Silifke), 291
Zeus Labrayndus, Temple of, Labraynda, 212
Zeus Olbious, Temple of, 293
Zeus Solymeus, Temple of, Termessus, 273
Teos, 179, 180
Tepekule, 173
Termessus, 273
Termessus Milli Park, 273
Teucer, 31, 136, 138
Texas A.M. University, 93, 217
Thales, 28, 32, 180, 208
Themistocles, 206
Thecla, 43
thermals, 100
Thessaly, 32
Thrace, (European Turkey), 23, 27, 30, 122, 125–127
Three Graces, 294
Thracians, the, 30
tirandil, 222
Tlos, 254
tombs
    Ajax, Tomb of, 137
    Alcetas, Tomb of (Termessus), 273
    Artemis (Ephesus), 187, 188
    Bellerophon, Tomb of (Lycian Hero), 254

Çifte Anıt Mezarları (Monument Tombs), 293
Dardanus Tumulus, 136
Fearless Satrap, Tomb of the, 294
Gazi Süleyman Pasha, Tomb of, Bolayır, 125
Güveç Dede, Tomb of, Milâs, 213
Harpies Tomb, the, Xanthus, 34, 92, 255
Has Yunus, Tomb of, Enez, 127
Hatun Türbe, Antalya, 270
Hıdırlık Kulesi, Antalya, 271, 291
Karaca Bey, Tomb of, Gelibolu, 126
Mound of Achilles, 137
Namık Kemal, Tomb of, Bolayır, 125
Neiried Monument, Xanthus, 256
Painted Tomb, 260
Pillar Tomb, Xanthus, 255
Royal Tomb, 254
Sarıca Pasha, Tomb of (Gelibolu) 126
Soldier's Tomb Termessus), 273
St. John, Tomb of (Ephesus), 198
Tumulus of Antilochus, 137
Tumulus of Patroclus, 137
Tumulus of Penelaus, 137
Tumulus of Protesileus, (Morto Bay), 127, 146
Xanthian Steele, the, (Xanthus), 256
Zincirkıran Mehmed Pasa Türbe, 270
Toprakkale, 305
Torba, Bodrum, 221
Tourism Ministry, 95
Tralles, Aydın, 201
Trek Travel, 267
Triopium, Palamut, 236
Tripolis, 47
Troad, the, 23, 30, 31, 135–139
Troy, 23, 26, 28, 34, 37, 38, 92, 123, 136, 140, 141, 142, 143, 144, 145, 146, 147, 274
Trojan Horse, 145, 146
Trojan War, 29, 30, 140–147, 158, 263, 287
Trojans, 29, 30, 31, 32, 138, 140, 141–147
Tros, 31, 136
tülüs (fighting camels), 184
Tunnel of Vespasian, 316
Turcomen tribes, 189
Turgut Özal Bulvarı, Adana, 301
Turgutreis, 221
Türkevleri, 227
Turkish Army, 130, 173

Turkish Employers' Association, 95
Turkish Historical Society, 92
Turkish Mafia, 93
Turkish Memorial, Anzac Cove, 129
Turkish Republic of Northern
    Cyprus, 291
Turkish Society for the Protection
    of Wild Life, 103
Turkish War Memorial, Morto Bay,
    129
Turquoise Coast, 23, 217
Turks, the, 49–53, 65–71
Turun, 232, 234
Turtle Beach, 249
Tuzla, 138, 229
Tyre, 47

u

Ugarit, 34
Ulu Burun Shipwreck, 34, 218, 257
United States, 93, 222
Urartians, 37
Urban II, Pope, 46, 49
Urfa, 47, 67
Urla Iskelesi, 178
Usak, 93
Uzuncaburç, 293
Üçagız, 259
Ürkmez, 180, 199
Üveycik, 137

v

Varsak, 272
Varius Baths, 193
V Beach, Gallipoli, 131, 133
Vedius, Gymnasium, 190
Venice, 46, 47, 51, 50, 138, 183
Via Egnatia, 125
Via Sacra (Sacred Way), 298
Vienna, 51, 65
Viransehir, 298
Virgin Mary, House of the,
    Ephesus, 199
Virgil, 146, 147

w

Walter the Penniless, 46, 47
War of Independence, Turkish, 27
Western Thrace, 67
wildlife
    Alabalık (trout), 117
    Anatolian Leopard, 101
    Egyptian Mongoose, 105
    European Ibex, 23, 104, 271
    Monk Seal, 103, 104
    Turtles, 102–104
Wishing and Asthma Cave, 238
Womens' Rights, 27
World War I, 23, 27, 65, 122, 126,
    129, 132, 135, 173, 268

World War II, 65, 67, 68, 132,
    176, 222, 228
World Wide Fund for Nature, 103
Xanthus (city), 23, 30, 92
Xanthus (the historian), 32
Xenophon, 158

y–z

Yahya Çavus 129, 133
Yalıkavak, Bodrum, 221
Yalvaç, 42
Yanartas (Chimera), 262
Yakacık, 305
Yapraklı Esik, 293
Yavuz Pasha, 305
Yenidogan, 206
Yenisehir, 137
Yesilköy, 53
Yesivot (Jewish high school),
    68
Yörük Turks, 68, 89, 90, 184
Young Turks, the, 27
Yozgat, 93
Yümüktepe, 31, 36, 298
Yüncü Tribe, 90
Yugoslavia, 50, 67
Yumurtalık, 23, 104, 105
Zerk-Altınay, 276
Zevi, Sabatai 68, 69, 176
Zeybek, 51, 70, 172